People in Touch

Assignments in Communication and Human Relations

John Pearce
Alan Cooper
Peter Leggott
Cyril Sprenger

Edward Arnold

© John Pearce, Alan Cooper, Peter Leggott
and Cyril Sprenger 1978

First published 1978
by Edward Arnold (Publishers) Ltd
41 Bedford Square, London WC1B 3DQ

Reprinted 1979, 1980

People in touch.
1. Communication 2. Communication in
management
I. Pearce, John, b. 1928
001.5′02′4658   P90

ISBN 0–7131–0223–3

Phototypeset in V.I.P. Palatino by
Western Printing Services Ltd, Bristol
and Printed in Great Britain by
The Pitman Press Ltd, Bath.

Preface

This book has been in preparation for a long time. In one sense it is a direct descendant of two parents: *Language in Use* (published by the same publisher in 1971), and the quite separate approach to English examining developed by the Local Government Training Board in the late 1960s. But it has been influenced by our experience in examining and assessing for O.N.C. English both in Business Studies and in Public Administration. Now these examinations are to be superseded by the courses of the Business Education Council, with demands which will seem exacting to most, new to many, revolutionary to a few – demands, however, which have been familiar to us and our colleagues for some years.

Our colleagues include lecturers who have tested earlier versions of our material and told us frankly of its errors. Their students have participated in these trials with forbearance and perception. We would like to mention Wendy Palmer (Derby CFE), Nona Bowring (Bournemouth C. of Technology), Sylvia Griffiths (Cambridge CFE), Sydney Bolt and Robert Crabtree (Cambridgeshire C. of Arts & Technology). We are indebted to Denis Brook for initiating our partnership and Cedric Blackman for revising the text. Several of Her Majesty's Inspectors deserve more credit for encouragement than their professional etiquette allows us to give them. Much more important than all of these, however, are the managers, junior executives, clerks, and secretaries, working in offices and factories and shops and local government, who have fed us material, put us right about the detail, and trusted us to reveal no identities.

If there be any virtue in these pages, our advisers and guides can justly claim some credit. The residual vices are ours.

JJP
AC
PL
CS

Contents

Assignments – Group C

Assignments – Group D

Using the Assignments – A Guide

"Where shall I begin, please your Majesty?"
he asked.

"Begin at the beginning," the King said,
gravely . . .

Alice in Wonderland

1 Communication

1.1   This book has been written primarily to
help lecturers and students engaged on the
course 'Communication and Human Relations' which is the compulsory Module 1 of
National Certificate courses under the Business Education Council. It is hoped that it may
also be of value to training staff in industry
and commerce, and to those teaching and
studying other courses where the level of skill
in communication is required to go beyond
that signified by a good grade in Ordinary
Level of the G.C.E.

1.1.2   The world of business and public
administration depends absolutely on having
an efficient communication system. Because
most communication passes between people,
the personal and human qualities of people
form an essential part of a communication system. This book, therefore, like the BEC core
module, rests on the belief that relating to
people and communicating with and through
them are two sides of the same coin.

1.1.3   We know that business studies students are just as often women as men, and
the same applies to their teachers. We know,
too, that senior posts in management are, and
always ought to be, open to women as readily
as to men. But it is simply clumsy, in a book
like this, to write 'he or she' and 'him or her'
every time we use a pronoun. We settle for
'he' and 'him' not because we are male
chauvinists (far from it), but because the language does not have a sex-neutral personal
pronoun apart from 'it' – and that would not
exactly convey our meaning.

1.2 Human Relations

1.2.1   There is a formal academic discipline
known as 'Human Relations', but we use the
term in its more ordinary sense of people making contact with one another to serve their
human, social, economic, and functional
needs. For a long time in Britain, and indeed

in some other parts of the English-speaking world, there has been a tradition that people communicated with people in one way, but business and other organisations communicated with each other in a different way. This tradition held that business letters, for example, should be written in a cold, formal style. Some examples were easy to make fun of, but the underlying purpose of this extreme formality was probably a kind of insurance policy. People who were not very sure of their own powers as users of written language were often led to use semi-official formulae. Indeed, there are organisations which to this day instruct their junior clerks to compose business letters by selecting particular sentences from a prescribed manual.

1.2.2 This kind of writing may protect the writer from the charge of allowing personal views or feelings to intrude on a business setting, but it also has the effect of keeping the reader at a distance. At its worst, this rigidly formal style is known as officialese. For example:

```
Madam:

I am required to inform you

that my company's lease of

this theatre will terminate

on the 22nd inst., and that

as from that date your

services will no longer be

required.
```

Thus was the box-office clerk of a theatre in the Midlands given the sack in 1921. The objection to such a letter is not that it is incorrect in any way, considered only as an example of language. It is, rather, that it is quite needlessly severe. Some would also regard it as an unacceptable way to treat a fellow human being, however junior he or she may be. But this is only one minor example of a practice and a style of business communication that has existed on an enormous scale for many years. There are very powerful reasons for believing that it is a style which needs to change.

1.2.3 Quite the strongest reason for seeking a more humane way of communicating in business is that ordinary men and women are no longer prepared to be addressed in a way which many of them think of as either condescending or hostile. They find writing of this kind at best stuffy, usually obscure, and at worst offensive. Among other reasons we may cite the fact that many senior businessmen today believe that excessively formal writing actually gets in the way of efficient communication. Industry, commerce, administration, and government, all alike, are concerned to secure the co-operation of people with people, and writing and speaking which approaches them as people is more likely to do that than a style which treats them as mere numbers.

That is why this book is not a collection of conventional English exercises or even a manual of correct usage. There are numerous 'books of rules' on the market, and some users of this book may need to possess one and use it. (In that case, the manual should be up-to-date.) Knowing all the formal rules and observing them, although necessary, is not sufficient. In order to relate successfully to other people, it is also necessary to master a flexible and sensitive use of speech and writing.

1.3 School English and Workplace English

1.3.1 People in offices do not spend the firm's time writing essays or answering comprehension questions. Few of them ever write summaries. What they do have to do is to read letters quickly and with accurate and inferential understanding, decide where to pass them on to, take telephone messages, answer queries, ask for time off, sort out a tangle, apologise for mistakes, accept a rebuke (just or unjust), and many other things which rest on skill with language. They may sound very easy and everyday tasks, but it is in these seemingly ordinary things that a successful career is based at every level of business employment. The notion that one does not have to get on well with people in order to succeed in business or administration is a novelist's myth.

1.3.2 In learning to do these and similar things successfully, one of the essentials is to identify and look closely at many things which most people take for granted. Listen, for example, to the immediate responses to the next four or five telephone calls you make. Some will be terse, even monosyllabic, even a mere angry 'Yes!' Others will say who they are or what post they have. Yet others will make some kind of gesture to show that you are not regarded as a nuisance or worse. In studying the way other people do ordinary things you have the opportunity to learn from their mistakes and improve your own performance.

1.3.3 The process of learning through a greater awareness of one's own performance of routine tasks is taken very seriously in this book. Many of the activities which we suggest will require systematic discussion in small groups, or the inspection of written drafts by groups of students, or the acting of sketches and simulations with follow-up discussion. This element in the book is there because it carries through the opportunity to look at ordinary activity in un-ordinary ways. This kind of learning is more productive than the assiduous taking of notes.

1.3.4 Doing the routine things well is important because life in businesses and public offices is apt to be unpredictable. One's boss may change suddenly, or the working conditions may vary. Offices and workshops are human institutions where people do human and unpredictable things like losing their temper or giving a severe rebuke to the wrong

person. The young employee who can use language skilfully in these situations is at a considerable advantage.

1.3.5 However, the opportunity to observe or practise situations of this kind does not always occur in school English. This is not a criticism of school English: on the contrary, most of the courses which will use this book require an above-average achievement in English at school level before the student can start. There are many skills in school English which this course will take further and develop, such as the ability to read a piece of writing accurately and the skill of writing material down in the patterns of sentence and paragraph which reflect the structure of ideas. In a business setting, however, one's skill as a reader is judged, not by answers to questions about words, but by what you *do* about the document in question. It is that practical emphasis which governs this book.

1.4 The Assignment Approach

1.4.1 English in business, as in most places outside school, always occurs in concrete settings. If we do not know the setting, and a great deal of apparently unimportant detail about it, we cannot communicate in it. In order to solve a problem it is necessary to know the facts which constitute the problem and which make it specific. Finding solutions means making decisions, and those need to be weighed up. An angry middle-aged woman brings some dress fabric back to the counter and claims she was served short measure: is she to be taken seriously or courteously told to jump in the proverbial lake? The decision depends on the customer, her credibility, the sales assistant, his or her status and experience, the firm's policy, and even the manners (or lack of them) shown by the customer in voicing her complaint. How to respond to her is a question answerable only when all the relevant details are known. (A situation not unlike this occurs in Assignment B9, Mrs Chillingworth's Cooker.) In principle, all language-use is like this: what is said or written relates to and depends on both the detail and the pattern into which it all fits.

1.4.2 To detach the communication skills from the circumstances in which they operate must make them artificial. Hence, the exercises in this book are first and foremost a set of circumstances. We have tried to make them realistic, and the aim has been to put the student in a position to use the situation, in all its detail, for the central purposes of communication. These are wider than the mere processing of information. In the light of the human relations perspective we must include the processes of persuasion, of co-operating and of negotiating with people, in addition to those of finding things out and setting them down for others.

1.4.3 A case-study approach brings about a change, then, in the nature of the teaching and learning work of the classroom. Conventional English tends to rely on using exercises where every student does the same task, has his work marked or assessed by the teacher, and bases his efforts to improve on what the teacher tells him. In case-study work the students learn from one another as well as from the teacher. Discussion in this setting is not a process of casual interchanges of casual ideas, but a process of working out the full meanings of a document, exploring the possible solutions to a problem, editing out the weaknesses of a draft, or sifting the ways in which a proposed draft or solution matches the details of the situation concerned. Activities of this kind happen in offices and in industry all the time, and there is no way of learning how to take part in them except by taking part in situations like them.

1.4.4 One consequence of using the case-study method is that the 'answers' cannot always be predicted. Rather, in most of the situations in these assignments, there is more than one acceptable way of carrying out each task. What matters is that the writing or speaking which is done in each situation should be appropriate rather than 'correct'. There can be many answers to some tasks which are perfectly correct, in the grammatical sense, but which are quite inappropriate. The sentences and the vocabulary may be as correct as any purist may wish, but if a letter intended to be persuasive is in fact abrasive, it will not be effective. The same holds for memoranda and reports: it is not enough to be correct, because it is also necessary to be concise. The process of learning to be concise, appropriate and tactful (as well as correct) is a slow one which involves discussion, editing, working out consequences, and many other activities which are provided for in these assignments.

1.4.5 There are some aspects of conventional 'business English' which we do not attempt to deal with in this book. The proper layout of letters and the etiquette of salutations in them are examples. There are two reasons for such omissions. One is that most such matters are (or will be) already catered for in General Level BEC courses or in the G.C.E. Ordinary Level English courses which will continue to constitute the main entry qualifications to courses using this book. The other is that while it is important to use correct layout and format, those features are not the only, or even the most important, aspects of business English. They are better treated as matters which call for attention when the student's work reveals the need for it.

1.5 The Assignments

1.5.1 This book contains 33 assignments arranged in four groups which have an approximate order of difficulty. In general, that is, Group B is a shade harder than Group A, and so on through the Groups. Within each group, too, the Assignments are roughly in ascending order of difficulty. But any arrangement of this sort is a matter of opinion, because a task is only difficult if one is unprepared for it or lacks the skills it calls for. Some students will find many tasks in Group D quite 'easy', while others will find some tasks early in Group A quite 'difficult'. This is one reason why the teacher has to do some selecting: only he can know what tasks will be difficult enough for his class to be worth working

4

on, without being so difficult as to make them feel frustrated.

1.5.2 An assignment, at its simplest, is a description of a situation and a number of tasks which a participant in it has to carry out. The situation is described in detail, for reasons we have already given (see 1.4.1–2). In some cases this detail is lengthy and complicated, because actual situations usually are like that. Some of the information is provided in the form of diagrams, maps, tables of figures, or other documents. So the first job of the students must be to study the account of the situation, which is written in such a way that they will need to read it twice before they can form a mental picture which takes account of the detail.

1.5.3 Each assignment has a similar structure:

1. References to the guide at the beginning of the book, of which this is the first chapter.
2. A description of a specific situation.
3. Opportunity for the teacher to insert tasks such as questions testing the students' understanding of the material. These tasks can only be devised by the teacher in the light of his knowledge of the class.
4. A set of **Tasks**, with the key instruction set **in bold type**.
5. Related documents which in many (but not all) cases form an appendix to the assignment.

All the assignments are based on events that have happened somewhere at some time, but the places and persons involved have been disguised, and any accidental resemblance to real people or places is unintentional.

1.5.4 The reading of the text of the assignment has to be done with care, because it is impossible to do the tasks adequately if the text has not been understood. For many students, the comprehension work involved may need to be more thorough than they are used to. Also, the descriptions provide a considerable amount of information about how business and public administration operates, in order to lessen the disadvantage of students who have no personal experience of employ-

ment. For the same reason, *the assignments never ask the student to invent or guess at important information.* We have assumed that specialist information should be given in the text, and we have normally gone to specialists to obtain it.

1.5.5 Each assignment provides four or, more usually, five tasks. It is for the teacher to decide both which assignments and which tasks to set. These selections will usually be made in the light of the needs of a class, and the programme of work that results may well vary from class to class and even from student to student. The work to be done may be oral or written, and the writing may take the form of letters, memoranda, notes, tables of figures, calculations, or (we hope) all of these in turn. Also, the tasks will vary in scale, some of them occupying no more than a few minutes in discussion, others taking as long as any homework set at school or college.

1.5.6 A further way in which the tasks will vary is in the range of communicative functions being served. The principal functions involved in this work are those of the National Certificate Core Module – informing, persuading, operating, and co-operating. (Operating refers to the way people in business settings know and make use of the internal structure or system of their place of work.) Some of these communicative functions involve simple, direct activity by an individual person, but most of them involve talking to or working with other people: all communication is communication with somebody. This explains why many of the tasks require students to work in small groups.

1.5.7 Communication work always has this dual purpose of handling the forms and formats of business communication and serving its main functions. For this reason it is not practicable to set up a programme of work as a formal list of items, a syllabus, to be worked through in some definite order. However, to help the teacher and the student to have some record of work, and plan future work we have suggested some sequences of Assignments in an appendix. The tasks are intended, of course, to be modified by the teacher in the light of the specific objectives being pursued.

1.5.8   The assignments have been assembled so as to escape from the rigid distinctions between Business Studies on the one hand and Public Administration on the other, or between either of these and Distribution Studies. There are assignment settings in all three areas and in others, and we hope that students who specialise in particular fields of study will nevertheless find useful material outside them.

1.5.9   The first assignment in each group is given with a set of suggested solutions, and with some notes on the solutions. The subject-matter of the assignments varies, and each group includes situations from industry, local government, and other settings. The subject-matter of the worked assignment, therefore, is not necessarily any indication of the kind of assignments that follow in the group. We have already said (in 1.4.4 above) that there is not usually any one right answer to the tasks, and the suggested solutions in assignments A1, B1, C1 and D1 are intended only as examples.

1.6 Using the Assignments

1.6.1   The assignments are intended to provide a bank of material for the teacher to draw on according to what he or she regards as the needs of the class. The assignments do not make, and are not intended to make, a continuous textbook to work through.

1.6.2   The assignments vary a great deal in the kinds of activity suggested for the student. The teacher is therefore in a position to select the emphasis he wants. The work can be strongly oral in emphasis, or almost entirely written. The writing can concentrate on very formal material or can include less formal work. The writing can concern itself largely with the use of conventional formats such as letter, memorandum, and report, or with the writing of functional documents for which the precise format is less important.

1.6.3   Some assignments are almost entirely oral in the activity which results (e.g. A6, The Medical Receptionist). Others are almost entirely designed to lead to writing (e.g. A3, Mrs Surtees' Bins). Some lead to extensive discussion (e.g. C4, C5, D3 or D7) while others require intensive analysis of the documents supplied (e.g. C6, Specialist Conference). This variety is provided to give the teacher choice. The teacher is also free, of course, to add other tasks of his own devising. For example, a college with the equipment for training students to use the telephone would find numerous opportunities in the assignments. Again, colleges with a specialist teacher of drama will build on opportunities provided in the text, such as the meeting described in the setting for D4, No Smoking, or a meeting of the local residents' group in C3, Wirkton Cutting.

1.6.4   The design of the BEC Core Module is likely to call for a year's work involving between ten and fifteen assignments. In many cases the assignments selected will have a particular emphasis, according to the Sector Board of BEC whose other modules are being followed – Business Studies, Finance, Distribution, or Public Administration. The assignment approach also lends itself to the preparation of students in a number of secretarial courses, where it has been in use for some years.

1.6.5   The student, then, is not expected to work through more than a selection of assignments, or necessarily through every task in each one. Obviously, there is no way of saying in advance how much time each assignment will take. Experience in the classroom trials of the assignments before publication suggested that a class unused to working in this way might need several hours to complete its first full assignment, whereas a class familiar with the approach might well complete several tasks in a 1½-hour period. Classes vary, too, according to their stage in the year. The trials also showed that a particular assignment may capture the interest of a class and provide material for much more extended work.

1.6.6 The terms 'note', 'letter' and 'report' need to be watched. An employer or a superior may not use them very precisely. 'Send a note . . .' will mean a letter if the recipient is outside the organisation, or a memorandum if he is inside it. As we make clear in 7.3 (page 20), there are several kinds of document which are often called reports but are in fact something else. Even when the term 'report' is appropriate, it may mean a short briefing note or a full advisory report. The task of deciding what the situation and the request really call for is a difficult but necessary one, about which it is not wise to be too literal-minded. We have deliberately not tried to make it easier. The text of the assignments sometimes does as people in real life do, using these labels loosely in order to pose the problem of what format to select in reply. The table in Appendix 2 sets out what we would expect, but in many cases alternatives would be acceptable.

1.6.7 Very few of the tasks in this book specify a word-limit, and then only because of printing or layout considerations. This is because word-limits in communications work are in reality a convenience for formal examinations. Industrial and administrative superiors rarely have the time to stop and count words, and if a document is rejected as too long or too wordy you may be sure it is so by a considerable margin. Deciding what the appropriate length for a document should be, as with its format, is something you need to learn by practice and experience. Moreover there is no merit in being so brief that you leave out important parts of the material altogether.

2 Meaning and Understanding

"When *I* use a word," Humpty Dumpty said in a rather scornful tone, "it means just what I choose it to mean – neither more nor less."

Alice Through the Looking Glass

2.1 We refer in Section 1.3 to the differences between English in school and the language activity of business. One of the most important aspects of this difference has to do with meaning and our understanding of it. In school work there is often great emphasis on what is known as 'comprehension'. This is a process of getting at the meanings of texts by exploring in detail the meanings of words. As the work develops, comprehension delves more and more into the meanings of words as they occur in particular contexts. But the underlying idea is that there is a meaning to get at, a meaning which can be discovered by looking hard enough at the text. In business things may be different: what a text means may depend on itself. What a letter means may depend on the letter it is answering.

2.1.1 Consider this example:

```
Dear Mr Clyde,

Thank you for your letter
about your firm's Series 2000
Planers dated March 9th.  I
very much appreciate your
continued interest in our
needs, but I feel I must have
rather more time to reach a
decision.  I hope to be able
to give you a more definite
reply in ten days' time.

        Yours sincerely,

        W P Martin
```

This letter seems to mean that Martin wants more time to think about a purchase of machine tools. Suppose, however, that Clyde's previous letter had given Martin four days to make up his mind, or the machines would be sold to another customer. In that case the meaning of Martin's reply is quite different: it is saying 'I cannot be pressured', or, perhaps, Martin thinks Clyde is bluffing.

2.1.2 But the context may be different again. Suppose that Martin is considering alternative makes, and Clyde has written to say that if he decides quickly he can have a substantial discount from his firm. In that case, Martin is saying something else: he is saying 'I don't respond to high-pressure salesmanship.'

2.1.3 This example illustrates a central principle about meaning. The full meaning of the letter is much more than the separate meanings of the individual words, obviously enough, but what the full meaning is *depends on the context*. This holds for individual words as well as for whole texts. For example, the term *capacity* usually means a container's space for holding a substance, but in the context of a planing machine it will mean the size of the piece it can hold for planing.

2.1.4 This principle means that conventional comprehension questions will not uncover the meaning of a document which depends on its context. That is why in this book you will find some very detailed accounts of contexts, but no comprehension questions. In fact, of course, every single assignment is a sustained and often difficult comprehension task, and the teacher will often treat the situations in the light of this. But the real test of how well the students have understood the situation described in each assignment must be how well they carry out the tasks which arise.

2.2 *Reading for Understanding*

2.2.1 Many of the assignments have been written in such a way that they reflect the comprehension problems of real life. Information in real life does not come with neat packages of comprehension questions to tell us which bits of it are important. On the contrary, it tends to come muddled up with all sorts of other information which may or may not be relevant. The job we have to do may depend on two or three tiny parts of the whole material, and the first part of the job is to find those parts and discard the rest. Digging out the relevant, setting aside the irrelevant, and using the material accordingly are central

tasks in most of the assignments, as they are in business life.

2.2.2 There are also numerous instances where vitally relevant material is not included, and its relevance may not even be stated. To use an example which does not occur in the assignments, a task relating to Sunday trading is likely to involve national legislation and local bye-laws. In Assignment C4 (The Withdrawal of the Rushton Bus), one of the key factors is the distances of the journeys, and it is up to the student to notice that the map is to scale and the scale is given. There are other instances where the use of outside information is vital to the comprehension process, and we have not tried to make it easy all the time.

2.2.3 Throughout the assignments there are two kinds of comprehension activity involved. One is, of course, the *literal* kind – the business of identifying the strict meaning of words and phrases. The other is *inferential* comprehension, which enables a reader to make inferences from the text to help his understanding. One example of the difference between the two kinds occurs in the opening paragraph of Assignment C3 (Wirkton Cutting). One of the sub-committees is called Environmental Services, and a straightforward study of the text will reveal that the *literal* comprehension of this term would include the idea that one of the services is refuse disposal. The same paragraph sets out some of the facts about the staff, and taken together they mean that the Head of Planning is the most senior officer in the whole Department (since there is neither a Director of Planning nor a Chief Executive). This is an *inference*. There are a great many such inferences to be made in reading the text of each assignment.

2.3 *Technical Language*

2.3.1 The kind of comprehension work involved in the assignments, however, goes beyond this. All the assignments, and thus all the tasks, are placed in particular settings –

business firms, local government departments, ordinary communities, schools, shops, and so on. In most settings of this kind the people who work there have a common fund of knowledge, and refer to it with language which they all share. Such language may often be very local, very particular to the setting. For example, one person mentioned in Assignment D5 is referred to as a 'beam handler'. The firm is in the textile trade, where the term 'beam' means the special roller on which fabric is rolled up before going through a process or as it comes out at the end of it. We have used such technical terms wherever they are appropriate, and students working the assignments are expected to come to terms with them. They will not always be found in a dictionary, or only in very large ones, but it will usually be possible to work out an approximate idea of the meaning or to find it out from students on other courses. There is no point in trying to avoid technical terms, because industry and commerce could not work without them.

2.3.2 There is another kind of usage which should also be mentioned. Many trades and situations use perfectly ordinary words in very special ways. 'Scale' is an ordinary enough word, but it has a special meaning for a heating engineer, and a quite different one, equally special, to a dentist. 'Property' in the insurance world refers to buildings and land only. In some cases ordinary words are invested with special meanings through the operation of law. The use of the term 'redundant' is a recent example, since the effect of the Redundancy Payments Act (1975) is to put the person formally declared redundant in a position to claim often substantial compensation. The whole field of labour legislation has become very greatly complicated in this way since 1972, and numerous seemingly ordinary words may now have peculiar force. This kind of meaning is a special case of the general feature of technical language. Most ordinary people refer to technical language as jargon, usually to deride it, but the job of the serious student is to understand it.

2.4 Language is Social

2.4.1 Language is used for other purposes than the conveying of meaning. It builds and sustains the social network. There is no escape from this social aspect of language, and there is no point in pretending that one can speak or write in a way which is totally free from social meanings. Every working person knows this from daily experience even in so simple a matter as the use of names. Except in a very limited set of circumstances it is almost universal for working colleagues of the same level of seniority to speak to one another by first names. This is now so general that to use title forms like Mr or Mrs is unusual enough to be regarded as deliberate. Such usage is nowadays understood as intended to keep someone at a distance, or to remind him of junior status. (There are exceptions, of course, like the Civil Service, the armed forces, and some commercial businesses.) The position in written language is rather different, but even here the rules are much more flexible and more relaxed than they were. Any organisation is likely to have individuals who prefer the old standards, of course, and such colleagues are entitled to have their preferences respected. As with so much else, it is necessary to watch for and learn the local customs in whatever organisation you join.

2.4.2 The naming habits of a group, however, are only a small part of the social meanings that language can convey. In one sense, every schoolboy knows this: every school pupil knows when his teacher is feeling bad-tempered or down-hearted without anything specific being said. But much the same can be said of the effects of language in all settings. Consider the two letters on page 10, both conveying the same basic message. The point about the contrast between these two letters is not merely that the one is cold and official in the bad sense, but that the other treats the applicant as a person: it addresses her by name, and tries to lessen her inevitable disappointment at not getting the job. One of the effects of such letters as the second one

Dear Sir/Madam,

I have to thank you for your application for the post of Housekeeper at Mounts Hill Old People's Home and inform you that the post has now been filled.

Yours faithfully,

Dear Mrs Welford,

Thank you for your application for the post of Housekeeper at Mounts Hill Old People's Home. We received an exceptionally strong set of applications, and have now made an appointment. I hope you will feel able to apply for other vacancies with us.

Yours sincerely,

must in the long run be to make employing organisations seem more human. It is of course quite futile to suggest that either letter is more correct than the other. It is reasonable to suggest that the second kind is more costly to send than the first, but it can still be a duplicated letter with the addressee's name written in and the sender's personal signature. (See the suggested solutions and notes to C1, G Smith & Sons, Printers.)

2.4.3 The wider issue of social meanings is bound up with the kind of society we all want to live in. Any language has the ability to serve its users in very varied ways, and in particular to enable people to increase or to lessen the distance which they maintain between each other. It used to be thought that the only correct kind of English was the very formal kind. This is now widely admitted to be an over-simplified view of a more complicated matter. It is not enough for a letter or any other docu-

ment to be correct in grammar and spelling and concise: it must also be courteous. What this means is the subject of Section 3.

2.4.4 All the examples and suggested solutions in this book are pieces of written English, but the approach to learning to communicate, and the principles underlying it, are the same for oral English as well. There is no virtue in being stiff and distant in speaking to people when your main need is to communicate with them. There will sometimes be teachers or superiors who believe that any degree of friendliness in speech is not quite correct. There will be some, too, who believe that in order to be correct in speech it is necessary to have a particular accent. It would be wise to disregard both viewpoints. One does not fall into a morass of slang merely by refusing to be formal, and there are many acceptable accents in English today besides those of the old BBC. In fact, Britain is not only much more tolerant of diverse accents than it used to be: it is also much more tolerant than it realises.

3 Us and Them

Father, Mother, and Me,
Sister and Auntie say
All the people like us are We,
And everyone else is They.
Kipling

3.1 We refer frequently below to the principle that a person in an official job has to be careful not to interfere in his colleagues' business. A counter-clerk in a pensions office often has to deal with enquirers about retirement. He may hear one of them say he is 59 and is intending to go on the dole until he can claim his pension. The clerk may know that this is questionable, even illegal, but the question of intent to deceive the department which pays unemployment benefit is not something the counter clerk can deal with. It is not his business, whatever his personal feelings may be. Rather, he should ask his superior to inform the other department.

3.1.1 The private individual is free to talk and write in ways which are not open to the official. This may sometimes be a problem for senior officers. An education officer, for example, may privately believe in comprehensive schools, but may work for an education authority which believes in separate grammar and secondary modern schools. He thus has to behave in one way as an individual and in another way as the holder of a post. If the conflict becomes too great, he may have to find another post, but the majority of public administrators accept this kind of conflict as an inevitable consequence of their chosen careers, and do their work with genuine integrity. The general need to keep one's personal views and one's official actions in separate compartments has a bearing on the language of official writing.

3.1.2 Official writing is not the same as officialese. Here are two ways of wording the same message, to the wife of a soldier wounded in action:

```
Dear Madam,

I regret to inform you that
your husband, Pte D L
Hardcastle 1239876 Royal Regt.,
was wounded in action on the
14th inst.  A bullet entered
the left fore-arm and came
into contact with the wrist-
bone.  Medical instructions
are that he remain in HQ
Hospital for some days prior
to recuperation home leave.

        Yours faithfully,

              etc.
```

```
Dear Mrs Hardcastle,

I am sorry to have to tell you
that your husband, Private
Derek Hardcastle, was wounded
in action yesterday.  He
received a bullet wound in the
left fore-arm which caused
minor splintering of a wrist
bone.  He is now in the
Headquarters Hospital, where
the doctor in charge assures
me that there will be no
permanent damage.  He will
then be given at least ten
days home leave.  You can
expect a telegram about his
time of arrival reasonably
soon after getting this
letter.

        Yours sincerely,
```

The first of these two letters is officialese, while the second is good official writing. The first is forced, cold, and leaves the recipient in anxiety because it does not tell her enough. It illustrates everything that the critics of officialese dislike, treating Mrs Hardcastle as the wife of a number. The second letter addresses her by name, uses her husband's name, and provides the answers to the questions she will naturally ask: how bad is the wound, will the damage be permanent, how soon will he be home, and how long for. It is, in short, humane, and it illustrates the point that it is perfectly possible to be official and humane at the same time.

3.1.3 It is worth pausing at this point to consider how the same letter would be written if the recipient was already known, personally, to the writer. It might go something like this:

```
Dear Mary,

I am sorry to have to say
that Derek was wounded in
action yesterday.  He got a
sniper shot in the left fore-
arm and the bullet caused a
minor splintering of a wrist
bone.  There won't be any
permanent damage, and he is
in good hands at the HQ
hospital.  He will have to
have a week there before home
leave (about ten days, I would
judge), and you'll be getting
the usual wire in a day or
two after this note.

        With best wishes,

            Yours sincerely,
```

This last example is written in a friendly style which can be given the label Casual Style. It is the normal style for writing between friends, or between people where the writer wishes to make a friend of the recipient. The first version of the letter is in Formal Style, and the second version is in Consultative Style. We can say, very broadly, that good business English is better written in a style between consultative and formal than in rigid formal style. Some business communications will be nearer to casual style than to formal: it all depends on the situation, the relationship between the writer and reader, and the needs of the task. There are some instances, for example in legal decisions and court evidence, where a very formal style is called for.

3.2 Levels of Formality

3.2.1 The simple classification of styles (more strictly, levels of formality) into formal, consultative, and casual is itself an over-simplification. In practice the levels of style shade off into one another, and particular examples often illustrate this combination of features of more than one style. Basically, stylistic variation of this kind is used for social purposes, which will underpin and support the communicative aims. If it will help your communication to be formal, then you should be formal: it will not serve you well to annoy a senior officer who likes formality by being deliberately casual in style. He is likely to suffer from the illusion that writing in casual style reflects a casual attitude. On the other hand, if you are developing a good relationship with a sales customer, your language usage may move towards less formal patterns. At the same time, English people are very sensitive to attempts to force the social pace by using casual style to make a relationship sound more cosy than it is.

3.2.2 The title of this section suggests that language has a good deal to do with the way in which people react to authority, and with the relationships between public bodies and the general mass of the population. We believe this is true. We also believe that there has been an immense change in the general climate in this matter in the past ten years. It is a change vastly for the better, and it is far from complete. There are still many local government servants who believe, as they were brought up to believe, that the only really correct use of English is formal and distant. There are still many offices where such language is expected of all staff in all external communications. But things are changing. For example, it is now very rare to see schools with notices at their gates forbidding parents to enter. By contrast, the posters advertising help for adult illiterates positively welcome contact and show how to achieve it. But the change has much farther to go.

3.3 The Society We Speak In

3.3.1 In the meantime, many of the students who use this book will have many opportunities, in their daily work, to improve the daily routine contacts between Us and Them. The thousands of individuals who make up the 'general public', thousands of people with names and not numbers, come to enquiry desks, call at the counter, ring up to make or change or cancel appointments, ask about schools, enquire about tax, seek help about their stamps, and hundreds of other things. In this daily traffic of question and answer, spoken and written, ordinary people need help in being understood and courteous consideration in being answered. They come to consult, and it is better not to be formal in style with them. The sum total of how they are treated adds up to a large proportion of the reputation of government, council, industry, banking, and commerce.

4 Simulations

"What is the use of a book," thought Alice, "without pictures or conversations?"

Alice In Wonderland

4.1 Three quarters of the assignments in this book include tasks which require students to participate in simulated meetings or discussions, and the purpose of this section is to explain what is intended by this and why.

4.1.1 The philosophy behind this book, and behind the BEC Module 'People and Communication', is that skill in the use of language cannot be separated from relationships with people. It is virtually impossible for a teacher to teach human relationships by instruction: they need to be explored in action. The same is true of large elements of language work, too. The only satisfactory way of making it possible to explore relationships in action is to set up specific situations in which the participants adopt particular roles. Simulation, therefore, is necessary for the fulfilment of some of the

most important of the objectives of the work. These include being able to explain a point of view and to present an argument, and, just as important, being able to listen constructively to others doing these things, with appropriate responses to them. It is important to be able to 'read' a conversation or a meeting, i.e. to understand and interpret non-verbal elements in communication, and for many people whose work includes periods at reception desks and enquiry counters it is essential to be able to help other people to say what they mean. This is part of the wider business of being able to see a problem through the eyes of another person, and, ideally, of being able to see oneself as other people do.

4.1.2 Simulations are, therefore, much more than 'mere' play acting. In the simulations in this book, especially in the earlier assignments, the nature of the roles to be adopted is set out in detail. The more this detailed prescription is studied, the easier it will be to enter imaginatively into the role concerned, but it is also valuable to study the prescriptions of the other roles in the situation. It should then be possible to use the material about the setting and the characters to produce a realistic discussion or interview. There is meant to be a great deal of scope for developing arguments and attitudes, but it is important that these be derived from the characters and settings. The principal purpose here is to gain practice in taking a role in a concrete situation while suppressing one's personal thoughts and prejudices. This is not an invitation to dishonesty or pretence: there are many occasions when one has to act or speak within the limitations of the role when, from a purely personal point of view, one might wish to speak and act otherwise.

4.1.3 For example, in Assignment B1, the official in the Education Department is asked a question about council housing, which is a matter for a different department. If the education official gives an answer which commits the housing department, positively or negatively, he is going beyond the proper limits of his role. He may know quite well that there is no hope of council housing for two years, but he has to bite his tongue off rather than say so: it is not his business. He may be able to quote the Housing Department in broad terms, but even there he has to be careful.

4.2 Guidelines

4.2.1 Taking part in simulated situations is something that one has to learn: it does not come naturally to everyone, but it is perfectly possible for the vast majority of people to learn how to do it. Even so, one should not expect one's first attempts at simulations to be splendid successes all at once. The ground-rules for successful simulation work are very simple:
1. Be clear about your own role and what the person in that role can and cannot do.
2. Know the available facts.
3. Be prepared to express opinions or views which are consistent with the role, even though personally you may hold quite different views.
4. Resist the temptation to 'ham it up' or over-act.

4.2.2 Most simulations will directly involve a limited number of students, which poses the problem of what the others in the group should be doing. In some cases the simulation will be one of several which will need to be compared, and the problem resolves itself. But in every simulation it is possible for observers to be taking notes, with a view to discussion afterwards or to preparing a Note for File, or to identify particular aspects of the exchanges.

4.2.3 It is exceptionally valuable, after a reasonably successful simulation, to be able to inspect it by playing back a sound or video recordings of it. It is better to start making recordings on sound only, because the microphone is intrusive until you are used to it, and this is even more true of cameras.

4.2.4 Many of the later simulations in this book bring in elements which have been treated separately elsewhere. For example, Task 4 of St Philip's Primary School (D3) is in reality part of a meeting of the school managers. As such, it is a committee which has to observe the rules of procedure, minuting, and so on which are summarised in Section 5. The bringing together of separate strands in the work is intentional, but may present difficulties at first. It is also important, however, because the human relations aspect has to be sustained whatever the pressures and demands of the communications aspect. Even in a committee where the chairman is running the meeting inefficiently, a member who tries to put him right will do more by kindness and tact than by trying to lay the law down. Also, the simulations develop in complexity because that brings them nearer to real life, and while only one participant will be speaking at a time, the depth and perception of the listeners' attention are vital parts of their communicative ability. It is just as important to be communicated with as it is to do the communicating.

5 Meetings

Those who cannot remember the past are condemned to repeat it.

Santayana

5.1 Meetings are gatherings of people. There are very many different kinds of meeting, but they fall into two broad categories – the one-off and the serial. One-off meetings include occasional public lectures, gatherings to say farewell to a retiring colleague, some kinds of election campaign meetings, and the like. Serial meetings are those which bring a group together more than once – groups like committees, councils, working parties, study-groups, boards of governors, and so on. It is with this latter kind that we are concerned here.

5.2 Order

5.2.1 Meetings of groups which meet more than once take place to serve the interests of a group or society, to solve a problem, or initiate and carry through some kind of group action. Even in the most closely knit group, there are bound to be differences of opinion, and in some groups there may be sharply conflicting views. Pursuing a group's purposes often requires a very strong sense of order. People are forgetful of facts, they get carried away, they cannot understand other opinions, or they cannot see the wood for the trees. So even in the most unlikely groups the possibility of conflict has to be catered for. The seemingly very formal arrangements which exist for the conduct of meetings are fundamentally devices for the control of conflict.

5.2.2 The purposes and nature of meetings vary. Some are formal, others very informal. Some such meetings are advisory, others are there to reach decisions. Some meetings occur all too regularly, others only occasionally. All meetings, however, need a framework which most participants know, and which newcomers can quickly learn. Beyond this, a number of meetings take place to conduct business which has some legal force, and in such cases it is necessary, in law, for the *basis*, *conduct*, and *record* of a meeting to be valid. Whether for legal purposes or not, these three requirements underly all meetings.

5.3 Principles of Meetings

5.3.1 First of all, a meeting must be properly *convened*. That means several things. The person who calls the meeting must have authority to do so, either as its chairman or as the secretary of the group concerned, or in accordance with a written constitution. The people entitled to attend it must know of the meeting, its time, place, and business, with reasonable notice. The person convening a meeting is usually responsible, too, for arranging accommodation for it and for circulating in good time any necessary documents. He is also responsible, as a rule, for preparing the agenda.

5.3.2 Secondly, a meeting requires to be properly conducted. It is a convention that everyone who speaks at a formal meeting addresses the chair. This often sounds stuffy and pretentious but the alternatives are not workable. If members of a meeting addressed one another, there would be no way of preventing the development of arguments or even abuse. In theory, indeed, nobody speaks at a formal meeting without the chairman's permission, and it is good meeting manners to indicate that you wish to speak and wait for the chairman to name you as the next person to speak. (Failure to use naming in this way is probably the most general weakness in chairmanship.) Such a practice retains in the hands of the chair the initiative in limiting or extending a discussion, and gives the chairman complete power to refuse to recognise a speaker, and to discipline him if he speaks without being recognised. Most meetings in England have a very strong intuitive belief that in matters of order and discipline the chairman must always be supported.

5.3.3 The proper conduct of a meeting requires the use of an agenda, a list of the items of business. This should usually be written, and if members do not have a copy of it the agenda should be read to them at the start. The agenda of a formal meeting will begin with apologies for absence, and approve or amend the minutes of the previous meeting (nowadays usually circulated in advance). It is usual for 'matters arising' to come next, and chairmen vary in their willingness to let this item wander. The good chairman will insist beforehand that the main agenda include most of the items likely to come up under 'matters arising', and will also insist that they come up in their proper place. A member bent on manipulating a meeting to push through a decision may bring up a string of small matters as technically 'arising' from the minutes in order to delay the conduct of business: his aim may be to ensure that only his supporters remain when 'Any other business' is reached. Firm chairmanship will see through such methods. (See Assignments C1 and D1.)

5.3.4 If officers have to be appointed, this item comes after Matters Arising, followed by the business in a logical order. The arrangement of the agenda is the Secretary's job, but in controversial matters he will consult with the chairman before circulating it.

5.3.5 The conduct of a meeting will usually depend on the rules and, more important, the customs of the body concerned. These vary so much that it is impossible to generalise, but it is foolish to regard a very formal procedure as the only correct one. Some organisations have sets of standing orders, and a chairman can often fall back on them to maintain order if he needs to. But a skilful chairman will avoid being as formal as that if he can.

5.3.6 There are three rules which are, however, almost universal.

1. Members of a meeting address the chairman, not each other directly, and usually do so by 'style and title' – i.e. by 'Mr Wilkinson' rather than by 'Joe there'. Any member of a meeting can modify its discussion by the way he uses names in referring to other members.

2. If a formal motion or resolution is proposed and seconded, it must be put in writing before being voted on, but if an amendment is proposed and seconded, the amendment must be voted on first.

3. A matter of procedure, when raised in the form of 'a point of order', and a question of fact, when raised as 'a point of information' have priority over other business. A good chairman may have to watch for abuse of this rule, and an example occurs in Assignment D1.

5.3.7 A meeting does not have to reach all its decisions by taking votes. Some meetings, notably Quaker business ones, reach their decisions by seeking and obtaining unanimity. Many well-run committees reach decisions by verbal assent, under chairmen who have a sensitive awareness of the 'sense of the meeting', but this power can be abused and some chairmen may push decisions through on that basis as a way of avoiding a formal vote.

5.3.8 Perhaps the commonest weakness of committees is that of going on discussing a particular item for too long. If a chairman allows this, it is always open to a member to move 'that the matter be put'; if this motion is seconded and approved the chairman must then close the item with a vote. In many cases chairmen welcome the support that comes from such motions. Where a committee vote is a tie, and there must be a decision, a chairman has a casting vote: that is, even if he has already voted as a member of the committee, he has a second vote as chairman to break the tie.

5.4 Minutes

5.4.1 The third basic requirement of a meeting is that its work be recorded. Such a record of a meeting is known as its 'minutes', a usage which goes back to the practice of recording each separate decision in a very terse summary of the reasoning behind it, known as a minute. (This usage of the term Minute continues to this day in the Civil Service.)

Minutes vary according to their context and purpose, but should follow the order of items in the agenda unless that is deliberately changed. In general, minutes do not seek to summarise everything that is said, unless the participants are representatives and need to be able to show their own constituents what they have said. Minutes should always record the meeting's decisions, but how far they go beyond this to summarise reasons or lines of argument is a matter for individual custom. Where a meeting hears a detailed briefing, it is best to summarise this in a separate document attached to the minutes. It is also quite common for meetings to become rather untidy and get agenda items confused, and in such circumstances the writer of the minutes has a duty to do some tidying up.

5.4.2 Minutes recording a meeting's decisions are usually recorded in the plural or in the passive: 'We have considered . . . and decide that . . .' or 'It was felt that . . .' or 'Mr So-and-so's request for such-and-such was agreed.' There is an example of this in Assignment B1 page 47.

5.5 Alternatives to Minutes

5.5.1 There are many different kinds of meetings, and those which need a formal procedure and minutes are a minority of them. A group which comes together, for example, to be briefed by a colleague, or issued with new instructions, or rebuked for a poor performance, is likely to have its structure and procedure already 'built in' by the authority relationships and the status of the person calling the meeting. In such cases the taking of minutes is superfluous, but a note for the file about what happened is a precaution taken by many senior staff.

6   Telecommunication

I do not mind lying, but I hate inaccuracy.
Samuel Butler

6.1 *Telos* is an ancient Greek word meaning 'distant'. It has been used in this century as a prefix in words describing many devices for communication over long distances – television, telegraph, teleprinter, telescope, and so on. It is easy to take telecommunications equipment for granted, but there are distinct skills in using some of it, skills that need development and practice as much as any other technique in communication.

6.1.1 The commonest piece of telecommunications equipment in the business world is the telephone, but organisations are also making increased use of Telex machines. These means of communication are as efficient as their users, and no more. Their users can also make them either relatively cheap or quite astonishingly expensive. In all telecommunication the key to efficient and economical use is preparation: you need to be adequately prepared, which means being ready either to talk or to leave a message.

6.2   Telephones

6.2.1 It is difficult to imagine business life without the telephone, but many people use it badly. It is easy to forget that if you were to read aloud a full page of this textbook over the telephone in the peak-rate period you might well spend more money than the cost of the whole book.

6.2.2 The telephone is a means of oral communication only. The other person cannot see you. It makes a great deal of difference, then, if the other person already knows you. Speaking for the first time to a stranger calls for a slow and careful approach: he may need to hear your name twice, will need time to get used to your accent and voice, and will certainly need to hear some explanation of who and what you are and why you are seeking to speak with him. In all this you do not have the advantage of face-to-face contact: you cannot see one another's eyes and facial expressions. The human voice can be a very flexible instrument in making up for these missing features, but its ability to behave in that way is much greater if it is relaxed. Any telephone call to or from a stranger begins with marked uncertainty on both sides. The caller has a duty to try to reduce that uncertainty, by establishing links (such as mutual concerns or acquaintances) and above all by stating his business clearly.

6.2.3 A telephone is technically a microphone, and its mouthpiece is a sensitive instrument which connects directly to the other person's earpiece. Speaking too loudly can cause discomfort, and speaking too close to the microphone can blur your message. Loudspeaker systems in public places are very often abused by the announcer speaking too close to the microphone, particularly on railway stations, where the blurring of the sound actually makes worse the problem the user is trying to solve.

6.2.4 Consider for a moment, if you are a regular user of the telephone, the way in which you identify yourself. Most users do this in one way when initiating the call and in another way when answering one. The rules of good manners lead some to feel they must start, when initiating a call, with 'Good morning' or some familiar formula. In general, business practice has moved away from this. When answering calls on behalf of an organisation you may have special instructions, but even here the financial factor has a bearing: a PBX operator who daily places two hundred calls in the peak-rate period will save the employer several hundred pounds a year by dropping the 'Good morning'. In answering calls on an office telephone, the freedom to say simply 'Hello' is a privilege for the very senior member of staff. It is now almost universal to name the department, and at the more senior levels to give one's name and department. Whichever you do, the voice-quality you use for this opening response may make a great deal of difference to the rest of your call.

6.2.5 An office telephone should always have a note-pad by it: a telephone is not a tape-recorder. If a message has to be taken, however, it is expensive and unnecessary to try to write it down, while listening, in the form in which it will be passed to the recipient: get the message down in rough, and write it out after the call. Messages arise because the person being sought is not at the telephone at the time, and it is not good practice to leave a telephone 'off the hook' in order to look for him. For one thing it may not succeed; it is (again) expensive; someone else may simply hang up; or the instrument will pick up other conversations taking place.

6.2.6 One aspect of telephone usage is the answering machine. It is not difficult for a college to set up a simple set of tape recorders which will serve as answering machines to practise on. Even if the device is unfamiliar, it is perfectly straightforward—provided the caller has prepared his message. If a response from such a machine comes as a surprise, it is usually wiser to ring off, prepare the message to dictate to the machine, and ring again. Here, too, the need for very clear statement of who you are is obvious, but there is no need to shout at an answering machine as many people do.

6.3 Telex

6.3.1 Many large organisations now rent Telex installations from the Post Office. Such machines transmit written messages typed out on the transmitting keyboard, and the receiving machine types them out in duplicate. Like photocopying machines, Telex machines need to be switched on, need filling with paper, and require periodic maintenance. ('Telex' is in fact a brand name, but like 'Hoover' the brand name has come to be used for the type of machine.)

6.3.2 There are two ways of using Telex:
1. direct transmission, i.e. typing your message through the keyboard. As the user pays for the time the machine is transmitting, most firms which rent Telex machines limit their use to quick and accurate typists;
2. tape transmission, whereby the typist or other user can type the message on a tape which is later run through the machine. The preparation of the tape may take as long as it needs without using the costly transmission time until it is ready.

6.3.3 Telex communication is one-way-only: it will not answer questions, or ask for clarification of them, so messages have to be explicit. It operates round-the-clock, which enables the user to send messages anywhere in the world without disturbing anyone's sleep. Telex messages are recorded in written form in the language of transmission, which forestalls the problems posed by recipients who may not be proficient in the sender's language.

6.4 Telegrams and Cables

6.4.1 The telegram is based, historically, on the use of Morse code for transmission over land lines or by radio. For that reason early cables were priced by the letter, but commercial convenience soon brought in a price structure based on so much per word. Modern technology has made other forms of communication cheaper and more generally available as more and more people have access to telephones. The greetings telegram endured for social reasons, but skilful use of telegraphic English is not called for very often. It is often thought that all one has to do is omit words, but changes in word order can save many more words. Or, in telegraphese, 'Word order changes cheaper than deletions'. It is often a useful exercise to work out a telegraphic version of a summary. One for this paragraph might run 'Telephonic developments made telegrams uneconomic'.

7 Writing reports

'Then you should say what you mean!' the March Hare went on. 'I do,' Alice hastily replied. 'At least—at least I mean what I say—that's the same thing, you know.' 'Not the same thing a bit!' said the Hatter.

Alice in Wonderland

7.1 Whole courses are conducted about report-writing, and there are textbooks on the subject. Most laymen, and a large number of businessmen, believe that learning to write reports is a very simple art which anyone can learn. This down-to-earth view is attractive, but we do not think it is quite true. Within an individual firm, or within a single government department for example, it will usually be possible to lay down the rules for report-writing in that one institution. But the reports governed by such rules are already specialised, dealing with a known range of problems. (As a matter of historical fact, the traditional report format which many textbooks put forward originated in just that way—in the Indian Civil Service early in the nineteenth century.) The problem with report-writing as a general technique is that the form and layout of a report needs to serve the report's purposes, and those purposes will depend on its content, context, and readership.

7.1.1 Our aim in this section is to explain why reports are a fact of business life and what factors influence how they should be written. We seek to distinguish between certain categories of report, and to define what kinds of document can or cannot properly be called reports. We then explain the way in which the type of report and its readership govern the structure of what is written.

7.2 Basic Features

7.2.1 To begin with practical realities, reports in business do not just happen; they are asked for. Anyone who writes a report does so in reply to an instruction, as part of a routine, or because the situation he is placed in makes it necessary or desirable. Any report must meet two fundamental requirements:
1. The recipient must be free to use it – e.g. to cite it, quote from it, or send it to a colleague.
2. The text must distinguish clearly between objective fact, personal opinion or judgement, advice, proposal, and surmise.

7.2.2 The first of these requirements creates a problem for the writer: he may not know who else, besides the original recipient, may see the text. This means that he may not be able to judge what assumptions to make about the readers he is writing for. It is always necessary to make an informed guess about this element, and many of the assignments in this book provide tasks in which the discussion of such questions enables the student to learn how to make such judgements independently.

7.2.3 In most practical circumstances the problem is relatively easy to solve. A report written in an electronics firm can assume a knowledge of technical terms like 'transistor' and 'impedance'. One written about a theatre for the benefit of a producer can refer to 'the flies' and know that the reader understands the term. But there are conditions where the judgement is much harder to make. An example is in writing for elected members of councils and committees in local government, who have to be assumed to be laymen in technical matters but are very sensitive about being patronised. This example underlines the need to make a conscious decision about the audience for which a report is being written.

7.2.4 The second basic feature is important because the reader of a report is entitled to know the status of each part that he reads. If an expression of opinion is located in otherwise factual material, it may be understood as fact. If the writer is later asked to provide evidence, it may be embarrassing to be able to provide none. If the writer has made clear that the point is a matter of opinion, his opinion is likely to be treated with whatever respect the rest of the report earns for him. The same applies to judgements which are not entirely opinions but which rely on the writer's well-informed experience and ability to analyse the evidence collated.

7.2.5 The central difficulty in learning to write reports is that most reports in business life are written by people who are in a position very different from students. They are writing about what they know or have access to, whereas students may not be. In particular, they know more than the reader for whom they are writing. In trying to simulate report-writing for students, it is easy to fall into the trap of asking students to write about material of which they know little, for the benefit of people who know it better, and so place the emphasis purely on the format. In the assignments in this book we have tried to avoid this, by providing a great deal of material to process, and by proposing readers who will not know about it. That is why the information given in the assignment, and the nature of the audience for whom each report is to be written, are set out in some detail.

7.3 What is NOT a Report?

There are many writing activities which are sometimes called reports, but which we prefer to identify by more precise labels. Students and teachers will be able to suggest others, but the three most common examples are:

1. Confirmations: decisions made or agreements reached at interviews or in conversations frequently have to be recorded, often in some detail, very shortly afterwards, partly to make sure they are not forgotten or obscured. Letters of confirmation are quite straightforward. The written 'note for the file' which records or summarises an oral exchange is in this book called a Note for File.

2. References: sometimes a superior says something like this: 'Joe Harter is applying for promotion and I need an up-date on his record. Would you do me a report, please?' A personnel assessment or staff appraisal document is a distinct activity in its own right, and it calls for special experience and some training. It is a dangerous fallacy to suppose that skill in writing reports automatically constitutes the ability to make such assessments.

3. Position statements: the same kind of request is often made about recently installed machinery, or the progress of an innovation. Such a request has two distinctive characteristics: the answer is most unlikely to go further than the person seeking it, and it would be ridiculous to go into the history of the matter since the recipient already knows it. Such a document is in many industrial firms handled by using a standardised form, and is best called a Position Statement, not a report.

There are several examples of confirmatory Notes for File in the assignments in this book. Personnel references are proposed in a smaller number of tasks, and are given with as much relevant detail as possible in order to allow discussion of the pitfalls of writing such items. Position-statements, like the forms on which they are often recorded, depend entirely on the technicalities of the workshops or offices in which they arise, and so cannot be treated in this book.

7.4 Types of Report

There are three main categories of report to consider.

7.4.1 *Informing reports* arise in the context of sequences of events where an individual carries out business for a superior and is required to inform him of progress, or to inform him of specific events if they occur. The writer and the reader share very similar degrees of knowledge of the contextual detail. The provision of the report is a matter either of periodic routine or of the reporting officer's initiative. His means of knowing what is contained in the report is taken for granted. The document contains only the barest essentials of what the recipient needs to know and does not know already, and the reporting officer can assume that if any decision arises his superior will not need or want advice in the form of recommendations.

For examples of assignment tasks which illustrate this and other categories of report, see the Table on p. 22.

7.4.2 *Briefing reports* arise when someone requires fuller information on a topic or problem, either for his own use or for the benefit of specified others, and commissions a junior to produce it. Here the writer can assume that his reader knows something of the topic and wants to know more. The provision of the report is a response to a request, which will be mentioned at the start. The means by which the writer knows the material contained in the report is of no great concern to the reader, since his designation of the writer to do the job carries an assumption that the writer would know how to proceed. The main substance of the report is thus a carefully organised presentation of the information requested. The organisation entails, as in all kinds of report, a clear indication of the dominant points, a clear articulation of subsidiary points to the main ones, and a segmenting or cutting up of the text to highlight these relative degrees of importance. The use of layout devices like paragraph numbering and indentation will serve the same purpose. The writer of such a report is asked to provide information, and is thus not expected to offer recommendations or even, unless asked for them, conclusions. If the information is of any length, say more than two sides of typescript, he would be wise to provide a summary, or synopsis.

7.4.3 *Advisory reports.* A specific issue or set of issues arises, on which an expert is called upon to marshal the relevant factual information, some of which may not be already known, and to make a considered assessment of its significance, leading to the appropriate advice. Here it is assumed from the start that the writer knows (or will find out) more than his intended readership, and in practice his readership is likely to be extensive (if only because advisory reports are usually internally commissioned or paid for in some way). Hence the report is being written for comparative laymen – but only comparative: they are not such ignorant people that they have not known whom to ask for the report. A report in these circumstances cannot begin by alluding to 'Your memo of. . .': it has to state explicitly why it is being written – that is, to give its terms of reference. For the same reasons, it has to state explicitly what the writer had to do in order to write the report: it must give its Procedure. It is often convenient to merge Terms of Reference and Procedure into a single section labelled Introduction. The factual information on which the report's advice is to be based has to be given in such a way as to carry the reader's thinking through to the later sections, and must be free from unidentified personal opinions or surmises. This central element in an advisory report is usually labelled as 'Findings'. The Findings lead logically to a set of Conclusions, which should be brief, and the writer then has to earn his keep by committing himself to the advice he has been called in to provide: his Recommendations.

7.4.4 The Table on page 22 sets all this out in a schematic form, but it cannot be overstressed that writing reports is not a matter of observing the right formula, or indeed any formula. The solution to Task 1 in Assignment A1 is an example of an Informing Report. In Assignment C1, the solution offered for Task 2 is an example of a Briefing Report. The difference between the two is one of scale, degree of detail, and the status of the writer.

7.4.5 There is a qualification to make about the format of Advisory Reports. The use of the section headings given in the Table is called for only in reports of some size. In shorter reports it is neither necessary nor desirable to

Basic features of the main types of written report

Features	Informing Reports	Briefing Reports	Advisory Reports (by experts)	Advisory Reports (student work)
Assumptions made about reader(s)	Relevant knowledge fully shared with writer	Some shared knowledge and desire to know more	Little specialist knowl. Rdrs. likely to be laymen and numerous	Text to be treated as a public document
Basis of writer's response	Routine, or specific request (which should be referred to).	Date, form, nature of request to be specified	Reason and background to be given as *Terms of Reference* or *Introduction*	Merge into a brief *Introduction*
Procedural aspect	Taken for granted	Writer is assumed to have or to have obtained the required material	Method of working to be given as *Procedure* or in *Introduction*	
Main Substance	Barest essentials. Abbreviation likely.	Information to be given in a sequence which can be followed	Material to be set out in numbered sections, each with a heading. Note-form layout permissible. To be headed *Facts* or *Findings*	To be headed *The Facts*
To be kept apart from Substance	Implications and opinions	Judgements or inferences	Opinions, surmise, conclusions, suggested action	As for other types
Outcomes	Implications may be added if situation so suggests	Brief summary including *Conclusions*	*Conclusions* — i.e. what the facts signify for the given readership. What the readership is to do about them should be set out separately, i.e. as *Recommendations*	To be headed *Conclusions* and kept brief
				If required, to be given briefly as *Recommendations*
Tasks to which answers would be examples:	B8 Task 1 D4 Task 2 D3 Task 3	A8 Task 3 C3 Task 1 C4 Task 3	C5 Task 2 D3 Task 1 D7 All	

use them as headings, although they can be very useful indeed as a guide to the writer in arranging material.

7.4.6 There is nothing sacred about the format of Advisory Reports given in these pages (or in any other textbook). The purpose of a format is to facilitate communication, and the format should never be allowed to get in the way. The layout in five parts (Terms of Reference, Procedure, Findings, Conclusions, and Recommendations) was originally devised as a guide for junior members of the Indian Civil Service in the early 19th century. It was passed on, down the generations, in the field manuals of the armed forces. However, until you are writing reports rather larger in scale than anything expected in this book, you would do well to use a simpler structure:

Introduction (combining terms of reference and procedure)

The Facts

Conclusions

Recommendations (if called for).

It is a useful exercise to try to do as many administrators have to do in practice; express the Introduction in one sentence, the Facts in (at most) two sentences, and the Conclusions and Recommendations in one sentence each. The result would be a single paragraph in which the taut structure is the more effective for not being immediately obvious.

7.5 Reports and Audiences

7.5.1 Any report, then, of whatever kind, needs to set out to communicate first, and worry about how well dressed it is afterwards. Obviously, if the situation is one where the likely readers of your document will not know what you are talking about, you have to write differently. As the Table suggests, the essential difference between this version and the previous one is in the amount of knowledge it takes for granted in the reader.

7.6 The substance of reports

7.6.1 This section has been about *writing* reports and how to organise the written document. More important and often more difficult is the business of preparing the material to be written. All serious report writing entails some process of investigation. How well you do the job depends above all else on your ability to ask questions which the brief or instruction does not spell out for you. The good investigator frames his own questions as well as reports the answers efficiently.

7.6.2 For example, in The Office Garden (A1), there are some questions about the under-gardener which are not spelled out for you. If the contract is accepted, what happens to him? If he is made redundant, the cost of his redundancy compensation has to be added in to the cost of taking the contract-gardening option. The investigator establishes the boy's wages, his length of service, and, from these facts, estimates his probable compensation. The skilful investigator will see this in advance, and by putting a figure on the compensation will keep a minor issue in proper proportion.

8 Memoranda

'The horror of that moment', the King went on, 'I shall never, *never* forget!'

'You will, though,' the Queen said, 'If you don't make a memorandum of it.'

Alice in Wonderland

8.1

```
MEMORANDUM

To:   Expert on business communication
From: Curious student    (Ref.A62/C9)

Subject:  Memoranda

Would you give me some simple advice on how
and how not to write memoranda, please.
```

8.2

```
MEMORANDUM                              FOR        PLEASE

FROM: Authors of People in Touch    ACTION     DISPLAY
                                    COMMENT     FILE
TO:   Readers of People in Touch    INFORMATION RETURN
                                    DISCUSSION  PASS TO:
DATE: February 1st, 19--                        ........
REF:- A62/C9.

SUBJECT: Nature and layout of memoranda.
```

1. Thank you for your undated note (ref.A62/C9) asking for guidance.

2. You will find the guidance you need in this memorandum, which is set out in accordance with the relevant rules. To make matters clearer, the rules are pointed out in a set of notes given below.

3. In order to write a memorandum successfully you need both (a) to understand the relevant rules
               (b) to apply them, if necessary adapt them, to the specific situation giving rise to the memo.

4. Please now write me a memorandum about an interesting item in this morning's post which shows me that you have now learned how to write a memorandum. This should reach me by tomorrow, February 2nd.

                    PCLS.

8.3   Notes on 8.2

FROM comes before TO, horizontally or vertically. DATE is essential, preferably in 'full' form. RECIPIENT'S REFERENCE if there is one. The order of items is constant:

1 From	5 Subject or brief title
2 To	6 Content
3 Date	7 Signature
4 Reference if any	

The content should include four elements:
1 A tie-in or link: the opening sentence should normally refer to a previous document, etc.;
2 What the writer wants known or done;
3 What the reader needs, as information or guidance, in order to do it or learn it;
4 A deadline for response.

Indicators: some memo-forms include a set of instruction terms. Some of these tell the reader what he is to do about the memo or the document attached to it. Some of them tell him what, if anything, he is to do with the piece of paper the memo is written on. Good memorandum forms keep these two kinds of indicator separate.

8.4   Further Examples

8.4.1   An example of a routine request to a superior:

```
From:    P R Johnson
To:      Manager, Finance Department

Date:    February 20, 19--

Subject: Leave of Absence
```

I am sorry to have to request leave of absence for half a day over and above the usual allowance of day-release. However, Standford College of Further Education is setting a complete 'mock' or trial examination for my HNC course, which cannot be conducted within the day of release, and the College insists that students take it. The half-day concerned is the afternoon of Thursday, February 28th. I am quite ready to make up the lost time by voluntary over-time if you wish.

            (Signature)

8.4.2   An example of a routine memorandum about a document unintentionally mis-directed:

```
From:    Purchasing Manager
To:      Finance Section (ref. PRJ/HG)

Date:    February 21, 19--

Subject: Invoices for Sanitary Fittings
```

I acknowledge receipt of your note attaching a set of nine invoices for purchases of washbasins and similar items. I did not initiate this purchase, but the Plant Maintenance Manager does his own purchasing of items, since my brief extends to purchasing only materials for use in production. I have passed your note and attachments to Mr Helpston.

            (Signature)

8.4.3   These two examples call for little comment. The request for leave of absence is accompanied by a tactful gesture to work off the time, but the purpose of it is to elicit an unambiguous ruling as to whether or not the leave has to count against the employee's holiday allowance. The second example is intended not to tell the recipient that the papers have been passed on, or to whom, since he will find that out soon enough. Rather, it is intended to explain the way the boundary between one kind of purchasing and another is drawn, so that the Finance Section does not repeat the mistake.

9 Notes

Notes are often necessary, but they are
necessary evils.

Samuel Johnson

This section is about how to lay out and write
notes for your own use. Since the essence of
the matter is the use of note-form, it is set out
in note-form.

1. NOTE-FORM: a graphic, i.e. <u>visual</u>, device
for setting down two features of information
more prominently than continuous prose can do:
    (a) the order of the parts
    (b) the relative importance of different
          parts

2. VISUAL PRESENTATION is achieved by layout
as well as the language, by
    (a) using sequences of numbers and
          letters to point up the serial
          relationships between items
    (b) using different sequences at
          different levels of importance so
          that
          (i) minor items are not confused
               with major ones
          (ii) items on the same level are
               visibly associated.

3. NUMBERING can be done in one of two ways:
    (a) using the pattern used on this page,
          which alternates numbers and letters
          (this section is thus 3 (a), and
          could be sub-divided further, e.g.
          into 3 (a) (i) etc.)
    (b) using numbers only, in the manner
          adopted for the rest of the
          introductory Guide in this book.

4. LAYOUT has a clear set of conventions:
    (a) where the pattern on this page is
          used, each step down in the
          numbering entails a further indent
          of the left-hand margin, so that
          (i) the items which belong on a
               particular level of
               importance can always be
               seen by position as well as
               by numbering
          (ii) the relationship of the items
               in a set to the set above and
               the sets below is always
               clear.

5. OPTIONAL features may be numerous. Within
the general pattern set out here, skilled note-
makers add many other devices:
    (a) note-fm allows wrtr to abbrev.,
          omit wds, use private shorthand,
          etc, BUT
          (i) private abbreviations may be
               forgotten
          (ii) they won't be accessible to
               others
          (iii) if taken down at speed they
               may need tidying-up
               immediately afterwards.
    (b) skilled note-makers can make
          extensive use of special punct.
          marks such as ** ?? ?! CAPS
          <u>underlining</u>
    (c) But the range of optional features
          does NOT extend to ignoring the
margin indentations (as this line does)

6. PUNCTUATION in notes is largely
unnecessary, since the layout is intended to
do the same job. Quotations, however, are an
exception. For similar reasons it is a good
habit to underline titles of books and
references to important sources such as case
law.

7. DICTATED NOTES are a contradiction in terms.
The term usually means, simply, dictation.

8. ORDER is vital to successful note making.
Some hints:
    (a) if a lecturer goes too fast, or
          seems to, you may be trying to note
          down too much of the material;
    (b) it is worth looking carefully at
          the notes made by an older student who
          does them well;
          (c) it is important not to wander
               about the page as this section
does.
    (d) good note-taking needs time and
          practice to learn.
    (e) Most notes need adding to or
          amending sooner or later.
          So give yourself and your later
          reader plenty of space up and down
          the page until you are really in
          command of the technique.

Assignments – Group A

A1 – The Office Garden

You work in a trainee administrative capacity with a commercial firm. Its Accounts, Sales, and Purchasing offices are housed in a Victorian villa which was originally a private house and has gardens of just over an acre. The warehouse, transport, and branch management staffs are housed elsewhere on a trading estate. The grounds of the house have been maintained for many years by a gardener and assistant, but the head gardener has announced his intention to retire. Your immediate superior, the office manager, who is new to the job, has suggested that you look into the merits of replacing the head gardener as compared with the use of a contract gardening firm of the sort which deals with the similar site next door, where a major insurance company has a computing division.

Task 1

In the course of investigation you discover the facts and figures given below. Work out the annual cost of employing the gardening staff, with overheads, and **present a short report** which sets the options before your superior as fairly as possible.

(a) P & A Gardens Ltd, which operates next door, has submitted estimate as follows:
Full maintenance of site to existing standards, inclusive of replacement planting, mowing, weeding, edge-trimming, pruning, fertilisers, maintenance of fencing, and all routine sundries:
£4,175 plus VAT, subject to annual review.

(b) Current costs of employing own staff:

Head gardener	£42.50 per wk
Boy assistant (17½)	£26.50 per wk
Luncheon vouchers for above	£160.00 p.a. approx
Maintenance of tools & eqpt	£36.00 p.a.
Equipment (mtce & deprec.)	£190.00 p.a.
New plants, shrubs, bulbs etc.	£80.00 p.a. approx
Employment & admin overhead	£550 p.a. (estimate)
Share of direct costs (toilets, canteen, etc.) @ £50 per head	£100.00 p.a.

Suggested solution to Task 1

```
From:      Administrative Assistant
To:        Office Manager

Subject:   Maintenance of Grounds
```

1. Further to your note requesting a comparison of the present arrangements with a contract gardening firm, I can now report the figures given below.

2. (a) Schedule of current costs:

```
     Staff  Head Gardener's salary            £2,210
            Non-contr.pension   12½%             276
            Assistant's wages                  1,378
            Luncheon vouchers                    160
                                              ───────
                                                          4,024

     Equipment
            Replacement & depreciation           190
            Maintenance                           36
            Plants, bulbs, fertilisers, etc.      80
                                              ───────
                                                            306

     Employment Overhead & direct costs                    650

     Total                                                4,980
                                                          =====

     (b)  Lowest of three estimates obtained:
     P & A Gardens Ltd:  contract price       £4,175
                         VAT @ 8%                334
                                              ───────
                                                          4,509
     Net redundancy cost (under-gardener)
                                                             60
                                              ───────
                           TOTAL
                                                          4,569
                                                          =====
```

3. Other factors.
The balance between the two is relatively close. I have received indications from Shieldsure Insurance Ltd that they are well satisfied with P & A Gardens Ltd's fulfilment of the current contract next door. I am uncertain whether it is correct practice to apply the employment overhead in this instance, as is done in assessing the costs of additional clerical staff, but the Gardener and his Assistant receive the full benefit of payment of wages, calculation of taxation, pension, holiday pay, use of toilet, canteen, and recreation facilities, and the company's medical care provision.

4. Conclusion.
Subject to assurances from the prospective contractor, it would seem slightly to our advantage to employ them.

Notes on Task 1

Recipient and Sender identified by title. In practice this report would be dated at the head. Likewise, the Office Manager's note mentioned in (1) would have its date given.

There is no merit, in a short Informing Report of this kind, in avoiding the first-person pronoun.

2. The schedule of current costs is contrasted with the contract estimate, and each is thus given a main sub-heading as (a) and (b)

respectively. Within (a), there are three main components, which could be similarly numbered as (i), (ii), etc., but this would be unduly fussy here, since the layout of the figures can do the same job effectively. The schedule follows standard accounting practice in presenting totals of sub-sections one column to the right. The two sum-totals to be compared are underlined accordingly.

3. The writer cannot quantify the value of the contract and furnishes what evidence is available. His other qualification to the figures given belongs in the same paragraph because the function of (3) is to record those aspects of the matter where the figures may not tell the whole story.

4. A recommendation is not specifically asked for, but it is a reasonable assumption that the recipient of this particular document would expect its writer to take some view of the matter.

Task 2

After you have submitted your report, George Grantley intervenes. He is the firm's personnel officer, a former assistant sales manager who has never really forgiven the firm for moving him into a job he regards as superfluous. Unknown to the Office Manager, Grantley has always treated the office gardens as his personal pride and joy, and in his previous job at the house was in fact responsible for them. Nobody has told him that they are now in the care of the new Office Manager, and his irascible temperament does not take kindly to the rumours he has heard. He rings you up from the trading estate site and refuses to listen to any explanation. He tells you quite simply to send him a copy of your report, explain why you wrote it, and adds 'And if you are thinking of changing the system I ran for over twenty years your reasons had better be good ones.' The Office Manager, on being consulted, says that he has to play it carefully: it is not worth alienating Grantley, who is senior to him, but he wants you to **write a covering note** for his own signature.

Suggested Solution to Task 2

```
From:     Office Manager, Grange Road
To:       Personnel Officer

Subject:  Maintenance of Grange Road Grounds

Thank you for your interest in this problem,
which I had not known about until now, and
which my assistant has mentioned.  Perhaps I
should explain that his balance between using
a contractor and going on with our own staff is
very close, so I would welcome your views.  The
figures are set out in the attached note.

The reasons for considering a contractor
seriously are clear enough.  We live in very
uncertain times, and as you know we are
required to scrutinise every post when it
becomes vacant because the costs of redundancy
and redeployment are now so high.  Secondly,
there was reason to believe that a contract
might well be a good deal cheaper.  As the note
shows, if one includes the employment
overhead this turns out not to be the case.
I am as concerned as you are, of course, to
ensure that if we do change to a contractor we
continue to provide the amenities we have
enjoyed until now.
```

Notes on Task 2

This is a memorandum, because it is internal to the firm. It deals with an angry intrusion by appearing to welcome the intruder's interest, and at the same time removes the pressure from the Office Manager's Assistant by taking responsibility. It departs from logical sequence in order to emphasize the writer's recognition of Grantley's concern. It goes on, with a tact which is not as hypocritical as it might appear, to invite Grantley's views – because such an invitation obliges Grantley to express them with moderation and to focus on the real issue rather than on the personal factors. It also makes it more likely that Grantley will be less hostile to whatever decision is ultimately reached. The note ends with a perfectly genuine assertion that the Office Manager and Mr Grantley have the same ends in mind.

Task 3

Grantley accepts the report, rather surprisingly. But he insists that the matter go before the firm's Administration Committee. This is chaired by the Managing Director, who has a rule that its agenda must be on a single page, with the essential substance of the point at issue under each item set down in a single paragraph of not more than 120 words. **Write the agenda item.**

Suggested Solution to Task 3

```
Administration Committee

Agenda item 4:
Maintenance of grounds, Grange Road site.
The 1-acre grounds at the Grange Road offices
have hitherto been maintained by employing our
own staff and equipment, under the supervision
of Mr Grantley until the Office Manager was
appointed last year.  The gross annual cost in
the last financial year was £4,980.  The
retirement of Mr Grundy, the Head Gardener,
raises the possibility of changing over to a
contract gardening arrangement, which Shieldsure
Insurance on the next-door site have used
satisfactorily for the last two years.  The
firm concerned has submitted the lowest of
three estimates, for £4,509 p.a. inclusive
of VAT, subject to annual review.  In the
light of the need to minimise direct-labour
recruitment, the Office Manager recommends the
contract option.
```

Notes on Task 3

The agenda item states the barest essentials of the issue and proposes a decision. The material is given in impersonal terms. Mr Grantley is identified by name because his supervision was a personal matter rather than part of his previous or present posts. The effect of the item as worded is intended:
(a) to enable the committee to decide quickly;
(b) to avoid confusing the committee with the issue of employment overheads;
(c) to enable the chairman to know which member of the committee will speak to the item.

Task 4

The Administration Committee is prepared to approve the use of a contract gardener, but wants assurances that the firm concerned will do the job properly. The Office Manager, who is a member of the committee, comes back and tells you to arrange a meeting with the firm. He also says it will be necessary to press them very hard about the value the company will get for its money, and Grantley will be hard to satisfy. He suggests that you **draw up a list of questions to put**, in the form of an interview-guide.

Suggested Solution to Task 4

Questions for discussion with P & A Gardening Ltd.
1. Frequency of routine visits for mowing etc. in season.
2. Policy on re-planting, considering trees, shrubs, ornamental beds separately.
3. Details of lawn-treatments included in contract.
4. Fertilisers, dressing, pest-control policies.
5. Hedge and fence maintenance. Creosoting?
6. Insurance cover on employees while on site.
7. Prices (if any) for special services such as removing windfall branches, lopping, etc. where not part of contract.
8. Paths and drive?
9. Any equipment to remain on site?
10. Any interest in buying our equipment?
11. Any significant differences from next door?

Notes on Task 4

This is a set of notes-for-own-use. There is nothing in the situation or in any rule-book to dictate the order of such items, but the more practical and immediate questions will naturally come first, and those on which agreement is least likely will be left until agreement has been reached on others. The set of notes is also as exhaustive as possible: it can waste a great deal of time to have to re-convene such meetings because some important issue was overlooked at the time.

A2 – APT Ltd

Read Section 6 of the Guide before attempting this assignment.

Allied Plastic Tubing Ltd, now known as APT, employs a total of 246 people, some 175 of whom are unskilled and semi-skilled manual workers. They are engaged in manufacturing rubber, plastic, and thermoplastic tubing and pipe, in diameters up to 5 cm., and the fittings and joints necessary for systems using the pipe. The firm's most successful line is garden hose-pipe, of which it is one of the four largest producers in the country. A subsidiary plant six miles away makes a patent and very profitable range of links, joints, nozzles and other fittings for the garden trade. The manual operatives are mostly on the day shift (09.00–17.00), but some thirty women work a short-day shift (10.00–15.00), and there is a small shift of 18–20 men who work nights (19.00–06.00) on the continuous process part of the production line.

Eleven weeks ago the firm which delivers APT's basic raw materials suffered a strike of delivery drivers. APT ran out of raw materials within a week, and laid off all the manual operatives except six maintenance men and all the office staff except 26 in the management, accounts, design and sales staff.

The strike has now been settled. The suppliers have informed APT by telephone that normal supplies of raw materials will be resumed within six hours. The raw material store at APT has capacity for four days' deliveries, but the production side will not be able to absorb more than 80% of normal for at least a week.

Work in groups of three or four on the following tasks:

Task 1

Work out the best means of informing employees of the date and time at which each shift will resume work. Assume that the town where the works is located has its own local paper, an evening daily, a local radio station, and a weekly paper published two days after APT is informed of resumption of deliveries. Formulate the text of the announcements to be made in particular media, and of other copy likely to be useful.

Task 2

The sales staff have learned that a small but significant proportion of their customers have switched to competing manufacturers, but most have remained loyal. APT has 220 main regular outlets for its garden products and sixty principal clients in the construction and related industries. Determine the best means of informing these customers of the resumption of work, using different messages for different groups if this seems desirable. **Draft the text of the messages** involved, one of which should be for sending by Telex.

Task 3

During the lay-off, six workers have taken jobs with other employers, but inform APT that they would rather return to their previous work if they can be allowed to work out their notice to the new employer. These employees have been entitled to lay-off pay on production of evidence that they have claimed unemployment benefit, but none of them has claimed. **Discuss** whether they should be allowed to return, or whether their taking other employment constitutes giving notice to APT.

Task 4

Five of APT's manual employees have taken other jobs during the lay-off, and announce that they will not be returning to APT. Technically they have left without giving notice, but their failure to claim lay-off pay has amounted to notice. APT advertises a vacancy for a supervisor, and one of the five, who would certainly have been promoted if he had stayed with APT, applies for the job. **Explore in discussion** the case for and against holding that the applicant's manner of leaving should disqualify him from the appointment.

Task 5

Inspect the available evidence to determine the urgency, or otherwise, with which APT should seek to replace the five who have left.

A3 – Mrs Surtees' Bins

You are a clerk with the Granet Metropolitan District Council, posted to the Engineer's Department to assist with the work involved in organising a new system of polythene liner-bags for dustbins. Each crew of dustmen is adding a quarter of its area each week for a month, to the handful of streets involved in a twelve-month pilot project. The work is a self-contained operation and you work on your own a good deal, referring direct to the Chief Engineer or his deputy when necessary.

One day a Councillor Gooch drops the following letter on your desk, saying 'I think we have heard from this lady before, and if she isn't on plastic bags yet you may want to anticipate any possible trouble.' Mr Gooch is an old and

wily individual: a hint of that sort is usually worth taking.

> 4 Pacific Avenue
> Billinton
> Granet
> June 14th
>
> Dear Mr Gooch,
>
> I really must complain about the dustmen in this area. They have been inconsiderate and un-cooperative for a long time, and I have had to speak to them often about being noisy early in the morning and leaving trails of refuse behind them. This morning I heard a lot of noise, and went out to find they had handled my bin so roughly the bottom fell out. All I got, as usual, was abuse – I can't write what they said. And they wouldn't take the refuse unless I found them another container to put it in.
>
> I know the bin was old, but it was perfectly sound. It is the Council's duty to replace it, and I hope you will support me about it.
>
> Yours sincerely
> B. Surtees (Mrs.)

You check the correspondence files under Complaints and find that Mrs Surtees has written twice before, seven months and eleven months ago, receiving non-commital replies. You check the crew's logs for the past year and find nine entries noting unfriendly exchanges, all of which are noted as started by Mrs Surtees. In every case the crew notes that they have a legitimate complaint against Mrs Surtees: in one instance the refuse included

31

ashes put in the bin immediately before the men called. She had alleged on the first visit of this crew that a new bin had been crushed in the truck's compressor, although it was not visibly damaged. Her refuse had often included a great deal of water. The crew's record had been carefully kept, through three changes of charge-hand. There was no evidence that the crew had allowed a difficult lady's provocation to upset them.

Task 1

Write a brief memorandum to the foreman in charge of the crews, asking for a quotation from the crew's log for June 14th, and for background information on Mrs Surtees. The note should not imply that you or your superiors are taking sides.

Task 2

Draft a reply to Mrs Surtees, which tactfully alludes to a record of strained relationships, expressing confidence in the crew. The letter should indicate that in deciding what they can or cannot take, the crew is obeying its instructions.

Task 3

The plastic bin-liner scheme is due to be extended to Pacific Avenue in ten days' time. The liners are issued free, and householders under the age of 60 are expected to close the bag and leave it at the roadside on the day of collection. Many householders who receive the circular announcing the change will be of limited reading ability, and others will have mixed feelings about local councils. **Write the text of the circular**, which should be friendly in tone, quite clear about the reasons for the scheme, and less than one side of typescript in length.

Task 4

Write a covering letter to Mrs Surtees personally, to seek her co-operation with a scheme designed to avoid several of the problems she has raised – noise, bin-damage, and the like. The letter should make clear that hot ashes will melt the bags and quantities of water would burst them.

Task 5

The Foreman who supplied the information in response to your Memorandum (Task 1) will wish to know what became of the matter. You are not allowed to send a copy of your letter out of the office. You telephone him, but he is out. The depot clerk offers to take a message and the matter does not justify writing a special note. **What do you say by way of a message the clerk can write down?** (See Guide, Section 6.2.)

A4 – The Filing Clerk

You are employed as a filing clerk at the local branch office of Shieldsure Insurance Ltd. This is a national company with offices in most large towns, and its usual practice is to maintain a branch filing room. Each of the main departments (Property, Personal Accident, Pecuniary Loss, Liability) has its own filing clerk who retrieves and replaces files from the Filing Room as may be necessary. Each clerk is trained to use the system of Absent Folder Cards with great care, and each department uses a distinctive colour of card, so that a missing file can always be traced not only to its department but to the member of staff using it.

The four filing clerks work as a service to their own departments, and carry out instructions from appropriate staff in them. In practice the Senior Clerk in each one is the filing clerk's day-to-day superior, but technically they are in the charge of Mrs Grattan, the head of the typing pool. She is a severe and widely feared woman of 55. The Office Manager, Charles Green, is her boss, but he is an unpredictable man who will sometimes meekly do whatever Mrs Grattan asks and at other times stubbornly refuse.

Task 1

Mrs Grattan insists, as a standard procedure which she regards as essential training, that the return of files at the end of the working day be done by first setting the folders to be filed in their proper numerical order. This is so that the clerks can follow one another in an orderly fashion rather than get in each other's way by hopping about from one part of the room to another. A typical day's set of file numbers is given in Document A. **Write down the set of numbers** in correct numerical/alphabetical order.

Document A

a	PE421567H44	m	KH989876B16
b	PA222482J11	n	KM111212D21
c	L962849M28	o	KM111212D19
d	PA222493K10	p	L963849M88
e	PA121888R67	q	BP752725Q64
f	BP725143Q91	r	PA131888P68
g	BP752525M58	s	KH989897M44
h	L964238A20	t	KM112112S25
j	PE863334R78	u	PE421654H38
k	PA222492J12	v	BP752752L12

Task 2

As space in the Filing Room is limited, it is a firm rule that the insertion of papers in files must be done in the departments, not the filing room. One of your fellow clerks is absent, and the stand-in, a typist from the pool who is senior to you, starts doing this work on a pull-out leaf in the filing room. **Discuss how**, if at all, **you should proceed** in such a situation, on the assumption that the typist has flatly rejected your own direct suggestion. Alternatively, **simulate the incident**.

Task 3

One of the claims assistants, a lady in her forties who is clearly senior to you, has developed the habit of coming for a file herself and omitting to leave the Absent Folder Card. She is in your own department and if the file is wanted elsewhere you will be held at fault. You ask Mrs Robinson to use the card, but she replies 'But the card is only a way of telling you what file I want, and you take so long about it.' **Explore in discussion** whether it is wiser to continue the discussion with Mrs Robinson or to proceed in some other way. Alternatively, **simulate the incident.**

Task 4

Your father is a small shopkeeper and has a minor fire in his backyard. His insurance claim was inspected by Mr Hallett, one of the claims inspectors employed in the Property Department at Shieldsure. Subsequently, your father sees Mr Hallett regularly delivering trays of eggs to neighbouring shops from a small van during working hours, and surmises that Hallett is running a small business 'on the side'. He suggests that you ought to report this as you work for the same firm. **Explore in discussion** whether you have such a duty, and on the assumption that you do, how you should proceed.

Task 5

A friend who is one of the other filing clerks sees that you are on the way to the toilet and asks you to bring back her purse, which she has left in her coat pocket. As you are getting it out, Mrs Grattan enters and jumps to the conclusion that you are engaged in stealing from it. You are 16, shy, afraid of your superiors, and very unwilling to get into a row or fight of any kind. Mr Green accepts Mrs Grattan's account, and asks you if you have anything to say. He does not give you enough time to reply, especially as he talks to you in front of Mrs Grattan, and does not ask your fellow-clerk for confirmation of your story. He sends you home at once, saying that your cards and wages will be sent after you. **Explore in discussion, and by reference to relevant guides to the Employment Protection Act, the nature of your rights** in circumstances like these and the proper stages at which to assert them.

Task 6

Your conditions of service allow you 18 working days' leave a year, and leave of absence at the Branch Manager's discretion for family emergencies. You know from previous experience that Mrs Grattan is not prepared to put such requests forward except for deaths and funerals of close relatives. However, it is November, you have used up your annual allowance of leave, and your twin sister is getting married just before Christmas. **Write the usual note** requesting leave of absence, in such a way that while Mrs Grattan cannot complain at your nerve in seeking leave with pay, she is given the option of doing you that favour.

A5 – Derwent Albion

Derwent is a small town in Lancashire. It is little known, except for its football team, Derwent Albion, which was founded over 90 years ago and is rightly proud of its history. The club had a good record, with occasional patches of real distinction, until recently, when it fell on very difficult times.

The Albion plays at St Jude's Park, Derwent, and was a Second Division league club until the mid-1920s, when it won promotion to the First Division. Its run of successes between the wars included winning the F.A. Cup and appearing in the final on two other occasions. After a decade in the Second Division it slipped into Division Three in 1962 and sank to the Fourth Division in 1967. A valiant effort in the early 1970s nearly gained promotion, but the steady decline in the club's fortunes continued.

The club's troubles have been greatly increased by the success of Oldchester United, a large city First Division club located only 15 miles away. Most young football enthusiasts support Oldchester United and travel to Oldchester rather than support Derwent. Knocked out of F.A. Cup and League Cup in early rounds, Derwent has debts of over £80,000 and is losing £1,000 a week. Average home attendance is only 1,700 for the season, with some gates down to 900, whereas an average gate of 3,000 is needed.

The club has now had to sell its star player to a Second Division club for £20,000 to stave off urgent creditors, and bankruptcy can be kept away only by the hard work of the Supporters' Club in fund-raising. It is now clear that the club will not survive the close season unless something drastic is done. You are an active member of the Supporters' Club, and at the Annual General Meeting you are asked to organise a 'Save the Albion' campaign because of your links with the Derwent business community.

Honorary Secretary of Derwent Albion Supporter's club.

Task 1

A local printer offers to run off 10,000 copies of a leaflet for you, provided it is kept to a single A4 size sheet set up as a four-page leaflet. You now have to:
(a) **work out the text** to be printed on it;
(b) **work out the design** for its layout;
(c) **decide how best and to whom it should be distributed.** *Appeal to the Public to help Save the club.*

Task 2

You are a member of the Derwent Junior Chamber of Trade, which publishes a monthly newsletter 'Firm News'. This is distributed to all local firms and organisations, and conversation with the editor suggests that an article of not more than 150 words would be printed. It should suggest why a successful football club is a commercial asset to a town like Derwent, and why the business community should help Albion to survive. **Write the article**.

Task 3

You decide to follow up the article by approaching local firms, asking to see a suitable person in order to discuss such matters as advertising at the ground or in the programme, sponsorship of particular events, etc. **Draw up a suitable letter** for this purpose (a) to a man you know reasonably well who runs the main department store in Derwent, or

(b) to the proprietor of the George Hotel, the only substantial hotel in Derwent, whom you have never met.

Task 4

A visit from a leading First Division Club in an early round of the F.A. Cup caused some ugly incidents among supporters, and residents near St Jude's Park have set up an Association. Their complaints about vandalism and hooligan behaviour have met with little response, and the Association has announced that it is going to campaign for matches at St Jude's Park to be stopped altogether. This is potentially a dangerous development for Albion, since the Residents' Association could well combine with the club's creditors to force the closure of the club and the sale of the ground. There is no question that some residents have suffered greatly over a number of years from the rough behaviour of visiting fans, and Charles Murphy, the aggressive interviewer for BBC Radio Oldchester, has made news stories of it before. He now rings you up: his early-evening programme 'Scene at Six' proposes a discussion between Mrs Brook, the chairman of the Residents' Association, and yourself, with Murphy in the chair. The programme lasts 12 minutes. **Work out in groups the line to be taken on each side.**

Task 5

Simulate the programme outlined in Task 4, recording it on tape, and discuss the recording's effectiveness.

A6 – The Medical Receptionist

Read Section 4 of the Guide before attempting this Assignment.

You are employed as a stand-by receptionist in the Out-patients Department of a small hospital. The Department normally runs three clinics at a time, for each of which a senior consultant and a second consultant are normally on duty. There is an Out-patients Sister, Mary Hackett, and an assistant to her who is usually brought in from the nursing staff to train in the work for a month. Mary Hackett is a gently spoken but very tough married woman in her fifties who runs the Department efficiently and yet amiably. She prefers to be addressed as Mary unless there are doctors or senior nursing staff in earshot, and will respond in kind unless she has been annoyed. She usually staffs two of the clinics herself and leaves the trainee nurse to handle the other. The duties there are to ensure that each doctor has the right record files on each patient, to clean and replace instruments, deal with removal and replacement of dressings, and signal to the receptionist that the next patient is required.

There are three clinics each day, except on Thursday. They start at 09.30 and are intended to run for 1½ hours. On Thursdays there is a fourth clinic, which in theory starts at 11.15 but in practice begins as soon as one of the three consulting rooms becomes available and a patient has arrived. It usually lasts 2 hours, sometimes longer. However, the Area Health Authority insists that all its out-patient work operates a block appointment system, and requires that for clinics of less than

2½ hours only one block be arranged. Normal clinic patients, therefore, are all summoned for 09.30, with the Ear, Nose and Throat clinic's list called for 11.00. Your duties as receptionist are to check that each patient down for an appointment relates to a record file sent down from Records Office; to sort the files into separate piles for each clinic; mark off each patient as he or she arrives; and keep each clinic's set of record files in order (usually, the order in which patients arrive, but Sister Hackett can change this if she wishes). You know from experience that the only times when you can secure Sister Hackett's attention are those when she comes out to signal that the next patient is required, and when she assists a departing patient to a chair. Once she has checked that each clinic has a sufficient 'list' for the session, she returns to what she describes as the full-time job of seeing that the consultants are not interrupted.

One very cold Thursday morning in winter the following are among the incidents which occur. (Your teacher may arrange for some of you to go out of the room and return one by one to present these or similar problems, while others observe or take the part of the receptionist.)

Task 1

A tall, well-dressed man arrives at 09.25 with an 09.30 call. There are eight others in this block appointment, on which the consultant has started early. This Mr Andrews waits until 09.50, when he comes up to complain that he is late being seen. He shows obvious disbelief when you tell him the clinic is ahead of schedule. At 10.10 he comes up again, and says that a string of other people have appointments to see him from 10.30 onwards. He says he cannot wait all day for a five-minute check for which he came punctually. He is angry and insists on being seen. From his point of view his complaint is wholly justified. **Discuss how this should be dealt with, or act out a number of solutions.**

Task 2

A lady in her sixties, walking with a stick and visibly in poor health, arrives at 09.40 with an 09.30 call – but for the next day: she has misread the date. There is an appropriate clinic going on, but the patient's file is upstairs and the list is already long. On the other hand, if she were told to come back next day the bus fare alone would be a problem. **Discuss how this should be dealt with, or act out a number of solutions.**

Task 3

The reception counter where you work is on a corridor, and the clinic's doors are along the corridor to the right, with the waiting room opposite them, so you cannot see the waiting room from your desk. At 11.15 a passing sister tells you that some patients are having to stand. From your knowledge of the lists and each clinic's progress you would not expect this. You go in and find five seats taken up by three elderly men from the locality who, when they can, use the place as a warm haven of rest where they can get free tea by pretending (not to you) to be out-patients. They are experienced and very clever at passing themselves off as genuine to the others waiting, thereby enlisting the waiting-room's occupants in support against the ruthless hospital that turns them out. **Act out a number of solutions** for the problem, bearing in mind that you do not know their names.

Task 4

A patient with a call for 11.15 arrives at 12.55, explaining that she is a midwife and was delayed at a confinement. The clinic's last patient has gone in, and there is no guarantee that Sister Hackett will re-appear before the consultant washes up before going. **Work out in discussion** what should be done.

Task 5

The eye clinic is on all morning, and Mrs West arrived on time for her 11.15 call. She is an old hand and knows she can expect to be seen at about 12.15. Six other partially-sighted patients have been seen and are awaiting transport home when you can arrange it, but the driver has been out on the road. At noon he arrives: Mr Routledge is a former ambulance team-leader who now does the round for walking patients, a stickler for the rules who has a booming voice audible only too clearly. He picks up his list, which his supervisor issued, and goes to the waiting-room. 'Mrs West, please!', he booms. When you go round to explain, he ignores the six waiting people and insists he must adhere to his list. He usually echoes everything you say to him. **Explore in discussion, or act out,** some solutions to the situation.

Task 6

For this task you should work in groups of four. The first member of the group acts as the receptionist, and works out a very crowded booking-sheet for a particular week. The second member acts as a patient who has been told by the consultant to make an appointment for that week, but the patient is himself a busy man with many appointments already. The receptionist and patient have to **negotiate a satisfactory outcome.** The other two members of the group repeat the negotiation, with a different set of constraints making it difficult to find a mutually agreeable appointment. The two negotiations are conducted in turn, and the nature of the problem common to both should be explored in discussion.

A7 – The Sports Club's Debt

Flextron Engineering Ltd is a substantial company in the business of plastic injection-moulding, and was one of the first companies in the development of bakelite and other early plastics. It is well established, with 600-odd employees, and has a good reputation as an employer. You are employed as a sales accountant, and as an active member of the cricket side you readily agreed to step into an unexpected vacancy for the post of Treasurer of the Sports Club.

Flextron gives good support to its welfare activities, but does not believe in subsidising their routine business. It helps the sports club by charging only a nominal rent for the ground and by including the sports ground in the schedules of its maintenance staff, but otherwise insists that the club be self-financing. About fifteen years ago the club demolished its old wooden pavilion after building a new, brick clubhouse of good size. The unexpected switch of club loyalties from soccer to rugby, and the sharp growth in activity on the women's side, have made the men's and women's showers inadequate.

The Sports Club has 220 members, 170 of whom pay £10 as playing members while 50 pay £3 p.a. as social members. The Club's annual income is made up approximately as follows:

Subscriptions	£1,850
Bar profits	700
Clubhouse lettings	200
Annual 'stars' cricket match	200
	2,950

The balance at the bank at the start of the current financial year is £2,600, and the accounts were presented and approved at the AGM in February. That meeting also decided, on the basis of its cash position, level of income, and ability to run a successful appeal, to enter into a contract for building an extension to the clubhouse, providing larger changing rooms and much more shower accommodation. An extension to and complete re-surfacing of the car park were included. The contract total came to £5,800, with an inflation clause for £500 and a penalty of £300 if payment is delayed more than six weeks (40 days) after acceptance of the works by the Club Secretary. The builder has not sought payment of instalments.

However, on your appointment as Honorary Treasurer you discover that things have gone badly wrong:
(a) the previous Treasurer has been ill from early in March until now (late June), but did not admit his inability to cope with the club's finances until a week ago. In consequence, while the banker's order subscriptions have come in, more than £1,300 of the current year's subscription income has still to be collected.
(b) The builder completed the work and, in the absence of the Treasurer, secured the signature of the club's Secretary on the Acceptance Note. The inflation clause has operated, and the delayed-payment clause, so that the debt is of £6,600. The builder has just written a formal letter to the Managing Director of Flextron Engineering requesting immediate payment in full.

Task 1

You have to circulate the members who have not yet paid their subscriptions, explaining that the matter is urgent. Because one of the members is the builder's son, your circular should give no reason for supposing that the debt is a bad one. **Write the letter.**

Task 2

You have to go to see the builder in order to explain the position you are in. You need to ask for time to put the club's affairs in order, and would hope to suggest an arrangement which the club could manage and the builder accept – but remember that the builder will see no reason why a firm of Flextron's size should not be able to settle at once. **Simulate the meeting.**

Task 3

You report the outcome of your meeting to the Club Committee, which decides that the debt should be paid by means of raising a loan. This presents a choice between going to a bank, which would charge the current interest rate for private loans, and the Company Treasurer, who would charge 2%–3% less but would impose rigid conditions on repayment. **Simulate the meeting** of the Club committee which decides which to seek, *or* **draft the document involved** (a memorandum seeking an internal loan, or a letter to the bank manager seeking a commercial one).

Task 4

The Committee finds that in order to meet the interest charges on a commercial loan, or to meet the stringent repayment terms of the internal loan, it has to increase the club subscription. It cannot do this without calling an Extraordinary General Meeting. The five members of the Committee are solidly behind you, but the members who come to the meeting are not pleased. Several of them argue that the real reason for the increase is the delay in paying the builder, and there is some evidence to support them. **Simulate the meeting,** at which the members accuse the Committee of negligence in having left the previous Treasurer without help for so long.

Task 5

The local newspaper has a weekly gossip column. Shortly after the Extraordinary General Meeting it prints this item:

COMPANY UNSPORTING
Flextron Engineering's sports club is bankrupt, and is being bailed out by Company Treasurer Martin Purvis. The club got in Kidman & Russell, the builders, to extend its club-house and car park, and found it couldn't foot the bill. Question: what is a well-run firm like Flextron, which made £1½m profit last year, doing with a sports club that goes broke over a mere £3,000?

The Managing Director instructs you, as the employee who knows more than anyone else about the club's finances, to go to see the Editor. He tells you that you should talk to the journalist who wrote the item, since a follow-up entry in the column would be easy to arrange. The journalist proves to be a trainee, a sensible young woman aged 18. **Simulate the conversation** in which you and she produce a text which can be published, not as a formal correction but as another 'newsy' entry in the column which, in passing as it were, sets the record straight.

A8 – Mr Farnsworth's Carport

Mr Jonas Farnsworth lives at 284 Calder Road, Westhanger. He is a gentle, quietly-spoken accounts clerk with one of the local firms. Westhanger is a smallish industrial town of narrow main roads and poor-quality ribbon development along them, of which Calder Road is typical. Much of the even-numbered side was developed as council housing in the 1930s, built in blocks of four with rear access for vehicles. There was space between each block of four to provide garages for the end houses in each block, and part of the gardens and rear access allowed garages for the inner pairs, but 284 was an exception. The houses were sold to existing tenants early in the 1970s, and the purchasers of 284 used their garage space to the side of the house to build a lean-to greenhouse. A year later the house was sold, with the vendor paying in the Council's share of the improved value. The new owners, Mr and Mrs Farnsworth, chose the house partly because of the greenhouse: they had a special interest in growing orchids.

In September 1974 Mr Farnsworth was involved in a serious accident which resulted in the loss of his left leg above the knee. He has retained his job, and with the help of the disabled persons' mobility allowance was able to buy a car, which greatly eased his problems of getting to work. He has applied for planning permission to build a carport in front of the greenhouse, claiming that he needs the car to get to work and does not wish to lose the greenhouse.

You are a general administrative assistant in the Planning Department of the Richworth District Council, dealing with committee business and the processing of planning applications. The application comes to you for consideration of whether it can be put before the Committee.

Task 1

Draft a reply to Mr Farnsworth explaining that when the former Urban District Council sold the houses, it imposed a restrictive covenant forbidding the erection of any structure beyond the building line. Mr Farnsworth's letter refers to 'a carport or platform', and you have to make clear that either of these is, for planning purposes, a structure.

Task 2

Mr Farnsworth telephones you on receiving your letter. He explains that he cannot park in the road because it is a restricted parking zone, and must have his car reasonably close to his house. He points out that a disabled colleague lives at 19 Acre Road just round the corner and has been allowed a similar platform. You promise to check the details and ring back.

You find that the essential difference between the two cases is that Calder Road is a bus route while Acre Road is not, and the restricted zone in front of Mr Farnsworth's house is in fact a lay-by bus stop. This makes any exceptional treatment out of the question, and the only possibility is to move the greenhouse.

Write to tell Mr Farnsworth this, in such a way that he does not feel himself unjustly treated.

Task 3

Councillor Mrs Hembry represents Mr Farnsworth's ward on the Richworth District Council. She is a member of the opposition party and loses no opportunity to attack the party in power. She takes up the case, alleging an inflexible and unsympathetic response from the Development Committee to a disabled person seeking to pursue his ordinary job. She also accused you personally of petty bureaucratic obstruction. The matter is placed on the agenda of the next meeting of the Development Committee, and you are instructed **to write the necessary briefing,** which must be objective, concise, and easily understood by the members (See Guide, Section 7.)

Task 4

The Committee discuss the issue at length, and conclude that unless Mr Farnsworth is prepared to move the greenhouse nothing can be done. You issue the usual formal notice of rejection of a request for planning permission and send it to Mr Farnsworth. The next day a very timid and distressed Mrs Farnsworth arrives at the office and asks to see you. She is clearly not used to dealing with officials, and she has come because she feels sure that somebody in the Town Hall does not understand the facts. She and her husband are devoted to their orchids, and giving up the greenhouse would be a terrible blow. She asks for the decision to be reconsidered. You for your part know that nothing further can be done. **Simulate the interview, which may be recorded for class analysis and discussion.**

A9 – The Hospital Opening

You are a member of the administrative staff of the South Helmshire Area Health Authority, on secondment for a year to the Abbey Hospital to assist the Hospital Administrator, Mr James Collett. A new wing of the hospital has been in use for some months as a purpose-built geriatric rehabilitation unit. The wing was a favourite project of the Hospital League of Friends, an unusually active and generous body of some 200 people under the Honorary Presidency of the Duchess of Chatterton. The League raised more than 65% of the cost of the new wing, over a period of six years, and Her Grace has a rather proprietary interest in it. The wing is, indeed, to be called The Chatterton Wing. The League has requested an official opening, so that those who contributed to it might see it in action and have some recognition of their work.

The opening is to take place on June 3rd, a Tuesday, and Mr Collett's outline programme is as follows:

```
1.50 p.m. Invited guests to be seated in the
Main Hall.
1.55 p.m. Arrival of platform party (bouquets
for ladies).
2.00 p.m. The Duchess of Chatterton will
introduce Mr Charles Bowen-Clarke, M.P.
(Conservative, Helmshire South), formerly
Secretary of State for Health and Social
Security.
2.15 p.m. Mr Bowen-Clarke will speak and un-
veil the Commemorative Plaque.
2.25 p.m. Blessing of the Wing by The Bishop
of Drewton.
2.30 p.m. Formal expression of thanks to
platform party by Mr Collett.
2.40 p.m. Guests to be escorted in groups of
15 on tour of new wing.
3.45 p.m. Tea served in cafeteria, at the
expense of the League of Friends.
Visitors are asked to remove their cars from
the Hospital grounds not later than 4.30 p.m.
```

Task 1

Draft formal letters confirming the arrangements and enclosing a copy of the programme to:
(a) The Duchess of Chatterton, Helmdale Hall, Drewton;
(b) The Right Rev. Cuthbert Vernon, M.A., D.D., Bishopscroft;
(c) The Rt. Hon. Charles Bowen-Clarke, O.B.E., M.P., House of Commons.

Task 2

You are asked to bring together and instruct the volunteer guides who will escort the visitors round the new wing. You can expect to have to deal with the platform party, which will include the named speakers and Mr Collett, and an audience of somewhere between 150 and 160. While twenty of the Friends of the Hospital have volunteered, some will miss the briefing and some may miss the opening. Your main problem is to brief the guides on techniques of getting their groups moving, and keeping them moving, without making them feel rushed on the one hand or late for tea on the other. (The note about removing their cars was Collett's method of having the canteen cleared in time for the hospital staff evening meal rush.) **Simulate the meeting.** (See Guide, 4.)

Task 3

About a week before the opening, some of your fellow union members express concern at what they see as public money being 'wasted' on the function. The Secretary of the branch calls a meeting, and as you have the facts and are a member, it falls to you to explain: public expenditure is minimal, as the League is paying for tea, and their fund-raising work is entitled to some kind of recognition. **Sketch out your notes for your speech,** bearing in mind that it is a speech, not a reading.

Task 4

On the day of the meeting, three days before the opening, the *Drewton Advertiser* prints the following leader:

Hospital Opening Wastes Money
We warmly welcome the addition of the Chatterton Wing at the Abbey Hospital. Local residents who have seen what proper rehabilitation can do for their elderly relatives are loud in its praise. But the Wing has been open for almost a year now, and we wonder whether an official opening is necessary – or appropriate. Good money is being spent on this pompous fuss. An M.P. is being brought from London, a Bishop is giving his blessing, and 200 people are being given tea and toast. Hospitals elsewhere in the area could well use all that money for equipment. Patients on long waiting lists will wonder about the hospital's priorities. The money could obviously be much better spent. We at The Advertiser say the hospital bosses should come to their senses and *call it off.*

After your success at the Union meeting, Mr Collett asks you to **draft a statement** on behalf of the Area Health Authority replying to the editorial. The paper is likely to print it *verbatim*, so it will have to withstand close scrutiny, but should be no longer than is absolutely necessary.

Task 5

The *Advertiser* sent a young journalist to 'cover' the opening, a man you knew at school. You sent him round with the best of the group guides and gave him tea yourself. During tea the Duchess calls you over, and refers to the M.P.'s speech. He had used the occasion, many thought quite tactlessly, to attack Government policy on the re-organisation of the Health Service. She says the Hospital is in line for a special grant, and it would not help this if the Hospital were found to have given a platform to opposition criticism. She suggests that you persuade the reporter to play down this aspect, since the grant would re-open a wing badly needed in the area.

Working in pairs or small groups, **work out the text of a newspaper report** which meets the need for interesting news without putting the hospital at risk. One member of each group should play the part of the journalist, and discussion may include distinctions between 'off the record' material and what can be published.

Assignments Group B

B1 – The Caretaker's Retirement

The Hedgeby Area Education Office serves an area covering a third of a scattered rural County. The Area Education Officer is in charge, and is served by the District Inspector, the Schools Officer, and the Administrative Officer. The Inspector is in charge of the six Advisers, the Area Educational Psychologist and his three colleagues, the Schools Meals Organisers (2), and the Youth Service team of four officers and a senior adviser. The Schools Officer runs the Schools Section, which includes administrative assistants dealing with teaching staff, non-teaching staff, courses, grants and awards, school transport, and 'miscellaneous duties'. The Administrative Officer is in charge of the office itself, including the typing-pool and the Finance Section, which has a Finance Officer and three clerical officers. Only the Area Education Officer has a secretary, all other clerical services being handled by the typing pool, which has a senior typist in charge of it and three other typists. There is a clerical assistant for the Advisers, one in School Meals, one in Youth, and one working direct to the Administrative Officer. The officer responsible for maintenance of playing fields over the whole County is attached to the Schools Section at Hedgeby.

Task 1

You are employed as the clerical assistant to the Area Administrative Officer. The new County Council has asked for a review of staff establishment in all offices, and as part of this process the Administrative Officer has to produce an organisation chart of the Area Education office. On the basis of the evidence given above, **draw this** for him.

Suggested Solution to Task 1

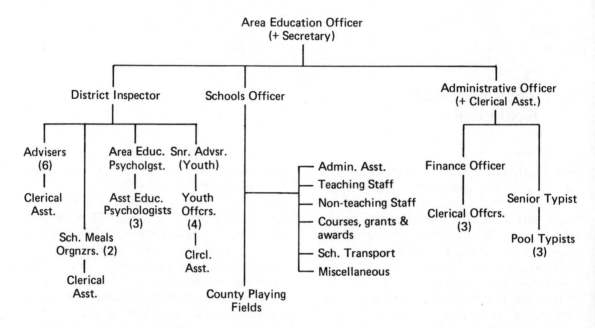

Notes on Task 1

Organisation charts may take several forms. The basic principles are:

(a) that posts at a given level appear at the same level on the chart;

(b) that the 'tree' lines indicate clearly the lines of responsibility.

In this example the bulk of the chart uses a horizontal pattern, while the central part of the tree uses a vertical one to save space.

This example is an organisation chart which does not carry any specific information about status or salary except to denote who is senior to whom within each sectional line. Organisation charts can of course be used to set out the relative status (i.e. in terms of salary) by treating the vertical axis as graduated by steps in the salary structure and 'placing' each individual accordingly.

In setting out any organisation chart, the fullest use should be made of the available space: allowing the text to become cramped can lead to a confusing layout.

Task 2

You come back from lunch one day to find this note on your desk from your boss, Jim Diamond, who is out. The first part of it is a telephone message to him, while the second part gives his notes on it for you:

Feb 14, 12.45 p.m.
Mr Diamond: Mr Wallace, Head of Shortbeach
Compr. rang. His caretaker, Hamblin, has now
decided to retire in July. Hamblin is asking
what his pension and lump sum will be; can
Council help w. housing, and does he have to
leave the school house as soon as he retires?

                                                LR

Jenny: ring Wallace and say we can't get a precise pension figure until Hamblin writes giving his date of retirement. But dig around with Will Smith at HQ salaries & he'll give you a provisional. I don't think there is a lump sum on Hamblin's pension. Margaret Sparrow at the Housing can give you the picture, but it has to go there himself. Have a word with Jim Wells, who knows the Hamblins. Then set up an OD reply to Hamblin, copy to the Head.

                                                JD

You establish that the pension figure will be roughly £24 p.wk., with no lump sum. Housing tells you there is little chance of suitable placement for July, but prospects look good in October. Jim Wells, the old hand who runs school transport in the Area, is out. On the basis of the information available, carry out Mr Diamond's instruction and **draft the letter.**

Suggested Solution to Task 2

Draft
J W Hamblin
Shortbeach Comprehensive School
Shortbeach
(c. to Headmaster)

Dear Mr Hamblin,

Mr Wallace has referred certain queries to me, and I write to answer them as best I can at this stage.

The Salaries Officer at County Hall cannot make a full calculation of your pension until he receives a copy of your letter stating your intention to retire. However, he thinks that the figure is likely to be approximately £24 per week, but this is an estimate only. No lump sum is payable to employees who joined the pension scheme after the age of 45.

About council housing, you should approach the District Council housing office, which is in the same building as this office. I understand that the position after October 1st is quite hopeful. The occupancy of the school house is for the School Governors to decide, in the light of County policy and the need of your successor for housing.

Notes on Task 2

Para 1: the use of the first person is not only not 'wrong' or objectionable: it is now generally accepted as sound practice—provided the person signing the letter is a responsible officer.

Para 2: The danger that an unofficial estimate may be taken as a final calculation has to be heavily guarded against. The requirement of a formal letter of notice protects the Salaries Officer from protest about the provisional figure.

Para 3: the text is assuming here that Hamblin knows what County policy is, which after sixteen years he ought to.

Throughout: the direct address to Hamblin as 'you' is adopted wherever possible. Any other mode of address would be ineffectively formal. Note also that any letter dealing with salary or pension figures should be marked Confidential.

Task 3

After you have drafted the letter requested in Task 2, Jim Wells returns to work, and Mr Diamond mentions the matter to him. In your hearing, Wells observes that Hamblin is retiring because his eyesight is failing a little (he is 63), but it is his wife who 'wears the trousers'. Mrs Hamblin is a local character, forceful, forthright, occasionally a troublemaker – and quite illiterate. Mr Diamond suggests that your draft letter may need revising and must in any case be typed with double-spacing. **Explore in class discussion** whether the text prepared needs changing in the light of this.

Suggested Solution to Task 3

```
Draft

Dear Mr Hamblin,
The Headmaster has told me of your decision to
retire, and while I shall be sorry to lose the
services of a faithful employee, I have to ask
you to let me have your notice in writing as
soon as possible.

The detailed statement of your pension depends
on a full calculation, and that is not done
until your notice is received.  I have been
given a provisional figure of about £24 per
week, but that is only a rough estimate.  I am
afraid there will not be a lump sum, because
you joined the pension scheme after the
starting-age.

Council housing is dealt with by the District
Council Housing Department. I know this is in
the same building as this office, but it is a
different Council from the Education Service.
I have mentioned the matter to them, and you
should go and see them as soon as possible.
Ask to see Mrs Sparrow.

The school house is for the new caretaker if
he wants it, and as it is rent-free it has to
be kept for employees of the Authority.
However, if the new caretaker does not want it
straight away the matter is up to the School
Governors, and you should give the Headmaster
a note about it.
```

Notes on Task 3

This version of the letter is designed to be read aloud to someone not used to dealing with official writing.
It therefore:
(a) separates the request for notice in writing into a paragraph on its own, and divides the contents of the previous version's third paragraph into two, giving the school house issue a paragraph to itself.
(b) changes a number of words and phrases into their less formal equivalents. Thus, the 'cannot make. . until. .' in para 1 becomes 'I have to ask. . .' in para 1 and 'and that is not done until. . .' in para 2. The word-order position of 'only' is changed. There are several other examples.
(c) makes implications explicit. 'I understand that the position after October 1st is quite hopeful' is an official hint that there is not much chance of anything before then, but the second version has to be definite and avoid hints. Hence, 'Ask to see Mrs Sparrow' and 'I have mentioned the matter to them' (which is not more than the plain truth). Similarly, the advice about approaching the Governors ('give the Headmaster a note about it') is explicit; the conditions under which the Governors can act are spelled out; and the reason why he cannot simply rent the house like a Council house is given in a form which the Headmaster can explain.

Task 4

At the end of May you are sent to represent the office at the termly meeting of the Governors of Shortbeach Comprehensive School. Item 6 on the agenda is dealt with in the brief discussion which your speedhand notes record as below – the Chairman is a man who pushes the business through very firmly.

Chairman: Now Item 6. Hamblin wants to stay in the house until October. Headmaster?
HM: Yes. The new caretaker lives locally and doesn't want to move in until January.

Hamblin has arranged a council flat but it's not free until mid-October.

Mrs Bennett: Does he pay rent?

HM: No, the house is rent-free. There's no rent book.

Mrs Bennett: So we wouldn't know what rent to charge?

HM: No.

Mr Darby: Hamblin hasn't been an ideal caretaker, with his refusal to do overtime.

Mr Hendrick (teacher representative): The staff have found him always pleasant but usually unhelpful – about chairs for assembly and evening performances and so on.

Chairman: Is there a County policy on this?

Cllr Aston: Not formally, but it's most unusual for anyone not in Council employment to occupy council property without paying rent.

Mrs Wilson: I'm sure the Hamblins could make arrangements for September and October, and don't see why they should stay.

HM: I agree, but time is a bit short for them.

Chairman: I propose we give them the month of August as a gesture, but tell them they have to be out by the start of the new term. It won't help the new man to have Hamblin breathing down his neck.

Pause.

Chairman: Is that agreed? (Murmurs of assent.) Thank you. Item 7 . . .

Record the Governors' decision as it would appear in the Minutes.

Suggested Solution to Task 4

```
6.  The request of the School Caretaker, Mr
Hamblin, to be allowed to occupy the school
house for a period beyond his retirement in
July.  Agreed that the request be granted for
the month of August only.
```

Notes on Task 4

Writing minutes is a skilled job, and there is much variation in the degree of detail demanded by the body concerned. Most people who are inexperienced at writing minutes suppose that minutes are a summary of what is *said* at a meeting. This is not so: minutes record the meeting's *decisions*, and summarise the other content of a meeting only where it is necessary for the benefit of future inquirers, absentees, etc. A talk from a specialist visitor, or a briefing report given orally, would often be summarised, but in very many cases the summary will be supplied by the speaker for distribution with the formal minutes. This particular task shows the main reason why minutes should not normally summarise discussion or name speakers: if they did, many participants would avoid speaking freely in case the minutes became known to the people concerned.

Task 5

Write the letter informing Mr Hamblin of the decision, which should come from the Clerk to the Governors (Mr Diamond).

Suggested Solution to Task 5

```
Dear Mr Hamblin,
The Governors considered your request to be
allowed to remain in occupation of the school
house until council housing becomes available.
The matter was discussed carefully, in the
light of the Council policy that school houses
can be occupied only by employees whose
conditions of employment include rent-free
housing.  I am sorry to have to tell you that
the Governors decided against your request,
but agreed that there would be no objection to
your remaining in the house until the end of
August on a rent-free basis.
             Yours sincerely,
```

Notes on Task 5

A straightforward 'business' communication which follows standard practice in:
(a) identifying the reason for the letter by referring to previous correspondence etc.;

(b) stating the dominant factor bearing on the decision;

(c) stating the decision itself humanely. (It is inexcusable not to offer regret about an unfavourable decision merely because the organisation making it is a company or an institution.)

Task 6

Early in July a presentation is to be held for Mr Hamblin to mark his retirement, and the Area Education Officer finds unexpectedly that he is unable to attend. He is a fatherly figure who likes to write warm, personal letters of appreciation to retiring servants of the Authority, however unco-operative they may have been. Hamblin has worked at Shortbeach since 1962, having been a police constable until a year or two before then. He has been efficient, honest, and reliable, but would very rarely work the overtime which the school's community education policy has often called for. He has been a very real influence for good in dealing with occasional vandalism by recruiting fifth-form boys to help clean up some of the results, but he has always regarded Saturday games fixtures as an intrusion into his week-end rest and his relations with the PE staff have therefore been strained. **Discuss how to draft** for the Education Officer's signature **a letter** of the kind which will be appreciated by Hamblin and be approved by the EO as in line with his style of doing things.

Suggested Solution to Task 6

Dear Mr Hamblin,

I am very sad to find that I shall not be able to attend the presentation held to mark your retirement at Shortbeach School on the 19th. I would very much have liked to associate myself publicly with this occasion, as one way of expressing my own, and the Authority's, deep appreciation of your long and faithful service.

We have, of course, had our disagreements, but sixteen years is a long stint, and few employees have put in such a time with such reliability. I recall with much pleasure the occasions when I have visited the school for public functions and have found it invariably tidy, and altogether shipshape.

I would also like to put on record the debt which we owe you for the way in which you have responded over the years to the occasional instance of vandalism at the school. Your skill in gaining the support of older boys in the work of tidying-up afterwards has clearly been a major factor in keeping the number of these unfortunate occasions to a very low level, and has built up a considerable loyalty among young people who might otherwise have contributed to the vandalism.

I know that retirement is often a difficult step to take, and hope that you and Mrs Hamblin will look forward to a well deserved and long period of happy release from daily effort. I hope also that you will feel able to recall your sixteen years with us as a time of satisfying service.

Notes on Task 6

This letter could be written in many different ways, and the usefulness of the Task would lie in discussion of the possible ways of saying things—and of whether to include some matters and omit others. However, such a letter cannot refer to the specific matters which have caused disagreement, although it may mention their existence as a way of heightening the value of other and better things. The letter stresses what can be praised and makes as much as possible of the positive virtues. The last sentence is genuine enough: although it does not suggest that the employers can look back on the time with absolute satisfaction, it offers a reasonable human concern that Mr Hamblin should do so. This is one of those occasions for leaving some things unsaid.

B2 – The TV Stand

You are a management trainee with the firm of Woodiwiss & Co. Established in 1928 as a household goods shop, the firm has grown into the largest department store in Dibden and has never sought to develop elsewhere. It concentrates on high quality household goods, fabrics, furnishings, appliances, sports goods and toys. It has no fashion or clothing trade, but its provision for home dressmakers is justly famous. The firm went through a depressed period until recently, and has recovered in every way under the new Store Manager, Philip Ashley, appointed three years ago. Part of his policy for the firm is to remedy the period of poor management which preceded his coming, by running a proper training scheme. Under this, you are spending six months in each of four departments, and are now assigned to the Appliances Department, whose manager is Miss Jennifer Peat, a woman who is completely at home with electronic equipment. You have been there for a month, and your recent work in the firm's training course has included the study of current literature issued by consumer organisations on the rights and duties of customers and traders under relevant legislation.

One Friday morning a customer comes in, evidently feeling cross about something, and demands to see 'the manager'. Miss Peat is in a meeting of department heads with Mr Ashley: you have to deal with the lady yourself. You explain this, which increases her annoyance. However, she pulls out a sales invoice of a transaction dated three months earlier, for the rental of a colour TV set. The invoice is inscribed 'Stand to mfr's spec. to be supplied when avail. (no chge)'. She has telephoned twice and called in twice, and feels she has been very patient. However, the maintenance technician who came the previous day to remedy a fault mentioned casually that she ought to have the proper stand; she complained to him, and he replied that he didn't know what could happen now because the model had already been replaced by a new model and there weren't any stands in stock any more. The customer, a Mrs Allison, tells you all this with increasing heat, and works up to say she will go to the Trading Standards people unless she gets immediate settlement of the problem. During her tirade, Mrs Allison also produces the operating instructions supplied with the set and points to one part which reads:

Cabinet Stands
Only the leg stand recommended by the manufacturer should be used with this model. . . The safety approval given to this product is invalidated if an unauthorised stand is fitted or if the stand is not fitted in accordance with the manufacturer's directions. . .

She asks if her occasional table is appropriate, and if not, whether the validity of her household insurance policy is affected.

If all that Mrs Allison says is correct, and you have every reason to think it is, the firm has made a significant blunder. You know that the proper stands are no longer available, and that the publicity which Mrs Allison is capable of giving to the matter would be unfortunate. You are no technician, and hesitate to go into the insurance problem. But Mrs Allison is in no mood for buck-passing.

Task 1

You cannot settle Mrs Allison's problem immediately, but you have to gain time for Miss Peat or Mr Ashley to resolve it, without letting Mrs Allison feel driven to making her complaint a formal one. **Simulate the interview** from the point where Mrs Allison says 'Well, what are you going to do about it?' (The interview should be tape-recorded.)

Task 2

You cannot interrupt Miss Peat at her meeting, but you can ask Ashley's secretary to take in a note when she takes in the coffee. **Write the note** giving Miss Peat the barest essentials and alerting her to the urgency of the problem.

Task 3

Mrs Allison now writes a personal letter to Mr Ashley about the matter, adding that when she came to the department the 'young person' on duty was obstructive and unhelpful. **Tape-record your reply to Mr Ashley's request** for a description of your conversation with Mrs Allison.

Task 4

The group should now consider the two accounts of the conversation, in the light of the two tape-recordings. Consider both the accuracy of the two versions, and the skill or otherwise of the trainee's handling of the interview.

Task 5

Miss Peat, after consultation with Mr Ashley, instructs you to arrange for the set to be replaced with a new model (complete with

manufacturer's recommended stand). In due course, by which time Miss Peat has left the firm, the finance director asks you to explain why a new set was installed without an installation charge, and the rental contract amended without charging the usual rental agreement fee or deposit. The finance director is a cold and distant man, but not hostile: he simply wants the facts, as objectively as possible. **Simulate the interview**, or **draft the necessary memorandum.**

B3 – Mr Garrett's House

The Woolston District Council caters for the city of Woolston (pop. 110,000) and its immediate environs in the County of Hundleshire. The Social Services Department of the County Council operates through four Area divisions, one of which includes the Woolston District. Housing, however, is a District responsibility, and you are employed as personal assistant to the Housing Manager. Since your training included a period with Social Services you tend to be given liaison work, and also to receive much of the complaints work. One day the Housing Manager hands you the letter opposite.

You know that Langley Road is a 1300-yard stretch of two-lane arterial road which regularly becomes heavily congested. You check with the Surveyor's Department and confirm that:
(a) The road is to be converted to dual-carriageway in two phases, one just about to start and the other due to start in 11 months' time;
(b) No. 81 is one of nineteen small

81 Langley Road
Woolston
24th April 19--

Dear Sirs,
    I think it's terrible the council knocking down these houses for widening the road. I've lived here forty years and at 81 I haven't long to go and don't want to be moved away from my friends and local.
    Everyone says were going to be moved, but how many of you council people did war service like me. The houses are quite alright, so my son's surveyor said, and I've never been behind with rent or rates. So turning me out won't happen without a fuss. I'll get onto my MP and the TV people as well. Others round here can afford to move but they aren't OAPs like me.
    Yours in disgust,
        J. Garrett.

houses scheduled for demolition for the second phase.

Your own departmental records reveal that the houses date from 1889 and were purchased with the road widening in mind as long ago as 1937; minor improvements were made in 1954 but all are structurally inadequate and in several cases unsafe.

You check with Social Services, and find that Mrs Harlow is the social worker who knows the occupants well. She tells you that:
(a) Garrett is a veteran writer of letters of protest;
(b) he invariably passes the replies round in the pub;
(c) being much more interested in being made a fuss of than in gaining what he calls his rights, he responds well to courteous and kindly treatment by officials.

Task 1

Write an appropriate reply to Mr Garrett. The letter should be in draft form for the Housing Manager's approval and signature.

Task 2

In July the tenants affected by Phase 2, one of whom is Garrett, have to be offered alternative housing. **Draft a letter** giving them eight months' notice of demolition and inviting them to come in to see you to discuss the alternatives—the sooner they do this the more choice they might have. Remember that their response will be coloured by anxiety.

Task 3

You receive the following memorandum:

> From: Area Officer, Social
>   Services Dept.
>
> To: Housing Manager,
>   Woolston.
>
> Date: 22 September 19--
>
> I am told by Mrs Harlow that you are seeking to re-house the occupants of 81 Langley Road. She suggests that you would wish to know that Mrs Garrett died on September 14th and that Mr Garrett is much distressed. She feels that the need for sheltered housing or old people's accommodation is now urgent, but is worried that he will suspect your department's motives and offers to assist.

You have to go and see Mr Garrett and it is a long and difficult interview, since he does indeed think you are really in league with the road-builders. Slowly and reluctantly he comes round to accepting that he ought to go into an old people's home. You arrange for a colleague to go with him to see Lowmoor House Senior Citizens' Home on October 5th. **Write up the note for the file** which records the substance of the interview.

Task 4

In the event, Mrs Harlow asks to help Mr Garrett over his move instead, and does so. Afterwards, she is obliged to ask her Chief Officer to notify your own superior that Lowmoor House had not expected them: the Warden had notified you in writing of the offer of a place on September 28th, but had not been told that the offer would be taken up. Your superior is quietly furious: he is known to care intensely about keeping his relations with other departments in good order. The fault is entirely yours: you have a system for these things but did not follow it. He sends you the memo and tartly invites you to comment (i.e. in writing). **Write the memorandum required**:

Task 5

Phase 2 work began on October 15th, a month early. The other occupants moved out in good time, but some of them suggest to the local District Councillor that Garrett was 'pushed around' by the Town Hall, and are worried lest they be treated likewise when they need residential care. The Chief Executive sends a guarded note of inquiry to your superior, who asks you to give him the bare facts in such a way that, without being defensive or apologetic about it, you show that all reasonable consideration was offered and that this is typical of the Department's work. **Write the summary.** (See Guide, 7.4.2.)

B4 – Roberts and Boon Ltd

Sam Roberts was demobilised from the Royal Air Force in 1946. He was 27 at the time, had been trained in the maintenance of the precision calibrators used in checking aircraft instruments, and had a gratuity of £450. With an RAF friend, George Boon, he set up a small business in Tamworth, Staffs, where, with a handful of technicians and skilled men, they developed a small range of precision instruments for use in hospitals and laboratories. The business gradually gained a name for quality and craftsmanship, especially in the fields of calibrating equipment, and its exceptional after-sales service secured many loyal customers. In the 1950s the business boomed and the firm expanded, but Roberts learned the hard way that products so intricate as these, requiring the most austere standards of accuracy, really require the discipline of a small firm to make them successfully. So although the payroll had once reached over 80, the partners held it down to 65 throughout the 1960s. The prospect of large-scale orders from Japan, which would have justified a complete new factory and doubled output, did not deter them from remaining small.

By 1970 Roberts & Boon Ltd were leaders in their field, with a stable, mature, very skilled and well paid workforce. The company became a co-operative: every employee with two or more years' service was allocated 20 shares, with two additional shares for each year of service. Sam and George avoided retaining enough shares between them to give them control. Shortly afterwards, however, Sam's wife developed a serious allergy which her doctor attributed to impurities in the air. She was advised to move to a less polluted atmosphere such as the south-west or the North Yorkshire coast.

Sam was now in his early fifties, and for the past four years had become increasingly absorbed in a new hobby. He shared this interest with four of his machinists: fine-scale model railways. With George Boon's support, they had started a small evenings-and-Saturday business making parts, accessories, and some rolling stock. They had been surprised at the market for these products, and had developed a small line of accurately detailed steam-powered locomotives. The wave of nostalgia for steam which followed the demise of steam locomotion on full-size railways created a far greater demand than Sam and his team could cope with.

At this point, Sam put to George and his group of colleagues the problem of Sheila's health. The outcome of their discussions was a decision to set up a subsidiary company. The small steam-pressure gauges which had been the origin of the new line remained, with other small parts, the heart of the business, but setting up as a separate firm would enable them to market the locomotives and to produce rolling stock to go with them. These could be sold in kit form or, for the more wealthy or less skilful, as assembled and painted finished models. The four men declared their willingness to move with the work, George Boon was willing to release several others, and the first task was to decide where to move.

Task 1

After much correspondence with estate agents and so on, Sam Roberts has drawn up a long list of nine sites to look at. The class should work in groups of three or four, and **each group should select one of the three sets of sites** given. Each group should then:
1. **study rail timetables and road maps** to determine whether Sam Roberts and his Works Manager should visit the sites by road or by rail;
2. **plan the journey concerned**, allowing $1\frac{1}{2}$ hrs for site inspection, 1 hr for local consultations with the agent, and $1\frac{1}{2}$ hrs for discussions with the local authority, for each site in the chosen set.

The sites listed are:

(a) A newly built factory on a trading estate at Falmouth; a warehouse next to the main railway station at Taunton; a 1960s-built factory/warehouse on the edge of Tavistock;

(b) A disused auction rooms near the centre of Hereford; a vacant yacht-builder's yard at Chepstow; a disused wool warehouse at Bradford on Avon.

(c) The empty premises of a former wholesaler in Whitby; a brand-new factory building in Northallerton; a vacant bowling-alley in Harrogate.

Task 2

The nine sites turn out to vary very little in labour costs and adaptation expenses. Housing is also available within reasonable distance and at appropriate price-levels except at Taunton and Bradford-on-Avon. However, there will have to be a weekly consignment from the main works, delivered by the firm's driver in its own van. Sam Roberts will also have to go to Tamworth once a week. The choice of location will be affected by the costs of these contacts, and by access to transport for raw materials and distribution.

Each group should select one of the three sites in its chosen set, as the most advantageous location for the new plant. It **should**

present its choice to the other groups for critical **analysis** and discussion. The work may lead to writing-up in the form of a note of record which summarises the differences of view or states the agreed choice.

Task 3

The firm needs to make further enquiries once a site has been chosen. Sam Roberts decides to go there for a week, leaving on a Monday, and to have his wife join him on the Thursday. Bearing in mind that they are a prosperous couple in their fifties, and using appropriate hotel guides, **write the letter seeking accommodation for the visit.**

Task 4

There are 66 employees, 52 of them shareholding partners, the others with less than two years' service. Thirteen of the partners are women married to other partners. Roberts, his wife, and four single men are already agreed on the move. **Work out how many remain who have to be told of the plan formally. Write the circular letter** which tells them of the scheme and invites additional volunteers.

Task 5

Until now the railway model accessories business has been conducted through informal contacts, clubs, and a small number of specialist shops. The serious business is done, however, through advertising in the specialist journals and orders by post. The business at the time of the move has 220 named customers in its files. **Draw up the text of the circular letter** which informs them that the firm will be moving, with relevant information about the move, and that its future contact with its clients will be through advertisements in the journals.

B5 – R & B Accessories Ltd

This assignment follows on from the previous one, and poses problems which arise five years after the creation of the subsidiary company led by Sam Roberts.

In the intervening five years, R & B Accessories Ltd has undergone considerable expansion. Sam Roberts had the insight to grasp that the oil-price crisis would have a lasting effect on the British economy. He therefore set out to make the firm almost entirely export-based. He knew that his market lay with two main kinds of customer: the well-off enthusiast who would buy one or more of most lines he produced, and the small hobbyist who treated the firm as a fellow-enthusiast and was usually a member of a local society. He advertised by taking a two-page spread in the specialist monthly journal, printing a stock-list rather than an advertisement, and refused all other kinds of advertising. His market had expanded all over Europe and the Commonwealth, and especially in the USA, where he charged premium prices in keeping with the firm's reputation as a quality manufacturer. The world-wide recession of the mid-1970s led the firm to watch for new markets, and the careful historical detailing of its products had won it an encouraging flow of orders from South America. The product lines had been extended to include principal locomotives of national railway systems in many parts of the world, with appropriate rolling stock. The locomotives were working steam-driven Gauge 0 scale models, of originals dating from between 1860 and 1914.

At the relevant time, you are employed in the sales office, dealing with invoices, payments, bad debts, mail-order items up to £50 value, and giving special attention to the South American market. It is for this reason that the Sales Manager hands you Document A.

Sales Clerk

THE GLOBE

12-16 Caxton Row
London EC4

19th August 19--

To Sales/Export Managers of small firms

Dear Sir,

As you may know, The Globe is a special sort of journal. It appears fortnightly, with a circulation of 155,000 in all parts of the world. It caters distinctively for English-speaking people in responsible positions in business, public life, and diplomatic work. It reprints articles of good quality from the British daily and weekly press, and survey articles by specialist reporters which are found valuable by readers who often know the subjects concerned very well.

The Globe is extending its services with a new venture, aiming to help small British businesses gain access to foreign markets. Once a quarter, the journal itself will be devoted to a particular area or continent, and at the same time a newspaper-style supplement will be issued with every copy - and with local major newspapers. The supplement will provide an outstanding advertising medium for firms unable to afford direct-mail or local media.

The first supplement will go to South America, where nine of the leading national newspapers have agreed to circulate it as a free addition to one of their own issues. The total circulation in Latin America alone is thus likely to exceed 450,000 over and above the readership of The Globe itself, which greatly exceeds its actual circulation through being standard provision in clubs and waiting rooms everywhere.

The advertising rates for the Supplement will be based on a figure of £100 per quarter-page, larger placings being reduced by 15% at half-page, full-page and double-page steps.

Final copy and blocks for our Small Industry Supplement are required by October 27th. In the meantime I should be happy to answer any questions you may have.

Yours faithfully,

Charles Purchase

Charles Purchase
Advertising Manager

Task 1

The circular from *The Globe* does not give enough detail to enable you to judge whether it would be worthwhile taking an advertisement of the kind proposed. Work out in discussion what additional information is needed, and **draft a letter** asking for the information needed. (21 August 1983)

Task 2

You conclude from the reply that on a page-size of 12″ × 9″ the most worthwhile choice would be a double page spread. You doubt whether Sam Roberts would agree to the cost, and you decide to explore sharing it with the parent company. **Draft the letter to the Tamworth sales manager** for your superior to sign.

Task 3

George Boon sees your letter and rings up Sam Roberts. Sam in turn calls you in and wants to know why you are in contact with the parent firm without keeping him informed. **Simulate the interview** in which you satisfy Sam Roberts of your good intentions.

Task 4

The Globe agrees to take a double page spread for the two firms. Sam, always the individualist, decides that the division should be diagonal across the two pages. You are asked to prepare copy for the R & B Accessories half, using not more than a third of the space for illustrations (good quality printing on art paper), and limiting your copy to 100 words about the firm, and a representative extract from the catalogue.

Propose a layout and suggest the text to go into the advertisement.

Task 5

The Small Industry Supplement is a success, and the Features Editor of *The Globe* asks for a 'potted history' of the firm, to form part of a series of six or eight examples of interesting export businesses in the UK. The readership is prosperous, up-market, conservative, concentrated in British communities overseas, powerfully nostalgic for the Britain they remember but cannot now find when they visit this country. You are asked to **provide the text of the article in about 500 words,** and are at liberty to fill out and embroider the facts available to you.

B6 – The Station Visitors

You are employed as assistant to the Station Master at Skilton Central, a large station of sixteen platforms on the London-Leeds main line which also deals with much commuter traffic in the East Midlands area. One morning the Station Master reminds you that the station is 'twinned' with Wurzburg as part of the activity of the Anglo-German Locomotive Society. The Deutsche Bundesbahn sends its trainees for two-week visits to Britain, and expects them to visit 'twin' stations for a day or two. In this case, Klaus Neuwieler and Götz Rändberg, both aged 20 and both able to speak good English, are coming from Wurzburg to Skilton. Neuwieler has been to England several times previously and is a Goods Scheduler, while Rändberg is Assistant Station Master.

The two young men are travelling on the night boat from Hoek van Holland and the daily boat train from Harwich to Manchester stops at Skilton at 09.50. They are due to arrive on Tuesday April 16th, have been booked in at the Central Hotel for the night, and are to catch the 16.50 to Nottingham on the 17th.

Task 1

The general instructions on exchange visits from the Society, issued through British Rail, mention that it is a normal courtesy to visitors to ensure that their personal names and that of their home town are correctly pronounced. **Find out how the names mentioned should be pronounced, and write down a sentence or two about this** for inclusion in a note to colleagues.

Task 2

The Station Master has approved your leaving your normal duties to act as host to the visitors, but you in fact arrange for Rändberg to spend most of Tuesday sharing in your daily routine, while Neuwieler visits the Goods Scheduling section. The next day there is a morning tour of departments and an afternoon run on the footplate to a nearby town (each visitor on separate trains, organised by Regional Control). **Write a memorandum** for the Station Master to issue to each section setting out the arrangements.

Task 3

Your memorandum is circulated, and you receive this note:

I know you wrote the memo about the Germans coming here. I want to let you know I'm disgusted with it. It's a disgrace: I was a POW in Germany for four years, and after all we had to put up with we don't want them here. The portering staff all think the same, and don't want to meet them.
H. Bestwick.

You refer the note to the Station Master, who promptly refers it to the branch convener of the relevant trade union. A meeting of the branch committee is called, and you and the Station Master are invited to attend. There are five members present, one of them Bestwick. The other four are torn between solidarity with their brother and their feeling that he is being unreasonable. **Simulate the meeting** at which the visit is described and Bestwick's objections are discussed.

Task 4

While the two visitors are being shown round the station (by you as their host), an urgent telephone message for them announces a change in their travel arrangements. **Work out and tape-record the text** of a loudspeaker announcement which will bring them back to the Station Master's office.

Task 5

The telephone message is that after reaching Nottingham on the 17th (at about 18.00), the visitors should travel on to Llandudno, reaching there as early as conveniently possible the next day. **Work out** from the relevant reference books **a suitable set of journey-times**, including a suggestion as to the most sensible point for an overnight stop.

B7 – Orange Lane Youth Club

The Humbria Police Authority covers the same area as the County of Humbria, and is a forward-looking organisation. In order to relieve trained police officers of clerical chores, and to ensure that the Authority does not commit 'maladministration', it is developing systematic support services. As part of this scheme, you are employed on AP2 as a Senior Clerical Assistant to the Superintendent of Police in Rowridge, the County's second town. In practice you work for his three Inspectors as well, among them George Beecham.

The town of Rowridge is a mixed one of 90,000 population, with industry, commuter-belt housing, extensive council estates, and an above-average proportion of retired people who have remained in the town because of its attractions. The education authority has had a large-scale programme of adult and community education which is now being run down, although the service remains in skeletal form. One of your spare-time activities has been to work as a voluntary part-time leader at a youth club in the large village where you live.

You are handed this message:

```
Telephone message

0945   17.5.7- Insp. Beecham

Mr Jones, 15 Orange Rd,
Rowridge.  Rang to complain
abt vandalism:  garden gate
thrown down, fencing damaged,
plants & ornaments knocked
about.  Several others in the
road likewise, he says.  Mr
Jones is over 70, has had the
trouble for a long time.
Most neighbours used to it,
believe the local youth club
is cause.  Late-night door
knocking has distressed Mrs
Jones and he feels he must
complain.  Sounded a very
genuine sort.
```

Inspector Beecham has added a note to you.

Ken: one for you, I think – you know about youth clubs, don't you?

57

The Inspector is right. Orange Lane Youth Club is a well-established one, and its sports teams used to win every competition in the area. It had gone downhill last year when it had no leader for seven months, but the present leader, Jim Breakspear, is one of the best there is. You know enough of him and the area to feel quite certain that Mr Jones' allegation is unfounded, but you cannot seem to take sides. Also, part of your job is to see that formal complaints are dealt with in such a way that the Authority can always show, later on, how they have been handled.

Task 1

[handwritten: Fully set out letter] [From Cumbria Police Authority Roundup Section] [To Orange Lane Youth Club Orange Lane Roundup]

Write an appropriate note to Breakspear (whom you know), inviting him to comment. Discuss first whether this note should mention the allegation or where it comes from.

Task 2

[handwritten: Note of Telephone Call] [Clear Headings] [Date Persons involved + disposition] [How it ended]

Breakspear telephones you: he is sure police intervention would do harm rather than good, and asks to be allowed to deal with it himself. *[handwritten: Set out like a diary]* You ask him what he proposes. He plans an 'adoption' scheme whereby some of his members make themselves useful to elderly residents – a scheme he has worked successfully elsewhere. Inspector Beecham regards youth club leaders as do-gooders being paid for what (in his view) could be done by volunteers. **Record the conversation** with Breakspear in a way which enables Beecham to see from the file how you dealt with his request.

Task 3 *[handwritten: July]*

Mr Jones telephones again, and is referred to you. After six weeks the adoption scheme is working well, and nobody now thinks the Club is responsible for the damage or the

[handwritten top margin: Say why Jim Inspector want the inspector to dissuade them from direct action. – they may resent the police interference]

door knockings. But both have continued. Breakspear, when you enquire, is worried: some of his members are quite likely to try to deal with the real offenders themselves, and he suspects a clutch of nine-year-old boys from an area of flats a mile away. He now wants a police officer to come and talk to his members to dissuade them from direct action. *[handwritten: Memo]* **Write the note giving Inspector Beecham the necessary background**, and a tactful suggestion or two about how to approach members of a youth club. *[handwritten: Don't go in uniform.]*

Task 4

[handwritten: Summary of event regarding...]

The Inspector agrees to go, but before he can do so there is a phone call from Councillor Russell to the Superintendent. Gary Russell, aged 9, has been 'beaten up' *[handwritten: alleged]* in Orange Road by 'two tearaways'. The case is passed to Inspector Beecham, who does not believe the father's plausible explanation of what a boy of that age is doing a mile from home at 10.15 in the evening. He obtains a statement from the two youths, in Breakspear's hearing, who allege that the boy has been the leader of a gang which they have watched for three nights that week. Beecham passes you a copy of the statement and asks you to **provide a factual summary** which the Superintendent can use when he interviews Councillor Russell. (The statement by the youths claims that they set out to frighten rather than harm, and that the only injury the boy received was caused when he tripped over the kerb on running away.) *[handwritten: Summarise the whole case study.]*

Task 5

Inspector Beecham still has to visit the Youth Club. He asks you to **work out the notes for his five-minute talk**, and suggest what questions can be predicted and how he should answer them. *[handwritten: Memo]*

B8 – Rothley Engineering Ltd

Production has been lost on a number of occasions at this firm by failures in the rolling machines in the High Pressure Fabrication Shop. Rothleys are a specialist engineering firm producing steel pipe for public works in Britain and abroad. They have been particularly successful in gaining overseas orders for large-diameter pipe capable of taking liquids under high pressure, and have numerous contracts for it in the distillation and desalination field. The labour force is highly skilled, especially in the foundry where the junctions, valves, and related hardware are made, and in the rolling and welding work in the HPF Shop. There, sheet steel is passed through rolling machines at an angle so that it is curved into a spiral; the edges are then welded to form the pipe. The principle of the rolling machinery is that one roller rotates slightly faster than the other and the pressure that this imparts to the sheet steel causes it to 'curl'.

You are employed as a clerk in the Works Manager's office, and your duties include routine liaison with the Shop Foremen. The HPF Shop foreman is Joseph Hunter, who is 'one of the old school' – i.e. a highly skilled craftsman of long experience, who can do every skilled operative's job better than most of his men, but with a certain intolerance of paperwork. He handles the progress-control and recording aspects of his duties quite competently, but views them as necessary distractions from what he sees as 'real' work, keeping the output going, preventing and repairing breakdowns, and checking constantly on quality. He has eight major machine tools in the shop, and keeps a clipboard for each of them on his office wall. The idea that anyone in the firm might not immediately understand any and every jotting he makes on these boards inspires him to laughter or contempt, so he does not have much time for clerks.

The two rolling machines are Blacker-Waring No 4s. You and Hunter know from experience that the rollers last about seven weeks. In the past year or so, too, a roller has occasionally been found to run slightly out of true – not because it is inaccurately machined, but because the weight of the roller's body is not quite evenly distributed round its central axis. This makes it run fractionally fast for one half and fractionally slow for the other half of each rotation. The effect on the spiral is no more than a millimetre or two, but it greatly increases the time and the difficulty of the welding process which follows because the edges to be welded do not 'marry' so easily. As a rule such a roller will do a satisfactory job if the machine is run below full speed until a replacement is fitted.

The record on Joe Hunter's clipboard for B/W4 No 2 reads as follows:

5/5	B roller refitted (during waiting time – stockflow off)
12/5	Press–test sec. rpts weld-spread; traced to skew in B Roller. Tested at ½ spd. O.K. Notice posted. Ordered replacemt Stevensons by phone.
19/5	Stevensons rang: new roller dely 26/5. Written order from WM.

24/5 Roller fractured 7.45 am. M. Andrews ran full spd. didn't see notice. Rang Stvsns to rush replacmt.

25/5 Stevenson's delivered spare A Roller. Rang them: didn't understand message. WM's clk conf. wr. order was for B.

26/5 B Roller fetched, Rothley transport.

27/5 Roller fitted (o'time); dummy run O.K.

28/5 ½ spd test a.m. O.K. Full spd test p.m. O.K. Checks.

2/6 Full use

Rothley's have standing instructions to operatives to look out for special instructions, especially when changing shifts or returning from time off. Hunter therefore did not feel it necessary to warn Andrews since he would have seen the notice in the changing room as well. Stevensons are a machine-tool manufacturer, and appear to have misunderstood Hunter's phone message as well as overlooked the detail on the confirmatory order.

A number of matters arise for you to deal with:

Task 1

The Works Manager asks for a written report on the loss of production in the HPF Shop in May. Hunter observes that this is your line of country rather than his, but you have to write for his approval and signature. **Draft a starkly factual account of events** in what Hunter calls 'your posh-school English'. (See Guide, 7.4.1.)

Task 2

Machine breakdown occurs in one department of the firm or another once a fortnight or so. The Works Manager looks at your report and decides he wants a standard form for the purpose. He asks you to look at report forms used in other firms for this job, and to **prepare a draft form** for discussion at the foremen's meeting next month.

Task 3

The meeting cannot be held and the next one will be in September, but the WM wants to get on with the form. He tells you to **write a short note**, to go with the draft form, setting out why one is needed. The note has to avoid incurring Hunter's derision, and somehow get him and the other foremen to see that a report-form is likely to suit them better than a demand to write a report.

Task 4

Explore in discussion the various possible ways in which the misunderstanding of the telephone message to Stevensons might have arisen. Bear in mind that Hunter would have had no difficulty if he had spoken to a technical man, and that Stevensons may have problems very like Andrews' failure to read the notice.

Task 5

Draft a letter to Stevensons pointing out the incorrect filling of the order for a B roller and inviting them to share the additional costs involved in fetching the right one. Rothley depends, absolutely, on the willingness of Stevenson's to supply parts accurately and quickly: the firm cannot afford to alienate a critically important supplier.

B9 – Mrs Chillingworth's Cooker

You are undergoing a traineeship with the Kingsford District Council, one stage of which is a three-month posting as Assistant to the Chief Executive, who passes on whatever work he thinks you can handle. One Thursday near the end of your time, the Chief Executive is out when an angry telephone caller insists on speaking to 'someone responsible' in the Chief Executive's office. The call is routed to you and goes as follows:

'Can I help you?'

'I certainly hope so! My cooker has been interfered with.'

'Well, Madam, can we begin with your name and address, please?'

'Mrs Chillingworth, 93 Grove Road, Lillington.'

'Thank you. Would you tell me what has happened?'

'I moved here two years ago and bought the cooker with the house. The pilot lights don't work, but I understand they often don't on natural gas. Otherwise it's a perfectly good cooker, but I went out this morning and some gas men called.'

'Do you know whether they were from the Gas Board or the Housing Department?'

'Well, the Gas Board say it wasn't them and put me on to you. Anyway, they dismantled the top of the cooker and left, saying it wasn't safe and needed new parts. That was yesterday, but they haven't been back.'

'If you were out, how did they get in?'

'My elderly mother let them in: they said they'd had a call. She wasn't to know, was she?'

'What type of cooker is it, Mrs Chillingworth?'

'A Glowplate 22.'

'Thank you, Madam. Can you let me have a couple of hours to investigate this for you?'

'Well, yes – but I want some action today!'

'Of course: so do I. And I would be grateful for your telephone number, please.'

'Lillington 62129.'

'Thank you very much. I'll come back to you on this as soon as I can.'

Mrs Chillingworth is obviously angry, and if she did not put in a service call she is entitled to be. In that event the Council is 'over a barrel'. You go down to the Housing Office to see the Direct Labour Supervisor. He is out, but his clerical assistant shows you the gas-fitters' call book. You find the call entry and trace it back to the request slip, which has pinned to it a telephone message and a confirmatory requisition received that morning. While the requisition records the address to be visited as 39 Grove Road, the telephone message has it as No. 93. The error could have occurred at either end of the phone call. You look at the Housing Department rent file and establish that 39 is a council house, but 93 is not. It had been, but was one of the earliest to be sold off by the former Lillington UDC in the 'sixties. The cooker is a make which you know to have been out of production for at least twelve years, so it had probably been installed for much longer.

You establish the whereabouts of the charge-hand gas-fitter and explain the problem. He grasps that because it is a private house the

Council is technically guilty of trespass and the cooker must be put right immediately. When he hears what make it is he observes that that means a trip to the Gas Board main depot ten miles away. You persuade him to go there, but there is no guarantee that the depot will have the spares. He also confirms that the gang which had done the gas conversion for the area had allowed Glowplate 22s to be converted when they ought to have been replaced. He mentions the small reserve stock of second-hand cookers kept by the Council to cater for such problems – but only for Council houses.

Task 1

You know from experience that the Chief Executive will always defend his staff but will never try to cover up for mistakes. **Draft the sort of letter of apology** to Mrs Chillingworth that you would expect him to approve and sign when he returns after lunch, marking it for delivery at once by the Direct-Labour Supervisor, and add the briefest possible explanation to the Chief Executive of why the letter is needed and what you have done about it so far.

Task 2

The charge-hand returns from the depot to say that no spares are to be had for a cooker which went out of production in 1961. At 4 p.m. Mrs Chillingworth herself arrives, in no way mollified by the letter: she demands the dismissal of the employee who made the mistake and the repair of her own cooker. **Simulate the conversation** between Mrs Chillingworth, yourself, the Chief Executive, and the charge-hand fitter who is called in to testify to the position about spares. **The rest of the group make notes** of how the Chief Executive persuades her to accept a replacement cooker without charge temporarily.

Task 3

The Chief Executive tells you to go along with the fitters to see that the replacement is in working order before you go home. While in the house you hear Mrs Chillingworth answer a telephone call which appears to be from the local newspaper. You can expect the paper to ask the Chief Executive for a statement: **draft one that he can dictate to the paper over the telephone**.

Task 4

The charge-hand reports next morning that, after you left, Mrs Chillingworth announced her intention of ordering a new cooker from Marshall's to replace the 'shoddy thing' just installed. 'Marshall's can make the Council pay much more easily than I can', she is reported as saying. Marshall's is a substantial firm which dominates the household appliance trade in the area but also does a great deal of contracting work for the Housing Department. Its Contracts Manager, Joe Leppard, is known to you. **Consider in discussion** how to approach him and what facts and arguments to put to him.

Task 5

Next morning, Mrs Chillingworth brings you Marshall's bill for the new cooker, which she is already using. Also, the local paper headlines her complaint, omits the Chief's statement and challenges the Council to pay for the new cooker. **Discuss the position of the Council** and **prepare a statement**. The Chief Executive tells you he has arranged with the editor for front-page placing, adding 'Facts only, no innuendos. Leave the reader to work out who is being difficult. And not more than 200 words.'

Assignments – Group C

C1 – G. Smith & Sons

In 1949 George Smith set up a small printing firm in Burrfield, and it was moderately successful. In due course two of his three sons, Jack and Edward, followed him into the firm – Edward as its accountant, and you, Jack, as a printing apprentice who worked from the shop floor up to Assistant Manager. Since your father had a heart attack in 1973 you have been in effective charge.

Apart from the two brothers, the firm employs three secretarial staff, two sales staff, a receptionist who operates the switchboard, two women packers who also do internal cleaning, a driver, and thirteen machine operators (eight men, five women) who are members of the appropriate printing union, together with the two supervisors who each run one of the two printing shops. The work which, in a larger firm, would be done by the company secretary, is done by Edward Smith, and you combine the functions of works manager, personnel officer, and quality control officer. It is a happy firm, with a long-serving staff, no record of difficulty over labour relations, and no sign of any resentment about your own steady promotion. Its main customers are Dartshire County Council, the local Area Health Authority, Burrfield District Council, and (more recently) I.S.T. Ltd, the large engineering employer whose works dominate the town and the labour market. But more than 40% of the business comes from printing bills, posters, programmes, handbooks, and headed stationery for dozens of local clubs, schools, small firms, and similar organisations.

Burrfield is a town of 89,000 people in the north Midlands. It has a low unemployment rate, since many of the small employers are sub-contractors for I.S.T. Ltd or for the motor industry, and a number of them have had major contracts with British Rail. In 1954 the local council set up the Elm Lodge Trading Estate seven miles to the east, equidistant from Burrfield and two other towns, to attract light industry, and the Estate is linked to Burrfield by an unusually good bus service. More recently the emphasis has been on improving the town itself: the Falcon Centre provides a shopping precinct and offices; parking meters were introduced; and the working-class housing area known as the Stanier Estate was designated as a General

Improvement Area with strikingly successful results. The more expensive housing lies across the river.

The last stage of the town improvement involves the redevelopment of the area between Stephenson Road and the River Burr. This area had been the victim of 'planning blight': with redevelopment expected, owners allowed their property to dilapidate. The exception was your firm, G. Smith & Sons, whose tenure of a corner site was a commercial asset, and who looked after that asset by keeping the property in good repair. However, the District Council now wishes to buy the firm out of the building in order to proceed with the redevelopment, and has never concealed that it would use compulsory purchase powers if necessary. The firm's record in maintaining the amenity of its corner site has led the Council to regard it as a valuable prospective tenant of a town-centre site if one can be found. Your main problem, and the tasks in this assignment, have to do with finding suitable alternative premises.

Document A is a diagrammatic map of the town centre. There are three realistic possibilities:

1. 48 Bishopgate. Originally a rather grand private house in a Georgian street which is part of a conservation area, this had been extended to the rear to accommodate a private nursing home. The front part is a listed building, but the road access for vehicles is good. The property is for sale at £47,000; necessary alterations internally in a building otherwise in excellent repair would cost £7,000; the District Council offers long-term loan facilities at 8% (renegotiable if market rates fall below that level); current rates are £1,950 p.a.

2. 126 Bridge Street. A mid-Victorian brick warehouse, formerly a British Rail Parcels depot, little used since 1960 and empty since 1971. Stands in a substantial site adjoining the station and goods yard, but is in need of extensive repairs. For sale at £29,500 and estimated to require expenditure on restoration etc. costing at least £30,000. Rates stand at £540 p.a. The same low-cost loan facility applies, but at $\frac{1}{2}$% more than for Site 1 (since the Council uses its interest-rate policy to induce occupancy of major sites).

3. Factory No. 11, Elm Lodge Trading Estate. This is a recently vacated small factory with suitable offices, one floor of workshop space with ample room for purpose-built additions, good parking, and regular bus-services. The site is to let at £7,900 inclusive of rates.

You and your brother have decided that in assessing the merits of the three sites, the employer must meet the cost of travel to the trading estate and regard that as one of the basic factors in the choice. The current fare for the return journey, for annual season tickets bought by the firm, is £105 per head.

Document A

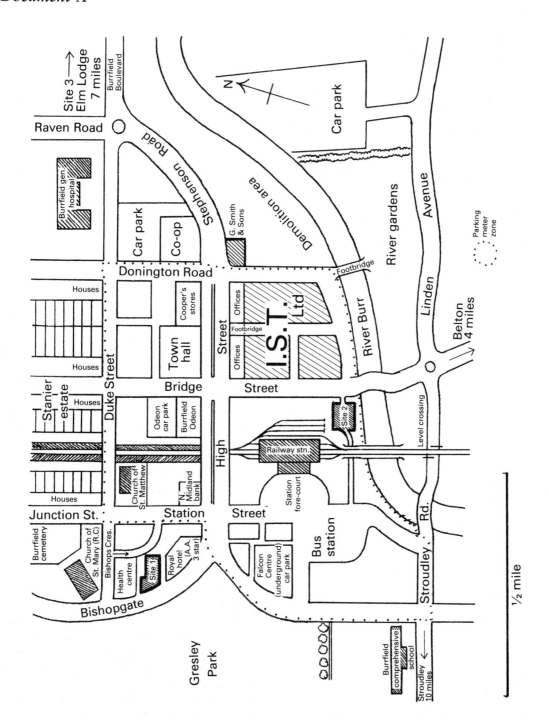

Task 1

It is necessary to secure the involvement of the whole of the workforce in the decision about the site. Their preferences are likely to have a marked effect on the success or otherwise of the move and on the firm's profitability afterwards. However, it is important for the staff's wishes to be based on sound information. **Set out the choices**, and the various factors which bear on the decision, in a way which the packers and the receptionist, as well as the skilled printers, would find helpful, and **include a simple form** on which they can express their views. The whole document should not be longer than one side of A4 typescript.

Suggested Solution to Task 1

```
Dear

As you know, we have been the only occupant of
the area surrounding our works for some time.
The Council owns the rest of the area, and
wants to build on it. The development needs
the whole site, and our company has to move
somewhere else. The directors of the company
do not think it would be of any use to try to
fight this proposal. However, we would like
to find out what each of the firm's employees
thinks about the other places we might go to.

There are three possibilities:

1. The former nursing home at 48 Bishopsgate,
opposite Gresley Park and next door to the
Royal Hotel. This is a beautiful building, in
good condition. It would not need much
alteration, and we could move in, with little
interruption of work, in about three months'
time. The building would not be perfect: it
has many steps and corridors, and our handling
problems might be difficult. There is no
parking for staff, except in the multi-storey
car-park. There is some traffic noise, but
the building would be easily recognised by our
customers.

2. The old railway parcels warehouse off
Bridge Street between the station and the
river. This would need a great deal of repair
and restoration, but the cost of this is off-
set by the much lower purchase price. There
is ample parking space, room for expansion,
and a building we could adapt. But we would
have to move in before the building work was
finished. There would be some noise from the
station, and some of you may think there will
be damp from the river.

3. Factory No. 11 on the Elm Lodge Trading
Estate, seven miles east of here. This is an
ideal building, since it is a modern factory
with good office space and plenty of parking,
all on one level. It is in the country,
```

```
quiet, clean, and by all accounts a place
where many people are happy to work in spite
of the journey involved. There is a very good
public bus service, and all employees using it
would be issued with season tickets purchased
by the company.

There is very little difference, on balance,
between the three sites so far as the costs
are concerned. The choice is one of
convenience and preference: your wishes are
a big factor in the decision we have to make.
Whichever place we choose, everyone's job is
guaranteed as long as we secure the work for
us to do.

Please tell us what you think: tear off the
slip below and let either of us have it.

                          Yours sincerely,
```

```
Which site do you prefer - first choice:
                                 . . . . . . . . . . . . .
                          second choice:
                                 . . . . . . . . . . . . .
What are your main reasons for your choice?
```

Notes on Task 1

The document should be a letter, and should be addressed to each recipient by name and signed by hand: there are only twenty-four people involved and personal relationships with that size of group are vitally important.

Secondly, the same letter should be used for all the staff. Thirdly, the letter should set out the basic reason for the move, and should describe the three choices without trying to suggest that one is better than the others. Above all, the letter needs to be clear without being unduly formal.

The use of the first person ('we') is less distant than using 'the company' throughout. The description of the town sites can reasonably assume that everybody will know and recognise these. The letter also has to forestall anxiety that the move might lead to redundancies.

This kind of letter can only be used in very particular circumstances. It is foolish to use this approach if the writers have no intention of being influenced by the response. Indeed, if the writers are suspected by the readers of using this kind of approach as a way of dividing the staff so as to get their own way more easily, such a letter will be dismissed cynically as worthless.

Task 2

The company's bank manager is entitled to be consulted about the move, and should be able to see a simplified but reasonably complete statement of the relative costs of the three sites. **Prepare such a statement**, and reach a provisional assessment of how important the financial factor is to the choice, on the assumption that the firm has already set aside £10,000 towards meeting the cost of the move. This should be set out as a briefing report.

Suggested Solution to Task 2

```
Assessment of alternative sites

A:  approximate cost estimates

Site 1:  48 Bishopgate

Purchase price:    £47,000    Annual rates:
Repairs etc.         7,000    Loan interest @ 8%      3,520
                   -------    Rates                   1,950
                    54,000    Repayment over 20 yrs   2,200
LESS cash in hand   10,000
                   -------       TOTAL               £7,670
Loan finance required:                              ======
                    44,000
                   -------


Site 2:  126 Bridge Street

Purchase price:    £29,500    Annual rates:
Repairs etc (est.)  35,000    Loan interest @ 8½%     4,633
                   -------    Rates                     540
                    64,500    Additional rates on
LESS Cash in hand   10,000      improved propty (est.)  500
                   -------    Repayment over 20 yrs   2,725
Loan finance required:
                    54,500       TOTAL               £8,398
                   -------                           ======


Site 3:  Elm Lodge Trading Estate

                    Rent & rates  £7,900
                    Bus Transport
                      (est*)       1,890
                                  ------
                                           9,790
                    LESS Investment
                    income on £10,000
                    @ 11% net:             1,100
                                          ------
                        TOTAL            £8,690
                                         ======

 * Estimate based on 18 staff not
   now driving to work, @ £105 p.a.
   season-ticket rate.
```

B: interpretation

For a firm of this size the differences between the direct site costs of the three sites are negligible. The margin between Site 1 and Site 3 is about 1% of turnover, and the higher cost of Site 3 would be offset by gains in handling costs on a flat-floor site.

The hidden costs and unpredictables are more difficult to assess. They would appear to include these:
(a) almost certain sharp increase in the rates on the improved property at Site 2 (cf the rates on Site 1);
(b) additional works transport and delivery costs of Site 3;
(c) the virtual certainty that labour would turn over more rapidly, with consequent increase in training costs, at Site 3;
(d) the considerable loss of production, perhaps up to £30,000 of turnover, entailed in the choice of Site 2.

In the absence of any factors we have overlooked, the state of staff opinion is genuinely relevant. If it prefers 1 or 2, I would choose 2 and look to the staff to put up with builders. If it is split between town and country, I would choose 3; if it is hopelessly divided, I would still recommend 2; but if it is decisive in favour of any site, that should settle the matter.

Notes on Task 2

The essential feature of any answer to this task must be the separation of the figures from the assessment/interpretation.

The statement of the costs is simplified, as called for in the Task, by the omission of factors which apply in roughly equal ways in all three sites. Thus, there must be redecorating costs at Site 3 which are omitted while repairs are included for the others, but to offset this both the other sites will involve payment of commission on the purchase price to the solicitors concerned.

The inclusion of the income on investing the cash in hand in the calculations for Site 3 is necessary, although it does not necessarily mean that the firm may use that sum in that way. Using it to assist with the purchase of Site 1 or 2 entails a loss of that income, and the corresponding gain is part of the cost-structure for Site 3.

The interpretation actually made is a matter of judgement. Why the interpretation is made, and how it is expressed, are more important.

Task 3

In due course one of the firm's regular meetings of the whole staff is to be held, at which the findings of the survey of preferences will be reported and discussed, and an assessment of the financial aspect of the move will be given by the Chief Accountant. It has emerged that several staff felt unable to give their true preferences on the reply slip because some of their colleagues had put pressure on them not to choose the Trading Estate (the colleagues did not want to make the bus journey). The existence of a serious possibility of a move to the estate has raised anxiety about redundancy. These and any other relevant matters can be brought up at the meeting. **Draw up an agenda** for the meeting which can be posted on the works notice board.

Suggested Solution to Task 3

G. Smith & Sons, Printers

Staff Meeting No. 64

A Meeting of the Directors and Employees of the Company will be held in the Conference Room on Thursday, February 28th at 4.15 p.m. Production and administrative departments will close at 4.10 p.m.

Agenda:

1. Minutes of Meeting No. 63 (posted)
2. Matters arising.
3. Alternative sites: to receive a report on the survey of staff preferences.
4. Alternative sites: to receive a report on the financial considerations affecting the choice.
5. Future employment prospects: to receive a statement by the Directors.
6. Alternative sites: to confirm any decision pursuant to the survey of staff preferences
       OR to discuss the position prior to a decision by the Directors.
7. Any other business.

E. Smith, Director.

Notes on Task 3

Apart from stating who is to meet, when, where, and why, agenda documents are more difficult than they appear. Their prime function is to state the business of a meeting, that is not merely to state what topics the meeting is to discuss, but to specify precisely what the function of the meeting is in relation to those topics. This particular example is a difficult one: the Directors are genuine in being willing to be bound by the staff preference, if it is clear – but the agenda has to provide for the possibility that it will not be clear.

The agenda must, in a serial committee, begin with minutes of the previous meeting, followed by such matters arising as are not in the following agenda items. (A skilful secretary will ensure that most matters likely to arise *are* in the main agenda.) The main items then have to specify a function – in this case 'to receive', or 'to confirm' or 'to discuss'. These function terms are important because the chairman of an unruly meeting can use them. If the agenda says 'to receive', the meeting can only receive or refer back (i.e. reject). If a finance committee has an item 'to approve', it can do so, or can refuse to do so. The wording of the agenda determines the powers of the chairman.

This may seem to be making a great deal out of a minor matter, but any organisation which is dealing with property, or with employment, is responsible in law for the proper conduct of its affairs, and those whose interests are harmed by that conduct can challenge the decisions in the courts if they are improperly taken or are taken by irregularly constituted bodies. For example, a sports club cannot, under an agenda item 'to receive the accounts', decide that because there is a deficit the groundsman must be declared redundant, and carry out the decision, without the matter appearing as an agenda item in its own right. On the larger scale of local government, the importance of correct procedure, minutes, agendas, and chairmanship is correspondingly greater.

Task 4

After due discussion of the choices, from which there will be a clear preference in the minds of individuals (and possibly the whole group), **write a news item** for the local evening paper's column 'Burrfield Burrbles' reporting the coming move in a fairly light-hearted way.

Suggested Solution to Task 4

SMITH'S TO MOVE

The Burrfield printing firm of G. Smith & Sons are to move. Their bright blue building on the corner of Stephenson Road is a local landmark, but it is the last remaining property on the site, and the Council starts re-development in the autumn.

Director Edward Smith, son of the firm's founder and well-known Burrfield character George Smith, told us today that democracy was the order of the day at Smiths. There had been three alternative places to move to, and the firm had polled the staff about them. They all wanted to stay in Burrfield, so the firm is buying the old nursing home in Bishopgate.

The firm's new home is a landmark, too. A listed building, its front half was built in 1795, along with the row of Georgian town houses which now form the Royal Hotel. The former nursing home, which shut down two years ago, built on the back in the 1950s, and the Smith brothers say the building will suit the firm beautifully.

Packer Annie Garden, who is 62 and has worked for Smiths ever since it began in 1949, said she was delighted. "We have to go, I suppose, but at least we don't have to go far, and it'll be nice looking out over the Park."

The purchase price is understood to be just under £50,000, and the purchase is being assisted with loan facilities from the Burrfield District Council. Full compensation for the old site has alreay been paid, and the move is expected to occupy three days at the end of June during the firm's extended summer closure.

Notes on Task 4

The style of 'journalistic' writing is often despised but has many virtues. This example exhibits four features of all good journalism:
1. It latches on firmly to the reader's existing knowledge.
2. It names names, and quotes people.
3. It packs a great deal of information into text which is divided into numerous short paragraphs.
4. Its sentence structures are relatively simple, using named persons or places as subjects, and avoiding subordinate clauses.

This kind of writing is well suited to its purpose, and some of its features are desirable in any kind of writing.

Task 5

Draw up the text of a circular to be addressed to the firm's customers telling them of the reason for the move, its date, and the firm's new address.

Suggested Solution to Task 5

G Smith & Sons – Printers

1 Stephenson Road
Burrfield

                              (date)

CHANGE OF ADDRESS

After almost thirty years in this building, Smiths of Burrfield are moving. As many of our customers will know, the Stephenson Road Site is to be redeveloped, and from July onwards Smiths will be at

      48 BISHOPGATE, BURRFIELD.

As already announced, our summer closure will be from June 16th to June 30th, and orders required for delivery in that period will be completed before the closure if copy is received by June 6th. To complete the move in the smoothest way we are running down some of our stocks, and one or two special paper sizes may take longer to supply in June and July.

Our new building is a Burrfield landmark, like our old one. Many customers will recognise it as the former Nursing Home near the Royal Hotel. We shall re-open for business on Tuesday July 3rd, with the same hours as before and the same telephone number. There will be no changes of staff, and we hope there will be no reduction in our service to all our customers.

              J. Smith
                     Directors
             E. Smith

Notes on Task 5

The resemblance between the tone of this circular and the piece of journalism is not accidental: Smiths know most of their customers by name, but they are too numerous to address individually. So the firm should use a tone which treats them as old friends, and should exploit their existing knowledge just as the news item does. There is no gain whatever in using formulaic language like 'We beg to inform' or 'We regret that owing to diminution of stocks it will be impossible to . . .'. Any business communication should be correct, concise, and complete, but it should also be *courteous*.

C2 – Death of a Grocer

You work as a hospital administrator in the north of England, and your wife, Carol, has very recently given birth to your first child. The day after the birth, you received news of the sudden death of Harold Goodnough, Carol's father.

Mr Goodnough trained as a grocer and became a branch manager with a chain just before the Second World War. He was able to use a legacy from his father and his service gratuity to buy a 'high class provision merchant' business in Lunceford, in the Thames Valley. This middle-class commuter village became very prosperous in the next two decades, and expanded enormously. Harold Goodnough's choice of site was thus a happy one, and his staid, courteous and kindly manner concealed an acute awareness of the value of customer loyalty in his kind of business. He had suffered less than most small grocers from the rise of the supermarket, but he was clear that he should wind up the business and retire. His wife, who had been something of a figure in the community, had died six years earlier, and when Harold died at the age of 64 he was within a year of retirement.

Before moving north, you had built up a very strong mutual trust with your father-in-law, and he had appointed you to be one of two Executors of his estate. The solicitor tells you when you go down for the funeral that apart from minor bequests the whole of the estate has been left to Carol. You ought, he suggests, to secure some time off work and come down to deal with urgent affairs. You arrange for a week's leave, and agree to clear any major decisions with Carol by telephone.

When you arrive for a week in Lunceford the solicitor takes you to see your late father-in-law's bank manager. There is enough evidence that the estate is sound to allow the bank to lend you £2,000. This sum would be repayable out of the estate, but should suffice to close the business. The bank manager requires you to keep a record of decisions made, and proper accounts. The solicitor adds that until the will receives probate it will not be possible to make use of the assets of the business, including any cash receipts which may come in. He describes the staff, and mentions that Mr Goodnough had intended to make a generous bequest to Miss Cazer, his long-standing assistant, but had died before carrying out this intention.

You are now faced with a number of duties, and your wife will need to be kept informed and, on major

decisions, to approve the decisions to be taken. You will have to tell the two members of the staff that the business is to close at once, although you will wish them to continue at work for two or three weeks to help dispose of stock, complete the accounts, and clear the premises.

Task 1

Alice Cazer is 56, a sedate, good-natured single woman who has been a hard-working employee ever since the shop opened. Like her employer, she has no relatives of her own generation, and had few outside interests. Only in the last two years had her health not been perfect, for which she had been allowed a lengthened lunch-hour without loss of pay. Her grasp of the trade, knowledge of customers and their preferences, and her unshakeable dignity made her an admirable employee, and Mr Goodnough and his daughter shared a profound regard for her. However, she could not hope to secure another job, and would reject anything smacking of 'charity' from you. The solicitor discusses the case with you and suggests that the best course would probably be to declare her officially redundant. **Find out the regulations governing redundancy, and calculate the level of redundancy pay** to which Miss Cazer would be entitled. (She has earned £57.50 per week for the past year, and has 31 years and 4 months' continuous service.)

Task 2

The other assistant, Mrs Yvonne Austin, is another matter. She joined the firm shortly after Mrs Goodnough's death as a part-time book-keeper. When her younger child went on to secondary school three years ago she became a full-time employee, although she works as much for the interest of the job as for the income. She has a keen mind, a good grasp of accounts, and a clear determination to make sure that you do not ride rough-shod over her and Miss Cazer. Mrs Austin's accounting skills make her indispensable to you in winding up the business. You have to make a decision about how long to continue employing her, on what terms, and what compensation for loss of employment to offer. These decisions will require knowledge of an employer's legal and other obligations to an employee. Assume that Mrs Austin is paid £52 a week, and has been employed for 2 years and 7 months for 25 hrs/wk and for 2 years and 11 months for 42 hrs/wk. Having reached your decisions and worked out their likely cost, **set up the brief notes** for a three-minute telephone call to your wife, and if possible simulate the conversation in which you tell her about your decisions relating to the staff.

Task 3

Mrs Austin takes you through the books and identifies four sizeable debtor accounts. Three are for sums between £80 and £100, and one is for £176. Mr Goodnough had ceased to supply to all four over a year before, but the solicitor has written twice to each with no effect. You receive a visit from a representative of a debt-collection agency, who follows the visit up with a letter offering £30 for the four debts. Two days later a meeting is arranged between your solicitor, yourself, and the representative, Mr Perana. You and the solicitor have decided that £80 is the minimum reasonable offer. Mr Perana is prepared to go higher, but his limit is below your minimum. It will be up to you to reject or accept his final offer, but you will have to account for the decision to Carol. **Simulate the meeting.**

Task 4

The cased stock and sundry canned goods are sold off for about £1,400, but this does not help your financial position. You hear from Mrs Austin that bills due within the next few days include those for electricity (£150) and the principal wholesale supplier who sends accounts every six months (£1,800, approx.). Your previous line of credit for £2,000 will not cover these items as well as salaries and compensation. You know the estate to be substantial and you can offer the bank good security for a further loan. Allow sufficient margin for contingencies, allow three months for probate of the will, assess the probable interest charges, and estimate the size of loan you require. The bank manager will be surprised by its size. **Simulate the meeting** with him.

Task 5

Before you leave Lunceford you receive the letter given below, and feel obliged to write a reply. **Draft the text** which will explain your decision as acceptably as possible.

```
Dear Mr Kenton,

On behalf of the Senior Citizens' Club here in
Lunceford, may I say how sorry we were to hear
of your father-in-law's sudden death. Mr
Goodnough was a real gentleman and he always
spent a bit of extra time serving the older
folk. He even allowed some of us credit, and
not many shops do that nowadays.

We hear that you are thinking of closing the
shop. This would be a tragedy for us. I know
many of the older people here dislike super-
market shopping. It is difficult to find what
you want. Sometimes one is knocked about by
the trolleys. And getting small quantities is
very hard (Mr Goodnough always let us buy 4oz
of butter or two eggs). It is an expensive
bus ride to the new precinct in Batsford, and
even the nearest Co-op has gone self-service.

So if you are thinking of closing down, please
bear the needs of old people in mind. I'm sure
Mr Goodnough would not have wanted us to be
treated this way.

              Yours sincerely,

              Celia Heath (Mrs).
```

C3 – Wirkton Cutting

The Carrside Metropolitan District Council is a local authority in a mainly urban area with a hinterland of rural and hilly countryside. It has main committees for Housing, Education, Finance & Resources, Planning, and Recreation & Leisure. The Planning Committee has sub-committees for Planning, for Environmental Services, and for Highways. Each of these sub-committees is served by a Head of Department, while the Director of Planning is Chief Officer for the three departments. Your post is that of Assistant (Admin) to the Head of Planning, who is the most senior of the three heads of department. Owing to a change of policy there is no longer a Chief Executive, and owing to financial cuts there has been some delay in filling the post of Director of Planning, which is still vacant.

The chief town in the Metropolitan District is Baughton, and the large village of Carley lies seven miles south of it. A mile or two west of Carley is the village of Wirkton. The landscape is hilly, and when the Great Northern Railway first drove its line from Baughton to New Maston it employed a large number of navvies. Some of these remained on the site for some time, and housing was built for them which became the nucleus of Wirkton. The village was fortunate in the subsequent find of an outcrop of brown limestone which gave rise to the development of a quarry and the building of a station on the railway. The quarry closed in 1939, the station in 1953, and the line itself in 1960, the tracks being taken up for scrap a couple of years later.

The new nylon spinning works in Carley and the big stock-rearing farms in the area provided alternative jobs. Temple Farm took over Ley Farm in 1966 and used much of the land to start market gardening for the Baughton market, but the farmhouse remained unoccupied. (See map overleaf.)

Wirkton originated as a settlement for navvies, and the creation of Wirkton Cutting was one of the more notable achievements of the great age of railway building. Its southern part was ordinary enough, running about 7 metres deep for just over 1 km. At the point where a bridge carried a minor road to the Common which gave the area its name, the cutting deepened sharply. For over 1.7 km it ran at 15 or 16 metres deep, and the sides of the cutting were immense. Their size and steepness caused repeated earth falls, which explained why some navvies were kept on after the building. The GNR eventually had to fence the top of the banks, and planted a dense line of trees and shrubs which occasional fires had kept down in the past. To the south of the cutting the steep fall in the land caused the railway to be set on an embankment, which was in places 22 m. high and was similarly fenced at the top to prevent accidents. To the north, the line ran through a short tunnel, but roof-falls had blocked it some years after the track had been removed.

The foregoing details may be checked on the plan of the area (Document A). Other relevant facts are:
(a) British Rail dismantled the bridge at A some years ago at the request of the owners of Hallston Farm. It still owns the other bridges, of

Document A

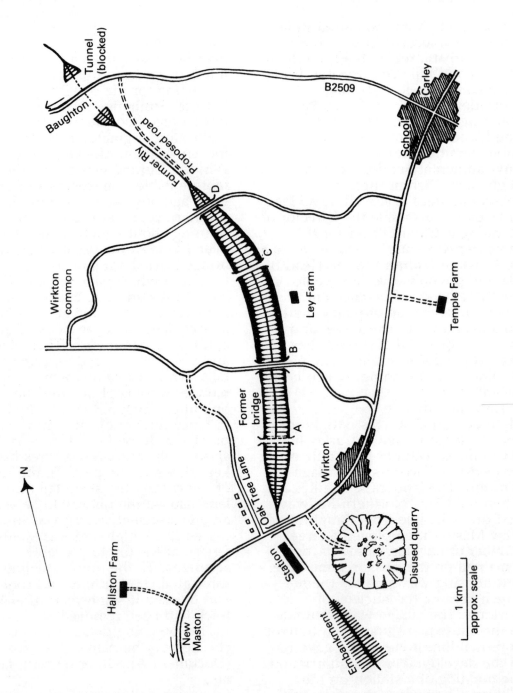

N

Tunnel (blocked)

Baughton

B2509

School

Carley

Former Rly

Proposed road

Wirkton common

D

C

Ley Farm

Temple Farm

B

Former bridge

A

Wirkton

Oak Tree Lane

Hallston Farm

New Maston

Station

Disused quarry

Embankment

1 km
approx. scale

74

which C was built to give light-traffic access to land north of the line which was then part of Ley Farm. Bridges B and D carry minor roads and are in good order.

(b) The former station was sold and converted into a private house in 1962.

(c) Of the five council houses adjacent to the Cutting at its southern end, the two northernmost have been vacant since 1971 because no tenant has been willing to live there.

Your superior greets you one morning with Document B and asks you to investigate. It is the first you or he have heard of the scheme. You make tentative inquiries by telephone in the Leisure and Amenities Department. It transpires that the scheme was first proposed by a member of the Environmental Services Sub-Committee as a solution to the problem of Baughton's refuse disposal, and was mentioned casually during a meeting of the Recreation & Leisure Committee next day. Another member of Recreation & Leisure appears to have thought it a much more fully developed scheme than it was, and in order to prevent it by causing a public outcry, leaked the story to the local radio station.

You report this to the Head of Planning, who instructs you to investigate formally on his behalf and report. He tells you that because the Director of Recreation is embarrassed by the leak of a mere suggestion as if it were a serious scheme, he is happy to co-operate on a joint report to both Committees. You glean these facts:

1. The incineration plant at Baughton was built to cope with a much smaller output of refuse, and

Document B

Countryside Association
New Maston Branch

12 October 19--

Director of Planning,
Carrside Metropolitan District Council
Council Offices
Baughton BH1 6ST

Dear Sir,

PROPOSED TIPPING AT WIRKTON CUTTING (ex-GNR)

The above proposal was reported in press and on radio on October 2, and a special general meeting of this branch was held to discuss it. 124 of our 176 members passed unanimously the following resolution:

> "This Association is totally opposed to the proposal to tip refuse at Wirkton Cutting and pledges itself to take every possible action to persuade the Carrside M.D.C. to withdraw the scheme."

I am directed to acquaint you with our reasons for objecting, viz:

1. Refuse tipping is a wasteful land-use anywhere, unless the in-filling is designed to create land useful for agriculture or other valuable purpose and the site to be filled cannot be used in any other way.

2. The Council's incineration plant is not far away, and its recovery of scrap metal yields revenue which tipping would deny.

3. We wish to see the line in question developed as a bridle-way, as has been done elsewhere with sites of similar recreational potential. At a time when such facilities are in short supply and increasing demand, we would regard tipping as the loss of a genuine opportunity to add to the District's amenities.

I hope you will consider these points before taking further steps to implement the proposal, and that you will consider a meeting between your officers and two or three representatives of our Association.

Yours faithfully,

D. Briggs
Secretary

Baughton needs tipping capacity of 200,000m³ over the next 20–25 years. A new incineration plant is too costly.

2. The Head of Environmental Services confirms that the suggestion gained some sympathy in committee, and was referred to him for further study. There had not yet been time for formal approaches to other departments.

3. The Recreation & Leisure Committee had considered the bridle-way proposal two years before and rejected it. The depth of the cutting, the height of the embankment, and the condition of the tunnel were felt to be hazards.

4. The Head of Environmental Services did not wish to commit himself formally, but felt that the deeper part of the Cutting would be ideal for tipping, and with mechanical impacting and proper dressing with topsoil land could be restored to agricultural use at a rate of 60–70 metres per year. This scale of operation would justify laying a road for the refuse trucks from the B2509 to the end of the Cutting.

Task 1

The chairman of the Planning sub-committee agrees to call an emergency meeting. He has a standing rule that preparatory documents must not exceed a single sheet of A4 paper. You need space for a plan, which leaves you **about 250 words in which to summarise the proposal,** state its advantages, outline the probable objections, and suggest how the latter might be met. You are not required to make recommendations, and are forbidden to mention the proposed road for the refuse trucks, since the landowner involved is a member of the sub-committee. (See Guide, 7.4.)

Task 2

You are handed Document C and are asked to **draft a reply**. The same restriction on mentioning the road applies.

Document C

```
                        35 Oak Tree Lane
                        Wirkton
                        New Maston
                        BH9 3MS

                        October 8  19--

Director of Planning
Carrside Metropolitan District Council

Dear Sir,

I have been asked to write on behalf of the
residents of Wirkton regarding your proposal
to tip refuse at Wirkton Cutting. We object
strongly to this proposal, and to the fact
that we have not been consulted in any way.
Residents close to the Cutting have many
objections to the proposal, but there is
general agreement about the following:

1.  The access roads are narrow with many
sharp bends. Regular use by large refuse-
disposal vehicles is bound to constitute a
danger, especially to children and old people
walking on the roads to get to the bus or
shops.

2.  A tip will attract vermin, and some of our
homes are only fifty to sixty feet away from
the Cutting.

3.  The work involved will cause nuisance from
noise and smell.

Copies of this letter are being sent to our
elected representatives on the District
Council, and we intend to raise the matter
with our M.P. when he holds his next meeting
in the locality.

                  Yours faithfully,


                  B. Shaw
                  Secretary, Wirkton Residents'
                  Action Committee
```

Task 3

The Chairman of the Planning Committee calls in you and the Head of Planning, in the absence of a Chief Officer, and instructs you to ensure that press leaks from the Environmental Services Sub-committee do not continue. Your boss objects that this is a matter between elected members, and points out that the offending councillor is very recently elected. The Chairman insists that something has to be done. The Head of Planning suggests that **a circular letter** from the Chairman to all members of the Committee (who constitute the sub-committees) would be in order. 'Very well. **Draft it.** But don't pull any punches and don't use town-hall cotton-wool stuff. Write the sort of thing *I'd* write!'

Task 4

The Chairman and Vice-chairman of the Wirkton Residents Action Committee meet the Head of Planning for discussion. They come to the conclusion that their members have very little ground for concern, but ask for help in writing a circular to tell them this. You are detailed to **write them a draft** which should state the relevant facts in as short and lucid a fashion as possible, remembering that the readership will be anxious and in some cases not very skilled readers.

Task 5

The scheme is approved and about to start. Between Ley Farm and the cutting is a group of barns and stables which the farmer does not use. You are instructed to **draft the text of a letter** to the farmer, T W Jameson, offering to lease the buildings from him for a three-year period to accommodate Council stores and equipment needed for the infilling work.

C4 – The Withdrawal of the Rushton Bus

The River Tene runs through a wide, low-lying plain in the County of Carraford. Much of the area where it passes the town of Fassett is a principal source of high quality gravel. Opposite the town, with the intervening spaces pitted with gravel workings, are the villages of Tollsworth, Leighton Darcy, Wattleford, and Rushton. A map of the area is given overleaf. Other relevant information is given below.

(a) The bridge over the river is a mediaeval landmark with a narrow carriageway 2.80m wide. One-way traffic alternates in each direction, controlled by traffic lights.

(b) Fassett North Primary School is a very good one, deservedly popular with parents, and the closure of Rushton Primary School in 1967 brought little objection as the few remaining pupils were sent to Fassett North. The school serves the other three villages as well.

(c) Local Education Authorities are obliged by law to provide school transport for children under the age of eight who live more than two miles from school, and for children up to the age of sixteen who live more than three miles from school. In this case, as no public bus service meets the need, a bus service is provided. It was statutory, but is now discretionary, for reasons which appear in the table on p. 79.

(d) Pupils attending Fassett Comprehensive School remain on the bus when the primary pupils alight, and are taken on the 500 yards additional journey.

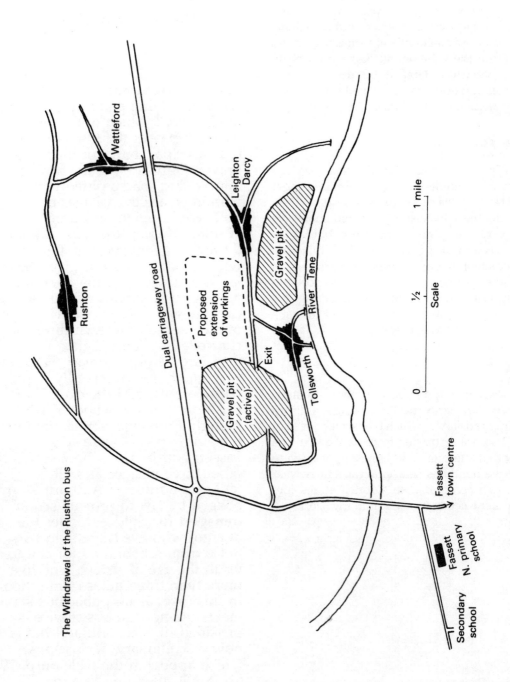

The Withdrawal of the Rushton bus

Wattleford

Rushton

Dual carriageway road

Leighton Darcy

Proposed extension of workings

Gravel pit

Gravel pit (active)

Exit

Tollsworth

River Tene

Secondary school

Fassett N. primary school

Fassett town centre

Scale

0   ½   1 mile

(e) Passenger statistics are as follows:

Village	1967 Children's ages				1979 Children's ages			
	5–8	8–11	11–16	Total	5–8	8–10	11–16	Total
Rushton	11	8	1	20	—	19	3	22
Wattlef'd	4	3	1	8	—		13	13
Leighton D.	3	1	—	4	—	4	3	7
Tollsw'th	4	2	—	6	—	3	3	6
Total	22	14	2	38	0	26	22	48

(f) LEA policy is to base routes on the most distant pick-up point and collect all children where buses have room.

(g) Harold Danbury, Area Education Officer, lives in Leighton Darcy. He has one child attending the primary and one child at the secondary schools referred to. His wife, with another member of the Fassett Primary School Parent-Teacher Association, runs the North Fassett Pre-school Play Group.

You are a parent of three of the Rushton children, and are a member of the PTA Committee. Other members are the Headmaster, the head of the Infant department (representing the staff), a father from Wattleford, and two mothers from Fassett, one who shares in the running of the Play Group. Early one February all the parents living in the four villages receive a circular letter from the Area Education Officer, explaining that the County Education Committee has instructed Area Officers to make savings of £15,000 on discretionary transport from April 1st. Accordingly, the Rushton service is to be withdrawn from the end of the current term. Mr Danbury's letter is apologetic but quite definite: the decision appears to be final.

Task 1

In groups of three or four, **explore in detail** the relationships between the data provided, the map of the area, and the Education Authority's obligations. Establish whether the Authority is correct in treating the bus service as discretionary. Interpret the available evidence to determine whether the parents might be able to base a case on other grounds.

Task 2

Either arrange a simulation of a meeting of the PTA Committee, bearing in mind that the Head and staff are not responsible for the cuts but cannot be expected to share in criticising decisions of their employing Authority; or the Committee ask you to **write to Mr Danbury**, making the strongest possible case for retaining the bus service, asking him to attend a meeting of parents, and sending a copy to County Councillor Neville.

Task 3

An angry protest meeting is held at Rushton Village Hall, where Mr Danbury defends the decision as one of several which would cause less hardship than others. He points out that savings of £15,000 p.a. have to be found in his own Area alone. The Rushton service costs £16 per head per term to run, and he claims that a major factor in his decision was that none of the pupils now lives within 'statutory distance'. Some parents claim in reply that he chose the Rushton bus in order to avoid the charge of favouring his own area which, otherwise, would have been made.

The meeting passes a resolution asking Councillor Neville to take up the matter. It turns out that he is annoyed at not having been invited to the meeting. He says to you 'I don't quite understand either side of this dispute. Would you set it all out for me so I can grasp why the LEA is stopping the bus, as well as the arguments for not stopping it?' **Write this** as concisely as possible.

Task 4

The replies to four inquiries seeking quotations for the transport of the children are given below. **Draw up a table** setting out the costs, and what is provided for the money in each case. On the basis of the table, select the best combination of costs and benefits.

MAHON BROS

Mini-bus Hire

Front Street
Fassett
Tel. 9133

347
March 16th 19--

Dear Sir,

Thank you for your letter. I must point out that we are a mini-coach firm, but we do have a coach suitable for your needs which we will be pleased to lease to you if required. We estimate the yearly cost to be £680 plus VAT and would be interested to meet you and discuss terms within the next seven days.

Yours faithfully
M. Mahon.

Tene Motor Traction Co Ltd
NATIONAL

Mrs Sarah Wicker
Elizabeth House
High Street
Rushton

PO Box 9
St Mears Way
Tenebridge TE8 2XY
Tel: Tenebr. 80490
Telegrams: Tenebus Tenebridge

QUOTATION
PRIVATE HIRE

Dear .... Mrs Wicker ....

Date .... 9 March 19-- ....

We thank you for your enquiry of ..6 March 19--.. for the hire of

1 x 49 .. to convey .. 48 .. passengers on .. school days .. from .. Rushton

to .. Fassett North Primary School .. outwards via .. Wattleford,

Leighton Darcy, Tollsworth, stopping at each

return via .. same route as outwards, stopping to set down at each

starting at .. 0810 .. hours and commencing the return journey at .. 1545 .. hrs.

WE HAVE PLEASURE IN QUOTING .. £760 per annum .. NET

PER VEHICLE SUBJECT TO A DEPOSIT OF .. £150 payable at start

of each term, and review of charges in August,
December, April.

All passengers extra to the number given above will be charged for additionally.
The quotation is made subject to the conditions printed on the back hereof.

Yours faithfully,

E & O E

Tene Motor Traction Co Ltd
Private Hire Supervisor

FORM OF ACCEPTANCE

Private Hire Supervisor
Tene Motor Traction Co Ltd
St Mears Way
Tenebridge TE8 2XY

Date ....

I accept your quotation for the hire of .... vehicles on ....

for the inclusive sum of .... subject to the conditions set out.

A deposit of .... is sent herewith.

Yours faithfully,

....

Address:

WHITE'S
LUXURY COACH SERVICES LTD
HESTON ROAD
FASSETT

(Established 1934)   Telephone Fassett 7486/7

Private hire quotation   Date: 14 Mar 1977

                         No: RB/794

Dear .... Madam ....

      Thank you for your enquiry. We have
pleasure in quoting as follows:

      For transporting approx 48 pupils to
....
Fassett North Primary School as per your
....
inquiry: £260 per school term. Discount 2½%
....
for payment in advance, 5% for annual contract.
....
Price subject to six-monthly review.
....

      We look forward to receiving your reply.

                  Yours faithfully,

                        J Temperley (Mrs)
                        Contracts Manageress.

      RSJ Travel, 54 Balcombe Street, Fassett

        Tel. Fassett 7213 (9 a.m. - 4.30 p.m.)

Dear Madam,

Thank you for your enquiry. We have pleasure

in offering either our 35-seater or our 44-

seater coach for the school year as per your

letter. On a self-drive basis the charge

would be £500, with a driver £720. Advance

payment of a yearly contract would be on a 6%

discount basis.

      We look forward to hearing from you.

                  Yours faithfully,

                  Ronald S Jones
                  (Manager)

Task 5

Explore in discussion the problems of arranging to collect parental contributions, paying the coach firm, securing payment from the forgetful or reluctant, and ensuring that the organisers are not out of pocket at the end of each school year. **Draw up a workable proposal** for action.

C5 – Flexible Working Hours

The General Star Assurance Company is organised on the basis of large regional offices, of which there are fourteen in all, each employing between 350 and 450 people, and housed in modern office blocks which are linked to a central computer. This assignment relates to the office in Barrdown, where the central computer is located. The town has just over 100,000 people and lies in a large rural county in the south west of England. Its principal industry was always engineering, but the development policy of the town council has brought in more than two dozen large office establishments like General Star's. The town is well laid out, with good roads, but there is an inevitable rush-hour problem since most of the office staffs can afford cars and use them.

  The company works a $39\frac{1}{2}$ hour week: 08.30–17.30 (17.00 on Fridays), with 12.30–13.30 lunch-hour. The Barrdown office staff of 430 includes 18 senior management, 20 porters, cleaners, and security staff, and 90 in the Computer Division. Until recently the company's Barrdown Manager refused even to consider requests for flexible working hours, on the grounds that the computer division had very expensive equipment and had to maximise the use of it. However, the pressure of computer work has led that division to change over to a shift system: staff work 06.00–13.30 or 13.30–21.00, and can generally have

Document A

their choice of remaining permanently on early or late shift or of alternating weeks or months. The vast majority have opted for alternating weeks.

The Barrdown office manager, for whom you work as Secretary and Personal Assistant, is allowed by the company to use the firm's recommended scheme for flexible working hours or an alternative (which must have the Board's approval). He suspects that the firm's recommended scheme is better suited to large-city offices than to Barrdown. The General Star scheme is set out as Document A. Your boss is a cautious man, and has learned that the only other branch to use an alternative scheme has had considerable trouble with it. He is prepared to hold extensive consultations with staff representatives (only the computer division is unionised), but likes to know most of the arguments each way before going into them.

He therefore draws up a questionnaire announcing to the staff that he is considering holding such discussions, but wants them to be based on accurate data concerning the staff's journeys to work. He receives 265 replies, and gives them to a trainee to analyse. He in due course presents the data set out in Document B.

Task 1

Assemble a small number of alternative schemes for flexible working hours. Each group of three or four students should study and compare, in considerable detail, at least three schemes including the General Star Scheme. The preferred schemes, not more than four, and preferably only two, should be subject to general discussion.

Document B

```
Questionnaire on travelling to work - 265
replies received.

Distance from home    Usual time of      Usual time of arrival
   to office             journey

0 - 1 m.      6        0-10m.      8      before 0800        3
1 - 4 m.    169        11-20min.  13      0800-0815         90
4 - 8 m.     47        21-30min. 191      0815-0830        161
8 -12 m.     39        30-45m.     9      after 0830        11
over 12 m.    4        over 45m.  44


Method of travel      Would flexible hours help
                        your travelling problems?      75%
public bus    64       would help          199*
train         37       would make no diff-
on foot       19         erence             49**   18.5%
own car      131
other's car   48       no reply/don't know 17    6.5%


  *    this figure includes 63 of those travelling
       by bus.

  **   38 added a note 'unless other offices in the
       area do the same' or words to that effect.
```

Task 2

In the light of this discussion, and the data in Document B, **draft the formal report** which the Office Manager is to lay before the Branch Manager. The purpose of the report is to inform the reader why change is being considered, what the alternatives are, which of them is to be preferred and why. The sub-sections of the report should have suitable headings, which should indicate the content of the section. The report should distinguish clearly between objective fact and the judgement or views of the writer. (See Guide 7.4.3–5)

Task 3

The Branch Manager decides that it would be a good idea to consult the other five major employers of office staff in the same sector of Barrdown. He tells the Office Manager to find out what the other firms are doing. Discuss which official should write such an inquiry and to whom it should be addressed. **Draft**

the text in such a way that the recipients are aware of the preliminary nature of the inquiry and treat it as confidential.

Task 4

Assume that one of the systems set out in the report made under Task 2 has been chosen. Like any flextime scheme, it has weaknessness which can only be avoided if the staff co-operate. Work out what those weaknesses are and **draft a persuasive circular** to the staff concerned.

Task 5

There are two established members of the typing pool who are disabled and drive invalid carriages. They point out in a reasonable memorandum that under flexible hours they will have parking problems: at present they arrive early to make sure of their parking places, which avoid placing steps between the car and the main entrance. The office manager tells you to go and see Tom Alcock, the head porter, and instruct him to mark out two parking places as reserved for the disabled. Alcock is a self-important character with a well-deserved reputation for being bossy to junior staff, wheedling to the top management and unco-operative with the rest. **Simulate your interview,** and if necessary explain, in another simulated interview with your boss, that you made no progress with Alcock.

C6 – Specialist Conference

This assignment is concerned with the administration of an international two-day meeting of specialists in a technical field. You are a management trainee with a medium-sized iron-founding company in the south-west. The firm is a keen supporter of the industry's own research association, which is based near Birmingham, and which occasionally mounts seminars and conferences for experts to share their findings. This particular meeting concerns toxic substances in foundry dusts, but you are involved because the research association's Research Information Officer, who normally handles such matters, is absent on overseas study leave, and the Associations's Director has asked to 'borrow' you for the job. You are to work two days a week for four months, full-time for the two weeks on either side of the meeting, and occasional days thereafter to deal with publication of the proceedings. The Director is the nominal Conference Secretary, but wishes to delegate the work to you, including accommodation, reservations, accounts, and publication of proceedings.

The meeting is arranged for September 24–26 inclusive, and you first visit the Association on May 10th. You find that the Director has already issued a circular to possible participants, and has had their replies tabulated as in Document A. He has secured options on accommodation at each of three large hotels, all of them able to handle the whole number likely to attend, all having simultaneous-translation facilities, and all willing to keep open the options until May 15th.

An American foundation which fosters scientific work has offered a grant of £5,000, but has imposed some conditions. It requires that at least eight nationalities be represented, and that five languages be available in simultaneous translation. Its papers refer to the exercise of reasonable economy, and suggest that most participants should pay the board-and-lodging share of their attendance. The organizers are free to invite visiting guest speakers (offering a suitable fee and expenses) if they are appropriate. However, the Director has himself agreed to speak the previous week at the major Congress of Metallurgical Sciences in Liège, and has invited two speakers, one local and one from India who is also attending in Liège and needs expenses only from there. Two technical journalists are invited to attend, but will follow usual practice in taking meals with the conference but paying for their own accommodation.

The form of the meeting is based on a series of short spoken contributions lasting 15–20 minutes each, such that the 22 participants who have offered contributions can

Participant number	Town of origin	Attending	Accomm. req'd.	Languages used* listening	speaking	Notes (*if not using English)
1	Izmir	full-time	+wife	Ger/Russ	Russian	
2	Brno	full-time	single		German	Wants to stay on 4 nights following
3	Gøteborg	day 1	none			) taking in conf. as part of study tour;
4	Oslo	day 1	none			) own hotel arrangements;
5	Cobnhavn	day 1	none		German	) meals req'd.
6	Gelsenkirchen	full-time	single		German	
7	Schaffhausen	full-time	single	German	German	
8	Torino	full-time	single	French	French	
9	Detroit	full-time	single			Wants rm. for 2 nts. + conf. pd. (with 17-18)
10	Hamilton, Ont.	full-time	single			
11	Osaka	day 2	single		Japanese	Bringing priv. sec. as interpreter (wants rm.)
12	Charleroi	full-time	single		French/Ger	
13	Eindhoven	full-time	+wife		German	diabetic diet
14	Sheffield	full-time	single			
15	Linwood	full-time	single			
16	Pont-à-Mousson	full-time	single		French/Ger	
17	Caracas	full-time	single	Span/Fre	Span/Fre	as 9 above
18	Rio de Janeiro	full-time	single	Spanish	Spanish	as 9 above
19	Teheran	full-time	single			treat as vegetarian
20	Stalingrad	full-time	single)	Ger/Russ	Russian	) Soviet embassy specifies double room only
21	Kharkov	full-time	single)	Ger/Russ	Russian	
22	KarlMarxStadt	full-time	single	German	German	As for 2 above
23	Birmingham	full-time	single			Conference Chairman; reception rm. req'd.
24	Pittsburg	full-time	+wife			Vice-Chairman. Wife diabetic.
25	Birmingham	day 1	non-res.			Guest speaker
26	Leningrad	day 1	single			Guest speaker. May bring wife.

Document A

be heard in the four main sessions, with the opening session devoted to the guest speakers, the second afternoon to a visit to the host Association's laboratories, and the closing session that evening to a plenary discussion. The participants have been led to expect a working session after dinner on the first day. The commitments involved in the advance publicity include providing coach transport for the visit (15 miles each way, leaving 13.30 and arriving back 17.00), a woman hostess/guide for participants' wives for the two days, and a shorthand-typist for the week to handle the transcribing of the proceedings.

Task 1

Study a hotel guide and town plan of a major city in your own region and **decide which of the major hotels to use** for the conference. Bear in mind accessibility to stations, and make use of available brochures and publicity material without approaching actual hotels.

Task 2

Draw up a schedule of accommodation requirements for the participants. (Assume that the hotel concerned has conference facilities which for a meeting of this kind are provided without additional charge.) **Draw up a separate schedule of meal requirements** for guests, organising staff, and others involved. On the basis of prices quoted in the hotel guide, VAT at current rates if not included, and 12½% service if not included, **calculate the total charge** for each schedule. **Draft the letter reserving the accommodation** and enclosing a 5% deposit.

Task 3

Set aside £1,500 for the printing and distribution of the published Proceedings, and allow fully for the costs of guests, overheads, translators (@ £25 per day each), and organising staff. Take account of the Foundation's grant, and **work out the fee per head** to be charged to participants so that the Conference account does not incur a deficit.

Task 4

In order to instruct the translation agency retained by the hotel it is necessary to **work out the translation requirements. Draft the letter which sets out your requirements**.

Task 5

At the end of July you learn that
(a) the Soviet and Czech participants will not be coming, and
(b) that a group of 15 unaccompanied men from the USA who will be at the Liège conference want to attend. **Make a list of the correspondence** entailed by these changes, and **calculate their effects** on (i) the translation requirements and (ii) the conference budget.

Task 6

The local paper rings up shortly before the conference and asks for a list of the nationalities taking part and an account of the conference which laymen could grasp. The reporter is particularly puzzled that there should be so few formal speakers. **Simulate the conversation or write him a piece of copy he can print as it stands.**

C7 – Hail Weston Ltd

You joined the clothing trade at the age of 17 as a trainee buyer with a large department store group. After fifteen months you have got a new job with Hail Weston, attached initially to its small headquarters staff. The firm began as a single boutique which merged with a competitor and did well enough to go on expanding, buying up a string of similar small shops in the teenage and young separates market. It now has nineteen wholly-owned boutiques and six associated ones. All twenty-five outlets are under contract to use Hail Weston's wholesale purchasing and distribution arrangements, although each boutique retains its original local name. The firm is run by a headquarters team of three directors and three buyers, but has begun to encounter problems in keeping all its outlets adequately managed without serious breaks in continuity. This has led to the appointment of two people, of whom you are one, called Assistant Buyers, whose real job is to stand in at the retail outlets when there is a gap in the local management. You are good at your job, but although it is quite usual in retailing for responsibility to fall on young people, you do not know the firm very well yet and are not always quite certain whether you will get backing for difficult decisions.

You are sent to take charge of the outlet in Reading, which has been one of the firm's best until recently. The manageress had given notice, but a miscarriage has led her to stop work before its expiry and inform the company that she would not be coming back. You arrive on a Friday, to find two members of staff. There should be three, and you find that your predecessor had sacked one of them on the spot the previous week. The two who remain are Mary Caudle and Jean Tewkes. There is also a Saturdays-only part-timer, Sarah Goodwin.

The tasks which arise concern (a) the existing staff and (b) the dismissal and replacement of Jennifer Rudge.

Task 1

Mary Caudle is 20. She has worked with the firm for a year, is interested in the business, reliable, good with shy customers, but with limited capacity for figures, so she says. She seems a competent salesgirl who dresses the part. Jean Tewkes is 18 and has been with the firm for six weeks: she left school shortly before that, and is intending to go to university in nine months' time. She is quick, acute, with an astonishing memory for the stock, and a tendency to push hesitant customers a shade too hard. You find in your in-tray the following notes:

> Manageress
> I should be grateful if you would reconsider the holiday arrangements for Easter. I am down to take one week then and two weeks in summer, but my fiancé's holidays have been changed and he now has two weeks at Easter. I don't want to lose my two weeks in Summer, so can I take an extra week at Easter without pay?
> M. Caudle.

Manageress

You said when I was taken on that I would be paid on my present rate for six weeks, and would then have a rise of £2.50 to bring me up to Miss Caudle's rate. The six weeks are now up and I would be glad to know the position.

J. Tewkes.

Both these notes were written to your predecessor. **Work out in small-group discussion how to deal with them**.

Task 2

Also in your tray is the following letter:

Dear Madam,

I refer to the recent dismissal of my daughter, Miss Jennifer Rudge. She tells me she was dismissed on the spot for misconduct, but that there was no action which would justify dismissal, you did not tell her why you were dismissing her, and did not give her any chance to ask or explain. In the circumstances I feel obliged to consult a solicitor in order to ascertain my daughter's rights under the Employment Protection Act. Before I do so I would be glad to receive any comments you may wish to make.

Yours faithfully,

P W Rudge

You consult each of the staff one at a time. Jean Tewkes tells you what happened: just after lunch, Jennifer and the previous manageress had emerged from the cloakroom, Jennifer in tears and very obviously having been caught in the act of doing something wrong. She was asked twice, and quite clearly, whether she had any explanation, but had shaken her head. Mary Caudle added the information that Jennifer had been suspected of stealing before, and had fallen into a trap prepared for her: coins had been marked with spots of paint and left in her own and Jean's coat pockets. The manageress found some in Jennifer's purse and in her hand. Mary confirmed that all three of them knew the firm's rules about dismissal, and that the rules had been observed. Jennifer had been given a formal warning previously, and had full opportunity to state her side of it. She had been paid, Mary thought, her previous week's wages and up to the end of the day of her dismissal. There was no explanation of why the previous manageress had not recorded the matter in the log book.

Work out and draft a suitable reply to Mr Rudge.

Task 3

You have to arrange for the replacement of Miss Rudge, for if the case were to go before an Industrial Tribunal, even a ruling in favour of Miss Rudge would not require reinstatement: the firm would pay compensation.

(a) **Draw up an outline job description** for a junior sales assistant.

(b) **Draft advertisements** suitable for insertion in your local evening newspaper and a local weekly advertising magazine.

(c) The whole class should **write applications for the post**, in reply to one of the advertisements drafted.

(d) A short-listing panel drawn from the group should **select four applicants**, on the basis of the letters, for interview.

(e) Working in groups, **prepare confidential references** on each of the candidates shortlisted for interview.

(f) **Simulate the interviews** and select a candidate for appointment (appointment is subject to confirmation by Head Office, but the manageress is expected to forward a recommendation).

(g) **Write a brief summary** of the foregoing process, including your recommendation, for the Head Buyer.

(The work of this Task is greatly enhanced if the interviews can be recorded, on tape or, ideally, on video-tape, and the playback studied in detail.)

Task 4

A well-spoken woman of about 26, with a charming manner, brings in a long dress which she says she bought ten days ago and has not worn. Mary tells you that this is an old routine which your predecessor had allowed, but she shows you that the dress has been worn and that the date on the sales slip appears to have been altered. **Simulate the conversation** in which you resist, or even match, the lady's charm and send her away with the dress.

C8 – The Bulleid Site at Churchward

You have just been appointed Assistant Site Manager on the Bulleid Development at Churchward, Moorshire, where your employers, HST Ltd, are building a large four-stage estate of two– and three-bedroom detached houses intended for 'first owners'. The firm is a large one, a top-rated share on the Stock Exchange, with some thirty such estate developments in progress at a time. While the site costing and timings are severely controlled, the firm is rightly proud of its good reputation for public

relations and for unusual considerateness to people living or working close to its sites. It is careful about planning procedures, but, once it has gained the necessary consents, its profitability lies in making sure that its work goes through on schedule. Those in the lower management grades know that to hold work up is the quickest way to loss of bonus if not of job.

One important feature of the firm is that it pays its site management well, and expects them to handle local problems with minimal support from head office. Indeed, 'head office' in this instance means just six people, two of them secretaries.

Churchward

The village of Churchward is an old country community which has grown in haphazard bursts, as industry in nearby towns has expanded and additional housing has been needed. It lies on the A123 running east to west, and now has a population of nearly 2,000. There is a belt of expensive housing to the north of the main road, but the heart of the village is from the junction of Lime Avenue and the High Street to the south end of the latter about 1.5 km away. The middle-class housing brought with it pressure for a sports club, which now owns the Recreation Ground next to the churchyard. Until recently the bulk of the rectangle formed by the main road, the High Street, and the two stretches of Lime Avenue was largely derelict. It had been the site of a country house which its eccentric owner had called Bulleid. He died in 1880 without heirs, and left the house and grounds to the Church. Until 1955 it had served as the Rectory, approached up a drive from the A123. It became too expensive for the Rector to maintain, and he moved into a house on the then new Council estate to the west of the High Street. For the next twelve years it stood vacant, the fields let to a local farmer as grazing. When HST Ltd approached the Church Commissioners with an offer, they were happy to sell: they had already sold one corner to the Recreation Ground Committee for the sports club, and the opposite corner to the Education Authority for a new school. (This would replace the 1885 building on Lime Avenue, which remained as a furniture store and was in due course to be the site for a new infants' school). The new primary school had grown steadily: the expansion of Churchward itself had been reinforced by the closure of two very small schools in villages to the east.

The village had been marked out in the County Council's Structure Plan for substantial further development, and HST Ltd had discussed its scheme in outline with the County Planning Department before approaching the Church about Bulleid. The plans afterwards went through the various stages of consent with little difficulty. Such housing would improve the balance of the community, which was awkwardly split between the 'posh' group and the Council tenants. The middle-class residents did not feel able to challenge the scheme as they were newcomers, while the 'old' village people and the Council tenants were too lacking in leadership and organisation to mount firm resistance. Hence, a development was approved which

would increase the population from 1,950 to 2,870 (approximately) in five years, add 231 houses to the existing total of 674, and generally transform the nature of the village. In compensation, HST Ltd had undertaken to provide and build a Village Hall, sited with a large car park for the use of the community shopping in the High Street. Subsequent discussions had modified some of the figures. The building would be phased, probably in two phases.

The Bulleid Site

The planning of the site was based on the principle of keeping direct access to and from main roads to a minimum, and laying out the site so as to preserve all major existing trees. The Site Manager at the time planned to build in two main blocks, but a wholly unexpected delay upset matters. The sewerage system provided for Churchward effluent to be piped to a main sewage works just off the A123 six miles to the east. A month before the site works were due to start, a mining subsidence broke the main sewer. The development was halted, but the break took almost a year to repair. During that year, the property boom collapsed, along with the economy. HST Ltd slimmed down its management even further, and all its developments were 're-phased'. The Bulleid site was kept going, but would be built in four phases, each phase taking a year.

At the time of your appointment, Phase 1, in two blocks of land at the eastern end of the site, had been virtually completed and sold. The site works for Phase 2 (see plan,

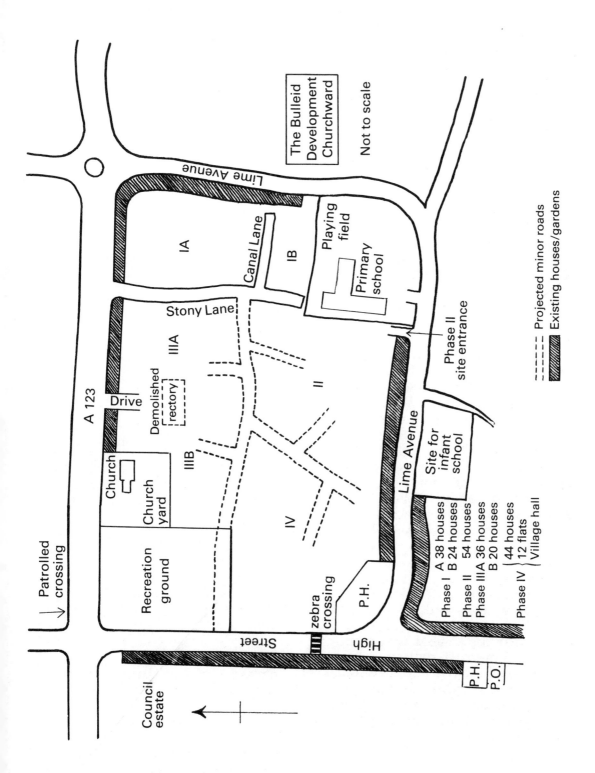

Document A

Document A) had started, using a site entrance immediately west of the school. The main site roads, which would form the boundaries of Phases 2, 3 and 4 had not been built: they would normally be put in first, but were to be put in towards the end of Phase 2, in order to ease the burden on the company's cash flow.

Other Information

The relevant local authorities have different functions. Churchward Parish Council has no planning powers, but would be entitled to consultation over the Village Hall and car park. Moorside County Council is responsible for Planning and Development, while detailed planning consents and consents under the Building Regulations come under Stalmore District Council. The County Council is the Highways Authority and the Education Authority, and the District Council has no delegated powers in either sphere.

The Site Manager hands you Document B. He comments:

'He probably has a case, but limiting deliveries in the way he suggests is simply not on: scheduling is difficult enough as it is! The phasing decisions were made by HQ, and we shall have to duck that one, but HQ will want to know what we can do now to improve matters. The gate is possible, but we'll have to ask the LEA. Hardcore in the entry we need anyway. But the main thing is to show him we're on the same side about safety.'

Document B

15 Ashlea Close
Churchward
Moorshire
MO4 6BC

14th March 19--

HST Ltd
14 Swannington Street
Manton
Moorshire
MO2 3AB

Dear Sirs,

<u>Bulleid Development, Churchward</u>

A number of parents of children attending Churchward School have discussed their alarm about the dangers created by your vehicles delivering materials to this site. They have asked me to write on their behalf, sending copies of this letter to the District Council for their comments.

There are two main dangers:

1. The main access to the site adjoins the school, and your vehicles use it at times when more than 240 children are arriving at or leaving the school. The access road has not been surfaced, and its condition leads children to walk in the road to avoid its deep mud. Some of the children, as you know, are of infant age.

2. The children who live west or north of Lime Avenue are required to use the zebra crossing to cross the High Street or the Patrolled crossing over the A123 at its junction with the High Street. If your firm would allow the PTA of the school to instal a gate at the school end of Stony Lane, these children (and others) would not need to use the Lime Avenue entrance at all.

The entrance proposed for Stony Lane would not solve the whole problem. We wish to suggest that since the site is a large long-term project you should close this access point and open a new one, preferably on the A 123. In the meantime, we wish to request that your delivery drivers avoid entering and leaving the site between 8.30 and 9.15 a.m., 12.15 and 13.45 p.m., and 15.20 and 16.15 p.m.

Yours faithfully,

C.M.Pickersgill.

Task 1

The kind of gate suggested by Pickersgill is among the amenities which HST expect to provide. **Write a letter** to the Moorshire

County Education Department (Sites & Buildings) asking permission to instal the gate. Make clear that local concern for safety suggests a need for quick action.

Task 2

Draft a reply to Mr Pickersgill.

Task 3

Write the paragraph in the Site Manager's weekly report to HQ which will deal with Pickersgill's letter and the matters it raises.

Task 4

A planning officer from the Stalmore District Council calls, and you mention the matter. Yes, he tells you, Pickersgill is a known trouble-maker: a questionnaire to the parents would soon show him up. Working in pairs, **devise a questionnaire** to test parental feeling without, if possible, arousing the very feeling it is seeking to test. Each pair should try out its draft by putting it to another pair for answer.

Task 5

HST send a note the following week as follows:

```
Actions re access and Pickersgill's letter
approved.  Our phasing plans envisaged use of
Lime Avenue route, but truck size prevented
this and you were correct in avoiding the A123
access which planning consents exclude.  Long-
term we proposed to buy derelict strip  8m x
170m on S side of Recreation Ground.  Please
proceed with purchase, via local solicitor,
offering re-planting of trees;  limit £1,250
including planting.
```

The Site Manager and you arrange to meet the Recreation Ground Committee to discuss the purchase. When you meet you find there are four members present, who include Mr Pickersgill and a satisfied customer of HST living in one of the new houses. The strip of land in question is a gravel outcrop, on which the stones cleared from the sports field were dumped. There are seven diseased elms along one side of it, and a thin beech hedge. **Simulate the discussion**.

Task 6

The Education Authority has ruled that it has no objection to the gate into Stony Lane, but that the Headmaster's views should decide the matter. He is not at all sure it is worthwhile, or even a good thing. He calls a group of interested parties together to discuss it: Mr Pickersgill, the keeper of the crossing over the A123 (an old Churchward character in his late sixties), a manager of the school who lives in Canal Lane, the Deputy Head (who lives on the estate north of the main road), and yourself. You go to the meeting having learned that the new site access along the back of 'the Rec' will not be ready for use until well into the Autumn term. **Simulate the meeting**.

Assignments – Group D

D1 – Committee Meeting

Study Section 5 of Guide in connection with this Assignment.

This Assignment takes the form of a transcript of part of a meeting of a local government committee, followed by a set of Tasks which arise in connection with the meeting. The transcript is a verbatim record. The committee involved is the Finance & Resources Committee of the Moorshire County Council, a powerful body which can over-rule the County Education Committee or other 'spending' committees so long as the Council itself can be counted on to endorse such decisions.

Present: *Elected members*: Mr Braithwaite, Mrs Budge, Mr Callender, Sir Henry Davis, Mr Elkington, Mr Gordon (vice-chairman), Mr Jelfs, Mrs Quinn, Mr Stetchworth, Mrs Tomblin, Mr Waters.
Co-opted members: Dr Hevens, Miss Killey, Rev. Canon Lowes, Mr Rilling.
Officers: Mr Howes (Cty Treasurer), Mr Cornwall (Dep. Ch. Educ. Offr), Mrs Target (Dir. Soc. Servs) Dep. Asst Cty Treas. as Clerk.
At 2.35

Mr Gordon (Taking the chair): Well, ladies and gentlemen, our Chairman asked us to proceed if he was unable to get here, and I think we should start. The minutes of the last meeting have been circulated, but as this is a special meeting perhaps members have not yet read them? (Murmurs of agreement.) In that case, we shall leave the formal approval of the Minutes until next time.
Mrs Orr: Mr Chairman, should we not record the apologies?
Mr Gordon: Thank you. I apologise – I am not exactly used to the procedure. I have mentioned the Chairman's apology. Any others?
Clerk: Mr Hall, Mr Wells, and Mr Young.
Mr Gordon: Thank you. It is not logical to take matters arising if we are not approving the minutes, but there has been some dispute locally about our application of the Pay Code, and Mrs Tomblin has asked for clarification. Would you care to put your question?
Mrs Tomblin: Some of my constituents, Council employees, are saying that they did not get the

maximum rises allowed under the old Pay Code. Those were 5% or £4 a week, whichever was the less. So they are asking why they cannot now be brought up to that maximum. For example, the teachers got £186 a year, which is a lot less than either figure. The position for clerical officers was even worse.

Mr Gordon: Mr Howes?

County Treasurer: Thank you, Mr Chairman. This is a quite understandable confusion, and there are two parts to the answer. One is that almost all the Council's employees are covered by national agreements, and we have no power to pay increases which depart from those agreements. But that does not explain why some of the agreements were for increases of less than either figure. The reason is that under the old Pay Code, which operated for 1976–77 and until well into 1977–78, the total increases, the total addition to the salary bill, for each group of employees, had to be within the limits. Teachers are a good example: they almost all get annual increments, and the cost of those had to be found within the limit. In theory the numbers retiring, who are on maximum, gives scope to cover the increments bill, but teaching is 'bottom heavy' in its age-structure. That is, there are many times more teachers in their twenties, entitled to increments, than there are coming up to retirement. The difference between the saving on retiring people and the increments bill comes out in the difference between £186 a year and £4 a week (or £208 a year). The same principle holds in every other wage agreement where there is an increment structure, although the amounts vary.

Mr Gordon: Does that answer your question?

Mrs Tomblin: Yes, thank you. But I doubt if I shall be able to remember the answer.

Mr Gordon: Would you be able to put it in writing for members, Mr Howes?

Mr Howes: Certainly. In fact Mrs Tomblin will find the full picture, with notes by me, in Appendix 4 to the 1976–77 Estimates, page 804 in the Committee's papers. If she would like me to simplify that paper for her constituents I would be happy to do so.

Mr Gordon: Thank you. I think we should leave other matters arising until we formally approve the minutes next time. This meeting has been called to consider the problem which faces us about cleaning. This affects Social Services and Education, mainly, since our own establishments are cleaned under a contract which is reviewed every six months, but it has become a very tricky problem. Perhaps the Director of Social Services would speak to her paper about it, as some of us only received it this morning. Mrs Target?

Dir. Soc. Servs: Well, Mr Chairman, it all arises from our own earlier decision on the Budget, that all manpower services except teaching staff would be cut by 2½%. That does not seem a big cut, but the nature of cleaning staffs is peculiar. There are three elements to the problem. In education we are still sorting out the differences between the three education authorities which were merged into the new County in 1974, in one of which heads of schools could decide for themselves how to get the school cleaned. We brought in a common system, but the agreement was for a three-year period of change-over and we are only half way through that. There were two separate authorities for Social Services, too, and one of them was one of the most generous in the country in its establishments for cleaning. We have only just completed the scheme for having schools and social services homes based on a common scale for cleaning staff hours. The third aspect is that this is a rural county, and a very high proportion of our cleaning staff are local women. Not only do they badly need the income, but there are no alternative jobs and many cleaners have held their jobs for very long periods. More than 45% of the school cleaners in the Northern District have done the job for over 20 years. So it is not easy to arrange a $2\frac{1}{2}$% cut. Natural wastage would give us less than $1\frac{1}{2}$% and would leave some small schools with no cleaner at all. Redundancy is therefore inevitable, and the union has reacted strongly. The Western Division schools have already had a one-day strike, and we have to decide today whether to proceed with this particular cut or find the money somewhere else.

Mr Callender: I'm sorry, but I don't see the problem. Why cannot every individual cleaner be asked to work $2\frac{1}{2}$% less time?

Mrs Target: In order to save $2\frac{1}{2}$% we would have to reduce the hours worked by between $3\frac{1}{2}$% and 4%, unless we did it by cancelling all overtime, which would shut down all evening functions in schools and colleges.

Mr Callender: Then why do we not cut 4% of hours across the board?

Mrs Target: For two reasons. One is that it is simply unrealistic to reduce

by 4% the hours of a cleaner who only works 4 hours a week as it is (and that is the average for the County). The other is, as some members know, the marked variation in cleaning staff between otherwise similar establishments. (Pause.) Shall I elaborate, Mr Chairman? (He nods.) Well, I can quote two homes for residential care of children which are roughly the same size, about 35 children and 6 resident staff. In one of them there is a weekly provision for 180 hours cleaning and in the other 55 hours. Mr Cornwall can quote schools with even greater variations.

Mr Jelfs: The Education Committee and the Social Services Committee both decided on selective redundancy?

Mr Gordon: I can speak for Education. Yes, we thought the overmanning in some schools quite glaring, and regard the Union's position as indefensible.

Dr Hevens: I was on the working party which Social Services set up to look into this. Mrs Target is quite right: we were unanimous that there would be no justification at all for an across-the-board cut in hours while these disparities remained. We asked the officers to work out a points system which would cover social services and education alike, and that is now ready. It is in the agenda papers for the next round of meetings.

Mr Elkington: And the proposed redundancies are based on the points system?

Dr Hevens: They are at the establishments where the overmanning is greatest.

Mr Elkington: Greatest on what basis? On the basis of a points system none of us have seen?

Dr Hevens: On the contrary: Social Services Committee and the Education Committee have both approved it.

Mr Elkington: But this Committee has not yet seen it, officially?

Dr Hevens: I would suppose not.

Mr Elkington: Mr Chairman, this really will not do. I propose that this meeting be adjourned, and re-convened when members have been able to read the document referred to. Then we can approve the document and impose redundancies in proper order, or reject it and find some other basis.

Mr Gordon: Could I ask the officers, please, whether the cases of over-manning which are envisaged for redundancy are in fact based on the points system not yet approved?

Mr Cornwall: In fact, sir, no. My department had identified the problem many months ago, and the points system was designed as an objective and fair way of establishing what was fairly obvious to everyone concerned in the office.

Mr Elkington: I have put a motion, Mr Chairman.

Mr Gordon: Yes, but it has not yet been seconded.

Mrs Budge: I second it.

Mr Gordon: Mr Elkington has proposed an adjournment until such time as this committee has reached a decision on the points system for assessing cleaning staff hours. Would those in favour please show. (Hands raised.) Those against? Thank you. Three in favour, eleven against. I declare the motion defeated.

Mrs Budge: The principal of the handicapped children's home near us says she'll have to get the children sweeping the floors if these cuts go through. I don't accept the cuts and I don't accept the consequences.

Mr Rilling: The statement is a gross exaggeration.

Mr Jelfs: It wouldn't be such a bad idea for children to help in their own housekeeping.

Mrs Budge: You don't know what you're talking about. Handicapped children sweeping the floors indeed – kids with no proper arms or unable to stand up straight. What sort of a Tory tyrant are you?

Mr Gordon: Ladies and gentlemen, We must conduct our work in an orderly fashion. Mrs Budge, I must ask you in future to address the chair. Would you now withdraw your last remark, please.

Mrs Budge: Why? It's true.

Mr Gordon: It was a question, and a very offensive one. Please withdraw it.

Mrs Budge: Very well. I withdraw.

Mr Gordon: Thank you.

Sir Henry Davis: On a point of information, Mr Chairman, is it true that children may have to help clean the homes?

Mr Gordon: With respect, Sir Henry, that is a point of substance rather than a point of information, but it is one we should pursue. Mrs Target?

Mrs Target: Many children already do as part of their training. I do have to record that one of the principals who has complained that the cuts will force him to put children to work already does this more than my staff would like.

Mr Braithwaite: Mr Chairman, I have listened to the discussion carefully, and have come to the conclusion that this is a matter on which our senior staff know what they are doing. They have in effect asked us to meet today and support them in a battle with the unions. The battle concerns nine posts, in full-time-equivalent terms, which our officers are quite convinced are surplus to real requirements. They have done their detailed homework, and the points system proposed is, I believe, a good one. The union representatives on the working party which devised it have signed the report. The point at issue, then, is not mainly one of cuts, but one of taking out some obvious and not disputed over-manning. The union publicity will represent it as the thin end of the wedge, but it will become that only if we are as badly treated on the Rate Support Grant next year as we have been these past two years. But the union publicity should not be allowed to put us off the real issue. That is that these staff are superfluous to requirements and should go. May I formally propose, Mr Chairman, that this Committee record its support for the policy being pursued by the officers?

Mr Jelfs: I second that.

Mr Gordon: I hesitate to cut short the discussion, but I feel that Mr Braithwaite has summed the matter up very well, and that we are probably ready to resolve it. The motion before you is that we record our support for the policy being pursued by the officers.

Mr Jelfs: On a point of order, I think the motion should be more specific. Could we add 'in declaring selective redundancies in clear cases of cleaning hours provision markedly greater than would apply under any agreed points scheme'.

Mr Gordon: Thank you. Those in favour: (hands). Those against? Twelve in favour, three against. The motion is carried. Thank you, ladies and gentlemen. The meeting is adjourned.

Task 1

Draw up the summons and agenda on which this meeting is based.

Suggested Solution to Task 1

```
        Moorshire County Council

You are requested to be present at County Hall,
Mardock, on Thursday November 19th at 2.30 p.m.
for a meeting of the Finance and Resources
Committee of the County Council, to transact
the undermentioned business:

AGENDA

1.  Apologies for absence
2.  Minutes of previous meeting (enclosed)
3.  Matters arising
4.  To consider - policy concerning cuts in
       cleaning staff at County establishments
       (paper enclosed).
5.  Any other business.

                       C W Power
                       Deputy Asst County
                          Treasurer,
Date                   Clerk to the Committee
```

Task 2

Write the minutes of the meeting. (A real Committee clerk would supply every member's initials from the official list, but this can be omitted here.)

Suggested Solution to Task 2

```
Minutes of meeting of

    Finance & Resources Committee

    held at County Hall, November 19th at

    2.30 p.m.

Present:  Mr Braithwaite, Mrs Budge, Mr
          Callender, Sir Henry Davis, Mr Gordon,
          Mr Jelfs, Mrs Quinn, Mr Stetchworth,
          Mrs Tomblin, Mr Waters, Dr Hevens,
          Miss Killey, Canon Lowes, Mr Rilling
          County Treasurer, Deputy Chief
          Education Officer, Director of Social
          Services.

In the absence of the Chairman, Cllr Gordon
took the chair.


1.  Apologies for absence were received from
    the Chairman, Messrs Hall, Wells and Young.

2.  Minutes of previous meeting.  Approval was
    deferred.
```

3. <u>Matters Arising</u>. Clarification was sought on the eligibility of employees to have their salaries brought up to the level implied by the maxima of the Pay Code, where the increases actually awarded had been less than those maxima. The County Treasurer explained that the employees concerned were governed by wage agreements negotiated nationally, from which the County had no power to depart. He referred inquirers to the fuller information available in Appendix 4 of the 1976-77 Estimates (p.804 of the Committee's papers for that year).

4. The Director of Social Services explained the nature of the problem outlined in the paper recently circulated (ref. FR/78/34). Cllr Elkington proposed, Cllr Mrs Budge seconded
   THAT this meeting be adjourned until such time as members can read the Report of the Joint Working Party on provision for cleaning in Authority establishments.
   The motion was defeated.
   Cllr Braithwaite proposed, Cllr Jelfs seconded
   THAT the Committee record its support for the policy being pursued by the Council's officers in declaring selective redundancies in clear cases of cleaning hours provision markedly greater than would apply under any agreed points scheme.
   The motion was carried.

5. Any other business: none.

Task 3

The Chairman was unable to attend the meeting. In order to find out what happened, he asked the Committee's clerk to write him a digest, not for publication and in confidence. He also asks Mr Stetchworth, a young councillor and estate agent who was present, for an account. For this task, work in pairs: one of each pair should **draft one of the two documents**, and the two should be compared for differences in approach.

Suggested Solution to Task 3

The Clerk's digest:

Dir.Soc.Servs spoke to her paper, seeking to show why we should not use an across-the-board cut. Members of both Education and Social Services Ctees spoke for their ctees'

preference for selective redundancy because of over-manning. Cllr Elkington sought to delay matters on the ground that the Working Party Report proposing a points scheme had not yet come to Finance & Resources; this was rejected 11-3 as a technicality. There was a flash of irritation over children allegedly doing the cleaning in homes for handicapped children. Cllr Braithwaite summed up and pointed out that the union representatives had signed the Working Party Report on the points scheme. Committee approved Cllr Braithwaite's motion of support by 12-3.

Mr Stetchworth's digest:

This was my first meeting of Finance & Resources. I had read Mrs Target's paper, which was clearer than her oral presentation, but she kept the over-manning point to the end of her piece. Elkington and Mrs Budge tried to get the whole thing adjourned on the grounds that we ought first to approve the Report of the Working Party on a points-based scheme for cleaners, but the Committee would not listen. Mrs Budge was then very rude to Jelfs for suggesting that it wouldn't hurt for children to help clean their own places, but Gordon sat on her firmly (and did a very good job as chairman, I thought). Most members had obviously read the paper and made up their minds. Mr Braithwaite sensed this, summed up beautifully, and proposed a motion of support which went through very easily.

Task 4

The Chief Education Officer has to instruct the Education Officer for the Western Division to proceed in the light of the Committee's decision. **Write the memorandum required.**

Suggested Solution to Task 4

```
            MEMORANDUM
FROM     Chief Education Officer
TO       Divisional Education Officer, Western
         Division
DATE     November 20th 197-
SUBJECT  Cleaning staff - redundancies

Finance & Resources Committee met yesterday to

consider the policy of selective redundancy in

the light of the recent one-day strike by

cleaning staff.  The Committee decided by a

substantial majority to endorse the policy.

This constitutes authority to proceed with the

six proposed redundancies set out in your

schedule (Ed/W/NT/44).

Please take the necessary steps, and inform the

Treasurer of your own estimates, in each case,

of the compensation involved, with a copy to

me.  This should reach the Treasurer by

December 10th.

                (Signature)
```

Task 5

Mr Braithwaite is a former chairman of the County Council. He and his colleagues who form the inner controlling group in the Council are seeking a new chairman for a major committee. Braithwaite's colleagues ask for a judgement on Gordon's chairmanship. By close analysis of the text, **work out in discussion** what that judgement would probably be.

Suggested Solution to Task 5

The focus of this task is the discussion of the transcript. It should reveal the following points:

Mr Gordon is as yet unfamiliar with some of the procedural aspects, such as omitting to take Apologies for Absence before the Minutes, and omitting to mention Any Other Business. However, he deals firmly with Mrs Budge's indiscipline, and is tactful in dealing with Sir Henry Davis' improper use of a Point of Information. He is clearly in control of the meeting, in that there is no instance of more than one member trying to speak at a time. He shows skill in referring matters to officers, who respect his position by keeping their contributions within reasonable bounds. His invitation to Mrs Target to reply to Mrs Budge's complaint is skilful, and he senses accurately that the Committee is ready to agree with Cllr Braithwaite's summing up. On balance, on this evidence, a promising performance.

D2 – The Publisher's Move

The Ephesus Press is a specialist publishing house owned by a university in a large British city. It publishes books of a highly specialised nature for the university market, and has built up its reputation and its financial stability by careful identification of its sales areas. It issues books which have relatively limited sales but a steady demand, in such fields as laser technology, urban traffic management, highway engineering, translation theory, and parliamentary history. Although the Press is expected to break even rather than make a profit, it has in fact shown a profit of over £50,000 a year for the last five years.

The firm relies on three main sources of income. One is its small number of new books, usually five or six each year, which if successful will sell between 750 and 1,000 copies to university and other libraries in the English-speaking world in their first two years, and about 150 copies yearly for the following five years before being outdated. It is vital for such books to secure a good set of reviews in the academic journals, and to relate directly to 'growth' areas of interest among scholars and students. The second source of income is the 'back list', made up of books which have a sales life of more than five years and sell well enough to justify a reprinting every two or three years. (A reprint of less than 1,000 copies is uneconomic.) There are sixty titles in the back list. The third source of income is the photographic re-print service: there is regular demand in higher education for out-of-print books which ordinary publishers do not find it economic to go on reprinting, but which Ephesus Press can reprint because its clients are not put off by the delay or the high prices charged.

The Press's pricing policy is based on conservative assessments of likely sales, related directly to the costs of production. The back list is re-priced each time a book is reprinted, and reprints and new books are thus priced at similar levels. The average price per volume in trade-price terms is about £7, so that books will retail in the UK at about £10 and at upwards of £15 overseas. The back list stock is maintained on the principle that reprints are ordered when a title goes out of stock, provided it has sold its previous printing in less than three years. In practice, on average two titles drop out of the back list every year and two other titles come into it from new and recent publications. Otherwise, on average half the back list is reprinted in lots of 1,000 copies every two years and the balance every three years.

The business is run by the Publisher to the University, who has a personal assistant, with a Senior Editor, Finance Officer/Accountant, Sales & Publicity Manager, Warehouse & Distribution Manager, and clerical and secretarial staff in each section. The professional staff salary costs amount to £45,000 p.a., while the clerical and manual wages costs total £40,000 p.a.

For the past nineteen years the Ephesus Press has been accommodated in buildings at the edge of the University site – a cluster of demountable offices on the site and a leasehold warehouse across the road from the offices. The final phase of university building is approaching and the offices have to be dismantled to make way for it. At approximately the same time the lease on the warehouse comes up for renewal. The Press pays a rent of £4,000 p.a. for its offices and the old lease on the warehouse was at a rent of £6,500. The owners of the warehouse have been offered £22,000 p.a. for the lease by another client, and similar accommodation elsewhere in the same locality would cost at least as much. Commercial office property would have to be taken in lieu of the existing offices, and would cost roughly the same as a new warehouse. The problem has been discussed by the University Senate, of which the City Development Officer happens to be a member, and he has pointed out that a factory building offering slightly more spacious accommodation for warehouse and offices can be rented on the Colditch Trading Estate for only £28,000 p.a. The Senate have therefore instructed the Publisher to explore the feasibility of moving there. The Board of Management of the Press (which is a sub-committee of the University Senate) have pursued the enquiries in confidence. An informed estimate of the staff situation suggests that only one of the manual and one of the clerical staff would be likely to make such a move with the firm, since Colditch is 17 miles away with the city centre in between. Prevailing wage rates at Colditch for manual and junior clerical staff are much lower, and the saving on the wage bill could reach £15,000 p.a. Further, the size of the warehouse would permit palletised storage and fork-lift handling, which could be operated

with a much smaller labour force. The professional staff would be required to move with the firm, of course, and the Board judges that all of them except the Publisher himself could reasonably claim compensation in some form for the additional cost of travelling to Colditch. They decide to include the Publisher and treat all five alike.

Task 1

Explore in discussion the various possible formulae on which compensation for additional travelling costs might be based for the five professional staff. Bear in mind that some forms of such payments are taxable, and that from the company's point of view the precise form of the compensation matters less than the need to combine a fair and workable scheme with both reasonable economy and flexibility in the face of inflation. It may be useful to compare a travel-expenses scheme such as the N.J.C. (i.e. Local Government) one with providing company cars. The gross cost of the scheme should be such that, after drawing up a schedule of the net saving accruing from the move, the Press still shows a substantial reduction in its overall costs as a result of moving out to Colditch instead of leasing property close to the University site.

Task 2

Work out in discussion in small groups the various ways in which the decision to move to Colditch can be made known to the 14 clerical and manual employees. Either at the initial stage or subsequently it will be necessary to inform them in writing that the posts at the new site will be adverised to existing staff first, and that they will be welcome to apply for them. In the light of the discussion, **draft the text** of such a document. The employees do not belong to a trade union.

102

Task 3

It is possible to derive from the foregoing material a reasonably clear picture of the contents of the book division of the warehouse. Assume that all the stock is of hard-back books of Crown 8vo size, packed in 10s. Work out a scheme whereby the Warehouse Manager can ensure that the removal firm and his own staff conduct the move with the minimum of disruption to the business and the minimum of handling and damage to the stock. **Write out the instructions** to the removal firm which arise from this scheme.

Task 4

The Press naturally has to inform everyone with whom it does business – customers at home and overseas, the book trade, authors, readers, advisers, printers, binders, etc. – of the timing of the move and the firm's new location. **Work out** whether a single mode of communication is feasible in these circumstances, and if not, develop a schedule of modes and an estimate of the costs involved. Then **design the text and layout** of the document which is intended for the largest single category of those to be informed.

Task 5

The firm's Senior Editor is an eccentric. He works very strange hours, doing most of his editorial work in the late afternoon and evening, spending long lunch-hours almost every day with lecturers and professors in the university. He works hard and has a flair which at times has a touch of genius, so his eccentricity is tolerated. However, the Publisher's personal assistant has to work hard herself to keep the Editor's administration in order, and he has a quirky habit of sending very emotional and often rather silly memoranda to the Publisher. Document A is a case in point, and it reflects its author's habit of going round and round each point so much that he gives away his own arguments. Identify the weaknesses in his arguments and **prepare the draft reply** which the Publisher's personal assistant is asked to provide.

Document A

```
Editor to Publisher

Charles -

This proposal to move out to Colditch really
is taking a quite unrealistic view of the way
we work.  Anyone would think our books are so
many tins of beans.  I don't in the least mind
the area - it's quite pleasant - but the notion
that we can run a university press from a site
away from the university is pure fantasy.

1.  Our present location enables us to keep up
with the big boys in terms of quick and very
well-informed advice about MSS sent to us for
publication.  If we moved away I would have to
spend my time nosing around for it, even in our
own university, and might even have to start
nosing around in others.  Is that a right use
of my time?

2.  Our other advantage over the big boys also
depends on our location:  early information on
major developments.  We are both members of the
Senior Common Room, and you know yourself how
much this lets us in on what the coming things
are.  I know this university hasn't quite the
glamour it once had, but it is our main source
of good material.

3.  About half our list originated as teaching
material with undergraduates.  Have you the
slightest idea of the nursing and observation
and re-writing that goes on in the process of
turning teaching notes into a decent book?  Do
you begin to realise the importance of being
on the spot for such work?

4.  George tells me that our own university
bookshop sells as much as 12% of our sales for
the better-selling half of our list, and 5%
of the total turnover.  Only two other book-
shops in the country do any better for us.  I
know this is really George's business as Sales
Manager, but are we wise to throw up such an
asset?

I can't see the house saving a penny piece by
this move:  every item I have mentioned will
add to our costs, and the savings must be pea-
nuts by comparison.

                              Esmond
```

D3 – St Philip's Primary School

A Church of England (voluntary aided) primary school in a suburban village three miles from an industrial town, St Philip's has 232 pupils and a staff of ten, two of whom teach part-time only. The numbers in each age group and their organisation in classes are set out in Table 1. The problems posed here have to do with the school meals provision, and the plan of the school is a principal part of the material.

The main school, built in 1927, houses the classrooms of the Junior department, the school offices, and the hall, which doubles as a gymnasium. In 1956 the meals service was improved by the building of a 'temporary' wooden building on a concrete foundation and with solid floors. It had a serving kitchen only: the food was to be cooked at another school three miles away and delivered by van in insulated containers.

In 1972 the County's policy of closing very small rural schools affected the neighbouring infants' school which sent its pupils on to St Philip's: it had been built in 1844, and the head teacher was retiring. A five-sided building was added at St Philip's, designed to provide four teaching bays (three infant classes and a nursery, or four classes) with a hall area. The combined schools, however, were too big to service by van meals. For the time being one bay of the new building was taken over as a cooking kitchen, and the whole school used the wooden building as a dining hall.

In 1976 the Managers complained to the Local Education Authority that no action had been taken to end this arrangement, and requested a

Table 1

Class	Room	No on roll 1978/9	1979/80	1980/81
Recep	A	26	21	15
2 Inf	B	30	26	21
3 Inf	C	29	30	26
J 1	3	28*	29	30
J 2	4	26	30	29
J 3	5	27	29	34
J 4	6	26	32	32
J 5	2	28	—**	—
Remed	1	12	14	—
Total		232	211	187
Staffing		HM 8 f.t.	HM 7 f.t.	HM 7 f.t.
		0.6 Rem.	0.8 Rem.	

* Five pupils due to be withdrawn owing to closure of neighbouring armed forces establishment

** Five junior classes re-organised into four to adjust to staff reduction through falling roll.

better, permanent provision. They based their complaint on several grounds:
1. the kitchen presented a fire risk to a building not designed to house it;
2. the lack of teaching space in the infant department was harming the development of the school's work;
3. the meals were of poor quality because of the lack of space and cooling on the way to the dining hall.

The LEA agreed to produce a new plan, and in due course proposed the following:

St. Philip's C. of E. Voluntary Aided Primary School

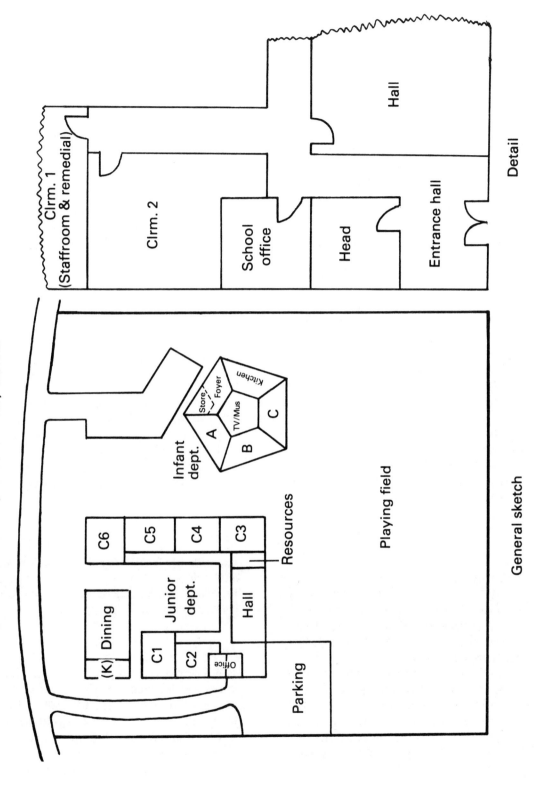

General sketch

Detail

1. to use the wooden building as a classroom;
2. to use the school hall as the dining room;
3. to remove the kitchen from the Infant building and install it in Classroom 2.

At this stage the Vicar, who was Chairman of the Managers, fell ill. The leading members of the managing body, apart from the Vicar, were Mrs Jacqueline Hardy, the deputy head and the staff representative, and Mrs Vivienne Hanscombe, one of the two parent managers, who had agreed to become vice-chairman without expecting it to involve any serious work. The other managers tended to stay away from meetings unless strongly pressed, because they did not much like the Vicar.

The deputy head put the proposals to the teaching staff, who rejected them flatly. They argued that:
1. the use of the wooden hut would break up the unity of the school and oblige them to break up the central resource area in order to equip it;
2. the Hall was vital to the school's activity in gymnastics and country dancing, for which it was well known. These could be run only at lunch-time as buses took many children home at 3.45.;
3. the location of a kitchen between the Head's office and the room which doubled as staff room and remedial room seemed damaging and unnecessary.

The managers met under Mrs Hanscombe's chairmanship and agreed with these objections. They asked for a meeting with the LEA, whose representatives told them:
1. the decision rested entirely with the Managers;

2. the funds would not be available after the current financial year;
3. the wooden building could not be used as a cooking kitchen under the Health & Safety at Work Act;
4. the situation could remain as it was, but the same law might cause serious problems in the future in that case;
5. van-service could be restored, from the Central Kitchen eight miles away.

Your role in the following tasks is that of Mrs Hanscombe, a parent-manager who left school at 16, qualified as a secretary, and is now acting chairman of the managers. There are eight other managers (two from the parish council, two from the District Council, two appointed by the LEA and the Vicar, and the representative of the diocese). The LEA nominees are a local shopkeeper and a county councillor who attends when she can. You should suppose that the tasks have to be completed between February and May of a given year, when the post of diocesan representative is vacant.

Task 1

Examine the Health & Safety at Work Act, or a reliable guide to its provisions, and **prepare to inform the Managers** orally of its consequences for this situation.

Task 2

The headmaster is a man of 34 who was appointed last year. He draws your attention to the school population forecast in Table 1. He suggests that the kitchen could be located in Classroom 3, and that the school could manage for a year until the falling numbers provide more space. The wooden hut could then be demolished in due course to make more playground space. However, the Head feels that the plan would be accepted more readily by the staff if it appeared to come from the Chairman rather than the Headmaster. **Simulate the discussion** in which, in the presence of the Head, you put this scheme to Mrs Hardy as if it were your idea and were new to the Head as well.

Task 3

Mrs Hardy and the Head suggest that the scheme should be set out in writing, in the form of a paper for discussion by the managers, with the staff being invited to submit comments on it to the meeting. **Write this paper** so that it faces the difficulties involved squarely, and is based on a diagram.

Task 4

The scheme is discussed in the staff room at length, on the whole very favourably. The staff ask, however, that a group of them discuss with the managers the proposal that the wooden building be retained as a specialist craft workshop, to provide for some cookery, woodwork, and especially for the school's very strong interest in pottery. Not being the Authority's representative, you have no power to commit the Authority to any spending, and have to bear in mind both fire regulations and the Health & Safety at Work Act. **Simulate the discussion** between two members of staff, the Headmaster, and the managers.

Task 5

Assume that this scheme is approved. **Draw up the text of a circular letter** to parents which explains the plan and seeks to enlist their support and co-operation in what is bound to be a trying first year.

D4 – No Smoking

Colin Thompson is 24, and works as a machine operator in the photogravure department of Ellis & Nock Ltd, printers, of Calton-on-Soar. One Friday at the end of April 1978, at 16.15 hrs, ten minutes before 'clocking off' time, he stopped his machine and surreptitiously lit a cigarette. Thompson is an experienced printer whose apprenticeship was successful and praiseworthy. He knew, therefore, very well indeed that in a printing works smoking always had been and still was forbidden: the presence of highly volatile inks constitutes a serious fire risk. Hence, the penalty for such an offence is instant dismissal.

The operator of the neighbouring machine was Norman Wainwright, a man of about 50 who was the 'father' of the machine operators' 'chapel'. He saw Thompson light the cigarette and immediately ordered him, with appropriate expletives, to put his ***** fag out or he would do it for him. Thompson refused, just as forcefully. Wainwright rushed at him to snatch the cigarette from his mouth and a scuffle ensued. Two other machine operators rapidly intervened and pulled the two men apart, by which time Wainwright had stamped the cigarette underfoot.

The shop foreman, Jim Wheeler, heard the noise and came into the machine room to ask what was going on. Wainwright, in some heat, gave the foreman the facts of the matter with creditably little exaggeration. Wheeler took Thompson to Frank McDonnell, the Photogravure Supervisor, and explained what had happened.

McDonnell immediately telephoned the Works Manager, Charles Wilson, who called McDonnell and Thompson to his office, severely berated the latter and reminded him firmly but politely of the penalty for smoking in the works. With Thompson's agreement he telephoned Arnold Yeomans, the Personnel Manager and one of the four most senior men in the Company. Yeomans came down to Wilson's office as the main body of the workforce were going home, listened to McDonnell's report and Thompson's concurrence with it, but firmly refused to hear any explanations or defence: 'No: I think everyone should go home for the week-end and calm down. Then we'll have you and your Union rep. in for a meeting in my office on Monday when we can look at it coolly.'

On his way home, Yeomans managed to intercept Thompson's shop-steward, Bill McManus, a good-hearted, mild-tempered man who took his union work very seriously. Yeomans had built up enormous respect among the shop-stewards for his diplomatic skill, and together he and McManus worked out a possible solution. McManus agreed to talk to the Area Officer of the union during the week-end.

The meeting took place in Yeomans' office on Monday at 10.30. Those present were Yeomans himself, McDonnell, Wilson, McManus, Wheeler, and Frank Burton, the Area Officer of the union. Thompson waited in the ante-room, and was called in for questioning. It transpired that Thompson was in difficulties at home: his wife had been seeing other men, and on the Friday in question she had been observed leaving home with a smartly-dressed man in his thirties driving an expensive car. This information had reached Thompson at 13.45, when he was starting a job requiring careful and constant attention and very fine adjustments of his machine. The afternoon proved one of increasing strain, and by 16.15 he felt it so severely that he could no longer stave off his craving for a smoke. Thompson complained that Wainwright's manner had been much too rough, and provoked him where a less aggressive approach would have got him to put it out immediately. Wainwright, called in for his side of it, defended his attitude by pointing to the risk of serious fire and said that Thompson's foolhardiness made him lose his temper. He had apologised to Thompson for his violence.

McManus pointed out that nobody was denying the right of the firm to dismiss Thompson, but he was a popular and very skilful worker whose mates knew something of his troubles and had indicated to McManus that the full penalty would be regarded as too severe in the circumstances. This was a guarded way of hinting that they might strike in protest, and Yeomans insisted, gently but firmly, that McManus be plain about it. A strike would be disastrous for a very busy firm, and the meeting eventually agreed with Yeomans' and McManus' suggestion: suspension without pay for five weeks. Thompson admitted that the decision would be fair, and thanked them for their consideration and leniency. McDonnell sought to insist that Thompson be forbidden to bring tobacco into the plant in future, but was over-ruled. Wilson asked that the report of the meeting which would go to the Managing Director record his view that Thompson should have been dismissed.

Task 1

Assume that you are Jim Wheeler, the machine room foreman. **Simulate the interview** with Thompson and Wainwright held at the side of Thompson's machine, including the questioning of the two operators who intervened.

Task 2

Prepare a report of this interview for the Personnel Manager to study over the week-end. (See Guide 7.4.1)

Task 3

Simulate the meeting between Yeomans and McManus who work out the possible solution to the problem of what to do about Colin Thompson, bearing in mind the view that Wilson has expressed.

Task 4

Yeomans asks Thompson for a written statement, giving him the facts of the incident and whatever reasons for his behaviour that are relevant. **Draft this statement**. (See Guide 7.4)

Task 5

Frank Burton, the Area Officer of the union concerned, is about to retire. He has had good reason to look on the record of relations with Ellis & Nock Ltd with satisfaction. This particular episode is characteristic of the pattern he has known. **Write the note for the** union's Area Office **file** which he writes for his successor in the union work, giving the essential facts of this episode and placing it in its context.

D5 – Hackworth & Locke Ltd

Hackworth & Locke Ltd are an old-established textile manufacturing concern employing about 300 people in warp knitting. The management consists of a Managing Director, a Finance Director, Works Manager, four department managers (in production departments), and managers for Sales, Purchasing, Accounts, and Technical (i.e. quality control); a personnel officer, an assistant works manager, a manager of progress who runs the materials handling teams and the despatch section, and eight foremen, one of whom is in charge of the eight skilled maintenance men. Handling and Despatch have thirty employees, all unskilled, there are six senior salesmen, and three assistant staff in each of personnel, sales, and purchasing. The Accounts office has four accounts clerks, and contains the typing pool of six girls. Each of the top management down to and including the Technical Manager has his own secretary. The total work-force is 303, including the management. Just over three quarters of the latter are women, and exactly a quarter of the total production staff are 57 or older, ten of them men and the rest women.

Entry into the EEC has greatly widened the firm's markets. It produces long runs of unpatterned fabric from plain or crimped yarn, and has specialised in handling man-made yarns knitted up for foam-backing and similar treatment. There is a steady demand for the product, and the firm provides a service to some much larger firms by producing test lengths of fabric from their experimental yarns. Hackworth

& Locke have always avoided contracts that would tie up more than a third of their business with a single customer. They are efficient both economically and socially, in the sense that while their costs are competitive, they are also small enough to have all the benefits of morale and loyalty that small enterprises often gain.

You are the senior of the three assistant staff in the Personnel Office. Your boss is a former department manager whose health showed signs of strain, and you have specialised in dealing with the employees and their union representatives. You come from the same background as the shop stewards (your father still works for a similar firm in the same town, as a beam-handler) and you get on well with them. The other members of the personnel staff are a woman welfare officer and a records clerk who should (in your opinion) be in the wages department. Interviewing for vacancies is done by whichever of the personnel staff is available.

In recent months a steady stream of papers has been passed on by the MD or the Works Manager, usually to the Personnel Officer, who gives them to you, on the subject of training. A guide to the Employment and Training Act of 1974 is one of these. There have been papers about the Industrial Training Board, the Manpower Services Commission, the Training Services Agency, and the need for improved skills in the industry. You have not paid much attention. However, two events have shaken you and your superiors out of this lethargy. Some months ago an employee who had been on the production staff for fifteen months

had been sacked for poor workmanship, and had appealed to an industrial tribunal. She won her case, and secured reinstatement, not because the firm was wrong in its judgement of her work, but because it failed to provide adequate training to help her improve. More recently, one of the department managers mentioned to the Managing Director, during one of his weekly tours of the works, that an employee retiring that week would be the first of twenty to be retiring at monthly intervals in that department alone. The MD demanded to know what was to be done about replacing them with workers of similar quality, let alone about building up the extra sixty likely to be needed for the growth in Europe.

Discussions followed, in which you were asked to draft out a Training Plan. Work in the plant was basically done on piecework in teams of four. When a vacancy occurred, an untrained employee would be slotted in to learn from the other three, and the team's wages would be 'made up' (i.e. paid on average earnings) until the output reached normal levels (usually in 3–3½ weeks). As vacancies occurred no more than twice a year, in normal times, this was reasonable. The 'making up' costs of such a system would be much more serious in trying to train perhaps a hundred new employees. Your proposal is to set up a small training shop: recruits would work there on basic rate for three weeks, and then join an existing gang of four, as a supernumerary on basic rate, for three weeks. At that stage the trainee joins a gang on normal piecework rates.

Task 1

Find out about the legal and administrative framework within which training schemes operate. You should examine the text of, or recommended guides to:
The Employment and Training Act (1974);
The Employment Protection Act (1975).

The literature of Industrial Training Boards, the Manpower Services Commission and Training Services Agency will also be worth consulting. In particular, establish whether the kind of training scheme proposed here would be eligible for grant or subsidy from the ITB or other sources.

Task 2

Set out the proposed training scheme **as a paper** for consideration by the company's Board of Directors. They will be very interested in its costs, and in the light of semi-skilled wage-rates in your own area you should try to assess the wage-costs of:
(a) trainees not yet producing at basic time rate because they are in the training shop;
(b) the supervisor of the training shop;
(c) the trainees while working as gang supernumeraries.

You should offset against these costs the benefit of giving up the present system. The trainee joins a gang, whose output falls so that their wages have to be made up to average wages. This is on average 30% of their earnings for three weeks, and three men are involved in each such gang. Data given at other points allows a reasonably accurate net costing of the labour side of the scheme. Anticipate the probable objections of the Board.

Task 3

The Board accept the scheme in principle and offer you the post of training supervisor. You refuse it because it needs close knowledge of the machinery. The Board ask you, however, to put the scheme to the unions next day. The six shop stewards are amiable but alert people who know you well. There is not time to prepare a briefing document. **Simulate the meeting** at which you put the scheme to them and invite comment and suggestions.

Task 4

The union representatives approve the scheme, and a training supervisor is appointed. However, the workforce in general know little of the coming expansion, and it would not be tactful to remind many of them that they will soon be retiring. It is now necessary to inform the whole workforce about the scheme, giving them good reasons, and reassurance about its effects on them, in language understood by people who mostly left school at 14. **Draft the letter** to be circulated.

Task 5

In readiness for a visit to a progressive employer with a vigorous training policy, **draw up a list of questions or study-guide** which will identify in advance the points on which you will need to obtain information during the visit.

D6 – Kynaston Park Motor Museum

This assignment relates to a country house and its substantial grounds. You should agree on a suitable location to use for the purpose, such as an actual country estate in your neighbourhood. Alternative locations which would serve the purposes of the exercise include:
1. the site of the large reservoir just NE of Daventry (Northamptonshire);
2. one of the reservoirs near Hemsworth, Yorkshire;
3. the grounds of several former colleges of education such as that at Newbold Revel, Warwickshire.
The site requires to be located in such a way that major road access is not difficult to within a few miles of it, while immediate access from major roads to the site presents real difficulties.

During the fifteen years after World War 2, the Earl of Kynaston assembled a collection of vintage cars and old racing cars in a group of outbuildings on his estate at Kynaston Park. The few enthusiasts and friends who were able to see it believed the collection to be of outstanding quality, but the Earl was a very private man who detested crowds. After his death in 1971 the will was the subject of legal dispute. Eventually the house and grounds and contents went to James Carteret, the late Earl's nephew, a man of 43 who owned an estate in the West Indies, was already wealthy, and believed the United Kingdom to be far advanced in decay.

However, Carteret saw business possibilities in the site. The Park included a racing circuit, too small and narrow for modern racing, but in sound condition and possessing a famous name in the record books of the thirties. He arranged to convert the estate into a limited company, whose task would be to open the Museum to the public, run a number of meets for restored old vehicles to race on the track, and provide other appropriate amenities and attractions.

Mr Carteret views the whole matter as a commercial proposition and wishes to avoid, so far as possible, having to come to England himself. He has appointed a general manager named Virgil Jarred, an American motor car enthusiast with sound business experience but no knowledge of English conditions. In particular, he has never heard of VAT, the Employment Protection Act, planning permission, or the Health and Safety at Work Act, and is unfamiliar with the English climate. His brief is to get the Museum and related amenities going for an April–September season, leaving the racing events until the Museum has become established.

Mr Jarred has appointed you as one of three employees to help get the business going. One is the estate's existing manager, responsible for maintenance and improvement of buildings and grounds; one is the firm's accountant, who also has charge of catering and the vehicle mechanics; while you are responsible for everything involving the visiting public, contacts with outside bodies, publicity, public relations, and what Jarred calls 'the commercial side'. This turns out to include selection and control of all staff except the

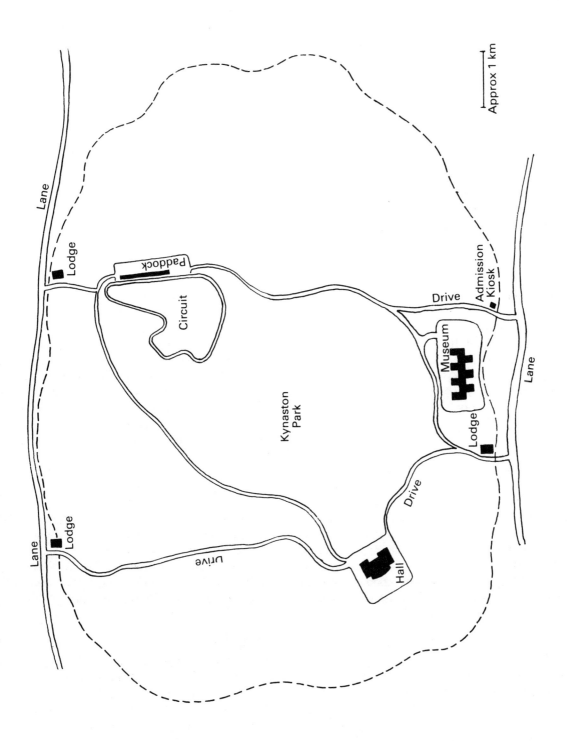

Lane

Lodge

Paddock

Circuit

Kynaston Park

Lane

Lodge

Drive

Drive

Lodge

Hall

Museum

Lodge

Drive

Admission Kiosk

Lane

Approx 1 km

113

mechanics, groundsmen, and caterers.

The essential features of the site are given on the map. The museum itself contains 74 vehicles, ranging from a 1926 Morris Minor to a pre-1914 Rolls Royce. There are no commercial vehicles. They are housed in eight separate galleries, all converted from barns and stables originally built for the Home Farm and all linked by concrete paths into a continuous circuit. Discussion with Jarred confirms that you will need to employ a security guard in each gallery throughout opening hours, each of whom has to be released for a lunch break and replaced during it. A ticket office will need to be provided and staffed, but a souvenir shop will be self-financing. The firm will need to employ a foreman to take charge of the security guards and toilet staff (there are to be four public toilets). All of these and other factors enter into the cost-structure of the business.

Task 1

Making use of suitable reference books (such as the annual *Historic Houses and Gardens*), **make a selection** of five or six approximately similar establishments, which will be smaller and less elaborate than the best-known and most publicised grand houses; **draw up a table** of their opening hours, admission charges, amenities, and other data **relevant to the central problem of deciding what admission charges to impose.**

Task 2

On the basis of the information given above, and other assumptions to be set out as you judge relevant, **make a schedule of staff** to be employed, giving hours and basing wages on unskilled-labour rates in your own area. Use this schedule to **work out the probable costs** of the Museum operation for a year. Jarred is working on a first-year target of 60,000 visitors, arriving by car at an average rate of 2.5 persons per car, and aims to achieve 100,000 in the second year. This flow of visitors will be required to yield a trading surplus of £65,000 per annum (after the first year) in order to pay for maintenance and staffing of buildings, grounds, and the vehicle mechanics. **Estimate the admission and parking charges** which will be necessary to achieve this by the end of the second season.

Task 3

One of your tasks is to stock the souvenir shop, which will require a stock of picture postcards. These can be made locally, but cards of adequate quality have to be made by one of two or three specialist firms. These take their own photographs, which require good weather, and normally expect to supply in lots of 5,000 copies. Delivery is normally twelve weeks. The firm you wish to deal with offers cards at 7p each for lots of 5,000 and 8¼p for lots of 1,000. There are over 40 cars which would make good pictures, but to secure the bulk discount you order cards for 18, adding one of the house and one of the museum exterior, making a total order of 100,000 cards. The order requires Jarred's approval, and he sends the order back with a note:
'What *are* you about? We can't possibly sink £8,500 in picture postcards at this stage and only get 18 of the cars for it.'

Jarred likes such notes to be answered in writing, but very briefly. Check your own and Jarred's figures and **write the reply.**

Task 4

Draft (a) a letter for Mr Jarred's signature informing the County Planning Officer of the intention to re-open the Park as a museum. The letter should invite the Planning Officer to comment, advise on any necessary procedures, and visit the site if he wishes.

(b) a covering memorandum to Jarred explaining why it is absolutely necessary to send such a letter. The last time you mentioned this to him he dismissed it with comment about the 'fuddy duddy British'.

Task 5

The County Planning Officer replies to the letter from Mr Jarred, and extracts from his reply are given in Document B. He refers to a letter from a local amenity society, and his extracts from it are given as Document C. You point out to Mr Jarred that unless the objections raised in the two letters can be met, the whole enterprise will collapse. **He asks you to draft a reply** and to list the implications for the firm.

Document B

Extract of letter from Planning Officer

Apart from the planning regulations, there are considerations under the broader heading of amenity. My department has a duty to take these into account, and in some circumstances they can be decisive.

Since a formal application for planning permission has not yet been made, I can let you have a copy of parts of a letter I have already received about your proposals. In our experience, many other letters of this kind must be expected, and we are obliged to pay careful regard to the points they raise.

Perhaps I should explain that major planning decisions are taken by the elected committee of the District Council, and while my advice is listened to I have no power of decision. Within that limitation, I have discretion to hold discussions with interested parties about any major proposal. I would be very grateful if you would indicate whether or not you would be willing to take part in such an informal meeting in the near future.

In the meantime, there is no possibility that the procedures for planning permission for change of use at Kynaston Park could be completed before the meeting of the Planning Committee on June 20th next. There are likely to be other questions to be resolved at a later stage, but I am sure you would wish to know the position on the central issue.

Document C

Extract from letter to Planning Officer from local branch of Countryside Association.

The recent report in the Courier of developments proposed at Kynaston Park causes us concern. If Mr Jarred is correctly reported, he hopes ultimately for 'well over 100,000 visitors a year'. We must assume that this means at least twenty coaches and two thousand cars every week in the season, or more than three hundred extra vehicles a day. We submit that the lanes leading to Kynaston cannot handle such traffic without grave risks.

Secondly, although major roads are only ten miles off, it requires expert map-reading to reach Kynaston from them without going through one or other of two small, peaceful towns. The impact of such traffic on either town would be very serious. In any case, we feel that a major enterprise of this sort would have found it tactful and in its own interests to enter into some discussion with other interested parties such as the District Council before making a press announcement.

Thirdly, we naturally welcome the additional employment which the proposal would bring, but feel that the main burden of the additional tourist traffic it would bring must fall on others. That most of them would come by car makes this burden immeasurably greater, and we view with the greatest anxiety the noise, litter, and other likely consequences.

Fourthly, we feel bound to express concern about the view taken by Mr Jarred when he was asked about facilities to be provided. He proposes picnic areas, but felt that restaurants could be left to private enterprise and toilet and parking provision in the area were for the local people to arrange. These views suggest a very limited understanding of the delicate balance of factors which make the English countryside what it is.

May we, therefore, register our anxiety about this scheme and express the hope that your Department will exercise the utmost vigilance. We also request that we be notified when application for planning permission is received.

D7 – Own and Run, or Buy In?

Read Section 7 of the Guide again before attempting this Assignment.

A problem which affects businesses and government organisations of all sizes is that of how to secure the provision of a specialised service. In ordinary private life, most young people who move from one flat to another can organise the removal by hiring a van and doing the work themselves. There comes a point, however, beyond which it is cheaper and safer to employ a firm of removers. The question of where that point comes can present itself in many different guises.

The first assignment in this book, The Office Garden (A1), is based on one particular form of the choice between buying in a specialised service, and owning and running the equipment oneself. The same basic issue is at work in the latent argument over alternative transport in The Withdrawal of The Rushton Bus (C5): do the parents rely on car-pools or hire a coach? Again, when G Smith & Sons (C1) have completed a move to an out-of-town site (supposing the staff had made that choice), the same question arises over issuing season tickets on the public service or buying a company mini-bus.

The layman is apt to suppose that if you need to have a job done regularly in a business, the simplest solution is to engage the labour and buy the equipment required. However, there are many jobs which almost every firm needs to have done occasionally, but not often enough to justify each firm in having its own staff and equipment for it. A specialist firm can provide the service more cheaply to each firm than any one of them could provide it for itself. This is the economic base for numerous service industries such as office cleaning, telephone hygiene, telephone answering, party catering, data processing, dance bands and discos, specialised printing, cash-collection, and large-scale advertising. The belief that, because there is money to be made in providing such services, those who provide them are exploiting their customers, may be mistaken.

At the other extreme, there are services which an organisation of any size would find uneconomic and unreasonable to put out to a specialist contractor. Examples would include stock control in a retail chain, the cooking of school meals, and quality control on an industrial production line.

Between these two extremes is a middle category of services where the balance is more even. Selection of staff for senior management may be one instance. Is it cheaper for a large local government office to contract out the catering in its canteen? Would a company employing nine or ten people whose conditions of service include the provision of a company car do better to buy this fleet or to rent it from a service firm? Should an education authority try to compete with commercial publishers of textbooks by publishing its own?

For this assignment the class should work in syndicates of four or five students. Each syndicate should appoint a chairman and:
1. select a business or situation described in a previous assignment;
2. identify a service needed in that context, for which the relative

cost-benefit (the balance of costs and gains) can be assessed;
3. establish, by investigation or by specifying the relevant assumptions, the set of factors on which the analysis has to be based;
4. confirm the results of the foregoing steps with the teacher;
5. assemble the data and estimates on which to base an advisory report;
6. draw up a report on the following terms of reference: to determine the balance of advantage for (the organisation) in providing (the service) by purchase from an outside contractor, as compared with providing it by employing staff and purchasing equipment for the purpose.

Examples of assignments and tasks appropriate for this purpose include:

Office cleaning in the type of offices described in Assignment A1 (The Office Garden).

The maintenance of driveways and grounds of a hospital like that in A9 (The Hospital Opening).

The use of a public relations firm to introduce a major change in a public service, such as the plastic bags in A3 (Mrs Surtees' Bins).

The provision of specialised packaging materials for the export trade of R & B Accessories Ltd (B5).

The provision of translators, or translation equipment, or both, at the Specialist Conference (C6).

The provision and maintenance of heavy equipment for impacting and earthmoving on the tip at Wirkton Cutting (C3).

Employing an Executor and Trustee Company, or the appropriate department of a bank, for disposing of Mr Goodnough's estate (C2).

The provision of clocking-in and related paperwork systems for operating Flexible Working Hours (C5).

Winter-time security or the supervision of car-parking at Kynaston Park Motor Museum (D6).

Appendix

This Appendix has two parts:

1. A set of 'pathways' or sequences of assignments which, in the authors' view, would constitute a rational basis for selecting assignments for the Core Module. Each of these suggests a basic sequence and a number of others which can be substituted for one or more in it. This pattern is repeated for each of the four BEC Boards. Here again the listing is intended only as a guide, since teachers will need to relate the emphasis of their selections to the class and its strengths and weaknesses, as well as to the course objectives. The sequences given should not be regarded as indicating the authors' recommendations or 'best buys'.

2. A table which sets out the principal forms and formats of work in English at this level, and shows how the tasks in each assignment relate to them. This is intended to show the teacher who prefers to plot his course through work in writing letters, memoranda, reports, and the like, which assignments will enable him to do this most readily.

Appendix 1: Pathways through the Assignments

A: Business Studies Sector

Main: A2 A7 B4 B5 B8 C6 D4 D5
D6 D7
Options: A5 B9 C2 C5 C8 D2

B: Financial Studies Sector

Main: A5 A7 B5 C2 C4 C5 C6 D2
D5 D6 D7
Options: B2 B4 B8 C3 C8 D4

C: Distribution Studies Sector

Main: A4 A6 B2 B5 B9 C2 C7 D4
D6
Options: A2 A3 A9 C5 C6 D7

D: Public Administration Sector:

Main: A3 A8 A9 B3 B6 B7 B9 C3 C8
D3 D7
Options: A4 A6 C4 C5 C6 D6

E: Mixed Groups

Main: A4 A6 A7 B3 B4 B9 C2 C3
C8 D4 D5 D7
Options: A2 A5 B7 B8 C4 C6 D2

Appendix 2 table — Forms and Formats of Communication in the Assignments. Column headings are the assignment titles (the rightmost column, "Orange Lane Youth Club", is cut off at the page edge).

Form / Format	The Office Garden	APT Ltd	Mrs Surtees' Bins	The Filing Clerk	Derwent Albion	The Medical Receptionist	The Sports Club's Debt	Mr Farnsworth's Carport	The Hospital Opening	The Caretaker's Retirement	The TV Stand	Mr Garrett's House	Roberts & Boon Ltd	R & B Accessories Ltd	The Station Visitors	Orange Lane Youth Club
Minutes, Agendas, etc	3									4						
Calculations	1			1												
Table or schedule													1/2		5	
Abstract/summary												5				
Report – advisory	1															
– briefing								3								
– informing																
Note for file/record										1		3				
Notes for own use	4								3							
Copy for the press						2	5		5				5			
Circular or publicity		1	3		1		1		4				4/5	4		
Letter (other)	2										5		3		5	
Letter to persuade			4		3			2	6			1		2		
Letter to inform								1	1	2		4		1		
Memorandum	1			5			3	1				2			2	
Leaving a message	2							5		2	5					
Broadcast or script		1			4/5											
Oral briefing				2/3		1–6		4	2		1				3	
Oral persuasion			1		2		2									
Assignment No	A1	A2	A3	A4	A5	A6	A7	A8	A9	B1	B2	B3	B4	B5	B6	

Appendix 2: Forms and Formats of Communication in the Assignments

Rotnley Engineering Ltd
Mrs Chillingworth's Cooker
G. Smith & Sons, Printers
Death of a Grocer
Wirkton Cutting
The Withdrawal of the Rushton Bus
Flexible Working Hours
Specialist Conference
Hail Weston Ltd
The Bulleid Site at Churchward
Committee Meeting
The Publisher's Move
St Philip's Primary School
No Smoking
Hackworth & Locke Ltd
Kynaston Park Motor Museum
Own and Run, or Buy In?

Code	Minutes, Agendas, etc	Calculations	Table or schedule	Abstract/summary	Report – advisory	– briefing	– informing	Note for file/record	Notes for own use	Copy for the press	Circular or publicity	Letter (other)	Letter to persuade	Letter to inform	Memorandum	Leaving a message	Broadcast or script	Oral briefing	Oral persuasion
B9		2																	
C1	1 2 3	1 2											5 4	1	5	2	2		
C2		1/4									5								
C3			1		1						5 2/4 3	5					1		
C4			4		3	3		4			2	5	2	5					
C5			2		2			3			4 3		4 3		5				
C6		2 2/3			5	5	6				4	2		4					
C7								3			3 3	2		2					
C8						3		3			2 1			4			4		
D1	1/2					3	3					4							
D2		3 1	1			3		4				5	4	5 2			5		
D3																		1	
D4				4	2	2	5	5				5 2							
D5					2				5			2			4			3	
D6		1 2	1											3 4					
D7				all															

IRISH MEDICAL CARE RESOURCES:
AN ECONOMIC ANALYSIS

Copies of this paper may be obtained from the Economic and Social Research Institute (Limited Company No. 18269). Registered Office: 4 Burlington Road, Dublin 4.

Price IR£12.50

(Special rate for students IR£6.25)

A. Dale Tussing is Professor of economics and Director of the Health and Society Program of the Maxwell Graduate School at Syracuse University, Syracuse, New York. He was on secondment to The Economic and Social Research Institute for 1979/81. The Paper has been accepted for publication by the Institute, which is not responsible for either the content or the views expressed therein.

IRISH MEDICAL CARE RESOURCES:
AN ECONOMIC ANALYSIS

A. DALE TUSSING

©THE ECONOMIC AND SOCIAL RESEARCH INSTITUTE

DUBLIN, 1985

ISBN 0 7070 0078 5

Acknowledgements

This work has benefited from the aid and kindness of many people. I want to try to acknowledge some of the help I have received.

My major study of economic aspects of the education system, *Irish Educational Expenditures — Past, Present and Future* (Tussing, 1978) was published in 1978. That same year, Professor Kieran A. Kennedy, Director of The Economic and Social Research Institute, suggested that I return to Ireland to "do for the health care system what [I had] done for the education system". I have Professor Kennedy to thank, therefore, not only for suggesting the present study, but for enabling me to develop my interest in the economics of health and health policy, an opportunity which has been valuable to my career. As one consequence I am, as I write a few years later, Director of the Health and Society Program of the Maxwell Graduate School at Syracuse University, Syracuse, New York.

I returned to Ireland in 1979 as Research Professor at The Economic and Social Research Institute to perform this new research. As explained in Chapter 1 of this report, I determined that I would need to conduct a national household sample survey to generate the data necessary for my analysis. The ESRI was sympathetic and encouraging, and approved my research proposal, but was unable to finance the extra costs entailed in the survey. As a consequence, it was necessary for me to spend the next several months in fund-raising efforts. I want to acknowledge the kind and valuable assistance of Mrs. Maura Dempsey, then Assistant Director (Administration), ESRI, in these efforts, which were ultimately successful.

The Central Bank of Ireland made a grant at a crucial time, permitting the project to go forward. Grants from the National Board for Science and Technology, the Voluntary Health Insurance Board, and the Health Education Bureau permitted completion of the survey. None of these grantors is responsible for any of the statements or judgements which appear in this report. The survey itself was conducted by the Survey Unit of the ESRI, at rates lower than those charged external clients. Hence the ESRI also contributed substantially to financing the costs of the survey. I am deeply indebted to these five institutions for their support; without them, this study would not exist.

A great many people were involved in the development of the survey instrument, the conduct of the interviews, and checking and coding responses, and it would be impossible to acknowledge each of them individually. Let me then attempt to acknowledge this debt at least by thanking the ESRI Survey Unit collectively. It is an extraordinarily competent, professional, co-operative and industrious group of people and my reliance on them was total.

Professor Brendan Whelan, Head of the Survey Unit, aided me in developing the survey instrument, a task at which I was a complete novice; and he selected the sample. Dr. Ian Graham of St. Vincent's Hospital gave freely of his time in helping me devise morbidity questions for the survey, questions which, however, had to be omitted (for reasons of time) from the final version of the questionnaire. Leslie Daly of University College, Dublin, was also very helpful at this stage. In acknowledging the help of these people, I do not mean to blame them for any errors in designing the survey instrument. Indeed, there are a number of things I would, in retrospect, have done differently. However, I can also state that the survey was quite successful and I have many people to thank for that.

While the survey instrument was in its developmental stages, I was also aided by commissions that the ESRI received for health-related research. The Institute for Public Administration asked me to prepare the health sections of *Poverty and Social Policy*, the Irish National Report presented to the Commission of the European Communities (Tussing, 1982c). The Oireachtas Joint Committee on State-Sponsored Bodies asked me to act as consultant for its review of the Voluntary Health Insurance Board (Joint Committee on State-Sponsored Bodies, 1980). These commissions were useful in building my knowledge base on the Irish medical care system and I want to acknowledge them.

Computer programming at this stage, involving the original creation and cleaning up of the data set, and aid with the initial analysis, was done by June Ryan of the ESRI, with additional work by John McGregor of Trinity College, Dublin (now of Ryerson Polytechnic Institute, Toronto). Their considerable and very competent contributions are gratefully acknowledged.

My ESRI appointment was for two years, 1979–1981. In that time, I was able to design the project, raise the funds necessary to conduct the survey, develop and conduct the survey, get the data cleaned and entered into the computer, perform some preliminary analysis and survey the relevant international literature. In addition, I completed the two commissions referred to earlier and performed some ESRI duties unrelated to the health project. Most of the statistical analysis and writing was done after I returned to my full-time lecturing and other duties in the Economics Department and the Health and Society Program at Syracuse University.

For more than three years, then, I continued this project, essentially contributing my time, after hours, on week-ends and during summer and holiday leaves. I was willing and indeed glad to do so because of my interest in and commitment to the project. While I am not sure that I would ever want to undertake a project of this scope under such terms again, I do not regret having done so in this instance.

Before leaving Ireland, I was able to discuss aspects of my work with friends, associates and colleagues in this country, to my very great profit. These included David Jacobson of AnCO (now of the National Institute for Higher Education, Dublin); Paul Turpin of the National Economic and Social Council (now with the Department of Industry, Commerce and Tourism); James Raftery, also of NESC; Joe Durkan of ESRI (now with the OECD, Paris); David Rottman and Miriam Wiley, also of the ESRI; Ruth Barrington and Shawn Trant, of the Department of Health; Jimmy Stewart of Trinity College; and Roger Cole, of *In Dublin* magazine. In addition, a number of people provided important help in specific ways. Miceal Ross of the ESRI provided me with data on per capita income by Health Board area and other county data from his own work. Sean Barrett of Trinity College gave me helpful comments on a paper which was an

ACKNOWLEDGEMENTS

early offshoot of this study. Richard Sommerville, also of TCD, gave me background information on the Irish medical care system and Anthony Coughlan, of the same institution, made available valuable research materials and gave me useful advice. John Horgan (now of NIHE Dublin) helped as a TD with parliamentary questions.

In addition, at this same time, Professor Alan Maynard of York University gave me very useful advice and encouragement and provided me with copies of studies not otherwise available to me.

During this period, my wife, Ann K. U. Tussing, a scholar and author in her own right, gave me useful advice and encouragement, assisted me in the construction of tables, read and improved my drafts and helped in many other important ways.

At Syracuse University, a number of people also contributed in significant ways to this study. My colleague Professor John Henning gave me advice on statistics and econometrics. Another colleague, Professor Stephen Long (now of the US congressional Budget Office), gave me advice on health economics questions, particularly in the sections dealing with the international literature and with physician-induced demand for medical care. Claire Rudolph, Professor of Social Work, and then Director of the Health Studies Program, gave me valuable administrative support. My Dean, Professor Guthrie Birkhead, supported a research assistantship for me, which made it possible for me to secure the aid of Martha Wojtowicz, who contributed enormously to this study with her computer and statistical work, as well as with her advice and patience. My computer programmers at Syracuse University, Mark Miller and Nelson Pardee, also contributed mightily to this work.

Several people in the US and in Ireland read part or all of various drafts of this study. I am deeply in the debt of all of the following: Denis Conniffe, Gerry Hughes, Kieran Kennedy, Robert O'Connor and Miriam Wiley, of the ESRI; Ruth Barrington and Shawn Trant, of the Department of Health; Paul Turpin of the NESC; Brendan P. Ryan of the Department of Finance; T. O'Grady Walshe of the Central Bank of Ireland; Eamon O'Shea of the Institute of Public Administration; Geoffrey Dean of the Medico-Social Research Board; Ann K. U. Tussing; and an anonymous referee. These advisers saved me from many errors of fact and judgement. Of course, any remaining errors in this study are mine and mine alone.

This is a large work and it went through many drafts and iterations. Consequently, a great many people helped with the typing and I cannot hope to acknowledge each of them personally. Instead, let me thank all of the staff of the ESRI general office, under Mary Cleary, and the secretarial staff of the Health and Society Program at Syracuse University, under Barbara Cico. My deepest thanks also are due to Mary McElhone of the ESRI Editorial Office for supervising the copy editing and printing.

Finally, I want to thank my patient and understanding family for help of many kinds and many kindnesses: my children, Kathy, Michele, Aaron, Nicholas, and Marri; and my wife, Ann, who is a part of me.

CONTENTS

LIST OF TABLES

LIST OF FIGURES

APPENDIX TABLES

This is a study of the Irish medical care system from the standpoint of health economics. Though there is some technical material, particularly in Chapters 6 and 7, for the most part the study is accessible to the general reader.

The medical care delivery and financing systems of Europe and North America grew up over the twentieth century with little concern for, or attention to, the implicit incentive structures they contained. Instead, the growth patterns of these systems depended on each country's unique history, as well as ideology, party politics, expediency, and the relative strengths of such factors as the medical professions, civil servants, and religious organisations. As a consequence of inattention to incentives, medical care systems grew increasingly inefficient in their overall economic rationality and explosively inflationary. In the past decade, in most of these countries there has been an intense re-examination of medical care structures and at least the beginnings of systematic reform.

The same has been true of Ireland, with one important exception. With minor qualifications, there is no health economics tradition in this country. There have been no health economists trained as such and pursuing that speciality, and there is no health economics literature, except for peripheral, non-empirical, or minor materials.

This study is intended to begin the process of building such a literature. As a consequence, its focus is broad: it concerns Irish medical care resources in general. The main methods have been (1) to subject the existing structure of the Irish medical care system to analysis from the standpoint of economics, which means concentrating on the incentives structure; and (2) to use statistical techniques to study the determinants of utilisation of medical care, such as physicians' services, hospital out- and in-patient care, pharmaceutical medicines, and dental care.

The study has another major dimension, one which is partly a means to the above end and partly an end in itself. The data base for systematic analysis of medical care resources and utilisation was found to have serious weaknesses and gaps. To help rectify this, and to provide the basis for quantitative aspects of the present study, the author organised a major national sample survey of Irish households. The main results of the survey are extensively reported in a statistical appendix. A great deal of information on Irish medical care utilisation appears for the first time in these tables, and its publication is an important purpose and result of the study. The survey also forms the basis of the statistical analysis of Chapters 6 and 7. The data can be made available to scholars for further analysis upon application to the author.

Because the data were collected from households, and not from doctors or hospitals, the analysis is of necessity households-oriented. This means that the present study is particularly concerned with primary care, and less so with hospitals, even though the Irish medical care system is strongly hospitals-oriented. In one way, this is a weakness in the study. Resource use and cost inflation have been strongly concentrated in the hospitals sector, and the incentive structure faced by hospitals and consultants needs study. After extensively reviewing the Irish medical care system, we conclude that the most important item remaining on the agenda of Irish health economics research is a study of the economics of the hospitals sector. In another way, however, it is a strength of the study. General practitioners, who give most primary care in Ireland, account for only a small fraction of total medical care expenditures; but as "gatekeepers" to the medical care system, and through their referral behaviour, they determine or strongly influence most of the rest. Our estimate, published in Chapter 6, is that spending on GP services accounted for only 5.2 per cent of all Irish medical care expenditures, public and private, in 1980, but that GP decisions conservatively accounted for 66.8 per cent of total expenditures.

This report is structured as follows. After an introductory chapter which among other things discusses the household survey and statistical techniques employed in the study, there is in Chapter 2 a review of the relevant Irish and international literature in health economics. This chapter might serve as a short introduction and review of health economics for university students and others. Chapter 3 constitutes a review of health, or rather of morbidity and mortality, in Ireland, with international comparisons. The Irish medical care system, including the distribution of resources, financing, and eligibility for public health services, is discussed in detail in Chapter 4.

Chapter 5 deals with Irish medical care expenditures. It discusses the recent Irish record concerning cost inflation in medical care and the apparent reasons for it. These reasons seem to concern the incentive structure in Ireland, so this is reviewed. Chapter 5 also presents new estimates, arising out of the survey, of household (private) medical care expenditures. These are combined with published State and Health Board data to yield new estimates of total (i.e., public and private) medical care expenditures.

Chapter 6 reports on extensive analysis of utilisation of general practitioner services, relying primarily on multiple regression analysis, both logit and ordinary least squares. We report on determinants of utilisation of GP services by samples of the whole population and of various sub-groups in the population; of household expenditures on GP services; of GP home visits as opposed to office/surgery consultations; of time spent in GPs' waiting rooms; and of physician-induced demand for medical care by GPs. In addition, we compare patterns of GP consultations between Ireland and Britain; and we compare patterns of GP referrals (return visits arranged, referrals to other doctors, prescriptions written, and referrals to hospital for admission) between persons with different levels of eligibility under the Irish public health services, as well as between Ireland and Britain.

Chapter 7 reports on analysis of utilisation of medical care other than GP services. We report on determinants of pharmaceutical prescription medicines, specialist consultations, visits to hospital out-patient departments, hospital in-patient admissions (discharges), and visits to dentists. We report also on determinants of household (private) expenditures on medical care. And we report on utilisation of a number of preventative services: asymptomatic physical examinations (examinations when one is not or does not believe one is ill or pregnant); immunisation; cervical cancer smear ("pap") tests; and blood pressure tests.

Finally, Chapter 8, Conclusions and Recommendations, has three purposes. First, it reviews a number of problem areas in the Irish medical care system, which require attention. Secondly, it reviews a number of alternative models which have been or might be proposed for the Irish medical care systems, systems toward which the financing and delivery structure might evolve and progress. And thirdly, the chapter and the study conclude with a number of specific proposed changes, meant for adoption now, to bring more economic rationality and cost containment in the Irish medical care system, without sacrificing quality of care or distributional equity.

Some Findings Highlighted

In the remainder of this General Summary, we highlight some of the findings of the study. We begin with a brief overview of the Irish medical care system. We then summarise the incentives structure, emphasising aspects which might contribute to over-utilisation and inefficiency. We then offer an overview of empirical findings. We conclude with some highlights of our recommendations.

The Irish medical care system is essentially a market-oriented system in which generous state subsidies play an important role. Individuals are eligible for free or subsidised care in a complex, three-tiered system of benefits. Approximately the lowest third of the income distribution are eligible in Category I, evidenced by Medical Cards. They receive essentially all medical care, including general practitioner services, free of charge. The next approximately 50 per cent of the income distribution are eligible in Category II. They must pay for GP services, but can have free specialist care, both out-patient and in-patient and free hospital accommodation. The latter, however, means accommodation in a public ward, not a private or semi-private room. The remaining group, at the top of the income distribution, are eligible in Category III. They must pay for both GP and specialist care. They can have free hospital accommodation, but again only in a public ward. Those in Category I receive free pharmaceutical medicines; others receive a subsidy toward the cost of such medicines.

The Voluntary Health Insurance (VHI) Board provides health insurance to those who pay for it, which covers services not provided free through the state, including specialist care for those in Category III, and hospital semi-private or, if one pays more, private accommodation. VHI covers out-patient care after a deductible is reached.

General practitioners provide primary care and act as "gatekeepers" to the whole system. They are remunerated on a fee-for-service basis, by the state for persons in Category I, and by the patient, at a higher rate, for all others. Consultant specialists practise from hospitals. They are paid salaries by the hospitals, and they also receive fees from their private patients. The latter include persons in Category III, who are not eligible for free specialist care; and they include persons in Category II and, occasionally, Category I, who prefer to be private rather than public patients. Junior doctors, who work under the supervision of consultants, are salaried by the hospitals in which they work.

The public health services in Ireland are provided mainly through eight regional Health Boards, who in turn receive most of their resources from the Department of Health. There are basically three kinds of hospitals: Public voluntary hospitals, run by religious orders and other non-profit organisations, who receive their budgets from the state; Health Board hospitals of various types and sizes, owned and funded by the Health Boards; and private hospitals, which are essentially financed by their own revenues.

There are important direct and indirect subsidies to private care, especially to private hospital care.

In terms of international comparisons, GP consulting rates are not extraordinarily high. However, GP referrals to other doctors, to hospital in-patient departments, and for hospital admissions, are very high, higher indeed than can easily be explained by the incentives structure. One possible explanation, arising out of the literature, is that Irish GPs, particularly those working in isolated solo practices, are unsure of their own diagnostic abilities and use referrals and hospitals to protect themselves (and their patients) in cases they are afraid they do not fully understand. For whatever reason, Irish hospital admitting rates are extraordinarily high. Hospital costs are high and rapidly rising, and are a large proportion of total medical care costs.

This appears to be a main reason why medical care costs in Ireland have risen at explosive rates. Between 1965/66 and 1980, the average annual rate of increase of Department of Health expenditures was 22.8 per cent, which provides for a doubling of expenditures every three years and four months. When expenditures are deflated by the Consumer Price Index, the average rate of increase over the same period was 10.25 per cent, a rate which means that expenditures double about every seven years. These are truly extraordinary rates of increase, to be sustained for such a long period of time. They are, however, not different in kind from increases sustained in other western countries.

There seems to be a general tendency in these countries for medical care costs to rise explosively. This tendency causes obvious difficulties for governments, insurers, taxpayers, premium payers and patients. The difficulties are exacerbated in times of fiscal stringency. Yet it is a safe guess that if the cost increases, even those as large as noted above, occurred in a context of rapidly rising benefits from medical care, such as occurred earlier in this century when infectious illnesses were brought under control, complaints would be few and muted. But the contrary is true. The cost explosion occurs at a point in history in which, statistically speaking, the benefits are difficult to discern at all.

This is one reason why economists would be inclined to describe the problem as one of economic inefficiency rather than of rising costs *per se*. There is increasing doubt that pouring more and more resources into the medical sector brings as much benefit to society — even in the form of health and life — as the same resources could bring if applied elsewhere. There is also increasing doubt that resources are efficiently distributed *within* medical care.

Because of the special character of medical care as a commodity, certain features are found in virtually all well-developed medical care systems which lead to a tendency for inefficient over-utilisation and cost inflation. In addition, there are features unique to the Irish system which further predispose this system to the same ills.

The need for medical care is unpredictable, and if patients must pay the costs from their own resources the consequences can be financially catastrophic. Hence there is a universal tendency of people to insure against medical care costs. In this context, social provision of medical care should be viewed as a compulsory form of health insurance. Because of the near-universal coverage by insurance, buyers' point-of-purchase prices for medical care are typically lower than average or marginal costs, and may even be nil. If, as economic theory tells us, buyers push their consumption of medical care to the point at which the benefit to them of the last unit is equal to its cost, they will over-utilise medical care in the presence of insurance.

Even in the absence of insurance, the economising role of buyers is weakened by the presumed ignorance of consumers regarding medical care. Most consumers are forced to rely on doctors to make medical care utilisation decisions, except for the initial decision to contact a primary care practitioner. This creates additional problems.

For one thing, in fee-for-service systems such as found in Ireland, providers are not paid for results but for resources used. Outside of medical care, most producers enter the market knowing that if they use fewer resources to produce a commodity, they will be rewarded with higher profits. There are positive incentives to economise. That is usually not the case with medical care, unless financing and delivery systems are carefully organised to achieve such a result (as is discussed in Chapter 8). Instead, any increase in resources used tends to be associated with an increase in revenues of providers.

Second, some providers face what amounts to a conflict of interest. The doctor who economises on patient or public resources faces the prospect of thereby reducing his or her own income as a result. There is a substantial literature in health economics on the subject of economically self-interested physician-induced demand for their own services. The incentive for this kind of over-utilisation disappears when the method of remuneration shifts from fee-for-service to some other method, though other problems can arise.

The structure of Irish charges, fees, insurance, remuneration and budgets is laid out in detail in Chapter 4. Here we review the incentives arising out of this structure, concerning ourselves primarily with general practitioners, pharmaceutical medicines, consultant specialists, hospitals, and VHI cover.

General practitioners are paid on a fee-for-service basis by the state for public

(Category I) patients, and at a somehwat higher rate by the patient for private (Categories II/III) patients. This remuneration technique encourages GPs to increase resource use. As discussed below, this study provides evidence that some Irish GPs apparently stimulate demand for their own services, in order to increase their own incomes. Not only are GPs provided with incentives to increase numbers of GP consultations, but it appears likely that that increased utilisation is correlated with other types, such as pharmaceutical medicines, laboratory tests and x-rays. To public patients, GP services are free. Thus at best these patients are not provided with incentives to economise on GP resources. Private patients, who do pay fees, do therefore have an incentive to economise on GP resources. If they have VHI cover, on the other hand, and have exceeded their annual deductible amounts, the incentive to economise disappears. No system in Europe or North America provides a greater incentive to resource use than that provided by the Irish system for Category I patients by the combination of services free to patients remunerated to providers on a fee-for-service basis.

As far as their public patients are concerned, the method by which GPs are remunerated offers no incentive for them to use "physician extenders" or paramedical aides. The same can be said of private patients and of reimbursement by the VHI.

Pharmaceutical medicines are furnished free to Category I patients and are subsidised for other patients. The nature of the latter subsidy (full reimbursement after a deductible is reached) is such as to provide little if any disincentive to use by patients. Category I patients have a significantly higher level of pharmaceutical consumption than other patients, even when we control for age, sex, social group *and GP utilisation*. This may be a consequence, at least in part, of the differences in patient incentives, but it is more likely to reflect physician than patient behaviour. Physicians, not patients, make most pharmaceutical use decisions (though they may take into account patients' economic as well as medical needs), and in general physicians do not bear the costs of such decisions. There is strong evidence of higher prescribing in all those European systems where GPs are remunerated on a fee-for-service basis than in those in which the capitation method is used, and here again the Irish system is predisposed to high resource use. Little in the Irish system encourages provider or patient to economise in the area of pharmaceutical medicines.

Specialists' incentive structures differ as between public and private care. For private patients, specialist consultants are remunerated on a fee-for-service basis, which provides the doctor with no motive to economise, and is likely on the contrary to encourage the opposite behaviour. The VHI publish a list of fee levels at which they will remunerate specialists, and evidently the large majority of specialists do charge the suggested fees. Thus patients have little opportunity to question charges, and fee level is not an aspect in the choice of doctor. Patients covered by VHI are in general given first-penny, 100 per cent reimbursement for in-patient specialist charges. For out-patient services, those covered by VHI are reimbursed in full after a deductible is reached, and it is the same deductible that applies to GP fees and prescription medicines. The level of the deductible is such that a patient who sees a specialist as a private out-patient is likely quickly to reach it, thus effectively cancelling any disincentive it provides. On the other hand, for private patients not covered by VHI, there may be a substantial motive to economise on specialist services. However, there is reason to believe that this is a very small fraction of the population. In sum, specialists have no motive to economise on the application of their services to private patients. Most private patients themselves have little or no motive to economise, though there will be a small motive for out-patient care for those covered by VHI, and a substantial motive for all care for those not covered by VHI.

The private patients referred to in the preceding paragraph are a considerably smaller fraction of the population than private patients of GPs. They consist of those with Category III eligibility, together with such others, mainly in Category II, who prefer private care. Approximately 85 per cent of the population are eligible for free specialist care, both in and out-patient. Consultant specialists providing public care are remunerated on a salary basis. These doctors are, therefore, given an important motive to economise on their own resources. However, they are also encouraged by this incentives structure to apply more resources in the form of junior hospital doctors (a resource provided them without cost) to public patients, and to shift their own energies, at the margin at least, to fee-paying private patients.

Some public patients have an unusually strong motive to use specialist services. For the approximately 50 per cent of the population with Category II eligibility, it is less expensive to see a specialist on an out-patient basis than to see a GP. This unfortunate incentives structure encourages patients to use higher cost specialist services, and shifts the balance away from primary, community care.

Finally, it should be noted that GPs who refer patients to specialists, or specialists who refer patients to other specialists, bear none of the costs of so doing.

Hospitals are, as noted, the main resource users in the Irish system. There is little difference between the situation facing private patients who have VHI cover and that facing public patients. The former are guaranteed full first-penny cover of in-patient charges. The latter pay no charges. None of these patients has significant economic motive, apart from the costs of time, to question a decision to admit them to hospital; to compare hospitals as to charges; to question extra hospital services; or to resist what may seem to them to be over-long stays in hospital. Private patients without VHI cover do have an incentive to economise, but even these motives are sharply reduced by the very considerable direct and indirect state subsidies to private care which are discussed in this report. These subsidies almost certainly induce higher demand for costly private as opposed to public care.

Doctors and not patients make the main hospital utilisation decisions and, in general, as they do not bear any of the costs they have no motive to economise on hospital resources.

The most important hospital resource use decisions are made, however, when hospitals are provided their annual budgets by the state. How budget decisions are made is somewhat obscure to the analyst, and this process is deserving of study.

VHI is the subject of a final comment regarding the incentives structure found in the Irish medical care system. Currently, people are encouraged to purchase VHI cover, and hence to use costly private care, by the nature of the incentives. Substantial tax relief on premia, more favourable than that available for unre-imbursed private costs, means that the exchequer pays one-third to one-half of VHI costs indirectly. All of the subsidies to private care, especially those to pri-vate hospitalisation, also have the effect of lowering premium rates, by reducing claim payments, and these hence induce people to buy VHI cover. The net effect is that VHI is now too large, from an efficiency standpoint, and this translates into inefficiently high demand for costly private care.

A review of the incentives structure facing providers and patients reveals, then, very few instances in which participants have a significant motive to economise on medical care resources, public or private, and more than a few in-stances in which there are inducements to use resources.

Empirical Results

A brief summary of empirical findings of this study follows.

1. The main correlates of general practitioner utilisation appear to be sex, age and Category of eligibility under the health services. Females use 27 per cent more GP services than males. Males 65 and over use 183 per cent more, and females 65 and over 131 per cent more, than males and females under 65. Persons in Category I, who are public patients of GPs, use 148 per cent more, nearly two and one-half times as much GP services as persons in Categories II and III, who are private patients of GPs. We also find that persons in farming and fishing families use fewer GP services than other persons.

2. These gross or simple relationships hold up, in general, when we use multiple regression analysis, which measures the net effect of these and other independent variables, whilst holding constant the influences of other variables. The analysis was done not only for all persons in the sample, but separately for persons in Category I, Categories II/III, Mothers, Males, Females, Persons aged 65+, and Persons Aged 0–16. In all cases, Category I strongly influenced not only whether people had GP visits, but also for those who did how many visits they had. Age and sex were also persistently strong. GP fee often has a negative in-fluence on visits in the partitioned versions. Farming/fishing families again often showed lower utilisation.

3. Household private expenditures on GP services correlated strongly with category of eligibility, VHI cover, Health Board area of residence and occupa-tion group. Persons in Category I spent on average extremely little, while those

in Categories II and III differed little from each other in spending about £8.50 per person in 1980. Those with VHI cover spent about 60 per cent more than those without. Those living in the Eastern Health Board area spent about 50 per cent more than those in the rest of the country. And people from families headed by professionals, managers and white collar workers spent more than those in working class and farming/fishing families.

4. Not all of these relationships showed up as significant in multivariate analysis. The main net influence was the interaction of Category I and no VHI. Households in areas with high per capita incomes spent more than those in other areas. And persons who had other help with medical care costs, provided through their places of employment, spent about £10 less than those who did not on GP services.

5. Those more likely to have home visits are the very young and the aged; persons other than from farming/fishing families; persons from areas with low ratios of doctors to population; persons from areas with low ratios of persons in Category I to population; and persons who pay low usual GP fees and/or high GP house call fees. In addition, persons in Category I were more likely to have house calls if they lived further from the GP; and persons in Categories II and III were more likely to have house calls if they were covered by VHI.

6. A comparison of Irish and British GP consulting rates shows similar levels overall, but it also shows Irish rates to be lower, relative to the Irish average, than British rates are to the British average, in the higher social groups, and higher in the lower social groups. These results are as predicted on the basis of incentives. Irish GPs appear to refer their patients more frequently to another doctor, to hospital out-patient departments, or to hospital for admission than British doctors. This pattern seems to run contrary to the incentives structure. British GPs are paid on a capitation basis, and it is traditionally held, on the basis of the incentives implicit in that system that doctors so remunerated are quicker than doctors paid on a fee-for-service system to refer their patients to others, since so doing reduces the workload without affecting incomes. One possible explanation for the fact that Irish GPs' referrals exceed those of their British counterparts is that Irish GPs are more likely to work in isolation from other doctors and to lack confidence in their own diagnostic abilities.

7. Irish referral behaviour also differed according to the category of eligibility of the patient. Among persons in Category I, 34.9 per cent of most recent GP consultations resulted in a return visit being arranged with the same GP; among persons in Categories II and III, only 16.5 per cent resulted in a return visit being arranged, giving a ratio of 2.12 to 1. This ratio seems surprisingly high. One reason is that persons in Category I are poorer and older than the rest of the population, and hence are more likely to have health problems requiring a succession of GP visits.

But this pattern of high return visits for persons in Category I is not repeated in the other referrals made by GPs. As compared with the 2.12 ratio of Category I to Category II/III return visit probability, we have the following ratios for other referrals: referred to another doctor 0.70; prescribed medicines, 1.15; referred to hospital out-patient department, 0.95; and referred to hospital for admission, 1.35. If illness and chronic conditions explained the high Category I return visit rate, one would expect similarly high ratios for other kinds of utilisation. Instead, some types of referral show more and some less for Category I than for other patients, but for no type of referral does the ratio approach that found for return visits. However, the result is consistent with what would be predicted on the basis of incentives. A possible explanation is that:

a. GPs wishing to increase their incomes arrange for return visits by persons in Category I. Those in Categories II and III, who must pay for GP services, are more likely to resist extra visits, and GPs may feel better about arranging extra visits for persons who are not charged for them. A specific test for physician-induced demand for medical care is discussed below.

b. Persons in Category II can avail of free out-patient hospital and specialist care, but must pay their GPs. For these patients, it is cheaper to be referred to a specialist or the out-patient department of a hospital than to return to their GPs. If physicians take into account their patients' economic situations they might refer some patients in the manner described.

8. The study includes a test for physician-induced demand by general practitioners. The argument is as follows. Where the supply of GPs is high relative to population, other things being equal, physician incomes will be depressed. If physicians attempt to compensate for reduced income, they will attempt to generate additional demand, in the form of repeated return visits. Thus one hypothesis is that return visits will be positively related to the ratio of GPs to population. In addition, where the (unstimulated) demand for GP services is lower, again physician incomes will be low, and if they compensate, GPs will generate return visits. Therefore, where per capita income is relatively low, we would expect, other things equal, reduced demand, and hence more return visits. Similarly, where the ratio of persons in Category I to population (the Medical Card ratio) is low, again we expect reduced demand for GP services, and reduced GP incomes, and an effort by GPs to stimulate more return visits. These hypotheses of return visits varying positively with ratio of GPs to population and negatively with area per capita income and ratio of Category I persons to population were borne out by our study. In addition, return visits varied with age, were higher for persons in Category I, and fell with increased distance to the GPs office/surgery. These results held not only for all persons in the sample, but generally for sub-groups in the population: males; females; all persons except women aged 20–40; persons in Category I only; and persons in Categories II/III only.

The results seem therefore to bear out the hypothesis of self-interested demand generation by some Irish GPs. This does not necessarily mean that *unnecessary* GP utilisation takes place, though it almost certainly means that some *uneconomic* utilisation does. That is, it would be wrong to conclude that the induced consultations can have no medical value, or rather no *probability* of medical value. But it is likely that they are not worth their cost — that the same resources, devoted to medical care elsewhere in the system, or to non-medical goods, would yield significantly more value to society.

9. Multiple regression analysis was used to seek the determinants of other kinds of utilisation than GP services, *viz.*, prescription items, specialist consultations, visits to hospital out-patient departments, and in-patient hospital admissions (discharges). All of these were strongly influenced by numbers of general practitioner visits, and usually by numbers of specialist visits as well. These independent variables influenced whether the individual received the service, and for those with any, how many units of the service he or she received. In addition, persons with Category I eligibility were more likely to have prescription medicines and among those with any had more. They also had average hospital stays about two weeks longer than other persons, when other variables were controlled for.

10. Utilisation of dentists' services was influenced by variables different from those affecting most other kinds of medical care. The chief influences were age and social class, the latter measured mainly by the age at which the head of household completed full-time education. Similar results were obtained when the analysis was restricted to children.

11. Household private expenditures on all medical care averaged £117.54 per household and £32.88 per person in 1980, according to our survey. The most important influence on this level was Category of eligibility under the health services. Those with Category I eligibility had extremely low expenditures; those with Category II eligibility had four and one-half times the expenditures that those in Category I had, while those in Category III had 163 per cent of those of persons in Category II. VHI cover, Health Board area of residence, and social group were also strongly related to household expenditures on medical care, but these presumably reflect mainly category of eligibility.

12. When multiple regression analysis is used, the strong effect of category of eligibility on household expenditures still holds. Households whose head had Category I eligibility and no VHI cover spent £70 less than households whose head had Category II eligibility and VHI cover. Per cent of household with Category III eligibility also had a strong and significant effect: a household with 100 per cent Category III spent £72 more than one with 0 per cent in that category.

13. A separate analysis was done of prevention-oriented medical care. In the survey, we asked, with respect to each household member, when he or she was last seen by a doctor. We asked who, in the previous year, had a physical examination when he or she did not suspect an illness or pregnancy; had been immunised against any illness; had a blood pressure test; or (for adult women only) had a cervical cancer smear ("pap") test. The results included the following:

a. Men were more likely to fail to see their GPs over long periods of time than women. Others likely to fail to see a doctor included persons with Category II eligibility (who must pay to see a GP); persons in the North-Eastern Health Board area; persons in households headed by unemployed persons or farmers/fishers.

b. Physical examinations rise consistently with age. Persons with Category II eligibility are the least likely to have had an examination, as are persons in households headed by the unemployed, or by semi-skilled or unskilled workers, and persons living in the North-Western Health Board area.

c. Immunisations follow a pattern opposite to age. Only one child in six, aged 0–14, was immunised against any disease in 1980, a figure which seems low, though of course every child does not need immunisation in any given year.

d. Women were about 50 per cent more likely to have blood pressure tests than men, even though men are more likely to be victims of high blood pressure and stroke. Most disturbing is the low rate for men aged 15–44, slightly less than half the rate for women at the same age. Public (Category I) patients are nearly twice as likely to have blood pressure tests as private (II/III) patients.

e. Only one adult woman in ten had a cervical smear test, which is an unfortunately low ratio. The most important influence on this form of preventative care appears to be social class. Low income and working class women are much less likely to avail of this test.

Conclusions and Recommendations

The report ends with a final chapter offering conclusions and recommendations. As it is recognised that many readers of this chapter will not read the full study, an effort was made to make Chapter 8 self-contained; but readers are reminded that the argument is made, and the conclusions are supported, by the study as a whole.

The conclusions and recommendations are divided into three parts. First there is a discussion of problem areas in the Irish medical care system. Second there is an analysis of alternative models for reforming the system fundamentally. And third, there is a set of proposed changes meant for more or less immediate adoption.

Problem areas are broken into four categories. First are weak spots in the quality of care. It is argued that general practice needs strengthening. The required strengthening involves group and team practice and greater use of non-doctor personnel, including clerical staff, technicians, nurses, para-medical aides, midwives, and social workers. Changes in the incentives structure can help bring about the desired strengthening. Another weak spot in primary care is the evident failure of outreach to the aged poor, and possibly to other disadvantaged or handicapped populations. Routine physical examinations for these

people are likely to be cost-effective. Other weak spots in the quality of care include the following: persons with Category II eligibility used significantly less
primary care, and less preventative care, than others; there are indications that
specialist care of public patients is inferior to that of private patients; and some
hospitals are too small to provide an adequate medical staff.

The second category of problem area concerns the amount and distribution of
resources. In general, these problems are minor. There may be mal-distribution
of GPs and, especially, specialist consultants, across regions. There appears to be
a mal-distribution of social workers and physiotherapists across Health Board
areas. There are too few dentists, especially Health Board dentists. There are
signs that the North-West Health Board area has too few hospital beds.

The third category of problem area involves anomalies in standards of
eligibility for the public health services. We suggest three changes: that
eligibility standards be indexed to a national earnings index, to reduce the erosion of benefits in inflationary periods, and to separate the correction of
eligibility standards for inflation from real changes in those standards, taking the
former out of the political process; that Category I entitlement be made a legal
right for those meeting eligibility standards; and that eligibility for Category II
be based on the family (i.e., on family income and family size) rather than the
individual earner.

The fourth problem area, that of explosive and irrational costs and expenditures, has been a major theme of the report. It concerns to a large extent the incentives structure, which has already been discussed in this general summary.
The main incentives problem is that those who make resource-using decisions
concerning medical care — patients and providers — frequently do not individually bear the economic costs of those decisions. This problem has a demand side
and a supply side.

The demand side refers to the influence of price on patient demand for
medical care. Cost-sharing, under which the patient pays at the point of use
some part of the cost of providing the care, can help control demand and hence
utilisation. However, the position taken in this report is that as a *general* technique for limiting utilisation it is liable to have the undesirable effect of limiting mainly or only the types of care which we least want to limit, *viz.*, self-
initiated primary care. Instead, we urge use of cost-sharing to shift utilisation
from high-cost and/or low-priority uses to their opposites — to alter the
pattern rather than the level of demand.

The supply side refers to the influence of remuneration techniques and other
incentives on resource-using medical care decisions made by providers. It is
generally conceded in health economics that supply side incentives are more
crucial than demand side incentives in influencing utilisation. Two arenas dominate the discussion: physician remuneration; and hospital budgeting or
reimbursement.

The main alternative to fee-for-service remuneration of physicians is capitation, under which physicians are paid according to the number of patients they

have, rather than the number of times they see them, or the number of services they provide. There is considerable evidence on a world-wide basis that capitation reduces utilisation, and further that it reduces pharmaceutical prescribing rates as well. An alternative is the reorganisation of medical care delivery into pre-paid group plans (PPGPs) such as health maintenance organisations (HMOs), under which patients purchase all medical care, and not merely physicians' services, on a capitation basis.

Methods by which hospitals are budgeted or reimbursed are as important as or more important than the ways in which physicians are remunerated. The report advocates some technique by which hospitals are budgeted by formulae so that their resource-using decisions are separated from factors influencing their incomes, so that they are rewarded for any economies and penalised for inefficiency. This is an area where further research in Ireland is required. Indeed, the report describes this as the most important single item on the Irish health economics research agenda.

In the next section, we review and assess four alternative models which have been or might be offered for the Irish medical care system: the insurance model; the incremental growth model; the competitive pre-paid group plan model; and the national health service model.

The insurance model, which roughly corresponds to systems in use in Belgium and Canada, was proposed a few years ago by a working party of the Irish Medical Association. The incremental growth model was once but is no longer advocated by the Irish Congress of Trade Unions, and approximates the past pattern of development of the Irish system. Both of these proposals contain attractive features which it would be desirable to incorporate in the Irish system. Both are rejected as models for reform, however, as they fail to improve upon the all-important incentives structure, and in some ways worsen it.

The same is not true of the two other models, both of which then warrant serious consideration. The competitive pre-paid group plan model is market-oriented and capitalistic, while the national health service model is centralised and socialistic.

Pre-paid group plans (PPGPs) are organisations established for the purpose of providing comprehensive medical care to their clients for a set annual pre-paid fee. The best-known and most common type of PPGP in the United States is the Health Maintenance Organisation or HMO. HMOs are growing and successful in the US, but still enrol only about 10 per cent of the population. They have incentives to keep their clients healthy, to use resources efficiently, and to emphasise preventative care. According to evaluation studies, they reduce costs 20 to 33 per cent, with the savings concentrated in hospitalisation.

Irish readers are familiar with the national health service model, as it obtains in neighbouring Britain and Northern Ireland. The term refers to a centralised, non-market system in which resource-using decisions are made administratively at the macro level, and made, as elsewhere, by physicians, through referral, prescribing, etc., decisions, at the micro level. Because in such a centralised system it is possible to determine total medical care spending in advance, and as well to determine its regional and functional allocation, it is possible to limit spending, and its growth, to any level.

The Irish system has grown by fits and starts in an *ad hoc* manner, without any apparent model or set of guiding principles in mind. While it is not suggested that there be immediate or fundamental change, such as adopting one of these models, it is suggested that an attempt be made to develop a national consensus on the goal toward which the system might progress in coming years.

The immediate goal is not, however, so much further development as rationalisation of the present system. The paper concludes with a set of proposals meant for present rather than ultimate consideration. These proposals include the following.

It is proposed that free general practitioner service be extended to everyone, and that GPs be remunerated by the state on a capitation basis. At the same time, it is proposed that charges be imposed for out-patient hospital and consultant specialist services, and for in-patient hospital care, for those who currently receive these services without charge. This set of changes, taken together, is intended approximately to balance in terms of overall expenditures, the added cost of free GP care being roughly equal to the increased revenues arising out of the new charges. None of the new charges is intended to cover full costs. In-patient hospital charges should be high enough to assert social priorities in favour of out-patient over in-patient care, and of primary care where possible.

It is proposed that the remaining subsidies to private care be reduced, that private hospital patients be charged the costs of all services provided to them, and that tax relief for VHI premia be abandoned. There are also proposals for medical audit and peer review; incentives to group practice and physicians' auxiliaries; enabling legislation for PPGPs; increases in dental resources; expansion of the conception of, and increased resources for, health education; and expanded funds for research. In the last category, we refer not to basic medical research, to which others will have to speak, but rather three other matters. First, we argue that the Department of Health should have a continuing research concern with air quality, occupational health and safety, prevention of poisoning in the home, road safety and other aspects of prevention. Second, we argue for improved collection of epidemiological data, more routine collection of morbidity data from general practitioners and periodic in-depth studies. Third, we argue that Ireland needs health economists and other social scientists trained in such disciplines as social policy analysis relating to health and medical care, not only in the public service and research institutions but in the universities.

The author is aware of the difficulties, especially the political ones, inherent in an attempt to make such significant changes in the medical care system. At the same time, he believes that the proposals will attract broad support, especially when their long-run as well as their short-run implications become fully clear.

Chapter 1

INTRODUCTION

This is a study of the use of medical care resources in the Republic of Ireland. This definition of our subject gives us two focuses; utilisation *per se*, that is, doctor consultations, hospital admissions and services, pharmaceutical prescription items, etc.; and expenditures as expressed in money terms, which reflect the opportunity costs of utilisation.

There are two important reasons for a study of medical care resources in Ireland.[1] One is that medical care is increasingly expensive in this country, and has been the subject of explosive expenditure growth in recent years. By our calculations (see Chapter 5), medical care used approximately 10 per cent of Gross National Product in 1980, a percentage which has itself been rising rapidly.[2] There is a widespread impression that this expenditure growth has not been accompanied by corresponding increases in the benefits from medical care, so that most of the increase is in a sense pure cost inflation. Even though there may be more resources (input) used, both labour and non-labour, there is no corresponding increase in product (output). Unlike general inflation, the cost inflation in this area uses resources. The price level increase in the medical care area has been very much more rapid than in the economy at large (as measured, e.g., by the Consumer Price Index). To that extent, medical care absorbs real resources transferred from elsewhere in the economy. Hence there is a need to examine the rationality and efficiency of medical care expenditures and resource use. We want to see whether structural characteristics within the Irish medical care financing and delivery scheme account or help account for this explosive growth. By implication, we want to see whether changes in the structure of the system can reduce the rate of cost inflation, and make the system more efficient and responsive. This study concludes that they can.

The second reason for a study of this sort is to be able to understand better the

[1] Unless otherwise noted, the terms "Ireland" and "Irish" in this study pertain to the 26-county Republic of Ireland.

[2] This measure differs from published ones, relating Department of Health expenditures to GNP, in a number of ways. It excludes non-medical care Department of Health expenditures. On the other hand, it includes private expenditures, estimated by the author, and it includes public capital expenditures. See Chapter 5.

operation of an extremely important sector of the economy. The medical care sector would in many respects be no less important if it used but 3 per cent of GNP. Its importance does not derive solely from its resource use; in a meaningful way, its resource use derives from its importance.

This study is addressed to several audiences. It is addressed to my fellow economists and social scientists and is meant to contribute to economic knowledge. It is also addressed to a more general audience, including politicians, civil servants, other policy-makers, journalists and the public. An effort has been made to keep the study accessible to this general audience, and, in general, it is. Some sections will be difficult for general readers, but the thread of the argument, it is hoped, will be clear.

The principal readership addressed is in Ireland. But it is also intended that this study fill a void in the international literature on the Irish medical care system. Therefore, pains are taken to describe the Irish medical care system in detail.

The first section of this chapter discusses the purposes and limits of the present study. The second section discusses the methods used. The latter includes a large nation-wide sample survey conducted for the author by the Survey Unit of The Economic and Social Research Institute. The third section discusses statistical method. The fourth describes the outline of the present volume. The fifth and final section deals with the author's preconceptions and opinions.

A. Purposes of the Study

When the author undertook an initial review of the Irish medical care system, he found the following four things:

1. *A good medical care delivery system.* The evidence at hand indicates that the Irish medical care system generally provides care of high quality, using up-to-date methods and resources, and that this care is, in general, available to all, whatever their income or social class, and whatever their region of residence. While there are weak spots in both the quality and the distribution of care, as there inevitably are in any system, Ireland has good reason to be pleased with the overall development of its medical care system. The organisation of medical care in Ireland is in general preferable to that of the United States of America, with which the author is also very familiar, though it of course lacks the latter's enormous resources.

2. *A complex medical care financing scheme.* The pattern of eligibility for free and subsidised medical care, the patterns of direct and indirect state subsidy, the intricacies of private insurance provided by a state-sponsored body, and the interaction of these with the fiscal system are so complex as to be understood by very few people, even within the system. To an extent, this complexity reflects an ingenious mix of the features found in other medical care systems, capitalistic and socialistic. To an extent, however, it also reflects unplanned and often uncontrolled growth, as influenced by

party politics, and by struggles amongst affected interest groups.

3. *Enormous data gaps.* Like most countries, Ireland collects and publishes data on its medical care system primarily where the statistics arise as a by-product of administering public programmes, mainly the health services. This leaves some very considerable and important gaps, particularly for economic analysis. Virtually all data on the private sector are absent, for example, general practitioner utilisation data for two-thirds of the population; and household expenditure data for the whole population.[3] Moreover, data on the public sector is provider based rather than household based, so we can usually infer very little about the distribution of or the determinants (or correlates) of utilisation, even in the public sector, from official data. Because of these gaps, it was determined that a national household survey of medical care utilisation and household expenditures was necessary. The survey is discussed in a later section.

4. *Little relevant literature.* As will be clear as we proceed, we are unable to build upon the base of an established Irish health economics literature, especially as regards empirical analysis. (The large international literature is reviewed in Chapter 2.) Much has been published on the edges of the topic. Culyer and Maynard wrote an extremely useful survey of the Irish system (NESC No. 29, 1977). The authors rank as two of the world's leading health economists, and their publication filled a major void. But no new empirical work was done, and the authors worked within the data gaps referred to above. There have been international comparative studies with chapters or sections on Ireland (e.g., Abel-Smith and Maynard, 1978); short articles (e.g., Barrett, 1979); policy papers (e.g., Dowling, 1978); and papers on closely related subjects (e.g., Kaim-Caudle, 1969, 1970a and 1970b). But there is neither a thorough-going review of the system nor any statistical or econometric study.[4]

We wanted to build upon this uncertain foundation and prepare a study which would contribute to the two objectives mentioned at the beginning: understanding better the important medical care sector of the economy, and finding whether the system could be made more efficient and less explosively expansionary. Given the foundation and the objectives, it was clear that the present study would have the greatest chance of success if it had the following

---

[3]There are, of course, published data on private care from the Voluntary Health Insurance (VHI) scheme (see Chapter 3). But without further data, we do not know how much private care is not financed by VHI, nor do we know the distribution through the population of VHI membership — how many persons, for example, with each level of eligibility under the health services have taken VHI cover. In addition, there are estimates of household expenditures from the Household Budget Survey (see Chapter 7); but again we lack correlates with category of eligibility and other important variables.

[4]This list excludes the author's own previous publications on the Irish medical care system and related topics, all of them prepared as by-products of the present study. See Tussing, 1980a, 1980b, 1981a, 1981b, 1982a, 1982b, 1982c, 1982d, 1983a, 1983b, 1983c, 1984a, 1984b and 1984c.

four characteristics: it had to be a broad and general study, essentially covering the whole of the system, rather than focusing more narrowly, while more deeply, on one aspect, such as hospital admissions. Second, it had to concentrate on the determinants of utilisation of the main parts of the system. Since many if not most utilisation decisions in medical care are made by physicians, this concentration implies some analysis of the economics of the behaviour of physicians, as well as of patients. Third, it had to be system-oriented and policy-relevant. In addition to empirical analysis of utilisation, it was thought to be important to review and examine the medical care system, as a system, with attention to the incentive structure, from an economic standpoint. And fourth, as already noted, it had to be based on new data, in addition to official sources. Indeed, the collection and publication of the data, apart from the analysis, was deemed by itself to be an important objective of the study. For this reason, a large part of the present paper is given over to the publication, in the Appendix, of utilisation and expenditure statistics, for the use of scholars, policy makers and the general public.

We do not, it is obvious, claim that this work is the last word in its subject area. It indeed comes closer to being the first. It is hoped that other economists and social scientists from other disciplines will follow, to correct the errors of omission and commission in this study, fill in gaps, address in detail issues only introduced in the present study, and ultimately, make the present study obsolete.

One difficulty, however, which stands in the way of such an outcome, is the fact that there are no health economists trained as such and acting as such in Ireland, in the civil service, in research institutes, or in the universities.[5] This is truly unfortunate and should be rectified. The medical care sector, as noted earlier, used 10 per cent of GNP in 1980; the health care sector, which is larger (see below), used still more. And medical care, as we argued earlier, is important in its own right, wholly apart from its large share in GNP. In such circumstances, that there should be no health economists in a country in which there is no shortage of economists is regrettable, and a reflection, in the end, on the universities.

While we have claimed breadth for this study, in one sense it is truly narrow. Our concern is only medical care, and not the economics of health; it is by and large limited to acute care; and it is by and large limited to traditional care.

It is customary to distinguish between "health care" and "medical care." Health care includes but is not limited to medical care. The latter involves the diagnosis, care and/or treatment by medical personnel of persons who are or might be ill or pregnant; and preventative services such as examinations and immunisations, given by medical personnel. Medical personnel are usually defined as doctors and nurses, or others under their supervision. Health care

---

[5]Since this was written, Mr. Eamon O'Shea, who had completed an M.Sc. in Health Economics at the University of York, joined the staff of the Institute of Public Administration, with duties including but not limited to health economics work. There was previously a trained health economist in the Department of Health, but he moved to a non-health economics position and was replaced by a successor not trained in health economics. There are some trained economists currently active in analysing health issues; but the number of even these is too small.

includes medical care, but adds to it some important health-related services outside of medical care proper. Prime responsibility for one's health rests with one's self, or one's parents or other responsible family members, with the aid and advice of authorities and trained personnel. Health care includes, then, nutrition, exercise, non-prescription preparations such as vitamins and analgesics and other health-related personal care and behaviour. It includes the contribution to fitness, healthy lives and health education, by schoolteachers, coaches, the media, the Health Education Bureau and others. Finally, it includes long-term care, outside of hospitals, of the handicapped and of the infirm aged.

These definitions are not precise and there are borderline questions. Are dentists, Health Board social workers and home helps, within the medical care system? The answer is not certain, but they are included in the present study, though they do not have a central role.

We have also stated that the present study is limited to acute care. Long-stay institutional care, including psychiatric care, is not covered. These are important topics and they are not omitted out of any denigration of their significance. Careful economic analysis of them is an important task facing social scientists in Ireland. But beyond a given point, additional breadth in a study such as this one, comes at enormous sacrifice of depth, and/or at such a cost in terms of time as to delay the culmination of the study beyond its likely usefulness. In addition, as will be noted later, the household survey method proved ineffective in obtaining accurate data concerning psychiatric hospital stays of household members.

We have stated, finally, that the present study is limited to traditional care. Some of what is often called "fringe" medicine is practised in Ireland, by personnel as varied as homoeopaths, acupuncturists and what might be called self-trained folk chiropractors. Nothing either positive or negative is implied by their omission from this study. It will readily be seen that methodological difficulties would have been faced attempting to incorporate these practitioners in the present study.

B. Methods: The Survey

As noted above, the author administered a national household survey on Irish medical care utilisation and household expenditures.[6] The survey was conducted by the Survey Unit of The Economic and Social Research Institute, under the direction of Brendan J. Whelan, director of the survey unit, by approximately 50 trained and experienced interviewers, under the supervision of Mrs. E. M. Colbert-Stanley.

The survey was supported, in part, by the Central Bank of Ireland; the Health Education Bureau; the National Board for Science and Technology; and the

[6]The author also conducted a small postal survey of some employers who were identified in the household survey as providing employees, and sometimes their families, with some kind of help with medical care costs (see Chapter 5).

Voluntary Health Insurance Board.[7] The author is profoundly grateful to these sponsors; without their timely aid, this study could not have been undertaken. It should be added that only the author is responsible for the content of this study; the sponsors neither asked for nor were offered the right to approve or disapprove methods or text at any stage.

The sample was selected using the RANSAM system as described in Whelan (1979). A sample of 65 primary sampling units (clusters) was randomly selected from the Electoral Register with probability proportional to the size of the cluster. Twenty individuals were then selected from each cluster by means of a systematic random sample. This gave an initial sample of 1,300 names, distributed in all eight Health Board areas (see Chapter 3). These names constituted an epsem (equal probability of selection) sample of persons from the Electoral Register.

The response rate was 82 per cent, providing data from 1,069 households, somewhat better than the target of 1,000. Most of the non-response arose from non-contact, person deceased, moved, etc.; the refusal rate was only 3.7 per cent.

Information was collected on each household member, so there are a maximum of 4,522 observations. However, for most purposes of this report, including all of the Appendix and text tables, an adjustment was made. Since the objective was to obtain a representative selection of individual household members for analysis, it was necessary to re-weight the data in order to obtain unbiased estimates of household characteristics. The probability of a given household cropping up in the sample was proportional to the number of electors in the household. Hence, the data from each household was re-weighted by a factor inversely proportional to the number of persons aged 18 and over in the household. This restored the representative character of the sample. Weighting reduced the number of individuals in the sample to 3,755, though the number of households remained at 1,069.

This weighted sample was used in text and appendix statistical tables, and in grossing up to yield some state-wide estimates. For purposes of statistical analysis, however, in most cases only one observation per household was used, as is described in the next section.

The survey was conducted in January, 1981, and dealt (with very few exceptions) with medical care utilisation and household expenditures occurring in the calendar year 1980.

The survey questions do not include any pertaining either to morbidity or to household or individual income. Both were included in a pilot survey conducted in November, 1980. Morbidity questions absorbed an enormous amount of interview time in order to obtain useful results, such that they would have displaced many important utilisation questions. Hence they were dropped from the

[7]The sponsors are listed alphabetically. The Economic and Social Research Institute also contributed to the survey and to the study as a whole. Also see the acknowledgements for others who assisted personally.

final questionnaire. It is unfortunate that this had to be. Morbidity data would have been extremely useful in our analysis of utilisation and expenditures, mainly as a control variable. Income responses in the pilot study provided undependable estimates; results, where apparently incorrect, were usually on the low side.[8] The survey does include a number of income proxies, such as category of health services eligibility (see Chapter 4), social group and education of head of household.

The survey questions included some pertaining to psychiatric in-patient care of household members. The results, when grossed up, yielded numbers smaller than 10 per cent of actual totals as reported in official sources. Evidently respondents did not want to tell interviewers about psychiatric care of relatives. The inference is that a large stigma attaches to psychiatric care, which is regrettable for many reasons. No similar difficulty arose with respect to any other category of medical care. Psychiatric care results were discarded and are not used in this study.

The survey questions were, for the most part, retrospective. Households were asked to recall numbers of general practitioner consultations, pharmaceutical prescription items, and other utilisation data, and household expenditures on medical care, for the previous year, without the aid of diaries or logs. Thus our results may be affected by errors of recall. In using the resulting data, we are implicitly assuming that these errors are both positive and negative and have a mean of zero. The questionnaire included numerous questions regarding utilisation, referrals, expenditures, etc., which served both as aids to memory and as cross-checks on responses. Each set of responses was subsequently checked for internal consistency and plausibility by an experienced team of interviewers and coders. An unknown number of errors of recall surely persist, which will reduce R^2, t, F and χ^2 statistics in our empirical work.

In addition to errors of recall, the survey is of course affected by sampling error. While the overall sample size is large, for sub-samples (e.g., for regions) sampling errors will be larger than for overall, national figures.

The main results of the survey are reported in Tables A.1 through A.42, in Appendix I. These tables are discussed briefly in that appendix. A summary version of the questionnaire, with means and frequencies, appears in Appendix III.

C. Methods: Statistical Analysis

The principal statistical method employed in this study is multiple regression analysis. Where the question involves *utilisation* of a particular type of medical care, analysis is usually carried out in two steps. First, we seek the determinants of whether there was any utilisation at all by the individual. Thus our equations

---

[8]Most of the respondents were housewives who, it is said, are in Ireland sometimes given a fixed household allowance by their husbands and do not actually know how much money income the household receives.

have a dichotomous dependent variable, taking the values of 0 (no utilisation in 1980) or 1 (any utilisation). Second, for persons with any utilisation only, we seek the determinants of the number of units of utilisation (number of general practitioner consultations, number of pharmaceutical prescription items, etc.). In this case, the dependent variable is continuous and can take values greater than one.

With respect to certain utilisation equations — specifically, those dealing with preventative care, such as blood pressure tests — the second step, above, is omitted, and the analysis is limited to the dichotomous step. Similarly, in regressions where the dependent variable measures whether, at the patient's most recent GP visit, a return visit was arranged, the analysis is limited to the dichotomous form. Where the dependent variable is household expenditures on medical care, as opposed to physical units of utilisation, there is no dichotomous step and only a continuous dependent variable appears.

We discuss below a number of issues pertaining to the dichotomous dependent variable equations. We then turn to issues relating to the continuous dependent variable equations. Finally, we discuss some matters pertaining to both.

Where the dependent variable is dichotomous, it is inappropriate to use OLS (ordinary least squares), for two reasons. One is that there is likely to be heteroscedasticity in the error term. (Heteroscedasticity is discussed later in this section.) The other is that, with OLS, there is no guarantee that the predicted values of the dependent variables will lie within the 0, 1 interval. Obviously values lying outside this interval are meaningless. In these cases, we have employed a procedure based on a cumulative logistic probability function, which we refer to throughout as a logistic regression, or logit. (For a discussion, see Section 8.1 of Pindyk and Rubinfeld, 1976; Section 12.5 of Theil, 1978; or Aldrich and Nelson, 1984.) The procedure produces a model χ^2 and χ^2 statistics for each coefficient, as well as an R^2 which measures the fit of the model. This R^2 is analogous to but not the same as the familiar OLS R^2. It has the value such that

$$R^2 = (\text{model } \chi^2 - 2v)/(-2L(O))$$

where v is the number of variables in the model excluding intercepts and $L(O)$ is the maximum log-likelihood with only intercepts in the model. There is a fairly serious penalty for loss of degrees of freedom, from adding variables to the model. If this $-2v$ correction is ignored, R has a value of 0 if the model is of no value and 1 if it predicts perfectly, and R^2 is the proportion of log-likelihood explained by the model. Many authorities believe that no such general, summary measure as this R^2 should be reported for logit (or probit) analyses and all recommend caution (Aldrich and Nelson, 1984). However, we report this R^2 in all cases. Where we have used OLS and logistic regressions for the same dichotomous dependent variables, in precisely the same models, they have produced essentially similar results, though OLS R^2s are usually higher than the logit R^2s (See Tussing, 1983a).

The left-hand side of logistic regressions are equal to log p/1 – p where p is the probability of the event (e.g., any utilisation). Thus the parameters estimated are difficult to interpret intuitively. To provide, in each case, an intuitively understandable counterpart of the regression, we have used the regression to calculate exemplary probabilities for the events predicted and these are reported in separate tables. In general, the procedure is to "plug in" specified values of the independent variables, multiplying them by their respective coefficients, adding the intercept term and solving for p. The specified values of the independent variables begin with the mean values of continuous variables and typical values for qualitative variables; and then we vary each of these, including, for continuous variables, at least their minimum and maximum values, and for qualitative variables, usually all of their possible values.

The OLS utilisation regressions for persons with any utilisation are candidates for two kinds of problems: sample selection bias and heteroscedasticity.

Sample selection bias arises because in these OLS regressions we have excluded all persons without utilisation and hence our sample is no longer a random one.

Heckman and others have shown that the bias amounts to omission of a right-hand-side variable and can be interpreted as an ordinary specification error, and that this can be dealt with by using the "Inverse Mills ratio" (or hazard rate) in an OLS regression as an additional regressor. The Inverse Mills ratio is produced as a by-product of a probit model with a dichotomous dependent variable. (Heckman, 1976; see also Gronau, 1974; Lewis, 1974; Stromsdorfer and Farkas, 1980). Because heteroscedasticity seemed probable with the OLS regressions, a Goldfeld-Quandt test was performed on these, and in about half of the equations significant heteroscedasticity was discovered. We have decided to bypass the usual solution for this problem, namely experimenting with various transformations of the variables until one producing homoscedastic error terms emerged. This decision was made on two grounds. One is that this study includes an extremely large number of regression equations, and repeatedly re-performing these analyses would have been prohibitively costly, in both time and money. Secondly, the parameters of equations with transformed dependent variables are extraordinarily difficult to interpret. Instead, we have adopted a different strategy. Heteroscedasticity does not bias the parameter estimates, though standard errors and t-statistics will be biased (in an uncertain direction). In equations with heteroscedasticity, we have added 10 per cent to the critical values of t (for reported significance levels of 1 and 5 per cent). This is in the same spirit as Theil's suggestion, in another context (in discussing regression strategy), that,

> Given the present state of the art, the most sensible procedure is to interpret confidence intervals, coefficients, and significance limits liberally when confidence intervals and test statistics are computed from the final regression of a regression strategy in the conventional way. This is, a 95 per cent confidence coefficient may actually be an 80 per cent confidence coefficient and a 1 per cent significance level may actually be a 10 per cent level (Theil, 1978).

This is a conservative approach, but as t-statistics are reported in all cases, the reader may adopt a more or less conservative one as suits his or her point of view.

We now discuss issues common to both dichotomous (logit) and continuous (OLS) dependent variable regressions.

As noted above, survey data were collected from 1,069 households, on 4,522 individuals. Because household members were not statistically or causally independent of each other, we included only one member per household in regressions (except the expenditure regressions, which were done on a household basis anyway). This adjustment was achieved by sampling our sample, randomly taking one observation per household. A number of such samples were taken, one for regressions including all persons, another for regressions limited to females, another for males, another for children aged under 16, etc. Because in each case sampling bias is introduced (in an all-child regression, for example, any individual child's chances of being included are inversely proportional to the number of children in the household), we include as a control variable the number of persons in the household from whom the sample is drawn (e.g., the number of children in the household, in the all-child sample).

In the regressions, we test specific hypotheses drawn from a theoretical model which is in turn drawn from the relevant literature. In each case we report results on the "full model," i.e., with all the independent variables in the model included. In addition, we report on the "5 per cent version," including only variables which meet a 5 per cent significance test.

We tested extensively for two-, three- and even four-way interactions amongst the variables in our models. Our interaction terms are two or more independent variables multiplied by each other. In general, only two kinds of interactions produced significant results. One was a four-way interaction of dichotomous independent variables (producing still another dichotomous independent variable), based on sex, age group, category of eligibility in the health services and whether the person had Voluntary Health Insurance (VHI) cover. (In regressions partitioned by sex, this of course collapses to a three-way interaction.) The other kind of successful interactions were created by multiplying regional variables: the ratio of GPs to area population; the ratio of persons covered by Medical Cards to area population; an index of per capita income; and, sometimes, the ratio of consultants to population.

Where a variable is included in a regression on its own (main effects) and in one or more interactions, and when the coefficients of these variables take different signs, the direction of the net effect of that variable is not obvious from the regression itself. Here the exemplary probabilities calculated from logistic regressions, discussed above, do double duty. As we vary the value of such a variable from its minimum, through its mean, to its maximum, holding other variables constant, we can observe the effect on the calculated probability. In effect, we have the partial derivative of probability with respect to the variable.

Where we have an interaction term, or where a variable is included in the form of a quadratic (as is the case with age: both age and age-squared are included in all regressions), we have calculated a joint test of the significance of the variable. Using the coefficients obtained from our regressions, e.g., the coefficients of age and age-squared, we construct a new variable for age and re-run the regression. The coefficient of the new variable is 1.0, and all other results are as in the previous version (except that we appear to have an added degree of freedom); but interest attaches to the t-test of the new, constructed variable, for that provides a joint test of the significance of that variable. In general, such joint tests produce stronger t-tests than the original, separate parameters, because the latter naturally are reduced by multicollinearity. This test measures the effect of including the variable in all its forms in the model, and is equivalent to an F-test comparing the residual sum of squares where the variable is included with that where the variable is excluded.

In general, our multiple regression equations explained between ten per cent and one-third of the variance in our dependent variables. These figures are about average for microdata, especially where medical care is concerned. They would have been raised, perhaps considerably, had we morbidity and income data.

D. Outline of the Paper

This volume has eight chapters, including this Introduction, which is Chapter 1, in addition to the Appendix, already discussed.

Chapter 2 introduces some economics of medical care. It discusses the ways in which medical care is similar to and different from other commodities produced and distributed in a market economy, and in particular how these relate to the peculiar ways in which medical care is financed. Medical care is provided in every country of which we have knowledge with point-of-use prices and fees which are either nil or far below cost, and we must explain both the reasons for and the consequences of that fact. Chapter 2 discusses the welfare economics of medical care, that is, how medical care fits into the traditional economics notion of optimality. And it reviews the international literature on the subjects of medical care utilisation and physician behaviour. Thus it sets the theoretical background for the present study.

Chapters 3 and 4 set the factual background, concerning Ireland in particular. Chapter 3 discusses Irish morbidity and mortality, in a European setting. Chapter 4 discusses in detail the organisation, financing and delivery of medical care services in Ireland. In the process, it discusses the incentive structure and other economic dimensions of the system.

Chapter 5 reviews the level and growth of expenditures — public, private and total — in three categories: medical care, health and Department of Health. The growth rate in expenditures has been extraordinarily high and appears unsustainable. Explanations for this rapid growth, especially those relating to the incentive structure, are offered and the details of this structure, as set out in Chapter 4, are gathered together to provide a concise analytic summary.

Chapters 6 and 7 report the main statistical findings of this study. Chapter 6 is devoted to general practitioner (GP) services, which are pivotal in the Irish system. Included is a major discussion of the problem of self-interested physician-generated demand for their own services by Irish GPs. Chapter 7 deals with all other kinds of care, with preventative services and with household medical care expenditures.

Chapter 8 is devoted to conclusions and recommendations. In it, some detailed recommendations are made with respect to particular features of the Irish system. Then four alternative models of fundamental reform or re-structuring are reviewed and assessed. Finally, the author sets out his own proposals for reform.

E. The Author's Point of View

The author has tried, successfully he believes, to prevent his views from unduly affecting his analysis. None the less, in a work of this kind, it seems appropriate for him to set out his views regarding medical care, and especially regarding the kind of health and medical care systems he would hope someday to see in Ireland.

It should be an ultimate goal, the author believes, of the development of the health services in Ireland and everywhere, that needed health care be available to all, without charge at the point of use. It is to be emphasised that this is not a conclusion of the present study, but an ultimate goal favoured by the author. Indeed, the conclusions, dealing with present problems, are rather different.

The author believes that the same quality of care should be provided to everyone, irrespective of income, social class, education, region, sex, or age. There should be effective outreach of the health services, so that those who are ill are assured of coming to the attention of the right practitioners and of being given treatment.

Health should not be the sole or even the primary domain of the medical profession. First responsibility for care should be with the individual. Expanded programmes of occupational and personal safety, preventative care and health education are needed, to reduce morbidity and mortality associated with modern living, such as from heart attack, stroke and cancer. People should be made conscious of the costs to them and to society of unhealthy lifestyles. Ireland needs, far more than exists today, a cost-conscious and health conscious population.

For this to occur, it will be necessary that physicians share more information with their patients, abandoning the authoritarian model in widespread use, in favour of a more modern one, which emphasises two-way communication between doctor and patient. The doctor and patient should work together, in partnership, rather than in subject-object relationship.

This work is being written in a time of fiscal crisis and budgetary stringency, no less in the medical care area than in others. The main focus of the present work is not on development of the health services, but as already noted on economising, on controlling, on stopping the explosive growth of medical care expenditures. Consequently, in spite of his long-run goals, the author proposes charges for a number of medical care services currently provided without charge (though there are also proposed shifts in the opposite direction). This study is not a brief for a visionary future system, but a careful and objective analysis of the current situation. But the author firmly believes that none of the objectives stated above is inconsistent with an efficient and economically rational medical care system. We will return to this theme in Chapter 8.

Chapter 2

SOME ECONOMICS OF MEDICAL CARE

Medical care is a commodity. It may differ in a number of respects from other commodities in its human significance, in its manner of production and consumption, and in other respects, but it remains a commodity. In Ireland, its production uses roughly an estimated 10 per cent of Gross National Product (1980), as we will see in Chapter 5, a figure which is both fairly typical for the developed world, and rising.

The concept of economic rationality or efficiency applies to medical care, as to other commodities. Economic efficiency requires that medical care have the right or optimal share of society's productive resources, that these be applied in an appropriate or optimal mix within medical care, and distributed across the component parts of medical care in an optimal manner. Using a conventional exercise in microeconomics, it can be shown that when certain conditions are met, economic efficiency so defined can be attained through the operation of the market, with medical care sold at prices equal to the added cost to society of providing one more unit. In general, according to this exercise, if a commodity is produced and consumed without major external effects in private markets under competitive conditions, there normally is no need for regulation or collective provision in order to ensure that approximately optimal quantities are provided. Individuals will compare the cost to them, which is also the cost to society, of incremental units of that product, with their benefits and arrive at individual optimum solutions. There are objections to this exercise, but they need not be discussed, as the necessary conditions are not met in the case of medical care: the market fails, because of the properties of medical care as a commodity. In this chapter, we will review the properties of medical care as a commodity, and the conditions of its delivery, as a background to our subsequent discussions and analysis of the Irish medical care system. First we will review the position of medical care in the economy as a whole, from the standpoint of welfare maximisation. This will take us briefly into the question of placing an economic value on human life. We will then review the ways in which medical care is thought to differ from most other commodities, especially within the context of market failure. One way in which it arguably differs is that doctors, who are suppliers of medical care services, also significantly influence demand. The economics of

29

physician behaviour will be examined in the next section. Following that, the possibility that a form of "Parkinson's Law" explains medical care demand will be reviewed. Finally, the empirical literature on medical care utilisation will be reviewed.

A. Medical Care and Welfare

Medical care enters into positive and normative economic models in ways which, even when they are reduced to their simplest, are somewhat intricate. Medical care presumably influences the state of health of the population, though it may not in fact be among the most important such influences. Via health, it influences the productivity of the labour force and hence the level of output. Therefore, medical care is capable of both direct and indirect influences on human welfare. Similarly, output has both direct and indirect influences on health. Best and Smith (1980) have presented a usefully compact way of displaying the role of medical care in the determination of social welfare.

First, we begin with what economists call a "production function" — the set of relationships that determine the amount of output in a firm, in an industry, or even in the economy as a whole. Our economy-wide production function is expressed in the most general possible way:

$$Q = Q(X, I) \tag{1}$$

which says that output (Q) depends on (is a function of) resources — capital, labour, technology, etc. (X), and of the level of illness in the system (I). Output is positively related to resources and negatively related to illness.

Output can be divided into medical care, M, and other output, C:

$$Q = M + C \tag{2}$$

Next, we have an illness production function,

$$I = I(C, M, Z) \tag{3}$$

which tells us that illness is a function of medical care and other output, and of Z. Z is a set of exogenous factors and attributes, such as age, sex, and genetic distributions, and the like. We withhold for a moment discussion of whether these relationships are positive or negative.

Finally, we have what economists call the welfare function (or objective function),

$$W = W(C, I) \tag{4}$$

which states that social welfare depends on non-medical output or C and on the level of illness. (Medical care, M, does not appear, because it is a means to an end rather than an end in itself.) This is a highly oversimplified view of what social welfare depends upon, but it will serve our purposes here. C increases social welfare and I reduces it.

It can be shown that welfare maximisation, as in (4), requires that the welfare benefits from additional non-medical output be equated with the benefits of additional medical care output:

$$\frac{\Delta W}{\Delta C} = \frac{\Delta W}{\Delta M} \tag{5}$$

The reasoning is simple. If they were unequal, there would be an opportunity to redistribute society's resources and get an improvement in welfare. If a pound spent on non-medical output added more to welfare than a pound spent on medical output, society could shift a pound from the latter to the former and increase total welfare. Only where they are equal is it impossible to increase welfare through resource shifts.

Equation (5) is more complex than it appears. The welfare effects of non-medical output are both direct and indirect, via illness. The welfare effects of medical output are *only* indirect. We can rewrite (5) as follows:

$$\frac{\Delta W}{\Delta C} + \frac{\Delta W}{\Delta I} \times \frac{\Delta I}{\Delta C} = \frac{\Delta W}{\Delta C} \times \frac{\Delta C}{\Delta I} \times \frac{\Delta I}{\Delta M} \tag{5a}$$

The left-hand side gives the direct effect of non-medical output on welfare, added to the effect of illness on welfare times the effect of non-medical output on illness. We will discuss in a moment the directions of these effects. The right-hand side gives the effect of medical output on welfare; this is the product (reading from right to left) of the effect of medical care on illness, the effect of illness on non-medical output, and the effect (again) of non-medical output on welfare.

Let us turn to an examination of the directions of these relationships. First, illness certainly reduces output and hence C. The direct effect of output, C, on welfare is always assumed in economics to be beneficial: C increases W. What is the effect of C on I? Until recent years, this relationship was always assumed to be negative. The higher the level of output and income in society, the better were presumed to be housing, sanitation, nutrition, and the like, and through them health. But we have reached a point in many industrial societies where the major causes of morbidity and mortality — heart disease, hypertension, cancers, motor vehicle accidents, other accidents and violence — can be interpreted as consequences to a considerable extent of either the production or the consumption, or both, of output. That is, we may have reached a point at which the relationship is changing from negative to positive. Best and Smith suggest that the relationship between I and C is ordinarily U-shaped, and that the "levelling out effect" in the USA and the UK began as long ago as 1930. For Ireland the 1950s or even 1960s would seem a better guess. (There may be a third stage, at which the sign becomes negative again. The USA, Canada and Finland, have through changes in lifestyle, managed to reduce the incidence of heart disease and stroke in the 1970s. But Ireland along with Britain and other countries seems to be far from this third phase.)

It is interesting as well to consider the relationship between I and M. Of course it is normally assumed that increasing the amount of resources devoted to medical care will reduce the level of illness in society, i.e., that the sign is negative. But there is little if any statistical or historical support for such an assumption. As Fuchs has stated,

> ... The connection between health and medical care is not nearly as direct or immediate as most discussions would have us believe. True, advances in medical science, particularly the development of anti-infectious drugs in the 1930s, '40s, and '50s, did much to reduce morbidity and mortality. Today however, differences in health levels (between developed countries or within them) are not primarily related to differences in the quantity or quality of medical care. Rather, they are attributable to genetic and environmental factors and to personal behaviour. Furthermore, except for the very poor, health in developed countries no longer correlates with per capita income. Indeed, higher income often seems to do as much harm as good to health, so that differences in diet, smoking, exercise, automobile driving and other manifestations of "life-style" have emerged as the major determinant of health. (Fuchs, 1974.)

No doubt expenditures on medical care account in numerous individual instances for reduced incidence and prevalence of disease, for shorter spells of illness, and for reduced mortality. But medical care expenditures are also reflected in convenience, comfort, amenity, dignity and other laudable objectives; in tolerance of and ability to "live with" illness, in ways which are not reflected in reduced morbidity statistics; and in incomes of medical professionals and other personnel. The relationship between I and M is almost certainly negative, but the strength of the relationship is probably smaller than is commonly assumed.

Best and Smith group the causes that might account for an increase in I, the level of illness, into three categories.

> First, illness might increase as a result of an increase in the prevalence of one or more of the infectious diseases. These diseases are those which arise as a result of exposure to a "disease agent" in the form of a specific pathogen. They include a number of familiar bacterial diseases such as whooping cough and typhoid fever, as well as viral diseases such as measles and influenza. Until as recently as 50 years ago, infectious diseases figured prominently amongst the most common causes of premature death in all industrialised countries. And while some infectious conditions persist as important causes of morbidity (e.g., the common cold and influenza; bronchitis and pneumonia) and premature mortality (e.g., certain respiratory conditions of early infancy), it is generally recognised that these conditions account for a declining proportion of the total disease burden in all industrialised countries.

> Second, illness might increase as a result of an increase in the prevalence

of conditions that are associated primarily with a natural or biological process. The most obvious conditions within this category are those that frequently accompany the ageing process ... Other conditions within this category include genetically contingent problems such as cystic fibrosis; congenital abnormalities; and certain "natural" complications of childbirth ...

Thirdly, illness may increase as a result of an increase in the prevalence of non-infectious conditions related primarily to lifestyle or other environmentally-determined factors. The conditions falling into this category have been variously labelled "the diseases of civilisation", "the diseases of modern economic development", or "modern epidemics". Included here are those conditions that are the most common causes of premature mortality in industrialised societies (e.g., ischaemic heart disease, accidents and many forms of cancer) as well as some of the most important causes of morbidity (e.g., smoking-related respiratory problems, many occupational illnesses and dental caries).

The third group of conditions have become the most common causes of premature mortality in most industrialised countries not only as a result of the unhealthy conditions and environmental influences of life in such countries, but also as a result of the decline, due both to income growth and to health and medical developments, in the first category, infectious diseases. The consequent lengthening of expected human life accounts for a larger number of aged persons, and consequently increases in the prevalence of conditions in the second group. Conditions in the second and third groups differ from those in the first in the degree of their apparent responsiveness to outlays on medical care, and it has been suggested that medical care is as a consequence now characterised by decreasing returns. It certainly is true that we have little if any improvement in mortality tables to show for the rapid expenditure increases in the last two decades (Barrett, 1979).

While recognising that the distinctions are over-simple and ignore interactions, Best and Smith note that the conditions in the first group are the most amenable to *cure* in the usual sense; those in the second group tend not to be cureable and usually require attention to rehabilitation and *care*; and those in the third group are also not often cureable in the usual sense, and require an approach emphasising *prevention*. The idea that the link between M and I may be weakly negative, and that returns to W and even I may be greater from concentrating additional resources on what Best and Smith call "C-centred measures" amounts to an updating of the old adage that an ounce of prevention is worth a pound of cure.

Evidence bearing on the magnitude, and even on the sign of the link between I and M is very limited. Auster Leveson and Sarachek (1969) analysed inter-regional differences in age-sex-adjusted mortality rates in the United States, in order to estimate the net elasticity of health with respect to medical services (i.e., the per cent change in mortality rates of American states with a one per cent change in medical services while controlling for other influences). They found an elasticity of –0.1. The elasticity for education (–0.2) was, however, higher. Positive net elasticities were found for cigarette smoking (+0.1) and, interestingly, family income (+0.2). The latter may bear on the question, raised earlier, of the direction of the link between C and I.

B. A Value on Human Life?

Equation (5), which states the conditions for welfare maximisation, says that the added contribution to human welfare of the last pound or penny spent on non-medical output must be the same as the added contribution of the last pound or penny spent on medical care. Welfare maximisation also requires that $\Delta W/\Delta M$ be the same throughout the system — that the final expenditure on hospitals in Cork yield the same benefit to society as the final expenditure on pharmaceuticals in Sligo and the final expenditure on medical education in Dublin.

While such criteria may seem appropriate in making judgements about, e.g., highways or drainage, it may seem novel to apply them to health care. After all, in the final analysis, is not the business of health care the saving of lives? How can the value of a human life be weighed against, e.g., a new car or a telephone? Can it be that economists are about the business of setting explicit or implicit values on human lives, and comparing such values with the benefits from consumer goods, public investment and the like?

The answer is that *society* places an implicit value on human life, a value incidentally which is far from infinity, and economists observe, note and report this. There exists a fairly sizeable literature in economics on the value of human life, and it is virtually all empirical — that is, it is based on observation of behaviour of society (cf. Bonamour, 1983).

The first step in the economics of the value of human life is to distinguish between the value of the life of a known individual and the value of an abstract or anonymous generalised human life. If we ask, how many lives per year can we save if we improve a dangerous turn in a highway, or buy a new ambulance, or enforce emission controls on motor vehicles, or operate blood pressure clinics, and if we decide on the basis of such calculations whether to undertake the necessary costs, we are implicitly placing a value on an abstract human life. Assuming that the whole population is equally at risk in each case, so that we are not making interpersonal or intergroup comparisons, economic efficiency would require that we treat human life as of equal value in each case — that we not spend more to save human life in medical care, for example, than in highway safety. On the other hand, however, if a specific child falls down a mine shaft, a yachtsman is lost at sea, or a particular patient requires an available but costly treatment, society will typically spend far more, and sometimes a virtually unlimited amount to save a life. It is an understandable quirk of human psychology that leads us almost without exception to value the known over the unknown individual. Economists of course regard the behaviour of society toward the abstract, anonymous person, and not that toward the known individual, as the accurate indicator of the value placed by society on human life generally.

It is worth pointing out that applying the concept of "economic efficiency" to health and medicine does not imply the subordination of medical considerations to budgetary or accounting ones, but rather means that (a) the level of medical care expenditure is such that the contribution to human welfare of the final expenditure on medical care is equal to that of the final expenditure on other goods; and (b) that the contribution to human welfare be the same for the final expenditure in each part or aspect of the medical care system. The first rule would be violated if either too much or too little of society's resources were expended on medical care. If medical expenditure were excessive, the final pound or penny spent on health care would add so little to human welfare, that a re-allocation to other human needs and wants, such as food, housing and recreation, would actually raise welfare. The "final" expenditure refers to the least urgent one — the one which would be sacrificed if the money were no longer available and if we were free to vary expenditures flexibly. If medical care expenditures were insufficient, then the contribution to human welfare of the last pound or penny would exceed that of any other activity, and a re-allocation in favour of medicine would provide for an increase in human welfare. The second rule would be violated if there were such an imbalance in the medical care system as the following. If there were too many resources devoted to hospital care, compared with infant screening, then the contribution of the last pound or penny to the latter would add more to human welfare than that of the former. Total welfare could be increased with a re-allocation of resources.

As noted, since society explicitly or implicitly sets a value on human life, then human life can be figured into this concept of efficiency. Let us assume for the moment that all human life is valued equally by society. This assumption is merely an expository convenience, and it is not argued that it is, or should be, true. If it were, then the two assumptions tell us, *inter alia*, that the same final resource expenditure would be made on the saving of lives by each branch of the medical care sector, and by and in the rest of society. This conclusion also means that the total number of lives saved is maximised. This obviously does not imply the subordination of medical considerations to economic ones.

If society decides to set a different value on the lives of different persons, that changes the outcome only in detail. If the rich, the young, senior politicians, etc., are to be favoured, then one can merely attach weights to the values of their lives (e.g., a cabinet minister is worth 1.5 ordinary persons, etc.) and the outcomes stated above are correct in terms of weighted lives.

We should not, of course, equate medical care with life-saving. A large and evidently increasing proportion of medical care is directed at improving the quality of life and not at life-saving *per se*.

C. How Medical Care Differs from Other Commodities

Medical care is one sector of the economy in which economic efficiency has in recent years been of major and growing concern. For a variety of reasons, most health care systems seem to contain major areas of irrationality from an economic standpoint; these manifest themselves in imbalances as well as in unrelenting cost increases. The irrationality shows up, e.g., in the extraordinary range of implicit values attached to a human life, depending on whether the concern is prevention or cure, what therapies are used, and where, in or out of the medical care system, the judgement is made.

In virtually every country in the world, medical care is delivered either free at the point of use[9] or at net prices (i.e., prices net of reimbursement or tax relief) which are not only below average costs, but almost certainly below marginal costs as well. In most of these, medical care is financed mainly by government, through either general revenues and exchequer payments, or social wefare contributions and trust fund payments. Even where the state's involvement is less (as, e.g., in the USA), private, voluntary insurance covers a substantial part of costs, leaving the user to pay either nothing or a small amount at the point of use. (In the USA, 70 per cent of medical care costs are covered by third-party payments, either public or private.) These practices suggest that medical care is either some kind of public good, or at least a special kind of private good.

It might be assumed by some that medical care is often financed or subsidised because it is *essential* to human life. Essentiality is not a characteristic which is either unique to medical care or true of all aspects of medical care. The market is used to distribute commodities such as food and clothing which are more certainly and generally essential to life. We look, then, to the theory of public goods for an explanation, but return to the question of essentiality later.

The theory of public goods (or of market failure) provides us with a number of categories of goods which may, to the extent there is demand for them, be provided through some type of public finance: pure public goods; quasi-public goods, which have significant external benefits; goods (such as products of public utilities) produced under conditions of decreasing costs; merit goods; and others.

It is clear that medical care does not meet the definition of a pure public good. Individuals can consume different amounts; there is rivalry in consumption (i.e., the consumption of medical care by individual A uses resources which then are unavailable to produce goods for individual B); and people can easily be excluded from consumption of medical care if, for example, they do not pay. Medical care is essentially a private good.[10]

Medical care is, however, certainly sometimes affected by externalities.

---

[9]When medical care is described herein as "free" or "free at the point of use" what is meant is that there is no fee or charge associated with use. Of course, medical care is never free in the resource or opportunity cost sense.

[10]This may not be true of some aspects of health care outside of medicine, especially such preventative services as food inspection, anti-pollution programmes, etc.

Individual A's medical care can figure in B's utility function in two important ways. First, infectious or communicable disease, from colds to cholera, involves obvious externalities, and there is clearly a social demand for the prevention, treatment, or isolation of cases of such diseases in individual A. These *public health* aspects of medical care have the most venerable tradition of public finance; and while as noted earlier infectious disease is absolutely and relatively less important in the health of nations today than it was one, two and three generations ago, our medical care delivery and financing arrangements today are dominated to a considerable extent by a picture of health and medicine based on those earlier conditions.

Only 2 per cent of Irish current public expenditure on health goes to prevention of infectious diseases, health education, food hygiene services, and child health examinations combined (Table 5.1 below). Other countries have similar findings. Barrett (1979) cites Lees as estimating that only 5 per cent of medical expenditures can be justified on the grounds of the benefits to third parties of disease prevention. This type of externality, then, does not appear to be the principal reason for the social finance of health care.

Arguments can also be made for some public intervention in the case of decreasing cost industries, which can never be effectively competitive, and where anything approaching marginal cost pricing implies losses. But no one seriously argues that medical care fits into this category.[11]

In a seminal paper, Arrow (1963) argues "the special economic problems of medical care can be explained as adaptations to the existence of uncertainty in the incidence of disease and in the efficacy of treatment". Uncertainty regarding the incidence of disease implies some type of *insurance* solution, and public finance of health care can with little loss in accuracy be regarded as a form of compulsory insurance. But why compulsory? This is a point to which we will return presently.

Uncertainty "in the efficacy of treatment" is a more complex and subtle point than would first appear. Medical care is a highly technical field of knowledge, and medical practice represents the culmination of an extraordinarily long training programme. Hence a vast gulf separates, or appears to separate, the general public from physicians, in terms of understanding of illness and its treatment. The public turn to doctors to determine whether they are in fact ill; to diagnose what illnesses they suffer from; to choose what is the appropriate treatment; and, to an extent, to determine whether the treatment has been successful. That is, the patient is likely to be uncertain regarding the quality of care received *before*, *during* *and after* the treatment.

This uncertainty, combined with the vital nature of the services provided, and their frequent personal and sensitive character, make it impossible for the buyer to deal in the market in any ordinary way with the providers of medical care. Instead, there has developed a unique sort of relationship between doctor and

[11]An exception of some practical importance concerns resource lumpiness or discontinuities, as, e.g., physicians in sparsely settled areas.

patient, requiring an extraordinary degree of trust. These factors mean, *inter alia*, (i) that the state or the medical profession have an obligation, met through licensing and related techniques, to assure that all doctors are at least minimally competent;[12] (ii) that price competition, advertising, etc., as among physicians, hospitals, etc., are viewed as inappropriate and even unethical; (iii) that primary care physicians not only advise patients but often actually decide on their behalf on the course of treatment, whether that involves return visits, referrals, pharmaceutical medicines, hospital admissions, or some other (resource-using) form of treatment; (iv) that the same applies as well to specialists and other doctors to whom patients invest their trust; (v) that the medical profession therefore is in a position of determining, to a unique degree, the demand for their own services; and finally (vi) that for all these reasons, reliance on an unregulated, unsubsidised market will not avail to provide economic efficiency in the usual sense. One of the basic conditions necessary for economic efficiency in a market solution is the independence of supply and demand, and medical care clearly does not meet this requirement.[13] (We return to physician behaviour later in the chapter.)

Rawls has argued in his celebrated book (1971) for a major degree of progressive income and wealth redistribution, approaching complete equality,[14] on the following grounds. Suppose we were able to decide the shape of society's income distribution without knowing our own positions, as individuals, in it. For example, let us imagine a conference held on the day before the universe is begun, of all potential populators of the universe; and one question addressed in the conference is the degree of economic equality or inequality to be achieved in society, *before* each of us knows our individual economic positions. Rawls argues that most people would insist on a risk-averting "maximin" strategy, of maximising the position of the poorest members of society, because of the possibility each person faces that he or she will be one of these persons. Redistribution is viewed as a form of insurance.[15]

Rawls' proposal is obviously only a philosophical abstraction, a *gedanken* exercise. But on a more practical level, social means for the provision of medical care are arranged in every country in large part on a similar basis. People know their positions in society's income distribution, but they do not know whether they

---

[12]The logic of this argument would appear to require periodical re-examination and re-certification of physicians, or some other technique to assure the public that its doctors remain competent. Nothing of the sort is done in Ireland, nor anywhere else, so far as it can be determined.

[13]Where supply and demand are interdependent, price may be indeterminant, and/or may not relate to marginal evaluations of buyers.

[14]Since any redistributive process can involve unavoidable disincentive effects on labour force participation, investment, etc., which in turn can reduce output, after some point attempts to transfer income to the poor may, paradoxically, reduce the income of the poor. Rawls would cease the redistributive process at that point. That is, the target is maximum income for the poorest, rather than equality of income *per se*.

[15]Arrow (1963) had some years earlier argued that "a good part of the preference for redistribution expressed in government taxation and expenditure policies and private charity can be reinterpreted as desire for insurance", on similar grounds.

will be ill, what illnesses they will face, or what the costs of those illnesses will be; so they insist on a medical care system which will provide adequately for their own care and treatment if the worst should happen. Again, public provision of medical care is viewed as a form of compulsory health insurance.

And again, why compulsory? The answer to that appears to reside in the concept of "merit good". Stripped of flowery and mystifying language,[16] a merit good is one provided by government even though it is essentially a private good, because leaders feel that consumers do not know what is in their best interests. Consumers may lack the technical expertise or the far-sightedness to provide adequately for their *own* needs, so benign and paternal government compensates by providing essentially private goods.

Public finance of medical care is in effect a provision of insurance. It is financed through mandatory payments (ordinary taxes and social insurance contributions), providing for universal eligibility (within defined economic groups) *because society is unwilling to accept the consequences of individuals' failure to insure.* Reliance on voluntary insurance would require that the fraction of the population who are so myopic as not to purchase cover, and who have no other resources to purchase medical care, simply be denied that care should it be required.[17] But such an outcome would be intolerable and unacceptable to a majority of the population, because medical care is viewed as *essential.* Society then insists that coverage be universal.[18,19]

The assumption that low-income persons might be more likely than others to fail to insure may account for the general view of national health services as progressively redistributive even in systems (such as the British NHS) where utilisation is significantly higher in the higher socio-economic groups (Black, 1980).

To summarise this section so far: (i) medical care today is basically a private good; (ii) however, the market cannot efficiently be used for its provision because

[16]"While consumer sovereignty is the general rule, situations may arise, within the context of a democratic community, where an informed group is justified in imposing its decision on others. ... These are matters of learning and leadership which are an essential part of democracy reasonably defined ..." (Musgrave, 1959).

[17]Though they are decidedly exceptional, there are some parts of the USA where fire brigades are supported by voluntary fee payments by householders; and occasionally one reads of the brigade being called out to watch the burning of houses owned by non-fee payers. (The brigade stands by, to prevent the fire spreading to houses owned by its clients). Most places in the world would reject such a system, because they would be unwilling to countenance the burning down of homes of those too myopic to pay fire brigade fees.

[18]This is true even of the USA, which relies primarily on "voluntary" health insurance rather than any state device. "Voluntary" is in inverted commas because for the most part it is provided as a product of collective bargaining contracts between unions and employers. Union negotiators prefer health insurance to higher cash incomes for their members because they too, are unwilling to accept the consequences of individuals' failure to insure, i.e., because medical care is a merit good, provided not through the state but through another vehicle.

[19]One might instead view the case as one of an altruistic or sympathetic externality, i.e., where the ability of individual A to avail of needed medical care figures in the utility function of individual B. The difference is mainly a semantic one, as the argument is essentially the same in both cases.

buyers lack sufficient knowledge; (iii) physicians, to whom buyers have implicitly delegated the role of agent, do not bear the resource costs of their decisions; (iv) uncertainty about future morbidity and its costs makes the provision of insurance necessary; and (v) such insurance is a merit good and hence health care is provided through some explicit or implicit form of compulsory insurance.

As a consequence of the foregoing, the market is either abandoned or interfered with, and much medical care is provided at a zero price, or at point-of-purchase prices which are well below social opportunity costs of providing the care. Let us, in the next few paragraphs, discuss the consequences of this in terms of zero prices, bearing in mind that prices and fees which are non-zero but below social opportunity costs have similar effects but to lesser degrees.

While one can argue, on the basis of the considerations discussed above, that prices ought to be zero, or (to phrase it positively rather than normatively) that prices *will* be zero in medical care, this outcome creates problems of economic efficiency. Where no decision maker, patient or provider, bears an added cost when a resource is used, such resources are apt to be treated by all concerned as free. This problem does not reside uniquely in public finance of medical care; it plagues private insurance — voluntary as well as compulsory — as well. In insurance, the problem is referred to as "moral hazard", the tendency of insurance to increase the likelihood of the contingency insured against. To take an example outside of the health area, one would probably be far more careful abour fire hazards if one's home or business were not covered by fire insurance. If fire insurance did not exist as an institution, some firms would go to extraordinary lengths to prevent or limit fire, and staffing procedures, building structures, and materials would all differ, as compared with the existing situation. It follows that the existence of fire insurance may mean that there are more fires, overall, than there would otherwise be. Likewise, the existence of health insurance, or its public-sector equivalents, means more utilisation and more cost (which are the contingencies insured against, not illness), than if full-cost fees were charged for each use of the health services, i.e., than if there were no insurance. Yet it does not follow that fees should therefore be charged, just as it does not follow that fire insurance should be abolished.

Economic theory tells us that where a product's price is effectively zero, users will push their use to the point where their marginal evaluation of the product is zero. (This abstracts from time costs, discussed in Section F.) An implication is that unless some other rationing device is employed, people may use the health services to deal with problems such as headaches, cramps, itches and other discomforts; with only mildly disturbing symptoms which do not portend serious illness; and with loneliness and isolation, where other, less socially costly solutions to the same problems are available and would be preferrable. Zero point-of-use pricing can lead to many situations in which social opportunity costs of medical care utilisation will exceed marginal social benefits.

There are three possible budgetary consequences of such excessive utilisation demands. One might be a corresponding increase in supply, requiring an increase in taxation (or in the government borrowing requirement). A second would also be a corresponding increase in supply, but financed by cuts elsewhere in the budget, e.g., in education or social welfare expenditures. If annual public medical care budgets are fixed by a process unrelated to such demands, then the third alternative consequence, that some members of the public be deprived of needed care, is more likely (Culyer, 1971). This point needs noting because some commentators might otherwise take the position that there is no such thing as excessive utilisation demand, and that efforts to curtail access through pricing or regulation are improper.

D. The Economics of Physician Behaviour

As noted, doctors either make or influence many, possibly most, resource-using medical decisions. It is important to consider how doctors make such decisions, and whether they make them, or can be led to make them, in ways which contribute to economic efficiency. We discuss theory here, and return to the subject again later when we deal with empirical studies of utilisation.

Primary-care physicians are the gateways to the medical system for most persons and in most cases. They provide access, often the only access, to specialists, hospitals and prescription medicines. They regulate such access, and their own services, according to patient need and possibly other criteria. Hence they have a rationing function, one which in many systems, especially those in which medical care is provided free at the point of use, is the dominant one in terms of resource utilisation. Commenting on this rationing function, Culyer and Maynard (NESC, No. 29, 1977) observed,

> In all countries with which we are acquainted, the rationing function has been left to physicians who not only (under any system of remuneration in current use) have a clear incentive to press always for more resources (except possibly physicians) in health care but who also do not have any clear instructions from society as to how their rationing function is to be discharged.

In an angry response, the physician-editor of the *Irish Medical Journal* (70:12, 1977) replied, "Perhaps no single sentence of the Report will illustrate the fundamental difference in philosophy between doctors and economists. ..." The editorial specifically denied that health services must inevitably be rationed. "Doctors do not ration services, nor will they readily submit to 'clear instructions from society'. A doctor has a fiduciary relationship with his individual patient. He is there to see that his patient gets the necessary treatment."

Doctors do of course ration services, in the sense above, which is the sense intended by Culyer and Maynard; what the editorial might have meant will be considered in a moment. The question at hand is *on what basis* doctors make decisions that have resource-utilisation implications.

There are three models of physician behaviour. It is likely that more than one,

and possible that all three, operate to some extent in explaining physician behaviour in all medical care systems. The three are the *agency* model; the *self-
interest* model; and the *medical ethics* model. Only the first two are represented in
the economics literature.

Agency model: Perhaps the most popular concept of physician behaviour in the
economics literature is that of the so-called "agency role of the physician",
which is due to Feldstein (1974). The patient indicates his or her financial position, insurance coverage, and relevant preferences to the doctor, who then uses
technical medical expertise to act for the patient as the patient "would for himself if he had the appropriate expertise". If and to the extent that the physician
acts in the sole interest of the patient, "it would be difficult if not impossible to
distinguish the agency relation from the traditional model of independent consumer behaviour on the basis of observed household consumption. ... If the
agency relationship is complete, it can essentially be ignored for the analysis of
demand." Though Feldstein concedes that the relationship is not complete, he
argues that "available evidence ... does seem to support the notion of a
generalised agency model of household demand for hospital services."[20]

Self-interest: Doctors are, among their other roles, economic beings, and in Ireland they are almost all independent professionals. It would be surprising indeed
if they did not act in their own economic self-interest. The notion that physicians
often do have their own economic self-interest at heart, even where it may conflict with that of the patient, has a considerable degree of support in the
empirical literature, as we will see below. Most of the empirical literature on
demand generation by physicians comes from North America, where the health
care delivery system differs from that found in Ireland. In North America,
specialists provide primary care, and GPs (general practitioners) are a vanishing
species. Primary care physicians who order hospitalisation, surgery, etc., are
often in the position of creating demand for their own services. In Ireland, none
of these is true: there is ordinarily no obvious self-interest on the part of general
practitioners to generate demand for hospital admission, surgery, or specialist
care. Instead, self-interest among general practitioners would lie primarily in
generating higher levels of GP consultations, especially arranging multiple
return visits. GPs, as we will see in the next chapter, are paid on a fee-for-service
basis by the state for those covered by Medical Cards, and by the patient, at a
higher average rate, for other members of the population.

Medical ethics: It is sometimes claimed that the medical profession has an

---

[20]A recent illustration of the agency model as articulated by an Irish physician appeared in a
recent *Irish Times* series on "the drug culture". "Look", the doctor is quoted as saying, "if I
prescribe a drug for a GMS (public) patient, I will prescribe the best available, which may or may
not be the most expensive. But if it is a private patient, who I know has a large mortgage and other
liabilities, then I will think harder before I prescribe a drug at all". The remainder of the doctor's
statement seems to be derived from some other model of behaviour, however, and not the
"medical ethics" model, either: "This [thinking harder before prescribing a drug for a private
patient] is partly because I have time to think about it, whereas the GMS scheme does not pay me
enough to give the same time and thought to the GMS patient", *Irish Times*, March 9, 1981.

obligation to treat the patient at hand without concern for economic considerations. An assertion that doctors follow this principle appears to lie behind the *Irish Medical Journal*'s assertion, quoted above, that doctors do not ration services. If doctors act on the basis of an ethical code requiring them to provide the care or treatment necessary to the patient at hand, whatever the cost, there may in fact be conflicts between medical ethics and economic efficiency. Examples are many of instances in which the medical care system has concentrated large amounts of resources on prolonging for short periods of time the lives of certain patients with poor prognoses, even when other aspects of the system have inadequate resources to provide for timely care for all who need it. Such behaviour conflicts with economic efficiency by attaching heavier implicit weights to the lives of persons known to the medical care system than to those not known. The fact that doctors and hospitals typically use whatever resources are necessary to treat the patients who present themselves with injuries and diseases, though the system may fail in some areas of prevention and effective outreach, constitutes another example of the rule that in the calculus of the value of human life, the known individual outweighs the abstract, statistical person several times over.

Putting these models into more familiar economics language, we might summarise them as follows: *Agency:* maximise each patient's utility or welfare, in so far as it relates to medical care. The marginal utility of medical and non-medical expenditures are equalised. *Self-interest:* maximise the doctor's own utility, a function (positive) of income, (negative) of work, and (probably negative) of demand inducing. *Medical ethics:* maximise the patient's health regardless of cost. The focus is on the patient, not on society.

In order to understand how economic factors may bear on physicians' decisions, we need to know how doctors' incomes are determined. There are basically three techniques for remunerating physicians: *fee-for-service, capitation* and *salary.* There are, of course, a number of possible hybrid combinations of these. Each method and its principal characteristics can be briefly described:

Fee-for-service: This is, in a sense, the original method. Doctors, as independent professionals, are paid so much per item of service, as are such other professionals as solicitors and accountants. When GPs are paid on a fee-for-service basis, they are normally paid, whether by the patient or by a third party, a predetermined fee for each consultation. A premium will typically be added for a home and/or after-hours' visit. Irish GPs are compensated in this fashion, as we will see in the next chapter. In some medical systems, the fee will vary according to what service the doctor provides (give injection, write prescription, etc.). For specialists, the nature of fee-for-service varies. For out-patient services, i.e., where patients are not admitted to hospital for at least an overnight stay, the fee is normally either per consultation or per time period. For in-patient services, i.e., where the patient is admitted to hospital, the fee is usually set according to the procedure or condition treated (e.g., so much for an appendectomy), though in some systems there have been doctors who were paid on the basis of the number of days the patient spends in hospital. This per diem technique is mentioned here, as it is regarded by the profession as a fee-for-service method, though strictly speaking it is not.

Capitation: This method is employed in a number of European medical care systems, most notably in the United Kingdom's National Health Service (NHS). In addition, some doctors employed in Health Maintenance Organisations (HMOs — see Chapter 8) are also paid on a capitation basis. Under the capitation approach, patients choose one general practitioner and are registered on that doctor's list of patients; and the GP is paid according to the number of such patients on that list, irrespective of the number of consultations. Normally, however, the GP will also be compensated on a fee basis for extra services, such as late hours, or home visits. Specialists can also be paid on a variant of the capitation method. In some systems, for example, patients see specialists only on referral from a GP, and patients are, in effect, put on a specialist's list for a month, once such a referral occurs. The one-month listing is indefinitely renewable. The specialist is then paid according to the number of patients on that monthly list, irrespective of the number or length of actual consultations.

Salary: General practitioners and other primary-care physicians are paid by salary in socialised systems in Israel, in Eastern Europe and in some HMOs. In addition, specialists in many systems and junior hospital doctors in almost all systems are also paid by salary. As with the capitation method, additional amounts, on either a fee-for-service or a time (e.g., hourly) basis, may be paid for additional work.

Characteristics: The medical ethics model of physician behaviour implies no difference in doctors' judgements arising out of method of remuneration. The agency model suggests that physician behaviour will vary according to the cost to the patient, but is silent on the effect of method of remuneration, except as this is related to patient cost. The self-interest model does imply differences in behaviour in different types of schemes.

If we assume (see section F, below) that doctors are like other people in wanting, within some limits, high incomes and low workloads, the self-interest model predicts the following, among other things. (1) There will be more physician-induced consultations, and hence more total consultations, per patient in a fee-for-service system than in others, *cet. par.* (2) As a corollary, if consultations per patient and per physician are higher in this system, then time per consultation may be lower. (3) In systems where the primary care physician also performs surgery and other in-patient procedures, as in North America, there will be more hospital admissions in fee-for-service systems than in others; and similarly, where the primary care physician also maintains a laboratory and a staff of technicians, as in Germany, there will be more out-patient tests than in other systems. (4) In capitation systems, doctors will try to maximise the size of their lists. (However, a limit is normally placed on list size.) (5) In capitation and salary systems, doctors will seek to minimise patient contact time, both in terms of numbers of consultation and in terms of their length. (6) There will be more referrals to other doctors by GPs in capitation or salary schemes, than in fee-for-service, to minimise the GPs' own efforts. (7) The fee-for-service system will tend to be the most sensitive to market influences, with the doctor losing incomes both through patients consulting less and by patients transferring to other doctors where patients are not satisfied. The capitation system is less sensitive, as doctors lose income only when patients seek another doctor. The salary system would be the least sensitive, as dissatisfied patients do not threaten doctor income at all, at least directly. For this reason, in a salary system, the doctor may require supervision; or, to put the point the other way around, one tends to find salaried doctors mainly where supervision is feasible.

(8) As a corollary of (1), certain other types of medical care than physician consultations, but not including referral to other physicians, may be subject to higher utilisation, *cet. par.*, under a system in which primary care physicians are paid on a fee-for-service basis. The reason is that a larger number of consultations implies more opportunity for, and more patient expectation of, physician-induced utilisations. Since primary care physicians are gateways to the whole medical care system, methods of remunerating them reverberate throughout the structure. In light of frequent doctor complaints that patients seem always to expect a prescription to be written at the end of each consultation, the self-interest model would especially predict more pharmaceutical prescriptions to be written under the fee-for-service system than the other two. On *a priori* grounds one would also expect such out-patient referrals as for x-rays and laboratory tests, which are strongly associated with doctor consultations, also to be higher in a fee-for-service system. (9) A related point is that another corollary of (7) is that patient expectations, e.g., for pharmaceutical prescriptions as an outcome of GP consultations, would have somewhat more force in the fee-for-service approach than the capitation method and considerably more than in a salary system.

Abel-Smith (1983) reports that 1975 doctor consulting rates in Western Europe showed an apparently strong effect of remuneration technique. Of four countries surveyed, England, with its capitation method of remuneration, had the fewest average consultations per year (3.5). The others, in ascending order, were Belgium (6.3), Italy (11.5), and FR Germany (12, 1976).[21]

Within the European Economic Community (EEC), there is wide variability in per capita pharmaceutical prescribing rates, ranging from 4.5 items per person per year in the Netherlands to 21 per cent in Italy. The six countries with the highest prescribing rates, ranging from 9 to 21 (with an unweighted average of 10.25) all remunerate doctors on a fee-for-service basis, and three countries with the lowest prescribing rates, ranging from 4.5 to 6.9 (with an unweighted

---

[21]As the present paper is drafted, three studies of medical care costs and expenditures in the European Community have been published; Abel-Smith and Maynard (1978); Michel (1978); and Abel-Smith and Grandjeat (1978). These concerned organisation and financing; cost of hospitalisation; and pharmaceutical consumption, respectively. No volume on primary health care has yet appeared.

average of 5.9), all use the capitation method (Abel-Smith, 1983).[22] Italy
recently completed a major reform in its health care system, shifting, *inter alia*,
from a fee-for-service system to a capitation one. During the transition, it was
found that "the number of consultations per patient under fee-for-service payment was on average greater than under capitation payment" (Abel-Smith and
Maynard, 1978).

There is evidence that hospitals are also affected by the method of
remuneration.

> Where hospitals are paid per day of care, there is an incentive on the
> hospital to extend the length of stay to secure payment for as high a propor-
> tion of staffed beds as possible unless patients are waiting to be admitted.
> Moreover, the cost falling on hospitals tends to be lower for later than
> earlier days of stay so that high occupancy is more profitably attained by
> longer stays than more admissions (Abel-Smith and Maynard, 1978).

E. A "Parkinson's Law" of Medical Care Demand?

It was once believed that some objectively defineable notion of health or
medical care "needs" existed, and that a medical care system, if it operated
properly, should be expected to match resources to those needs. Such ideas seem
naïve today.

Instead, it appears that demands for health care are in effect insatiable, at
least in the aggregate. There is no objectively defineable and limited concept of
medical need, nor is there an objectively defineable and limited concept of
appropriate care of treatment. Consequently, economists have begun to talk of
"an advanced form of Parkinson's Law" operating in the medical care area
(Office of Health Economics, 1979). The original "law", due to C. Northcote
Parkinson, was that work expands to fill the time available. In medical care,
there appear to be two versions of the "law".

According to the first, "it appears that to whatever extent health care facilities
are expanded they will generally still all be used; and at the same time there will
remain a steady pool of 'unmet' demands" (Office of Health Economics, 1979).
There is impressive evidence for this within the British NHS. Culyer (1976) shows
that despite rather large changes in the throughput capacity of British hospitals
(defined as number of hospital beds available, divided by the average length of
hospital stay), the total waiting list has remained remarkably constant, and the
waiting list per capita even more so, over a 16-year period. Culyer cites two
reasons for this phenomenon.

---

[22]Based on 1973, 1974, 1975, or 1975 data depending on country; hence Greece is not included.
The Irish figure was for public patients only. The Italian figure was for doctors paid on a fee-for-
service basis under the main health insurance scheme. However, under that scheme, doctors paid
on a capitation basis prescribed less than doctors paid on a fee-for-service basis (Abel-Smith,
1983).

First, the increase in throughput capacity has come about primarily through a fall in the average length of stay. This means that even though hospitalisation is free in the NHS, the "time-price" or cost of medical care in terms of one's own sacrifice of valuable time, had fallen, thus inducing an increase in utilisation as a movement along a demand curve. This, however, is the less important of the two explanations offered by Culyer.

Much more important, however, is the fact that the demand for care is mediated by doctors whose perception of need, operationally and at the level of the individual patient, is what really decides whether a patient is admitted. Since doctors also control supply, the usually convenient separation of resource allocation problems into a demand side and a supply side (the two blades of Alfred Marshall's 'scissors') ceases to be valid, for the factors affecting one side can no longer be supposed to be independent of the factors affecting the other: a necessary prerequisite for the valid application of demand/supply analysis. Supply increases, therefore, instead of reducing the excess demand (as mediated by doctors), tend not only to enable the meeting of existing demands, but encourage GPs to refer more patients to hospital, and hospital doctors to assign more people to the waiting list, until a more or less "conventional" waiting time is again reached.

According to the second notion of Parkinson's Law, an increase in the quantity of physician services in relation to population will give rise to a compensating rise in per capita physicians' services. In contrast to the first version, where physicians are regulating the use of *other* medical care resources, here physicians are argued to be stimulating or accepting increased utilisation of their *own* services, in order to maintain their incomes.

Figure 2.1, based on two diagrams employed by Reinhardt (1978), illustrates the concept of provider-induced demand, and permits a distinction between it and price-induced demand. The initial supply curve (S_0) and demand curve (D_0) provide the initial equilibrium price (P_0) and quantity (Q_0). Then it is supposed that there is an outward shift in supply (to S_1) caused, e.g., by an increase in the number of doctors (relative to population). If the market is competitive and supply and demand are independent, price falls (to P_1) and output rises (to Q_1). An increase in the ratio of doctors to population results in an increase in the rate of consultations per capita. This is not what is meant by supply-induced increases in demand. It might be called price-induced demand, and it represents an ordinary adjustment process, found in conventional markets. If doctors influence demand in this case, they do so only within the context of an agency model.

This solution indicates a fall in average physician incomes. The rise in the number of doctors, if it is indicated by the rightward shift in S, exceeds the rise in Q, indicating that the average doctor's workload has fallen. The unit price has also fallen. Therefore, average physician income has fallen. Again, this is the result expected in a normally competitive market.

Now let it be supposed that doctors are willing and able to induce a compensating increase in demand for their own services and that the demand curve shifts outward to D_{1A}. In this case, which represents true provider-induced demand, quantity rises (to Q_{1A}) and so does price (to P_{1A}). Empirically, the market looks very much like one with an upward-sloping demand curve: increases in supply are associated with increases in price. If we observe such a positive correlation between the doctor-population ratio, and doctors' fees, assuming that we have controlled for other influences, we could take it as evidence that we have a self-interest model of physician-induced demand.

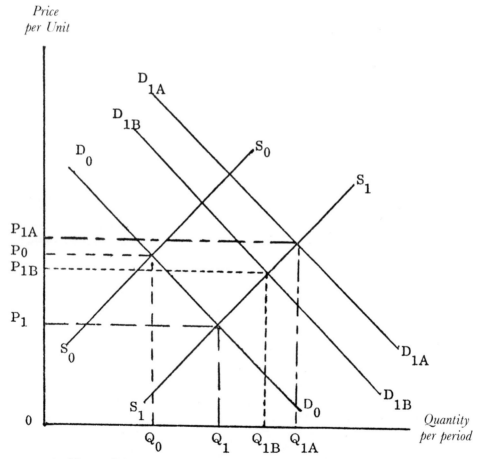

Figure 2.1: *Provider-Induced Demand vs. Price-Induced Demand*

However, it needs to be added that a *negative* correlation between the physician-population ratio and fees does not provide evidence contrary to the self-interest model. The rightward induced shift in demand may be affected by, e.g., limits to doctors' market power, patient resistance, or doctor distaste for self-interested demand induction. If the demand curve shifts only, e.g., to D_{1B}, which is a compensating shift within the self-interest model, price will rise only to P_{1B}, and we will observe a negative correlation between the physician-population ratio and price, just as in the price-induced case.[23] There is no *a priori* way to determine whether fee levels will actually rise (Anderson, House and Ormiston, 1981). Hence we may well find no significant relationship between fee levels and physician supply, even where we control for demand-influencing variables.

Some of the empirical evidence on self-interested behaviour will be reviewed in a moment. Health economists have been described as falling into two groups, the "Ns" (for narrow) and "Bs" (for broad), the latter, unlike the former, assuming that the physician "is a predominant force in determining utilisation patterns due to his/her ability to form consumer/patient preferences and to provide information on which patient choices are made" (Evans, 1976). Sloan and Feldman (1978), whose paper when read in conjunction with Reinhardt's (1978) interpretation, is the most thorough review of the empirical literature available, and who regard themselves as Ns, comment that the difference between the two groups is one of degree and not of kind, and note that *neither* view is well supported by the empirical literature:

> There are substantial differences between economists who espouse the supply-created demand view, the B's, and the neo-classical economists, the N's. The former stress anomalies of the health care market while the latter rely on formal theoretical methods and econometrics and emphasise similarities with other markets. Though less formal, the B's have called attention to features of the industry that the N's might miss. Frequently, the N's have met the challenges. Even so, applied econometric studies based on the standard theory often report low R^2s, and some of the variables are only proxies for the theoretical concepts. ...
>
> Supplier-induced demand is not an "all or nothing" matter in which opponents of the supplier-induced demand notion are forced to find evidence ruling out supplier-induced demand shifts entirely. Rather, at issue, is whether supplier-induced demand represents a major demand determinant. We find that the B's have been much too hasty in concluding it is.

Sloan and Feldman's views to the contrary notwithstanding, those policy-makers and budget drafters responsible for developing techniques to control health care cost expansion appear to have concluded that a form of Parkinson's Law operates with respect to both hospitalisation and to physician services. The neo-classical model would be consistent with *expanding* the number of physicians in order to reduce medical care costs. In the USA, it has come to be accepted that *restricting* the number of physicians is a technique which belongs on a list of "mutually reinforcing strategies" for controlling health care costs, not only in

[23]The discussion of Figure 2.1 is based on the discussion by Reinhardt (1978).

order to limit the utilisation of physician services themselves, but also to limit other medical care expenditures influenced by physicians (Raskin, Coffey and Farley, 1980). In the USA, it has been estimated that 70 per cent of personal medical care expenditures are controlled by physicians, and that in 1972, the average physician generated an average expenditure of $240,000, which is equivalent to approximately IR£330,000 in 1981, taking account of inflation and the exchange rate. (Raskin, Coffey and Farley, 1980.) (See Chapter 6 for an estimate of Irish physician influence.) A number of countries in the European Community are reported to be restricting the number of medical students, because:

> it is widely believed that an increase in the number of doctors per thousand population results in higher costs of health care, quite apart from the cost of the remuneration of the extra doctors, because of the costs they generate in their prescribing of medicines and their authorization of diagnostic tests, hospital admissions and therapeutic procedures (Abel-Smith and Maynard, 1978).

The Netherlands, Denmark, France and Germany are pursuing this course of action, as is, in a sense, Ireland.[24]

Similarly, both the USA (Raskin, Coffey and Farley, 1980) and all members of the European Community (Abel-Smith and Maynard, 1978) restrict hospital construction and expansion in order to limit the number of beds, per thousand population, as a cost-containment method.

A related implication is that hospital budgets should not be allocated on the basis of utilisation. In the NHS, it was shown (Feldstein, 1967) that regions with more beds hospitalised more people, who had longer average stays. In other words, "the supply of beds created its own demand" (Maynard and Ludbrook, 1980). If then budgets were allocated according to "need", and if the latter were defined in terms of utilisation and average stay, then existing patterns would merely be reinforced and replicated. While this analysis was based on a non-market medical care system, it appears to apply generally.

Thus the notion of a medical "Parkinson's Law" is an extremely important development in both the conceptualisation of markets for medical care and in the control of health care expenditures. While not all economists are equally convinced of the self-interest aspects, none seems to be advocating increases in

---

[24]In 1978, the size of the entering medical school class in Ireland was cut by 15 per cent. But this appears to have been more addressed to the decline in overseas opportunities than to control of Irish health expenditures. Legislation in the US and in Canada in 1976, limiting the entry of foreign medical graduates (devices adopted in *those* countries to control the growth of health expenditures), reduced access to what theretofore had been major outlets for the Irish doctor surplus; the reduction in class size should be seen as a response. In spite of the cut, Irish medical schools continue in the early 1980s producing from 350 to 370 graduates per year, when only 200 to 250 will be needed, according to a survey conducted by the Royal College of Physicians in Ireland. The survey also indicated that 80 per cent of medical graduates did not have permanent posts five years after graduating, *Irish Times*, 5 June, 1981.

the physician or hospital-bed stock as a way of controlling expenditures and quite a large number advocate the opposite policy.

F. Empirical Studies of Utilisation

There is a growing empirical literature on the determinants of utilisation of medical care. Many studies show utilisation to depend on *health* status and proxies for health, including age, sex and social class; on *income* and proxies for income, including social class and educational attainment; on *price*, and proxies for price, including insurance cover, distance to medical facilities, waiting times, sex and age; on *availability* of medical care resources, especially hospital beds; and on *physician* characteristics and market conditions. Each of these is discussed in turn.

Health. Where data are available, health status explains much of the person-to-person variation in medical care utilisation. (Bice and White, 1969; Rutten, 1978; van der Gaag, 1978; Held and Manheim, 1980). Many empirical studies are, however, conducted where health data are not available. Some close substitutes are sometimes available, such as days lost from work (May, 1975). In other cases, weaker proxies must be employed. Age is presumably correlated with health problems, and most types of medical care utilisation are positively correlated with age (see, e.g., Feldstein, 1967; Held and Manheim, 1980), except that, with respect to some, a U-shaped relationship holds instead, with utilisation high in infancy, then falling through early childhood and rising again. Hence age squared is often used along with age (Rutten, 1978; van der Gaag, 1978). Many studies show that females use more medical services than males (e.g., Feldstein, 1967; Rutten, 1978; van der Gaag, 1978). This is mainly a matter of morbidity and pregnancy, but sex, and to an extent age, may be proxies for price, as will be discussed below. Many studies show social class to be related to utilisation (Feldstein, 1967; Bice and White, 1969; Bice, *et al.*, 1973; Rutten, 1978; van der Gaag, 1978) though the relationship may be complex. Persons of lower social class presumably have more health care problems. It is known that in Ireland, at least, they smoke more tobacco, are more likely to be overweight and to exercise less (Mulcahy, Graham, Hickey and Daly, 1980). But social class is also related to income, and as well to attitudes, preferences and other similar influences on utilisation.

Income. Income has, for reasons just mentioned, a positive association with preference for medical care and negative relationships with need. Thus it is useful to be able to measure the impact of income whilst controlling for the influence of health (or its proxies). Most studies have found a significant positive income elasticity for medical care consumption (e.g., Feldstein, 1967; Andersen and Benham, 1970; Phelps and Newhouse, 1975), though the elasticities are low (0.1–0.4). Mean regional income also has a similar effect (Held and Manheim, 1980). Social class may act as a proxy for income. Where social class is measured by occupational category, it reflects characteristics other than income. For example, the morbidity and behavioural differences between farmers and urban workers are not limited to income alone. In the event, occupational category has been found in the United States to have a significant relationship to utilisation, with middle class workers using more medical services than the highest or the lowest category workers, while agricultural workers had far lower consumption than non-agricultural workers (Bice, *et al.*, 1973). Educational attainment is often used as an alternative to occupational level as a measure of class. Conceptually, it has some advantages over occupational level as a measure of class.[25] One US study (Bice, Eichhorn and Fox, 1972) found a positive relationship between educational attainment and medical consumption.

Price. Prices consist of money prices, which are not relevant to all medical care systems, and time prices, which are relevant to all. A difficulty in measuring money-price elasticity is that output is not always easily defined in homogeneous units. For example, if price and quality are correlated, price elasticities will be underestimated (Feldstein, 1974). Specification of net price is a problem where there are co-insurance, deductibles, tax relief, etc. None the less, most studies indicate negative price elasticities (e.g., Fuchs and Kramer, 1972), but there are exceptions, subject to interpretation. Feldstein (1970) finds a positive relationship between price and utilisation, which he interprets as showing a permanent excess demand for medical care, though others have disagreed with his interpretation. The extent or type of insurance cover may substitute for or complement price data in arriving at net price where the latter are not available (Fuchs and Kramer, 1972; Rutten, 1978; van der Gaag, 1978). Time prices are costs of utilisation, in the form of travel time (as measured by distance to doctor, hospital, etc.) and time in waiting room, etc. (Phelps and Newhouse, 1975). These may be measured indirectly by doctor-area density or doctor-population ratios (see physician behaviour, below). Where private insurance and/or public entitlement to health services are extensive, time prices may be more important than money prices (Acton, 1973). The opportunity cost of time spent in travel or waiting rooms may be higher for the employed than for the unemployed, those not in the labour force and the retired. Where utilisation is higher for these groups — e.g., for women or the aged — that fact may reflect a lower opportunity cost, as well as health status.

Availability. The availability of medical care resources, especially hospital beds but also including physicians (see physician behaviour, below) has such a strong effect on utilisation that it often overwhelms the other variables. This effect lends support to a supply-creates-demand or "Parkinson's Law" hypothesis as discussed in the preceding section (Feldstein, 1967, 1971, 1971a; May, 1975; Rutten,

[25]Low income may be a consequence as well as a cause of health status. To a lesser extent, occupational level may as well. Educational attainment, however, does not vary as a person's health varies and consequently has some advantages in empirical work.

1978; van der Gaag, 1978; Held and Manheim, 1980). The availability of resource A (e.g. physicians) also influences the utilisation of resource B (e.g., hospital admissions), though resources that appear as substitutes in one study show up as complements in another, and often results are counter-intuitive (e.g., Feldstein, 1967, 1976; Davis and Russell, 1972, May, 1975).

Physician. Rutten (1978) and van der Gaag (1978) show that individual doctors vary considerably in the utilisation they order or generate for their patients, even where all the variables discussed above, and others, are controlled for. Given sex, occupational level, nature of insurance cover (in the Dutch system), presence or absence of serious disease, and of psycho-social problems, and given type of residence, the maximum difference between GPs of similar age and identical sex practising in the same area with similar clientele was 30 per cent for number of GP contacts and around 40 per cent for probability of referral to a specialist. These are differences not associated with any model of physician behaviour described above, reflecting only differences in individual physicians' training, experience, methods, attitudes, etc. The differences are quite significant, and point to considerable doctor influence over patient utilisation. They help explain as well the low R^2s found in most studies, where it is impossible to control for individual physician influence.

G. Physician-induced demand

Most empirical studies of physician behaviour focus on testing the self-interest hypothesis. Two main propositions are tested in this literature. One is that where doctors are paid on a fee-for-service basis, utilisation levels are higher than where capitation or salary methods are used, where similar clientele are served. The basis of this proposition was discussed above, in Section D. The other is that where the ratio of physicians to population is high, a situation which by itself would depress physician incomes, physicians stimulate compensatory increases in the demand for their own services. The latter proposition is limited, for obvious reasons, to physicians working in fee-for-service systems. The basis of this proposition was discussed above, in Section E. These two branches of the empirical literature will be discussed in turn.

Monsma's (1970) study in the United States is an important early one in the remuneration literature. He found a higher level of surgery in an American fee-for-service institutional arrangement than in an otherwise identical system under which the doctors were salaried; and evidence is produced suggesting that all appropriate surgery was, in fact, performed in the salaried case. The apparently excess surgery concentrated on the removal of putatively redundant organs: appendicectomies, tonsillectomies and hysterectomies. Rutten (1978) and van der Gaag (1978) found higher utilisation levels in The Netherlands, in fee-for-service than in capitation systems, controlling for patient characteristics and other variables.

Health Maintenance Organisations (HMOs) are private medical care providers found mainly in the United States. Patients pre-pay for medical care on an annual fee basis, so that they in effect pay for all medical care and not merely GP services, on a capitation basis. A large literature shows lower utilisation, especially hospitalisation, under HMO arrangements. (For a review, see Luft, 1978). HMOs will be discussed in more detail in Chapter 8.

On the other hand, it also appears that similar patterns of variability, albeit at different levels, exist in different countries for common surgical practices, irrespective of method financing. McPherson, Wennberg, Hovind and Clifford (1982) examined surgery rates for tonsillectomy, haemorrhoidectomy and five other common procedures in three states in the north-eastern United States and in Norway and England. They found that while surgery rates were quite a bit higher in the United States, where a fee-for-service system generally obtains, patterns of variability were the same in the three countries, suggesting a less important role for method of finance than shown in other studies.

On balance, the evidence points strongly to higher utilisation levels where fee-for-service methods are used.

However, Ireland, which generally employs the fee-for-service method, probably has lower levels of self-interested physician-generated demand than other fee-for-service countries. This is because the strict separation of general practice from hospital-based specialist care, and the fact that Irish GPs do not generally provide x-ray or pathology services as do primary-care physicians in many other countries, means that there are severe limits on practical opportunities for physician-generated demand. That is, the propensity of physicians to pursue their own economic self-interest when carrying out their agency roles depends not only on the method of remuneration, as traditionally argued, but also on the method of delivery of medical care (Tussing, 1983c). Delivery of medical care in Ireland is discussed in Chapter 4.

We turn now to the second proposition in the literature, that of compensatory physician-induced demand. If markets for physician services were conventional, doctors would be more or less evenly distributed geographically, subject to two qualifications to be noted presently. If there were a disproportionate tendency of doctors to locate their practices in favoured locations (e.g., Dublin), that would drive down physician fees and lower their incomes; lower physician densities in more remote areas (e.g., Donegal) would raise fees and incomes. These incentives would induce physicians to relocate (e.g., from Dublin to Donegal), thus smoothing out the regional distribution of physicians. The qualifications are as follows: If patients in one area had a stronger preference or need for medical care, and hence a higher demand, that would, *ceteris paribus*, raise demand and fee levels in that area, meaning that it could support more physicians. Thus physician densities should relate to community health needs. If physicians had strong locational preferences, such that they might be willing to accept lower incomes were they to locate in favoured areas, that could explain uneven geographical distributions of physicians.

Fuchs and Kramer (1972) and Fuchs (1978) find that doctors in the US tend to locate their practices according to community amenity levels, and to the availability of hospital beds, without relation to community health needs. Fuchs and Kramer estimate a simultaneous four-equation system in which the doctor-population ratio is endogenous, and has a negative effect on workload, and a positive effect on doctor services per capita. The utilisation equation controls for net money price, so the model is not that of price-induced demand but rather supplier induced demand, as in Figure 2.1. Fuchs, whose 1978 study will be discussed further below, shows that physician supply is in part determined by factors unrelated to demand, especially by the attractiveness of the area as a place to live — ingeniously measured by per capita hotel receipts in the locality.

There are essentially two branches of this literature, depending on the theoretical device used to *limit* physician-induced demand in the model. If doctors have the ability to shift patients' demand curves, as in Figure 2.1, and if they are profit-maximisers, as is implied in the self-interest hypothesis, they might be expected to shift demand as much as they are able, irrespective of doctor-population ratios. Such behaviour would be inconsistent with the compensatory demand stimulating hypothesis, and would moreover be virtually impossible to detect empirically. In the literature, two devices are relied upon to limit or constrain doctors' demand stimulation in self-interest models. One is the assumption that doctors aim for exogenously determined "target incomes" (linked, e.g., to the incomes of other professionals in the community). If doctors' locational decisions are also exogenously determined, target incomes can be achieved or approached by compensatory demand stimulation. Examples of target income studies are Evans (1974); Evans, Parish and Sully (1973); Fuchs (1978); Fuchs and Kramer (1972); Hixson, *et al.* (1980); Newhouse (1970); and Sweeney (1982).

The other device, used in the context of a theoretically more elegant utility-maximising model, is to assume that doctors have a distaste for demand stimulation. That is, utility is increased by income, reduced (within the relevant range) by work, and reduced by unnecessary or excessive treatment or other demand stimulation. This model also yields compensatory demand stimulation. (Wilensky and Rossiter, 1980; Sloan and Feldman, 1978). The two models yield similar predicted physician behaviour.

Evans (1974) wrote an early and important article in the compensatory literature. Using Canadian data, he showed that physicians appear to have target income and workload levels, based on their training, expectations and previous experience, and that discrepancies between these targets and actual experience lead to adjustment behaviour, if income and workloads are below target, demand generation takes place. If physicians feel over-worked and underpaid, prices are raised either through upward revision of fee schedules, or through independent adjustments in billing behaviour. He also found a general tendency for physician prices to be higher in regions where physicians are plentiful than where they are scarce, a finding consistent with the shift to demand curve D_{1A} and price P_{1A} in Figure 2.1. The elasticity of utilisation with respect to the physician-population ratio was estimated to be on the order to 0.4, which is relatively high.

Held and Manheim (1980) found that in Quebec the GP-to-population ratio is positively associated with cost and the revisit rate, though the elasticities are small; and the specialist-to-population ratio has an even smaller negative effect on cost and the revisit rate. Their study concerns hypertension, which they argue is "a medical condition which allows considerable discretion to the physician in determining treatment mode, and patient initiation of care is considerably less than in many other chronic conditions. It would therefore appear to be a natural candidate for testing the hypothesis of physician inducement." Their results show that the cost of treatment for hypertension is not independent of local physician supply, but increases as the number of general practitioners increases, and decreases as the number of specialists increases. "The magnitude of both these effects, however, tends to be fairly small. Interestingly, the change in costs is associated more with the cost per visit than with the number of visits." They conclude, "The results presented here suggest that if physician inducement is present, the magnitude is not large." The low positive elasticity for GPs and low negative elasticity for specialists is not as damaging to the hypothesis as the authors believe, however, in light of Reinhardt's analysis (Figure 2.1). A small increase or even decrease in utilisation associated with a rise in the number of physicians (in a cross-section sense) is consistent with a significant amount of compensatory physician demand generation, as in the shift to D_{1B} in Figure 2.1. As Reinhardt notes, a positive relationship between price and supply is more damaging to the "N" (or agency) model than a negative relationship (especially a small one) is to the "B" (or self-interest) model.

Fuchs (1978), already cited above in relation to physician location, studied the supply of surgeons and the demand for operations in the USA. Surgery in America provides an especially useful test of the self-interest model. Operations are more well-defined than many other medical procedures, and thus provide a better quantity measure, though quality can still vary with price. The "excess demand" interpretation (of, e.g., Martin Feldstein) can be ruled out, as US data unequivocally point to an excess supply of surgeons. It was noted above that the physician-population ratio might be interpreted as a proxy for time-price. A higher ratio implies a shorter distance to travel, and/or a shorter wait in the office, thus encouraging more utilisation without a need to resort to demand generation for the explanation. But Fuchs argues that time costs "are likely to be less relevant for in-hospital operations because the psychic costs of surgery and the time costs of hospitalisation are likely to be large relative to the time costs of search, travel and waiting". The results provide impressive support for the thesis that surgeons shift the demand for operations. Other things equal, a 10 per cent increase in the surgeon/population ratio results in about a 3 per cent increase in per capita utilisation. A higher surgeon/population ratio is associated with higher fees (as in P_{1A} in Figure 2.1).

Most of the studies cited have employed aggregated cross-section data, which regress, for example, mean utilisation rates on doctor densities for metropolitan areas or other regions (including whole American states). Mitchell, Cromwell and Dutton (1981) use individual patient data, and also find evidence of compensatory demand inducement amongst U.S. surgeons, affecting surgery rates and, especially, fees. However, they find no inducement in rural areas and considerable inducement in densely populated urban areas.

Pauly, in an important book (1980), and Pauly and Satterthwaite (1980), emphasise the significance of information in individual patient-based empirical models. Patients with adequate information on price and quality of medical care — taken to be persons with more education, or persons who live in rural areas — do not show significant compensatory demand-inducing effects in Pauly's test of a target-income model. Only less-educated urban residents, whose access to information is most limited, are subject to significant inducement as measured by utilisation levels. Pauly and Satterthwaite advance the theory that physicians' monopoly power increases as the number of physicians in a market (measured by the ratio of physicians to area, rather than to population) increases, because the increase in numbers is associated with a fall in the amount and quality of consumer information (especially as regards alternative providers). They find physician-to-population ratios strongly correlated with physician-to-area ratios, and speculate that the former may just be a proxy for the latter in many demand-inducement models. However, Mitchell, Cromwell and Dutton, cited above, with a larger and more varied data set, in which the correlation between the two ratios is lower, find that the inclusion of the physician-to-area variable actually increases the significance of the physician-to-population variable, in explaining utilisation levels.

All of these studies are affected, more or less, by the identification problem referred to earlier: it is necessary to infer the existence of physician-induced demand from utilisation levels (aggregate or individual) because we have no way of directly observing physician behaviour, and consequently, we cannot discern a shift in demand, especially from D_0 to D_{1B}, from movement along a more gently sloped demand curve. An important exception is the study of Wilensky and Rossiter (1981), whose unique data set from the USA includes "... a direct measure, from the patient's perspective, or the perspective of a member of the patient's household, of who initiated the demand for each visit..." the doctor or the patient. They also have extensive data on physicians, linked to the household sample. They found 39 per cent of consultations to be physician initiated. Their empirical work uses the probability that a visit is physician-initiated, rather than utilisation itself, as the dependent variable. Wilensky and Rossiter found a strong relationship between physician initiation and local physician density. There was also a strong relationship between physician initiation and proportion of the doctor's bill paid by the family, which the authors believe also supports the self-interest model, though it would appear to be consistent with the agency model as well. Other interesting relationships discovered provide additional evidence for the self-interest model. For example, young doctors are significantly more likely to initiate consultations than older doctors. For primary care physicians, as physician age increases from 25 to 65, which is perhaps the plausible range of most practising physicians' ages, the probability of physician initiation falls from 0.51 to 0.39, holding constant other influences at their means. And for non-primary care specialists, outside (non-practice) doctor income significantly influences physician initiation. As outside income increases from 0 to $25,000 per year, the likelihood that a consultation will be self-initiated by the physician declines from 0.76 to 0.65, *ceteris paribus*. These results seem strongly supportive of the self-interest model.[26]

It is worth noting one final aspect of these empirical studies of utilisation and of physician-induced demand. They often have low adjusted R^2s, sometimes as low as .050, though more usually in the range .100 or .250, in spite of the presence of a number of highly significant coefficient estimates. While the analyses reported obviously bear on the hypotheses tested, it would be hard to argue that we have gone very far in explaining the person-to-person or region-to-region variability in utilisation with the types of equations estimated.

These results, taken together, are not definitive. Empirical results are always subject to interpretation, and more high-powered and rigorous models and tests will undoubtedly come in the future. One important step, for example, would be to replicate compensatory physician-induced demand studies in a capitation system such as Britain. If we were to find that in Britain, physician density was significantly associated with return visits or physician-initiated visits, we might have to discard our interpretation that the source of the observed behaviour was physician economic self-interest (Tussing, 1983c). But the evidence is mounting that the doctor's own income and workload are an important consideration when she or he influences utilisation patterns. The evidence is strong enough to conclude that medical care systems should give attention to organising themselves — their methods of service delivery, their methods of finance, and their methods of remunerating providers — so that, consistent with other objectives, excessive utilisation is not encouraged, while appropriate utilisation is not discouraged. In the remaining chapters of this study, and especially Chapter 6, Irish data will be analysed, the determinants of utilisation in this country will be estimated, and attention will be given, along with other issues, to physician initiation. The subject of changes in the organisation, financing and delivery of medical care will reappear in Chapter 8.

---

[26]Wilensky and Rossiter use all the independent variables discussed previously in this section. Their work had not been referred to above because their equations predict physician initiation, not utilisation *per se*. They find that patient age does not significantly influence the probability that a visit is physician initiated, but that sex does, with a higher rate of physician initiation among female patients. Poor health status is associated with higher probability of physician initiation. Educational attainment affects physician initiation outside of primary care, among specialists seen on referral. Family income has a significantly negative effect on physician initiation.

H. Summary and Conclusions

Expenditures on medical care have an association with the extending of life that is weak and growing weaker. The types of morbidity and mortality which are increasingly predominant in Western societies are not as amenable to medical intervention as was the case in the past, and decreasing returns appear to apply to the use of economic resources for medical care. The past two decades have seen rapidly rising medical expenditures in virtually every country, but little progress in life expectancy. It is difficult, however, to make any but the most general statements about returns to medical expenditures, because of the general lack of scientific studies of the efficacy and cost-effectiveness of existing medical procedures.

The concept of economic rationality applies to medical care as a commodity and to human life as well. But it is evidently accepted in all countries that economic rationality in these areas cannot be achieved in the market, with buyers paying prices equal to social opportunity costs for medical care services. Though medical care appears to be a private good, with only limited external benefits, the market fails because the vital condition of independence of supply and demand is absent. Instead, the physician — the most important supplier of medical care services — either influences or controls a large part of the demand for it, on behalf of the buyer. Two other problems limit use of the market. Because of the uncertainty that most members of the public face concerning the timing and extent of their future use of medical care, they require and demand some form of insurance cover. A consequence is a significant element of moral hazard when and if markets are relied upon. Even if there were to be no government intervention and even if medical care were priced at marginal costs, there would be a tendency for over-utilisation, because of moral hazard. Second, medical care appears to be a merit good. Society refuses to accept the consequences of some members' failure to insure voluntarily; thus medical insurance is made compulsory, through government or some other institutional device.

The special characteristics of the institutional techniques for the delivery of medical care services have led to theoretical and empirical search for understanding of the determinants of utilisation, and in particular for understanding the behaviour of the physician, a central figure. Medical care utilisation appears to depend in predictable ways on the patient's health, age, sex, income and social class, as well as on price, etc. It also appears to depend, in a way analogous to a Parkinson's Law applied to medical care, on the available supply of medical care resources, especially physicians and hospital beds. In addition, there is considerable evidence that doctors exercise their influence over patients' medical care decisions at least in part in such a manner as to maximise their own self-interest, especially their incomes, when that is made possible by the financing and delivery arrangements in a particular society.

A number of problems are created by the following, taken together: the interdependence of supply and demand, with at least some applicability of the self-interest model; a money price below marginal cost, with a limit of zero, and attendant moral hazard; use of alternative, non-market rationing techniques; and the medical Parkinson's Law. One consequence is economic irrationality. Medical care resources appear to be distributed in ways that do not equate the marginal benefit, in life-saving or other terms, of final expenditures across all aspects of medical care systems. Some patients apparently over-use certain medical care resources, with the likely consequence that others either must queue for more crucial services, or not avail of them. Another consequence is medical harm. Over-surgery, over-prescribing and excess application of other medical procedures are not only inefficient and costly; they are bad for patients. And finally, these problems help explain, though they do not fully explain, the rapidly rising costs of medical care in virtually all industrialised societies.

Chapter 3

MORBIDITY AND MORTALITY IN IRELAND

This chapter discusses Irish morbidity and mortality. Chapter 4 reviews the organisation, financing, and delivery of medical care services in Ireland, and Chapter 5 discusses Irish medical care expenditures and their growth.

Ireland may appear rather typical with respect to all three subjects. The Irish death rate from all causes ranks second lowest, along with Italy, in the European Community.[27] The medical care system has been accurately described as "as good as the next" (Nowlan, 1977). Like almost all other Western countries, Ireland has experienced rapidly rising medical care costs in recent years, both absolutely and relatively to Gross National Product or Gross Domestic Product (GNP or GDP).

These statements, though they are true, conceal much. For Ireland has a unique pattern of morbidity and mortality, different from those of its European neighbours. It has a unique system or organisation and financing of medical care, reflecting this country's history, needs and politics. And Ireland faces particularly difficult problems today and in the future in attempting to control health expenditures.

Public health services in Ireland are delivered through a decentralised organisation consisting of eight regional, multi-county Health Board areas. Though it is not yet time to discuss organisation (see Chapter 4), as some of the data to be presented are given by Health Board area, it is useful briefly to introduce the areas. The eight areas are listed in Table 3.1 and shown in Figure 3.1.[28] Their populations ranged in 1981 from 202,146 in the Midlands to 1,194,735 in the Eastern Health Board area. Those aged 65 and over, who are particularly significant to the health services, ranged from 8.4 per cent of the population in the Eastern region, to 14.5 per cent in the North-Western Health Board area, in 1979.

[27]References to the European Community are to the nine nations who were members in 1980, prior to the accession of Greece.
[28]The eight Health Board areas are identical to the eight Planning Regions, except that County Meath is in the North-Eastern Health Board area and the Eastern Planning Region, and Roscommon is in the Western Health Board area but in the Midland Planning Region. (The Health Board area called "Southern" is the same as the Planning Region called "South-Western.")

Table 3.1: *Health Board Areas: Constituent Counties, 1981 Population and Area*

Health Board	Constituent Counties	Population 1981	Area, sq. mls.
Eastern	Dublin	1,194,735	1,792
	Kildare		
	Wicklow		
Midlands	Laois	202,146	2,519
	Longford		
	Offaly		
	Westmeath		
Mid-Western	Clare	308,212	3,038
	Limerick		
	Tipperary North Riding		
North-Eastern	Cavan	288,980	2,448
	Louth		
	Meath		
	Monaghan		
North-Western	Donegal	208,195	3,147
	Leitrim		
	Sligo		
South-Eastern	Carlow	374,575	3,631
	Kilkenny		
	Tipperary South Riding		
	Waterford		
	Wexford		
Southern	Cork	525,235	4,695
	Kerry		
Western	Galway	341,327	5,328
	Mayo		
	Roscommon		

For comparison purposes, Irish data on mortality, morbidity and medical care are sometimes shown together in this chapter with figures for the other members of the European Community. It is recognised that there are considerable differences among these countries, with respect to their populations, areas, incomes, industrial structures, age compositions, meteorological conditions, etc., and that direct comparisons may often be misleading. But data on deaths per 100,000 population by cause, or on hospital beds per 1,000 population, or on per cent of GNP devoted to health services, are difficult to interpret apart from a comparative context. Hence, such comparisons, when cautiously interpreted, serve a useful purpose. Cultural, linguistic and meteorological similarities make comparisons with the United Kingdom particularly apt.

Figure 3.1: *Health Board Areas.*

A. Morbidity and Mortality in Ireland

Our discussion begins with mortality and morbidity, so it is worth a reminder that the relationship between them and medical care or health expenditures does not appear to be a strong one. Evidence from among the developed countries gives us no reason to believe that those nations spending more, either per capita or in relationship to income, on medical care or health programmes will necessarily experience observably better health conditions (See Chapter 2).

The Irish life expectancy at birth, shown with comparable statistics from other countries in Table 3.2, is high. Female life expectancy in 1970 was, however, the lowest in the Community, at 73.5; male life expectancy was above the median, at 68.8. As Table 3.3 shows, there has been a substantial improvement in both of these figures between 1925–27 and 1970–72. Male life expectancy at birth has increased by 19.9 per cent; for females, the increase has been 26.9 per cent. A closer look at Table 3.3 reveals that the improvement, for males, has been greatest in the early years of life, especially the first year. During the same 45 year period, male life expectancy at 25 increased by only 9.2 per cent; and life expectancy at 65 and 75 actually fell during the period. For females, the improvement has been spread more evenly over the years of age, partly reflecting reductions in maternal mortality. Note also the comparison between 1960–62 and 1970–72. For males, life expectancy at every age except 0 and 75 actually *fell* during the period. For females, life expectancy at every age continued to grow at a modest pace.

Table 3.2 also records infant and maternal mortality rates. The reported 1980 Irish rate of infant mortality of 11.2 deaths per 1,000 is the Community median.

Table 3.2: *Selected mortality statistics*
European Community

State	Infant mortality per 1,000 births, 1980	Maternal mortality per 1,000 births, 1975 or (1974)	Life expectancy at birth, 1970 male	female
German Federal Republic	12.6	0.39	67.4	73.8
France	10.0	0.25 (c)	68.3	75.9
Italy	14.3	0.25	69.0	74.9
Netherlands	8.6	0.11	70.7	76.5
Belgium	11.0	0.04 (c)	67.8	74.2
Luxembourg	11.5	(a)	67.0 (e)	73.9
United Kingdom	12.1	0.14 (d)	68.6	74.9
Ireland	11.2	0.07 (f)	68.8 (b)	73.5 (b)
Denmark	8.4	0.06	70.5	75.4

Notes: (a) Absolute number too low to establish meaningful rate. (b) 1971. (c) 1972. (d) 1973. (e) 1974. (f) Source: *Statistical Abstract of Ireland, 1976.*
Source: Eurostat, *Social Indicators for the European Community* except as in (f).

Table 3.3: *Irish life expectancies, 1960-62, 1970-72; comparison between 1925-27 and 1970-72*

		1970-72	1960-62	Percentage change between 1925-27 and 1970-72
Males:				
Number of additional years a				
person can expect to live at age	0	68.8	68.1	+19.9%
	1	69.2	69.3	+13.1%
	5	65.5	65.7	+10.1%
	25	46.3	46.4	+9.2%
	45	27.6	27.8	+4.2%
	65	12.4	12.6	-3.1%
	75	7.3	7.1	-5.2%
Females:				
Number of additional years a				
person can expect to live at age	0	73.5	71.9	+26.9%
	1	73.8	72.7	+21.4%
	5	70.0	69.0	+18.2%
	25	50.5	49.5	+19.1%
	45	31.4	30.7	+16.3%
	65	15.0	14.4	+11.9%
	75	8.5	8.1	+1.2%

Source: Irish Statistical Bulletin, Various issues, as cited in Dept. of Health (1980).

The maternal mortality rate, quite low at 0.07 in 1975, rose a bit to 0.14 in 1979, and fell to provisional figures of 0.04 in 1980 and 0.00 (nil) in 1981. (Some problems of international comparison of perinatal and infant mortality are discussed in Kirke (1981) and Kirke and Brannick (1981)).

In Chapter 2, it was noted that in developed countries, morbidity and mortality due to infectious diseases had declined drastically over the past two generations, while conditions associated either with natural or biological processes (mainly ageing), and especially conditions relating primarily to lifestyle or other environmentally-determined factors, were increasing in significance, both absolutely and relatively to other causes. This is true no less in Ireland than elsewhere. Mortality associated with smallpox, scarlet fever, whooping cough, measles, typhoid and other infectious diseases has fallen dramatically. The most striking and important improvement has involved tuberculosis, once a major killer in Ireland, and today a relatively minor one. In 1925, the Irish tuberculosis death rate was 156.6 per 100,000 population. In 1935, the rate was still as high as 126.9 and in 1945, 125.1. It was at that point that the significant drop began. By 1955, the death rate was only 30.4 per 100,000; by 1965, 11.6; and 1975, 5.0. Indeed, as Table 3.4 indicates, the death rate for all infective and parasitic diseases stood at only 10.5 (males) and 8.3 (females) per 100,000 in 1979. On the other hand, cancer was in the 1960s and 1970s the single fastest rising cause of death in Ireland. Though the death rate from cancer (neoplasms) was among the lowest in the Community, Table 3.4 shows it to be second only to heart disease as a cause of death in Ireland. Both cancer and heart disease are regarded as significantly influenced by lifestyle and environmental conditions, though heart disease is also strongly associated with the ageing process. The death rates for lung cancer place Ireland higher (worse) in the "league table" than those for cancer in general, perhaps reflecting the fact that Ireland is reported to have the second highest, and possibly the highest, cigarette consumption rate in the Euro-

Table 3.4: *Deaths in Ireland by selected causes, per 100,000 population, 1979, with European Community rank (from lowest)*

Cause	Deaths per 100,000		Ireland's EC Rank	
	Male	Female	Male	Female
Infectious and parasitic diseases	10.5	8.3	5	8
Neoplasms	204.0	170.8	1	2
of which lung cancer	37.3	20.4	3	8[a]
Ischaemic heart disease	313.5	181.4	7	6
Respiratory system, diseases of	139.9	108.2	8[a]	8[a]
of which bronchitis	44.7	22.6	5[a]	8[a]
Digestive System, diseases of	28.4	24.8	2[a]	1[a]
of which cirrhosis of the liver	4.2	2.4	1	1
Other diseases	81.9	76.2	4[a]	3[a]
External causes of injury	77.8	33.6	3[a]	1[a]
of which motor vehicle accidents	27.9	9.3	4	2
of which suicide	8.6	2.9	2	1
All causes	1,104.1		4	3

Note: Except as in Note a, below, rank order based on 1974 data for Italy; 1976 for Germany, France, Netherlands, Belgium, Denmark, and the United Kingdom; 1977 for Luxembourg; and 1979 for Ireland.

[a]Rank order based on 1972 data for Italy; 1974 for Belgium, Luxembourg, France, and the United Kingdom; 1975 for Germany, Netherlands, and Denmark; and 1979 for Ireland.

Sources: For Ireland, *Report on Vital Statistics 1979*, Central Statistics Office, Dublin, 1983. For other countries (for ranks), Eurostat, *Social Indicators for the European Community, 1980*, except as in note a, 1977 edition.

pean Community.[29] Essentially, a non-industrial city, Dublin experiences air pollution comparable to that found in the most industrial cities of Europe (Walsh and Bailey, 1979). Ireland is also said to have the highest bowel cancer mortality rate in the Community. Death rates from heart disease, while as noted higher than those from any other cause, appear to have stabilised in the last decade.

After heart disease and cancer, the third most important cause of death in Ireland is respiratory disease, which consists primarily of pneumonia and bronchitis. This cause of death is worthy of particular attention, because the Irish rate, together with the British, stands apart from those of other developed countries, in the European Community or outside. Ireland and the UK have very similar mortality rates from respiratory illness; the other seven members have rates which are considerably lower. Irish meteorological conditions, which are in general shared with those of Britain, are important in explaining this exceptional mortality experience. Cigarette consumption and air pollution also play a part.[30] As will be noted below, respiratory problems are particularly acute in Dublin.

The Irish death rates for diseases of the digestive system are, by contrast, among the lowest in the Community, in fact in the world. The reported Irish death rate from cirrhosis of the liver, a disease associated with excessive alcohol consumption, is the lowest in the Community. (This contrasts with the reported alcoholism rate; see Table 3.7). The Irish rate for external causes of injury — accidents, violence, suicide, etc., is quite low, and the rate of suicide is the lowest

---

[29]Figures for 1978 showed, in descending order of magnitude, the following Community "league table" for cigarette sales per person: Luxembourg, 3,019; Ireland, 2,398; United Kingdom, 2,247; Germany, 2,008; Netherlands, 1,693; Belgium, 1,625; Italy, 1,573; France, 1,554; and Denmark, 1,454. (*Irish Times*, January 29, 1980). However, it should be noted that these statistics relate to sales, rather than consumption; and as Luxembourg has a lower rate of tax than adjoining states — indeed, the lowest rate of cigarette tax in the Community — it is possible that its sales figures are inflated by large sales to foreign consumers. Thus, it appears likely that per capita consumption may be higher in Ireland than in any other member state.

[30]A 1975 international study to determine the effects of air pollution on respiratory disease pointed to particularly severe problems in Dublin (Medico-Social Research Board, 1977). The Medico-Social Research Board, which conducted the Irish part of the study, reported on results in 19 urban areas, including Dublin, Cork and Galway in Ireland. Primary school children, chosen as to be sensitive indicators of the respiratory health of the whole population, were surveyed to determine the prevalence of the following respiratory symptoms: cough; breathlessness; wheezing; asthma. The children were categorised as to whether there was a tobacco smoker in the same household. The highest prevalences of respiratory symptoms in the entire survey were found in Dublin and in the three English cities in the study, all of them highly industrial: Hartlepool, Middlesbrough and Stockton. The Dublin rate was the highest in the study for the categories, boys with a smoker in the home, and girls with no smokers; and was third highest for girls with a smoker in the home. The rates exceeded those of such highly industrialised cities as Lyon, Paris, Milan and Venice. Setting aside rankings, the actual rates were alarming. More than one-third of Dublin boys and girls with a smoker in the home, and of girls with no smoker, reported respiratory symptoms. Cork and Galway reported about half the respiratory symptoms reported in Dublin.

reported in the Community, though more reporting errors are thought to affect suicide than any other cause of death. The rate for motor vehicle accidents is somewhat higher, and while below the Community average, is none the less cause for concern.

In Table 3.5 death rates for selected causes are compared among the eight Irish Health Board areas. It will be seen that the North-Western Health Board area has the highest death rate at 12.2 per 1,000 population, 27 per cent higher than the rest of the country. This is explained in part by demographic differences; 14.9 per cent of the North-West's population is aged 65 or more, as compared with 11.1 for the country as a whole. This contributes to an explanation of the higher circulatory (including heart) disease and cancer death rates. The North-Eastern area has a motor vehicle accident death rate which is almost double that of the rest of the country (28.1 per 100,000 in the North-Eastern, as compared with 15.9 in the other seven regions, and 17.0 for the country as a whole).

Irish morbidity data show similar patterns to those shown by mortality data. In 1980, 543,698 patients were treated in Irish public (Health Board and Voluntary Public) hospitals, and another 41,483 were treated in private hospitals (Table 3.6). This amounts to one discharge for every six persons. Of the total, 372,899 are included in the Hospital In-Patient Enquiry (or HIPE), which are the best morbidity data available. (The difference is due to non-reporting by some hospitals. There are no data on ambulatory morbidity.) The 1980 HIPE data are shown in Table 3.7. Accidents, poisonings and violence accounted for the largest number of hospital stays (discharges) followed by diseases of the respiratory system.

In addition to respiratory disease, some diseases and congenital conditions are known to be particularly prevalent in Ireland. Coeliac disease occurs in Ireland at three times the rate in England and Wales, and is particularly prevalent in the West of Ireland. There is a region of endemic goitre in South Tipperary. A condition called "farmer's lung," caused by inhaling material from mouldy hay, is common in North-West Ireland (Shelley, et al., 1979). Schizophrenia is also more common in Ireland: among males aged 25–34, the Irish rate is treble that of England and Wales.[31] "Dublin shares with Belfast," O'Donovan (1976) reports, "the unwelcome distinction of having the highest frequency of neurological malformations (anencephalous and spina bifida) in any community in which records are available."

A number of conditions show marked differences between rural and urban prevalences, and these for the most part relate to lifestyle and environmental influences, especially what appear to be higher rates of alcohol consumption and cigarette smoking, and poorer air quality, in urban areas, especially Dublin. HIPE data show five conditions for which the reported prevalences among men

---

[31]However, schizophrenia prevalences are sensitive to the particular definition employed and cross-national comparisons are not always valid.

Table 3.5: *Mortality: numbers and rates by selected causes of death by Health Board area, 1979*

	Eastern	Midland	Mid-Western	North-Eastern	North-Western	South-Eastern	Southern	Western	Ireland
Total deaths	9,294	2,049	2,856	2,700	2,501	3,855	5,616	3,919	32,790
Crude death rate (per 1,000 population)	8.0	10.4	9.5	9.6	12.2	10.5	10.9	11.7	9.7
INFANT MORTALITY									
Total deaths	344	53	91	76	42	107	133	52	898
Rate (per 1,000 live births)	13.3	12.4	14.2	12.1	10.2	13.1	12.2	8.2	12.4
NEO-NATAL MORTALITY									
Total Deaths	221	29	76	56	24	67	93	27	593
Rate (per 1,000 live births)	8.5	6.8	11.9	8.9	5.8	8.2	8.5	4.3	8.2
CIRCULATORY SYSTEM									
Total deaths	4,260	1,147	1,599	1,389	1,342	1,994	2,878	2,238	16,847
Rate (per 100,000 population)	365.7	579.4	531.6	494.4	656.6	543.6	557.2	666.0	500.2
CANCER									
Total Deaths	1,907	318	494	490	413	693	1,025	605	5,945
Rate (per 100,000 population)	163.7	160.6	164.2	174.4	202.1	188.9	198.5	180.0	176.5
MOTOR VEHICLE ACCIDENTS									
Total deaths	202	37	32	79	22	67	84	48	571
Rate (per 100,000 population)	17.3	18.7	10.6	28.1	10.8	18.3	16.3	14.3	17.0

Source: Central Statistics Office, as cited in Department of Health (1981).

Table 3.6: *Patients treated in hospital, average stay and total patient-days,*
1973–1981

Year	Patients treated, public hospitals[a]	Patients treated, private hospitals	Public hospitals		
			Average stay (days)	Patient days (× 1000)[b]	Patient days per capita
1973	418,279	(n.a.)	12.4	5,187	1.7
1974	441,011	(n.a.)	11.3	4,983	1.6
1975	456,140	40,240	11.4	5,200	1.6
1976	472,898	41,535	10.8	5,107	1.6
1977	489,533	39,268	10.3	5,276	1.6
1978	512,261	40,968	10.4	5,404	1.6
1979	519,654	41,231	9.6	4,989	1.5
1980	543,698	41,483	9.7	5,274	1.6
1981	559,563	(n.a.)	9.4	5,260	1.5

[a] Health Board Hospitals plus Voluntary Public Hospitals.
[b] Patients treated (col. 2) multiplied by average stay (col. 4).
Source: Department of Health.

in Dublin County Borough was greater than 150 per cent of that in rural districts in 1970–72. In all five cases, Dublin prevalence rates exceeded those in the remaining urban districts, with rural rates still lower. The five, in descending order of excess Dublin prevalence over rural rates, were cancer of trachea, bronchus and lung, 202 per cent; cirrhosis of liver, 192 per cent; tuberculosis of respiratory system, 161 per cent; pneumonia, 158 per cent; and bronchitis, emphysema and asthma, 157 per cent.[32] Of the five, four are respiratory conditions, the exception being cirrhosis of the liver. That condition, pneumonia, and tuberculosis are associated with high consumption of alcohol, while lung cancer and chronic bronchitis are well known correlates of high cigarette consumption. Adult males in the Dublin area smoked 36 per cent more cigarettes than rural men in 1971, and alcohol expenditure was 48 per cent higher, per capita, in urban than rural households in 1973 (Ward, Healy and Dean, 1978). This study was conducted more than a decade ago, and conditions may well have changed in the intervening years.

Neither mortality nor morbidity data are recorded on a socio-economic class basis (except psychiatric admissions, discussed below). There is some crude evi-

---

[32] Among women, no excess prevalence exceeded 150 per cent, but the following exceeded 125 per cent: pneumonia, 145 per cent; benign and unspecified neoplasms, 143 per cent; cancer of trachea, bronchus and lung, 141 per cent; and bronchitis, emphysema and asthma, 129 per cent. Thus Dublin women have higher rates of respiratory illness than rural women, though the difference is not so great as among men. In 1971, adult females in the Dublin area smoked 90 per cent more cigarettes than rural women (Ward, Healy and Dean, 1978).

Table 3.7: *Hospital in-patient enquiry: number of discharges and average duration of stay by diagnostic category, 1980*

Diagnosis	Number of cases	%	Average duration of stay
Accidents, poisoning, and violence	50,650	13.6	8.1
Diseases of the respiratory system	39,510	10.6	11.4
Symptoms and ill-defined conditions	36,627	9.8	7.8
Special admissions and consultations	33,845	9.1	5.7
Diseases of the digestive system	35,062	9.4	9.3
Diseases of the circulatory system	33,539	9.0	17.1
Diseases of the genito-urinary system	27,690	7.4	7.6
Neoplasms	18,383	4.9	15.9
Diseases of the nervous system and sense organs	20,415	5.5	10.5
Infective and parasitic diseases	13,615	3.7	12.4
Diseases of the musculo-skeletal system and connective tissue	15,041	4.0	15.4
Diseases of the skin and subcutaneous tissue	9,977	2.7	8.1
Endocrine, nutritional and metabolic diseases	8,553	2.3	11.8
Congenital anomalies	6,890	1.8	10.6
Diseases of the blood and blood forming organs	3,715	1.0	9.2
Miscellaneous	19,387	5.2	8.8
Total	372,899	100.0	10.2

Note: The Hospital In-Patient Enquiry does not cover all discharges from hospitals. See Table 3.6.
Source: Hospital In-Patient Enquiry, Medico-Social Research Board.

dence pointing to higher prevalences of certain conditions among persons of lower incomes. These include diseases of the digestive system; neoplasms; diseases of the respiratory system; diseases of the circulatory system; and accidents, poisonings and violence.[33] There is also independent evidence pointing to higher rates of heart disease among lower socio-economic groups (Mulcahy, Graham, Hickey and Daly, 1980).

In 1983, approximately 4,000 women giving addresses in Ireland had legal

[33]These are conditions reported at least one-third more frequently in HIPE than in comparable reports from the Voluntary Health Insurance Board, the latter being drawn from a somewhat higher socio-economic group, though the two groups substantially overlap (see Tussing, 1982c).

abortions performed in England. Nearly 60 per cent were from County Dublin, though only about one-third of Irish women aged 15–29 lived in Co. Dublin at the time of the 1981 Census (Medico-Social Research Board, 1984).

In 1980, there were 27,098 reported admissions to psychiatric hospitals and units of general hospitals,[34] approximately one admission for every 124 persons. Over one-fourth of the admissions (26 per cent) were for the diagnosed conditions alcoholism or alcoholic psychosis. Nearly as many, 24 per cent, were for schizophrenia and 21 per cent were for manic-depressive psychosis. The Medico-Social Research Board (1981) reports on admission rates per 100,000 population, by socio-economic group, as established by the reported occupation of the head of household. Reported admission rates are strongly associated with social class. The unskilled manual rate of 1,621.6 admissions per 100,000 population, dominated by the same three conditions (led however by schizophrenia rather than alcoholism), implies one admission for every 62 persons in this group. Their rate is more than twice the national average. In descending order, the three socio-economic groups with the next highest admission rates were other non-manual (1,057.7 per 100,000); other agricultural (975.1); an intermediate non-manual (950.3). These are also relatively low socio-economic groups. It is clear that reported admission to psychiatric hospital or unit is consistently and significantly inversely related to socio-economic status (Medico-Social Research Board, 1981).

Irish emigrants to England show a similar pattern of psychiatric admissions, decidedly different from that of UK residents. "Irish male immigrants had twice and female immigrants 1.7 times the expected number of first admissions to psychiatric hospitals in South-East England in 1976 when expected number was based on the age- and sex-standardised rates of first admission of the population born in the United Kingdom living in the region. Admission for alcoholism and alcohol psychosis was five times higher in men and four times higher in women, and for schizophrenia 2.4 times as high in both sexes ... Marital state, socio-economic group, and occupation may partly account for the high number of admissions for alcoholism and schizophrenia ..." (Dean, Downing and Shelley, 1981).

A health and mental health problem of significant though localised proportions which has apparently arisen only recently is the high use of addictive illegal narcotic drugs in areas of high unemployment and disadvantage in Dublin City, especially in the North-Central region (Medico-Social Research Board, 1982).

The following stand out in our review of Irish mortality and morbidity: Life

---

[34]The psychiatric survey was said to be nearly complete in 1979. All psychiatric units and hospitals, with the exception of a unit in one voluntary general hospital reported (O'Hare and Walsh, 1979). "The year of the survey, 1977, was the first year since the War in which there was an overall decline in the number of admissions to psychiatric hospitals. This is partly attributed to a greater provision of community-based psychiatric services. It could be that higher socio-economic groups make more use of these facilities and this could account for the relative drop in their rates of admission," (Tussing, 1982c).

expectancy at birth is high in Ireland, though the level for women is the lowest in the European Community. Infant and maternal mortality are low and seem to be falling. Like other European countries, Ireland has experienced significant improvements in infant mortality, and in the toll of infectious and parasitic diseases, in the twentieth century. The death rate for cancer is the lowest in the Community, but this is the most rapidly growing cause of death in this country. The second fastest rising cause is motor vehicle accidents. Heart disease is the single leading cause of death, cancer the second and respiratory disease is the third. The last stands out as uniquely high in both Ireland and Britain. Respiratory illness seems to be suffered in Ireland more by low- than high-income persons, and more by urban than rural populations. Cancers in general and accidents and violence also appear to be suffered disproportionately by members of lower-socio-economic groups, as are all reported causes of admission to psychiatric hospitals or units. In addition, lung cancer and cirrhosis of the liver appear to be more prevalent in urban than in rural populations.

Chapter 4

THE IRISH SYSTEM OF MEDICAL CARE

The Irish system of medical care can be described in the following terms. It is a "dual" system, with both public and private components. The two parts contain large elements of cross-subsidisation, and the nominally private side is financed largely, perhaps mainly, by government. The public side is decentralised in administration, at least far more than is common elsewhere in the Irish public service. However, as the regional Health Boards have virtually no independent sources of income, and receive practically all their funds from the Department of Health, the system is more centralised than in many other countries having local health authorities. The private system has an effectively functioning Voluntary Health Insurance Board, a state-sponsored body.

The public scheme provides for three classes of eligibility, with the number of free services or the extent of subsidisation depending (mainly) on one's income. It is intended that no one be deprived of needed care for economic reasons, and this goal is close to being met.

The standard of care is high, and medical personnel have available to them all modern methods and materials, though there are specific problems, e.g., those arising out of the organisation of general practice and out of the age of some of the main hospitals. Primary care is provided by general practitioners; specialists are seen mainly on referral; and though lip-service has been paid to community care, the system remains strongly a hospital-centred one.

As the foregoing implies, the Irish system of medical care consists in fact of a number of constituent sub-systems: an organisation structure for the public health services, centred on regional Health Boards; a scheme of entitlement to publicly financed services; a structure for private care; a scheme for private, voluntary insurance; and a system for the delivery of medical care services. These constituent sub-systems will be examined, in turn, below.

A. *The Organisation of Public Health Services*

Figure 4.1 shows the administrative structure of the health services. The Minister for Health is a member of the Government, which draws its authority from the Houses of Parliament (the Oireachtas). He or she heads a Department of

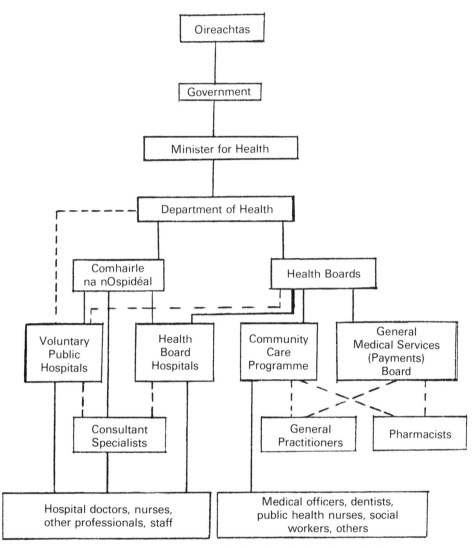

Figure 4.1: *Organisation of Public Health Services of Ireland.*

Health which has primarily a planning, budgeting and reporting function, and which itself spends only about one per cent of current public health outlays. Services on the ground are provided by and through the eight regional Health Boards (Hensey, 1979). This description probably understates the strong controlling power the Department has over the Health Boards and other health agencies.

Each Health Board runs a hospital programme and a community care programme. Community care consists of preventative health services, the general practitioner services, dental and public health nursing services and social work. Most of these are operated at a local (usually county) level rather than at a Health Board level. The Director of Community Care must be a qualified doctor, and under him or her there are employed medical officers, dentists, public health nurses, health inspectors, community welfare officers, social workers, midwives and home helps.

In addition, general practitioner (GP) services come under Community Care. The GPs are not, however, Health Board employees, but are independent professionals who provide services on a fee-for-service basis. Those persons eligible for free GP care (see below) have their fees paid for them by the state. Claims for fees in respect of services provided are submitted monthly by doctors to the General Medical Services (Payments) Board and doctors are paid directly by the Board. The Board is nationwide, established jointly by the eight Health Boards. The GMS (Payments) Board also pays pharmacists who dispense pharmaceutical medicines for the same clients. (Broken lines to GPs and pharmacists in Figure 4.1 indicate that they are not public employees but rather independent, private professionals, even though they are part of the system providing public medical care.)[35]

There are, broadly speaking, three kinds of hospitals in Ireland. Health Board hospitals are owned, financed and operated by the Health Boards. Voluntary Public Hospitals are owned in the main by religious orders and receive their budgets directly from the Department of Health. Private hospitals, discussed later, do not appear in Figure 4.1. Within the Health Boards, a distinction is made between general hospitals and special hospitals, the latter including hospitalisation for psychiatric, geriatric and mentally handicapped patients. Consultant specialists in Voluntary Hospitals, though they may receive a salary (as discussed later), like to think of themselves as independent professionals with contractual rather than employer-employee relationships with the hospitals. Junior doctors, nurses, physiotherapists, and other hospital staff are, on the other hand, Health Board (or Voluntary Hospital) employees.

The one remaining box in Figure 4.1 is that of Comhairle na nÓspidéal, the hospital council, which regulates the types and numbers of consultants appointed to Voluntary Public and Health Board hospitals, and also acts as a general advisory body on the hospital services. The line running from Comhairle na nOspideal to consultant specialists in Figure 4.1 might well be thought of as running in the opposite direction, as the consultants dominate the council. The Department of Health seems inclined to establish independent agencies to carry out aspects of its work which for one reason or another it feels cannot be done

---

[35]Certain former permanent District Medical Officers have guaranteed incomes and a small number claim salaries instead of fees. Other such doctors have guaranteed incomes but opt for fee payment. In addition to fees paid by the GMS (Payment) Board, fees to former District Medical Officers and allowances to other doctors participating in the scheme are paid by Health Boards. See Note 47.

within the departmental framework. Other examples, besides Comhairle, include the Health Education Bureau, the Post-graduate Medical and Dental Council and the National Social Service Board.

As will be discussed in Chapter 5, hospitals account for approximately 75 per cent of public health expenditures (general hospitals something over 50 per cent, and the special hospitals something over 20 per cent); Community Health Services about 15 per cent; other Community Care and Preventive Services together account for another approximately 5 per cent; and administrative costs about 5 per cent.

The Department of Health provides the Health Boards with annual budgets from which they make their own allocations. The Department also provides money directly to Voluntary Hospitals, "on behalf of" Health Boards. (This relationship between Health Boards and Voluntary Hospitals explains the broken line between them in Figure 4.1.)

The System of Entitlement

The Irish health care system provides a complex system of entitlement to free or subsidised medical care. Basically, there are three groups of services or benefits. There are, first, those to which all persons, regardless of income or situation, are entitled. There are, second, some additional services or benefits to which all but approximately the highest 15 per cent in the income distribution are entitled; and there are, third, the comprehensive benefits — consisting of virtually all medical care services, provided free of charge at the point of use — to which the lowest third of the income distribution are entitled.

The pattern of entitlement is shown in Figure 4.2. (Figure 4.2 is intended to show the principal services and does not include every type of service and there are qualifications to some of the items shown. See the current leaflet published by the Department of Health, "Summary of Health Services." For a useful handbook on entitlement, see Gormley, 1980.) Note that everyone in Ireland is entitled to free hospital accommodation, in a public ward only. In addition, all persons are eligible for free specialist out-patient services, including x-ray and diagnostic procedures, if these are carried out at a public hospital, even though the person may be a patient in a private room, ward, or hospital. There are free services available to victims of infectious diseases, and chronic illnesses, and to children suffering from mental illness, mental handicap, or acute leukaemia. In addition, all persons are entitled to assistance with the cost of pharmaceutical medicines, though the form of assistance varies with category of eligibility. Persons in Category I are provided all prescribed medicines free of charge, while those in Categories II and III are eligible for subsidies.[36] The benefits available to

---

[36]As of March, 1980, households bore the cost of the first £8 of prescribed medicines in a month and were reimbursed by their Health Boards for an outlay in excess of that amount. As of 1984, the refund was the excess over £28.

Figure 4.2: *Medical care entitlement under the Health Services – Categories I, II,
and III**

Category I　　　　　　　　　Category II　　　　　　　　Category III

General practitioner
care.

- - - - - - - - - - - - - - - - - - -

Dental, Ophthalmic, and
aural services.

Maternity: medical, surgical, and midwifery
  services.

Infant welfare service.

- -

Consultant specialist services, out-patient
  and in-patient.

Prescribed medicines:　│　Prescribed medicines: subsidy toward cost of
provided free.　　　　　│　　those not provided free (below).

Hospital accomodation (exclusive of doctors' fees) in public ward of
  public hospital.

Specialist out-patient services including x-ray and diagnostic procedures (excluding consultants' fees - see above) if carried out at a
  public hospital (even for patients of private hospitals).

- -

Infectious diseases: immunisation, hospital treatment.

Chronic illness: all persons, prescribed medicines; children only,
  certain illnesses, hospital treatment.

Mental handicap, mental illness: children only, hospital services.

Mental illness and acute leukaemia: Children only, prescribed
  medicines.

- -

Infant screening and child health examinations.

*Category I eligibility covers roughly the lowest third of the income distribution, and Category III
roughly the highest 15 per cent. See text.

all, including the drugs subsidy scheme, are the only benefits available to persons in Category III.[37]

There are two differences between Categories II and III. The main one is that persons in Category II receive free consultant specialist services, while those in Category III must be private patients of consultant specialists, whether on an in-patient or an out-patient basis, except of course for the infectious or chronic illnesses for which all services are free to all. In addition, maternity care is available from GPs under the mother and infant scheme without charge to persons in Category II but not to those in Category III.

Those in Category I receive all the services available to those in Category II, and in addition receive free GP care and dental, ophthalmic, and aural services, including the cost of dentures, eyeglasses and hearing aids. In addition, as noted above, the full cost of prescription medicines, and not merely a partial subsidy, is provided to persons in Category I.

In general, persons in all three Categories use the same facilities and see the same doctors. Persons in Category I are entitled to choose their own general practitioners, and most GPs with public patients have private patients as well, and vice versa. However, it has sometimes been argued that GPs spend less time with public patients.[38] Private patients pay fees which are, in general, roughly 1.6 times those paid on behalf of public patients. Private patients of consultant specialists are almost always treated by the consultant personally, while public patients may well be treated by a junior doctor working under the consultant. Public patients may have to wait longer for admission to hospital, while private patients can "queue-jump", though our survey showed no difference in wait for admission either by eligibility category or Voluntary Health Insurance cover (see Appendix Table A.42).

As indicated in Figure 4.2, persons in Category I are eligible for free dental care from dental officers employed by the Health Boards or from dentists in private practice who render their services on a fee-per-item basis to the Health Boards. In addition, children are eligible, where the dental problem came to light in a school health examination, or at a health clinic or health centre.[39] However, patterns of eligibility for free or subsidised dental care are more complex than this indicates. Complications arise from two facts. (1) There never have been enough Health Board dentists to provide a comprehensive dental service to all who are eligible. Hence services are provided on a priority basis to such groups as pre-school and National School children, nursing and expectant mothers, the aged and the handicapped. Those with Category I eligibility falling outside these groups find that as a practical matter they cannot avail of dental

---

[37]Tax relief for VHI premiums and for most unreimbursed private medical expenditures, discussed somewhat later, constitute important forms of public aid for medical care not shown in Figure 4.2.

[38]See Note 20, Chapter 2.

[39]The children eligible are those referred under the Health Act, 1970, broadly speaking pre-school and National School children.

services for which they are nominally eligible. (2) There is another scheme for dental care, operated by the department of Social Welfare. Workers (but not their dependants) qualify through Social Welfare contributions and receive free or subsidised care from a private dentist who is on the Department's Dental Panel.[40] Thus, many persons with Category II or III eligibility qualify for or receive free dental care.

Category II eligibility is determined quite differently from Category I. Category I eligibility is based on income, number of dependants, household expenses and exceptional expenses involved in travel to work. In addition, any other consideration such as chronic illness can be taken into account at the discretion of the CEO (Chief Executive Offices) of the Health Board. In Category II, only earnings are considered. Thus a single person with a given earnings and a family of ten with the same earnings are deemed to have the same need. This approach may create hardships for a large family with earnings above the Category II eligibility threshold, who have large consultant specialist bills. As no adjustments are made for living or commuting expenses, the difficulty could be acute for some families with large household costs, etc. It seems more appropriate to take family size into account.

If there is only one earner in the family, the Category II limit applies to that person, and eligibility extends to everyone in the family. But if both husband and wife have incomes, each one's eligibility is determined by her or his own earnings, and the children are deemed to be dependants of the parent with the higher income. This creates the anomaly that should a spouse take work, thus raising family income, he or she might thereby gain Category II eligibility previously lacking because the other spouse's income was too high. In other words, a rise in income can be the occasion for a gain in entitlement.

As of June 1983, the Category II eligibility cut-off was £11,000. Let us assume a hypothetical family consisting of husband, wife and children, with £12,000 annual income. If one parent earned the entire £12,000, no one would be eligible under Category II. If one parent earned £9,000 and the other £3,000 then the whole family would be in Category II. In Chapter 8, some changes in this scheme are suggested.

Beginning in 1983, farm income has been assessed factually for both Category I and Category II eligibility.

Among our 1980 survey respondents, approximately 33 per cent were covered in Category I, 49 per cent in Category II and 18 per cent in Category III. However, these distributions did not apply to individual age groups. For example, in the 65 and over age category, 76 per cent were in Category I, 21 per cent in Category II and only 3 per cent in Category III.

---

[40]Persons under 21 years of age need at least 26 social welfare contributions, and persons over 21 need at least 156 contributions, of which 26 are in the year immediately preceding the claim. Filling, scalings and extractions are free, while dentures, crowns, inlays and bridges are subsidised (Gormley, 1980).

There were also significant regional differences in the distributions of eligibility. Category I eligibility varied from 20 per cent (in the Eastern) to 46 per cent (in the Mid-Western). The Category II range was smaller, varying from 37 per cent (in the North-Eastern) to 54 per cent (in the Eastern). Category III representation ranged from only 7 per cent (in both the Midland and the Western) to a high of 26 (in the Eastern). The Eastern Health Board area was the least typical in the country, having either the highest or lowest in each category. By contrast the South-Eastern area was the most representative, with its profile neatly matching that of the Republic as a whole. (See Appendix Tables A.36 and A.37 for details.)

The Private Sector

When we refer to the "private sector" of the Irish medical care system, we refer to that part in which fees or charges are imposed, and where patients may not avail of the service unless they pay for them. Public bodies can act in the private sector (e.g., one might take a private or semi-private room in a public hospital), and private providers can offer services in the public sector (e.g., GPs, who are independent private professionals, provide services in the Medical Card population). As used here, "private sector" does not necessarily imply that the fee or charge covers the full economic cost, average or marginal, of providing the service. Such a strict definition would mean that the private sector would probably not exist in Ireland, as subsidies to the private sector, as defined here, are quite important.

The private sector, so defined consists of the following:
— General practitioner care for persons in Categories II and III (roughly two-thirds of the population).
— Dental, ophthalmic and aural services for about 30 per cent of the population.
— Maternity care for women in Category III.
— Consultant specialist services for persons in Category III.
— Maternity care, consultant specialist services and other services for persons eligible for free care but who elect private or semi-private accommodation.
— Prescription medicines for persons in Categories II and III. (As noted, significant subsidies apply; hence one might wish to regard the "private sector" component as consisting of the net cost to consumers.)

Subsidies to the private sector are discussed presently. Estimates of private household medical care expenditures in 1980 appear in the next chapter.

Seven per cent of households in our survey reported that other bodies or organisations, mainly employers, provided them with help toward their medical care costs. Estimates of the money amount of this aid, which forms part of private medical care expenditures, appear in the next chapter.

VHI: Voluntary Health Insurance

Private medical insurance, i.e., insurance purchased by individuals against private medical costs, is available through the Voluntary Health Insurance Board. The VHI, as it is known, is a state-sponsored body, organised by the state, and run by a Board whose members are appointed by the Minister for Health. It is characteristic of the blending of private and public sector in Ireland that private insurance for private medical bills is provided by a state enterprise. The VHI by virtue of its enabling legislation (Voluntary Health Insurance Act, 1957) has a virtual monopoly on private health insurance in Ireland.

Approximately 25 per cent of the population of Ireland are covered by VHI insurance (see Table 4.1). This coverage is not uniform across the categories of eligibility under the Health Services, however. Only about 4.6 per cent of persons with Category I eligibility, and 19.8 per cent of those with Category II eligibility have cover, according to our survey. By contrast, 77.7 per cent of those with Category III eligibility have cover. Those with only Category III eligibility, and without VHI cover, amount to only about 4 per cent of the population. Thus when both health services eligibility and VHI cover are considered, 96 per cent of the population are assured of first-penny protection against cost of hospitalisation, both with respect to hospital charges and with respect to doctors' fees.

Membership in VHI is proportionately higher among persons in Category III, not only because they must pay their own consultant specialist bills, in-patient and out-patient, but also presumably because they have a higher demand for private care.

Since the inception of VHI, cover has concentrated on hospital bills. Under the scheme introduced in April 1979, coverage has two sections. One covers doctors' fees when subscribers are hospitalised. Coverage is so designed that in the

Table 4.1: *VHI Cover by category of Health Services eligibility, 1980, per cent of population by age and sex*

	Category I	Category II	Category III	All persons
Males	4.3	17.4	77.2	24.2
0–14	2.5	17.0	75.9	27.9
15–44	8.8	16.0	74.9	25.1
45–64	1.4	17.3	87.6	27.0
65+	3.3	31.0	51.4	11.9
Females	4.8	22.6	78.2	26.8
0–14	2.7	18.0	84.0	31.4
15–44	10.4	22.8	68.4	30.0
45–64	2.0	27.8	78.8	25.6
65+	4.1	32.8	20.0	9.8
All Persons	4.6	19.8	77.7	25.5

vast majority of cases doctors' bills are covered in full.[41] The doctors' fees section of benefits can be purchased jointly with a hospital plan, or separately under the name, "Public Ward Scheme." Only about 3 per cent of subscribers opt for that scheme, however; that is, about 97 per cent choose one or another of three hospital plans. This implies that most people who buy VHI cover do want private (or semi-private) hospital accommodation and private consultant care. Under the three hospital plans, subscribers are covered, respectively, for charges for semi-private or private rooms in public hospitals; private rooms in public hospitals or semi-private rooms in private hospitals and nursing homes; and private rooms in any hospital or nursing home. When a hospital plan is purchased, the VHI guarantees to cover 100 per cent of hospital maintenance charges (at the type of accommodation chosen). Thus the VHI normally provides its subscribers with first-penny coverage of hospitalisation. That is, when a VHI subscriber enters hospital, she or he can be confident that the VHI will cover all costs. In other countries, by contrast, health insurance funds usually require some form of subscriber cost-sharing, normally either a flat charge unrelated to the size of the bill; a percentage share; or a deductible. We will comment further on this point in the next chapter.

In addition to hospital maintenance, the hospital plan section of coverage also provides for a number of out-patient benefits. "Day surgery", i.e., surgery performed without admission to hospital for an overnight stay, is covered on the same terms as in-patient surgery, i.e., on a first-penny basis. General practitioner and out-patient specialist fees, and prescription medicines to the extent not provided or subsidised by the Health Board, are covered subject to an annual deductible and an annual ceiling.[42] The deductible has the property that before it is reached, medical expenses are born in full, and after it is reached, they are wholly free.

For an analysis of VHI benefits, see the Report of the Joint Committee on State-Sponsored Bodies (1980). In it, the committee commented:

> The structure of the ... scheme, together with its active and successful promotion, may generate an increase in demand for semi private and private rooms in public hospitals, and rooms in private hospitals, so that at any given time the demand may exceed the supply.

In other words, the more successful the Board is in selling its policy, the less likely any individual member is to receive the benefits contracted for. This is so, of course, only if new private and semi-private capacity is not added to the Irish hospital system; continued rapid growth in VHI membership certainly could

---

[41]As of 1983, subscribers were required to purchase 18 units of cover in this section and could buy as many as 30. The VHI recommends at least 24. As an example, each unit provided £1 of cover for a specialist consultation.

[42]As of 1983, the deductible was £120 for a family and £72 for an individual; the annual ceiling was £800, £1,000 and £1,200, respectively, in the three plans.

translate into the provision — mainly by the state — of more such private accommodation. Our survey revealed that, for whatever reason, half of
hospitalised patients with VHI cover in 1980 were in rooms containing five or
more beds (Appendix Table A.40).

Though the VHI is a state enterprise, the state has never provided it with any
direct financial assistance, nor does it stand ready to underwrite losses. The state
does, however, provide the VHI with an important form of indirect assistance.
Subscribers are permitted to deduct premia, in full, against taxable income. The
Joint Committee commented,

> The effect of this provision is the same, in terms of cost to the Exchequer and
> in aid to VHI and its members, as an explicit cash grant equal to the
> amount of tax reduction experienced by the members. No estimate exists,
> however, of the amount. The Deputy General Manager of the VHI told the
> Committee that he believed there was a "substantial sum involve." To any
> individual subscriber, the cash value of the income tax provision is equal to
> the amount of the subscription premium multiplied by the subscriber's
> marginal income tax rate, be it 25, 35, 45, 55, or 60 per cent. Because the
> VHI draws its membership disproportionately from among those with
> higher incomes . . . , it is fair to assume that many subscribers have relatively
> high marginal income tax rates. Hence it is conservative to estimate that
> income tax relief provides an indirect subvention to the VHI of at least one-
> third of its subscription income.

(Income tax rates have since been revised and are now 35, 45, 55, 60 and 65
per cent; the implicit subsidy is presumably somewhat higher.)

We argue in the next chapter that the VHI is now too large, in its membership
subscriptions, its excessive growth in part a consequence of indirect subsidies.

There are some important economic consequences to be noted of the VHI's
monopoly in Ireland. According to the literature on the economics of health
insurance, there are two predictable differences between competitive and
monopoly situations in the provision of health insurance (P. J. Feldstein, 1979).

Where there is competition, sub-groups in the population with a low probability of a claim (the low-user population) pay lower premia than those with a
high probability of making a claim (the high-user population). For example,
premium levels often depend on age. In the USA, smokers are often required to
pay higher premia than non-smokers. Insurance companies are forced by
competition to equalise the benefit-premium ratios (the ratios of total benefits
paid to total premia collected) for major sub-groups in the population.

By contrast, monopoly health insurance underwriters tend to establish a
single set of premia which apply to the whole population — a so-called "community rate". This is precisely what is done by VHI. In that case, benefit-
premium ratios for sub-groups are not equalised. Instead, the low-user population has a low benefit-premium ratio and the high-user population has a high
benefit-premium ratio (probably higher than 1.0). Hence there is a redistribu-

tion from the former to the latter. While one effect is probably to put health insurance within reach of more people, and in particular to make it accessible to more aged people, this pricing policy of health insurance has been criticised by economists on efficiency grounds:

> Depending upon the price elasticity of demand for insurance, low-user groups would, under community rating, demand less insurance. Like an excise tax that is placed on some goods and services and hence distorts their relative prices, a community rate is a tax on the insurance premium of a low-risk person (Feldstein).

The second difference between competition and monopoly in the provision of health insurance is that where the former prevails, the public will normally be presented with choices regarding the benefits for which they would like to buy insurance and regarding the amount of co-payment (deductibles, co-insurance). Monopoly insurers, by contrast, are more likely to offer a single plan or "package" for all insured. Like the community rating system, the single plan also involved implicit patterns of cross-subsidisation.

As noted, the VHI offers three plans — A, B and C — for different types of hospital accommodation. In addition, they offer the so-called "public ward scheme" which only provides for doctors' fees. These options provide an extremely narrow choice set, exactly as health insurance theory predicts. Moreover, as the plans A, B and C are not separately funded, there may be cross-subsidisation of one plan by another. This could include subsidisation of subscribers generally using private hospitals (Plan C and some Plan B subscribers) by those generally using public hospitals (Plan A and some Plan B subscribers).

Subsidisation of the Private Sector

As has been noted, higher-income persons do not have the same entitlement to the state health services that medium and low-income persons have. There is a three-tiered system of benefits, tapering away as income rises. In spite of that fact, the state may in Ireland be more generous with the upper-income person with respect to medical care than in, e.g., the UK, where the National Health Service is available to all, irrespective of income, as paradoxical as that may sound.

The reason is that in the UK, the NHS endeavours to make a sharp separation between public and private sectors and to avoid aiding the latter. Hence the state aids high income persons in the UK only to the extent that they use services which are common to all. (However, according to the UK's "Black Report" (Policy and Planning Unit, 1980), high-income persons make more, and more effective, use of the NHS than do low-income persons.) In Ireland, while high-income persons do not qualify for the whole range of public services they can avail of substantial subsidies for private services. Private medicine thrives in Ireland in part because it receives much public aid.

It is beyond the scope of the present study to make quantitative estimates of these subsidies. Such estimates are in principle possible and would be a useful research topic. Here we will content ourselves with a listing and description of the main subsidy elements.

The principal subsidies are in private hospitalisation, i.e., where persons are private patients of the consultant specialist, and take accommodation in private or semi-private rooms in public hospitals, or any accommodation in private hospitals.

If such patients choose private or semi-private rooms in public hospitals, the room charge does not recover the cost incurred by the hospital in providing the room. The difference is an implicit subsidy. There is also a small subvention to private nursing home and private psychiatric hospital care.[43]

Public hospitals are today built and expanded on the basis of state capital grants. The pay of junior doctors, nurses, other professional and non-professional staff comes from the state. These facilities are put at the disposal of consultant specialists, to use for their private patients, without charge to the doctor. It is understood to be an implicit part of the remuneration of consultant specialists who work in public hospitals that the consultant's private patients will be served by hospital equipment and staff.

As was indicated in Figure 4.2, private patients receive free out-patient specialist services, including X-ray and diagnostic procedures, from public hospitals, even if they are patients at private hospitals.

Finally, there are two important kinds of tax relief available to private patients. First, there is tax relief on VHI premia, by which according to the conservative estimate quoted above of the Joint Committee on State-Sponsored Bodies the state provides the VHI and its subscribers with an amount equal to at least one-third of its subscription income. Secondly, tax relief is available on unreimbursed medical expenses in excess of £50 for an individual or £100 for a family.[44] This provision seems little known, and in 1979 only 1,681 refunds were made to claimants, for a total of £296,342 (Dáil Proceedings, 28 May, 1980).

Given the foregoing, an educated guess is that the state pays, directly or indirectly, over half the cost of private care.

---

[43]As of 1983, the following schedule of daily room charges prevailed for private and semi-private patients in public hospitals: Health Board regional hospitals and Voluntary Public teaching hospitals, private, £55 and semi-private, £40; Health Board County Hospital and Voluntary Public non-teaching hospitals, private £40 and semi-private £33; and Health Board District Hospital, private £21 and semi-private £16. (Source: Department of Health.) As of 1983, the subsidies to daily charges were as follows: homes providing nursing care only, £4.75; mainly for old people, £4.50; and private psychiatric hospitals, teaching, £2.25; and non-teaching, £1.30 except no subsidy for short-stay patients. (Source: Department of Health.)

[44]Unlike the tax relief on VHI premia, that on unreimbursed medical expenses is retrospective. Taxpayers file a form (MED. 1) and receive a refund — from the Inspector of taxes, not from the Department of Health — equal to their own tax rates times the eligible expense, after the deductible amount. For purposes of this provision, the following are not considered to be qualifying health expenses: routine maternity care, routine ophthalmic treatment, or routine dental treatment.

B. *Delivery of Medical Care*

Medical care systems have been described as having four levels (Rutten, 1978). At the first level, that of primary care, there stand the general practitioners (see Figure 4.3). GPs provide two kinds of services. They provide a large fraction of out-patient care, to patients with more common and routine problems or conditions — infectious illnesses, orthopaedic problems, routine obstetrics, etc. The GP also "plays an important role as the person who decides whether or not a patient will be treated at a higher and more costly level of care" (Rutten, 1978). In other words, patients typically enter the system at the first level. Most go no further, but a fraction are referred to a specialist at the second level. According to our survey, 7.1 per cent of 1980 GP consultations involved a referral to another doctor. Certain specialists provide primary care. That is,

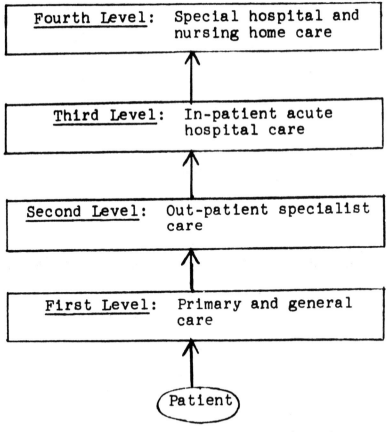

Source: Adapted from Rutten, 1978.

Figure 4.3: *Levels of the Medical Care System*

patients may go to them directly, without first seeing a GP. These primary-care specialists include paediatricians, gynaecologists, obstetricians and psychiatrists.

At the second level is out-patient specialist care. This care is usually provided in a clinic or office located at a hospital, by the consultant specialist or by a junior hospital doctor working under the former's direction. In 1980, according to our survey, the average person in Ireland had 3.6 consultations with a general practitioner and 0.4 consultations with a specialist. However, as we will see in Chapters 6 and 7, where utilisation is discussed, there is considerable variability in utilisation, according to age, sex, category of eligibility under the Health Services, etc.

Table 4.2 shows Ireland with 12.0 doctors per 10,000 population, though adjusting Eurostat data to correct the population estimate would raise the figure to 12.6. Either figure places Ireland near the bottom of the European Community, with only Luxembourg reporting a lower ratio of doctors to population. It must be emphasised that this does not necessarily reflect against the Irish medical care system. The "Parkinson's Law" phenomenon discussed in Chapter 2 suggests that an increase in supply of physicians could generate more "need" for physicians' services. There seems to be no basis for asserting that there is a doctor shortage in Ireland, though there may be problems with the geographic distribution of doctors, with the North-Western area at a particular disadvantage.

Non-doctor health professionals — dentists, nurses, social workers, opticians,

Table 4.2: *Doctors, nurses and dentists per 10,000 population, European Community, 1976*

State	Doctors per 10,000 population	Nurses per 10,000 population	Dentists per 10,000 population
German Federal Republic	19.9	30.0	5.2
France	16.3	40.2	5.1
Italy	22.5	36.0	(c)
Netherlands	16.6	31.0	3.3
Belgium	20.4	35.9[a]	3.1
Luxembourg	11.3	47.2[b]	3.2
United Kingdom	13.8	41.5	2.4
Ireland	12.0	59.1	2.7
Denmark	19.5	58.8	8.8
Ireland's Rank (from lowest)	2	9	2[d]

Notes: [a] 1971; [b] 1970; [c] Not available; [d] Rank of eight; (Italy not available.)
Source: Eurostat, Social Indicators for the European Community, 1960–1978.

chiropodists, etc. — also practice in Ireland, some on a referral basis, some providing primary care, some as supporting staff. Table 4.2 shows Ireland to have the highest ratio of nurses to population in the European Community. This ranking probably reflects, in part, the hospitals orientation of the Irish system, as compared with community care, and probably also reflects some substitution of nursing for physician personnel. Table 4.2 also shows Ireland to be second lowest (after the United Kingdom) in ratio of dentists to population. There are acknowledged deficiencies in the Irish dental care system, with an inadequate number of dentists overall, especially Health Board dentists.

The third level of the medical care system consists of acute or general hospitals. Ideally, patients enter hospitals as in-patients only on the basis of a referral by a specialist. The fourth level consists of long-stay or special hospitals, and nursing homes, and similar residential facilities. Comparative statistics do not report on hospitals in precisely this manner. Table 4.3 shows Ireland to have among the lowest ratios in the European Community of hospital beds (other than psychiatric) to population, but to be among the highest in the rate of hospital admissions. These seemingly contradictory statistics require efficient use of beds, and Table 4.3 does show Ireland to be lowest in average stay and highest in cases treated per bed per year (both in ties with Denmark). On the other hand, Ireland leads the Community, and by a very wide mark, in ratio of psychiatric beds to population.[45]

These statistics, which are from *Eurostat*, have been criticised on the criterion of comparability. Irish-UK comparisons from Table 4.3 are particularly suspect, as the Irish figure is limited to acute beds only (including maternity), while the UK figure includes nursing homes. Table 4.4, which was compiled by James Raftery of the National Economic and Social Council, and published in NESC No. 73 (1983), compares Ireland (i.e., the Republic) with Northern Ireland, England, Scotland and Wales, by type of bed use. Ireland has more acute beds per head of population than England, Scotland, or Wales, and somewhat fewer than Northern Ireland. Ireland has significantly more long-stay beds, and more beds of all types, per head, than any of the UK countries (NESC No. 73, 1983).

The progress of individual patients through the medical care system does not always follow exactly the idealised four-level model. As noted, according to our survey, 7.1 per cent of all general practitioner consultations in 1980 led to a referral to another doctor (usually a specialist), while 14.1 per cent of all specialist consultations led to a referral to another doctor. Of all specialist consultations, 85 per cent were either return visits or referrals from other doctors; and of first visits (i.e., excluding return visits), 80 per cent were referred by other

---

[45]These statistics need some qualification. Ratios of beds to population have not been adjusted for population age distribution. The patient population in Irish psychiatric hospitals includes a large number of persons who are not mentally ill, viz., mentally handicapped adults and geriatric patients for whom more appropriate facilities are not available. Because of such differences in bed use, international comparisons can be misleading if inappropriate inferences are drawn, e.g., concerning the comparative prevalence of mental illness.

Table 4.3: *Selected indicators of hospital facilities and use, European Community, 1976*

State	Hospital[a] beds per 1,000 population	Hospital[a] admissions per 1,000 population	Average stay in hospital[a] (days)	Cases treated per bed per year[a]	Psychiatric beds per 1,000 population
German Federal Republic	10.0	163	18	17	1.8
France	8.1	168	14	22	2.5[e]
Italy	8.6	171	13	20	2.0[d]
Netherlands	5.2	104	15	20	1.8
Belgium	6.4	(c)	12	(c)	2.7[d]
Luxembourg	7.1	119[d]	13	19	3.8
United Kingdom	8.7[.b]	115[b,e]	22[b]	14[b]	3.0
Ireland	5.8	162	11	28	4.9[d]
Denmark	6.4	172	11	27	2.1
Ireland's Rank (from lowest)	2	4[f]	1/2[g]	8[f]	8

Notes: [a] Excludes psychiatric; [b] Includes nursing homes; [c] Not available; [d] 1975; [e] 1974; [f] Rank of eight (Belgium not available); [g] Tied for first, second.

Source: Eurostat, *Social Indicators for the European Community, 1960–1978.*

Table 4.4: Occupied[a] beds in hospitals and residential centres, numbers per 1,000 population, UK and Ireland, 1979

	England	Wales	Scotland	Northern Ireland	Ireland
Acute specialities[b]	2.1	2.1	2.5	3.5	3.2
	(2.8)	(3.1)	(3.5)	(4.2)	(3.8)
Maternity per 1,000 females aged 15–44[c]	1.4	1.4	1.9	2.2	2.2
	(1.9)	(2.1)	(2.6)	(2.9)	(2.7)
Psychiatric mental illness[d] mental handicap	3.1	3.1	4.7	3.8[g]	5.2
	(3.5)	(3.4)	(5.1)	(4.6)	
Geriatric[e] per 1,000 persons aged 65+	24.7	31.3	30.7	33.3	39.5
Other[f]	—	—	—	—	0.4
Total beds per 1,000 population	9.1	10.3	11.9	11.4[g]	13.5

Notes:
[a] "Occupied" rather than "available" bed population ratios have been used because data on the latter are not collected in all cases. The figures in parentheses show ratios for "available" beds, where possible.
[b] UK data from Regional Trends 1982, HMSO, Table 4.4. Ireland's data from Statistical Information Relevant to the Health Services 1981, Table G1, excluding maternity, psychiatric and geriatric assessment beds, all district hospitals, cottage hospitals and all private hospitals.
[c] UK data as (b). Ireland's data: Statistical Information Relevant to the Health Services.
[d] UK data by combining Table 4.4 and 4.15 Regional Trends 1982. Ireland's statistic was derived by combining Health Board Psychiatric Hospitals and Units, Special Psychiatric Hospitals, acute psychiatric beds, Special Residential Centres for the Mentally Handicapped.
[e] UK data as for (d). Ireland's statistic was derived by combining acute geriatric assessment beds, longstay District Hospitals and the 1980 data on Health Board Geriatric Units (including private and voluntary Hospitals and Homes) in Statistical Information Relevant to the Health Services, 1982.
[f] "Other" comprises Short Stay District Hospitals and Cottage Hospitals, which do not fit easily into any of the other categories.
[g] Northern Ireland's statistic excludes mentally handicapped.
Sources: Health Services: The Implications of Demographic Change, National Economic and Social Council, No. 73, Dublin, November, 1983.

doctors. Of all hospital admissions, 58.5 per cent were originated by general practitioners and only 21.7 per cent by other doctors. Hence GPs appear to have a greater role in hospital admissions than the model would indicate. These and other aspects of utilisation and referral patterns are discussed in greater detail in Chapter 6 (see also Appendix Tables A.28 through A.35).

In the following sections, we will discuss, in turn, general practitioners, specialists, other professionals, general hospitals and special hospitals.

General Practitioners

Though Irish medical care revolves around the General Practitioner, only about 7 per cent of total medical care expenditures (about 5 per cent of public and 15 per cent of private expenditures) are for GP services (see next chapter). Approximately 42 per cent of Irish doctors with medical practices are general practitioners; the remainder are specialists (about a quarter of the total), most of whom base their practices in hospitals, and junior hospital doctors (about a third) (see Table 4.4). These statistics again reflect the strong hospitals orientation of the Irish medical care system and its relative weakness in community primary care.

Results of our survey show that private patients (those in Categories II and III) paid a usual fee averaging £3.75 per consultation in 1980 (see Table 4.4). The mean charge ranged from £3.39 in the North-Western Health Board area to £3.95 in the Eastern. The usual fee for a home visit averaged £5.38, and ranged from £5.03 in the Midland area to £5.70 in the North-Eastern, reflecting a premium of roughly £1.50 for house calls. About 20 per cent of all consultations are home visits.

Fees for public (i.e., Category I) patients, paid by the state, are considerably lower. From October, 1980, to the end of the year, the basic fee was £2.34, or 62 per cent of the average private fee, for office visits within normal hours. A schedule of fees payable for house calls, according to the distance from the doctor's surgery, and the time of day, could bring the fee up to as high as £17.66 (for a call after midnight to a home more than ten miles distant). The 1980 schedule of fees is found in the Appendix. The overall average payment in 1980 per consultation reflecting fee schedules (which changed twice during the year) was only £2.63, about 64 per cent of the overall average private fee of £4.08. Payments are made by the General Medical Services (Payments) Board (See Figure 4.1).[46]

---

[46]As of 1977, 75 per cent of GPs in the General Medical Services choice-of-doctor scheme were paid wholly on a fee basis; another 19 per cent were paid on a fee basis, subject to a guaranteed minimum annual payment; and 6 per cent were paid entirely by salary. Prior to the choice-of-doctor scheme, those persons covered by Medical Cards were treated by District Medical Officers under the so-called dispensary system; when the change took place District Medical Officers were given some choice as to remuneration, and the latter two groups of GPs not paid wholly on a fee basis are former District Medical Officers who chose the remuneration methods indicated. GPs in their private practices work entirely on a fee basis, except for a handful, mentioned earlier, who supply GP services for employers and are remunerated on a capitation basis.

While the fee level was, then, significantly higher for private than public patients, the public rate is in a sense compensated for by the very much higher consulting rates among patients in this category, as we will see in Chapter 6.

Prior to 1972, public patients were treated in dispensaries by salaried practitioners known as District Medical Officers (who also might have had significant private practices). In 1972, the "Choice of Doctor" scheme was introduced, by which public patients were permitted to select their own GPs, subject to the latters' acceptance, from among those in the area who were participants in the scheme. Most doctors who participate have private patients as well. Though these GPs remain private, independent professionals and cannot in any sense be considered as state employees, they do not have free entry into the scheme. Instead, they may enter an area and accept Category I patients only when a vacancy occurs, and in that case the position will be advertised and a number of applicants may compete. GPs are usually limited to 2,000 Medical Card patients, thus helping assure a more even geographical distribution of doctors. This rule is not applied in some (Western) areas with low ratios of doctors to population.

When the Government proposed the "Choice of Doctor" scheme in a White Paper in 1966, it stated a preference for the capitation method of remuneration (see Chapter 2), the technique then found in the UK and two other EEC countries, and recently adopted by Italy as well (Stationery Office, 1966). "For the Department [of Health], capitation had the main advantage of being relatively cheap and difficult to abuse. It was also easy to calculate expenditure from year to year. ... The Department ... disliked fee-for-service because they feared it would prove too expensive and would be abused by unscrupulous doctors" (Barrington, 1973). The organised medical profession argued and lobbied strongly for fee-for-service, and the disagreement held up the major health legislation of which the scheme was a part. In the end only a change of Ministers after a General Election broke the deadlock, in favour of a fee-for-service system.

There are no statistics on utilisation under the dispensary system, but it is generally agreed that the change to the new system of fee-reimbursed private GPs was associated with a major rise in uptake and utilisation. In the first year of its operation, the General Medical Services (Payments) Board proved to be seriously underbudgeted; in other words, predicted utilisation levels, based on scattered bits of data from the dispensary scheme and from private practice, fell short of actual levels.

Table 4.5 shows that in 1975 there were 4.8 general practitioners in Ireland for each 10,000 persons in the population. This ratio varied from 4.3 (in the Mid-Western area) to 6.0 (in the Midland area). These ratios presumably reflect doctors' locational preferences more than policy decisions. The doctor shortage in the North-Western area is rather more severe than that area's reported 4.5 ratio would indicate, as the population in that three-county region (Donegal, Sligo, Leitrim) has a materially higher proportion of aged persons than any other and average distance to the doctor is greater. it is well known that medical

Table 4.5: *Doctors in Ireland and their distribution amongst Health Boards, 1975, together with average fee levels, surgery and home consultations, 1980*

	Eastern	Midland	Mid-Western	North-Eastern	North-Western	South-Eastern	Southern	Western	Ireland
No. of GPs – total	527	112	123	124	87	161	223	156	1,513
GPs – Choice of Doctor scheme	453	84	91	93	87	127	199	142	1,276
No. of Consultants	446	24	51	37	25	143	48	79	853
No. of Junior Doctors	682	34	71	66	35	171	51	149	1,259
No. of Public Health Doctors	36	10	22	10	10	17	15	12	132
Total Doctors	1,691	180	267	237	157	554	275	396	3,757
GPs per 10,000 population	4.9	6.0	4.3	4.7	4.5	4.6	4.6	4.8	4.8
Consultants per 10,000 population	4.2	1.3	1.8	1.4	1.3	2.9	1.4	2.4	2.7
Doctors per 10,000 population	17.1	10.1	9.9	9.7	8.4	11.9	8.4	12.7	12.6
Average GP fee – surgery (£)	3.95	3.53	3.57	3.62	3.39	3.84	3.77	3.44	3.75
Average GP fee – home (£)	5.51	5.03	5.47	5.70	5.12	5.22	5.09	5.53	5.38
Average no. of home visits as per cent of consultations	23.2	17.3	17.7	18.1	22.9	23.7	21.0	16.9	20.6

Source: GP fees and home visits, author's survey. Other data, Department of Health, 1982, and NESC No. 29, 1977.

care needs (and utilisation rates) of aged persons are significantly greater than those of the rest of the population. While 10.7 per cent of Ireland's 1979 population were aged 65 and over, 14.5 per cent of the North-Western area's population (and only 8.4 per cent of the Eastern area's) fell in that age group. The North-Western area has only about half the ratio of GPs to aged population as is found in the Eastern Health Board area.

A price may be paid for the doctor shortage in the North-West area. Our survey shows that people in this area are least likely, by far, to have physical examinations when they do not suspect they are ill pr pregnant. Preventative care is discussed in Chapter 7.

There is general agreement that some aspects of Irish general practice need strengthening. Doctors should make more use of clerical and ancillary or para-medical help. At present, there is no financial incentive for them to do so, as the GMS (Payments) Board will only pay for consultations with GPs and not with other medical or para-medical personnel. Few doctors are involved in any form of group practice. Perhaps 30 per cent of GPs are in practices of two or more doctors.

A study of general practice, initiated and planned by the South of Ireland (i.e., Republic of Ireland) Faculty of the Royal College of General Practitioners, and carried out by GPs in the early 1970s, concluded:

> With few exceptions, general practice in Ireland is a free enterprise type of medical care. It has been described as having cottage industry qualities, and because single-handed practices predominate, consulting hours, quality and variety of services vary enormously ... Shortage of money in many areas leaves the doctor practising from his home, or a rather ramshackle outlying dispensary. Advances in technical medical care, surgery premises, [and] doctor grouping are, of course, developing in the cities, but, by and large, general practitioners outside these areas continue to practice from their homes, using little or no ancillary help, relying heavily on wives for quasi-secretarial and other administrative services.
>
> There are some indications, especially from referral rates, that the level of acute medical care is more haphazard than in the United Kingdom, and Irish doctors still having a too ready recourse to direct hospital admission to solve their patients' problems (Gowen, 1972).

This last comment is in reference to the alleged tendency of some GPs, uncertain of their diagnostic abilities, to refer their non-routine cases to hospital for tests or admission. Whatever the reasons, the Irish rate of admission to hospital is high by European standards, as we have seen (Table 4.3). The situation on the ground is known to have improved since 1972, when the above was written, but in 1976, an authoritative commentator noted,

> The isolation of the Irish general practitioner both geographically and intellectually needs urgent attention (Shannon, 1976).

On the other hand, some GPs are beginning to practice in Community Health Centres, such as the modern and progressive centre operated out of the District Hospital in Dungloe, Co. Donegal. In that centre, the district medical officer, public health nurse, and other health board community care personnel, have their offices, whilst the area's GPs, paying rent as private tenants, also maintain their offices and surgeries there. The adjoining hospital provides x-ray and other facilities.

Research elsewhere indicates that the optimal organisation of physician practices involves two or more doctors practising together, using a variety of "physician extenders" such as nurse practitioners and physician assistants. These studies indicate, however, that most physicians employ less than the optimal number of aides, and that their practice sizes (in terms of physicians) are sub-optimal. While the results cannot readily be translated to Ireland, in the absence of such research, it may fairly be assumed that Irish practice sizes and use of physician extenders are frequently sub-optimal as well (P. J. Feldstein, 1979.)

GP consulting and prescribing rates are considerably higher for public than for private patients, a fact which probably reflects both the demographic and socio-economic differences between the two groups and the economic incentives facing physicians, as will be discussed in greater detail in later chapters. Also discussed later will be some evidence pointing to demand stimulation by GPs, especially of public patients, for reasons relating to the GPs' own economic self-interests. The GMS (Payments) Board monitors consulting and prescribing rates, and refers excessive rates to a peer review group who, after investigation, are empowered to impose penalties which can include warnings, reduced remuneration, or termination of a doctor's GMS contract. (GMS (Payments) Board, 1980.) These penalties are sometimes imposed,[47] but those penalised are not identified. "Excessive" or "abnormal" consulting and prescribing rates are defined by reference to average patterns. Hence any systematic *general* tendency of doctors to over-prescribe or to stimulate excessive consulting rates would not come under scrutiny under this review procedure, nor would behaviour which resulted in statistical results still within the range considered normal.

As Table 4.6 indicates, where consultations took place — in the GP's office/surgery or in the patient's home — varied according to the distance between these. Home visits appear to have risen with distance until the latter reached 5 miles, then to have fallen rather precipitously, possibly reflecting increasing doctor resistance to long trips. Table 4.7 suggests that there may be a somewhat greater propensity for home visits for public (Category I) patients than for private patients, but no difference according to presence or absence of VHI cover.

---

[47]In 1980, cases involving 17 doctors were referred for investigation, and in 15 of these remuneration was reduced. In addition, one case referred in 1979 resulted in 1980 in a contract termination (General Medical Services (Payments) Board, 1981).

Table 4.6: *Where most recent GP consultation took place, as per cent of consultations, by distance from GP's office or surgery*

Distance to GP (first that applies)	Patient's home	GP's office or surgery	Elsewhere
Under 1 mile	17.6	80.4	2.0
Under 2 miles	17.3	80.6	2.1
Under 3 miles	21.6	77.8	0.6
Under 5 miles	27.0	71.9	1.1
Under 10 miles	17.0	82.5	0.5
Over 10 miles	11.3	88.2	0.5
All persons	19.1	79.5	1.4

Table 4.7: *Where most recent GP consultation took place, as per cent of consultations, by category of eligibility and VHI cover*

Eligibility and VHI cover	Patient's home	GP's office or surgery	Elsewhere
All VHI	1.91	80.0	0.9
All non-VHI	19.1	79.3	1.6
All Category I	23.1	75.8	1.1
VHI	25.7	73.3	1.0
non-VHI	22.9	75.9	1.1
All Category II	15.5	82.7	1.8
VHI	17.2	81.8	1.0
non-VHI	15.0	83.0	2.0
All Category III	19.7	79.3	1.0
VHI	19.7	79.7	0.6
non-VHI	19.5	78.0	2.5
All persons	19.1	79.5	1.4

Table 4.8 reports on how long patients had to wait in waiting rooms, etc., to be seen by their GPs.[48] Roughly one person in six had to wait more than an hour. No apparent difference exists between public and private patients in this regard.

[48]In general, as explained in Chapter 1, although the respondent in our survey is the housewife, data pertain to each member of the household. However, it was felt that the respondent would be unlikely to know about waiting times of other household members, so all data pertaining to waiting times, including all data in Table 4.7, pertain to the respondent only. This may introduce a bias. Persons found in the home by survey interviewers are probably less likely than other household members to have outside employment or to be full-time students. Thus, they may be able to schedule their visits to the doctor so as to minimise waiting time. Whether this is the case is, of course, not known.

Table 4.8: *Waiting time at GP's office or surgery, by category of Health Services entitlement and VHI cover, 1980 – per cent distribution*

	Up to 30 minutes	Up to 1 hour	Up to 2 hours	Over 2 hours	Total persons[b]
All VHI	64.0	28.8	4.4	2.8	100.0
All non-VHI	52.0	29.2	13.9	5.0	100.0
All Category I	52.9	31.5	11.4	4.3	100.0
VHI	61.2	36.8	2.0	0[a]	100.0
non-VHI	52.5	31.2	11.9	4.5	100.0
All Category II	52.4	29.2	13.8	4.6	100.0
VHI	60.6	30.6	7.3	1.5	100.0
non-VHI	50.3	28.9	15.4	5.4	100.0
All Category III	65.8	24.4	5.4	4.3	100.0
VHI	66.7	26.6	2.6	4.1	100.0
non-VHI	62.8	17.0	15.1	5.0	100.0
All Persons	55.0	29.1	11.5	4.4	100.0

[a] Less than 0.05 per cent.
[b] Totals may not add due to rounding.

Persons with VHI cover, for reasons which remain unclear, had significantly less waiting time than persons without, irrespective of income group (as indicated by category of eligibility). One possible explanation is that GPs who are not in the choice-of-Doctor scheme may cater to those with VHI cover and may have shorter waiting times. Another is that those with VHI cover may be more likely to have telephones, permitting them to avoid long waits by making advance appointments. Table 4.9 indicates a very considerable range in Health Board area percentages of patients waiting more than one hour at a GP's office or surgery, from a quite acceptable 5.1 per cent in the Midland area, to a quite un-acceptable 39.1 per cent in the North-Western, reflecting the latter's low ratio of doctors to population, especially aged population.

These Health Board area differences in waiting time reflect underlying differences in doctor-to-population ratios; utilisation levels; and population characteristics such as social class. Further statistical analysis of waiting time, reported in Chapter 6, shows no net explanatory effect of Health Board area when such underlying differences are controlled for.

A review of general practice in Ireland, as regards Category I patients, with up-to-date information, analysis and recommendations for change, appears in the Report of the Working Party in General Medical Service (1984), which was published too late to be systematically discussed in the present report. Some of the recommendations are, however, reviewed in Chapter 8.

Table 4.9: *Per cent of patients waiting more than one month for admission to hospital, and per cent of patients waiting more than one hour at GP's office or surgery, by Health Board area, 1980*

Health Board Area	Hospital	GP Surgery
Eastern	6.1	16.4
Midland	0[a]	5.1
Mid-Western	0[a]	11.8
North-Eastern	10.0	17.1
North-Western	2.3	39.1
South-Eastern	9.0	9.1
Southern	1.9	16.7
Western	7.8	13.8
Ireland	7.8	14.6

[a] Less than 0.05 per cent.

Specialists and Other Hospital Doctors

Most specialists are consultants and base their practices in hospitals. Comhairle na nOspidéal, the hospital council (see Figure 4.1), regulates the numbers and types of consultants in health board and public voluntary hospitals and determines qualifications for those appointments.

Consultants whose specialities make it appropriate (physicians, surgeons, obstetricians, gynaecologists, etc., but not anaesthetists, pathologists, radiologists, etc.) control certain beds in the hospitals in which they practise. With rare exceptions, only their patients occupy these beds; and these doctors control the flow of these patients through the hospital.

In 1983, a new common form of contract for all hospital consultants was introduced. For consultants practising from Public Voluntary Hospitals, the new arrangement replaced the widely-criticised "pool" system.[49] All consultants are now salaried and they have liberal benefits — pensions, annual leave, sick leave, study leave, etc. — as well as tenure. Their salaries remunerate them for their public-patient work. They are paid on a fee-for-service basis by their private patients.

The VHI distributes to consultants a schedule of fees for various surgical and medical procedures at levels at which they are prepared to remunerate those with VHI cover. It would be extraordinary for a consultant to charge less than

[49]The Health Boards, under this now abandoned system, paid the hospitals for public patients on a patient-day basis, for in-patient care. While the Department left it to the hospitals to divide out the payment, not concerning itself with the method by which consultants were individually remunerated, in fact, the consultants were known to be remunerated on a patient-day basis. This system was alleged to lead to excessively long (and inter-regionally varied) hospital stays (Kelly, 1976).

the amount listed by VHI. Some may charge more, but as the patient must pay the full difference between the fee and the VHI rate, such specialists are in the minority. The VHI periodically up-dates their "suggested" fee schedule, which is a significant influence on consultant fees in Ireland.

As Table 4.5 indicates, there is considerable variation in the ratio of consultants to population, from a low of 1.3 per 10,000 in the Midland and North-Western to a high of 4.2 in the Eastern Health Board area.[50] These patterns reflect the distributions of hospital beds and, in particular, the concentration of major teaching hospitals in Dublin. While geographic parity is neither practical nor desirable, the more than three to one disparity probably means excessive inter-regional inequities, and these deserve review by the medical profession as well as by Comhairle na nOspidéal and the Department of Health.

Specialist doctor care may be an important exception to the general rule that medical care of equal quality is available to persons in all categories of eligibility. Private patients are more likely to be cared for personally by the consultant, while public patients are served by junior hospital doctors. More seriously, a 1975 Irish Medical Association Working Party questioned whether the latter were competent to deal with their patients' problems (Mulcahy, et al., 1975). This issue is discussed further in Chapter 8.

Dentists

Persons eligible in Category I are entitled to free dental care from dentists employed by Health Boards and paid by salary. In addition, persons eligible under the Social Welfare scheme can get free or subsidised dental care from private dentists, who are remunerated by the Department of Social Welfare on a fee-for-service basis. The remainder of the population pay for private dental care, on a fee-for-service basis, out of their own resources.

As noted earlier, many persons with Category I eligibility find themselves for practical purposes unable to avail of free dental care, while some better off people with Categories II and III eligibility qualify for the Department of Social Welfare Dental Benefit Scheme. Table 4.10, based on our survey, shows that 53.6 per cent of reported most recent dental visits were free. Of those persons covered in Category I, 70.4 per cent had free dental visits, as did 53.6 per cent of those in Category II and 41.5 per cent of those in Category III. The average fee paid by those paying fees was £16.45.

Fees vary, of course, according to the treatment, as indicated in Table 4.11, which also indicates that dental visits for check-up only were more likely to be free than those for any other purpose.

VHI does not at present cover dental care, apart from some surgery and in

---

[50]These figures do not reflect subsequent expansion of Letterkenny Hospital and the related increase in consultants. Comhairle na nOspidéal report that in May, 1983, the ratio of consultants to population was 1.9 per 10,000 population in the North Western and 4.1 in the Eastern Health Board areas.

Table 4.10: *Dental visits, free and fee, by category of Health Services entitlement*

Category of Entitlement	% Whose most recent dentist visit was free	% Paying for most recent dental visit	Average fee recent dental visit, excluding free visit
I	70.4	29.6	(a)
II	53.6	46.4	(a)
III	41.5	58.5	(a)
All	53.6	46.4	£16.45

(a) The differences among these means were not statistically significant.

cases of accident, but it is of interest none the less to compare those with and those without VHI cover. Table 4.11 indicates that 40.3 per cent of dental visits were by persons with VHI cover (though they formed only 25.5 per cent of the population). This figure varies by type of treatment from a low of 29.2 per cent for dentures to a high of 54.4 per cent for check-up only. Fees were paid for 55.6 per cent of visits by those with VHI cover; for those without, the figure was 40.3 per cent.

Table 4.11 also gives the main purpose of each person's most recent dental visit. Something of the crisis intervention nature of Irish dental care is indicated by the fact that 22.7 per cent of visits were for the purpose of extraction!

Table 4.12 reports on the geographic distribution of practising dentists and dentists employed by Health Boards. Dental resources are not evenly distributed, especially when one takes into account areas as well as populations to be served.

Table 4.11: *Type of treatment and per cent fee-paying, by VHI cover, and average fee by type of treatment, most recent dental visit*

Treatment[a]	VHI		Non-VHI		Total			
	% of Total	% Fee paying	% of Total	% Fee paying	% of Total	% fee paying	Average fee (£)[b]	% of visits
Check-up only	54.4	44.9	45.6	18.3	100.0	32.8	6.58	17.0
X-ray	46.2	50.0	53.8	57.1	100.0	55.8	23.97	1.1
Filling	45.1	55.9	54.9	44.1	100.0	49.4	14.87	44.2
Extraction	25.0	63.8	75.0	48.3	100.0	52.2	13.66	22.7
Dentures	29.2	67.9	70.8	30.9	100.0	41.7	37.85	9.3
Other	39.7	60.9	60.3	45.7	100.0	51.7	27.85	5.7
All	40.3	55.6	59.7	40.3	100.0	46.4	16.45	100.0

(a) If a visit had more than one purpose, then treatment given is main purpose of visit except "Check-up only" is chosen only where there was no other treatment.
(b) Excluding free visits.

Table 4.12: *Practising dentists, 1983, number and per 1,000 population, and Health Board dentists, 1981, number and per 1,000 eligible persons, by Health Board area*

Health Board	Number of practising dentists (1983)	Dentists per 1,000 population[a]	Health Board dentists (1981)	Health Board Dentits per 1,000 eligible persons[b]
Eastern	445	0.37	66	0.24
Midland	38	0.19	11	0.12
Mid-Western	57	0.18	18	0.17
North-Eastern	55	0.19	16	0.14
North-Western	47	0.23	11	0.09
South-Eastern	93	0.25	22	0.14
Southern	182	0.35	43	0.25
Western	58	0.17	27	0.15
Ireland	975	0.28	214	0.17

[a] Dentists in 1983 divided by 1981 populations.
[b] Persons eligible in Category I, from Dept. of Health.
Source: Department of Health.

Table 4.12 shows that there are 0.28 dentists per 1,000 persons, which amounts to one dentist for every 3,500 persons; and 0.17 Health Board dentists per 1,000 persons eligible in Category I, which amounts to one dentist for every 5,900 eligible persons. Both figures are low; the latter figure is critically so. By contrast, Norway and Sweden have approximately one dentist for every 1,000 persons; the USA and France have about one to every 2,000 persons; and Italy has one for every 5,000 persons (Wiley, 1984). As seems often to be the case with health and medical resources, the North-Western Health Board area has a significantly lower resource level, per eligible person, than any other region; the Southern and Eastern Health Board areas are the most favoured.

Clarkson (1982) reports that the average number of persons served by one dentist in Ireland fell from 4,130 in 1971 to 3,330 in 1980, an important achievement, though much more progress is necessary. He reports comparative European figures which range from about 1,000 (Norway and Sweden) to 5,000 (Italy), though most countries seem to be in the area of 2,500. Table 4.2, above, which does not include Italy, indicates that in the European Community only the United Kingdom had a lower ratio of dentists to population than Ireland in 1976 and that all other states had considerably higher ratios.

The reason for the shortage concerns economic incentives for dentists, rather than under-production by Irish dental schools. Indeed, there is a well-established pattern of emigration by Irish dental graduates (Wiley, 1984).

A thorough review of the Irish dental care system, as well as of the relevant international literature, appears in Wiley (1984).

Other Personnel

As we will see in Chapter 7, approximately one person in four sees her or his dentist at least once each year, and approximately one person in six uses the services of personnel other than a doctor or a dentist — a nurse, a social worker, a physiotherapist, etc. — at least once a year. Sometimes these professionals are seen on referral from a physician; sometimes they in effect provide primary care.

Table 4.13 reports on the distribution of nurses, social workers, physiotherapists and home helps, as provided by Health Boards, among the eight Health Board areas. Nurses are more uniformly distributed across the country than are doctors. The Eastern Health Board area, as is so often true of medical care resources, has a significantly higher ratio of social workers and of physiotherapists to population than elsewhere, approximately treble the rest of the country in the case of social workers, and more than double in the case of physiotherapists.

General Hospitals

The third level of medical care, as indicated in the schematic diagram of Figure 4.3, is in-patient hospital care. We turn to a discussion of the system of acute hospitals.

As is indicated in Table 4.14, there are several types of hospitals, but these break down into three main categories: *Health Board (or Public) Hospitals*, which are owned and managed by the state, through the Health Boards, and which receive most of their funds from the exchequer; *Public Voluntary Hospitals*, which, like public hospitals, receive most of their funds from the state, and which are under some state jurisdiction, but which are owned and managed by private charitable bodies, mainly religious orders or congregations; and *Private Hospitals*, which, like public Voluntary Hospitals are owned and managed, on a not-for-profit basis, by private charitable bodies, mainly religious, but which are not under the aegis of the state, except that private hospital patients are eligible for services provided by specialist departments of public hospitals.

Of the three, the oldest are the Public Voluntary Hospitals, established as charities either by philanthropic individuals from the early eighteenth century or under enabling legislation of the Irish Parliament in 1765. The first charitable hospital was founded in 1718 and still exists as Jervis Street Hospital in another building. Public Voluntary Hospitals are concentrated in and around Dublin and, to a lesser extent, Cork. Indeed, more than 75 per cent of Dublin's hospital beds are in Voluntary Public Hospitals. Of 44 Voluntary Public Hospitals, 16 are teaching hospitals and these have an average of 280 beds each. The remaining 28 have an average of 140 beds each. Public Voluntary Hospitals receive grants from the Department of Health, "on behalf of" the Health Boards in the respective areas.

There are five types of Health Board Hospitals. The largest, with the greatest number of specialised units, are the Regional Hospitals, most of which are teaching hospitals. They averaged 270 beds in 1979. They are located in Dublin, Cork, Galway, Limerick, and Waterford, i.e., in all Health Board areas except the Midland, the North-East, and the North-West. (The North-East has, how-

Table 4.13: *Distribution of nurses, social workers, physiotherapists, and home helps, total and per thousand population,*(a) *by Health Board area, 1979*

Health Board	Nurses						Social Workers						Physio-therapists		Home Helps	
	Hospital				Non-hospital		Com-mun-ity care									
	Hospital total	per 1,000 pop.	Public health	Other	Total non-hospital	per 1,000 pop.	Com-mun-ity care	Medical	Psychi-atric	Other	Total	Per 1,000 pop.	Total	Per 1,000 pop.	Total	Per 1,000 pop.
Eastern	7,470	6.41	367	722	1,089	0.93	86	86	31	108	311	0.35	194	0.17	1,823	1.56
Midland	1,087	5.48	97	101	198	1.00	13	0	1	9	23	0.12	12	0.06	317	1.60
Mid-Western	1,768	5.87	109	183	292	0.97	8	0	0	29	37	0.12	16	0.05	343	1.14
North-Eastern	1,332	4.74	115	248	363	1.29	9	2	1	10	22	0.08	16	0.06	493	1.75
North-Western	1,277	6.26	107	111	218	1.07	26	2	1	10	39	0.19	16	0.06	838	2.98
South-Eastern	2,028	5.52	155	63	218	0.59	17	0	0	35	52	0.14	29	0.08	287	0.78
Southern	3,165	6.13	153	147	300	0.58	33	2	4	19	58	0.11	45	0.09	829	1.61
Western	2,478	7.37	169	85	254	0.76	35	0	4	20	59	0.18	35	0.10	732	2.18
Ireland	20,552	6.10	1,272	1,660	2,932	0.87	227	92	43	240	601	0.18	363	0.11	5,662	1.68

(a) Census of Population, 1979.
Source: Dail Proceedings, 24 June, 1980

Table 4.14: *Beds in acute hospitals, by type of hospital, distribution by Health Board area, December 31, 1979.*

Health Board Area:	Health Board Hospitals					Voluntary Public	Total Public	Private	Total beds	Beds per 1,000 persons
	Regional	County	District	Other[a]	Total					
Eastern	165	277	428	283	1,153	6,481	7,634	682	8,316	7.01
Midland	0	413	231	0	644	114	758	90	848	4.24
Mid-Western	524	229	183	120	1,056	190	1,246	70	1,316	4.31
North-Eastern	0	596	39	82	717	383	1,100	0	1,100	3.85
North-Western	0	477	222	0	699	0	699	28	727	3.51
South-Eastern	265	587	464	140	1,456	136	1,592	75	1,667	4.48
Southern	877	424	764	299	2,364	676	3,040	428	3,468	6.63
Western	603	339	216	183	1,341	204	1,545	141	1,686	4.97
Total Beds	2,434	3,342	2,547	1,107	9,430	8,184	17,614	1,514	19,128	5.59
Number of hospitals	9	24	54	11	98	44	142	16	158	

Notes: [a] Fever and orthopaedic.
Source: Department of Health.

ever, a large Voluntary Public Hospital, and the North-West has a large County Hospital.)

County Hospitals averaged 140 beds in 1979. Only one County Hospital, that in Manorhamilton, Co. Leitrim, had fewer than 100 beds (it had 66). But as a rule County Hospitals have fewer specialised units than either Regional or Voluntary Public Hospitals. The 54 District Hospitals, on the other hand, are extremely small, averaging fewer than 50 beds in 1979. The two other categories, grouped under "Other" in Table 4.12, are Fever Hospitals and Orthopaedic Hospitals, together averaging 100 beds.

In addition to Voluntary Public and Health Board Hospitals, there are also Private Hospitals, which comprise about 10 per cent of the hospitals, but account for only 8 per cent of the beds.

There are two issues regarding the size and distribution of hospitals. One pertains to the distribution of hospital beds per capita. As of December 31, 1979, there were in the Republic 5.59 beds for every 1,000 persons. As Table 4.3 above indicates, this put Ireland on the low side, as far as European comparisons are concerned. But 5.59 per 1,000 is by no means an inadequate number of beds. A standard adopted in the United States in 1978 was that *no more than* four hospital beds should be available per 1,000 population, except that larger numbers might be required in more sparsely settled rural areas, or where there were large numbers of elderly persons.[51] Although this standard is excessively mechanical and cannot be directly transplanted to Irish conditions in any case, it does provide an interesting benchmark. As Table 4.14 shows, the Eastern and Southern Health Board areas exceeded it somewhat in 1979. The Midland, Mid-Western, and South-Eastern Health Board areas had fewer than 4.5 beds per 1,000; the North-Eastern area came closest to the US standards; and only the North-Western Health Board area fell significantly short. The addition of 59 beds at Letterkenny Hospital since then, assuming no reductions elsewhere in the North-Western area, will have raised that area's bed total (Table 4.14) to 786, and the beds per 1,000 population (using 1981 population) to 3.78 — still the lowest in the state. Many people in the North-Eastern Health Board area live reasonably close to the major Dublin hospitals, and indeed our survey disclosed that 38 per cent of those resident in the North-Eastern Health Board area who were discharged from hospital in 1980 had been patients in hospitals in the Eastern Health Board area (see Appendix Table A.41). The same cannot be said of the North-Western Health Board area, which on the population density

---

[51]U.S. Department of Health, Education, and Welfare, *National Guidelines for Planning Goals*, reprinted in Rapoport, Robertson and Stuart (1982). The standard applies to "short-stay" beds only. Adjustments are permitted where the ratio of persons aged 65 years and over to population exceeds 12 per cent. In Ireland, the North-Western is the only Health Board area in which the aged population exceeds 12 per cent. The standard also provides for an adjustment where a majority of the residents would otherwise be more than 30 minutes travel time from a hospital. Aside from upward adjustments, "4.0 beds per 1,000 population is a ceiling, not an ideal situation."

criterion (the area includes large sparsely settled areas) might merit a higher ratio of beds of population. In addition, the North-West has the largest proportion of population aged 65 and over, which normally implies a higher demand for hospital services. The North-West, in spite of recent expansion, may still be underserved by hospital facilities.

The unequal distribution of beds is explained partly, but only partly, by the concentration of specialised beds in regional urban centres. The Eastern Health Board area not only has a higher ratio of specialised beds to population, but also a higher ratio of general medical and surgical beds as well. Data for 1972 cited by Maynard (1976) show 1.85 general medical beds per 1,000 population in the Eastern area, as opposed to 1.26 for Ireland as a whole and only 0.58 for the North-West area (the lowest).

It is sensible that more specialised units be found only in regional urban centres, and this explains some of the inter-regional differences in bed-to-population ratio. According to our survey, of 394 reported hospital admissions (discharges) in 1980, 46 (or 12 per cent) involved a person resident in one Health Board area using the services of a hospital in a different Health Board area. The Eastern Health Board area, unsurprisingly, was the only net recipient: 35 of its 155 patients (23 per cent) came from elsewhere, mainly from the North-Eastern area. The Southern area was neither a net sender nor a net recipient; it "broke even." All other areas sent patients to other areas, mainly to the Eastern. (See Appendix Table A.41.)

Of course, we do not know how much of this migration for hospital care was the result of regional centralisation of specialised facilities and how much was due simply to the mal-distribution of beds. The ratios reported give us merely the results of these processes. As Culyer and Maynard, commenting on the unequal distribution of hospital beds in Ireland, state,

> The causes of such inequalities are complex. History is an important explanatory variable. Hospital bed stocks are often aged and built to serve populations which have long since either declined or migrated to other areas. Geographically unequal incomes and the geographically unequal philanthropic propensities of past generations are two other important variables. Another factor is that because of economies of scale, specialised units are small in number, tend to be located in the East and people travel there to use them. These inter-regional flows blur the character of the crude statistics ... but they do not account for the magnitude of the inequalities. ... (NESC, 29, 1977).

The second issue regarding these data concerns the fact that there are a great many very small hospitals in Ireland. Table 4.14 reports that there are 89 hospitals with fewer than 100 beds, of which 52 have fewer than 50 beds. In 1968, the Fitzgerald Report (Stationery Office, 1968) argued,

> We consider that the small hospital of less than 200 beds with one surgeon and one physician is no longer capable of adequately meeting public needs.

While in some instances there will be special local factors to justify having a smaller hospital, we recommend that the broad policy should be to establish General Hospitals of not less than 300 beds.

As Table 4.15 indicates, only 13 of Ireland's 158 hospitals have more than 300 beds. These account for approximately 25 per cent of total acute beds. When hospitals are too small, they will either be inadequately staffed and equipped, or they will be inefficient and costly, or both. A minimal hospital should have x-ray and pathology departments; it should have two or preferably three surgeons and physicians, and two obstetricians, to provide 24-hour coverage and to allow for annual leave, illness, etc. If this minimal staff is not employed in a small hospital, it will not provide adequate service; if it is employed, the small hospital will not have enough patient activity to utilise them efficiently.

Moreover, there are indications from US research that larger hospitals may provide higher output quality. Hospitals where fewer than 200 open-heart operations were done in a year had death rates 24 per cent higher than the average (adjusted for severity of case mix); those where more than 200 such operations were performed had death rates 23 per cent below the average (Luft, Bunker and Enthoven, 1979).

In a sense, approximately half of the District Hospitals are not truly acute hospitals. The Department of Health classifies District Hospitals according to average length of stay. There were 26 District Hospitals in 1979 whose average length of stay was under 30 days, and the group average length of stay was 15.7 days (compared with 8.3 for Regional Hospitals, 7.3 for County Hospitals, and 9.6 for Voluntary Public Hospitals). The remaining 28 with average lengths of stay of 30 or more days had a group average of 113.3 days. These hospitals' services more nearly resemble those of institutions providing skilled nursing, convalescent and geriatric care than acute or short-stay care.

The Fitzgerald report recommended that most of the small hospitals be down-

Table 4.15: *Acute hospitals, size distribution (numbers of beds) by Health Board area, December 31, 1979*

Health Board Area:	1–50	51–100	101–200	201–300	301–400	401–500	501–600	601–700	Total
Eastern	4	10	17	6	5	2	—	1	45
Midland	4	3	4	—	—	—	—	—	11
Mid-Western	4	4	4	—	1	—	—	—	13
North-Eastern	3	1	4	—	1	—	—	—	9
North-Western	5	2	1	1	—	—	—	—	9
South-Eastern	13	5	3	2	—	—	—	—	23
Southern	16	8	8	1	1	—	1	—	35
Western	3	4	3	2	—	1	—	—	13
Total	52	37	44	12	8	3	1	1	158

Source: Department of Health

graded to nursing homes, health centres, etc., but there was considerable resistance at local level to the loss of a hospital facility. In the mid-1970s it was decided that each Health Board would determine which of its County Hospitals it would develop as a general hospital for the region and which it would downgrade. Hospitals were selected and planning and building began. But local pressure in the localities where hospitals were to be downgraded proved to be greater than the will to rationalise the system, and it was agreed that practically every County Hospital would provide the minimum requirements of a general hospital. The *Irish Times* has stated that "the policy of a 'hospital within sight of every polling booth' has triumphed" (December 11, 1978). Though politics are not the only reason for the retention of so many undersized hospitals, it can hardly be doubted that many of these hospitals provide an inadequate acute hospital service to their communities.

It has been estimated that approximately 25 per cent of Irish hospital beds are either in private accommodation (only one bed in the room) or "semi-private" accommodation (two to four beds), the remainder being in public wards with five or more beds (Joint Committee on State-Sponsored Bodies, 1980). This accords with our survey, in which 10.8 per cent of patients reported only one bed in their rooms, and 16.1 per cent reported two to four, for a total of 26.9 per cent private and "semi-private." Females of all ages except middle age (45–64) are more likely than males to take private accommodation (Appendix Table A.39). As noted earlier, all persons are eligible for hospital in-patient care in a public ward, but (as Appendix Table A.40 shows) only 85 per cent of persons with Category I eligibility, 70 per cent with Category II eligibility and 54 per cent with Category III eligibility were in rooms with 5 or more persons. As also noted, many people purchase VHI cover in order to be entitled to private or semi-private accommodation. Among those with VHI cover, almost exactly half had private or "semi-private" accommodation, and half were accommodated in larger wards. Among those without VHI cover, only 20 per cent were in private or "semi-private" accommodation.

Table 4.9 above, reports that 7.8 per cent of patients had to wait one month or more to be admitted to hospital. Of these, 1.6 per cent had to wait more than a year (not shown in Table 4.9). These figures do not indicate a serious problem in aggregate though there may be local problems in some areas. By Health Board area, the numbers waiting at least a month ranged from insignificantly small to 10.0 per cent. It is sometimes argued that people buy VHI cover, at least in part, in order to avail of private (or "semi-private") care precisely in order to "queue-jump" and avoid long waits for admission. Our survey shows no difference between VHI and non-VHI patients in length of wait (Appendix Table A.42). Likewise, no difference is indicated according to category of health services eligibility.

Table 4.3, above, shows Ireland with the shortest average length of general hospital stay in the European Community (tied with Denmark) in 1976, and with the highest number of cases treated per bed per year. Department of Health data show a general downward trend in average stay, which stood at 10.4 in 1979 (averages by type of hospital have already been cited above). It would not be correct, however, to conclude that length of stay is not a problem. Lengths of stay vary considerably around the country for the same diagnosis and treatment (Kelly, 1976) indicating the likelihood of excessive stays in some cases. Length of stay should be the object of attention from the Department of Health, as part of a strategy aimed at strengthening and encouraging primary and other community care, and shifting resources away from costly hospitalisation. We will return to this question in the final chapter.

Another source of concern is admitting rates, which are high and rising. Table 4.3 shows there to be a low group (UK, Netherlands, Luxembourg) and a high group (the others), the latter including Ireland. The Irish rate rose from 141 per 1,000 in 1975 to 162 in 1976. In 1978 and again in 1979, there were 166 hospital discharges for each 1,000 persons in the population. A high rate of hospital admissions (or discharges) may be evidence of too ready resort to hospitalisation by doctors, and represents a high-cost alternative (and often a medically inferior one as well) to community care. Admitting rates, too, should be the object of the Department's attention, as part of the same strategy aimed at shifting the centre of gravity in the direction of primary care in the community, as will be discussed in the final chapter.

Special Hospitals

The special hospital programme forms only a small part of the present study. For reasons mentioned in Chapter 1, our survey results are unreliable in the area of psychiatric hospitals and units and are not presented. Questions were not asked concerning long-stay care of mentally handicapped or other handicapped, or of the aged. Analysis of this sector of care would require special analysis and tools not employed here.

For adults, eligibility follows the same principles in psychiatric as in general hospitals. For children under sixteen, psychiatric services are free, irrespective of family means. As with general hospital care, psychiatric care in private hospitals is subsidised by the state. Roughly one-eighth of current health expenditure goes for psychiatric care. As of the end of 1980, as Table 4.16 indicates, there were approximately 13,000 patients in psychiatric hospitals and psychiatric units of general hospitals in Ireland, a figure which appears to be decreasing steadily each year. The total number of long-stay psychiatric patients in Irish hospitals has fallen from 16,400 in 1970, to 15,000 in 1975, to 13,343 at the end of 1980. The scope for further reductions in the psychiatric hospital in-patient population over time is reflected in the fact that no less than 3,000 or about 22 per cent of the total, are over 65 years of age and have spent more than five years in hospital. The development of community-based psychiatric services, along with the development of specialist geriatric and mental handicap services, will all combine to reduce the total number of in-patients. The numbers of mentally handicapped adults in psychiatric hospitals has shown a consistent decline over recent years.

Psychiatric beds are as unequally distributed as acute beds — though rather differently. The Department of Health does not publish numbers of psychiatric beds, but rather patients on register. The national average for December, 1980, as shown in Table 4.16, was just under four patients per 1,000 population; but three Health Board areas (the Eastern, North-Eastern and Southern) had fewer than three patients per 1,000, and four (the Midland, North-Western, South-Eastern, and Western) had more than five. The ratio of the highest to the lowest exceeds two to one. Where long-stay patients tend to stay in facilities far from their homes, difficulties are imposed for family members and friends who might visit them.

Table 4.16 also reports on admissions, which appear except in recent years to have risen consistently, a trend which is reconciled with declining numbers of patients in residence by falling lengths of stay, due in part to modern methods of treatment. It will be observed that admissions are somewhat less unequally distributed than patients. Admissions to psychiatric hospitals and units now appear to have reached a plateau, having risen consistently in every year from 1945 until 1977.

Table 4.16: *Psychiatric in-patients, admissions 1980, and patients in psychiatric hospitals/units December 31, 1980 – numbers and numbers per 1,000 population, by Health Board area*

Health Board Area	Admissions in 1978		Patients in Hospital, December 31, 1980	
	Number	Number per 1,000 population	Number	Number per 1,000 population
Eastern	8,069	6.77	3,337	2.80
Midland	1,492	7.39	1,164	5.77
Mid-Western	3,309	9.87	1,369	4.44
North-Eastern	2,118	7.33	709	2.45
North-Western	2,183	10.51	1,090	5.25
South-Eastern	3,641	9.72	2,183	5.83
Southern	3,623	6.90	1,464	2.79
Western	2,774	8.14	2,027	5.95
Ireland	27,098	7.88	13,343	3.88

Note: Numbers per 1,000 population are ratio of numbers of patients in area, whatever their Health Board area of original residence, to population resident in Health Board area. Of the 12 private psychiatric hospitals in the country, eight, including all of the large ones, are situated in the Eastern Health Board area, and accommodate about 1,000 patients, who would be drawn from all parts of the country. The Eastern area numbers and rates may be significantly inflated as a consequence. Rates per 1,000 population are based on 1981 census figures for 5th April, 1981. Total admissions of 27,098 include 159 non-national admissions.

Source: Admissions, Medico-Social Research Board; Patients in hospital, Department of Health.

It is worthwhile commenting on the role alcoholism and alcohol-related disorders play in psychiatric admissions. Alcoholism and alcohol psychosis accounted for 15 per cent of admissions in 1970, while only ten years later alcohol-related psychiatric disorders accounted for 26 per cent of admissions. Indeed, there was an increase between 1970 and 1980 of about 16.3 per cent in non-alcohol related admissions, compared with a 33 per cent increase in all admissions over the same period. Alcoholism has therefore assumed the proportions of a major and central problem in so far as the psychiatric services are concerned.

In this chapter, we have reviewed the system of medical care in Ireland. We have examined the organisation of the public health services and of the private sector; the system of eligibility for free and subsidised medical care; the Voluntary Health Insurance scheme; and the system for delivery of medical care, including professionals — doctors, dentists, and others — and institutions — general and special hospitals. We have seen that some important medical care resources seem to be mal-distributed across the country. The North-West Health Board area, in particular, seems to suffer in inter-regional comparisons.

In recent years, medical care — public and private — has absorbed an increasing share of Gross National Product, as both costs and utilisation levels have risen dramatically. We turn in the next chapter to medical care expenditures, how they are financed and how they are rising.

Chapter 5

HEALTH AND MEDICAL CARE EXPENDITURES

Health and medical care costs and expenditures appear to be rising significantly faster than the average level of all prices and GNP, respectively, in virtually all developed countries, whatever their form of organisation and financing of their health services. And all countries appear to be earnestly searching for methods of controlling and rationalising their health and medical care expenditures.

Ireland is no exception to this global rule. Indeed, recent increases in health expenditures in Ireland are large, even by world standards. In this chapter, we review data on expenditures in part A; and we discuss the sources of cost inflation and expenditure growth and possible techniques to deal with them in part B.

A. A Look at Health and Medical Care Expenditures

In this part, we review Irish health and medical care expenditures, their composition, regional distribution and recent growth. In the process, we report new estimates of private medical care expenditures. First, however, we must distinguish between health expenditures and medical care expenditures, and between either of them and Department of Health expenditures.

"Health Care" vs. "Medical Care"

As noted in Chapter 1, it is conventional to distinguish between "health care" and "medical care." The former is the broader category and includes the latter. *Medical care* involves the care and/or treatment of ill (or pregnant) persons by medical personnel, usually defined to include doctors and nurses (and possibly others, but usually under the supervision of or on referral from doctors or nurses), or in medical facilities such as hospitals; and preventative services (including examinations) by or under the supervision of medical personnel or in medical facilities. As a rule of thumb, medical care virtually always involves doctors, though that is not a definitional necessity.

Health care includes medical care, but adds to it the following: (1) Care of one's self, through nutritious diet, exercise, administration of (usually non-prescription) medicines and other therapies, and such. (2) Preventative services

113

and treatment outside the aegis of medical personnel, as by or through health education (in school or by such organisations as the Health Education Bureau), nutritionists and dieticians, food hygiene inspectors and numerous others. (3) Long-term care, outside of hospitals, of the handicapped and of the infirm aged.

These definitions are imprecise and, in application, arbitrary. Are dentists, psychologists, or social workers "medical personnel"? When is research to be defined as part of "medical care"? Are nursing homes sometimes to be considered "medical facilities", and if so, when? Yet, in spite of imprecision and arbitrariness, the point can safely be made that medical care constitutes the core of health care and certainly involves doctors, nurses, prescription pharmaceutical medicines and hospitals.

If we distinguish between health care and medical care, so too must we distinguish between health care expenditures and medical care expenditures. To these two categories we must add a third: *Department of Health Expenditures*. This last is not really a definitional category, but rather an administrative device. In Ireland, it includes, for all practical purposes, virtually all *public* health care expenditures. It omits, however, a small volume of public expenditures outside the Department of Health, such as the Dental Care Scheme of the Department of Social Welfare, which might be considered health expenditures.[52] It omits, of course, *private* health care expenditures. It includes, on the other hand, some related expenditures not usually considered health care expenditures, such as a variety of welfare or transfer programmes which for historical reasons are administered by the Department of Health. In 1980, these expenditures, collectively known as the Community Welfare Programme, amounted to £46.835m, or more than 6 per cent of Department of Health current expenditures.

Department of Health expenditures are thus not an entirely satisfactory measure of health or medical care expenditures, both for what they omit (private and other public health care expenditures) and for what they include (non-health care expenditures such as the Community Welfare Programme). Yet, they are frequently used as a proxy for either health care or medical care expenditures and they will be so used here in much of our discussion. The reason is that Department of Health expenditures provide the only conveniently available, reasonably consistent series covering a number of years.

Department of Health Expenditures

Table 5.1 reports on estimated current (non-capital) Department of Health expenditures in 1980. Also reported are three concepts of the total, together with three sets of percentages of the total. Total A, £732.000m, is the estimated total of

---

[52]It also does not include medical care and other health care expenditures made outside the Department of Health or Health Boards by state or local public agencies on behalf of their own employees, including the Defence Forces, nor does it include the costs of a variety of health (not necessarily medical) related functions of public bodies, ranging from sanitary services under the Department of the Environment to in-school health education or to services provided by County Councils to Travelling People.

Table 5.1: *Estimated non-capital Department of Health expenditure by programmes and services, 1980*

Programme and Service	Expenditure £ million	Per cent of total[a]		
		A	B	C
Community Protection Programme				
Prevention of infectious diseases	3.150			
Child health examinations	6.100			
Food hygiene and standards	1.400			
Drugs Advisory Board	0.220			
Health Education	1.500			
Other preventive services	0.630			
Total	13.000	1.8	1.9	1.5[b]
Community Health Services Programme				
General Practitioner Service (including prescribed drugs)	56.000			
Subsidy for drugs purchased by persons ineligible under 2.1 above	6.500			
Refund of cost of drugs for long-term illnesses (including hardship cases)	3.500			
Home nursing services	12.000			
Domiciliary maternity services	1.200			
Family planning	—			
Dental Services	8.500			
Ophthalmic Services	2.400			
Aural Services	0.300			
Total	90.400	12.3	13.2	14.5
Community Welfare Programme				
Cash payments to disabled persons	25.750			
Mobility allowances	0.150			
Cash payments to persons with certain infectious diseases	0.560			
Maternity cash grants	0.150			
Allowances for "constant care" of handicapped children	2.185			
Cash payments to blind persons	0.590			
Home help services	4.300			
Meals-on-wheels services	1.400			
Grants to voluntary welfare agencies	3.800			
Supply of free milk	0.800			
Boarding out of children	0.750			
Payments for children in approved schools	2.800			
Welfare homes for the aged	3.600			
Total	46.835	6.4	—	—
Psychiatric Programme				
Service for diagnosis, care and prevention of psychiatric ailments	90.000			
Payments for patients in private psychiatric hospitals	3.500			
Total	93.500	12.8	13.6	15.0

Table 5.1: *Continued*

Programme and Service	Expenditure £ million	Per cent of total[a] A	B	C
Programme for the Handicapped				
Care in special homes for mentally handicapped	33.600			
Care of mentally handicapped persons in psychiatric hospitals	13.100			
Care in day centres for mentally handicapped	1.800			
Assessment and care of blind	0.900			
Assessment and care of deaf	0.700			
Assessment and care of persons otherwise handicapped	7.100			
Rehabilitation service	2.450			
Total	59.650	8.1	8.7	—
General Hospital Programme				
Services in regional hospitals	83.200			
Services in public voluntary hospitals	160.000			
Services in health board county hospitals and homes	80.500			
Contributions to patients in private hospitals	8.800			
Services in district hospitals	17.300			
Services in health board long-stay hospitals	35.000			
Ambulance services	9.000			
Total	393.800	53.8	57.5	63.3
General Support Programme				
Central administration	4.415			
Local administration (Health Boards)	18.000			
Research	1.100			
Superannuation	7.800			
Finance charges (including interest on borrowings, insurances), etc.	3.500			
Total	34.815	4.8	5.1	5.6
Gross Non-Capital Total — All Programmes (£M)	732.000	732.000	685.165	621.765
Income				
Charges for maintenance in private and semi-private accommodation in public hospitals and other income of health agencies	31.000			
Net Non-Capital Total	701.000			

Notes:

[a] Total A consists of all items, and equals £732.000m. Total B omits Community Welfare Programmes and equals £685.165m. Total C equals Total B, minus Programme for the Handicapped, and the last four items under Community Protection Programme, and equals £621.765m. Details may not add to totals because of rounding.

[b] Prevention of infectious diseases plus child health examinations, as a per cent of Total C.

Source: Data from Department of Health.

all Department of Health expenditures in 1980. It will be seen that the General Hospital Programme accounted for 53.8 per cent of Total A. Total B, which omits expenditures on the Community Welfare Programme, amounts to £685.165m. The General Hospital Programme accounted for 57.5 per cent of Total B. Total C omits not only expenditures on the Community Welfare Programme, but also those on the Programme for the Handicapped, and on the non-medical components of the Community Protection Programme, *viz.*, the last four items shown. Total C, then, is £621.765m, and the General Hospital Programme accounts for 63.3 per cent of that total.

It will be recognised that Total A is the same as Department of Health expenditures (excluding capital expenditures), and that Totals B and C are approximations, respectively, of *public* health expenditures and *public* medical care expenditures, as defined above, though omitting non-Department of Health public expenditures.

The percentage breakdowns in Table 5.1 are striking. The Community Health Services Programme, which is roughly equivalent to primary care, used only 14.5 per cent of Total C in 1980, and of that only about 9 per cent for GP (general practitioner) services *and* prescription medicines for persons with Category I eligibility. (Eligibility is discussed in Chapter 4.) The biggest user of resources, by far, was the hospital system. The General Hospital Programme spent an estimated £393.8m, or (as noted) 63.3 per cent of Total C. These figures show how strongly hospital-oriented are the public health services in Ireland. Moreover, in spite of talk about strengthened community care, the share of (all three versions of) total expenditures devoted to the General Hospital Programme has been creeping upward in recent years. They increased by more than five percentage points in the three years 1977–80 (National Economic and Social Council No. 53, 1980), but levelled off in 1983, as will be seen presently. In order to control the growth of medical care expenditures, it will be necessary to control outlays under the General Hospital Programme. This will probably require strengthening primary, community care.

The Department of Health and the Health Boards have a reputation for skilled and efficient administration, and that appears borne out by Table 5.1, which shows only 4.8 per cent of Total A (the relevant total in this case) spent on the General Support Programme (of which only 0.6 per cent, about one-eighth, is spent on central administration in Dublin, and 2.5 per cent, slightly more than half, on Health Board administration). On the other hand, this same item shows a pitifully small amount, 0.15 per cent of Total A, spent on research.

It will be noted that the £732.0m, spent in 1980 by the Department of Health was partially offset by income of £31.0m, so that net expenditure, i.e., the amount provided from the Exchequer for current Department spending, was £701.0m. The income figure is surprisingly low.

The same hospitals orientation applies, unsurprisingly, to capital expenditures of the Department of Health, as reported in Table 5.2. General hospitals spent about 64 per cent of the total and virtually all the rest went to psychiatric

Table 5.2: *Department of Health Capital Expenditure, 1980*

	× £1000	Per cent[a]
General hospitals, total	22,447	64.1
of which Health Boards	11,770	33.6
of which Voluntary Public	10,677	30.5
Psychiatric hospitals	1,375	3.9
Mental handicap	6,521	18.6
of which Health Boards	405	1.1
of which Voluntary bodies	6,116	17.5
Geriatric accommodation	1,229	3.5
Others, miscellaneous, and minor schemes	3,430	9.8
Total capital expenditure	35,002	100.0

Notes: [a] Detail do not add to 100 per cent because of rounding.
Source: Department of Health.

hospitals and long-stay facilities.

A fuller account of public health-related expenditures would add £4.6m in dental care and £0.2m in aural and optical care expenditures of the Department of Social Welfare to all three totals.

We have concentrated on 1980 for comparability with our survey results, and with some detailed Health Board income and expenditure data, which are both for that year. The percentage distributions have changed little in subsequent years. As percentages of Total A, expenditures changed as follows between 1980 and 1983, with estimated 1984 outlays in parentheses: community protection, 1.8 per cent to 1.6 per cent (1.6 per cent); community health services, 12.3 per cent to 12.7 per cent (12.8 per cent); community welfare, 6.4 per cent to 7.9 per cent (8.1 per cent); psychiatric services, 12.8 per cent to 12.6 per cent (12.7 per cent); services for the handicapped, 8.1 per cent to 10.4 per cent (10.3 per cent); and general hospital services, 53.8 per cent to 54.8 per cent (54.5 per cent). (Department of Finance, 1984.)

Sources of Funds

Ireland is one of the few countries in Europe not to finance a significant portion of its public health services through social insurance contributions. While those with Category II and III eligibility are required, as noted in Chapter 4, to pay health contributions, these financed only 6.5 per cent of current Department of Health expenditures in 1980. Of the remainder, 92.0 per cent came from the Exchequer, 1.3 per cent from the European Community and 0.2 per cent from the Hospitals Sweepstakes. In the capital programme, 1.4 per cent derived from the Hospitals Sweepstakes, and the remainder from the Exchequer.[53]

The fact that health contributions are levied at a low rate on a taxable income which reaches a ceiling (1 per cent on the first £11,000 of income in 1983) means that there is some potential for increasing income from this source. As it stands, once the ceiling is reached, health contributions become, in effect, a per capita tax on earners, and hence are extremely regressive. While on the surface it might appear that this income group, which corresponds to Category III, receives much more limited services than others, hence justifying the contributions ceiling, in fact the considerable subsidies, direct and indirect, to private care (as discussed in Chapter 4) warrant consideration of applying this tax to all incomes. However, it must be conceded that the added revenues would be modest in comparison with the resources required to finance the health services.

As will be discussed below, current net expenditures of the Department of Health constituted 8.1 per cent of Irish Gross National Product in 1980. When capital outlays are included, the share rises to 8.5 per cent. (It is appropriate to add capital outlays because current expenditures do not include a depreciation item.)

Regional Distribution

All except about 2 per cent of Department of Health current expenditures are in the form of grants, either to the eight regional Health Boards (70 per cent of grants) or to voluntary agencies (30 per cent), mainly Voluntary Public hospitals. The grants to voluntary agencies are made "on behalf of" the appropriate Health Boards.

Table 5.3 reports on grants to Health Boards, other income of Health Boards, and Health Board expenditures, on a total and per capita basis, for 1980. Per capita Health Board expenditures in Ireland averaged £197.92 in 1980, and ranged among Health Boards from a low of £180.48 in the North-Eastern area, to a high of £239.92 in the Western area (line 6, Table 5.3).

Table 5.3 also shows (line 1) the distribution of grant payments made to or on behalf of Health Boards to have averaged £196.23, with a range of from £178.18 (North-Eastern area) to £237.36 (Western area). Per capita grants are not

---

[53]As the Sweepstakes are associated in the minds of many with the finance of Irish hospitals, a brief review in a footnote seems appropriate. The Hospitals Trust Fund was established by legislation in 1933, with its income to be derived from sweepstakes on horse racing, and its outlay to be used for capital expenditures by and to cover current operating deficits of the Voluntary Public Hospitals. In its day, the Trust Fund made a major contribution to health care finance, especially to capital expenditure. As late as 1966, the Government could state in a White Paper, "The main source of funds for capital expenditure on the health services has been the Irish Hospital Sweepstakes. From 1 April 1948 to 31 March 1965, capital expenditure on the provision of hospitals and other institutions amounted to £34.9 million. Of this, £21.6 million was provided from the Sweepstakes." (Stationery Office, 1966.) But Sweepstakes income has not risen with the cost of medical care, and its relative role has been eroded significantly since then, and it is no longer an important source of hospital finance.

Table 5.3: *Per capita income and expenditure of Health Boards*[a], *1980, together with per capita household medical expenditure, 1980*

| | Health Board | | | | | | | | |
	Eastern	Midland	Mid-Western	North-Eastern	North-Western	South-Eastern	Southern	Western	Ireland
1. Per capita grant payments made to or on behalf of Health Boards[b]	180.20	215.49	191.21	178.18	236.73	193.20	197.75	237.36	196.23
2. Per capita income of Health Boards	184.86	229.99	201.70	186.60	247.41	203.17	207.56	250.63	204.95
3. Per capita hospital expenditures, Health Board[b]	127.38	134.41	106.59	112.59	128.13	120.99	130.22	151.14	127.95
4. Per capita expenditure on General Practitioner Services and General Medical Services, Health Boards	22.63	32.48	24.45	25.28	51.37	24.64	26.55	47.27	28.60
5. Per capita community care expenditure, Health Boards	34.13	46.49	38.29	38.28	64.61	36.39	41.40	62.13	41.56
6. Per capita health expenditure, Health Boards, total	184.10	220.48	190.70	180.48	233.03	188.84	195.60	239.92	197.92
7. Per capita household medical expenditures[c]	44.65	18.39	22.59	29.48	20.40	23.44	31.94	35.30	32.88
8. Per capita public and household medical expenditures[c]	228.75	238.87	213.29	209.96	253.43	212.28	227.54	275.22	230.80

Notes:

[a] Income (line 2) and expenditure (line 6) differ primarily with respect to timing. Per capita income (line 2) consists of grant payments (line 1) plus other income. The Department of Health provides grants to Health Boards, and to others (mainly Voluntary Hospitals) on behalf of Health Boards. Health Board expenditure can be grouped into General Hospital expenditure, Special Hospital expenditure, Community Care, and others. Line 3 includes both General and Special hospitals. General Medical Services (line 4) are part of Community Care (line 5). The total (line 6) is the sum of hospital expenditure (line 3), Community Care expenditure (line 5), and other. Central Department of Health and VHI administrative costs excluded.

[b] Includes payment to Voluntary Hospitals and others on behalf of Health Boards.

[c] Sum of lines 6 and 7.

Source: Lines 1–6 are derived from Department of Health data; Dail Proceedings, 5 May, 1981. Line 7 is derived from our own survey. Line 8 combines the two.

expected to be equal among Health Board areas, but rather should reflect proportion of the population with Category I (and, to a lesser extent, Category II) eligibility; population density; age distribution of population; the array, in terms of size, age and distribution, of hospitals with which each area is endowed; etc. Line 2 reports per capita total income, the difference between that and line 1 being other income, mainly hospital room charges. Line 3 reports on per capita hospital expenditures, which is the sum of Health Board expenditures and Department grants to voluntary hospitals in each area.[54] Per capita hospital expenditures of £127.95 are 64.6 per cent of per capita total Health Board expenditures. The range is somewhat greater than expected, from a low of £106.59 in the Mid-Western area to a high of £151.14 in the Western. Line 4 reports on expenditures on the General Practitioner Services and General Medical Services, i.e., GP care and prescription medicines, for those with Category I eligibility. The range here seems to reflect the distribution of the Medical Card population throughout the country. The striking thing about this line is the relatively low level of these expenditures. Per capita GMS expenditures (note: not per eligible person, but per head of population) of £28.60 was only 14.5 per cent of all expenditures made by or on behalf of Health Boards. Line 5, community care, includes line 4 together with the rest of the Community Health Services Programme. Lines 7 and 8 concern private, household expenditures, and will be discussed later in this chapter.

These data are not routinely published by the Department of Health, and surfaced only as the result of a parliamentary question posed in the Dail. It is recommended that data on grants to, income of and expenditures of Health Boards be published regularly.

Household Medical Care Expenditures

In order to provide the basis for estimates of private, household expenditures on medical care, our survey included questions of the following sort:

> Would you please try to estimate how much money, altogether, the household spent on general practitioners' fees in 1980?

Similar questions were asked in nine other categories, including "other".

Four things should be noted about these questions. First, as noted in Chapter 1, they are retrospective, and thus may be affected by errors of recall, though we have tried to minimise this problem in the design of the survey.

Second, the data are for a whole calendar year. Thus there is no need to attempt seasonal adjustments.

Third, data are for whole households, not for individuals. Thus we cannot

---

[54]It will be noted that this statistic is something of a hybrid, in that *net expenditures* of Health Board hospitals are added to *grants* to Voluntary Hospitals in each area. It would have been conceptually more appropriate to have added net expenditures by Health Board hospitals to net expenditures of Voluntary Hospitals, but the latter data were not available.

report on expenditures by age or sex, except by age or sex of the head of household. Because we know the number of persons in each household, we are able to
divide each household's medical care expenditures by that number to obtain
medical care expenditures per person; but this is not the same, obviously, as
having expenditure data on each individual.

The fourth point to be noted concerning these survey questions is that households were not asked to deduct VHI or Health Board reimbrusement and then to
report *net* expenditures on medical care. It was determined that such procedure
would be excessively confusing and could result in additional error. As VHI and
Health Board reimbursement data are available in aggregate, it was not thought
to be necessary to ask these questions. Instead, households were asked to provide
gross medical care expenditure information. Data reported here should be read
with that understanding.

The results are reported in summary form in Table 5.4 and in detail in
Appendix Tables A.19 through A.30. It is estimated that in 1980, households
spent an average of £117.54, or an average of £32.88 per person, on medical care.
This is grossed up to a national total of £107.4m, after the deduction of £6.5m for
Health Board reimbursement for pharmaceutical medicines (the latter a
Department of Health statistic). The largest component was prescription medicines (before the deduction of Health Board reimbursement), at £8.90 per
person, £30.77 per household and £30.8m nationwide (£24.3m net). The second
largest component of gross, and the largest component of net, household medical
care expenditures is hospital and specialist charges, out-patient and in-patient
combined, which were £28.38 per household, £7.95 per person and £27.6m
nationally. The third largest was general practitioner fees, which were £20.69
per household, of £5.68 per person and £19.7m nationally. These three — prescription medicines, hospital charges and specialist fees and GP fees — constituted 68.6 per cent of gross and 66.7 per cent of net medical expenditure by
households. The relatively low share of hospital and specialist charges in the
total reflects the patterns of eligibility for public health services, as well as the
considerable public subsidisation of private hospitalisation (both discussed in
Chapter 4).

Other Estimates of Household Expenditures

The Central Statistics Office, in its Household Budget Survey (HBS), collects
information on household medical care expenditures. Its methods and definitions are different from ours, but some comparisons are useful. The HBS leaves
log books with households and they record all of their weekly expenditures. The
survey is continuous, so some households are sampled in every month. The
expenditures are net and can be combined with VHI premia to yield a total defined somewhat differently from ours.

The two surveys are compared in Table 5.5. The averages for the state are
remarkably similar, as indeed are the estimates for most of the Health Board
areas. Sampling differences as well as methodological and definitional differ-

Table 5.4: *Household expenditure on medical care, 1980, Ireland, by type of expenditure: per person, per household and national total*[a]

Type of Expenditure	Per person (£)	Per household (£)	National total (£m)
General practitioner fees	5.68	20.69	19.7
Hospital and specialist charges, total	7.95	28.38	27.6
Of which:			
Specialist fees, out-patient	1.86	7.53	6.5
Hospital charges, out-patient	0.28	1.05	1.0
Hospital and specialist charges, in-patient[b]	5.81	19.80	20.1
Prescription medicines[c]	8.90	30.77	30.8
Non-prescription medicines	3.02	10.58	10.5
Dentists' fees and charges	4.08	16.43	14.1
Other health professionals[d]	0.98	3.17	3.4
Eyeglasses	2.11	7.02	7.3
Other medical expenditure[e]	0.15	0.50	0.5
Total	32.88	117.54	113.9
Substract Health Board reimbursement for pharmaceutical medicines, 1980			−6.5
Net household medical care expenditure			107.4

Notes: [a] Excludes expenditures made by employers on behalf of employees and dependents. [b] Includes ambulance transport and any ancillary charges relating to hospitalisation. [c] Ignores Health Board reimbursement for pharmaceutical medicines, estimated at £6.5m in 1980. Net household prescription medicine expenditure estimated at £24.3. [d] For a partial list, see Table A.7, Appendix. [e] Includes medical, surgical and nursing devices and equipment, hearing aids, etc. *Source:* Author's survey (see Ch. 1), except Health Board reimbursement for pharmaceutical medicines, for which source: Department of Health.

ences account for the differences. Note that ESRI figures are gross medical expenditures, without deducting VHI reimbursements, but without adding VHI premia; while HBS figures are for net medical expenditures, after deduction of VHI reimbursement, to which we have added VHI premia. The two figures are conceptually the same, therefore, except that VHI administrative expense is included in the HBS figures, and there are timing differences.

The similarities in the state averages increases our confidence in the totals, reported in Table 5.4.

It is also useful to compare our estimates of total household medical care expenditures with claims against the VHI. The VHI reporting year begins 1 March and ends 28/29 February, while our figures are on a calendar year basis.

Table 5.5: *Household medical care expenditure, 1980: ESRI estimates compared with household Budget Survey, weekly, by Health Board area (£)*

Health Board Area	ESRI	HBS		
		Medical Expenses	*VHI Premia*	*Total*
Eastern	3.10	2.28	0.75	3.03
Midland	1.26	1.54	0.31	1.85
Mid-Western	1.38	1.42	0.49	1.91
North-Eastern	2.25	1.49	0.40	1.89
North-Western	1.36	1.22	0.21	1.43
South-Eastern	1.70	1.56	0.34	1.90
Southern	2.31	1.96	0.58	2.54
Western	2.04	1.30	0.30	1.60
Ireland	2.26	1.80	0.52	2.32

Sources: ESRI: Present Survey; HBS, David Rottman, "The Distributive Effects of Public Expenditure and Taxes: Policy Implications." Forthcoming.

However, the VHI estimate an approximate two-month average lag between the incurring of medical care expenses and their payment of claims, so our 1980 data are roughly comparable with their reporting period ending 28 February, 1981.

In that year, the VHI paid claims of £27,532,000. These are mainly but not entirely in-patient hospitalisation expenses. We have estimated £27,600,000 in in- and out-patient hospital specialist charges, of which £20,100,000 is for in-patient care. Part of our estimated £19,700,000 in GP fees and £24,300,000 in net prescription costs may also have been recoverable from VHI. Our conclusion is that our estimates are consistent with VHI reported claims.

Other Private Medical Care Expenditures

As noted in Chapter 4, some employers and others provide help in a variety of ways for employees, dependants, members and others, with their medical bills. We were able to make only the most approximate estimates of non-household private medical care expenditures.

Survey respondents were asked,

"In addition to the VHI or the Health Board, is there any other body or organisation that helps you with your medical care costs?"

If the answer was yes, they were asked to identify the organisation. Seven per cent of respondents answered in the affirmative. All the organisations identified were contacted and asked what services or benefits they provided; who was covered (e.g., employees only, pensioners, spouses, other dependants); how many persons, total, were covered; and what was the annual cost.

In all, 29 organisations were identified and contacted of which 13 responded with information, but only 7 responses were usable in estimating outlays. Fortunately, these 7 included employers of great range in size (from 400 employees to 20,000), and they included public, semi-state and private organisations. It is difficult to generalise regarding the types of services offered. The average annual cost or outlay was estimated at £9.96 per household member, or £35.17 per household. There was less variation in the average cost than in the nature of the services provided. These amounts gross up to an estimated £2.385m for Ireland in 1980. If we add an estimated 10 per cent administrative overhead, we get a total for non-household private medical care expenditures of £2.624m.

Total Medical Care Expenditures

In Table 5.6, private medical care expenditures (Column 1) can be compared with public medical care expenditures, as defined earlier (Column 2) and with total expenditures (Column 3). Private medical care expenditures are estimated at 15.2 per cent of the total. This percentage varies widely, however, when we examine the five main components: general practitioner care, prescription medicines, hospitals (combining in- and out-patient, and hospital and specialist charges), dental care, and other. (Note that non-household private is included in "other" because it was impossible to allocate by type or purpose of expenditure.) Household expenditure was 51.2 per cent of GP fees; 33.3 per cent of prescription medicine costs; only 5.4 per cent of hospital and specialist charges; 51.8 per cent of dental care costs; and 41.6 per cent of other medical care costs. These figures once again reflect the hospitals orientation of the public system, which can be criticised as reflecting perverse incentives, encouraging use of costly hospital and specialist care as compared with primary, community care by GPs.

The distribution of total medical care expenditures is worthy of review. The largest share is given over to hospital care, 69.1 per cent. Prescription medicines are next, at 9.8 per cent, followed by "other," 7.8 per cent. Only 5.2 per cent of total public and private medical care outlays went to general practitioner care, which is the linchpin of the system. An even smaller amount, 3.7 per cent of the total, went to dental care, a part of the system in need of attention.

In Chapter 4 (Table 4.5), it is reported that there were 1,513 General Practitioners in 1975. We have no figure for 1980, but if it is assumed the number had risen to 1,600, our estimate of £38.5m in total GP fees yields an average GP income of £24,000. The typical full-time GP probably received more, as some of our estimated 1,600 GPs had only part-time practices. The estimate does not, of course, take account of the costs of operating a practice; net income is less.

We can combine the figures presented thus far in some other ways to yield interesting aggregates. If we add the estimated £113.1m of private medical care expenditures to Department of Health current expenditures and to Department of Social Welfare dental, aural and optical expenditures, to create a rather heterogeneous "total health expenditure" (one which includes non-medical

Table 5.6: *Total current medical expenditures Republic of Ireland, 1980*[a]

Type of Expenditure	(1) Private[b]	(2) Public[c]	(3) Total
	£m	£m	£m
General Practitioner	19.7	18.8	38.5
Prescription medicines	24.3	48.6	72.9
Hospital: total	27.6	487.3	514.9
Dental care	14.1	13.1	27.2
Other[d]	24.1	33.9	58.0
Overhead[e]	3.3	30.3	33.6
Total	113.1	632.0	745.1

Notes:

[a] Medical expenditures differ from health expenditures or Department of Health expenditures. See text.

[b] Household expenditure only, except £2.4m other private included in "Other" and £0.2m in "Overhead."

[c] In addition to Department of Health medical expenditures, this column includes £4.6m of Department of Social Welfare expenditures on dental care, and (under "Other") £0.2m of Department of Social Welfare aural and optical care expenditures. In addition, £0.5m, or 10 per cent, is added for estimated administrative overhead in the Department of Social Welfare.

[d] "Other" expenditure included in Column (1) includes private, non-household expenditure, unallocated by type; household expenditure on health professionals other than doctors or dentists; eyeglasses; medical, surgical and nursing devices and equipment; hearing aids; etc. "Other" expenditure included in Column (2) includes other Community Health Services Programme, £24.4m (home nursing, home maternity, dental, ophthalmic, aural services); and part of Community Protection Programme, £9.24m (prevention of infectious diseases, child health examinations); and £4.8m in Department of Social Welfare expenditures (see note (c)).

[e] Total Department of Health overhead of £34.815m (central administration, local or Health Board administration, research, superannuation, and finance charges) allocated between medical and non-medical expenditures according to amounts in these. £0.5 is added for estimated Department of Social Welfare overhead (see note (c)). Private overhead is the sum of household and non-household, where household is estimated VHI administrative cost for calendar year 1980 and non-household is based on the assumption that it is 10 per cent of medical expenditures.

Sources: Column (1), author's survey; Column (2), Department of Health.

Department of Health expenditures, but excludes non-medical private health expenditures), the total of £849.9m is 9.8 per cent of GNP. We have no estimate of non-medical private health expenditure, but if we assume these to be the same percentage, 15.2 per cent, of total health care expenditures that private medical care expenditures are of total medical care expenditures, we obtain an estimate of £152.1m for private health care expenditures, which gives an estimate of total health care expenditure of £1,002.0m, or 11.6 per cent of GNP. This is a less heterogeneous and more conceptually defensible measure, but because it relies on untested assumptions it is of problematic accuracy.

If we then add £35.0m in public capital expenditure (from Table 5.2) to this total, we obtain a grand total of £1,037.0m in health care expenditure for 1980, which was 12.0 per cent of GNP. This figure excludes private capital spending, on e.g., private hospitals, GP surgeries, dispensing chemists' facilities, etc., but in the private sector capital costs (in the form of depreciation charges, etc.) presumably are (or should be) explicitly or implicitly provided for in the setting of charges, and adding them again at this point would involve double-counting. Conceptually, this is our best figure, and though it includes some components that are only estimated, the results are not very sensitive to different assumptions used in making these estimates. Hence we are justified in saying that in 1980, health care used "about" 12 per cent of GNP and that medical care used "about" 10 per cent.

We can return briefly to Table 5.3 above. The estimated household medical care expenditure of £32.88 varies regionally (line 7). The low is £18.39 in the Midland region, while the high is £44.65 in the Eastern region. It is not surprising to find that the regional variation in total public and household per capita medical care expenditures (line 8) is much less than in public (line 6) or household (line 7) individually. Indeed, the two largest regions, the Eastern and the Southern, have total per capita expenditures which are very close to the national average. The range is from £209.96 in the North-Eastern to £275.22 in the Western. Only the Western region is above the national average in both public and household per capita expenditures. Four regions — the Mid-Western, the North-Eastern, and the North-Western and, very slightly, the Southern — are below both national averages.

Average household and per capita expenditures also vary by age and sex of household head; category of public health services eligibility; VHI cover; and labour market status, occupation group and education of the head of household. Detailed statistics on these appear in Appendix Tables A.19 through A.24 (household averages) and A.25 through A.30 (per person averages). We review these figures briefly.

Per household and per person comparisons are useful for different purposes. These comparisons may diverge where numbers of household members vary. For example, households with male heads spent £139 per household and £35 per person, while those with female heads spent £46 per household and £26 per person. Male-headed households spent 302 per cent of female-headed household expenditures, but because female-headed households are smaller, on a per person basis the ratio was only 135 per cent (Appendix Tables A.19 and A.25).

As might be expected, category of eligibility appears to make the greatest difference in household expenditures. This is so, as noted in Chapter 4, for two reasons: first, those with Category III eligibility are eligible for fewer public services than those in Category II, while those in Category II are eligible for fewer than those in Category I. Hence more private expenditures are required in Category III than II, and more in II than I. Second, those with higher incomes are expected to have higher demands for medical care in general, and private care in particular, even apart from eligibility for public services.

These surmises are borne out in Tables A.20 and A.26. The latter shows per capita spending of approximately £67 in Category III, £41 in Category II and only £9 in Category I. As might be anticipated, the difference between Categories III and II is the greatest for hospital costs and that between II and I is the greatest for GP fees.

It is to be emphasised that Tables A.20 and A.26 cannot be used to determine either what Category I or II eligibility is "worth," or the "cost" of lesser eligibility in Category II or III. Differences in per capita expenditures reflect not only differing eligibility, but different needs (including those associated with demographic aspects) and preferences.

The same tables show some differences according to VHI cover. Per capita spending for those with VHI cover was £60 whilst that for those without VHI cover was only £24. However, this probably exaggerates the difference, since VHI cover is strongly correlated with category of eligibility. Within each Category of eligibility, the difference between VHI and non-VHI is less (only £18, for example, in Category III).

It is not surprising to find (in Table A.28) that per person medical expenditures are greater where the head of household is employed than when that person is unemployed, retired, or has some other labour market status. We find (Tables A.23 and A.29) apparent class differences in household medical expenditures, with the highest outlay by those in households whose head is classed as a professional, manager, or employer (£71); the next where that person is a salaried employee or intermediate non-manual worker (£47); and then relatively smaller differences among the other four groups, which are, in descending order, skilled manual worker (£28); other non-manual worker (£26); farmer, agricultural worker, or fisher (£22); and semi-skilled or unskilled manual worker (£19). Again it must be noted that these differences can reflect differences in eligibility and VHI cover, in demand (for both medical care and private care), and medical need (though the pattern appears contrary to morbidity patterns, to the extent we know them).

Social class differences are also reflected in Appendix Tables A.24 and A.30, which report expenditures by the age the head of household completed his or her full-time education. The regularity of this association is striking, with a nearly unbroken rise in expenditures with educational level.

In order to capture the *net* influence of these differences in persons — their category of eligibility and VHI cover, the age, sex, labour market status, occupation and education of the head of the household, and of Health Board area — it is necessary to use multiple regression analysis or some equivalent form of multivariate analysis. Results of such are presented in Chapters 6 and 7. (To the extent that these independent variables are correlated with each other, however, we will not be able to capture the net influence of each through multivariate analysis.)

Growth in Expenditures

As noted, we do not have reasonably consistent series for either medical or health care expenditures covering a number of years, so for comparisons over time we are forced to rely on Department of Health expenditures.

The rapid rate of general inflation in Ireland in the 1970s and 1980s may tend to mask the extraordinary rate of cost and expenditure growth in the health care area. Table 5.7 shows how really explosive the latter growth has been.

In Table 5.7, Column 1 reports on nominal (i.e., current price) growth in Department of Health expenditures. These expenditures have risen *seventeen times* in just under fourteen years. The average annual rate of increase between 1965/66 and 1980 was 22.8 per cent, a rate which provides for doubling every three years and four months!

Table 5.7: *Department of Health current expenditure, in current and constant (1970) prices, 1965/66–1980*

Year[a]	(1) In current prices £m	(2) In constant 1970 prices, £m[b]	(3) % change in (2) from previous year	(4) As % of GNP
1966/67	41.0	51.5	9.8	3.8
1967/68	44.9	54.8	6.4	3.8
1968/69	50.6	58.7	7.1	3.8
1969/70	59.2	64.1	9.2	3.9
1970/71	76.2	76.2	18.9	4.4
1971/72	86.6	80.8	6.0	4.4
1972/73	108.1	91.3	13.0	4.5
1973/74	142.8	108.3	18.6	5.1
1974	179.6	116.5	7.6[c]	6.0
1975	242.6	130.2	11.8	6.5
1976	274.6	124.9	-4.1	6.0
1977	328.0	131.3	5.1	6.0
1978	400.0	148.7	13.3	6.4
1979	505.0	165.7	11.4	6.9
1980	701.0	197.0	18.9	8.1

Notes:
[a] Year ending 31 March through 1973/74; year ending 31 December thereafter. Figures shown for 1973/74 and 1974 overlap for three months.
[b] Deflated by Consumer Price Index. Years ending 31 March deflated by index for year ending previous 31 December.
[c] Compares 12 months ending 31 March 1974 with 12 months ending 31 December 1974.
Source: Department of Health (Column 1). *National Income and Expenditure*, various issues (GNP, CPI).

This rather remarkable rate of increase reflects: (a) the increase in *prices* or unit costs of health care services (e.g., the rise in physician fee levels, or in hospital room daily charges); (b) the increase in *quantity* or volume of health care services (and other Department of Health services) provided; and (c) the transfer of certain health care expenditures from the private to the public sector and from local authorities to the state. The implication of (c) is that the rate of increase in total, as opposed to state, health care expenditures, were it known, would almost certainly be less than the reported figure for public expenditures.

Increases in price or unit cost, as in (a), are not known, as there is no index of health care prices in Ireland. Analytically, these increases are the product of the general price increase, as measured, e.g., by the Consumer Price Index, and the rise in health care prices relative to the average, which is not known. The latter, unknown increase reflects real resource shifts to health care from the rest of the economy. When the price of a commodity rises relative to other prices, typically it means that in order to maintain the same output quantity or volume relationships it is necessary to shift resources from elsewhere in the economy to the production of that commodity. Hence these changes are not merely nominal "inflationary" movements. Column (2) reports Department of Health current expenditures in constant 1970 prices, i.e., adjusted for the rise in consumer prices generally and not for increases in prices in the health sector. Column (3) shows the percentage change in inflation-adjusted health care expenditures from the previous year. The average annual rate of increase between 1965/66 and 1980 was 10.25 per cent. This rate and the rate of increase of nominal expenditures cited earlier are averages of annual increases, and are not disproportionately affected by the beginning and ending values. This is a truly extraordinary real rate of increase, particularly to be sustained for such a long period of time. It is much more economically significant, and hence striking, than the higher rate of increase in nominal or current-price expenditures. It provides for a doubling the ratio of Department of Health expenditures to the CPI every seven years and one month.

Column (4) reports on Department of Health expenditures as a per cent of Irish Gross National Product. This represents another way, alternative to Column (3), of representing real expenditure growth. This rapid increase is also remarkable and is presumably unsustainable. The figures reported exclude capital outlays. They also exclude private health care expenditures. As noted earlier, it is estimated that total health care expenditures were 12.0 per cent of GNP in 1980, as compared with the 8.1 per cent reported in Table 5.7 for Department of Health expenditures relative to GNP.

Care should be taken not to read more into Table 5.7 than appropriate. The rise in real Department of Health expenditures, and in Department of Health expenditures as a percentage of GNP, is certainly not wholly a bad thing. As said earlier, part of it reflects expansion of services, much of which was in response to real needs. But it must also be said that the increase of the last several years is unsustainable, and it will clearly be necessary to bring under control what in a number of ways seems to have been uncontrolled growth. It also almost certainly reflects, to an extent, an irrational pattern of expenditures. We will comment on these issues below.

B. Causes of Expenditure Growth

Health expenditures are the product of prices and quantities. Because so many health expenditures are governmental, and because in any case we lack an index of private health service prices, we cannot decompose recent health expenditure growth into its price and quantity components. Consequently, we do not know what part of the expenditure growth is volume (e.g., patient days in hospital) and what part is price. One reason it is particularly difficult to make this separation is that volume growth includes quality change. For example, if the number of services routinely provided by hospitals to patients increases over any period of time, or if the same services are provided by persons with more training, then to that extent the rise in patient-day costs reflect volume rather than price, even though to all intents it presents itself to us in the form of a price change.

Our general inability to separate the price and quantity components of expenditure growth is less troublesome, however, than it might at first appear. It is really expenditure growth and not merely price inflation that constitutes the central fiscal problem; expenditure growth in the health area requires the transfer of resources from elsewhere in the economy.

In Ireland, real (CPI-adjusted) Department of Health expenditures have risen 318 times in $13\frac{2}{3}$ years (Table 5.7). In the United States, where there are health price index data, medical care prices rose 2.0 times in 13 years (1965–78), a comparable period. In the US, price increases were led by nursing homes and hospitals. Nursing home unit prices rose 3.4 times in the same period and led all other categories. Hospital unit prices rose 2.5 times, but were of greater absolute significance than nursing home costs. When one surveys other countries, the US result appears universal: hospital costs have been the main source of medical care cost inflation in recent years.

It seems reasonable to suppose that similar patterns have been followed in Ireland. As we have seen, hospital costs are a high *and rising* proportion of total Department of Health, health and medical care expenditures. The public General Hospital Programme was responsible for 53.8 per cent of Department of Health expenditures, 57.5 per cent of estimated public health expenditures and 63.3 per cent of public medical care expenditures in 1980, and the first of these rose more than five percentage points in three years. O'Hagan and Kelly (1984) note that between 1966 and 1979, average cost per patient week in Irish hospitals, relative to GDP per capita, increased from 3.386 to 6.929, an increase of 104.6 per cent, which they describe as "quite dramatic".

There are no published studies of Irish hospital costs. Elsewhere, the causes of hospital cost inflation appear to concern, first and foremost, a major and continuing increase in *resource intensity* per patient (P. J. Feldstein, 1979). While adaptation to technological change in hospitals plays a role, in the sense that new technology is expensive to implement and raises per patient costs, that is neither the sole nor even the major explanation for rising resource intensity. Instead, the explanation seems to lie in the following: First, there appears to be a continuing increase in diagnostic tests, pathology, x-rays and the like, associated with each medical or surgical procedure for which a patient might be hospitalised. That is, instead of many wholly new procedures involving new equipment and/or therapies, there appears to be more use of existing ones. Secondly, there appear to be more specialised and highly qualified personnel performing existing functions, a change which may not appear to be, but is, an example of increased resource intensity.

The move to a new hospital usually speeds up these processes. In old hospitals, older and less resource-intensive methods are used. When a new hospital comes into use, per-patient charges may suddenly rise by as much as one-third, a rule of thumb often used in Britain and in continental Europe. The changes are not avoided, however, by continuing to use older hospitals; they are only made gradual and steady rather than discontinuous.

To describe this form of hospital cost inflation is not to explain it. The ultimate causes of rapid medical care cost increases appear to lie in the incentive structures facing patients and providers, combined with the open-endedness of medical care. Moreover, this explanation extends beyond hospitalisation to cover most other aspects of medical care as well. These problems were discussed in Chapter 2 and we will return to them in the next section.

In addition to rising resource intensity, hospital cost inflation elsewhere is explained by rising wage rates. Where products are produced under conditions of slower-than-average productivity growth (with productivity measured in terms of resources used per patient day, or other similar measure), then the price of that product (also measured in patient day or similar terms) will necessarily rise relative to all prices. This phenomenon, sometimes called "Baumol's Disease," appears to apply to services (i.e., intangibles, as distinguished from physical commodities) in general and to health and medical care in particular. "Baumol's Disease" itself probably accounts for, and will continue to account for, from 2 to 3 per cent growth in relative prices in the medical and health care areas, even apart from other influences.[55] Though these are price changes, they do not resemble general price inflation, because they do involve real resources. Other things held constant, they involve a rise in the share of society's economic resources devoted to medical and health care.

The Incentive Structure

Alain Enthoven, Professor of Economics at Stanford University in the USA, in a heralded and widely-quoted book on health care cost increases and cost con-

---

[55]Baumol's Disease, in the context of rising educational expenditures, was discussed in Tussing (1978), pp. 68–71.

tainment in that country, stated,

> Many factors contribute to the cost increase: general inflation in the economy, ... better and more widespread insurance coverage, new technology, an ageing population, ... and others. Some contributors have been surprises. In the 1960s we almost doubled the number of students entering our medical schools, only to find in the 1970s that more doctors mean more doctoring and higher fees. Overall, there has been much overuse of services (excessive hospital stays, duplication of tests), overinvestment, and waste.
>
> I believe, however, that the *main cause* of the unnecessary and unjustified increase in costs is the complex of perverse incentives inherent in our predominant system for financing health care. The "fee-for-service", or piecework, system by which we pay doctors rewards the doctor with more revenue for providing more, and more costly, services, whether or not more is necessary or beneficial to the patient. Physician gross incomes account for only (a small share) of total health care spending ..., but physicians control or influence most of the rest. They admit people to the hospital, order tests, and recommend surgery and other costly procedures. Yet our system assigns them very little responsibility for the economic consequences of their decisions. Most physicians have no idea of the costs of the things they order — and no real reason to care.
>
> Hospitals are paid on the basis of either their costs or charges based on costs. The net effect is that more costs mean more revenue. Those who make the decisions concerning the use of hospital services, doctors and insured patients, have no reason to be cost-conscious. Most medical bills are paid for by "third-party payors", insurance companies and government agencies that pay the bills after the care has been given and the costs incurred. ... Consumers' insurance gives them free choice of doctor and hospital and little or no incentive to seek out a less costly doctor or style of care. ... This system embodies many cost-increasing incentives and virtually no rewards for economy (Enthoven, 1980).

Enthoven's comments were addressed to the US system and not to this country's. However, his remarks apply with equal force here. Indeed, it can be argued that the incentive structure in the Irish health and medical care systems is in some respects even more perverse to economical resource use than in the United States.[56]

As we saw in Chapter 2, many of the problems referred to by Enthoven result from the unique economic character of the commodity, medical care. Uncertainty in the incidence and cost of medical care leads to a need for some form of insurance, public or private; and the character of medical care as a merit good

---

[56]Enthoven's scheme for controlling medical care cost and expenditure inflation is discussed in Chapter 8.

leads many societies to impose that insurance as compulsory. (It will be recalled from Chapter 2 that social provision of medical care through government can best be viewed as a form of compulsory health insurance.) Thus point-of-purchase prices are often lower than average or marginal costs, and may even be zero, though time prices can be important. Usually we expect consumers of commodities to be economisers, carefully comparing benefits with costs at the margin; but that role is weakened because insurance drastically alters the usual market mechanism.

That role is further weakened by the presumed ignorance of consumers regarding medical care. Most consumers are forced to rely on providers, especially doctors, to make medical care utilisation decisions. This imposes two additional problems.

First, providers are typically paid not for results but for resources used. Outside of medical care, most producers enter commodity markets knowing that if they use fewer resources to produce a commodity, they will be rewarded with higher profits. There are positive incentives to economise. That is usually not the case with medical care, unless financing and delivery systems are carefully organised to achieve such a result. Instead, any increase in resources used tends to be associated with an increase in revenues of providers.

Second, some providers face what amounts to a conflict of interest. The doctor who economises on patient or public resources faces the prospect of thereby reducing his or her own income as a result. Professor A. J. Culyer has argued that "... the agency role of the doctor, if it is to operate most perfectly in accord with the health interests of patients, requires the clear separation of the exercise of professional judgement from the earnings of the professional's income" (Culyer, 1980). In a fee-for-service system, that separation does not exist.

The structure of Irish charges, fees, insurance, remuneration and budgets was laid out in detail in Chapter 4. Drawing on that background, let us review the incentive structure and cost-containment devices used in the Irish system of medical care, asking as we go along about each detail of the system, holding other influences constant, whether for any of the participants it provides a motive to *use* resources; is *neutral* with respect to resource use; or provides a motive to *economise* in resource use.

We will concern ourselves primarily, and in order, with general practitioners; pharmaceutical medicines; consultant specialists; hospitals and VHI cover.[57]

General practitioners are paid on a fee-for-service basis by the state for public (Category I) patients, and at a somewhat higher rate (on average 60 per cent higher) by the patient for private (Categories II/III) patients. This remuneration technique encourages GPs to increase resource use. In the next chapter we will review evidence that some Irish GPs apparently stimulate demand for their own services, in order to increase their own incomes. Not only are GPs provided

---

[57]Parts of the following discussion are based on Tussing, "Financing the Health Services", in McCarthy and Ryan (1982).

with incentives to increase numbers of GP consultations, but it appears likely that increased utilisation that is correlated with GP consultations, such as higher amounts of pharmaceutical medicines, laboratory tests and x-rays, should also be induced. To public patients, GP services are free, though there may be time costs. Thus at best these patients are not provided with incentives to economise on GP resources. Private patients, who do pay fees, do therefore have an incentive to economise on GP resources. If they have VHI cover, on the other hand, and have exceeded their annual deductible amounts, the incentive to economise disappears. No system in Europe or North America provides a greater incentive to resource use than that provided in the Irish system for Category I patients by the combination of services free to patients remunerated to providers on a fee-for-service basis.

As far as their public patients are concerned, the method by which GPs are remunerated by the GMS (Payments) Board offers no incentive for them to use "physician extenders" or paramedical aides. The same can be said of private patients and reimbursement by the VHI.

Pharmaceutical medicines are furnished free to Category I patients and are subsidised for other patients. The nature of the latter subsidy (full reimbursement after a deductible is reached) is such as to provide little if any disincentive to use by patients. As will be seen in the next chapter, Category I patients have a significantly higher level of pharmaceutical consumption than other patients, even when we control for age, sex, social group *and GP utilisation*. This may be a consequence, at least in part, of the differences in patient incentives, but it is more likely to reflect physician than patient behaviour. Physicians, not patients, make most pharmaceutical use decisions (though they may, following an agency model of behaviour, take into account patient incentives), and in general physicians do not bear the costs of such decisions.[58] As noted in Chapter 2, there is strong evidence of higher prescribing in all those European systems where GPs are remunerated on a fee-for-service basis than in those where a capitation system is used, and here again the Irish system is predisposed to high resource use. Little in the Irish system encourages provider or patient to economise in the area of pharmaceutical medicines.

Specialists' incentive structures differ as between public and private care. For private patients, specialists are remunerated on a fee-for-service basis, which provides the doctor with no motive to economise, and is likely, on the contrary, to encourage the opposite behaviour. The VHI publishes a list of fee levels at

---

[58]The reader can better understand what is meant by the concept of physicians bearing the costs of their decisions in such areas as the prescribing of pharmaceutical medicines by considering the HMO (Health Maintenance Organisation), discussed in Chapter 8. HMOs are organisations for the group practice of medicine usually owned by co-operating physicians. They charge their patients an annual fee and in exchange undertake to provide all required medical care, including primary physician care, specialist care, hospitalisation, pharmaceutical prescriptions, etc. Thus doctors who refer patients to specialists, prescribe medicines, or send patients to hospital, in effect bear the cost, collectively.

which they will remunerate specialists and evidently the large majority of specialists do charge the suggested fees. Thus patients have little opportunity to question charges and fee level is not an aspect in the choice of doctor. Patients covered by VHI are in general given first-penny, 100 per cent reimbursement for in-patient specialist charges. For out-patient services, those covered by VHI are reimbursed in full after a deductible is reached and it is the same deductible that applies to GP fees and prescription medicines. The level of the deductible is such that a patient who sees a specialist as a private out-patient is likely quickly to reach it, thus effectively cancelling any disincentive it provides.[59] On the other hand, for private patients not covered by VHI, there may be a substantial motive to economise on specialist services. However, there is reason to believe that this is a very small fraction of the population.[60] In sum, specialists have no motive to economise on the application of their services to private patients. Most private patients themselves have little or no motive to economise, though there will be a small motive for out-patient care for those covered by VHI and a substantial motive for all care for those not covered by VHI.

The private patients referred to in the preceding paragraph are a considerably smaller fraction of the population than private patients of GPs. They consist of those with Category III eligibility, together with such others, mainly in Category II, who prefer private care. Approximately 85 per cent of the population are hence eligible for free specialist care, both in- and out-patient. Specialists providing public care are remunerated on a salary basis. These doctors are, therefore, given an important motive to economise on their own resources. However, one might speculate that they are also encouraged by this incentive structure to apply more resources in the form of junior hospital doctors (a resource provided them without cost) to public patients, and to shift their own energies, at the margin at least, to fee-paying private patients. A 1975 Irish Medical Association Working Party claimed that public patients attending out-patient clinics "are often seen by residents who may not be competent to deal with their problems" (Mulcahy, *et al.*, 1975). This problem is discussed further in Chapter 8.

Public patients have an unusually strong motive to use specialist services. For approximately 50 per cent of the population with Category II eligibility, it is less expensive to see a specialist on an out-patient basis than to see a GP. This unfortunate incentive structure encourages patients to use higher cost specialist services and shifts the balance away from primary, community care.

Finally, it should be noted that GPs who refer patients to specialists, or

---

[59]In 1980, the deductible amount was £60 for a family or £40 for an individual. If a patient saw his or her GP, was referred to a specialist, saw the specialist once or twice, was given a prescription for medicines or was referred for some other out-patient therapy, he or she would be well on his or her way to a £40 deductible.

[60]Our survey indicates that 77 per cent of persons with Category III eligibility have VHI cover. Persons with Category II eligibility can avail of completely free hospitalisation, but some of them may prefer private care. Only 17 per cent of these people have VHI cover. See Chapter 4.

specialists who refer patients to other specialists, bear none of the costs of so doing.

Hospitals are, as noted, the main resource users. There is little difference between the situation facing private patients who have VHI cover and that facing public patients. The former are guaranteed full first-penny cover of in-patient charges. The latter pay no charges. None of these patients has significant economic motive, apart from time costs, to question a decision to admit them to hospital; to compare hospitals as to charges; to question extra hospital services; or to resist what may seem to them to be over-long stays in hospital. Private patients without VHI cover, who are a very small fraction of the total, do have an incentive to economise, but even these motives are sharply reduced by the very considerable direct and indirect state subsidies to private care. These subsidies almost certainly induce higher demand for costly private as opposed to public care.

Doctors, rather than patients, make the main hospital utilisation decisions, and, in general, as they do not bear any of the costs, they have no motive to economise on hospital resources.

The most important hospital resource use decisions are made, however, when hospitals are provided their annual budgets by the state. How budget decisions are made is somewhat obscure.[61] The Department of Health provides operating budgets which are meant to cover costs of approved beds, equipment and personnel. Requests for new equipment, added capacity and new personnel are carefully and critically evaluated by the Department, on an individual basis. The Department resists unnecessary expansion and seeks economical resource use. However, the budgetary and political circumstances of the Government of the day are important and variable, which means that Department stringency vs. liberality must also vary. Further, it is widely believed that the negotiating skill, audacity and personal influence of hospital administrators, consultants and Health Board officers are also critical in the budgetary process. Though these budgetary methods are of uncertain effect, in terms of the set of incentives they provide for resource economy, the steady growth in hospital costs, both absolutely and as a proportion of Department of Health expenditures, do not provide strong testimony in favour of the *ad hoc* methods employed.

VHI is the subject of a final comment regarding the incentive structure found in the Irish medical care system. Currently, people are encouraged to purchase VHI cover, and hence to use costly private care, by the nature of the incentive structure. Substantial tax relief on premia, more favourable than that available for unreimbursed private costs, means that the exchequer pays one-third to one-half of VHI costs indirectly. All of the subsidies to private care, especially those

---

[61]It must be emphasised that the procedure is obscure not because of any disposition of the Department of Health to make it so, or to withhold from the public or researchers vital information concerning the procedures or the outcomes. Instead, the procedures are *ad hoc* rather than automatic or formula-based and are inherently difficult to model. This budget process warrants research.

to private hospitalisation, also have the effect of lowering premium rates, by reducing claim payments, and these hence induce people to buy VHI cover. The net effect is that VHI is now too large, from an efficiency standpoint, and this translates into inefficiently high demand for costly private care.

A review of the incentive structure facing providers and patients reveals, then, very few instances in which participants have a significant motive to economise on medical care resources, public or private, and more than a few instances in which there are inducements to use resources.

Administrative Devices

In the case of medical care, the market, far from providing an institutional device for controlling costs and utilisation, appears to encourage expansion in these. The market often seems to be part of the problem, not the solution.

Most medical care systems employ a number of non-market administrative devices, to substitute for or supplement the market in rationing resources, limiting utilisation, achieving efficient resource use and achieving other objectives. We will discuss three types of administrative techniques: cash budget limits; supply or input restrictions; and quality review. In the process, we will note the techniques used elsewhere and those used in this country.

Cash Budgets Limits

One can distinguish between two types of health care financing systems: those in which services are mainly government financed, as in the United Kingdom or in most Scandinavian countries, and those where services are mainly insurance financed, as in Germany or France. The Irish system is mixed. In government-financed systems, particularly centralised systems (e.g. the UK, but not Sweden), it is possible for the state to impose strict controls on the resources used in the medical care system. In the UK, for example, regional health authorities are provided with budget limits which cannot normally be exceeded; and UK governments have shown that they are prepared to stand by such limits in spite of widespread complaints. As a consequence, the UK stands out in international comparisons as one of very few countries in which health care costs have not exploded in recent years, in amount or relative to GNP. It is up to the regional authorities to determine expenditure priorities within the cash limits. Though restrictive budgets have been in effect since 1975/76, their effects on medical care delivery have not been fully evaluated. Some individual problems have appeared, but in general, evidence of harm to medical care is thus far lacking. However, some types of medical care are rationed (Aaron and Schwartz, 1984). The effect on expenditures are clear: costs have been controlled.

Few other countries have the degree of central control over expenditures necessary to impose such strict limits. At a recent World Health Organization workshop on health care cost control, in which experts from 17 countries (14 from Europe, plus the United States, Canada and Israel) took part, of the 17 only the UK, Hungary and Greece had the necessary degree of centralised control[62] (World Health Organization, 1982). However, a number of other countries, including Ireland, exercised some degree of central control through cash budget limits.

In Ireland, the eight Health Boards, and as well 52 Voluntary Hospitals and others who deliver health services and related services are given budgets fixed in annual terms. Two differences between the Irish and British cases must be noted. First, in the case of Ireland, GPs and through them pharmacists have what amounts to an open-ended claim to funds for the Medical Card population, through the GMS (Payments) Board. Hence a budget for the General Medical Services is strictly speaking an estimate, not a cash limit. In capitation and salary systems, such as in the UK, it is possible precisely to budget GP expense; in fee-for-service systems, it is not. There are other open-ended aspects of the Irish scheme: for example, the subsidy to prescription pharmaceuticals for Category II and III persons and the subvention to private hospitals. Secondly, it has been the practice frequently in Ireland (though less so in recent years) to provide supplementary funds during the year to Health Boards and voluntary agencies; hence the annual budgets cannot be and are not viewed in all cases as fixed cash limits.

In spite of these qualifications, budget limits do exist in Ireland, and they are said to have constituted the most effective control of Irish public health care expenditures.

As already noted, how budget decisions are made is obscure, and so necessarily is the degree of efficiency or rationality of the resulting mix of services.

Supply or Input Restrictions

Supply or input restrictions are particularly suited to insurance-based systems, where cash limits are not possible. France and the United States, for example, endeavour to control utilisation by such techniques. France's controls concentrate on the hospital sector. In that country,

> in 1972, a "hospitalization map" was introduced which described both what existed and what was desirable as regards such factors as bed/population ratios, distribution of expensive capital equipment, etc. By 1979 the major goals had been achieved and the Ministry of Health began to restrict hospital investment and development. Planning of the system now includes, for example, the closing of beds or departments where excess capacity exists. Acute beds have also been reclassified as long-stay beds. In addition, consistent with the general approach of controlling inputs, entry to medical schools is controlled (WHO, 1982).

The aspect of control mentioned in the last sentence reflects changed thinking. Not long ago it was agreed that medical care costs might be controlled by *increasing* the numbers of physicians, while now some argue that *restricting* their num-

---

[62]The author attended and took part in the conference.

bers is necessary in order to achieve the same objective. The rationale lies in the notions of a medical Parkinson's Law, as discussed in Chapter 2, as well as in the notion of physician-induced demand for medical care, discussed in Chapters 2 and 6.

The US system is less centralised than the French, and comparable controls are not possible, though a regulatory system exists to limit hospital construction and expansion. A change in both the United States and Canada of some significance to Ireland is that since the middle 1970s both countries have limited entry of foreign medical graduates. Both North American countries were important markets for the graduates of Irish medical schools. In this country, though medical school entering classes have been significantly reduced in recent years, the annual supply of new doctors is still excessive and there is continuing evidence of an oversupply.[63]

Quality Review

Quality review procedures are directed primarily at the appropriateness of medical (and other professional) judgements and only secondarily at resource use. The most extensive such set of procedures is in the United States, where Professional Standards Review Organizations (or PSROs) must be established by physicians to "apply professionally developed norms of care, diagnosis, and treatment ... as principal points of evaluation and review," to qualify for eligibility under major Federal government reimbursement programmes. It appears that the resource-saving implications of PSROs are less than had been at one time hoped. However, as a technique for establishing norms and standards for practice, and for resource efficiency, PSROs have been strongly endorsed by a well-known Irish consultant who has experience under both the American and the Irish systems (Kelly, 1976).

Many other countries, notably Austria, the Netherlands, France, and the German Federal Republic, maintain quality review procedures of a more or less

---

[63]The Royal College of Physicians in Ireland recently released results of a survey they had conducted of Irish medical graduates of 1971, 1973 and 1975. The following quotation is from a summary of their findings provided to the author by the RCPI: "Of all Irish doctors who responded to the survey, 63 per cent were living in the Republic of Ireland at the end of the survey; 21 per cent were in the United Kingdom and Northern Ireland; and 11 per cent were in North America. ... At five, seven, and nine years after graduation, only 33 per cent, 61 per cent, and 80 per cent respectively of the graduates were in permanent posts. The remainder were still in post-graduate 'training' posts. ... Over one-third of the women doctors with children living in Ireland who responded to the survey are not in medical employment. A further 43 per cent are working part-time, usually on a sessional basis with poor career prospects. ... At present Irish Universities produce approximately 350 medical graduates each year, half of whom will eventually make a career in General Practice, although annual requirements at present for this speciality are only 75 doctors." Note that the most recent class in this study is that of 1975, prior to the cut-back in North American willingness to take Irish medical graduates. See also the discussion by the Working Party on the General Medical Services (1984), who recommend "that steps be taken as a matter of urgency to reduce substantially the annual intake of Irish students to medical school."

extensive sort. None of them reports significant resource savings, however (World Health Organization, 1982).

In addition, in most countries there are local and in-hospital review committees of physicians, e.g., bed utilisation committees, to monitor physicians' referral, prescribing, hospital bed utilisation and other practices.

In Ireland, quality review is quite limited. Only a small number of hospitals appear to have established drugs committees or bed utilisation committees of physicians.

The General Medical Services (Payments) Board reviews and disciplines general practitioners for violations, as we saw in Chapter 4, but there are limits to the scope of this type of review. The Voluntary Health Insurance Board, as was said in Chapter 4, does not engage in any form of medical audit, and does not question the need for or medical efficacy of any procedure for which they reimburse beneficiaries. There is no PSRO-like effort by the medical profession to devise even voluntary or suggested norms of care, diagnosis or treatment. There is room for expansion of this type of technique in Ireland and we will return to this subject in Chapter 8.

There are seemingly inevitable and irresistible aspects to the explosive rise in medical care costs and expenditures. Wages and salaries inexorably rise. Equipment, procedures and personnel training become more complex and costly. And yet it appears in Ireland as elsewhere that the system itself is a main reason for the rapidity with which expenditures and costs are rising. The market provides few incentives to economical and rational resource use. Both patients and providers, though in different ways, benefit from medical care outlays and both share in the decisions concerning utilisation. Yet neither bears a cost which comes close to reflecting the social cost of medical care utilisation. Moreover, the incentive structure in the Irish scheme in many instances favours physician care over equally effective but less costly care by other professionals and para-professionals; costly private care over public care; consultant specialist care over general practitioner care; and hospital care over community care. With the exception of cash limits from the exchequer, which have been inconsistently applied, there is little if any supporting system of administrative devices to supplement the market and compensate for its weaknesses. Unless there is some fundamental change in the system, it will undoubtedly continue to expand rapidly, both absolutely and as a share of GNP.

Chapter 6

UTILISATION OF GENERAL PRACTITIONER SERVICES

We saw in Chapter 5 that, of an estimated total medical care expenditure of £745.1m in 1980, only £38.5m, or 5.2 per cent, was devoted to General Practitioner services. (See Table 5.5; the summary data are repeated here, in Column (4) of Table 6.1). It would appear, on this basis, that General practitioner services are a relatively unimportant component of the Irish medical care system, at least with respect to economic impact.

Such a conclusion would be an erroneous one. GPs serve, as we saw in Chapter 4, as gatekeepers to the entire system of medical care. Not only do they deliver medical care services of the utmost importance themselves, but they prescribe medicines, suggest non-prescription medicines, prescribe other devices or implements, and refer patients to specialists and others and send them to hospital for out- or in-patient services. The amount of medical care services and expenditures they decisively influence vastly exceeds, in money measure, the amount they deliver directly.

Estimates of this influence are quantified in Table 6.1. In our survey, we asked respondents, with respect to each household member's most recent utilisation (of GP services, specialist services, out-patient hospital services, in-patient hospital services, dentists' services and prescription medicines) whose idea it was, or who first suggested that the service be utilised. (A return visit arranged at a consultation with a physician is deemed to be that physician's idea). The results of this question are spelt out in detail in Appendix Tables A.30 through A.35. They are summarised in Columns (1) and (2) of Table 6.1. The methods used in calculating Table 6.1 are set forth in Appendix II. General Practitioners were responsible for initiating nearly a third (32.7 per cent) of all GP consultations, mainly through arranging return visits; over half (51.6) of all specialist consultations; well over half (58.5 per cent) of all hospital admissions; and nearly all (94.5 per cent) prescription medicine items. Another doctor (typically a specialist) was responsible, as indicated in Column (2), for much of the remaining utilisation.

In Column (3), these figures are adjusted to take account of indirect GP influences as well. For obvious reasons, GPs can be deemed to be responsible for 100 per cent of GP services. For specialists, we attribute to GPs not only their direct share, as in Column (1), but an identical proportion of return visits. For

Table 6.1: *General Practitioner responsibility for medical care utilisation and expenditures, 1980*

Type of Service	(1) (2) % of utilisation for which a doctor is responsible		(3) GP's adjusted share	(4) Total expenditure £m	(5) GP share of expenditure £m
	GP	Other			
General Practitioner	32.7	0.5	100.0	38.5	38.5
Specialist	51.6	33.5	65.2 ⎤		
Out-Patient Hospital	60.6	17.1	71.7 ⎬	514.9	364.7
In-Patient Hospital	58.5	21.7	72.6 ⎦		
Dentist	1.9	0.8	2.4	27.2	0.7
Prescription Medicine	94.5	4.9	97.7	72.9	71.2
Other	—	—	—	58.0	—
Overhead	—	—	—	33.6	22.4
Total Expenditure				745.1	497.4

Note: See Appendix II for methods of calculation.

the remaining kinds of utilisation, the proportion for which GPs are directly responsible is augmented to reflect their indirect responsibility for the services prescribed by the specialists to whom the GPs referred patients.

The adjusted shares in Column (3) are then applied to total medical care expenditures, as brought forward from Table 5.5 to Column (4) of Table 6.1. The results are given in Column (5), which show that GPs are directly and indirectly responsible for an estimated £497.4 million in medical care expenditures, or 66.8 per cent of the total public and private medical care expenditures of £745.1 million. The actual figure is undoubtedly higher, as we have used conservative assumptions, especially as regards the "other" category and by including dental expenditures in the denominator.

For these reasons, the utilisation of general practitioner services is itself an important subject for detailed review and is the subject of this chapter. Arguably, the influences which bear on GP utilisation in turn affect utilisation throughout the entire medical care system. We begin with the determinants of GP utilisation. We then look at the determinants of household (i.e., private) expenditures on GP fees. We also analyse the factors bearing on house calls (vs. office/surgery consultations) and the length of wait in GPs' waiting rooms. We conclude with an extended treatment of referrals by GPs, including referrals to themselves, i.e., return visit behaviour. In this last part we deal with the important and sensitive issue of physician-induced demand for their own services.

A. Determinants of GP Utilisation

As Table 6.2 shows, GP utilisation varies with sex, age, category of Health Services entitlement, VHI cover, and whether the head of household is a mem-

Table 6.2: *General practitioner utilisation, 1980, by sex, age group, category of health services entitlement, VHI cover and head of household farmer or non-farmer*

	GP consultations			
	Per year, per 1,000	% with any	Per year, persons with any	Prescription items per GP consultation
All persons	3,616	66.1	5.47	0.888
Males	3,186	61.3	5.20	0.813
under 65	2,630	58.4	4.45	0.648
65+	7,443	83.2	8.94	2.062
Females	4,036	70.8	5.70	0.962
under 65	3,417	67.8	5.00	0.846
65+	7,892	89.8	8.79	1.686
Category I	6,082	77.3	7.87	1.185
Categories II, III	2,450	60.8	4.01	0.748
VHI	2,270	74.2	3.54	0.929
No VHI	4,084	66.8	6.11	0.875
Farmer	3,138	60.8	5.16	0.701
Non-Farmer	3,370	67.8	5.55	0.952

Source: Appendix Tables A.1–A.5.

ber of the occupation group, farmer, farm worker, or fisher. Females have more than 25 per cent more GP consultations than men, a result both of a greater likelihood of any GP consultations and of more consultations among those who have any. Age is even more strongly associated with this form of utilisation. Men over 65 have nearly triple, and women over 65 double, the utilisation of their younger counterparts. Again, the higher utilisation arises both out of a greater likelihood of any contact and greater contact among those with any.

Category of entitlement also is strongly associated with GP consultations. Those with Category I entitlement, who have free GP services, had two and one-half times as many GP consultations as those with Category II or III entitlement, who had to pay their GPs. Those with VHI cover had much fewer consultations than those without that cover. We also include in Table 6.2 the differences between the utilisation of those living in households headed by farmers and those headed by others. Farm household members use somewhat fewer GP services.

Table 6.2 also reports on the number of prescription items per GP consultation in 1980, for the same groups in the population. It will be seen that, in general, those with high utilisation of GP services also consume larger quantities of prescription items — females more than males, the aged more than the non-aged, those with Category I entitlement more than those with other categories and those from farmer households fewer than those from non-farmer households.

The one exception is VHI cover: those with VHI cover consumed more prescription items per consultation, even though they were less likely to have consultations.

More detail on GP utilisation is to be found in Appendix Tables A.1 through A.6.

The relationships reported in Table 6.2 are "simple" or "gross." The population classifications are overlapping and it is hazardous to infer causation or influence. For example, it seems unlikely that those without VHI cover consume more GP services *because* they lack private, voluntary insurance; instead, the reason is more likely to lie in correlates of VHI cover. It is known that those with Category I entitlement are unlikely to have VHI cover, and this fact undoubtedly explains much of the difference shown in Table 6.2.

Though simple or gross relationships as shown in Table 6.2 are important, in that they tell us of the actual differential utilisation of groups in the population, for purposes of uncovering the net influence of such variables as age, sex, entitlement, etc., it is preferable to use some kind of multivariate analysis. Multiple regressions of GP utilisation, as a dependent variable, were run on a set of independent variables, including those found in Table 6.2. Before turning to those regressions, let us first sketch out the underlying theory.

The Utilisation Model

The utilisation model employed here derives from the literature, which is discussed at length in Chapter 2. General practitioner utilisation, X_g, is subscripted for individual i. In general, medical care utilisation is taken to be a function of H_i, the individual's health status; Z_i, the individual's taste for medical care; P_i, the set of relevant medical care prices facing the individual; A_i, the availability of medical care services to individual i; and D_i, the individual's *doctor's* tastes, preferences, attitudes and philosophy. Regarding the last of these, as seen in Chapter 2, it is well established in the literature that doctors on occasion may pursue their own economic self-interests when making utilisation decisions for or suggesting them to their patients, in addition to which, quite apart from self-interest, individual doctors often have quite different approaches to medical care, reflecting differences in their training, backgrounds, expertise or ability and personal philosophies.

The price variable includes both money price and time price. The latter has frequently been shown significantly to influence the demand for medical care. Indeed, as noted in Chapter 2, it is not uncommon for time price to loom larger for many people than money price.

Our basic medical care utilisation model, then, as applied to GP services, is:

$$X_{gi} = X_{gi}(H_i, Z_i, P_i, A_i, D_i)$$

Because of data limitations and in some cases conceptual problems, proxy variables often have to be used to represent the independent variables. In regression analyses, where the dependent variable is patients' general practitioner utilisation, the following independent variables are used:

Sex: Table 6.2 shows more utilisation among females than males. It is well established in the literature that for many kinds of medical care, utilisation is greater amongst females, presumably reflecting morbidity patterns. Therefore, sex appears in empirical models mainly, in effect, as a proxy for health status.

Age and age-squared: Similarly, Table 6.2 and the relevant literature show utilisation to rise with advancing age. In addition, for some kinds of services, infants and/or young children appear also to be greater than average users. Including age-squared along with age permits the relationship to take a curvilinear form (including U-shaped where both the very young and the very old have higher than average utilisation). Age is also, then, mainly a proxy for health status.

Age and sex as proxies may represent other causal variables in our basic model, however, in addition to health status. Employed and self-employed persons may pay a higher time price for medical care than others. Persons with heavy household duties may, as well, pay a higher time price than retired persons or children. Age and sex may also represent the Z or taste variable. If males and females, or young and old traditionally have differing utilisation patterns, these may affect social expectations and ultimately attitudes and behaviour.

Head of household farmer or non-farmer: Occupation group, education and labour force status of head of household are characteristics presumed to be associated with Z, taste for medical care. In some literature, the higher the status of the head's occupational group, the greater the utilisation, other things being equal. Similarly, the more years of education the head has had, the greater the utilisation. These associations are usually presumed to reflect differences in outlook. Another interpretation sometimes offered is that higher-class or more-educated persons have longer time horizons and are hence more apt to go for routine medical care, or attend to minor problems, before illness reaches crisis levels. Others note that these higher-class/more-educated persons and their doctors are more likely to be drawn from the same social classes, thus making medical care an easier and more comfortable experience than for the rest of the population. Those of lower occupation group status, and/or less education, tend to feel less comfortable in doctors' surgeries, hospitals and other care facilities, and limit utilisation accordingly. Labour force status — whether one is employed, unemployed, retired, has full-time home duties, etc. — may also reflect similar attitudes, but time price is likely to be involved as well.

These background or socio-economic variables, as is shown in the appropriate Appendix Tables (A.4–A.6) are related to several kinds of utilisation. Evidently, however, this is largely due to their correlation with other causal variables. When they were incorporated in our multiple regression models, which shows their *net* contribution to explaining utilisation, holding constant other influences, they are very rarely of significance, because of their collinearity with other model independent variables. The single most important exception is where the head of household is a farmer, a farm worker, a farmer's relative, or a fisher. That occupation group's utilisation, as will be seen, was frequently significantly different from those of other groups, even when other relevant causal variables (or their proxies) were controlled for. Consequently, in the final equation form estimated and reported here, these variables, except farmer, do not appear. This is also why farmer, and not the others, appears in Table 6.2.

Category of health services entitlement: Like several of the other variables discussed thus far, category of health services entitlement is a proxy for several of the causal variables in the basic model. First and foremost, it is a price variable. Those with Category I eligibility are entitled to all medical care services, including GP consultations, without charge, and they should hence be expected to consume more medical care services than those with categories II or III. Similarly, those with Category II eligibility should be expected to consume more of certain services (though not GP care) than those with Category III eligibility. In addition, category of eligibility, as it reflects income, may also represent health status (morbidity appears to move inversely with income, as noted in Chapter 3), and also, in the opposite direction, taste for medical care. Finally, as will be noted later, there are reasons to believe GPs may be more likely to attempt to induce medical care utilisation for their own economic ends among persons in Category I. Thus there are three causal forces pointing to higher utilisation among Category I persons — price, health status and doctor influence — and one pointing to lower utilisation — income-associated taste for medical care. Price is expected to dominate and the net association is expected to be positive.

GP fee: GP fee appears, presumably, both in patients' demand functions, where utilisation is a decreasing function of fee, and also in doctors' supply functions, where utilisation is an increasing function.[64] Since we are in effect estimating reduced form equations, we face an identification problem: a priori, it is not obvious whether utilisation should vary positively or negatively with fee. If, for example, patients in the neighbourhood or area served by a given GP have in common a higher-than-average demand for relative to supply of medical care, because (e.g.) of Z or H reasons, both utilisation and fee may be high. In that case, as demand varies, we observe supply. On the other hand, if physician density (the ratio of general practitioners to population) varies from place to place (relative to demand), fees will vary, and to the extent the public responds with varying utilisation to such fee differentials, we observe a negative association between fee and utilisation, i.e., we observe the demand curve. GP fees are, one would suppose, considerably more significant economically to doctors than to patients, and, on that ground at least, are intuitively more likely to affect doctors' than patients' behaviour. That would argue for a positive association.

---

[64]In the case of Category I patients, fee charged the patient is nil, and that is the amount used in this variable, whilst the fee received by the physician, while significantly lower than that received for Category II/III patients, is positive. Thus to the extent the equation represents a supply function, it is somewhat mis-specified.

There is still another possibility. Suppose GPs engage in compensatory demand-inducing behaviour. This possibility will be dealt with more extensively in a later section. For now we will only note that if physician density is high, we would expect, *ceteris paribus*, lower fees and physician incomes. But if GPs are able and willing to stimulate demand — arrange for extra return visits, etc. — in order to maintain target incomes, so that a lower patient-to-doctor ratio is compensated by higher utilisation per patient, then we may observe no clear correlation or association between fee and utilisation. Supply variation will be matched, more or less, by demand variation, and the relationship between utilisation and fee will depend on the degree or extent of compensatory demand stimulation. (This discussion is continued later in the chapter.)

House call fee: We also include as an independent variable the house call fee, the amount normally paid for a home as opposed to office/surgery consultation. For patients who are infirm, indisposed, etc., and who require a home visit by the GP, the house call fee arguably influences demand. However, it also may appear in the physician's supply function.

No VHI: GP fees and other out-patient care are covered by VHI, but only after a deductible is reached.[65] Hence VHI cover is a proxy for price in patients' demand functions. As such, VHI cover should be positively associated with utilisation. (Note that this is counter to what is reported in Table 6.2.) Those with VHI cover may differ in important respects from other people, and this variable may hence reflect more than merely price. For example, as is shown in Appendix Table A.2, those with VHI cover have considerable more dentist visits than those without, even when one controls for category of health services eligibility and hence (broadly) for income group. This is so despite the fact that dental care is not covered by VHI. Perhaps those people who buy voluntary health insurance are more health-conscious, or have longer time horizons, or have greater taste for medical care, than those who do not.

As the variable in the empirical model is "no VHI," a negative association is hypothesised. Because of the deductible, this variable is expected to be only weakly associated with GP utilisation, or indeed with other out-patient utilisation. VHI cover does not causally affect doctors' incomes, so there is no identification problem here.

Distance: Distance from the patient's home to the GP's office/surgery is included as a measure of time-price. GP utilisation should vary inversely with distance.

Density: Density is defined as the ratio of general practitioners to population in a Health Board area. If demand is given, higher density should result in lower fee and higher utilisation. If GPs in high-density areas engage in compensatory demand stimulation to maintain incomes in the face of these tendancies, as discussed later in the chapter, still higher utilisation will result. Thus in both circumstances, in the absence or presence of physician-stimulated demand, there

[65]See Chapter 4.

should be a positive association between density and utilisation, and the presence of the variable in this model does not provide a test of physician-induced demand. There are reasons, however, not necessarily to expect significant results. Density is measured within Health Board areas. While it is suspected that between-area variation in density exceeds within-area variation, the latter is none the less important and will weaken the estimated relationships. Variability in demand will also influence utilisation and may overwhelm the influence of density. A superior test of physician-induced demand appears later in the chapter.

Medical Card ratio: The proportion of the population in a Health Board area with Category I entitlement, or Medical Card ratio, plays a part in our test for physician-induced demand, and will be discussed in more detail later. Briefly, the higher is this proportion, the higher will be average utilisation levels, and, other things equal, the higher will be GP workloads and incomes. Consequently, the higher this ratio, the less the need for demand stimulation, and the lower will be the utilisation of the ith patient, X_{gi}. Thus we hypothesise a negative relationship. As with density, we expect stronger and more relevant results in a somewhat different test, later in the chapter.

Other help: As noted in Chapter 5, some respondents reported that they received help with their medical care expenditures from their employer or some other group. Other help is included as a dichotomous variable, for control purposes.

Persons in household: Because each person's chance of being selected in our sample depended on the number of persons in the household, and because one's utilisation arguably is influenced by numbers of persons in the household, persons in the household was included as a control variable.

Other household members' GP utilisation: It was hypothesised that any individual's utilisation of medical care services would be positively associated with that of other household members. There are many reasons for this hypothesised relationship, and unravelling them statistically seems virtually impossible. First, household members frequently share the same tastes for medical care, so this variable is in effect a proxy for Z. Indeed, the household member making or most strongly influencing utilisation decisions may be the same for several household members. (A mother who is concerned with routine preventive care for one of her children, for example, will be likely not only to be concerned with it for other children, but also for herself and she may also urge it on other adult household members as well.) Secondly, several household members will frequently see the same GP, and consequently will be similarly affected by his or her tastes, attitudes, philosophy and/or economic needs. Hence this variable may also be a proxy for D. Third, this variable may also stand in for H, as there are likely to be positive correlations among the health statuses of household members because of infective illnesses and because they share many of the same genetic and environmental influences.

It might be objected that other household members' GP utilisation is endogenous — that is influenced by many of the same variables, such as eligibility, VHI cover, GP fee, farmer–non-farmer, as are already in the model. This is not always the case; most of our variables vary by individual, even within the household. Including the variable permits us to control for some important background and doctor variables. We deal with this possible econometric objection, here and in other models reported later, by reporting regressions both including and excluding other household members' GP utilisation.

Interactions: Because relationships amongst our independent variables may be multiplicative rather than additive, we have included a number of interactions in the model, as discussed in Chapter 1. In preliminary work, we tested a large number of two-, three-, and even four-way interactions, and found, in general, two types to yield good results frequently enough to be included in our models. One is an interaction between sex, age, eligibility Category I and no VHI cover, a dichotomous variable. For example, Woman-I-No VHI carries the value of one where the person is female, aged 45–64, has Category I eligibility, and does not have VHI cover. The other is an interaction amongst the regional variables in the model. In the present model, the only regional variables are Density and Medical Card Ratio; their interaction is included as an independent variable. (Other regional variables included in other models are the Consultant Density and an Index of per capita Income.)

Other variables: Other variables were included in versions of the estimating equation not reported here. In general, they did not improve results (i.e., they did not contribute except trivially to R^2s and t-statistics were low.) These other variables included Health Board area of residence. Appendix Table A.3 shows differences in GP utilisation among Health Board areas, with persons in the Southern area averaging only 3.4 consultations per year, whilst those in the North-Western area averaged 4.0. But these differences are apparently due to such influences as age and category of entitlement, as Health Board variables (introduced as seven dichotomous variables) were almost never significant. The same is true of occupation of head of household, as noted, with the exception of the farmer category. And the same is true of the year of age the head of household completed his or her full-time education. It was decided that it would add little if anything to publish these equations in full.

The Results

The analysis was done on all persons and on seven major sub-groups in the population, the members of which arguably might be expected to have different utilisation behaviour. Those with Category I eligibility do not have to pay for medical care, including GP services. Those with Categories II and III pay for varying proportions of their medical care, but they are all alike in having to pay GPs.

"Mothers" are female adults who are parents of other household members. Their morbidity patterns, and hence their utilisation, varies from that of the rest of the population. Separate equations are also estimated for males only, females only, the elderly (persons aged over 64) and children (persons aged under 16), because the literature indicates different morbidity and utilisation patterns among these groups.

For all persons and for each sub-group, three tables are reported. The first (e.g., Table 6.3), reports on a logistic regression in which the dependent variable is dichotomous, whether the person had any GP consultations at all in 1980. As noted in Chapter 1, the left-hand side of these logistic regressions is equal to log $(p/1-p)$, where p is the probability that a person had a GP consultation. Thus the parameters do not have a direct, common-sense interpretation, as those in OLS (ordinary least squares) regressions, for example, do, though signs and significance levels have the same meaning as elsewhere. Therefore, we report a second table (e.g., Table 6.4), based on the first, which uses the logistic regression results to calculate probabilities based on specified values of the independent variables. The third table (e.g., Table 6.5) reports on OLS regressions of the numbers of GP consultations, for those persons having any. Because there is a chance of sample selection bias, we have included the inverse of the Mills ratio as an independent variable, as discussed in Chapter 1.

In both logistic and OLS regressions, we report on both a "full model", in which all independent variables for which relationships are hypothesised are included, and a "5% version", in which only those variables from the full model meeting a 5 per cent significance test are included. The variables significant in the former may vary somewhat from those in the latter, mainly because of colinearity amongst independent variables. We also report on the significance of the whole equation (a χ^2 test in logistic regressions, an F test in OLS regressions), and on $\bar{R}^2$ (adjusted in all cases for degrees of freedom), which measures the percentage of the variance in the dependent variable explained by the equation. In general, our equations are very significant but the R^2s are low. This can be interpreted as meaning that economic and demographic variables have a relatively small effect on utilisation — generally 10 per cent or less — but that they have effects is statistically quite certain.

Results are given in Tables 6.3–6.26. Note that where a variable is dichotomous, representing a quality, the absence of that quality is reflected in the intercept term. For example, sex = female is a variable. Sex = male is included in the constant term. Likewise, included in the constant term are eligibility = Category II, VHI cover = yes, other help with medical costs = no, and occupation of Head of Household = non-farmer. Where sex-age-eligibility-VHI cover variables are included in the Model, the absence of the specified properties is included in the intercept term. For example, in Tables 6.3–6.5, the intercept term includes utilisation of persons with VHI cover, in Categories II/III, aged 0–4 or 18–39.

We will first discuss the results for all persons, i.e., Tables 6.3, 6.4, and 6.5. We will then review the results for sub-groups in the population, by comparing them with the experience of all persons.

Table 6.3 shows sex to be a very significant influence, in all versions, on

Table 6.3: *Logistic regression of any general practitioner consultations in 1980 (dichotomous variable) on selected independent variables, all persons*[a]

	Full Model[b]		5% Version[b]	
	(1)	(2)	(3)	(4)
$\bar{R}^{2}$[c]	.059	.070	.058	.063
N	1,068	1,068	1,068.00	1,068
Equation χ^2	122.69**	139.51**	91.30**	112.00**
Intercept[d]	-2.645	-3.544	1.430	2.703**
	(.24)	(.42)	(2.66)	(8.05)
Sex = Female	.476**	.514**	.481**	.499**
	(9.31)	(10.63)	(11.57)	(12.76)
Category III	-.571**	-.555**	-.437	-.437*
	(6.44)	(5.99)		(3.97)
Category I	.205	.172	.845**	.687**
	(.11)	(.08)	(23.40)	(15.78)
Persons in household	-.067*	-.056		
	(3.73)	(2.56)		
Age	-.020	-0.21		
	(2.38)	(2.49)		
Age squared ÷ 1,000	.311	.347*	.174**	.196**
	(3.01)	(3.71)	(17.05)	(23.17)
No VHI	-.557**	-.610**		-.560**
	(7.10)	(8.31)		(8.21)
Distance to GP	.025	.026		
	(.27)	(.27)		
GP Fee	.019	.039		
	(.10)	(.40)		
House Call Fee	.051	.043		
	(2.05)	(1.43)		
GP Density	8.121	9.442	-4.013*	-5.359**
	(.44)	(.58)	(4.52)	(8.21)
Other Help	.277	.277		
	(1.09)	(1.06)		
Medical Card Ratio	14.301	15.991		
	(1.27)	(1.56)		
Farmer	-.284	-.236	-.334*	
	(2.21)	(1.51)	(4.54)	
Category I - No VHI	.330	.342		
	(.23)	(.25)		
Girl-I-No VHI[e]	-.363	-.326	-.830*	
	(.62)	(.49)	(4.03)	
Woman-I-No VHI[e]	1.271*	1.219*		
	(5.83)	(5.31)		
Lady-I-No VHI[e]	.748	.661		
	(2.05)	(1.44)		
Boy-I-No VHI[e]	.155	1.72		
	(.10)	(.12)		
Man-I-No VHI[e]	1.300*	1.243*		
	(5.14)	(4.63)		

Table 6.3 (*contd.*)

	Full Model[b]		5% Version[b]	
	(1)	(2)	(3)	(4)
$\bar{R}^{2(c)}$	.059	.070	.058	.063
N	1,068	1,068	1,068	1,068
Equation χ^2	122.69**	139.51**	91.30**	112.00**
Gent-I-No VHI[e]	1.116	.951		
	(4.22)	(3.05)		
GP Density-Medical Card	−30.745	−34.544		
Ratio Interaction	(1.19)	(1.47)		
Household GP Utilisation	—	.083**		.091**
		(13.68)		(16.94)
Joint Tests				
Age	(3.11)	(4.29)*		
GP Density	(4.85)*	(5.54)*		
Medical Card Ratio	(1.53)	(1.79)		

Notes: [a]χ^2 in parentheses beneath parameter estimates. [b]Columns (1) and (3) exclude, and Columns (2) and (4) include, household GP utilisation variable in model. [c]$\bar{R}^2$ adjusted for degrees of freedom. [d]Intercept term includes in full model: sex = male; eligibility = Category II; VHI cover = yes; other help = no; head of household a farmer = no; and age = 0–4, or 18–39. [e]"Girl", "Boy" = age 5–17; "Woman", "Man" = age 40–64; "Lady", "Gent" = age 65+.
Significance: *0.01 < p ≤ 0.05; **p ≤ 0.01.

whether a person saw a GP in 1980, females being more likely to have consultations than males. Category of eligibility is also quite significant. Category I eligibility is significantly positive in the 5 per cent versions, whilst the Category I - No VHI interactions are significant in the full models. Category III is significantly negative in most cases (Category II being reflected in the intercept term). As persons in both Categories II and III are ineligible for free GP services, this latter difference in utilisation cannot be attributed to price. Rather, it must reflect either health status or background (income, class) differences. This suggests that the higher utilisation of persons in Category I, where there is a price effect, may also reflect similar non-price differences.

Age is negative but not significant, while age squared is significant and positive, suggesting a U-shaped relationship.

However, the appropriate significance test where two versions of a variable (in this case age and age squared, in other cases main effects and interaction) are included in the model is a joint test, as discussed in Chapter 1 and such a test has been performed and is reported at the foot of the table.

No VHI is negative and significant in most models, which is the same as saying that persons with VHI cover are *more* likely to have GP consultations, where the other variables in the model are controlled for.

GP density is positive and insignificant in the full model, but negative and significant in the 5 per cent version. If the latter is credited, it runs counter to the

Table 6.4: *Probability of any GP consultations, all persons, 1980 (based on logistic regression)*[a]

	Household utilisation is	Probabilities			
		Excluded		Included	
		Full Model	5% Version	Full Model	5% Version
Baseline probability applies when the following variables are set equal to their means, as below:[b]	*Baseline probability* *	.63	.69	.64	.67
Age = 38.5	*Other probabilities* **				
Distance to GP = 2.6	*Sex* = male	.51	.58	.51	.55
GP fee = £2.43	*Age =*				
House call	min = 1	.70	.63	.70	.60
fee = £2.78	10	.66	.64	.66	.61
GP density = .462	20	.64	.65	.64	.62
Medical Card	30	.63	.67	.63	.64
ratio = .370	40	.63	.69	.64	.67
Household GP	50	.65	.73	.66	.71
utilisation = 3.34	60	.68	.76	.70	.75
Persons in household = 4.23	70	.72	.80	.75	.80
and when the following	max = 95	.85	.89	.88	.90
qualities obtain:[b]	*Eligibility =*				
sex = female	Category I	.74	.84	.70	.80
eligibility = Category II	Category III	.49	—	.50	.57
VHI cover = no	*VHI cover* = yes	.75	—	.76	.78
other help = no	*Distance to GP*				
farmer = no	min = under 1 mile	.61	—	.62	—
	max = more than 10 miles	.65	—	.66	—
**Other probabilities*	*GP fee*				
apply when variables are	min = £0	.62	—	.61	—
changed, one by one (the	max = £7	.65	—	.68	—
others held constant as above)	*House call fee*				
to the values and/or qualities	min = £0	.60	—	.61	—
indicated.	max = £10	.71	—	.71	—
	GP density				
	min = 0.429	.67	.72	.68	.71
	max = 0.555	.58	.60	.59	.55
	Other help = yes	.69	—	.70	—
	Medical card ratio				
	min = 0.232	.65	—	.66	—
	max = 0.586	.66	—	.66	—
	Farmer = yes	.56	.61	.58	—
	Persons in household				
	min = 1	.68	—	.68	—
	max = 14	.47	—	.50	—
	Household GP utilisation				
	min = 0	—	—	.57	.60
	max = 40	—	—	.97	.98

Notes: [a]See Table 6.3. [b]For 5% version, applies only to variables in the model; for household utilisation, applies only to model including that variable.

Table 6.5: *Regression of annual numbers of general practitioner consultations, 1980, on selected independent variables, ordinary least squares, persons with any consultations only*[a]

	Full Model[b]		5% Version[b]	
	(1)	*(2)*	*(3)*	*(4)*
$\bar{R}^{2[b]}$	0.185	0.220	0.185	0.225
N	729	729	729	729
Equation F	10.219**	12.437**	55.01**	23.19**
Intercept[c]	0.903	0.766	-2.795	-0.354
Sex female	0.547	0.896	—	—
	(0.799)	(1.439)		
Age	-0.029	-0.046	—	—
	(0.580)	(1.011)		
Age squared ÷ 1,000	0.405	0.729	—	0.549**
	(0.603)	(1.243)		(3.922)
Category I	1.891	2.327*	—	2.129**
	(1.618)	(2.185)		(2.950)
Category III	-0.196	-0.292	—	—
	(0.205)	(0.332)		
No VHI	1.663(*)	1.237	2.268**	1.310(*)
	(2.039)	(1.684)	(3.718)	(2.032)
GP Fee	-0.290	-0.181	—	—
	(1.218)	(0.787)		
House Call Fee	0.287	0.307*	—	0.225*
	(1.965)	(2.234)		(2.182)
Other help	-0.636	-0.470	—	—
	(0.630)	(0.495)		
Farmer	-1.357	-1.371*	—	-1.635*(*)
	(1.995)	(2.311)		(2.827)
Persons in household	-0.136	-0.189	—	—
	(0.931)	(1.476)		
Girl-I-No VHI[d]	-3.189(*)	-3.219	—	—
	(1.705)	(1.769)		
Woman-I-No VHI[d]	4.275	5.413**	—	5.654**
	(1.780)	(3.920)		(5.511)
Lady-I-No VHI[d]	0.369	0.521	-2.154*	—
	(0.191)	(0.341)	(2.272)	
Boy-I-No VHI[d]	-2.771	-3.135	—	—
	(1.399)	(1.617)		
Man-I-No VHI[d]	3.325	3.876*	—	3.403*(*)
	(1.618)	(2.409)		(2.602)
Gent-I-No VHI[d]	3.224	3.275(*)	—	2.580*
	(1.601)	(2.097)		(2.406)
Inverse Mills	0.450	0.017	1.860**	
	(0.795)	(0.295)	(10.955)	

Table 6.5 *continued*

Table 6.5 (*contd.*)

	Full Model[b]		5% Version[b]	
	(1)	*(2)*	*(3)*	*(4)*
$\bar{R}^{2[b]}$	0.185	0.220	0.185	0.225
N	729	729	729	729
Equation F	10.219**	12.437**	55.01**	23.19**
Household Utilisation		0.271**		0.285**
		(4.281)		(5.775)
Joint Tests:				
Age	(1.847)	(1.795)		

Notes: [a]Figures in parentheses beneath parameter estimates are t-statistics. Columns (1) and (3) include, and Columns (2) and (4) exclude, household utilisation (GP utilisation of other household members). [b]$\bar{R}^2$ adjusted for degrees of freedom. [c]Intercept term in Full Model includes sex = male; eligibility = Category II; VHI cover = yes; Other help = no; Household Head a Farmer or Fisher = no. [d]"Girl", "Boy" = 5–17; "Man", "Woman" = 40–64; "Lady", "Gent" = age 65+.
Significance: *0.01 < p ≤ 0.05. **p ≤ 0.01.
(*)Parentheses around asterisk indicate parameter did not pass t-test adjusted for heteroscedasticity; see Chapter 1.

Table 6.6: *Logistic regression of any general practitioner consultations in 1980 (Dichotomous Variable) on selected independent variables, persons in category I only*[a]

	Full Model[b]		5% Version[b]	
	(1)	*(2)*	*(3)*	*(4)*
$\bar{R}^{2[c]}$	.079	.095	.093	.106
N	556	556	556	556
Equation χ^2	79.51**	90.61**	56.08**	65.28**
Intercept[d]	.581	–2.484	.014	–.258
	(.01)	(.09)	(.01)	(1.38)
Sex = Female	.166	.179		
	(.15)	(.18)		
Category I persons in household	.005	–.025		
	(.01)	(.18)		
Age	.003	.006	.031**	.030**
	(.02)	(.04)	(50.28)	(47.89)
Age squared ÷ 1,000	–.291	–.295		
	(.88)	(.89)		
No VHI	–.730	–.820		
	(2.79)	(3.50)		
Distance to GP	–.129	–.124		
	(2.52)	(2.25)		
GP Density	6.771	10.671		
	(.14)	(.34)		
Other help	–.423	–.585		
	(.69)	(1.29)		
Medical Card Ratio	7.516	12.303		
	(.16)	(.42)		

Table 6.6 (contd.)

	Full Model[b]		5% Version[b]	
	(1)	(2)	(3)	(4)
$\bar{R}^{2(c)}$	.079	.095	.093	.106
N	556	556	556	556
Equation χ^2	79.51**	90.61**	56.08**	65.28**
Farmer	.462	.531		
	(2.49)	(3.25)		
Girl[e]	-.563	-.504		
	(1.54)	(1.21)		
Woman[e]	2.224**	2.089**		
	(7.83)	(6.82)		
Lady[e]	2.854**	2.683**		
	(6.98)	(6.12)		
Boy[e]	-.598	-.593		
	(1.84)	(1.75)		
Man[e]	2.030**	1.842*		
	(6.77)	(5.42)		
Gent[e]	2.733**	2.411*		
	(7.13)	(5.50)		
GP Density-Medical Card	-18.306	-28.755		
Ratio Interaction	(.20)	(.47)		
Household GP Utilisation	—	.113**		.095**
		(8.43)		(7.21)
Joint Tests:				
Age	(2.14)	(1.87)		
GP Density	(.27)	(.64)		
Medical Card Ratio	(.53)	(.74)		

Notes: [a]χ^2 in parentheses beneath parameter estimates. [b]Columns (1) and (3) exclude, and Columns (2) and (4) include, household GP utilisation variable in model. [c]$\bar{R}^2$ adjusted for degrees of freedom. [d]Intercept term includes in full model: sex = male; VHI cover = no; other help = no; head of household a farmer = no; and age = 0-4, or 18-39. [e]"Girl", "Boy" = age 5-17; "Woman", "Man" = age 40-64; "Lady", "Gent" = age 65+.
Significance: *0.01 < p ⩽ 0.05; **p ⩽ 0.01.

physician-induced demand thesis, as discussed in Chapter 2, where a positive relationship between the two is hypothesised. However, GP density is not only not significant, but a long way from being so, in all the regressions reported below for sub-groups in the population. A more direct and apposite test of the thesis appears later in this chapter.

Finally, in those versions including other household members' GP utilisation, this has an extremely significant association with the dependent variable.

As noted, the values of the parameters of Table 6.3 are incapable of straightforward interpretation. The regressions reported in that table are used in calculating Table 6.4, where we report probabilities of any GP consultation, based on specified values of the independent variables. (Similar calculations are reported in this chapter and the next wherever a logistic regression function is used, i.e., wherever the dependent variable is dichotomous.)

The first figure reported is the "baseline probability". This is the probability (0.63 in the full model, with household utilisation excluded) where *quantitative* variables are set equal to their *mean* values and where the following *qualities* are specified: The person is female, with Category II eligibility, no VHI cover, no other help, and not a member of a farming or fishing household.

In the remainder of Table 6.4, these specifications are changed, one by one, to determine their effects on the probabilities. For example, where we change sex from female to male, leaving all else unchanged, the probability of any GP consultations drops very considerably from 0.63 to 0.51. Similarly, where we change eligibility to Category I, the probability jumps to 0.74; where we change it to Category III, it drops to 0.49.

The U-shaped effect of age shows clearly in those probabilities. The positive effect of VHI cover proves to be a large one. On the other hand, the effects of many of the variables, including GP fee, and density, and the Medical Card ratio, appear to be quite small.

Table 6.4 reports only a small fraction of all possible probabilities. For example, the reported probability for males is only for males of average age and other characteristics measured by quantitative variables, with Category II eligibility, no VHI cover, no other help, and not a member of a farming/fishing family. Information is provided in Table 6.4 which the reader can use in conjunction with Table 6.3 to calculate any desired probability. The procedure, regrettably somewhat laborious, is to multiply the coefficients in Table 6.3 by the chosen specified values of the variables (the means, minima and maxima, are found in Table 6.4). The total will equal $\log (p/1-p)$. The last step is to solve for p, the desired probability. (All dichotomous variables are 0, 1, except for sex male = 1, female = 2 and VHI cover yes = 1, no = 2.)

Table 6.5 reports on OLS regressions of the numbers of GP consultations amongst persons with any in 1980. Because we have excluded all persons with no GP consultations, we have a non-randomly selected sample. A technique which tests for sample selection bias, and corrects for it if it exists, is to include as an independent variable in the OLS regression an "Inverse Mills ratio", derived from a probit regression. This technique is discussed more fully in Chapter 1. (The Inverse Mills ratio is included in the full models in Table 6.5 and other OLS regressions; it is included in 5 per cent versions only if it satisfies the 5 per cent inclusion criterion.)

According to a Goldfeld-Quandt test, the error terms in the OLS regressions reported in Table 6.5 are heteroscedastic. Accordingly, we have increased by 10 per cent the critical values of t for 5 per cent and 1 per cent significance levels. One and two asterisks indicate 5 per cent and 1 per cent significance levels, using unadjusted critical t values; but where a parentheses has been placed around an asterisk, as (*), the interpretation is that the parameter did not pass the adjusted t-test. This correction is also discussed in Chapter 1.

The R^2s are relatively high for this kind of analysis and the equations are quite significant. None the less, few parameters in the full models are significant, presumably because of multicolinearity. In the model including household utilisation, that variable is quite significant and positive and several other variables are significant. Persons with Category I eligibility have about two more consultations per year, when other influences are held constant, than those with Cate-

Table 6.7: *Probability of any GP consultations, 1980, Category I only (based on logistic regression)*[a]

		Probabilities			
		Excluded		Included	
	Household utilisation is	Full Model	5% Version	Full Model	5% Version
Baseline probability applies when the following variables are set equal to their means, as below:[b]	*Baseline probability**	.54	.82	.58	.83
	*Other probabilities***				
Age = 48.26	*Sex* = male	.48	—	.88	—
Distance to GP = 2.66	*Age =*				
GP density = .468	min = 1	.66	.51	.67	.53
Medical Card ratio = .396	10	.53	.58	.56	.60
Household GP utilisation = 3.76	20	.65	.65	.67	.67
Category I persons in	30	.62	.72	.65	.73
household = 2.60	40	.93	.78	.93	.79
and when the following	50	.91	.83	.92	.83
qualities obtain:[b]	60	.89	.87	.89	.87
sex = female	70	.91	.90	.92	.90
VHI cover = no	max = 95	.96	.95	.79	.95
other help = no	*VHI cover* = yes	.71	—	.76	—
farmer = no	*Distance to GP*				
	min = under 1 mile	.62	—	.66	—
***Other probabilities*	max = more than 10 miles	.43	—	.48	—
apply when variables are	*GP density*				
changed, one by one (the	min = 0.429	.56	—	.61	—
others held constant as above)	max = 0.555	.54	—	.59	—
to the values and/or qualities	*Other help* = yes	.43	—	.44	—
indicated.	*Medical Card ratio*				
	min = 0.232	.59	—	.65	—
	max = 0.586	.50	—	.55	—
	Farmer = yes	.65	—	.70	—
	Persons in Category I in household				
	min = 1	.54	—	.59	—
	max = 11	.55	—	.53	—
	Household GP utilisation				
	min = 0	—	—	.48	.77
	max = 36	—	—	.98	.99

Notes: [a]See Table 6.3. [b]For 5% version, applies only to variables in the model; for household utilisation, applies only to model including that variable.

gory II eligibility, represented in the intercept term. Women aged 40–64, with Category I eligibility and no VHI cover, have about 5.5 more consultations per year.

There is a significant positive relationship between the house call fee and utilisation, a result evidently due to Category II/III persons in the sample. (In the various analyses which follow, relating to partitioned sub-groups in the population, in only the version including only those persons is this variable significant, and in that version it is quite significant.) The positive association is as hypothesised earlier. In this set of regressions and elsewhere, house call fee usually has a better fit than usual GP fee, suggesting that it is more sensitive to market conditions.

Many variables are included in the full models because of a desire to test hypotheses. The 5 per cent versions presumably reduce multicollinearity and to that extent reflect more accurately the significance of the individual variables in the model. Note that both $\bar{R}^2$s and equation Fs rise in the 5 per cent versions, as compared with the full models. For every 10 GP consultations of other household members, one's own GP consultations rise by nearly 3. Controlling for household utilisation also improves the performance of several other variables.

The Inverse Mills is significant only in the 5 per cent, no household utilisation model, suggesting that in the other variables in the full model, and in the household utilisation, we control for factors associated with whether persons will see their GPs, i.e., with selection.

Category I eligibility is consistently strong, in its main effects and/or in interaction terms, both in influencing *whether* a person sees his or her GP, and, among those who do, *how many* visits there are.

Tables 6.6 through 6.26 report similar results for various sub-groups in the sample: persons with Category I eligibility only, who can avail of free general practitioner care; persons with category II or III eligibility, who must pay for GP services; mothers; males; females; persons aged 65 years and over; and children aged under 16 years.

Table 6.27 summarises the results of the 5 per cent versions of these regressions, with respect to sign and significance. The most striking thing in Table 6.27 is the consistency with which Category I eligibility influences GP utilisation. In every regression in which the variable appears (it is excluded, of course, in Category I and Category II/III partitions), either Category I, or (in the case of females) Category I — no VHI interaction, positively and significantly influences the probability of any GP contact. With the further exception of children aged under 16, it also invariably positively and significantly influences numbers of visits for those with any.

The significantly negative effect found for Category III in the all-persons case is not repeated for any of the sub-groups.

Age in some guise (age, age squared, and/or age-sex-Category I-No VHI interaction) influences GP utilisation in every case as well. Either GP fee or House Call fee (but never both) positively influences utilisation in many cases, as

Table 6.8: *Regression of annual numbers of general practitioner consultations, 1980, on selected independent variables, ordinary least squares, persons with any consultations only – Category I only*[a]

	Full Model[b]		5% Version[b]	
	(1)	*(2)*	*(3)*	*(4)*
$\bar{R}^{2}$[b]	0.095	0.145	0.095	0.152
N	312	312	312	312
Equation F	3.520**	4.769**	10.75**	13.84**
Intercept[c]	3.664	-1.349	4.717	3.172
Sex female	2.791	1.705	—	—
	(0.897)	(0.654)		
Age	-0.268	-0.126	0.085**	0.078**
	(1.414)	(0.875)	(4.009)	(3.77)
Age squared ÷ 1,000	3.059	0.976	—	—
	(1.288)	(0.700)		
No VHI	4.055	3.399	—	—
	(1.540)	(1.327)		
Other help	0.283	-0.174	—	—
	(0.097)	(0.063)		
Farmer	-4.417**	-2.587*	-2.770**	-2.505*
	(2.512)	(2.380)	(2.516)	(2.345)
Girl[d]	-7.051*	-4.883	—	—
	(2.032)	(1.744)		
Woman[d]	6.775	6.793	3.953**	4.243**
	(1.904)	(1.997)	(2.987)	(3.303)
Lady[d]	6.180	3.570	—	—
	(1.292)	(0.819)		
Boy[d]	-3.984	-3.673	—	—
	(1.261)	(1.216)		
Man[d]	6.738*	6.247	—	—
	(1.933)	(1.841)		
Gent[d]	9.050*	6.570	—	—
	(2.032)	(1.594)		
Inverse Mills	-2.192	-0.353	—	—
	(1.508)	(0.747)		
Household Utilisation		0.418**		0.386**
		(3.939)		(4.584)
Joint Tests:				
Age	(1.122)	(1.079)	—	—

Notes: [a]Figures in parentheses beneath parameter estimates are t-statistics. Columns (1) and (3) include, and Columns (2) and (4) exclude, household utilisation (GP utilisation of other household members). [b]$\bar{R}^{2}$ adjusted for degrees of freedom. [c]Intercept term in Full Model includes sex= male; VHI cover = yes; Other help = no; Household Head a Farmer or Fisher= no. [d]"Girl", "Boy" = age 5-17; "Man", "Woman" = age 40-64; "Lady", "Gent" = age 65+.
Significance: *0.01 < p ⩽ 0.05. **p ⩽ 0.01.

Table 6.9: *Logistic regression of any general practitioner consultations in 1980 (Dichotomous Variable) on selected independent variables, persons in Categories II and III only*[a]

	Full Model[b]		5% Version[b]	
	(1)	(2)	(3)	(4)
$\bar{R}^{2[c]}$	.040	.051	.034	.048
N	803	803	803	803
Equation χ^2	83.65**	96.66**	45.18**	65.09**
Intercept[d]	1.420	1.726	-.522	-.720
	(.05)	(.08)	(3.23)	(4.21)
Sex = Female	.895**	.955**	.575**	.623**
	(14.30)	(15.83)	(14.94)	(16.89)
Category III	-.508*	-.502*		
	(5.06)	(4.87)		
Category II, III persons in household	-.063	-.030	-.082*	
	(2.22)	(.46)	(5.06)	
Age	-.060**	-.062**		-.039**
	(9.53)	(10.17)		(7.34)
Age squared ÷ 1,000	.953**	1.035**		.644**
	(9.39)	(10.90)		(10.39)
No VHI	-.507**	-.578**		
	(6.34)	(8.02)		
Distance to GP	.079	.081		
	(2.02)	(2.11)		
GP Fee	.138*	.152*	.170**	
	(4.65)	(5.51)	(12.18)	
House Call Fee	.029	.017		
	(.65)	(.23)		
GP Density	-2.096	-3.686		
	(.02)	(.07)		
Other help	.541*	.535		
	(3.75)	(3.61)		
Medical Card Ratio	2.704	1.561		
	(.04)	(.01)		
Farmer	-.557**	-.509*	-.555**	-.547**
	(6.83)	(5.60)	(11.29)	(10.42)
Household GP Utilisation	—	.075**		.074**
		(10.42)		(11.46)
Girl[e]	-.697*	-.705*		
	(4.32)	(4.37)		
Woman[e]	-.738	-.799*		
	(3.20)	(3.69)		
Lady[e]	-1.111	-1.237		
	(1.64)	(2.01)		
Boy[e]	-.404	-.374		
	(1.84)	(1.55)		

Table 6.9 (*contd.*)

	Full Model[b]		5% Version[b]	
	(1)	*(2)*	*(3)*	*(4)*
$\bar{R}^{2(c)}$	.040	.051	.034	.048
N	803	803	803	803
Equation χ^2	83.65*	96.66**	45.18**	65.09**
Man[e]	−.039	−.060		
	(.01)	(.02)		
Gent[e]	−.649	−.707		
	(.61)	(.72)		
GP Density-Medical Card	−5.482	−2.696		
Ratio Interaction	(.03)	(.01)		
Joint Tests:				
Age	(10.17)**	(11.37)**		(12.54)**
GP Density	(2.34)	(2.73)		
Medical Card Ratio	(.10)	(.15)		

Notes: [a]χ^2 in parentheses beneath parameter estimates. [b]Columns (1) and (3) exclude, and Columns (2) and (4) include, household GP utilisation variable in model. [c]$\bar{R}^2$ adjusted for degrees of freedom. [d]Intercept term includes in full model: sex = male; eligibility = Category II; VHI cover = no; other help = no; head of household a farmer = no; and age = 0–4, or 18–39. [e]"Girl", "Boy" = age 5–17; "Woman", "Man" = age 40–64; "Lady", "Gent" = age 65+.
Significance: *$0.01 < p \leqslant 0.05$. **$p \leqslant 0.01$.

Table 6.10: *Probability of any GP consultations, 1980, Categories II and III only (based on logistic regression[a])*

		Probabilities			
	Household utilisation is	Excluded		Included	
		Full Model	5% Version	Full Model	5% Version
Baseline probability applies when the following variables are set equal to their means, as below:[b]	Baseline probability*	.70	.70	.70	.65
	*Other probabilities**				
Age = 31.77	Sex = male	.49	.57	.47	.50
Distance to GP = 2.61	Age =				
GP fee = £3.18	min = 1	.85	—	.85	.77
House call fee = £3.64	10	.64	—	.64	.71
GP density = .458	20	.72	—	.72	.67
Medical Card ratio = .357	30	.70	—	.70	.65
Household GP utilisation = 3.18	40	.54	—	.53	.67
Category II/III persons in	50	.60	—	.61	.71
household = 3.79	60	.70	—	.72	.77
and when the following	70	.76	—	.77	.84
qualities obtain:[b]	max = 84	.91	—	.93	.92
sex = female	*Eligibility* = Category III	.58	—	.58	—
eligibility = Category II	*VHI cover* = yes	.79	—	.80	—
VHI cover = no	*Distance to GP*				
other help = no	min = under 1 mile	.65	—	.65	—
farmer = no	max = more than 10 miles	.75	—	.75	—
	GP fee				
***Other probabilities*	min = £0	.60	.58	.59	.54
apply when variables are	max = £7	.80	.82	.80	.77
changed, one by one (the	*House call fee*				
others held constant as above)	min = £0	.68	—	.68	—
to the values and/or qualities	Max = £10	.74	—	.72	—
indicated.	*GP density*				
	min = 0.429	.73	—	.73	—
	max = 0.555	.62	—	.60	—
	Other help = yes	.80	—	.80	—
	Medical Card ratio				
	min = 0.232	.70	—	.69	—
	max = 0.586	.71	—	.72	—
	Farmer = yes	.57	.58	.58	.52
	Persons in Categories				
	II/III in household				
	min = 1	.74	.75	.72	—
	max = 11	.60	.57	.65	—
	Household GP Utilisation				
	min = 0	—	—	.65	.60
	max = 52	—	—	.99	.99

Notes: [a]See Table 6.9. [b]For 5% version, applies only to variables in the model; for household utilisation, applies only to model including that variable.

Table 6.11: *Regression of annual numbers of general practitioner consultations, 1980, on selected independent variables, ordinary least squares, persons with any consultations only – Categories II and III only*[a]

	Full Model[b]		5% Version[b]	
	(1)	*(2)*	*(3)*	*(4)*
$\bar{R}^{2\,[b]}$	0.064	0.078	0.064	0.075
N	416	416	416	416
Equation F	2.784**	3.072**	7.06**	6.69**
Intercept[c]	6.119	2.151	-0.863	-0.478
Sex female	2.141*	1.423*	—	1.144*
	(2.115)	(2.082)		(2.512)
Age	-0.180**	-0.130**	—	—
	(2.847)	(2.934)		
Age squared ÷ 1,000	2.376*	1.835*	—	—
	(2.417)	(2.399)		
Category III	-1.466	-0.553	—	—
	(1.640)	(0.932)		
No VHI	0.293	0.774	1.312**	0.936**
	(0.410)	(1.475)	(2.905)	(2.00)
GP Fee	-0.541*	-0.326	—	—
	(2.339)	(1.685)		
House Call Fee	0.360**	0.296**	0.231**	0.251**
	(3.349)	(2.957)	(2.740)	(2.978)
Other help	-0.142	-0.388	—	—
	(0.192)	(0.541)		
Farmer	-0.962	-0.425	—	—
	(1.450)	(0.756)		
Girl[d]	-3.862**	-2.675**	—	-2.172**
	(3.119)	(3.030)		(2.78)
Woman[d]	0.361	0.088	—	—
	(0.326)	(0.080)		
Lady[d]	1.165	-0.858	—	—
	(0.470)	(0.395)		
Boy[d]	-1.862*	-1.370	—	—
	(1.937)	(1.514)		
Man[d]	1.614	1.203	—	—
	(1.291)	(1.007)		
Gent[d]	0.396	-1.559	-2.261*	—
	(0.154)	(0.706)	(1.970)	
Inverse Mills	-1.159	-0.084	0.931**	—
	(1.342)	(0.943)	(3.633)	
Household Utilisation		0.192**		0.142**
		(2.707)		(2.793)
Joint Tests:				
Age	(3.488)**	(3.707)**	—	—

Notes: [a]Figures in parentheses beneath parameter estimates are t-statistics. Columns (1) and (3) include, and Columns (2) and (4) exclude, household utilisation (GP utilisation of other household members). [b]$\bar{R}^2$ adjusted for degrees of freedom. [c]Intercept term in full model includes sex = male; eligibility = Category II; VHI cover = yes; Other help = no; Household Head a Farmer or Fisher = no. [d]"Girl", "Boy" = 5-17; "Man", "Woman" = 40-64; "Lady", "Gent" = age 65+.
Significance: *$0.01 < p \leqslant 0.05$. **$p \leqslant 0.01$.

Table 6.12: *Logistic regressions of any general practitioner consultations in 1980 (Dichotomous Variable) on selected independent variables, mothers only*[a]

| | Full Model[b] | | 5% Version[b] | |
	(1)	(2)	(3)	(4)
$\bar{R}^{2[c]}$	.032	.036	.036	.045
N	766	766	766	766
Equation χ^2	60.39**	65.87**	35.73**	45.17**
Intercept[d]	−.019	−1.115	.643**	.458*
	(.00)	(.03)	(12.73)	(5.78)
Category I	1.803	1.826	1.162**	1.006**
	(2.57)	(2.62)	(26.01)	(18.83)
Category III	−.332	−.304		
	(1.43)	(1.19)		
Mothers in household	−.263	−.274		
	(.42)	(.46)		
Age	−.119**	−.104*		
	(7.17)	(5.46)		
Age Squared ÷ 1,000	1.010*	.883*		
	(4.96)	(3.78)		
No VHI	−.088	−.090		
	(.11)	(.12)		
Distance to GP	.110	.107		
	(2.84)	(2.66)		
GP Fee	.072	.085		
	(.67)	(.92)		
House Call Fee	.099*	.087*	.114**	.105**
	(4.80)	(3.74)	(10.21)	(8.60)
GP Density	8.978	10.280		
	(.35)	(.46)		
Other Help	.496	.482		
	(2.04)	(1.90)		
Medical Card Ratio	12.973	14.127		
	(.67)	(.79)		
Farmer	−.465	−.447	−.553**	−.511**
	(3.54)	(3.26)	(8.34)	(7.02)
Category I-No VHI interaction	−1.045	−1.089		
	(.78)	(.84)		
Woman-I-No VHI[e]	.910	.798		
	(3.43)	(2.60)		
Lady-I-No VHI[e]	.824	.707		
	(1.61)	(1.17)		
Medical Card Ratio-GP Density Interaction	−30.087	−32.724		
	(.74)	(.87)		
Household GP Utilisation	—	.081*		.105**
		(4.54)		(7.49)
Joint Tests:				
Age	(11.17)**	(8.43)**		
GP Density	(1.87)	(1.89)		
Medical Card Ratio	(1.03)	(1.19)		

Notes: [a]χ^2 in parentheses beneath parameter estimates. [b]Columns (1) and (3) exclude and Columns (2) and (4) include, household GP utilisation variable in model. [b]$\bar{R}^2$ adjusted for degrees of freedom. [c]Intercept term includes in full model: eligibility = Category II; VHI cover = no; other help = no; head of household a farmer = no; and age = 18–39. [e]"Woman" = age 40–64; "Lady" = age 65+. *Significance:* *$0.01 < p \leqslant 0.05$. **$p \leqslant 0.01$.

Table 6.13: *Probability of any GP consultations, 1980, mothers only (based on logistic regression)*[a]

	Household utilisation is	Probabilities			
		Excluded		Included	
		Full Model	5% Version	Full Model	5% Version
Baseline probability applies when the following	*Baseline probability**	.68	.73	.69	.75
variables are set equal to their	*Other probabilities***				
means, as below:[b]	*Age =*				
Age = 45.82	min = 18	.90	—	.90	—
Distance to GP = 2.63	20	.95	—	.88	—
GP fee = £2.77	30	.80	—	.80	—
House call fee = £3.21	40	.72	—	.73	—
GP density = 0.460	50	.66	—	.68	—
Medical Card ratio = .366	60	.64	—	.66	—
Household GP utilisation = 2.81	70	.67	—	.68	—
Mothers in household = 1.001	max = 88	.81	—	.80	—
and when the following	*Eligibility =*				
qualities obtain:[b]	Category I	.92	.90	.92	.89
eligibility = Category II	Category III	.60	—	.63	—
VHI cover = no	*VHI cover =* yes	.70	—	.71	—
other help = no	*Distance to GP*				
farmer = no	min = under 1 mile	.61	—	.63	—
	max = more than 10 miles	.75	—	.77	—
***Other probabilities*	*GP Fee*				
apply when variables are	min = £0	.63	—	.64	—
changed, one by one (the	max = £6	.73	—	.75	—
others held constant as above)	*House call fee*				
to the values and/or qualities	min = £0	.61	.66	.63	.68
indicated.	max = £10	.80	.86	.81	.86
	GP density				
	min = 0.429	.71	—	.73	—
	max = 0.555	.66	—	.68	—
	Other help = yes	.78	—	.79	—
	Medical Card ratio				
	min = 0.232	.72	—	.74	—
	max = 0.586	.66	—	.67	—
	Farmer = yes	.57	.61	.59	.64
	Mothers in household				
	min = 1	.68	—	.70	—
	max = 2	.62	—	.63	—
	Household GP utilisation				
	min = 0	—	—	.64	.69
	max = 39.66	—	—	.98	.99

Notes: [a]See Table 6.3. [b]For 5% version, applies only to variables in the model; for household utilisation, applies only to model including that variable.

Table 6.14: *Regression of annual numbers of general practitioner consultations, 1980, on selected independent variables, ordinary least squares, persons with any consultations only – mothers only*[a]

	Full Model[b]		5% Version[b]	
	(1)	*(2)*	*(3)*	*(4)*
$\bar{R}^{2[b]}$	0.147	0.166	0.175	0.173
N	151	151	151	151
Equation F	3.166**	3.314**	15.75**	15.58**
Intercept[c]	9.188	5.797	4.934	4.853
Age	-0.271	-0.026	—	—
	(0.861)	(0.747)		
Age squared ÷ 1,000	3.021	2.416	—	—
	(0.863)	(0.873)		
Category I	7.790*	7.126*	8.681**	—
	(2.074)	(2.228)	(5.613)	
Category III	-2.333	-1.914	—	—
	(0.935)	(0.800)		
No VHI	0.563	0.770	—	—
	(0.255)	(0.366)		
GP Fee	0.003	0.094	—	—
	(0.005)	(0.144)		
House Call Fee	0.448	0.332	—	—
	(1.159)	(0.909)		
Other help	0.144	0.179	—	—
	(0.053)	(0.068)		
Farmer	-2.114	-1.693	—	—
	(1.133)	(1.053)		
Woman-I-No[d]	3.382	1.973	—	8.015**
	(0.710)	(0.573)		(4.785)
Lady-I-No[d]	-6.130	-7.497	-6.161**	—
	(1.437)	(1.779)	(2.850)	
Inverse Mills	-0.329	-0.053	—	—
	(0.282)	(0.623)		
Household Utilisation		0.428		0.352**
		(1.625)		(2.492)
Joint Tests:				
Age	(2.652)**	(1.944)*	—	

Notes: [a]Figures in parentheses beneath parameter estimates are t-statistics. Columns (1) and (3) include, and Columns (2) and (4) exclude, household utilisation (GP utilisation of other household members). [b]$\bar{R}^2$ adjusted for degrees of freedom. [c]Intercept term in full model includes eligibility = Category II; VHI cover = yes; Other help = no; Head of Household Farmer or Fisher = no. [d]"Woman" = age 40-64; "Lady" = age 65+.
Significance: *$0.01 < p \leqslant 0.05$. **$p \leqslant 0.01$.

Table 6.15: *Logistic regressions of any general practitioner consultations in 1980 (Dichotomous Variable) on selected independent variables, males only*[a]

	Full Model[b]		5% Version[b]	
	(1)	*(2)*	*(3)*	*(4)*
$\bar{R}^{2}$[c]	.068	.061	.063	.073
N	975	975	975	975
Equation χ^2	115.87**	126.53**	92.58**	109.99**
Intercept[d]	6.533	6.718	.988**	1.199**
	(1.44)	(1.50)	(8.20)	(10.65)
Category I	1.442	1.447	.940**	1.047**
	(1.77)	(1.79)	(29.25)	(26.55)
Category III	-.452*	-.420		
	(3.92)	(3.37)		
Males in household	-.105	-.086		
	(3.50)	(2.32)		
Age	-.042**	-.043**	-.033**	-.037**
	(9.21)	(9.62)	(7.04)	(8.50)
Age Squared ÷ 1,000	.638**	.665**	.613**	.618**
	(11.04)	(11.87)	(13.57)	(13.46)
No VHI	-.550**	-.581**	-.344*	-.418**
	(6.96)	(7.69)	(4.18)	(6.27)
Distance to GP	-.077	-.081		-.094
	(2.45)	(2.69)		(5.12)
GP Fee	.099	.111		
	(2.37)	(2.91)		
House Call Fee	-.015	-.024		
	(.19)	(.45)		
GP Density	-11.277	-12.097		
	(.84)	(.96)		
Other Help	.341	.341		
	(1.73)	(1.71)		
Medical Card Ratio	-5.764	-6.663		
	(.21)	(.27)		
Farmer	-.092	-.032	-.344*	
	(.24)	(.03)	(4.89)	
Household GP Utilisation	—	.061**		.065**
		(9.23)		(10.89)
Category I-No VHI	-.452	-.479		
	(.16)	(.18)		
Boy-I-No VHI[e]	-.376	-.407		-.698*
	(.83)	(.96)		(3.91)
Man-I-No VHI[e]	.724	.669		
	(2.69)	(2.27)		
Gent-I-No VHI[e]	.422	.256		
	(.71)	(.26)		
GP Density-Medical Card Ratio Interaction	14.865	16.770		
	(.28)	(.35)		
Joint Tests:				
Age	(11.23)**	(12.23)**	(25.53)**	(18.37)**
GP Density	(4.06)*	(4.12)*		
Medical Card Ratio	(1.39)	(1.35)		

Notes: [a]χ^2 in parentheses beneath parameter estimates. [b]Columns (1) and (3) exclude, and Columns (2) and (4) include, household GP utilisation variable in model. [c]$\bar{R}^2$ adjusted for degrees of freedom. [d]Intercept term includes in full model: eligibility = Category II; VHI cover = no; head of household a farmer = no; and age = 0-4, or 18-39. [e]"Boy" = age 5-17; "Man" = age 40-64; "Gent" = age 65+.
Significance: *0.01 < p ≤ 0.05. **p ≤ 0.01.

Table 6.16: *Probability of any GP consultations, 1980, males only (based on logistic regression)*[a]

	Household utilisation is	Probabilities			
		Excluded		Included	
		Full Model	5% Version	Full Model	5% Version
Baseline probability applies when the following variables are set equal to their means, as below:[b]	Baseline probability*	.43	.47	.43	.45
	*Other probabilities***				
	Age =				
Age = 36.91	min = 1	.60	.57	.60	.58
Distance to GP = 2.64	10	.52	.51	.52	.51
GP fee = £2.50	20	.46	.47	.46	.46
House call fee = £2.894	30	.43	.46	.43	.45
GP density = .462	40	.44	.49	.44	.46
Medical Card ratio = .371	50	.47	.54	.48	.51
Household GP utilisation	60	.54	.62	.55	.58
= 3.74	70	.64	.72	.65	.68
Males in household = 2.33	max = 90	.85	.90	.87	.88
and when the following	*Eligibility =*				
qualities obtain:[b]	Category I	.67	.70	.67	.70
eligibility = Category II	Category III	.33	—	.33	—
VHI cover = no	*VHI cover =* yes	.57	.56	.58	.56
other help = no	*Distance to GP*				
farmer = no	min = under 1 mile	.48	—	.49	.52
	max = more than 10 miles	.37	—	.37	.38
***Other probabilities*	*GP Fee*				
apply when variables are	min = £0	.37	—	.37	—
changed, one by one (the	max = £7	.54	—	.56	—
others held constant as above)	*House call fee*				
to the values and/or qualities	min = £0	.44	—	.45	—
indicated.	max = £10	.40	—	.39	—
	GP density				
	min = 0.429	.47	—	.47	—
	max = 0.555	.30	—	.30	—
	Other help = yes	.52	—	.52	—
	Medical Card ratio				
	min = 0.232	.38	—	.38	—
	max = 0.586	.48	—	.48	—
	Farmer = yes	.41	.39	.43	—
	Males in household				
	min = 1	.47	—	.46	—
	max = 9	.27	—	.30	—
	Household GP Utilisation				
	min = 0	—	—	.38	.39
	max = 80	—	—	.96	.97

Notes: [a]See Table 6.15. [b]For 5% version, applies only to variables in the model; for household utilisation, applies only to model including that variable.

Table 6.17: *Regression of annual numbers of general practitioner consultations, 1980, on selected independent variables, ordinary least squares, persons with any consultations only – males only*[a]

	Full Model[b]		5% Version[b]	
	(1)	*(2)*	*(3)*	*(4)*
$\bar{R}^{2[b]}$	0.258	0.3031	0.233	0.287
N	322	322	322	322
Equation F	9.620**	11.004**	32.28**	32.06**
Intercept[c]	5.295	3.117	−0.181	1.503
Age	−0.136(*)	−0.098	—	—
	(2.082)	(1.732)		
Age squared ÷ 1,000	2.082*	1.475(*)	—	0.613**
	(2.177)	(1.954)		(3.480)
Category I	2.218	1.139	—	3.908**
	(1.442)	(0.916)		(5.083)
Category III	−0.413	−0.081	—	—
	(0.341)	(0.071)		
No VHI	0.624	0.601	1.629(*)	—
	(0.625)	(0.648)	(2.066)	
GP Fee	−0.321	−0.382	−0.500*(*)	—
	(1.059)	(1.329)	(2.702)	
House Call Fee	0.240	0.196	—	—
	(1.296)	(1.098)		
Other help	1.898	1.580	—	—
	(1.513)	(1.308)		
Farmer	−1.901*	−1.020	—	—
	(2.247)	(1.424)		
Boy-I-No VHI[d]	−2.730	−2.612	—	−4.440*(*)
	(1.463)	(1.477)		(2.765)
Man-I-No VHI[d]	5.685**	4.452**	—	—
	(3.244)	(2.858)		
Gent-I-No VHI[d]	4.516*(*)	3.159	—	—
	(2.532)	(1.851)		
Inverse Mills	−0.571	0.099	1.585**	—
	(0.897)	(0.610)	(6.970)	
Household Utilisation		0.252*(*)		0.336**
		(2.782)		(5.380)
Joint Tests:				
Age	(3.520)**	(3.794)**		

Notes: [a]Figures in parentheses beneath parameter estimates are t-statistics. Columns (1) and (3) include, and Columns (2) and (4) exclude, household utilisation (GP utilisation of other household members). [b]$\bar{R}^2$ adjusted for degrees of freedom. [c]Intercept term in Full Model includes eligibility = Category II; VHI cover = yes; Other help = no; Household Head a Farmer or Fisher = no. [d]"Boy" = age 5–17; "Man" = age 40–64; "Gent" = age 65+.
Significance: *$0.01 < p \leqslant 0.05$. **$p \leqslant 0.01$.
(*)Parentheses around an asterisk indicated parameter did not pass t-test adjusted for heteroscedasticity; see Chapter 1.

Table 6.18: *Logistic regressions of any general practitioner consultations in 1980 (Dichotomous Variable) on selected independent variables, females only*[a]

	Full Model[b]		5% Version[b]	
	(1)	*(2)*	*(3)*	*(4)*
$\bar{R}^{2[c]}$	.049	.059	.058	.066
N	1,000	1,000	1,000	1,000
Equation χ^2	93.48**	106.91**	82.75**	*89.09**
Intercept[d]	-2.887	-2.941	.463	.341
	(.25)	(.26)	(2.88)	(1.86)
Category I	-.256	-.234		
	(.22)	(.19)		
Category III	-.228	-.178		
	(.94)	(.57)		
Number of Females in household	-.184**	-.170**	-.209**	-.200**
	(8.96)	(7.62)	(14.26)	(13.16)
Age	-.020	-.020		
	(2.10)	(1.99)		
Age Squared ÷ 1,000	.310	.322		
	(2.53)	(2.73)		
No VHI	-.075	-.084		
	(.12)	(.15)		
Distance to GP	.118*	.119	.118*	
	(4.63)	(4.63)	(4.93)	
GP fee	.132*	.168*	.172**	.189**
	(3.70)	(5.84)	(10.47)	(12.47)
House Call Fee	.041	.029		
	(1.15)	(.57)		
GP Density	8.025 7.367			
	(.38)	(.32)		
Other Help	.598*	.600*	.602*	.590*
	(4.08)	(4.03)	(4.25)	(4.21)
Medical Card Ratio	12.265	11.721		
	(.82)	(.74)		
Farmer	-.596**	-.543**	-.561**	
	(8.18)	(6.74)	(8.20)	
Household GP Utilisation		.083**		.086**
		(10.59)		(12.14)
Category I-No VHI	1.386*	1.355*	1.570**	1.418**
	(4.65)	(4.41)	(41.63)	(34.23)
Girl-I-No VHI[e]	-.905*	-.874*	-1.333**	-1.237**
	(4.41)	(4.08)	(15.37)	(13.13)
Woman-I-No VHI[e]	.366	.293		
	(.66)	(.42)		
Lady-I-No VHI[e]	.489	.351		
	(.82)	(.42)		
GP Density-Medical Card Ratio Interaction	-26.216	-25.072		
	(.76)	(.69)		
Joint Tests:				
Age	(2.57)	(2.95)		
GP Density	(1.89)	(1.92		
Medical Card Ratio	(1.00)	(.90)		

Notes: [a]χ^2 in parentheses beneath parameter estimates. [b]Columns (1) and (3) exclude, and Columns (2) and (4) include, household GP utilisation variable in model. [c]$\bar{R}^2$ adjusted for degrees of freedom. [d]Intercept term includes in full model: eligibility = Category II; VHI cover = no; head of household a farmer = no; age = 0-4, or 18-39; and other help = no. [e]"Girl" = age 5-17; "Woman" = age 40-64; "Lady" = age 65+.
Significance: *0.01 < p ≤ 0.05. **p ≤ 0.01.

Table 6.19: *Probability of any GP consultations, 1980, females only (based on logistic regression)*[a]

Household utilisation is	Excluded Full Model	Excluded 5% Version	Included Full Model	Included 5% Version
Baseline probability*	.66	.68	.66	.66
Other probabilities**				
Age =				
min = 1	.72	—	.72	—
10	.69	—	.69	—
20	.67	—	.67	—
30	.65	—	.66	—
40	.66	—	.66	—
50	.67	—	.68	—
60	.70	—	.71	—
70	.74	—	.76	—
max = 95	.86	—	.88	—
Eligibility =				
Category I	.85	—	.86	—
Category III	.60	—	.62	—
VHI cover = yes	.67	—	.68	—
Distance to GP				
min = under 1 mile	.58	.60	.59	—
max = more than 10 miles	.74	.76	.75	—
GP Fee				
min = £0	.58	.57	.56	.55
max = £7	.78	.82	.81	.82
House call fee				
min = £0	.63	—	.64	—
max = £10	.72	—	.71	—
GP density				
min = 0.429	.69	—	.69	—
max = 0.555	.64	—	.64	—
Other help = yes	.78	.79	.78	.78
Medical Card ratio				
min = 0.232	.67	—	.68	—
max = 0.586	.68	—	.69	—
Farmer = yes	.51	.54	.53	—
Females in household				
min = 1	.70	.73	.71	.71
max = 9	.35	.34	.38	.33
Household GP Utilisation				
min = 0	—	—	.60	.59
max = 40	—	—	.98	.98

*Baseline probability applies when the following variables are set equal to their means, as below:[b]

  Age = 38.66
  Distance to GP = 2.60
  GP fee = £2.50
  House call fee = £2.87
  GP Density = .461
  Medical Card ratio = .367
  Household GP utilisation = 3.44
  Females in household = 2.24

and when the following qualities obtain:[b]

  eligibility = Category II
  VHI cover = no
  other help = no
  farmer = no

**Other probabilities* apply when variables are changed, one by one (the others held constant as above) to the values and/or qualities indicated.

Notes: [a]See Table 6.18. [b]For 5% version, applies only to variables in the model; for household utilisation, applies only to model including that variable.

Table 6.20: *Regression of annual numbers of general practitioner consultations, 1980, on selected independent variables, ordinary least squares, persons with any consultations only – females only*[a]

	Full Model[b]		5% Version[b]	
	(1)	(2)	(3)	(4)
$\overline{R}^{2[b]}$	0.142	0.1702	–0.148	0.166
N	406	406	406	406
Equation F	6.174**	6.984**	23.27**	26.76**
Intercept[c]	1.601	0.550	–0.757	3.803
Age	0.010	–0.006	—	—
	(0.120)	(0.099)		
Age squared ÷ 1,000	0.052	0.377	—	—
	(0.044)	(0.427)		
Category I	2.641	3.226	—	—
	(1.324)	(1.911)		
Category III	–1.046	–0.856	—	—
	(0.762)	(0.664)		
No VHI	1.462	1.340	2.204*	—
	(1.184)	(1.189)	(2.371)	
GP Fee	–0.197	–0.031	—	—
	(0.547)	(0.087)		
House Call Fee	0.330	0.325	—	—
	(1.536)	(1.601)		
Other help	–2.030	1.823	—	—
	(1.354)	(1.279)		
Farmer	–1.759	–1.794(*)	—	—
	(1.584)	(1.934)		
Girl-I-No VHI[d]	–3.883	–3.983	—	—
	(1.656)	(1.760)		
Woman-I-No VHI[d]	4.620	4.544*	3.473*(*)	7.801**
	(1.716)	(2.420)	(2.629)	(7.095)
Lady-I-No VHI[d]	0.854	0.161	—	4.082**
	(0.383)	(0.075)		(4.102)
Inverse Mills	0.125	–0.010	0.985**	—
	(0.180)	(0.177)	(4.194)	
Household Utilisation		0.290**		0.277**
		(3.048)		(3.776)
Joint Tests:				
Age	(0.682)	(0.962)	—	

Notes: [a]Figures in parentheses beneath parameter estimates are t-statistics. Columns (1) and (3) include, and Columns (2) and (4) exclude, household utilisation (GP utilisation of other household members). [b]$\overline{R}^2$ adjusted for degrees of freedom. [c]Intercept term in Full Model includes eligibility = Category II; VHI cover = yes; Other help = no; Household Head a Farmer or Fisher = no. [d]"Girl" age = 5-17; "Woman" = age 40-64; "Lady" = age 65+.
Significance: *0.01 < p ≤ 0.05. **≤ 0.01.
(*) Parentheses around an asterisk indicated parameter did not pass t-test adjusted for heteroscedasticity; see Chapter 1.

Table 6.21: *Logistic regressions of any general practitioner consultations in 1980 (Dichotomous Variable) on selected independent variables, persons aged over 64 only*[a]

	Full Model[b]		5% Version[b]	
	(1)	*(2)*	*(3)*	*(4)*
$\bar{R}^{2[c]}$	.038	.036	.049	.049
N	374	374	374	374
Equation χ^2	42.76**	43.90**	20.34**	20.34**
Intercept[d]	−45.025*	−46.873*	.021	.021
	(5.50)	(5.87)	(.0)	(.0)
Sex = Female	.749*	.785*	.612*	.612*
	(5.30)	(5.75)	(4.30)	(4.30)
Category I	1.068**	1.007*	1.117**	1.117**
	(6.56)	(5.74)	(14.36)	(14.36)
Category III	−1.053	−1.032		
	(2.75)	(2.65)		
Aged Persons in Household	.00	−.116		
	(.00)	(.13)		
Age	1.302**	1.312**		
	(8.56)	(8.56)		
Age squared ÷ 1,000	−8.591**	−8.658**		
	(8.67)	(8.66)		
No VHI	−.996	−.999		
	(3.27)	(3.31)		
Distance to GP	−.040	−.035		
	(.12)	(.09)		
GP Fee	−.194	−.186		
	(2.22)	(2.04)		
House Call Fee	.052	.052		
	(.40)	(.39)		
GP Density	−2.640	.770		
	(.01)	(.0)		
Other Help	.862	.889		
	(.59)	(.62)		
Medical Card Ratio	.800	4.041		
	(.00)	(.02)		
Farmer	.049	.067		
	(.02)	(.03)		
GP Density-Medical Card Ratio Interaction	−4.036	−11.515		
	(.00)	(.04)		
Household GP Utilisation		.039		
		(.95)		
Joint Tests:				
Age	(8.63)**	(8.62)**		
GP Density	(.77)	(.75)		
Medical Card Ratio	(.40)	(.51)		

Notes: [a] χ^2 in parentheses beneath parameter estimates. [b] Columns (1) and (3) exclude, and Columns (2) and (4) include, household GP utilisation variable in model. [c] $\bar{R}^2$ adjusted for degrees of freedom. [d] Intercept term includes in full model: sex = male; eligibility = Category II; VHI cover = no; other help = no; and head of household a farmer = no.
Significance: *$0.01 < p \leqslant 0.05$; **$p \leqslant 0.01$.

Table 6.22: *Probability of any GP consultations, 1980, persons aged over 64 only (based on logistic regression)*[a]

	Household utilisation is	Probabilities			
		Excluded		Included	
		Full Model	5% Version	Full Model	5% Version
Baseline probability applies when the following variables are set equal to their means, as below:[b]	Baseline probability*	.85	.78	.86	.78
	*Other probabilities***				
	Sex = male	.73	.65	.74	.65
Age = 72.6	*Age =*				
Distance to GP = 2.74	min = 65	.70	—	.71	—
GP fee = £1.69	68	.79	—	.80	—
House call fee = £1.96	71	.84	—	.85	—
GP density = 0.46	74	.86	—	.87	—
Medical Card ratio = 0.393	77	.86	—	.87	—
Household GP utilisation = 3.84	80	.84	—	.85	—
Persons over 64 in household = 1.31	max = 95	.21	—	.22	—
and when the following qualities obtain:[b]	*Eligibility =*				
	Category I	.94	.91	.94	.91
sex = female	Category III	.67	—	.69	—
eligibility = Category II	*VHI cover* = yes	.94	—	.94	—
VHI cover = no	*Distance to GP*				
other help = no	min = under 1 mile	.87	—	.87	—
farmer = no	max = more than 10 miles	.84	—	.85	—
	GP fee				
**Other probabilities* apply when variables are changed, one by one (the others held constant as above) to the values and/or qualities indicated.	min = £0	.89	—	.89	—
	max = £6	.71	—	.74	—
	House Call Fee				
	min = £0	.84	—	.85	—
	max = £10	.90	—	.90	—
	GP density				
	min = 0.429	.87	—	.88	—
	max = 0.555	.80	—	.82	—
	Other help = yes	.93	—	.94	—
	Medical Card ratio				
	min = 0.232	.87	—	.89	—
	max = 0.586	.83	—	.83	—
	Farmer = yes	.86	—	.87	—
	Persons over 64 in household				
	min = 1	.85	—	.87	—
	max = 3	.85	—	.84	—
	Household GP utilisation				
	min = 0	—	—	.84	—
	max = 60	—	—	.98	—

Notes: [a]See Table 6.21. [b]For 5% version, applies only to variables in the model; for household utilisation, applies only to model including that variable.

Table 6.23: *Regression of annual numbers of general practitioner consultations, 1980, on selected independent variables, ordinary least squares, persons with any consultations only, aged over 64 years only*[a]

	Full Model[b]		5% Version[b]	
	(1)	*(2)*	*(3)*	*(4)*
$\bar{R}^{2[b]}$	0.070	0.139	0.078	0.163
N	176	176	176	176
Equation F	2.207*	3.377**	14.82**	16.95**
Intercept[c]	−153.677	−100.663	4.526	3.755
Sex female	−1.520	−0.500	—	—
	(0.785)	(0.434)		
Age	4.180	2.710	—	—
	(1.730)	(1.218)		
Age squared ÷ 1,000	−28.213	−17.909	—	—
	(1.705)	(1.206)		
Category I	3.016	3.820(*)	5.351**	4.271**
	(0.910)	(2.121)	(3.850)	(3.155)
Category III	1.380	0.597	—	—
	(0.285)	(0.132)		
No VHI	3.966	2.355	—	—
	(1.439)	(1.111)		
GP Fee	−0.517	−0.403	—	—
	(0.886)	(0.714)		
House Call Fee	0.165	0.323	—	—
	(0.385)	(0.873)		
Other help	−2.477	−0.997	—	—
	(0.553)	(0.259)		
Farmer	−1.126	−1.728	—	—
	(0.657)	(1.434)		
Inverse Mills	0.427	−0.028	—	—
	(0.388)	(0.735)		
Household Utilisation		0.383**		0.355**
		(3.289)		(4.204)
Joint Tests:				
Age	(3.950)**	(4.049)**		

Notes: [a]Figures in parentheses beneath parameter estimates are t-statistics. Columns (1) and (3) include, and Columns (2) and (4) exclude, household utilisation (GP utilisation of other household members). [b]$\bar{R}^2$ adjusted for degrees of freedom. [c]Intercept term in full model includes sex = male; eligibility = Category II; VHI cover = yes; Other help = no; Head of Household a Farmer or Fisher = no.
Significance: *$0.01 < p \leqslant 0.05$. **$p \leqslant 0.01$.
(*) Parentheses around an asterisk indicates parameter did not pass t-test adjusted for heteroscedasticity; see Chapter 1.

Table 6.24: *Logistic regressions of any general practitioner consultations in 1980 (Dichotomous Variable) on selected independent variables, persons aged under 16 only*[a]

	Full Model[b]		5% Version[b]	
	(1)	*(2)*	*(3)*	*(4)*
$\overline{R}^{2(c)}$	.095	.116	.109	.131
N	560	560	560	560
Equation χ^2	99.66**	117.24**	90.61**	106.73**
Intercept[d]	−1.279	−.007	2.027**	1.149**
	(.03)	(.00)	(20.83)	(6.28)
Sex = Female	.369	.422*		.407*
	(3.61)	(4.55)		(4.37)
Category I	1.230**	.996**	1.096**	.513*
	(11.74)	(7.60)	(15.37)	(4.18)
Category III	.154	.246		
	(.27)	(.66)		
Children in household	−.121	−.079	−.129*	
	(3.16)	(1.30)	(3.96)	
Age	−.133	−.111		
	(1.72)	(1.14)		
Age Squared ÷ 1,000	−3.078	−4.013	−10.704**	−10.089**
	(.26)	(.43)	(65.70)	(58.65)
No VHI	−.292	−.267		
	(1.04)	(.85)		
Distance to GP	−.010	−.011		
	(.03)	(.03)		
GP Fee	.011	.042		
	(.01)	(.18)		
House Call Fee	.081	.057	.091*	
	(2.61)	(1.25)	(4.85)	
GP Density	8.108	3.654		
	(.24)	(.05)		
Other Help	−.139	−.092		
	(.14)	(.06)		
Medical Card Ratio	7.283	1.979	−1.792*	−2.141**
	(.18)	(.01)	(4.48)	(6.39)
Farmer	−.072	.002		
	(.08)	(.00)		
GP Density-Medical Card Ratio Interaction	−19.681	−8.239		
	(.27)	(.05)		
Household GP Utilisation		.147**		.158**
		(13.13)		(15.60)
Joint Tests:				
Age	(63.04)**	(56.43)**		
GP Density	(.30)	(.06)		
Medical Card Ratio	(2.01)	(2.08)		

Notes: [a]χ^2 in parentheses beneath parameter estimates. [b]Columns (1) and (3) exclude, and Columns (2) and (4) include, household GP utilisation variable in model. [c]$\overline{R}^2$ adjusted for degrees of freedom. [d]Intercept term includes in full model: sex = male; eligibility = Category II; VHI cover = no; other help = no; and head of household a farmer = no.
Significance: *$0.01 < p \leqslant 0.05$. **$p \leqslant 0.01$.

Table 6.25: *Probability of any GP consultations, 1980, childreno aged under 16 only (based on logistic regression)*[a]

| | Household utilisation is | Probabilities | | | |
| | | Excluded | | Included | |
		Full Model	5% Version	Full Model	5% Version
Baseline probability applies when the following variables are set equal to their means, as below:[b]	Baseline probability*	.63	.65	.66	.73
	Other probabilities**				
	Sex = male	.54	—	.56	.64
Age = 8.29	Age =				
Distance to GP = 2.612	min = 1	.85	.79	.85	.84
GP fee = £2.84	4	.78	.76	.79	.82
House call fee = £3.32	7	.68	.70	.70	.77
GP density = .460	10	.55	.57	.58	.66
Medical Card ratio = .366	13	.40	.39	.43	.49
Household GP utilisation	max = 15	.30	.26	.33	.36
= 3.19	Eligibility =				
Persons under 16 in household	Category I	.86	.85	.84	.82
= 2.50	Category III	.67	—	.71	—
and when the following	VHI cover = yes	.70	—	.71	—
qualities obtain:[b]	Distance to GP				
sex = female	min = under 1 mile	.64	—	.66	—
eligibility = Category II	max = more than 10 miles	.62	—	.65	—
VHI cover = no	GP fee				
other help = no	min = £0	.62	—	.63	—
farmer = no	max = £6	.64	—	.69	—
	House call fee				
**Other probabilities*	min = £0	.57	.58	.61	—
apply when variables are	max = £10	.75	.77	.74	—
changed, one by one (the	GP density				
others held constant as above)	min = 0.429	.64	—	.66	—
to the values and/or qualities	max = 0.555	.67	—	.68	—
indicated.	Other help = yes	.60	—	.64	—
	Medical Card ratio				
	min = 0.232	.70	.70	.72	.78
	max = 0.586	.55	.56	.57	.63
	Farmer = yes	.62	—	.66	—
	Persons under 16 in household				
	min = 1	.67	.69	.68	—
	max = 8	.47	.48	.55	—
	Household GP Utilisation				
	min = 0	—	—	.54	.62
	max = 32	—	—	.99	.996

Notes: [a]See Table 6.24. [b]For 5% version, applies only to variables in the model; for household utilisation, applies only to model including that variable.

Table 6.26: *Regression of annual numbers of general practitioner consultations, 1980, on selected independent variables, ordinary least squares, persons with any consultations only – aged under 16 years only*[a]

	Full Model[b]		5% Version[b]	
	(1)	(2)	(3)	(4)
$\bar{R}^{2[b]}$	0.061	0.170	0.058	0.200
N	147	147	147	147
Equation F	1.868*	3.502**	9.03**	18.11**
Intercept[c]	13.972	7.082	6.381	3.980
Sex female	1.058	0.708	—	—
	(0.534)	(0.645)		
Age	-0.962*	-0.837*	-0.337**	-0.325**
	(2.155)	(1.991)	(3.005)	(3.133)
Age squared ÷ 1,000	40.674	35.674	—	—
	(1.407)	(1.312)		
Category I	5.462	1.740	—	—
	(1.339)	(0.861)		
Category III	-2.665	-1.453	—	—
	(1.006)	(0.946)		
No VHI	-1.231	-1.106	—	—
	(0.471)	(0.681)		
GP Fee	-0.083	-0.103	—	—
	(0.155)	(0.211)		
House Call Fee	0.398	0.107	—	—
	(1.301)	(0.397)		
Other help	4.026	2.085	—	—
	(1.721)	(1.193)		
Farmer	-2.596	-1.203	—	—
	(1.483)	(0.914)		
Inverse Mills	-4.211	-0.981	—	—
	(1.031)	(0.972)		
Household Utilisation		0.781**		0.646**
		(3.439)		(5.067)
Joint Tests:				
Age	(5.282)**	(4.806)**		

Notes: [a]Figures in parentheses beneath parameter estimates are t-statistics. Columns (1) and (3) include, and Columns (2) and (4) exclude, household utilisation (GP utilisation of other household members). [b]$\bar{R}^2$ adjusted for degrees of freedom. [c]Intercept term in full model includes sex = male; eligibility = Category II; VHI cover = yes; Other help = No; Head of Household a Farmer or Fisher = No.
Significance: *$0.01 < p \leqslant 0.05$. **$p \leqslant 0.01$.

hypothesised. No VHI, wherever it has a significant effect, somewhat paradoxically reduces the probability of any visit, while raising the number of visits for persons with any.

Head of household, a farmer or fisher reduces utilisation for everyone except children and the aged.

Other household members' utilisation increases the probability of any visits for all except the aged, and as well increases the number of visits in every model.

Finally, the Inverse Mills is significant and positive, indicating (and correcting for) selection bias, only in two cases, the all-persons model and the males only version.

It should be added that heteroscedasticity was found in the OLS regressions for males, females and the aged, thus requiring the same adjustment as discussed earlier in critical t-values.

Household Expenditures on GP Fees

We saw in Chapter 5 that an estimated £19.7m was spent by households in 1980 on GP fees, as compared with £18.8 spent by the General Medical Service on the same service for persons covered by Medical Cards. This household or private expenditure averaged £20.69 per household and £5.68 per person.

GP fee expenditures per household and household per person[66] are reported by a variety of characteristics of the households and household heads in Table 6.28. (More detail is provided in Appendix Tables A.16 through A.27).

It will be seen in Table 6.28 that category of health services eligibility has a marked effect on this type of expenditure. Households in Category I spent considerably less than other households; this is hardly surprising, as persons in Category I can avail of free GP care. Perhaps a little more surprising is that the figure was not nil.[67] Notable, too, is the extent to which households in Category III spent more than those in Category II. As this difference applies to household expenditures but not household per person, we can infer that household size varies between the two groups.

The figures given in Table 6.28 are gross, in the sense that VHI reimbursement is not deducted. Persons with VHI cover can gain reimbursement for outpatient care, including GP fees, only after a large deductible is reached, and it is not thought that VHI reimbursement looms very large in any case. Table 6.28 indicates that those with VHI cover spent about £10.00 more per household, and £3.00 more per person, than those without; but this difference is likely to reflect category of entitlement and socio-economic differences more than VHI cover itself.

---

[66]"Household per person" means household expenditures, divided by the number of persons in the household. We do not have data on expenditures for each individual in a household.

[67]One possible reason is that category of eligibility in Table 6.6 is that of the person reported as head of household. There are some households headed by persons with Category I eligibility, which contain persons with Category II or III eligibility and who therefore must pay their GPs.

Table 6.27: *Summary of logistic and OLS regression results, GP utilisation, 5% Version*[a]

	All persons		Category I		Cat. II/III		Mothers		Males		Females		Aged 65+		Aged 0–16	
	0,1	No.	0,1	No.	0,1	No.	0,1	No.	0,1	No.	0,1	No.	0,1	No.	0,1	No.
Sex female	++	++			++	+							+		+	
Age	+++	+++	+++	+++	-				---	---					+	- - - -
Age-squared	+++	++	++		++		+++	++	+++	++			++			- - -
Category I	+++	++					+++	++	+++	++++			++	+++ ++	- - -	+++
Category III	-								---	---		+				
No VHI	-- ++	(+)			++	+++	++ ++	++	---	---					+	
No. in household[b]									---	(+)	+					
Distance	-	-(-)	--	-(-)						-						
GP Fee	-				++ ++	+ +++	++ ++			-(-)		+				
House Call Fee		+									++				+	
Other help											++	--				
Farmer		-(-)	-(-)		--	-	---	---		-	---	---				
Girl-I-No VHI[c]	-		---	---	---											
Woman-I-No VHI[c]	++		++	+++			++				+(+)	++				
Lady-I-No VHI[c]		-										++				
Boy-I-No VHI[c]				-							++					
Man-I-No VHI[c]	+(+)								-	-(-)						
Gent-I-No VHI[c]	+															
Category I-No VHI	++										++	+++				
Household utilisation	++	++	++	+	++	++	++	++	++	++	++	++		++	++	++
Medical Card Ratio			++	+	++		++		++				++		+++ ++	-- - - -
GP Density	+++									++						
Inverse Mills	++					++										

Notes: [a] Based on Tables 6.3 through 6.26. 0,1 Column summarises logistic regressions of any GP consultations; No. Column summarises number of consultations, persons with any. ++ = significant at 1%, positive; + = significant at 5%, positive; – – = significant at 1%, negative; – = significant at 5%, negative. Second column includes household utilisation. [b] Number of persons, number of persons in Category I, number of males, etc., as appropriate. [c] Girl, Boy = aged 0–14; Woman, Man = aged 40–64; Lady, Gent = aged 65+. In Category I, Cat. II/III partitions, variables are Girl, Boy, Woman, etc. (rather than Girl-I-No VHI, Boy-I-No VHI, Woman-I-No VHI, etc.).

Table 6.28: *1980 household expenditures on general practitioner fees, per household and household per person*[a]*, by selected household characteristics*[b]

	Per household	Household per person[a]
	£	£
All Households	20.69	5.68
Category of eligibility:[c]		
Category I	4.58	1.29
Category II	28.96	8.55
Category III	36.60	8.31
VHI cover:[c]		
VHI	28.82	7.84
Non-VHI	18.04	4.98
Health Board area of residence:		
Eastern	29.11	7.97
Midland	11.06	3.06
Mid-Western	15.66	6.01
North-Eastern	20.13	5.23
North-Western	12.95	3.38
South-Eastern	14.94	3.32
Southern	21.94	5.87
Western	14.38	4.14
Occupation group:[c]		
Professional, managerial, or employer	28.09	7.34
Salaried or intermediate non-manual	22.41	6.98
Other non-manual	19.11	5.69
Skilled manual	24.45	5.80
Semi- or unskilled	19.38	4.79
Farmer, farm worker, or fisher	15.53	4.92

Notes: [a]Household expenditure divided by number of persons in household. [b]Expenditures are gross in the sense that VHI reimbursements are not subtracted. [c]Characteristic pertains to head of household.

Table 6.28 also reveals large differences in average expenditures in the various Health Board areas, ranging from a low of £11.06 in the Midland area to a high of £29.11 in the Eastern area. (It is to be emphasised that we are referring to Health Board area as a matter of residential location; these are private, not Health Board expenditures.)

Finally, Table 6.28 reveals differences among social or occupation group of heads of household. The range is perhaps smaller than might be expected, from £15.53 per household for farm households to £28.09 for professional, managerial, or employer. The per-person range is from £4.79 for semi-skilled or unskilled manual worker households, to £7.34 for professional, managerial, or employer.

Again, regression analysis permits us to determine the net or partial contribution of these and other independent variables to variability in the dependent variable, in this case household GP fee expenditures. Table 6.29 reports on such a regression equation, using ordinary least squares. The parameter estimates are in pounds and pence per household. Thus Table 6.29 tells us that households in the Eastern Health Board area spent £4.39 more than those in the Midland, Southern, or Western areas (whose expenditures are included in the constant term), and that the difference was not significant, statistically speaking when controlling for the other variables included in the model.

The significant variables in the model are the number of children aged 0–16 in the household (each child adds £3.34 to annual household GP expenditures in the full model and £3.83 in the 5 per cent version); the number of persons aged 17–64 (each adds £1.88 in the full model, £2.49 in the 5 per cent version); a dummy for an individual living alone (which reduces GP expenditures by £6.38 in the full model only); a dummy for other help with medical bills (which reduces expenditures by £9.58 or £9.85 — about half of average household expenditures); the index of per capita income (each one-point increase raises expenditures by 23p or 35p); and a dummy for the head of household having Category I eligibility without VHI cover (which reduced GP outlays by £19.52 or £20.42, very significantly).

There are few surprises in this regression. One might be that the number of persons aged over 64 reduced (though insignificantly) GP outlays. Another might be that per cent female of persons in the household also reduced (though also insignificantly) GP outlays.

Persons in Category I do not have to pay GP fees. In the regression reported in Table 6.30, we report on a household GP outlay regression for persons in Categories II and III only. In general, the results parallel those in Table 6.29.

The only significant variables in the model are the number of children aged 0–16 in the household (each child adds £5.04 in the full model and £5.51 in the 5 per cent version); the dummy variable for an individual living alone (which reduces expenditures by £13.62 in the full model, where it is significant at a 6 per cent level, and by £16.17 in the 5 per cent version); other help (which reduces expenditures by £11.40 or £10.57); and, in the 5 per cent version only, the index of per capita income (each one-point increase raises expenditures by 39p).

Possible surprises in Table 6.30 are, again, the negative but insignificant effects of numbers of persons aged over 64 and per cent female.

House Calls

As Table 4.6 (in Chapter 4) indicates, 19.1 per cent of GP consultations in 1980 were domiciliary, or house calls, a figure slightly higher for Category I (23.1 per cent) and lower for Category II (15.5 per cent). As Table 4.5 (also Chapter 4) indicates, house calls vary in an inverted U-shaped manner with distance, peaking (at 27.0 per cent) in the three-to-five mile category. It is lowest for the over-ten-miles category, at 11.3 per cent.

Table 6.29: *Regression of 1980 household general practitioner expenditures on selected independent variables – ordinary least squares*[a]

	Full Model	5% Version
$\overline{R}^{2[b]}$	0.156	0.162
N	1,045	1,045
Equation F	10.652**	40.09**
Intercept[c]	-2.52	-13.82
Persons Aged Over 64	-1.58	—
	(0.763)	
Persons Aged Under 17	3.34**	3.83**
	(4.472)	(5.536)
Persons Aged 17–64	1.88*	2.49**
	(2.249)	(3.49)
Dummy for Living Alone	-6.38	—
	(1.459)	
Eastern Health Board Area	4.39	—
	(0.974)	
Mid-Western Health Board Area	0.22	—
	(0.047)	
North-Eastern Health Board Area	0.78	—
	(0.191)	
North-Western Health Board Area	3.99	—
	(0.758)	
South-Eastern Health Board Area	-1.21	—
	(0.307)	
Per Cent Category III	6.80	—
	(1.593)	
Per Cent No VHI	-0.97	—
	(0.267)	
Other Help	-9.58*	-9.85*
	(2.189)	(2.326)
Occupation of Head:		
Professional, Manager Employer	1.93	—
	(0.406)	
Other Non-Manual	-1.23	—
	(0.244)	
Skilled Manual	4.37	—
	(0.937)	
Semi- or Unskilled Manual	6.16	—
	(1.396)	
Farmer or Fisher	1.60	—
	(0.361)	
Per Cent Female	-3.72	—
	(0.773)	
Index of Per Capita Income	0.23	0.35**
	(1.675)	(4.61)
Head Category I-No VHI	-19.52**	-20.42**
	(6.835)	(8.29)

Notes: [a] t-statistics in parentheses beneath parameter estimates. [b] $\overline{R}^2$ adjusted for degrees of freedom. [c] Intercept term in Full Model includes: individual living alone = no; Health Board Area = Midland, Southern or Western; other help = no; occupation of head = salaried employee or intermediate non-manual worker; and eligibility of head = Category II or III, with VHI cover. In 5% version, intercept term includes: other help = no; and eligibility of head = Category II or III, with VHI cover.

Significance levels: *0.01 < p ≤ 0.05. **p ≤ 0.01.

Table 6.30: *Regression of 1980 household general practitioner expenditures on selected independent variables – categories II and III only – ordinary least squares*[a]

	Full Model	5% Version
$\overline{R}^{2}$[b]	0.079	0.089
N	663	663
Equation F	3.996**	16.170**
Intercept[c]	3.43	-12.61
Persons Aged Over 64	-3.61	—
	(1.040)	
Persons Aged Under 17	5.04**	5.51**
	(4.884)	(5.608)
Persons Aged 17–64	0.86	—
	(0.727)	
Dummy for Living Alone	-13.62	-16.17**
	(1.896)	(2.466)
Eastern Health Board area	5.47	—
	(0.912)	
Mid-Western Health Board Area	-2.81	—
	(0.381)	
North-Eastern Health Board Area	0.53	—
	(0.089)	
North-Western Health Board Area	3.15	—
	(0.387)	
South-Eastern Health Board Area	-1.72	—
	(0.298)	
Per Cent Category III	5.00	—
	(1.004)	
Per Cent No VHI	-0.25	—
	(0.057)	
Other Help	-11.40*	-10.57*
	(2.147)	(2.100)
Occupation of Head:		
Professional, Manager, Employer	1.11	—
	(0.194)	
Other Non-Manual	-1.89	—
	(0.284)	
Skilled Manual	5.72	—
	(0.923)	
Semi- or Unskilled Manual	9.57	—
	(1.575)	
Farmer or Fisher	0.43	—
	(0.073)	
Per Cent Female	-6.03	—
	(0.825)	
Index of Per Capita Income	0.20	0.39**
	(1.046)	(3.818)

Notes: [a]t-statistic in parentheses beneath parameter estimate. [b]$\overline{R}^{2}$-adjusted for degrees of freedom. [c]Intercept term in Full Model includes: individual living alone = no; Health Board Area = Midland, Southern, or Western; other help = no; and occupation of head = salaried employee or intermediate non-manual worker. In 5% version, intercept term includes individual living alone = no; and other help = no.
Significance levels: *$0.01 < p \leq 0.05$. **$p \leq 0.01$.

In Tables 6.31 (all persons), 6.32 (Category I only) and 6.33 (Categories II/III only), we report logistic regressions of a dichotomous variable, measuring whether the individual's most recent GP consultation was a home visit, on relevant independent variables. Because incentives affecting GPs vary considerably as between Category I and other patients, separate regressions are reported for the two groups. It can be argued, on plausible a priori grounds, that the probability that the most recent visit was a home visit will have a U-shaped relationship to age, being higher for small children and the aged, and smaller for those in-between. That surmise is borne out in Tables 6.31 and 6.32, which show both age (negatively) and age squared (positively) to be highly significant independent variables for all persons and persons in Category I. For persons in Categories II and III, while the signs are the same, the age variables are not significant. However, in that version, "Lady," a dummy for females aged 65+, is significant and positive.

Because persons in Category I do not pay GP fees, and are unlikely to have VHI cover, the variables No VHI, GP Fee and House Call Fee are most meaningful in the Category II/III version. No VHI is negative and very significant, indicating that persons with VHI cover are significantly more likely to have house calls than others with Category II/III eligibility, though the reason is not obvious. The most recent consultation, a home visit, was significantly negatively associated with usual GP fee and positively with house call fee. On first examination, these results appear to reflect physician self-interest and this may very well be correct. Assuming the usual and house call fees are set in a somewhat competitive process over which the individual physician has little control, doctors might well respond to the incentive structure they face by choosing to make more house calls, for which they are paid more, when usual GP fee is too low and when house call fee is high. But causation may run in the other direction as well: in markets in which the demand for house calls is high, the house call fee should be expected to be higher.

In all three versions, we have controlled for important marketwide supply and demand factors by including GP density, consultant density, and the Medical Card ratio (ratio of persons with Category I eligibility to total population), as main effects and in interactions. These are significant in the all persons model, nearly so in the Category I version, and not in the Category II/III version. Because of the interaction terms, interpretation is not straightforward, and we postpone discussion briefly.

When we control for other influences, members of farming and fishing families are less likely to have had house calls, possibly reflecting lack of access to a telephone, and in spite of the results of Table 4.5, discussed earlier, distance to GP proves to have no significant net effect on house calls.

Once again, the parameters of these logistic regressions cannot easily be interpreted, and the effects of variables included in interaction variables are hard to discern, so once again we report, in Tables 6.34, 6.35 and 6.36, on illustrative probabilities based on these regressions. It will be seen that the variables having

Table 6.31: *Logistic regressions of most recent 1980 GP consultation a home visit (Dichotomous Variable), on selected independent variables*[a]

	Full Model	5% Version
$\bar{R}^{2}$[b]	0.087	0.084
N	1,003	1,003
Equation χ^2	125.24**	83.64**
Intercept[c]	19.821*	-0.749**
	(3.75)	(13.05)
Sex Female	-0.055	—
	(0.03)	
Age	-0.083**	-0.095**
	(21.52)	(48.56)
Age Squared ÷ 1,000	1.150**	1.307**
	(29.02)	(63.77)
Category I	0.167	—
	(0.38)	
Category III	0.437	—
	(2.14)	
No VHI	-0.211	—
	(0.66)	
Distance to GP	0.084	—
	(1.81)	
GP Fee	-0.236**	—
	(6.17)	
House Call Fee	0.166**	—
	(7.68)	
Farmer or Fisher	-0.890**	—
	(11.92)	
GP Density	-41.423	—
	(3.65)	
Medical Card Ratio	-52.592*	—
	(4.61)	
Persons in Household Who Saw GP	0.036	—
	(0.40)	
Girl[d]	0.250	—
	(0.45)	
Woman[d]	0.077	—
	(0.03)	
Lady[d]	0.646	—
	(2.09)	
Boy[d]	0.199	—
	(0.26)	
Man[d]	0.208	—
	(0.33)	
Medical Card Ratio-GP Density Interaction	110.436*	—
	(4.38)	
Consultant Density-GP Density Interaction	-10.194**	—
	(7.51)	
Times Seen by GP in 1980	0.009	—
	(0.62)	
Joint Tests:		
Age	(30.98)**	(76.85)**
GP Density	(7.68)**	
Medical Card Ratio	(5.43)*	

Notes: [a]χ^2 in parentheses beneath parameter estimates. [b]$\bar{R}^2$ adjusted for degrees of freedom. [c]Intercept term in Full Model includes: sex = male; eligibility = Category II; VHI cover = no; other help = no; head of household a farmer = no; and age = 0-4, or 18-39. [d]"Girl," "Boy" = age 5-17; "Woman", "Man" = age 40-64; "Lady" = age 65+.
Significance: *$0.01 < p \leqslant 0.05$. **$p \leqslant 0.01$.

Table 6.32: *Logistic regressions of most recent 1980 GP consultation a home visit (Dichotomous variable), on selected independent variables, persons in Category I only*[a]

	Full Model	5% Version
$\bar{R}^{2}$[b]	0.130	0.155
N	401	401
Equation χ^2	90.71**	75.33**
Intercept[c]	26.057	-0.920
	(3.08)	(3.67)
Sex Female	-1.229	—
	(1.76)	
Age	-0.178**	-0.124**
	(22.21)	(24.62)
Age Squared ÷ 1,000	2.115**	1.704**
	(28.42)	(35.90)
No VHI	0.769	—
	(1.26)	
Distance to GP	0.209*	0.272**
	(4.25)	(8.37)
Farmer or fisher	-1.255**	-1.207**
	(11.69)	(11.71)
GP Density	-53.982	—
	(2.98)	
Medical Card Ratio	-63.937	—
	(3.31)	
Persons in Household Who Saw GP	0.057	—
	(0.49)	
Girl[d]	0.267	—
	(0.10)	
Woman[d]	1.554	—
	(2.22)	
Lady[d]	1.813	—
	(3.28)	
Boy[d]	-1.685	—
	(2.88)	
Man[d]	0.941	—
	(2.89)	
Medical Card Ratio-GP Density Interaction	138.417	—
	(3.36)	
Consultant Density-GP Density Interaction	-10.727	—
	(4.30)	
Times Seen by GP in 1980	-0.010	—
	(0.36)	
Joint Tests:		
Age	(31.03)**	(53.64)**
GP Density	(4.54)*	
Medical Card Ratio	(3.41)	

Notes: [a]χ^2 in parentheses beneath parameter estimates. [b]$\bar{R}^2$ adjusted for degrees of freedom. [c]Intercept term in Full Model includes: Sex = male; eligibility = Category II; VHI cover = no; head of household a farmer = no; and age = 0-4 or 18-39. [d]"Girl", "Boy" = age 5-17; "Woman", "Man" = age 40-64; "Lady" = age 65+.
Significance: *$0.01 < p \leqslant 0.05$. **$p \leqslant 0.01$.

Table 6.33: *Logistic regressions of most recent 1980 GP consultation a home visit (Dichotomous variable), on selected independent variables, persons in Categories II and III only*[a].

	Full Model	5% Version
$\overline{R}^{2}$[b]	0.034	0.054
N	602	602
Equation χ^2	55.31**	39.73**
Intercept[c]	8.979	-0.581
	(0.34)	(1.08)
Age	-0.038	-0.016**
	(2.74)	(6.60)
Age Squared ÷ 1,000	0.417	—
	(1.78)	
No VHI	-0.649**	-0.650**
	(6.49)	(7.18)
Distance to GP	0.002	—
	(0.00)	
GP Fee	-0.267*	-0.250*
	(4.67)	(4.55)
House Call Fee	0.216**	0.213**
	(9.10)	(10.54)
GP Density	-13.064	—
	(0.16)	
Medical Card Ratio	-29.320	—
	(0.63)	
Farmer or Fisher	-0.764	—
	(3.62)	
Sex Female	-0.131	—
	(0.11)	
Times Seen by GP in 1980	0.051*	0.046*
	(4.40)	(4.17)
Persons in Household Who Saw GP	-0.029	—
	(0.11)	
Girl[d]	0.513	—
	(1.34)	
Woman[d]	0.115	—
	(0.05)	
Lady[d]	1.556*	1.939**
	(4.16)	(14.78)
Boy[d]	0.489	—
	(1.22)	
Man[d]	-0.163	—
	(0.09)	
Medical Card Ratio-GP Density Interaction	52.686	—
	(0.43)	
Consultant Density-GP Density Interaction	-11.884*	—
	(4.36)	
Joint Tests:		
Age	(2.93)	
GP Density	(5.57)*	
Medical Card Ratio	(5.03)*	

Notes: [a]χ^2 in parentheses beneath parameter estimates. [b]$\overline{R}^2$ adjusted for degrees of freedom. [c]Intercept term in Full Model includes: sex = male; VHI cover = no; head of household a farmer = no; and age = 0-4 or 18-39. [d]"Girl", "Boy" = 5-17; "Woman", "Man" = age 40-64; "Lady" = age 65+.
Significance: *$0.01 < p \leqslant 0.05$. **$p \leqslant 0.01$.

Table 6.34: *Probability that most recent GP consultation was home visit, all persons, based on logistic regression* [a]

| | | Probabilities | |
		Full Model	5% Version
Baseline probability applies when the following variables are set equal to their means, as below:[b]	*Baseline probability**	.07	.08
Age = 39.64	*Other probabilities***		
Distance to GP = 2.60	*Sex* = male	.07	—
GP fee = £2.43	*Age* =		
House call fee = £2.80	min = 1	.24	.30
GP density = .461	10	.17	.17
Medical card ratio = .369	20	.09	.11
Persons in household who saw	30	.07	.08
GP = 2.86	40	.07	.08
Annual no. of GP consultations	50	.09	.10
= 5.86	60	.13	.15
and when the following qualities	70	.34	.27
obtain:	max = 95	.80	.89
sex = female	*Eligibility* =		
Eligibility = Category II	Category I	.08	—
VHI cover = no	Category III	.10	—
Farmer = no	*VHI cover* = yes	.08	—
***Other probabilities* apply when	*Distance to GP*		
variables are changed, one by one	min = under 1 mile	.06	—
(the others held constant as	max = more than 10 miles	.09	—
above) to the values and/or	*GP fee*		
qualities indicated.	min = £0	.12	—
	max = £7	.02	—
	House Call Fee		
	min = £0	.04	—
	max = £10	.20	—
	GP Density =		
	min = 0.429	.06	—
	max = 0.555	.04	—
	Medical Card ratio		
	min = 0.232	.06	—
	max = 0.586	.04	—
	Farmer = yes	.03	—
	Annual GP consultations		
	min = 1	.07	—
	2	.07	—
	6	.07	—
	12	.07	—
	24	.08	—
	max = 60	.11	—

Notes: [a]See Table 6.31. [b]For 5% version, applies only to variables in the model.

Table 6.35: *Probability that most recent GP consultation was home visit, Category I only, based on logistic regression*[a]

		Probabilities	
		Full Model	5% Version
Baseline probability applies when the following variables are set equal to their means, as below:[b]	Baseline probability*	.02	.11
Age = 51.06	Other probabilities**		
Distance to GP = 2.60	Sex = male	.08	—
GP density = .471	Age =		
Medical Card ratio = .403	min = 1	.44	.42
Persons in household who saw	10	.17	.22
GP = 2.78	20	.06	.12
Annual no. of GP consultations	30	.03	.08
= 8.81	40	.02	.08
	50	.02	.10
and when the following qualities obtain:[b]	60	.04	.18
	70	.10	.37
Sex = female	max = 88	.66	.89
VHI cover = no	VHI cover = yes	.01	—
Farmer = no	Distance to GP		
Other probabilities apply when variables are changed, one by one (the others held constant as above) to the values and/or qualities indicated.	min = under 1 mile	.02	.06
	max = more than 10 miles	.05	.23
	GP density =		
	min = 0.429	.02·	—
	max = 0.555	.02	—
	Medical Card ratio		
	min = 0.232	.01	—
	max = 0.586	.02	—
	Farmer = yes	.01	.04
	Annual GP consultations		
	min = 1	.03	—
	2	.02	—
	6	.02	—
	12	.02	—
	24	.02	—
	max = 60	.02	—
	Number of persons in household who saw GP		
	min = 1	.02	—
	max = 14	.05	—

Notes: [a]See Table 6.32. [b]For 5% version, applies only to variables in the model.

Table 6.36: *Probability that most recent GP consultation was home visit, Categories II and III only, based on logistic regression* [a]

		Probabilities	
		Full Model	5% Version
Baseline probability applies when the following variables are set equal to their means, as below:[b]	*Baseline probability* *	.07	.10
Age = 32.03	*Other probabilities* **		
Distance to GP = 2.60	*Sex* = male	.09	—
GP fee = £3.44	*Age* =		
House call fee = £3.95	min = 1	.15	.15
GP density = .455	10	.11	.13
Medical card ratio = .346	20	.09	.11
Persons in household who saw GP = 2.91	30	.08	.10
	40	.07	.08
Annual no. of GP consultations = 3.88	50	.07	.07
	60	.08	.06
and when the following qualities obtain:[b]	70	.09	.05
	max = 95	.17	.04
Sex = female	*VHI cover* = yes	.14	.17
VHI cover = no	*Distance to GP*		
Farmer = no	min = under 1 mile	.08	—
** *Other probabilities* apply when	max = more than 10 miles	.08	—
variables are changed, one by one	*GP fee*		
(the others held constant as above)	min = £0	.17	.20
to the values and/or qualities	max = £6	.04	.05
indicated.	*House call fee*		
	min = £0	.03	.04
	max = .23	.28	
	GP density =		
	min = 0.429	.06	—
	max = 0.555	.08	—
	Medical Card ratio		
	min = 0.232	.11	—
	max = 0.586	.02	—
	Farmer = yes	.04	—
	Annual GP consultations		
	min = 1	.07	.09
	2	.07	.08
	6	.08	.11
	12	.11	.13
	24	.18	.21
	max = 50	.46	.48
	Number of persons in household who		
saw GP			
	min = 1	.08	
	max = 9	.06	

Notes: [a] See Table 6.33. [b] For 5% version, applies only to variables in the model.

the greatest absolute impact on house calls were age (especially for children); for Category I, GP density; and for Category II/III, GP fee, house call fee and annual GP consultations.

GP density has an ambiguous effect in these regressions. It is positively associated with the probability that the most recent visit was a house call in the all persons version, where the effect is small, and in the Category I version, where it is large. Its effect is negative, small and insignificant in the Category II/III version, though it is significant in the important joint test in this version. The positive relationship found in the former versions could reflect physician self-interest. By itself, high GP density should reduce fee levels and physician incomes. If physicians seek to compensate, in part, by seeking house calls, GP density will vary positively with the probability of house calls. A somewhat different interpretation is that where GP density is low, doctors will be less pressed for time, and will have more freedom to go on home visits, where these are indicated by other criteria.

The Medical Card ratio also has an ambiguous effect. It is significant in the joint tests in the all persons and Category II/III versions, but not in the Category I version. Tables 6.34 and 6.36 show that the effect is negative in both cases in which it is significant, but non-trivial only in the Category II/III version. Among other things, a high Medical Card ratio means higher demand for GP services in an area, given the higher utilisation of persons covered by Medical Cards. These findings tell us that where doctors have large numbers of patients covered by Medical Cards, they cut back considerably on their house calls to persons in Categories II and III, though house calls to persons in Category I are not affected. Where they have fewer patients covered by Medical Cards, they increase their house calls to patients in Categories II and III.

Comparisons with Britain

In 1979, the annual British GP consulting rate was 4.0, somewhat higher than our reported 1980 Irish rate of 3.6. The two countries have similar morbidity patterns, climates and cultures. Their medical care systems are different, in two important respects relevant to the present comparison. In Ireland, all but those in Category I must pay for GP consultations (excepting that those with VHI who have passed a significant deductible may also claim reimbursement). In Britain, the whole population can avail of free GP care. Secondly, British GPs are paid on a capitation basis, which means that their incomes are unaffected directly by their consulting rates, whilst Irish GPs for both public and private patients, are remunerated on a fee-for-service basis, which obviously means that their incomes are affected by their consulting rates. (This statement must be qualified somewhat, as British GPs are paid on a fee basis for certain services, such as night visits, immunisations, family planning services and others.)

Table 6.37 compares consulting rates by sex and age group. British rates are higher amongst both males and females. They are higher than Irish rates for males under age 65, and markedly lower amongst males 65 and older. They are higher than Irish rates for females under 45, but much lower for middle-aged and older

Table 6.37: *Average annual general practitioner consultations by sex and age, Ireland vs. Britain*

	Ireland[a]	Britain[b]
All Males	3.2	3.5
0–14	2.6	3.4[c]
15–44	2.1	2.7[d]
45–64	3.9	4.4
65+	7.4	4.7
All Females	4.0	4.5
0–14	2.4	3.3[c]
15–44	3.4	4.8[d]
45–64	5.3	4.3
65+	7.9	5.4
All Persons	3.6	4.0

[a]1980, present survey. [b]1979, Office of Population Censuses and Surveys, *General Household Survey*. [c]In this case the age range is 0–15 instead of 0–14 as for Ireland. [d]In this case the age range is 16–44 instead of 15–44 as for Ireland.

women. Irish consulting rates for persons aged 65 and over are well over 50 per cent higher than British rates for the same age group. Since morbidity is presumably similarly high in this age group in both countries, a possible explanation lies in the fact that a large proportion of Irish persons in this group are eligible in Category I. (As noted earlier, the Category I consulting rate is 6.1, much higher than the overall British rate; the rate for the rest of the Irish population is only 2.5, much lower than the overall British rate.)

It is sometimes argued that the Irish Category I consulting rate is high in part because large numbers of aged persons are in this category. Comparison with Britain points up the possibility that the causation may work, in part, in the opposite direction: older Irish people have high consulting rates because they have Category I eligibility.

More light is shed on the comparison by Table 6.38 which reports on Irish and British consulting rates by social group (occupation group of head of household). In Ireland, consulting rates rise sharply, from 68 per cent of the national average to 144 per cent, as one goes down the socio-economic ladder. The only exception to a continuous rise in consulting rates with a fall in social group is the extraordinarily low consulting rates in Irish farming and fishing families. (The latter loom larger in the Irish than the British population and help explain the difference in overall consulting rates.) In Britain, there is little difference in consulting rates as one moves through the ranks of social groups. In particular, the lower social groups, corresponding to the Irish Medical Card population, have consulting rates approximately equal to the British average.

Table 6.38: *Average annual general practitioner consultations by social group, Ireland vs. Britain*

	Consultations	*% of average*
Ireland[a]	3.4	100
Professional, manager, or employer	2.3	68
Salaried employee, or intermediate non-manual worker	3.2	94
Other non-manual	3.7	109
Skilled manual worker	4.1	121
Farmer, farmer's relative, farm manager, other agricultural worker, or fisher	3.1	91
Semi-skilled or unskilled manual worker	4.9	144
Britain[b]	4.0	100
Professional	3.0	75
Employers and managers	3.5	88
Intermediate and junior non-manual	4.0	100
Skilled manual and own account non-professional	4.1	103
Semi-skilled manual and personal service	4.5	113
Unskilled manual	4.2	105

[a] 1980, present survey. [b] 1979, Office of Population Censuses and Surveys, *General Household Survey.*

In short, Irish rates are lower, relative to the average, than British rates in the higher social groups, and higher in the lower social groups.

The reasons lie in part in the incentive structures in the two countries. The British professional, manager, and employer receives free GP care, whilst the Irish counterpart must pay. The Irish GP, unlike her or his British counterpart, is paid on a fee-for-service basis and has a motive to stimulate demand. It is sometimes argued that physicians working under a capitation system, as in Britain, not only have no motive to stimulate demand for their own services, but actually seek to reduce their workloads by referring their patients to others, mainly specialists. Comparison between Irish and British GP referral behaviour, discussed in a later section, does not appear to bear out this thesis. (See also McCormick and Allwright, 1977).

The Working Party on the General Medical Service, who had access to our data and to the comparisons discussed here between Ireland and Britain, read these numbers differently. They conclude that "Irish visiting rates by socio-economic group ... are not very different from those in Britain, but the visiting rates for the elderly are very much higher in Ireland" (Working Party on the General Medical Service, 1984). From this reading, they attach less significance to method of remuneration than we, or most economists, do.

Wait for GP

In Chapter 4, it was seen that the length of time patients wait in GPs' waiting rooms varies considerably from region to region. Multiple regression analysis reveals that region-to-region variation in such factors as the ratio of physicians to population accounts for the regional differences.

In Table 6.39 wait up to one hour, a dichotomous (or dummy) variable, was regressed on a number of relevant independent variables. Note should be taken of the fact that respondents only are included in this particular analysis, and not other members of households, as with the utilisation analysis. These respondents were mainly women, usually housewives, and the waiting times of other household members might be different.[68] A negative coefficient means longer waiting times; a positive coefficient, shorter times.

The variables which seem most to influence utilisation — sex, age, time-price (distance) and category of health services eligibility — do not significantly affect waiting time. Instead, the significant variables are:

1. VHI cover: Those without VHI cover seem more frequently to have to wait more than one hour. For a discussion, see item 4 below.

2. GP density: It is far from surprising to find that areas with high ratios of GPs to population have short waiting times, whilst those with low ratios have longer waiting times. This is the most significant relationship found. It is reflected in interaction as well as main effects variables. For overall significance, see the joint tests.

3. Consultant density: consultants may here be regarded as substitutes (competitors) for GPs in the sense that a low consultant population ratio will help fill GP waiting rooms.

4. Occupation group: respondents from households headed by other non-manual workers are significantly more likely to have to wait more than an hour. VHI (above) may also reflect social class. One explanation for this relationship may be that persons in lower social groups are less likely to have telephones, in which case they would be unable to make appointments.

The regression reported in Table 6.39 was also run adding Health Board areas as separate, additional dichotomous independent variables. These coefficients were consistently insignificant. This does not mean that waiting time does not vary from region to region; indeed, it has already been seen (Table 4.8, Chapter 4) that the variation is considerable. Instead, it means that the variation is explained by the variables in the model reported in Table 6.39.

The $\bar{R}^2$ in Table 6.39, 0.004, is very low. While the five variables discussed above are significantly associated with waiting time, the equation as a whole only explains about 0.4 per cent of the person to person variability in the probability that one will have to wait more than (or less than) an hour. The 5 per cent version explains less than 2 per cent. Both equations are, however, very significant.

---

[68]It was assumed in designing the interviews that the housewife would be likely to know about the GP utilisation of other household members but not necessarily their waiting times.

Table 6.39: *Logistic regressions of wait up to one hour (Dichotomous Variable) in GP's waiting room, most recent 1980 consultation, on selected independent variables*[a]

	Full Model	5% Version
$\bar{R}^{2(b)}$	0.004	0.017
N	1,073	1,073
Equation χ^2	36.30**	21.85**
Intercept[c]	−6.095	2.879**
	(2.43)	(52.40)
No VHI	−0.721**	−0.798**
	(7.37)	(14.18)
Distance to GP	−0.030	—
	(0.29)	
GP Density	19.519**	—
	(6.00)	
Category I	−0.006	—
	(0.00)	
Category III	0.055	—
	(0.03)	
GP Fee	0.061	—
	(0.68)	
House Call Fee	−0.081	—
	(3.39)	
Medical Card Ratio-GP Density Interaction	−0.596	—
	(0.03)	
Consultant Density	31.055*	—
	(3.69)	
Consultant Density-GP Density Interaction	−66.793*	—
	(3.71)	
Times Seen by GP in 1980	0.006	—
	(0.25)	
Executive, Professional, or Employer	−0.005	—
	(0.00)	
Other Non-Manual Worker	−0.632	−0.508*
	(3.35)	(4.86)
Skilled Manual Worker	−0.095	—
	(0.08)	
Semi- or Unskilled Worker	−0.229	—
	(0.53)	
Farmer or Fisher	0.038	—
	(0.01)	
Joint Tests:		
GP Density	(6.44)**	
Consultant	(3.71)*	

Notes: [a]χ^2 in parentheses beneath parameter estimates. [b]$\bar{R}^2$ adjusted for degrees of freedom. [c]Intercept term in Full Model includes: eligibility = Category II; VHI cover = no; and occupation of head of household = salaried or intermediate non-manual employee.
Significance: *$0.01 < p \leqslant 0.05$. **$p \leqslant 0.01$.

We have used the regression reported in Table 6.39 to calculate illustrative probabilities, and these are reported in Table 6.40. The probabilities relate to wait *up to* one hour. Thus, a low probability corresponds to a greater likelihood of a long wait. Table 6.40 shows that while GP density's effect may be statistically significant, the strength of the effect is quite small.

Table 6.40: *Probability of wait up to one hour in GP's waiting room, based on logistic regression*[a]

| | | Probabilities | |
		Full Model	5% Version
**Baseline probability applies when the following variables are set equal to their means, as below:[b]	Baseline probability*	.80	.78
	*Other probabilities*****		
Annual no. of consultations = 4.37	*Eligibility =*		
Distance to GP = 2.61	Category I	.80	—
GP fee = 2.44	Category III	.81	—
House call fee = 2.78	*VHI cover =* yes	.89	.89
GP density = .461	*Distance to GP*		
Consultant density = .271	min = under 1 mile	.81	—
and when the following qualities	max = more than 10 miles	.78	—
obtain:[b]	*GP fee*		
Eligibility = Category II	min = £0	.78	—
VHI cover = no	max = £7	.84	—
Occupation of head = salaried	*House call fee*		
employee or intermediate	min = £0	.83	—
non-manual employee	max = £10	.69	—
**Other probabilities apply when	*GP density*		
variables are changed, one by one	min = 0.429	.78	—
(the others held constant as above)	max = 0.555	.80	—
to the values and/or qualities	*Consultant Density*		
indicated.	min = 0	.78	—
	max = .387	.79	—
	Annual GP consultations		
	min = 0	.80	—
	2	.80	—
	6	.80	—
	12	.81	—
	24	.82	—
	max = 52	.84	—
	Occupation of head		
	managerial/professional	.80	—
	Other non-manual	.68	.68
	Skilled manual	.78	—
	Semi- and unskilled	.76	—
	Farmer, farm worker, fisher	.81	—

Notes: [a]See Table 6.39. [b]For 5% version, applies only to variables in the model.

GP Referrals and Revisits

As has been emphasised throughout this study, general practitioners are economically and medically important not alone for the significant primary care health service they provide to patients, but also for their roles as gate-keepers and decision-makers with respect to further utilisation of the system. It is to this function that we now turn.

Table 6.41 reports the coefficients of (simple) correlation among main types of medical care utilisation. The annual number of GP consultations correlates with other types of utilisation in the range, 0.209–0.484. All correlations are extremely significant (at the 0.0001 level).

The role of GPs in utilisation decisions was discussed above in connection with Table 6.1 (see also Appendix Tables A.30 through A.35). Another way of viewing GP referral behaviour is based on the following questions, asked in our household survey:

> I want to ask you just one more question about the *most recent time* each member of the household was seen by a *general practitioner* in 1980. If you can, try to remember the outcomes of those visits — what further care or treatment the doctor prescribed, suggested, or ordered, or what he told the member to do as a result of the visit. *Did the doctor . . .*
>
> . . . arrange for a return visit — for the member to see the same doctor another time?
>
> . . . refer the member to *another doctor*, such as a specialist?

and so forth, for seven additional categories or types of utilisation including "other". The answers to these questions provide a unique insight into GP consultations, and are given in detail, by Category of Health Services eligibility, and by VHI cover, in Appendix Table A.28, and summarised in Table 6.42. Of all persons' most recent GP consultations, 23.5 per cent resulted in a return visit being

Table 6.41: *Correlation Matrix: Medical Care Utilisation, 1980*[a]

	(2)	*(3)*	*(4)*	*(5)*	*(6)*
(1) GP consultations	0.284	0.484	0.271	0.217	0.209
(2) Specialist consultations		0.203	0.334	0.279	0.335
(3) Prescription items			0.151	0.188	0.190
(4) Out-patient hospital visits				0.180	0.202
(5) No. of times hospital in-patient					0.572
(6) Length of hospital stay					

[a]All correlations significant at 0.0001 level. N = 4,522.

arranged with the same GP; 7.1 per cent resulted in a referral to another doctor, usually a specialist; 77.2 per cent in one or more pharmaceutical medicines being prescribed; 10.0 per cent in a referral to a hospital out-patient department; and 5.3 per cent in hospital admission.

All of these rates appear high. Indeed, British physicians, operating under a capitation system which is sometimes argued to encourage referral, appear to have much lower referral rates. British data are organised differently from ours, but the following per consultation referrals seem comparable: admission to hospital, Ireland, 5.1 per cent, Britain, 0.6 per cent; specialist and out-patient, Ireland 16.2 per cent, Britain, 6.9 per cent; and other health professionals, Ireland, 2.5 per cent, Britain, 0.1 per cent.[69] (British data from HMSO, Morbidity Statistics from General Practice, Second National Study, 1970–71, London, 1974.)

The high Irish referral rates warrant some comment. In Chapter 3, we quoted the Gowen Report, a self-survey of Irish general practice by the Royal College of General practitioners, as stating, "There are some indications, especially from referral rates, that the level of acute medical care is more haphazard than in the United Kingdom, and Irish doctors still having a too ready recourse to direct hospital admission to solve their patients' problems" (Gowen, 1972).

Lest one think this problem to be exclusively a rural one, we also quote a Dublin GP, from a survey of his own practice published in a leading medical journal: "Some of my general practitioner friends will consider that sending one in every five patients for investigations would seem to be overdoing it. It is possible that this reflects my lack of confidence in my clinical acumen" (Berber, 1974).

---

[69]In 1970/71, British persons saw their GPs an average of 3.2 times per year. There were 240 referrals per 1,000 population, which works out to .075 referrals per consultation. These referrals consist of the following: *in-patient* (direct admission to hospital), 18.2 per 1,000 population, and .006 per consultation; *out-patient* (where a patient was sent for specialist opinion or service), 92 per 1,000, and .029 per consultation; *investigation* (where the GP initiated or stipulated the investigation or service she or he required for the patient, irrespective of whether a specialist reported on the result), 115.9 per 1,000, .037 per consultation; *local authority* (where services run by a local authority were invoked on behalf of the patient), 6.5 per 1,000 and .002 per consultation; *multiple* (where two different referral codes were required for the same consultation, e.g., investigation and local authority), 3.5 per 1,000 and .001 per consultation; and other (e.g., optician, chiropodist, dentist, etc.), 3.9 per 1,000 and .001 per consultation. The Irish data cannot be derived directly from the tables published here because of overlapping categories. Differences between the Irish and British data should be noted. In our survey in Ireland, we asked about referrals at each household member's most recent GP consultation. British data provide consultations per 1,000 population and referrals per 1,000 population, and the referral rate is obtained by dividing the latter by the former. Irish respondents reported that 5.1 per cent of most recent GP consultations resulted in a referral to hospital for admission, even though in general GPs do not have this authority. It is likely that in certain instances, GPs made what amounted to *de facto*, but not *de jure*, referrals to hospital for admission; the lower British rate may reflect the fact that it is based on official data sources, and comes from GP rather than household records, and hence may reflect *de jure* rather than *de facto* referrals.

Table 6.42: *General practitioner referrals and return visits arranged: per cent of consultations (most recent visit) resulting in further care or treatment ordered, prescribed, or suggested, 1980*

	(1)	(2)	(3)	(4)
				Ratio,
	Category	Categories	All	Col. (1)
	I only	II/III only	persons	to Col. (2)
Return visit arranged	34.9	16.5	23.5	2.12
Referred to another doctor	5.6	8.0	7.1	0.70
Prescribed medicine(s)	84.1	72.9	77.2	1.15
Referred to out-patient department	9.8	10.3	10.0	0.95
Referred to hospital for admission	6.2	4.6	5.3	1.35

Source: Appendix Table A.31.

The situation of Irish general practice has undoubtedly improved since the early 1970s, but our results suggest that the problems referred to in these quotations still exist. One suspects that the underlying problem is more one of isolation and self-confidence than of competence on the part of Irish GPs. One possible solution is organisation of group practices wherever possible, so that GPs can more readily consult and interact with each other. We return to this problem in Chapter 8.

In Table 6.42, special interest attaches to the differences in physician behaviour as regards Category I patients, whose medical care (including GP services) is free to them, and other (Categories II and III) patients, who must pay something for medical care, including fees for GP services. Column (4) reports the ratio of the percentage for persons in Category I to that of persons in Categories II and III combined. It reveals a striking pattern. Among persons in Category I, 34.9 per cent of most recent GP consultations resulted in a return visit being arranged with the same GP; among persons in Categories II and III, only 16.5 per cent resulted in a return visit being arranged, giving a ratio of 2.12 to 1.

This ratio seems surprisingly high. It relates, of course, to the regression results reported in Tables 6.3–6.26 which showed that controlling for age, sex and other important variables, persons in Category I had significantly more GP consultations in 1980 than other persons. The possibility arises, of course, that persons in Category I, who are, in general, poorer in income terms and more likely to be aged, had more health problems requiring a succession of GP visits than had other people. For example, chronic conditions often require repeated consultations. But if illness and chronic conditions explained the high Category I return visit rate, one would expect similarly high ratios in Column (4) for other kinds of utilisation. One would expect those in Category I to have appreciably more referrals to other doctors, such as specialists; more pharmaceutical medicines prescribed; more referrals to out-patient departments of hospitals; and more referrals to hospital, for admission, than those in Categories II and III.

This is not what one finds, however, in Column (4). Instead, there are *fewer* referrals to specialists for Category I than for Category II/III patients. This ratio, 0.70 to 1, is the lowest reported in Table 6.42. Pharmaceutical medicines are somewhat more likely to be prescribed (the ratio is 1.15 to 1),[70] and patients are more likely to be referred to hospital for admission (1.35 to 1), but there are slightly fewer referrals to out-patient departments (0.95 to 1). In short, some types of referral show more, and some less, for Category I than other patients, but for no type of referral does the ratio approach that found for return visits.

One possible explanation lies in the incentive structure in the Irish medical care system. Table 6.42 does not prove but it is consistent with the following:

1. GPs wishing to increase their incomes arrange for return visits by persons in Category I. Those in Categories II and III, who must pay for GP services, are more likely to resist extra visits and GPs may feel better about arranging extra visits for persons who are not charged for them. This point is developed further below.

2. Persons in Category II can avail of free out-patient hospital and specialist care, but must pay their GPs. For these patients, it is cheaper to be referred to a specialist or the out-patient department of a hospital than to return to their GPs. A physician acting in the manner predicted by the agency model (see Chapter 2) might refer patients in the manner described.

If they are true, both patterns of physician behaviour are uneconomic. The first results in increased return visits for persons in Category I, as well as in whatever other types of utilisation arise because of these return visits. (A discussion of "necessary" vs. "unnecessary" utilisation appears later in the chapter.) The second means that more costly specialist and hospital services are substituted for less costly primary GP care among persons in Categories II and III.

Taken together, they help us understand why Irish and British average GP consulting rates are similar overall but differ in detail. Irish rates are lower relative to the average than British for upper social groups and higher for lower social groups. The Category I rate exceeds and the Category II/III rate is exceeded by the overall British average. Though other explanations are possible, these patterns are precisely those one would predict on the basis of incentives.

The issue raised here is of medical as well as economic significance. Table 6.42 suggests that persons with Category I eligibility are more likely than others to be *kept* by the GP while those with Category II/III eligibility are more likely to be *referred on* to specialists and hospital. One wonders which, if either, are getting the medically most appropriate treatment.

---

[70]This ratio reflects the probability that *any* medicines were prescribed, rather than the number of items prescribed.

Physician-Induced Demand by Irish GPs

The following discussion of physician-induced demand by Irish GPs is based on a theoretical model published elsewhere (Tussing, 1983a, and Tussing and Wojtowycz, forthcoming). The reader is referred to those sources for the formal argument. The empirical results are presented here in full.

As we have seen in Chapter 2 and elsewhere, two types of study in the health economics literature point to self-interested physician-induced demand for their own services. One set of studies shows method of remunerating physicians influences utilisation. Where doctors are paid on a fee-for-service basis, utilisation rates are higher than where capitation or salary methods are used, even where similar or identical clientele are served. Another set of studies shows that where physician density (the ratio of physicians to population) is high, a relationship which by itself would depress physician incomes, high density is compensated for by higher per capita utilisation, believed to be physician-induced. This latter behaviour is called compensatory demand stimulation.

In Ireland, GPs are paid on a fee-for-service basis, so we have no opportunity to conduct the first type of study. We do, however, have data on physician density and relevant physician behaviour. Thus what follows is a test of compensatory demand stimulation by Irish GPs.

It will be recalled that Irish GPs do not have access to patients in hospital, do not perform significant amounts of surgery, do not have x-ray or pathology facilities as parts of their practices, and do not work in partnership with specialists or non-physician professionals. Hence if Irish GPs stimulate demand for their own services, it must be almost entirely by generating return visits.

It is important to note how much more limited the scope for physician-induced demand is in Ireland than in other countries using fee-for-service remuneration, particularly the USA and Canada, from which most of the relevant empirical literature emanates. To the extent that it exists, physician-induced demand is a much smaller problem in Ireland than other fee-for-service countries, though of course a larger one than in capitation countries.

In brief, the argument is as follows. Where the supply of GPs is high, other things being equal, physician incomes will be depressed. If physicians compensate for reduced income, they will attempt to generate additional demand, in the form of repeated return visits. Thus, we hypothesise a positive relationship between physician density and return visits. In addition, where the (unstimulated) demand for medical care is lower, again physician incomes will be low, and if they compensate, GPs will generate return visits. Therefore, where per capita income is relatively low, we would expect, other things equal, reduced demand and hence more return visits. Similarly, where the ratio of persons in Category I to population (the Medical Card ratio) is low, again we expect reduced demand for GP services and reduced GP incomes, and an effort to stimulate more return visits. Return visits should be positively related to GP density, and negatively related to per capita income and the Medical Card ratio.

In the analysis which follows, the dependent variable is a dichotomous one, set equal to one where a future return visit was arranged at the present visit. The dependent variables are hypothesised to influence the *probability* that the present visit leads to a return visit.

The independent variables in the model are the following:

Age, and age squared;
Distance to GP from patient's home;
GP density;
Medical Card Ratio;
Area index of per capita income;[71]
Women-Category I-No VHI (interaction);
Per capita income-GP density (interaction);
Per capita income-GP density-Medical Card ratio (interaction).

We will discuss the role of each of these variables in the model and its hypothesised sign.

Each independent variable relates to the agency model, the self-interest model, or both (see Chapter 2). The agency model states that physicians will take the patient's health status, preferences and economic circumstances into account in ordering medical care (such as return visits), acting on the patient's behalf as the doctor believes the patient would act if the latter had the doctor's knowledge, experience and authority. Therefore the agency model involves both health status variables (or their proxies) and economic variables (relating to patient preferences and economic circumstances).

We discuss the independent variables in turn.

Women-Category I-No VHI.   As utilisation is typically significantly higher among females than males, sex is a health status and preference proxy and we hypothesise a positive sign for females. Sex may also be a proxy for lower time price, again arguing for a positive sign. Category I is both an agency and a self-interest variable. Persons in Category I are poorer and, on average, older, and therefore should have higher morbidity. They should therefore have more return visits than the rest of the population. Moreover, they pay nothing for GP services; and therefore, a GP pursuing his or her agency function will order more services for them, other things being equal. Thus the agency model predicts a positive relationship between Category I and return visits. On the other hand, because they do not pay fees for GP services, persons with Category I eligibility are less likely to resist extra return visits than those in the population who do have to pay for them. Indeed, following Wilensky and Rossiter (1981), as discussed in Chapter 2, we might argue that physicians derive disutility (e.g., guilt) from undue demand generation; and in the Irish case disutility will certainly be less where the patient pays no fee. Hence the self-interest model also predicts a positive relationship between Category I and return visits. Because both agency and self-interest models predict a positive relationship, this variable is not useful

[71]The author is indebted to Dr. Miceal Ross of ESRI for this series.

in distinguishing between them. Women-Category I-No VHI performed better than sex and Category I separately, indicating an interaction among these three variables.

Age and age squared. Like sex female, age with age squared is first and foremost a health status proxy and secondarily a proxy for time price. The signs should be negative and positive, respectively, to yield a U-shaped relationship.

Distance to GP. This is a time-price variable, and a physician taking time-price into account and pursuing an agency role will order more return visits for his or her more nearby patients. Hence a negative relationship is hypothesised. This variable assumes considerable importance in the present study, as a control variable. If it were not included, then physician density could conceivably act as a proxy for time-price (on the plausible assumption that the lower the physician-to-population ratio, the further, on average, each patient would have to travel to a GP).

GP density. This is the most important variable in the model. For reasons set forth above, we hypothesise a positive relationship on the basis of the self-interest model. However, such a positive relationship does not point uniquely to the self-interest model. If an area has a high demand for medical care (e.g., because of preferences, social class, income, or health status), it will be likely to have both more return visits and a higher GP density. Thus it is important to control for the factors which influence demand for medical care. One weakness in the present study is the lack of measures of health status. We are unable to state whether there are areas with, e.g., a high prevalence of chronic conditions which might explain a positive relationship between return visits and GP density without resort to physician-induced demand. We do have a number of proxies, however, as noted. Moreover, we have two other variables, *viz.*, Medical Card ratio and per capita income, which relate to the self-interest hypothesis.

Medical Card ratio. On the basis of the self-interest model, we hypothesise a negative relationship, for reasons stated earlier. It will be noted that Category I eligibility has quite different effects when viewed from the individual patient perspective and when viewed from the standpoint of the area average. A patient with Category I eligibility is a *more* likely candidate than those in Categories II or III for demand stimulation, while a high regional ratio of Category I patients to population *reduces* the probability that any given patient, whatever be his or her own eligibility, will be the target of demand-stimulating efforts.

Area index of per capita income. On the basis of the self-interest model, we also hypothesise a negative relationship here, for reasons stated earlier. Again, there is a difference between the effect of patient income and that of area per capita income. The higher is the patient's income, the more return visits will be predicted, on the basis of the agency model. However, high per capita income, by raising the demand for GP services, will reduce the need for and hence the probability of economically-motivated, physician-stimulated return visits.

Interactions. In addition, the regional variables – GP density, Medical Card ratio, and index of per capita income — were combined in two- and three-way interactions, on the hypothesis that these variables may combine multiplicatively as well as (or instead of) additively, in their effects on return visit behaviour.

Empirical Estimates

Because the dependent variable is dichotomous, it is interpreted as relating to probabilities, and the model was estimated using a logistic multiple regression model.[72] Regressions were run on six sets of cases, namely:[73]

All persons;
All persons, except females aged 18–40
Males only;
Females only;
Persons with Category I eligibility only; and
Persons with Categories II or III eligibility only.

Females aged 18–40 were excluded in one version in order to delete most series of obstetrical return visits.[74] The model was partitioned by sex because of the known differences in morbidity and medical care utilisation between males and females. As those with Category I eligibility have free GP care while those with Categories II and III eligibility do not, the two groups arguably have quite different return visit behaviour.

The results are given in Tables 6.43 through 6.54. In all instances, tables reporting logistic regression results are followed by tables reporting illustrative probabilities calculated from the regressions.

The results strongly support the hypothesis. GP density, Medical Card ratio, and index of per capita income are all statistically very significant and their signs are in the hypothesised directions (positive, negative and negative, respectively).

To assess the effects of these three critical variables in the model, it is not sufficient to examine the main effects alone; interactions must also be considered. An example is GP density. In the all persons version of the regression (Table 6.43) the sign of the GP density variable in the full model is negative, which would appear to run counter to the hypothesis. But GP density also appears in two interactions, per capita income — GP density (positive) and per capita income — GP density — Medical Card ratio (negative). The question is the net combined effect of GP density on the dependent variable, or in other words, the sign of the partial derivative of the probability that a return visit was arranged at the most recent GP visit with respect to GP density. That the sign is positive is clear when one examines the probabilities in Table 6.44: as GP density varies

---

[72]The model was estimated by the LOGIST procedure in SAS. See footnote 66, above. However, some OLS regressions were run on the same model, yielding essentially similar results. See Tussing, 1983a.

[73]In addition, earlier versions of the same model were run for children aged 16 and under, and for persons aged 65 and over, with essentially similar results.

[74]The author is indebted to his former colleague, Professor Stephen H. Long of Syracuse University, for suggesting this version.

Table 6.43: *Was return visit arranged at most recent GP visit? – Dichotomous variable, logistic regression – all persons*[a]

	Full Model	5% Version
$\overline{R}^{2}$ [b]	0.136	0.123
N	1,003	1,003
Equation χ^2	183.70**	160.54**
Intercept	30.824	-9.313
Age	0.028*	0.021**
	(3.87)	(36.92)
Age Squared ÷ 1,000	-0.083	
	(0.25)	
Distance to GP	-0.098	-0.112*
	(3.54)	(5.46)
GP Density	-86.887**	21.701**
	(12.62)	(36.35)
Medical Card Ratio	29.055**	
	(15.12)	
Category I	0.697**	0.680**
	(14.22)	(15.22)
Per Capita Income	-0.623**	
	(21.10)	
Interactions		
Woman[c]-Cat. I-No VHI	0.611*	0.711**
	(4.32)	(6.83)
P.C. Income-GP Density	1.629**	
	(21.89)	
P.C. Income-GP Density-Medical Card Ratio	-0.967**	
	(22.14)	(23.18)
Joint Tests:		
Age	(37.96)**	
GP Density	(49.35)**	(36.49)**
Medical Card Ratio	(38.94)**	
Index of Per Capita Income	(29.44)**	

Notes: [a]χ^2 in parentheses beneath parameter estimates. [b]$\overline{R}^2$ adjusted for degrees of freedom. [c]"Woman" defined as female aged 40-64.
Significance: *$0.01 < p \leqslant 0.05$. **$p \leqslant 0.01$.

from its minimum value (0.429) to its maximum (0.555), holding constant other variables at their means (and qualitative variables at the values specified), the predicted probability varies positively, and quite considerably, from 0.08 to 0.91.

Table 6.44: *Probability that most recent GP visit resulted in a return visit being arranged, all persons, based on logistic regression* [a]

		Probabilities	
		Full Model	5% Version
Baseline probability applies when the following variables are set equal to their means, as below:[b]	Baseline probability*	.20	.20
Age = 39.64	Other probabilities**		
Distance to GP = 2.60	Age =		
GP density = .462	min = 1	.08	.10
Medical Card ratio = .369	10	.11	.12
Index of per capita income	20	.14	.14
= 99.04	30	.17	.17
	40	.20	.20
and when the following qualities	50	.24	.24
obtain:[b]	60	.28	.27
Eligibility = Category II/III	70	.31	.32
VHI cover = no	max = 95	.40	.44
Other probabilities apply when	Eligibility =		
variables are changed, one by one	Category I	.34	.33
(the others held constant as	VHI cover = yes	—	—
above) to the values and/or	Sex-age-eligibility-VHI cover[c]		
qualities indicated.	Woman-I-no = yes	.54	.50
	Distance to GP		
	min = under 1 mile	.25	.25
	max = more than 10 miles	.15	.15
	Index of per capita income		
	min = 73	.40	—
	max = 122	.11	—
	GP Density =		
	min = 0.429	.08	.13
	max = 0.555	.91	.53
	Medical Card ratio		
	min = 0.232	.54	—
	max = 0.586	.01	—

Notes: [a]See Table 6.43. [b]For 5% version, applies only to variables in the model. [c]"Woman" defined as female aged 40–64.

The appropriate significance test for this combined effect of GP density is the joint test, reported below the regression results in Table 6.43. The reported χ^2 value is extremely high, meaning that the effect is very significant indeed.

In the other, partitioned versions, GP density (main effects only) is always very significant, but in the full model it is sometimes positive and sometimes negative. However, the partial derivatives are always positive and in absolute values quite strong; and the joint tests show the effect of GP density to be considerable in all cases.

Table 6.45: *Was return visit arranged at most recent GP visit? – Dichotomous variable, logistic regression – All persons except women aged 18-40*[a]

	Full Model	5% Version
$\bar{R}^{2}$ [b]	0.147	0.136
N	863	863
Equation χ^2	175.79**	156.79**
Intercept	30.598	-10.009
Age	0.031*	0.020**
	(4.29)	(32.99)
Age Squared ÷ 1,000	-0.125	
	(0.49)	
Distance to GP	-0.102	-0.126*
	(3.25)	(6.01)
GP Density	-84.455**	24.187**
	(10.16)	(39.41)
Medical Card Ratio	26.386**	
	(10.90)	
Category I	0.791**	0.772**
	(16.21)	(17.26)
Per Captia Income	-0.615**	
	(17.60)	
Interactions		
Woman[c]-Category I-No VHI	0.556	0.680**
	(3.39)	(6.07)
P.C. Income-GP Density	1.597**	
	(18.00)	
P.C. Income-GP Density-Medical Card Ratio	-0.919**	-0.187**
	(17.62)	(27.37)
Joint Tests:		
Age	(34.45)**	
GP Density	(47.01)**	(39.41)**
Medical Card Ratio	(38.21)**	
Index of Per Capita Income	(24.79)**	

Notes: [a]χ^2 in parentheses beneath parameter estimates. [b]$\bar{R}^2$ adjusted for degrees of freedom. [c]"Woman" defined as female aged 40-64.
Significance: *$0.01 < p \leqslant 0.05$. **$p \leqslant 0.01$.

Table 6.46: *Probability that most recent GP visit resulted in a return visit being arranged, females 18-40 excluded, based on logistic regression* [a]

| | | Probabilities | |
		Full Model	5% Version
Baseline probability applies when the following variables are set equal to their means, as below:[b]	Baseline probability*	.21	.20
Age = 41.47	Other probabilities**		
Distance to GP = 2.61	Age =		
GP density = 0.463	min = 1	.08	.10
Medical Card ratio = 0.373	10	.11	.12
Index of per capita income	20	.14	.14
= 98.53	30	.17	.17
and when the following qualities	40	.20	.20
obtain:[b]	50	.24	.23
Eligibility = Category II/III	60	.27	.27
Sex-age-eligibility-VHI cover	70	.30	.31
= not woman-I-no[c]	max = 95	.36	.42
Other probabilities apply when	Eligibility =		
variables are changed, one by one	Category I	.37	.35
(the others held constant as	Sex-age-eligibility-VHI cover[c]		
above) to the values and/or	Woman	.50	.52
qualities indicated.	Distance to GP		
	min = under 1 mile	.26	.26
	max = more than 10 miles	.16	.14
	Index of per capita income		
	min = 73	.41	.34
	max = 122	.11	.10
	GP Density		
	min = 0.429	.07	.12
	max = 0.555	.91	.56
	Medical Card ratio		
	min = 0.232	.59	.42
	max = 0.586	.01	.04

Notes: [a] See Table 6.45. [b] For 5% version, applies only to variables in the model. [c] "Woman" defined as female aged 40-64.

Table 6.47: *Was return visit arranged at most recent GP visit? – Dichotomous variable, logistic regression – Males only*[a]

	Full Model	5% Version
$\overline{R}^{2\,b}$	0.146	0.147
N	453	453
Equation χ^2	92.89**	83.35**
Intercept	–14.916	–7.930
Age	0.050*	0.029**
	(5.06)	(31.83)
Age Squared ÷ 1,000	–0.272	
	(1.07)	
Distance to GP	–0.163*	
	(3.95)	
GP Density	30.777**	18.121**
	(9.83)	(16.22)
Medical Card Ratio	3.508	–8.218**
	(0.20)	(26.41)
Category I	0.895**	0.782**
	(11.03)	(9.27)
Per Capita Income	0.025	
	(0.75)	
Interactions:		
P.C. Income-GP Density-Medical Card Ratio	–0.338	
	(2.63)	
Joint Tests		
Age	(27.84)**	
GP Density	(16.64)**	
Medical Card Ratio	(20.80)**	
Index of Per Capita Income	(3.55)	

Notes: [a]χ^2 in parentheses beneath parameter estimates. [b]$\overline{R}^2$ adjusted for degrees of freedom. *Significance:* *$0.01 < p \leqslant 0.05$. **$p \leqslant 0.01$.

Table 6.48: *Probability that most recent GP visit resulted in a return visit being arranged, males only, based on logistic regression* [a]

		Probabilities	
		Full Model	5% Version
**Baseline probability* applies when the following variables are set equal to their means, as below:[b]	*Baseline probability**	.19	.18
Age = 37.72	*Other probabilities***		
Distance to GP = 2.62	*Age =*		
GP density = .461	min = 1	.05	.07
Medical Card ratio = .373	10	.08	.09
Index of per capita income	20	.11	.11
= 98.07	30	.15	.15
	40	.20	.19
and when the following qualities	50	.24	.23
obtain:[b]	60	.28	.29
Eligibility = Category II/III	70	.32	.36
VHI cover = no	max = 88	.34	.48
**Other probabilities* apply when	*Eligibility =*		
variables are changed, one by one	Category I	.37	.32
(the others held constant as	*VHI cover* = yes	—	—
above) to the values and/or	*Distance to GP*		
qualities indicated.	min = under 1 mile	.27	—
	max = more than 10 miles	.12	—
	Index of per capita income		
	min = 73	.31	—
	max = 122	.08	—
	GP Density		
	min = 0.429	.10	.11
	max = 0.555	.53	.54
	Medical Card ratio		
	min = 0.232	.51	.41
	max = 0.586	.02	.04

Notes: [a]See Table 6.47. [b]For 5% version, applies only to variables in the model.

Table 6.49: *Was return visit arranged at most recent GP visit? – Dichotomous variable, logistic regression – females only*[a]

	Full Model	5% Version
$\bar{R}^{2\,[b]}$	0.135	0.111
N	550	550
Equation χ^2	111.45**	83.06**
Intercept	42.461	-6.971
Age	0.008	0.015**
	(0.15)	(11.99)
Age Squared ÷ 1,000	0.112	
	(0.24)	
Distance to GP	-0.091	
	(1.64)	
GP Density	-118.999**	10.842**
	(13.80)	(17.09)
Medical Card Ratio	39.730**	
	(14.23)	
Category I	0.636*	0.632**
	(5.68)	(6.98)
Per Capita Income	-0.795**	
	(19.89)	
Interactions		
Woman[c]-Category I-No VHI	0.696*	0.707*
	(3.99)	(5.80)
P.C. Income-GP Density	2.075**	
	(20.25)	
P.C. Income-GP Density-Medical Card Ratio	-1.186**	
	(17.08)	
Joint Tests:		
Age	(13.84)**	
GP Density	(31.80)**	
Medical Card Ratio	(19.89)**	
Index of Per Capita Income	(19.32)**	

Notes: [a]χ^2 in parentheses beneath parameter estimates. [b]$\bar{R}^2$ adjusted for degrees of freedom. [c]"Woman" defined as female aged 40–64.
Significance: *$0.01 < p \leqslant 0.05$. **$p \leqslant 0.01$.

Table 6.50: *Probability that most recent GP visit resulted in a return visit being arranged, famales only, based on logistic regression*[a]

| | | Probabilities | |
		Full Model	5% Version
Baseline probability applies when the following variables are set equal to their means, as below:[b]	Baseline probability*	.19	.21
Age = 41.22	*Other probabilities***		
Distance to GP = 2.58	*Age =*		
GP density = .462	min = 1	.13	.13
Medical Card ratio = .366	10	.14	.14
Index of per capita income	20	.15	.16
= 99.83	30	.17	.18
and when the following qualities	40	.19	.21
obtain:[b]	50	.22	.23
Eligibility = Category II/III	60	.25	.26
Age-eligibility-VHI cover	70	.30	.29
= Not Woman-I-No[c]	max = 95	.45	.38
**Other probabilities* apply when	*Eligibility =*		
variables are changed, one by one	Category I	.31	.33
(the others held constant as	*Age-Eligibility-VHI cover*[a]c		
above) to the values and/or	Woman-I-No = yes	.47	.54
qualities indicated.	*Distance to GP*		
	min = under 1 mile	.23	—
	max = more than 10 miles	.15	—
	Index of per capita income		
	min = 73	.41	—
	max = 122	.11	—
	GP Density		
	min = 0.429	.06	.16
	max = 0.555	.95	.42
	Medical Card ratio		
	min = 0.232	.48	—
	max = 0.586	.00	—

Notes: [a]See Table 6.49. [b]For 5% version, applies only to variables in the model. [c]"Woman" defined as female aged 40–64.

Table 6.51: *Was return visit arranged at most recent GP visit? – Dichotomous variable, logistic regression, Category I only*[a]

	Full Model	5% Version
$\overline{R}^{2(b)}$	0.089	0.072
N	401	401
Equation χ^2	66.76**	49.44**
Intercept	40.363	-7.099
Age	-0.020	0.018**
	(0.71)	(14.78)
Age Squared ÷ 1,000	0.441	
	(2.81)	
Distance to GP	0.143	-0.176**
	(3.48)	(6.75)
GP Density	-100.844**	18.174**
	(9.89)	(14.01)
Medical Card Ratio	23.685*	
	(5.50)	
Per Capita Income	-0.672**	
	(14.26)	
Interactions:		
Woman[c]	0.962**	0.719**
	(8.98)	(7.14)
P.C. Income-GP Density	1.693**	
	(13.80)	
P.C. Income-GP Density-Medical Card Ratio	-0.821**	-0.135**
	(8.87)	(9.24)
Joint Tests:		
Age	(19.10)**	
GP Density	(23.46)**	(14.01)**
Medical Card Ratio	(18.58)**	
Index of Per Capita Income	(16.68)**	

Notes: [a]χ^2 in parentheses beneath parameter estimates. [b]$\overline{R}^2$ adjusted for degrees of freedom. [c]"Woman" defined as female aged 40–64.
Significance: *0.01 [a]$\langle$ p $\leqslant$ 0.05. **p $\leqslant$ 0.01.

Table 6.52: *Probability that most recent GP visit resulted in a return visit being arranged, Category I only, based on logistic regression*[a]

		Probabilities	
		Full Model	5% Version
Baseline probability applies when the following variables are set equal to their means, as below:[b]	Baseline probability*	.31	.39
Age = 51.06	Other probabilities**		
Distance to GP = 2.60	Sex = male	—	—
GP density = .471	Age =		
Medical Card ratio = .403	min = 1	.28	.21
Index of per capita income	10	.25	.24
= 94.63	20	.24	.27
and when the following qualities	30	.25	.30
obtain:[b]	40	.27	.34
sex = female	50	.31	.38
VHI cover = no	60	.37	.43
**Other probabilities* apply when	70	.46	.47
variables are changed, one by one	max = 88	.68	.55
(the others held constant as	VHI cover = yes	—	—
above) to the values and/or	Distance to GP		
qualities indicated.	min = under 1 mile	.40	.50
	max = more than 10 miles	.22	.26
	GP Density =		
	min = 0.429	.13	.27
	max = 0.555	.84	.66
	Medical Card ratio		
	min = 0.232	.75	—
	max = 0.586	.03	—
	Index of Per Capita Income		
	min = 73	.49	
	max = 122	.18	

Notes: [a]See Table 6.51. [b]For 5% version, applies only to variables in the model.

Table 6.53: *Was return visit arranged at most recent GP visit? – Dichotomous variable, logistic regression, Categories II-III only*[a]

	Full Model	5% Version
$\bar{R}^{2}$[b]	0.067	0.075
N	602	602
Equation χ^2	55.59**	52.31**
Intercept	-19.972	-11.478
Age	0.064**	0.062**
	(8.89)	(9.57)
Age Squared ÷ 1,000	-0.508*	-0.489*
	(3.84)	(3.87)
Distance to GP	-0.035	
	(0.24)	
GP Density	37.088**	25.247**
	(15.49)	(22.89)
Medical Card Ratio	12.412	
	(2.54)	
Per Capita Income	0.037	
	(1.90)	
Interactions		
Woman[c]	-0.171	
	(0.31)	
P.C. Income-GP Density-Medical Card Ratio	-0.500*	-0.185**
	(5.99)	(13.97)
Joint Tests:		
Age	(21.52)**	(24.88)**
GP Density	(21.56)**	(23.26)**
Medical Card Ratio	(15.17)**	
Index of Per Capita Income	(8.02)**	

Notes: [a]χ^2 in parentheses beneath parameter estimates. [b]$\bar{R}^2$ adjusted for degrees of freedom. [c]"Woman" defined as female aged 40–64.
Significance: *0.01 [a]< p ≤ 0.05. **p ≤ 0.01.

Table 6.54: *Probability that most recent GP visit resulted in a return visit being arranged, Categories II/III only based on logistic regression* [a]

| | | Probabilities | |
		Full Model	5% Version
Baseline probability applies when the following variables are set equal to their means, as below:[b]	Baseline probability*	.20	.20
Age = 32.03	Other probabilities**		
Distance to GP = 2.61	Age =		
GP density = .455	min = 1	.06	.06
Medical Card ratio = .346	10	.09	.09
Index of per capita income	20	.14	.14
= 101.98	30	.19	.19
and when the following qualities	40	.24	.24
obtain:[b]	50	.28	.27
Sex-age = Not Woman[c]	60	.29	.29
**Other probabilities* apply when	70	.29	.28
variables are changed, one by one	max = 95	.20	.20
(the others held constant as	Sex-age[c]		
above) to the values and/or	Woman = yes	.24	—
qualities indicated.	Distance to GP		
	min = under 1 mile	.22	—
	max = more than 10 miles	.19	—
	Index of per capita income		
	min = 73	.40	—
	max = 122	.08	—
	GP Density		
	min = 0.429	.11	.13
	max = 0.555	.58	.63
	Medical Card ratio		
	min = 0.232	.40	—
	max = 0.586	.01	—

Notes: [a]See Table 6.53. [b]For 5% version, applies only to variables in the model. [c]"Woman" defined as female aged 40-64.

A similar story can be told concerning the Medical Card ratio and the index of per capita income. Both are hypothesised to vary inversely with the dependent variable. When we look at the main effects, these variables sometimes have a positive effect. But again when we look at the partial derivatives, as indicated by the probabilities inferred from the regressions, the effect is always strongly negative.

When these regressions were run without interactions (not reported here), the signs of the coefficients of GP density, Medical Card ratio, and index of per capita income were as hypothesised — i.e., positive, negative, and negative respectively — and they were significant at better than the 5 per cent level, usually at better than 1 per cent.

When one compares the full models with the 5 per cent versions, one sees a similar effect. In all three instances in which GP density (main effects) has a negative sign in the full model, i.e., in Tables 6.43, 6.45 and 6.49, it "turns around" and becomes positive, and still very significant, once the per capita income-GP density variable is eliminated.

It should be noted that, in each case, we are assessing the effects of each independent variable, assuming the others are held constant at their means even though in the real world they tend to vary together. For example, the Medical Card ratio and the index of per capita income have a zero-order correlation of −0.85. This explains how the predicted probabilities can vary so greatly. In the real world, the effects of these variables work against each other, more or less.

The other variables in the model may be of interest.

Age is always significant (when the joint test is noted) and positive. The magnitude of the effect is large, though least so in the Category II/III version.

Category I eligibility raises the probability of a return visit from 0.20 to 0.34 in the all persons version; the effects are almost identical in the other versions. This result is consistent with both agency and self-interest models of physician behaviour. If the person in Category I is a woman aged 40–64, without VHI cover, the probability in the all persons case rises to 0.54, again with similar effects in other versions of the model.

Excluding women aged 18–40 adds about ten points to the R^2. Apart from that, the results of that version are virtually the same as in the all-persons version. Partitioning by sex seems to improve the regressions; partitioning by category of eligibility worsens them.

In general, these equations explain 10 to 15 per cent of the person-to-person variation in the probability that his or her most recent GP consultation led to a return visit being arranged. Of course, if we had health status information on the patient, or information on the doctor, these R^2s would be higher. None the less, using essentially demographic, economic and market-related data, we are able to explain an important part of physician behaviour. We are left with the conclusion that Irish GPs do engage in compensatory demand stimulation.

"Necessary" vs. "Unnecessary" Utilisation

All of the foregoing discussion of self-interested demand stimulation by Irish GPs may leave the impression that much unnecessary utilisation — GP consultations and other utilisation correlated with them — must be taking place.

The notion that there is a dichotomy between "necessary" and "unnecessary" utilisation is based on a simplistic and excessively mechanical interpretation, both of medicine and of economics. When a doctor orders a return visit which he or she would not have ordered under other incentive arrangements, it would be wrong to conclude that the visit can have no medical value, or perhaps it should be said no *probability* of any medical value. Medical value is not an either-or quality, but a question of degree and of judgement. A major problem in health care systems, not only in Ireland but around the world, is the tendency, arising out of moral hazard and provider incentive structures, to push medical care utilisation beyond the point where its benefits are as great as its costs. In most systems, that in Ireland included, decision makers in medical resource utilisation — mainly patients and physicians — do not bear the costs, individually, of their decisions. Unless other checks are introduced, excessive utilisation results. In fee-for-service systems, as in Ireland, incentives are actually perverse, encouraging still further excessive utilisation.

This excessive utilisation might best be described as *uneconomic* rather than unnecessary. Individual consultations arising out of self-interested demand stimulation by GPs may sometimes be of medical value; taken together in aggregate, all such visits almost certainly are. But it is almost certain that they are not worth their cost. The same resources, devoted to medical care elsewhere in the system, will yield significantly more medical value.

Having said this, it is important to add that *some* physician-stimulated utilisation is probably actually unnecessary. Indeed, because in medical care it is not always true that "more is better", some such utilisation may actually be harmful. Presumably, this is the rare exception, rather than the rule.

Conclusion

In Chapter 5, we discussed the reasons for believing the incentive structure in the Irish medical care system to be often perverse. Those a priori propositions have been borne out in this chapter. Consumer incentives are perverse, in the sense that persons in Categories II and III are encouraged to make excessive use of high cost specialist and hospital services, which are often cheaper to the patient than GP care. Provider incentives are perverse, in the sense that they induce GPs to generate excessive return visits, particularly amongst the Category I population. A systematic review by policymakers of this incentive structure is appropriate. Some suggestions are made in Chapter 8.

First, however, we turn to utilisation of services other than general practitioner care.

Chapter 7

UTILISATION OF OTHER MEDICAL CARE SERVICES AND PREVENTION-ORIENTED CARE

In Chapter 6, we reviewed the utilisation of general practitioner services, including household expenditures on GPs, and the issue of physician-induced demand for medical care by GPs. In this chapter, we examine the utilisation of medical care other than general practitioner services: specialist care; pharmaceutical prescriptions; out-patient and in-patient hospital care and services; and dental care. All except the last, as will be seen, are strongly linked to the utilisation of GP services. In a second section, we examine the determinants of household expenditures on medical care services. In a third and final section, we review the utilisation of prevention-oriented care.

A. Utilisation of Other Medical Care Services

In Chapter 6, we introduced a general model for the demand for or utilisation of medical care services and applied it to GPs. The same model can be applied, in general, to other services. For GPs, individual utilisation is a function of his or her health status (H_i); background variables affecting taste for or attitude to medical care (Z_i); money-price (P_i); time-price (T_i); and availability of the service (A_i). For services other than GP care, we add a fifth variable to the model, viz., physician referral or prescription (R_i). This is, of course, strongly correlated with H_i, but it was thought to be better to indicate it specifically and separately, as health status and referral are not the same, and the latter deserves explicit reference. Thus, for pharmaceutical prescription medicines (for example), subscripted p, the model is written

$$X_{pi} = X_{pi}(H_i, Z_i, P_{pi}, T_{pi}, A_{pi}, R_{pi})$$

and for other services the subscripts merely change.

As before, we do not have health status data, and must use proxies, mainly sex and age. General practitioner (and in some equations specialist) utilisation, which mainly represent R, also indirectly reflect health status. Occupation group and education are the main Z variables. P is represented primarily by category of health services eligibility, VHI cover, and other help with medical bills, though usual GP fee levels are included in several equations. Time price is

222

measured again by distance to GP, and in some cases by whether there is a large (300-bed) hospital nearby. Availability is also measured by the nearby hospital variable and by the ratio of persons eligible in Category I to the population. The "Nearby Hospital" variable is a dichotomous one: "Is there a 300-bed hospital within 10 miles?" On the theory that persons in Category I have higher utilisation levels for most medical care services, the ratio of those persons to population is an index of demand pressure on the available services and hence of availability. R is measured by GP utilisation and by specialist utilisation.

The results are reported in Tables 7.1 through 7.16, inclusive, for pharmaceutical prescription items, specialist consultations, out-patient hospital utilisation, in-patient hospital utilisation and dentist visits, respectively. For each type of utilisation (except dental visits for reasons to be noted), there are three tables. In the first, we report on a regression in which the dependent variable is dichotomous, taking the form, "Were there any pharmaceutical medicines prescribed (specialist consultations, dentist visits, etc.) in 1980?" As elsewhere in this study, where a dichotomous dependent variable is used, the form of regression analysis used is a logistic function. In the second table, following each logistic regression, there are reported illustrative probabilities, as in Chapter 6, because the parameters of the logistic regressions themselves are almost impossible to interpret intuitively. In the third table, we report on regressions in which only those persons with any 1980 utilisation are included, and the dependent variable is the number of pharmaceutical items prescribed, specialist consultations, etc., or in the case of in-patient admissions, the length of stay. The dependent variable is continuous and OLS (ordinary least squares) regression analysis is used. Because of the limited dependent variable, there is a chance of selection bias, and accordingly we include as an independent variable the inverse Mills ratio, as discussed in Chapters 1 and 6.

The tables reporting OLS regressions show both full models and 5 per cent versions, and also models including and excluding other household members' GP utilisation. See Chapter 6 for a discussion. This means there are four columns in each OLS table when the household utilisation variable is significant at the 5 per cent level or better, and three if it is excluded from the 5 per cent version.

The reader will find it instructive to compare the findings in Tables 7.1–7.16 with the data on utilisation found in Appendix Tables A.1 through A.6. Table 7.1 indicates that sex has essentially no *net* relationship to pharmaceutical prescriptions. This is in spite of the fact that Appendix Table A.1 shows that females had nearly 30 per cent more pharmaceutical prescription items per person in 1980, and indeed nearly 20 per cent more prescription items per GP consultation. Evidently, these male-female differences are completely explained by other variables in the model, especially GP utilisation.

The same can also be said for age. Appendix Table A.1 shows an important influence on pharmaceutical prescriptions for this variable, especially as between persons aged 65 and over, and the rest of the population. Part of this is due to higher GP utilisation among this part of the population, but Appendix Table

A.1 also shows a very much higher number of prescription items per GP consultation — about twice as high — for aged persons as for the rest. Hence age has its own effect. In Table 7.1, where both GP and specialist consultations, as well as other variables correlated with age (such as category of entitlement), are controlled for, age does not significantly influence whether there were any prescribed pharmaceutical items in 1980. However, Table 7.3 shows age to influence the number of prescription items, for persons with any, in the 5 per cent version.

Appendix Table A.2 shows pharmaceutical prescriptions to be considerably higher for persons in Category I than for those in II or III; and the same holds true of prescription items per GP consultation. The logistic regression in Table 7.1 shows persons in Category I to be significantly more likely to have any prescriptions filled even where such other varibles as age and GP utilisation are controlled for. However, Table 7.2 shows the magnitude of this effect to be small. In Table 7.3, women aged 40–64, with Category I eligibility and no VHI, have nearly four more prescription items per year than other persons who have any, in the 5 per cent version.

Easily the most powerful effect on pharmaceutical prescriptions as judged by χ^2 and t-statistics, is, of course, GP utilisation itself. This leads us to note again the point made in Chapter 6, that general practitioner services are important not only in themselves but in the other resource-utilising medical care decisions linked to them causally and statistically. As might be expected, specialist consultations are also significantly associated with prescriptions, though less strongly than GP consultations.

Table 7.2 shows how strong the relationship between GP and specialist consultations and the likelihood of a prescription is. Table 7.3 shows that, amongst persons with any prescriptions, each GP consultation adds approximately 1.2 prescription items, and each two specialist visits add about one prescription item.

Table 7.3 shows the Inverse Mills ratio to be significant though small in magnitude.

The regressions reported in Table 7.3 suffered from heteroscedasticity in the error variance, leading us to adjust the critical values of the t-statistics, as discussed in Chapter 1.

The $\bar{R}^2$s shown in Tables 7.1 and 7.3 are higher than most of those reported in this volume, and are relatively high for this kind of microdata analysis. Our equations explain more than a third of the person-to-person variability in prescriptions.

Tables 7.4, 7.5 and 7.6 report on determinants of specialist consultations. A review of the three tables will quickly make clear that they are all dominated by the influence of GP consultations. This is not surprising and it again points up the crucial role of GPs in subsequent utilisation. However, Table 7.5 shows each GP consultation to have a relatively small effect on the probability of a specialist consultation and Table 7.6 shows that the *number* of specialist visits was not significantly influenced by the number of GP visits.

Table 7.1: *Logistic regressions of any prescribed pharmaceutical items in 1980 (Dichotomous Variable)*[a]

	Full Model	5% Version
$\overline{R}^{2\,[b]}$	0.371	0.362
N	1,068	1,068
Equation χ^2	532.35**	512.17**
Intercept[c]	0.132	-1.185**
	(0.01)	(101.05)
Sex Female	0.238	—
	(2.02)	
Age	-0.014	—
	(0.98)	
Age Squared ÷ 1,000	0.197	—
	(1.19)	
Category I	0.469*	0.392*
	(4.91)	(4.63)
Category III	-0.008	—
	(0.00)	
No VHI	-0.143	—
	(0.43)	
Other help	0.297	—
	(1.04)	
GP Density	-2.856	—
	(0.74)	
Medical Card Ratio	-0.180	—
	(0.02)	
Consultant Density	0.259	—
	(0.05)	
Woman-I-No VHI[d]	-0.261	—
	(0.22)	
Times Seen by GP	0.799**	0.820**
	(150.82)	(164.45)
Times Seen by Specialist	0.112	—
	(1.58)	
Joint Tests:		
Age		(1.25)

Notes: [a]χ^2 in parentheses beneath parameter estimates. [b]$\overline{R}^2$ adjusted for degrees of freedom. [c]Intercept term in Full Model includes: Sex = male; eligibility = Category II; VHI cover = no; and other help = no. [d]"Woman" = 40–64.
Significance: *$0.01 < p \leqslant 0.05$. **$p \leqslant 0.01$.

Table 7.2: *Probability of any prescribed pharmaceutical medicines in 1980, based on logistic regression* [a]

		Probabilities	
		Full Model	5% Version
Baseline probability applies when the following variables are set equal to their means, as below:[b]	*Baseline probability* *	.90	.91
Age = 38.50	*Other probabilities***		
GP density = .462	Sex = male	.87	—
Consultant density = .462	*Age =*		
Medical Card ratio = .370	min = 1	.92	—
Annual no. of GP consultations	10	.91	—
= .381	20	.90	—
and when the following equalities	30	.90	—
obtain:[b]	40	.90	—
sex = female	50	.90	—
eligibility = Category II	60	.91	—
VHI cover = no	70	.92	—
Other help = no	max = 95	.94	—
**Other probabilities* apply when	*Eligibility =*		
variables are changed, one by	Category I	.93	.94
one, (the others held constant as	Category III	.90	—
above) to the values and/or	*VHI cover* = yes	.91	—
qualities indicated.	*GP density =*		
	min = 0.429	.91	—
	max = 0.555	.87	—
	Consultant Density		
	min = 0	.89	—
	max = .387	.90	—
	Other help = yes	.92	—
	Medical Care ratio		
	min = 0.232	.90	—
	max = 0.586	.89	—
	Annual GP consultations		
	min = 0	.23	.23
	2	.60	.61
	6	.97	.98
	12	1.00	1.00
	24	1.00	1.00
	max = 60	1.00	1.00
	Specialist consultations		
	min = 0	.89	—
	2	.91	—
	6	.94	—
	12	.97	—
	max = 25	.99	—

Notes: [a]See Table 7.1. [b]For 5% version, applies only to variables in the model.

Table 7.3: *Regression of annual number of prescribed pharmaceutical items, 1980, on selected independent variables, ordinary least squares, persons with any items only*[a]

	Full Model		5% Version
	(1)	*(2)*	*(3)*
$\bar{R}^{2}$[b]	0.373	0.375	0.382
N	641	641	641
Equation F	28.263**	26.681**	78.61**
Intercept[c]	3.437	3.889	-2.394
Sex Female	0.440	0.317	—
	(0.493)	(0.355)	
Age	0.071	0.069	0.091**
	(0.966)	(0.946)	(5.080)
Age squared ÷ 1,000	0.206	0.204	—
	(0.234)	(0.233)	
Category I	1.501	1.653	—
	(1.347)	(1.481)	
Category III	2.111	2.052	—
	(1.410)	(1.373)	
No VHI	0.417	0.484	—
	(0.338)	(0.393)	
Other Help	-0.243	-0.084	—
	(0.154)	(0.053)	
GP Density	-17.674	-17.872	—
	(1.139)	(1.153)	
Medical Card Ratio	1.677	1.937	—
	(0.353)	(0.408)	
Persons in Household	-0.034	-0.028	—
	(0.161)	(0.133)	
Woman-I-No VHI[d]	3.470	3.359	3.950*(*)
	(1.900)	(1.841)	(2.466)
GP Visits	1.179**	1.211**	1.200**
	(13.906)	(14.003)	(14.649)
Specialist Visits	0.529(*)	0.516	0.508(*)
	(2.011)	(1.965)	(1.990)
Household Utilisation	—	-0.163	—
		(1.769)	
Inverse Mills	-5.276*(*)	-0.000[e]**	-0.000[e]*(*)
	(2.716)	(2.823)	(2.751)
Joint Tests:			
Age	(5.657)**	(3.981)**	

Notes: [a]Figures in parentheses beneath parameter estimates are t-statistics. Columns (1) and (3) include, and Column (2) excludes, household utilisation (GP utilisation of other household members). [b]$\bar{R}^2$ adjusted for degrees of freedom. [c]Intercept term in Full Model includes sex = male; eligibility = Category II; VHI cover = yes; Other help = no. [d]"Woman" = age 40-64. [e]Less than |0.0005| but not zero.

Significance: *0.01 < p ≤ 0.05. **p ≤ 0.01.

(*) parentheses around an asterisk indicates parameter did not pass t-test adjusted for heteroscedasticity; see Chapter 1.

Table 7.4: *Logistic regressions of any specialist consultations in 1980 (Dichotomous Variable) on selected independent variables*[a]

	Full Model	5% Version
$\bar{R}^{2}$[b]	0.030	0.039
N	1,068	1,068
Equation χ^2	49.00**	38.97**
Intercept[c]	−0.956	−2.176**
	(0.62)	(29.60)
Sex Female	0.535**	0.468**
	(7.44)	(6.10)
Age	0.022	—
	(1.73)	
Age Squared ÷ 1,000	−0.353	—
	(2.77)	
Category I	0.083	—
	(0.11)	
Category III	−0.120	—
	(0.16)	
No VHI	−0.341	—
	(1.78)	
Other Help	0.206	—
	(0.41)	
Medical Card Ratio	−2.189	—
	(0.16)	
Woman-I-No VHI[d]	−0.551	—
	(1.49)	
Medical Card Ratio-GP Density Interaction	−1.795	−4.144**
	(0.04)	(8.03)
Consultant Density	−1.927	—
	(1.56)	
Times Seen by GP in 1980	0.063**	0.051**
	(25.46)	(22.33)
Joint Tests:		
Age	(4.05)*	
Medical Card Ratio	(5.79)*	

Notes: [a]χ^2 in parentheses beneath parameter estimates. [b]$\bar{R}^2$ adjusted for degrees of freedom. [c]Intercept term in Full Model includes: Sex = male; eligibility = Category II; VHI cover = no; and other help = no. [d]"Woman" = age 40–64.
Significant: *$0.01 < p \leqslant 0.05$. **$p \leqslant 0.01$.

Table 7.5: *Probability of any specialist consultations in 1980, based on logistic regression*[a]

| | | Probabilities | |
		Full Model	5% Version
Baseline probability applies when the following variables are set equal to their means, as below:[b]	Baseline probability*	.17	.15
Age = 38.50	Other probabilities**		
GP density = .461	*Sex* = male	.10	.10
Consultant density = .271	*Age* =		
Medical Card ratio = .370	min = 1	.13	—
Annual number of GP	10	.15	—
consultations = 4.24	20	.16	—
and when the following qualities	30	.17	—
obtain:[b]	40	.17	—
sex = female	50	.15	—
eligibility = Category II	60	.13	—
VHI cover = no	70	.11	—
Other help = no	max = 95	.05	—
**Other probabilities* apply when	*Eligibility* =		
variables are changed, one by one	Category I	.18	—
(the others held constant as	Category III	.15	—
above) to the values and/or	*VHI cover* = yes	.22	—
qualities indicated.	*GP density* =		
	min = 0.429	.17	.16
	max = 0.555	.16	.13
	Consultant density		
	min = 0	.25	—
	max = .387	.14	—
	Other help = yes	.20	—
	Medical Card ratio		
	min = 0.232	.23	—
	max = 0.586	.09	—
	Annual GP consultations		
	min = 0	.13	.12
	2	.15	.13
	6	.18	.16
	12	.25	.21
	24	.41	.32
	max = 60	.87	.75

Notes: [a]See Table 7.4. [b]For 5% version, applies only to variables in the model.

Table 7.6: *Regression of annual number of specialist consultations 1980, on selected independent variables, ordinary least squares, persons with any consultations only*[a]

	Full Model		5% Version
	(1)	*(2)*	*(3)*
$\overline{R}^{2[b]}$	0.246	0.2639	0.293
N	141	141	141
Equation F	4.544**	4.61**	58.00**
Intercept[c]	-2.953	-2.567	-1.280
	(0.791)	(0.745)	
Sex Female	0.446	0.502	—
	(0.747)	(0.889)	
Age	0.045	0.048	—
	(0.997)	(1.106)	
Age squared ÷ 1,000	-0.547	-0.564	
	(0.934)	(0.983)	
Category I	0.013	-0.034	—
	(0.020)	(0.052)	
Category III	-0.641	-0.705	—
	(0.795)	(0.886)	
No VHI	-0.111	-0.211	—
	(0.156)	(0.302)	
Other help	-0.437	-0.384	—
	(0.512)	(0.456)	
Medical Card Ratio	0.045	-0.096	—
	(0.010)	(0.023)	
Woman-I-No VHI[d]	-0.987	-0.913	—
	(0.834)	(0.783)	
Persons in Household	-0.214	-0.149	—
	(1.600)	(1.115)	
Specialist Density	3.250	3.012	—
	(0.795)	(0.756)	
GP Visits	-0.008	-0.027	—
	(0.102)	(0.405)	
Inverse Mills	7.012*(*)	6.114**	5.850**
	(2.801)	(3.455)	(7.616)
Household Utilisation	—	0.043	
		(0.548)	
Joint tests:			
Age	(0.632)	(1.142)	

Notes: [a]Figures in parentheses beneath parameter estimates are t-statistics. Columns (1) and (3) include, and Column (2) excludes, household utilisation (GP utilisation of other household members). [b]$\overline{R}^2$ adjusted for degrees of freedom. [c]Intercept term in Full Model includes sex = male; eligibility = Category II; VHI cover = yes; Other help = no. [d]"Woman" = age 40-64. *Significance:* *0.01 $p \leqslant 0.05$. ** $\leqslant 0.01$.
(*) parentheses around an asterisk indicates parameter did not pass t-test adjusted for heteroscedasticity; see Chapter 1.

Sex had an unusually potent influence on the probability of a specialist consultation (though not the number). Indeed, the "average" woman represented in the baseline probability in Table 7.5 had a 17 per cent probability of a specialist visit, whilst a man with the same characteristics had only a 10 per cent probability. This variable was quite significant.

The Medical Card ratio appears in the logistic regression in main effects and interaction versions and is significant in joint tests. Table 7.5 shows the effect to be negative. (This is the sign obtained for Medical Card ratio when no interaction terms are included, in regression results not reported here.) The interpretation is that the larger the percentage of persons in an area who have Category I eligibility the less likely *each* person is to see a specialist.

The $\bar{R}^2$ in the logistic regression is very small, while that in the OLS version is fairly high. In the latter, *only* the Inverse Mills ratio was statistically significant and again the error variance was troubled by heteroscedasticity.

Tables 7.7, 7.8 and 7.9, which report on utilisation of services of hospital out-patient departments, show a similar pattern. Tables 7.7 and 7.8 are dominated by GP consultations, again showing the importance of primary care, and equally by specialist consultations. A very interesting finding in this table is that the presence of a nearby large hospital *does* have a significantly positive effect on the probability of any utilisation, while distance to GP has a negative though insignificant relationship to number of visits. There may be some element of substitution between GP services and hospital out-patient clinic care, such that those who live far from GPs and/or near to hospitals use the latter in place of the former, and vice versa. It is notable that sex and category of eligibility have no influence on the probability of any out-patient utilisation, except that women aged 65 and over, with Category I eligibility and no VHI cover, are *less* likely to attend an out-patient department. Category I does strongly influence the number of out-patient visits, for those with any.

The regression reported in Table 7.9 suffers from heteroscedasticity in the error variance. The number of out-patient visits varies with the number of specialist visits and with the region's Medical Card ratio. The Inverse Mills ratio is also very significant.

We turn to Tables 7.10, 7.11 and 7.12, which deal with in-patient hospital care.[75] The equation reported in Table 7.10 is dominated by GP and specialist consultations, again pointing up the importance of the physician in medical care utilisation. Among persons with any hospital admissions, only Category I eligibility significantly influences length of stay, and its influence is very large. This could be the influence of diagnosis and severity, though it should be noted that we control for age, sex and GP and specialist visits.

Dentist care, reported in Table 7.13 for all persons and 7.15 for children,

---

[75]As elsewhere in this study, if a hospital stay involved two different calendar years, i.e., the end of 1979 and the beginning of 1980, or the end of 1980 and the beginning of 1981, it is treated as a 1980 stay in hospital if the discharge occurred in 1980.

Table 7.7: *Logistic regression of any visits in 1980 to hospital out-patient department (Dichotomous Variable)*[a]

	Full Model	5% Version
$\overline{R}^{2[b]}$	0.75	0.91
N	1,068	1,068
Equation χ^2	97.78**	87.74**
Intercept[c]	-2.971**	-2.498
	(7.20)	(273.08)**
Sex Female	0.154	—
	(0.54)	—
Age	0.020	—
	(1.36)	—
Age Squared ÷ 1,000	-0.166	—
	(0.59)	—
Category I	0.026	—
	(0.01)	—
Category III	0.051	—
	(0.03)	—
No VHI	0.030	—
	(0.01)	—
Distance to GP	-0.083	—
	(1.64)	—
GP Fee	-0.018	—
	(0.08)	—
Other Help	0.223	—
	(0.48)	—
Medical Card Ratio	-0.713	—
	(0.30)	—
Consultant Density	1.419	—
	(1.07)	—
Woman-I-No VHI[d]	-0.216	—
	(0.25)	—
Lady-I-No VHI[d]	-1.601**	-1.300**
	(7.82)	(6.95)
Times Seen by GP in 1980	0.071**	0.073**
	(27.34)	(35.55)
Nearby Hospital	0.343	0.685**
	(2.05)	(13.64)
Times Seen by Specialist in 1980	0.203**	0.218**
	(11.97)	(13.40)
Joint Tests:		
Age	(3.20)	

Notes: [a]χ^2 in parentheses beneath parameter estimates. [b]$\overline{R}^2$ adjusted for degrees of freedom. [c]Intercept term in Full Model includes: sex = male; eligibility = Category II; VHI cover = no; other help = no; head of household a farmer = no. [d]"Woman" = age 40–64; "Lady" = age 65+. *Significance:* *$0.01 < p \leqslant 0.05$. **$p \leqslant 0.01$.

Table 7.8: *Probability of any visit in 1980 to out-patient department of hospital, based on logistic regression*[a]

		Probabilities	
		Full Model	5% Version
Baseline probability applies when the following variables are set equal to their means, as below:[b]	Baseline probability*	.18	.19
	Other probabilities**		
Age = 38.50	*Sex* = male	.16	—
Distance to GP = 2.61	*Age* =		
GP fee = £2.43	min = 1	.12	—
Consultant density = .271	10	.14	—
Medical Card ratio =.370	20	.16	—
Annual number of GP	30	.17	—
consultations = 4.24	40	.18	—
Annual number of specialist	50	.19	—
consultations = .381	60	.20	—
and when the following qualities	70	.19	—
obtain:[b]	max = 95	.17	—
sex = female	*Eligibility* =		
eligibility = Category II	Category I	.19	—
VHI cover = no	Category III	.19	—
Other help = no	*VHI cover* = yes	.18	—
Nearby hospital = yes	*Distance to GP*		
	min = under 1 mile	.22	—
	max = more than 10 miles	.15	—
	GP fee		
	min = £0	.19	—
	max = £7	.17	—
	Consultant density		
	min = 0	.13	—
	max = .387	.21	—
	Other help = yes	.22	—
	Medical Card ratio		
	min = 0.232	.20	—
	max = 0.586	.16	—
	Annual GP consultations		
	min = 0	.14	.15
	2	.16	.17
	6	.20	.22
	12	.28	.30
	24	.48	.51
	max = 60	.92	.93
	Specialist consultations		
	min = 0	.17	.18
	2	.24	.26
	6	.41	.45
	12	.70	.75
	max = 25	.97	.98
	Nearby hospital = no	.14	.11

Notes: [a]See Table 7.7. [b]For 5% version, applies only to variables in the model.

Table 7.9: *Regression of annual number of visits to hospital out-patient departments, 1980, on selected independent variables, ordinary least squares, persons with any visits only[a]*

	Full Model		5% Version
	(1)	*(2)*	*(3)*
$\overline{R}^{2[b]}$	0.428	0.4321	0.473
N	153	155	153
Equation F	8.155**	7.849**	38.88**
Intercept[c]	0.861	0.173	−1.493
	(0.234)	(0.047)	
Sex Female	1.309	1.403	—
	(1.470)	(1.577)	
Age	−0.020	−0.024	—
	(0.282)	(0.343)	
Age squared · 1,000	0.512	−0.596	—
	(0.568)	(0.663)	
Category I	−3.419*(*)	−3.292	—
	(2.584)	(2.486)	
Category III	−1.136	−1.141	—
	(0.810)	(0.817)	
No VHI	0.085	−0.030	—
	(0.069)	(0.024)	
Distance to GP	−0.310	−0.310	—
	(1.090)	(1.094)	
GP Fee	−0.599(*)	−0.542	—
	(1.974)	(1.770)	
Other Help	−1.268	−1.224	—
	(0.911)	(0.883)	
Medical Card Ratio	6.770	7.400	8.804*(*)
	(1.527)	(1.664)	(2.514)
Lady-I-No VHI[d]	−0.132	−0.757	—
	(0.055)	(0.311)	
GP Visits	0.027	0.004	—
	(0.538)	(0.079)	
Nearby Hospital	−1.140	−1.052	—
	(1.045)	(0.966)	
Household Utilisation	—	0.121	—
		(1.393)	
Specialist Visits	0.601**	0.598**	0.550**
	(3.285)	(3.280)	(3.110)
Persons in Household	−0.004	−0.006	—
	(0.017)	(0.023)	
Inverse Mills	1.322**	1.353**	1.379**
	(6.810)	(6.940)	(8.601)
Joint tests:			
Age	(0.107)	(1.123)	

Notes: [a]Figures in parentheses beneath parameter estimates are t-statistics. Columns (1) and (3) include, and Column (2) excludes, household utilisation (GP utilisation of other household members). [b]$\overline{R}^2$ adjusted for degreess of freedom. [c]Intercept term in Full Model includes sex = male; eligibility = Category II; VHI cover = yes; Other help = no. [d]"Lady" = age 65+. *Significance:* *$0.01 < p \leqslant 0.05$. **$p \leqslant 0.01$.
(*) Parentheses around an asterisk indicates parameter did not pass t-test adjusted for heteroscedasticity; see Chapter 1.

Table 7.10: *Logistic regressions of any in-patient hospital utilisation (any discharges) in 1980 (Dichotomous Variable) on selected independent variables*[a]

	Full Model	5% Version
$\bar{R}^{2}$[b]	0.096	0.106
N	1,068	1,068
Equation χ^{2}	92.85**	79.52**
Intercept[c]	-2.446**	-2.676**
	(9.70)	(387.72)
Sex Female	0.184	—
	(0.65)	
Age	-0.033	—
	(3.37)	
Age Squared ÷ 1,000	0.340	—
	(3.48)	
Category I	0.131	—
	(0.20)	
Category III	0.089	—
	(0.06)	
No VHI	0.010	—
	(0.00)	
Other Help	-0.405	—
	(0.79)	
Woman-I-No VHI[d]	0.142	—
	(0.10)	
Boy-I-No VHI[d]	-6.965	
	(0.12)	
Times Seen by GP in 1980	0.045**	0.052**
	(11.33)	(18.99)
Nearby Hospital	-0.303	—
	(1.62)	
Times Seen by Specialist in 1980	0.438**	0.415**
	(38.53)	(37.72)
Joint Tests;		
Age	(3.50)	

Notes: [a]χ^{2} in parentheses beneath parameter estimates. [b]$\bar{R}^{2}$ adjusted for degrees of freedom. [c]Intercept term in Full Model includes: sex = male; eligibility = Category II; VHI cover = no; other help = no; and 300-bed hospital within 10 miles = no. [d]"Boy" = age 5–17; "Woman" = age 40–64.

Significance: *$0.01 < p \leqslant 0.05$. **$p \leqslant 0.01$.

Table 7.11: *Probability of any in-patient visits to hospital (discharges) in 1980, based on logistic regression*[a]

| | | Probabilities | |
		Full Model	5% Version
Baseline probability applies when the following variables are set equal to their means, as below:[b]	Baseline probability*	.06	.09
Age = 38.50	Other probabilities**		
Annual no. of GP consultations	Sex = male	.05	—
= 4.24	Age =		
Annual no. of specialist	min = 1	.12	—
consultations = .381	10	.09	—
	20	.07	—
and when the following qualities	30	.07	—
obtain:[b]	40	.06	—
	50	.06	—
sex = female	60	.07	—
eligibility = Category II	70	.09	—
VHI cover = no	max = 95	.18	—
Other help = no	Eligibility =		
**Other probabilities* apply when	Category I	.07	—
variables are changed, one by one	Category III	.07	—
(the others held constant as	VHI cover = yes	.06	—
above) to the values and/or	Other help = yes	.04	—
qualities indicated.	Annual GP consultations		
	min = 0	.05	.07
	2	.06	.08
	6	.07	.09
	12	.09	.13
	24	.14	.22
	max = 60	.45	.64
	Specialist consultations		
	min = 0	.05	.07
	2	.12	.16
	6	.44	.50
	12	.92	.93
	max = 25	.99	.99
	Nearby hospital = no	.08	—

Notes: [a]See Table 7.10. [b]For 5% version, applies only to variables in the model.

Table 7.12: *Regression of length of hospital stay, persons discharged from hospital in 1980, ordinary least squares*[a]

	Full Model		5% Version
	(1)	(2)	(3)
$\bar{R}^{2\,(b)}$	0.109	0.1003	0.177
N	111	111	111
Equation F	2.134*	1.952**	23.70**
Intercept[c]	11.043	10.951	6.950
Sex Female	0.989	1.075	—
	(0.285)	(0.303)	
Age	-0.034	-0.032	—
	(0.133)	(0.124)	
Age squared ÷ 1,000	0.456	0.412	—
	(0.146)	(0.131)	
Category I	12.757**	12.759**	14.262**
	(3.068)	(3.053)	(4.868)
Category III	1.237	1.172	—
	(0.198)	(0.186)	
No VHI	-0.120	-0.200	—
	(0.022)	(0.036)	
Other Help	-0.045	-0.045	—
	(0.006)	(0.006)	
GP Visits	0.057	0.047	—
	(0.269)	(0.212)	
Nearby Hospital	-3.681	-3.770	—
	(1.087)	(1.092)	
Specialist Visits	-0.276	-0.271	—
	(0.313)	(0.307)	
Persons in Household	-1.007	-1.009	—
	(1.228)	(1.224)	
Inverse Mills	0.737	0.765**	
	(0.287)	(0.296)	
Household Utilisation	—	0.060	—
		(0.147)	
Joint tests:			
Age	(3.993)**	(0.132)	—

Notes: [a]Figures in parentheses beneath parameter estimates are t-statistics. Columns (1) and (3) include, and Column (2) excludes, household utilisation (GP utilisation of other household members). [b]$\bar{R}^2$ adjusted for degrees of freedom. [c]Intercept term in Full Model includes sex = male; eligibility = Category II; VHI cover = yes; Other help = no.
Significance: *$0.01 < p \leqslant 0.05$. **$p \leqslant 0.01$.

Table 7.13: *Logistic regressions of any dentist visits in 1980 (Dichotomous Variable) on selected independent variables, all persons*[a]

	Full Model	5% Version
$\overline{R}^{2}$[b]	0.112	0.112
N	1,061	1,061
Equation χ^2	160.26**	147.44**
Intercept[c]	–3.556**	–4.466**
	(15.82)	(45.06)
Sex Female	0.299*	0.347*
	(3.70)	(5.47)
Age	0.062**	0.056**
	(18.96)	(16.11)
Age Squared ÷ 1,000	–1.174**	–1.121**
	(35.97)	(33.97)
Category I	0.220	—
	(1.27)	
Category III	0.198	—
	(0.73)	
No VHI	–0.302	—
	(2.31)	
Age Head Completed Education	0.152**	0.186**
	(12.31)	(25.02)
Boy-I-No VHI[d]	0.542	—
	(1.44)	
Man-I-No VHI[d]	–1.884	—
	(3.30)	
Skilled Manual Worker	0.089	—
	(0.18)	
Joint tests:		
Age	(61.54)**	(68.05)**

Notes: [a]χ^2 in parentheses beneath parameter estimates. [b]$\overline{R}^2$ adjusted for degrees of freedom. [c]Intercept term in Full Model includes: sex = male; eligibility = Category II; VHI cover = no; head of household a skilled manual worker = no. [d]"Boy" = age 5–17; "Man" = age 40–64. *Significance:* *0.01 < p ≤ 0.05. **p ≤ 0.01.

proves to be somewhat different from other types of utilisation, as one might expect. The only question our regression analysis was capable of answering was what determines whether someone sees a dentist. The equation reported in Table 7.14 explained about 11 per cent of the person-to-person variability in probability of seeing a dentist and that reported in Table 7.15 explained about 20 per cent amongst children. On the other hand, our OLS regressions, which do not seem worthwhile presenting, explained less than 1 per cent of the variation in

Table 7.14: *Probability of any dental visits in 1980, all persons, based on logistic regression*[a]

| | | Probabilities | |
		Full Model	5% Version
Baseline probability applies when the following variables are set equal to their means, as below:[b]	*Baseline probability**	.36	.40
Age = 38.50	*Other probabilities***		
Age at which head finished	*Sex* = male	.29	.32
full-time education = 15.44	*Age* =		
and when the following qualities	min = 1	.24	.30
obtain:[b]	10	.33	.39
	20	.39	.44
sex = female	30	.40	.44
eligibility = Category II	40	.35	.38
VHI cover = no	50	.25	.28
Occupation of head = not skilled	60	.15	.17
manual	70	.06	.07
**Other probabilities apply when	max = 95	.00	.00
variables are changed, one by one	*Eligibility* =		
(the others held constant as	Category I	.41	—
above) to the values and/or	Category III	.40	—
qualities indicated.	*VHI cover* = yes	.43	—
	Age head completed education =		
	min = 13	.28	.29
	max = 20	.53	.61
	Occupation of head =		
	skilled manual	.38	—

Notes: [a]See Table 7.13. [b]For 5% version, applies only to variables in the model.

numbers of visits amongst persons with any. Wiley, using our survey data, but employing techniques for analysis of dental utilisation which are beyond the scope of the present study, explained much more in her OLS regressions, and the reader is referred to her important study (Wiley, 1984).

Tables 7.13 and 7.14 show that females are significantly more likely to see their dentists than males. This is an interesting phenomenon, for which there is no ready physiological explanation. This result suggests the possibility that higher medical care utilisation of many types by females may be in part a cultural and attitudinal phenomenon. While pregnancy and the use of oral contraceptives reduce calcium and hence affect teeth, Table 7.15 shows that the difference applies amongst children. The sex female variable is positive but not significant; the interaction term, boy-Category I-No VHI is significant and negative, and in its absence the sex female term is significant and positive.

Age has the strongest effect in both versions (see especially the χ^2 statistics in the joint tests). Utilisation rises with age, peaks (between ages 20 and 30) and then declines. Social class, as measured by the age the head of household completed his or her full-time education, also has a major influence. Where the head of household left school at age 13, the probability of a dental visit is 0.28 (assum-

Table 7.15: *Logistic regressions of any dentist visits in 1980 (Dichotomous Variable) on selected independent variables, children under 16 only*[a]

	Full Model	5% Version
$\bar{R}^{2\,(b)}$	0.192	0.201
N	558	558
Equation χ^2	152.89**	147.53**
Intercept[c]	-8.961**	-9.798**
	(31.09)	(59.14)
Sex Female	0.118	—
	(0.24)	
Age	1.076**	1.049**
	(44.95)	(43.83)
Age Squared ÷ 1,000	-47.191**	-45.389**
	(32.00)	(30.99)
Category I	0.388	—
	(1.40)	
Category III	0.307	—
	(0.88)	
No VHI	-0.290	—
	(0.89)	
Boy-I-No VHI[d]	-1.213*	-1.052**
	(5.71)	(7.68)
Age Head Completed Education	0.221**	0.259**
	(11.17)	(20.47)
Skilled Manual Worker	0.158	—
	(0.31)	
Number of Children in Household	-0.069	—
	(0.83)	
Joint Tests:		
Age	(66.98)**	(67.16)**

Notes: [a]χ^2 in parentheses beneath parameter estimates. [b]$\bar{R}^2$ adjusted for degrees of freedom. [c]Intercept term in Full Model includes: sex = male; eligibility = Category II; VHI cover = no; head of household a skilled manual worker = no. [d]"Boy" = age 5–16.
Significance: *$0.01 < p \leqslant 0.05$. **$p = 0.01$.

ing the other characteristics specified in Tables 7.14 and 7.16); but where the head remained in full-time education until age 20, the probability rises to 0.53 (0.65 for children).

Of persons in our sample, only 27 per cent saw their dentists in 1980. Among children aged under 15 years, this was only 26 per cent among boys and 34 per cent among girls. Those who did not see their dentists are evidently in the lower socio-economic groups. This constitutes an important national problem.

All of these tables, except the last four, show again the great importance of the

Table 7.16: *Probability of any dental visits in 1980, children aged 0–15 only, based on logistic regression* [a]

		Probabilities Full Model	5% Version
Baseline probability applies when the following variables are set equal to their means as below:[b]	*Baseline probability**	.41	.45
Age = 8.29	*Other probabilities***		
Age at which head finished full-time education = 15.59	*Sex* = male	.39	—
	Age =		
Children in household = 2.51	min = 1	.01	.01
and when the following qualities obtain:[b]	4	.08	.09
	7	.31	.34
sex = female	10	.50	.55
eligibility = Category II	13	.50	.55
VHI cover = no	max = 15	.38	.44
occupation of head = not skilled manual	*Eligibility =*		
	Category I	.51	—
	Category III	.49	—
***Other probabilities* apply when variables are changed, one by one (the others held constant as above to the values and/or qualities indicated.	*VHI cover* = yes	.49	—
	Age head finished education		
	min = 13	.28	.30
	max = 20	.65	.72
	Occupation of head =		
	skilled manual	.45	—
	Children in household		
	min = 1	.44	
	max = 8	.33	

Notes: [a]See Table 7.15. [b]For 5% version, applies only to variables in the model.

general practitioner in influencing subsequent medical care. Table 7.17 reports on zero-order correlations among the types of further medical care utilisation arising out of each individual's most recent GP consultation, i.e., referrals by GPs. Return visit arrangements are correlated with the prescription of medicine, as discussed earlier; referral to a hospital out-patient department, presumably because x-rays and diagnostic tests lead to further consultations for interpretation and treatment; and referral to another doctor, such as a specialist.

B. Household Expenditures on Other Medical Care

Tables 6.29 and 6.30, in Chapter 6, reported on household expenditures on general practitioner fees in 1980. This section reports on total household expenditures on medical care in the same year, inclusive of GP fees.

Table 7.18 shows that the average household spent £117.54 on medical care in 1980, or £32.88 per person. This amount varied considerably by the category of health services eligibility of the person identified as head of household, with the Category III household spending ten times as much as the Category I household and twice as much as the Category II household; and with the Category II household spending five times as much as the Category I household. The household whose head is covered by VHI spends very considerably more than the non-

Table 7.17: *Correlation matrix: Further medical care utilisation arising out of most recent GP consultation*[a]

	Return Visit	Another Doctor	Other Professional	Rx Medicine	Non-Rx Medicine	Other Device	Out-Patient	In-patient
Return Visit Arranged								
Referred to Another Doctor	0.153							
Referred to Other Professional	0.102	0.127						
Prescribed (Rx) Medicine	0.300	0.084	0.079					
Suggested Non-Rx Medicine	0.070	0.022[c]	0.086	0.043				
Prescribed Other Device	0.066	0.095	0.130	0.039	0.042			
Referred to Out-Patient Dept.	0.167	0.243	0.111	0.081	0.052	0.068		
Hospital Admission	0.074	0.283	0.130	0.044	0.014[c]	0.048	0.178	
Other Treatment	0.117	0.132	0.091	0.037[b]	-0.001[c]	0.102	0.110	0.128

[a] All correlations significant at 0.01 level except as indicated, N = 4,522. [b] Significant at 0.05 level. [c] Not significant at 0.05 level.

Table 7.18: *1980 household expenditures on medical care, per household and household per person*[a], *by selected household characteristics*[b]

	Per household	Household per person[a]
	£	£
All households	117.54	32.88
Category of eligibility:[c]		
Category I	27.01	9.12
Category II	137.04	41.34
Category III	283.79	67.18
VHI cover:[c]		
VHI	223.28	60.19
Non-VHI	83.04	23.97
Health Board Area of residence:		
Eastern	161.39	44.65
Midland	65.70	18.39
Mid-Western	72.00	22.59
North-Eastern	116.79	29.48
North-Western	70.61	20.40
South-Eastern	88.25	23.44
Southern	120.09	31.94
Western	106.16	35.30
Occupation group:[c]		
Professional, managerial, or employer	242.33	71.06
Salaried or intermediate non-manual	150.37	46.92
Other non-manual	86.81	25.70
Skilled manual	109.75	27.64
Semi- or unskilled	72.95	18.83
Farmer, farm worker, or fisher	85.46	22.36

Notes: [a]Household expenditure divided by number of persons in household. [b]Expenditures are gross in the sense that VHI reimbursements are not subtracted. [c]Characteristic pertains to head of household.

VHI household, but this probably reflects category of eligibility as much as or more than VHI cover. There is also considerable variability from Health Board area to Health Board area, with the Eastern at the high end, at £161.39 per household, and the Midland at the low, at an average of £65.70. Finally, Table 7.18 shows considerable variability by occupation group of household head, with white collar occupations in general spending much more than blue collar or farming households.

Tables 7.19 and 7.20 report on regressions in which these same variables, and some others, are used as independent variables in explaining household expendi-

Table 7.19: *Regression of 1980 household medical care expenditures on selected independent variables – ordinary least square*[a]

	Full Model	5% Version
$\bar{R}^{2}$[b]	0.107	0.119
N	1,061	1,061
Equation F	7.374**	23.84**
Intercept[c]	80.38	62.20
Persons Aged Over 64	9.98	—
	(0.841)	
Persons Aged Under 17	12.02**	11.16**
	(2.832)	(2.820)
Persons Aged 17–64	16.30**	15.52**
	(3.432)	(3.844)
Dummy for Living Alone	−14.09	—
	(0.552)	
Eastern Health Board Area	22.32	—
	(0.866)	
Mid-Western Health Board Area	−1.09	—
	(0.041)	
North-Eastern Health Board Area	3.76	—
	(0.161)	
North-Western Health Board Area	2.28	—
	(0.075)	
South-Eastern Health Board Area	−33.06	−42.54*
	(1.482)	(2.112)
Per Cent Category III	64.40**	71.57**
	(2.636)	(3.263)
Per Cent No VHI	9.66	—
	(0.464)	
Other Help	−29.87	—
	(1.201)	
Occupation of Head:		
Professional, Manager, Employer	39.86	57.11**
	(1.482)	(2.769)
Other Non-Manual	−26.97	—
	(0.934)	
Skilled Manual	−20.98	—
	(0.788)	
Semi- or Unskilled Manual	−10.77	—
	(0.427)	
Farmer or Fisher	−12.81	—
	(−0.509)	
Per Cent Female	10.85	—
	(0.390)	
Index of Per Capita Income	−0.225	—
	(0.285)	
Head Category I-No VHI	−73.07**	−70.23**
	(4.454)	(4.822)

Notes: [a]t-statistics in parentheses beneath parameter estimates. [b]$\bar{R}^{2}$ adjusted for degrees of freedom. [c]Intercept term in Full Model includes: individual living alone = no; Health Board Area = Midland, Southern or Western; other help = no; occupation of head = salaried employee or intermediate non-manual worker; and eligibility of head = Category II or III, with VHI cover. In 5% version, intercept term includes Health Board Area = not South-Eastern; occupation of head = not professional, managerial, or employee; and eligibility of head = Category II or III, with VHI cover.
Significance Levels: *0.01 < p ≤ 0.05. **p ≤ 0.01.

Table 7.20: *Regression of 1980 household medical care expenditures on selected independent variables – Categories II and III only – ordinary least squares*[a]

	Full Model	5% Version
$\bar{R}^{2}$[b]	0.046	0.061
N	676	676
Equation F	2.712**	10.87**
Intercept[c]	121.09	39.08
Persons Aged Over 64	10.38	—
	(0.482)	
Persons Aged Under 17	18.85**	18.54**
	(2.954)	(3.092)
Persons Aged 17–64	18.69**	18.67**
	(2.563)	(2.909)
Dummy for Living Alone	−39.60	—
	(0.856)	
Eastern Health Board Area	29.20	—
	(0.781)	
Mid-Western Health Board Area	−2.51	—
	(0.054)	
North-Eastern Health Board Area	−5.89	—
	(0.158)	
North-Western Health Board Area	−4.59	—
	(0.090)	
South-Eastern Health Board Area	−54.57	—
	(1.526)	
Per Cent Category III	55.69	63.20*
	(1.791)	(2.311)
Per Cent No VHI	13.34	—
	(0.492)	
Other Help	−34.96	—
	(1.061)	
Occupation of Head:		
Professional, Manager, Employer	37.25	63.79*
	(1.05)	(2.398)
Other Non-Manual	−34.10	—
	(0.823)	
Skilled Manual	−36.67	—
	(0.947)	
Semi- or Unskilled Manual	−14.20	—
	(0.372)	
Farmer or Fisher	−14.85	—
	(0.407)	
Per Cent Female	15.68	—
	(0.34)	
Index of Per Capita Income	−0.73	—
	(0.614)	

Notes: [a] t-statistics in parentheses beneath parameter estimates. [b] $\bar{R}^{2}$ estimates adjusted for degrees of freedom. [c] Intercept term in Full Model includes: individual living alone = no; Health Board Area = Midland, Southern, or Western; other help = no; occupation of head = salaried employee or intermediate non-manual worker. In 5% version, intercept term includes occupation of head, professional, manager, or employer = no.
Significance: *$0.01 < p \leqslant 0.05$. **$p \leqslant 0.01$.

tures, with results somewhat different from those shown in Table 7.18. The unit of analysis in these regressions is the household, rather than (as in utilisation regressions) the person. Separate regressions are reported for all households and for households in which the person identified as head of household had either Category II or III eligibility. Persons with Category II or III eligibility are likely to have more household medical care expenditures than persons with Category I eligibility. Note, however, that not all persons in a household will necessarily have the same eligibility; hence there will be persons in Category I even in the households reported on in the regression Table 7.20.

The number of persons aged under 17, and the number of persons aged 17–64, significantly influenced expenditures; the number of persons aged over 64 did not. The three coefficient estimates, though two of them were significantly different from zero, were not significantly different from each other, at the 5 per cent level. Similarly, the fact that a household consisted of a single person living alone did not separately affect expenditures significantly, apart from the effect of number of persons.

Though Table 7.18 shows major differences among Health Board areas of residence, Tables 7.19 and 7.20 indicate that there was no significant *net* influence of Health Board area. In other words, the differences shown in Table 7.18 are accounted for by other influences, such as age, eligibility, etc. The single exception to this statement is that, in the 5 per cent version of the all persons model (Table 7.19), after 14 variables are eliminated from the full model, households in the South-Eastern Health Board area spend significantly less than the areas (Midland, Southern, Western) included in the intercept term — £52.54 less.

The proportion of the household with Category III eligibility had a strong influence on expenditures. (Category II is included in the constant term.) A household in which *all* the members had Category III eligibility spent £64.40 more than the all-Category II family. In the Category II/III-only model (Table 7.20), the difference is £63.20 — approximately the same. The dummy variable Head Category I-No VHI produced better fits than per cent Category I to represent the expenditure behaviour of that group. A household whose head had Category I eligibility and no VHI cover spent £73.07 less than the Category II household. No-VHI does not significantly affect expenditures except in the interaction term Head Category I - No VHI. This appears to validate our surmise, stated above, that the simple relationship shown in Table 7.18 between VHI cover and medical care expenditures reflects other influences (such as eligibility) and not VHI cover.

The influence of social group (occupation group of head of household) as shown in Table 7.18 shows up again in the net or *ceteris paribus* relationships of Tables 7.19 and 7.20. Only one such relationship is significant: Persons in "professional, manager, employer" households spend significantly more than others. It is to be noted that this is a net influence of social group, controlling for numbers of persons and their ages, category of eligibility, VHI cover, Health Board area of residence, etc., and hence appears to reflect social group only.

C. Prevention-Oriented Care

"An ounce of prevention is worth a pound of cure", states an old proverb. The ratio is surely even higher today, given the cost of hospitalisation and specialist care. Prevention can save money: measures taken to prevent, or to detect early, illnesses and injuries, can in many instances cost far less than treating them. More important, prevention can save needless pain, discomfort, economic loss and death.

Ireland appears to be behind many other countries in Western Europe and North America in prevention-oriented measures and programmes. Cigarette consumption is high by world standards, and non-smokers are forced to become captive, "passive smokers" in cinemas, pubs, buses and other places. Automobile and bus emissions, trash burning, and the use of soft coal and turf as heating fuels have made Dublin as polluted as several highly industrialised cities in Britain and Europe (Medico-Social Research Board, 1977; Walsh and Bailey, 1979). Motor vehicle laws seem only sporadically enforced, and pedestrians and cyclists are at extreme risk. Motorcyclists lose their lives more frequently in accidents than in most other countries. There is no requirement of child-resistant containers for medicines and hazardous household products, though such requirements have saved lives in other countries.

Health education seems to be having a minor impact on cigarette consumption, obesity, tooth decay, etc., at least in part because so little money is spent. Similarly, any national campaign of prevention must be based on better epidemiological data than are collected in this country.

Our concern in this study is not so much with nutrition, fitness, personal care, safety, or the like, however, as with medical care. Prevention-oriented medical care consists primarily of appropriate routine screening or examinations, and secondarily of immunisations, especially of children, against infectious illnesses. In our survey, we collected data on several types of prevention-oriented care. We asked, with respect to each household member, when he or she was last seen by a doctor. We asked who, in the previous year, had had a physical examination when he or she did not suspect an illness or pregnancy; had been immunised for any illness; had had a blood pressure test; or (for adult women only) had had a cervical cancer smear ("pap") test. By including these types of prevention-oriented care, we are not suggesting that they are, in all cases, efficient or cost-effective methods. They are indices of preventive care which could conveniently and usefully be studied on the basis of a household sample survey. In addition to these variables, our results on dental care reported above (see Table 7.13–7.16) might be considered reflective of prevention-oriented care.

The results are given in full in Appendix Tables A.10–A.15. It will be seen that approximately one-third of the population did not see a general practitioner in the past year, of whom half had not seen a GP in the past two years; and that 7.6 per cent had not seen a GP within the past five years (including never). Men are more likely to fail to see their GPs than women; 13.7 per cent of men aged 15–44 and 9.4 per cent of men aged 45–64, had not seen a GP in the past five years (including never). For women, the corresponding percentages were 6.8 and 7.5. Those most likely to fail to see a GP for long periods of time were: persons with Category II eligibility (9.5 per cent); persons in the North-Eastern Health Board area (14.7 per cent); persons in households headed by unemployed persons (9.7 per cent) and farmers, agricultural workers, or fishers (9.9 per cent).

Similar statistics emerged concerning physical examinations. These rise consistently with age, as is appropriate. Persons with Category II eligibility are the least likely to have had a physical examination, as are persons in households headed by the unemployed or semi-skilled or unskilled workers, and persons living in the North-Western Health Board area. Only 1.7 per cent of those living in that area reported a physical examination in 1980, compared with 8.1 per cent for the country as a whole, in spite of the North-West's high concentration of aged persons.

Immunisations follow a pattern opposite to age, as is appropriate. Only one child in six, aged 0–14, was immunised against any disease in 1980, a figure which seems low, though of course every child does not need immunisation in any given year.

Blood pressure tests rise with age in a striking fashion. Among men, 60 per cent of those aged 65 and over had a blood pressure test in 1980; 47 per cent of those aged 45–64; and 16 per cent of those aged 15–44. Among women, the corresponding figures were 71, 54 and 32. Overall, women were about 50 per cent more likely to have blood pressure tests than men, even though men are more likely to be victims of high blood pressure and stroke. Most disturbing is the low rate for men aged 15–44, slightly less than half the rate for women at the same age. Blood pressure tests do not have to be administered by a physician or even a registered nurse, and there appears to be a need for free blood pressure clinics, conducted perhaps at places of work. Occupational and regional differences in blood pressure tests seem minimal, or related to age and/or sex. Public (Category I) patients are nearly twice as likely to have blood pressure tests as private (II/III) patients.

Only one adult woman in ten had a cervical smear test in 1980, which is an unfortunately low ratio. The percentage falls from about 15 (ages 15–44), the years of child-bearing and frequent gynaecological examinations) to 2.5 (ages 65 and over), which is too low. The most important influence on this form of preventive care appears to be social class. The likelihood of an adult woman having a smear test rises with the years of education of the household head, from under 2 per cent (head completed full time education at age under 14) to over 25 per cent (age 19). Those from households headed by white-collar workers were about twice as likely to have smear tests as the rest of the population. Similarly, those with VHI were nearly twice as likely as those without, and the likelihood rose with category of entitlement, from 6 per cent (Category I) to 10 per cent (II) to 19 per cent (III) — clearly a reflection of income rather than price. Given the importance of these examinations, more effort must be made to reach working class women.

Another way of looking at the same data is with the aid of multiple regression analysis, using a model similar to that used earlier in this chapter and in the previous chapter. Table 7.21 reports on a logistic regression of no GP consultation within the past 5 years (including never) on selected independent variables. The equation explains only a small part of the variability in the dependent variable, but a number of significant influences were none the less found, including negative relationships with Category I eligibility and house call fee premium. Persons in Category I are less likely not to have seen their doctors. We have found previously that the house call fee premium appears on occasion to reflect the ratio of GP demand to supply. Since the dependent variable measures the failure to see one's GP over long periods of time, the negative sign, again, indicates a positive relationship between the independent variable and preventive care. Table 7.22 shows the magnitude of both effects to be moderate. Category I reduces the probability from 0.10 to 0.02 that one did not see a GP.

Table 7.21 shows GP density and the Medical Card ratio, as main effects and in an interaction term, very significantly to affect the individual's probability of not seeing a GP for 5 years. Table 7.22 shows the net effect of GP density to be positive and large, a somewhat paradoxical effect: the *higher* the ratio of GPs to population, the *more* likely it is that a person will fail to see his or her GP for extended periods. Medical Card ratio proves to have a negative effect, which is much more understandable: the higher the Medical Card ratio in an area, the greater the overall demand for GP services and the less time is available for each person in the community.

Tables 7.23–7.32 report on logistic regressions of the other forms of prevention-oriented care: physical exminations, immunisations (separate regressions are reported for all persons and children under 16 only), smear tests (adult women only) and blood pressure tests (persons aged over 15 only). These equations explain a larger fraction of the variability in the dependent variable than that reported in Table 7.21, particularly immunisation (20.7 per cent) and blood pressure tests (14.1 per cent). Probabilities based on these regressions appear in Table 7.17.

Sex female significantly influences blood pressure tests considerably raising the calculated probability from 29 to 43 per cent. Age is important for all types of utilisation. Table 7.30 shows the probability of a pap test to rise with age to about age 40 and then to decline rapidly. Category of eligibility is significant only for blood pressure tests. No VHI has a significantly negative effect, as might be expected, on the probability of a blood pressure test. Girl (age 5–15)-Category I-No VHI has a significantly positive effect on immunisation amongst children. Paradoxically, the *more* adult females there are in a household, the *less* likely each is to have a pap test.

Through main effects and/or interactions, GP density and the Medical Card ratio significantly affect some types of preventative care. The higher is GP density, the lower, oddly, is the likelihood of an asymptomatic physical examination (though the magnitude of the effect is small), and the higher is the probability of a women having a pap test (the magnitude of the effect is large). On the other

Table 7.21: *Logistic regression of no GP consultation within past 5 years, including never (Dichotomous Variable), on selected independent variables*[a]

	Full Model	5% Version
$\bar{R}^{2\,[b]}$	0.046	0.054
N	1,068	1,068
Equation χ^2	50.29**	32.61**
Intercept[c]	-40.007**	-1.737**
	(11.59)	(84.57)
Sex Female	-0.266	
	(1.08)	
Age	0.027	
	(1.30)	
Age Squared ÷ 1,000	-0.411	
	(1.74)	
Category I	-1.714**	-1.784**
	(15.97)	(23.95)
Category III	0.061	
	(0.03)	
No VHI	0.092	
	(0.08)	
Distance to GP	0.033	
	(0.17)	
GP Fee	-0.066	
	(0.45)	
House Call Fee	-0.123*	-0.164**
	(4.31)	(11.85)
Other Help	0.199	
	(0.23)	
GP Density	86.892**	
	(10.46)	
Medical Card Ratio	84.770**	
	(9.31)	
Medical Card Ratio-GP Density Interaction	-191.980**	
	(9.33)	
Joint Tests:		
Age	(1.97)	
GP Density	(11.29)**	
Medical Card Ratio	(9.33)**	

Notes: [a]χ^2 in parentheses beneath parameter estimates. [b]$\bar{R}^2$ adjusted for degrees of freedom. [c]Intercept term in Full Model includes: sex = male; eligibility = Category II; VHI cover = no; other help = no.
Significance: *$0.01 < p \leqslant 0.05$. **$p \leqslant 0.01$.

Table 7.22: *Probability of no GP visit in 5 years (including never), based on logistic regression* [a]

		Probabilities	
		Full Model	5% Version
Baseline probability applies when the following variables are set equal to their means, as below:[b]	Baseline probability*	.10	.10
	Other probabilities**		
Age = 38.50	Sex = male	.12	—
Distance to GP = 2.61	Age =		
GP fee = £2.43	min = 1	.07	—
House call fee = £2.78	10	.08	—
GP density = 0.462	20	.09	—
Medical card ratio = 0.370	30	.10	—
and when the following qualities	40	.10	—
obtain:[b]	50	.09	—
sex = female	60	.07	—
eligibility = Category II	70	.06	—
VHI cover = no	max = 95	.02	—
Other help = no	Eligibility =		
Other probabilities apply when	Category I	.02	.02
variables are changed, one by one	Category III	.10	—
(the others held constant as	VHI cover = yes	.09	—
above) to the values and/or	Distance to GP		
qualities indicated.	min = under 1 mile	.09	—
	max = more than 10 miles	.11	—
	GP fee		
	min = £0	.11	—
	max = £7	.07	—
	House Call Fee		
	min = £0	.13	.15
	max = £10	.04	.03
	GP Density =		
	min = 0.429	.10	—
	max = 0.555	.46	—
	Other help = yes	.11	—
	Medical Card ratio		
	min = 0.232	.25	—
	max = 0.586	.08	—

Notes: [a]See Table 7.21. [b]For 5% version, applies only to variables in the model.

Table 7.23: *Logistic regression of any asymptomatic physical examination in 1980 (Dichotomous Variable) on selected independent variables*[a]

	Full Model	5% Version
$\overline{R}^{2[b]}$	0.078	0.056
N	1,068	1,068
Equation χ^2	77.18**	39.01**
Intercept[c]	34.932**	–3.555**
	(17.84)	(177.67)
Sex Female	0.002	—
	(0.00)	
Age	0.057**	0.028**
	(6.55)	(35.33)
Age Squared ÷ 1,000	–0.311	—
	(1.73)	
Category I	0.194	—
	(0.37)	
Category III	–0.538	—
	(1.50)	
No VHI	–0.495	—
	(2.48)	
Distance to GP	0.106	—
	(2.32)	
GP Fee	–0.104	—
	(1.03)	
House Call Fee	0.028	—
	(0.20)	
Other Help	0.684	—
	(2.63)	
GP Density	–86.778**	—
	(21.42)	
Medical Card Ratio	–91.387**	–
	(22.43)	
Medical Card Ratio-GP Density Interaction	203.975**	
	(23.01)	
Joint Tests:		
Age	(27.81)**	
GP Density	(23.05)**	
Medical Card Ratio	(23.57)**	

Notes: [a]χ^2 in parentheses beneath parameter estimates. [b]$\overline{R}^2$ adjusted for degrees of freedom. [c]Intercept term in Full Model includes: sex = male; eligibility = Category II; VHI cover = no; other help = no.
Significance: *$0.01 < p \leqslant 0.05$. **$p \leqslant 0.01$.

Table 7.24: *Probability of asymptomatic physical examination in 1980. Based on logistic regression* [a]

| | | Probabilities | |
		Full Model	5% Version
Baseline probability applies when the following variables are set equal to their means, as below:[b]	Baseline probability*	.07	.08
Age = 38.50	*Other probabilities***		
	Sex = male	.07	—
Distance to GP = 2.61	*Age* =		
GP fee = £2.43	min = 1	.01	.03
House call fee = £2.78	10	.02	.04
GP density = .462	20	.03	.05
Medical card ratio = .370	30	.05	.06
and when the following qualities	40	.07	.08
obtain:[b]	50	.09	.10
sex = female	60	.11	.13
eligibility = Category II	70	.13	.17
VHI cover = no	max = 95	.14	.29
Other help = no	*Eligibility* =		
***Other probabilities* apply when	Category I	.08	—
variables are changed, one by one	Category III	.04	—
(the others held constant as	*VHI cover* = yes	.10	—
above) to the values and/or	*Distance to GP*		
qualities indicated.	min = under 1 mile	.05	—
	max = more than 10 miles	.09	—
	GP fee		
	min = £0	.08	—
	max = £7	.04	—
	House Call Fee		
	min = £0	.06	—
	max = £10	.08	—
	GP Density =		
	min = 0.429	.05	—
	max = 0.555	.01	—
	Other help = yes	.12	—
	Medical Card ratio		
	min = 0.232	.03	—
	max = 0.586	.07	—

Notes: [a]See Table 7.23. [b]For 5% version, applies only to variables in the model.

Table 7.25: *Logistic regressions of any immunisations in 1980 (Dichotomous Variable) on selected independent variables, all persons*[a]

	Full Model	5% Version
$\bar{R}^{2[b]}$	0.166	0.207
N	1,068	1,068
Equation χ^2	94.26**	88.92**
Intercept[c]	-21.126	-0.501*
	(2.67)	(3.84)
Sex Female	-0.020	—
	(0.00)	
Age	-0.208**	-0.202**
	(60.41)	(64.68)
Age Squared ÷ 1,000	2.233**	2.158**
	(48.72)	(53.14)
Category I	-0.009	—
	(0.00)	
Category III	-0.080	—
	(0.02)	
No VHI	-0.140	—
	(0.09)	
Distance to GP	0.033	—
	(0.11)	
GP Fee	-0.148	—
	(0.98)	
House Call Fee	0.049	—
	(0.31)	
Other Help	-0.316	—
	(0.31)	
GP Density	49.320	—
	(2.82)	
Medical Card Ratio	48.139	—
	(2.45)	
Medical Card Ratio-GP Density Interaction	-112.124	—
	(2.66)	
Joint Tests:		
Age	(66.56)**	(70.97)**
GP Density	(2.82)	
Medical Card Ratio	(3.43)	

Notes: [a]χ^2 in parentheses beneath parameter estimates. [b]$\bar{R}^2$ adjusted for degrees of freedom. [c]Intercept term in Full Model includes: sex = male; eligibility = Category II; VHI cover = no; other help = no.
Significance: *$0.01 < p \leqslant 0.05$. **$p \leqslant 0.01$.

Table 7.26: *Probability of any immunisations in 1980, all persons, based on logistic regression*[a]

		Probabilities	
		Full Model	5% Version
Baseline probability applies when the following variables are set equal to their means, as below:[b]	*Baseline probability**	.01	.01
Age = 38.50	*Other probabilities***		
Distance to GP = 2.61	*Sex* = male	.01	—
GP fee = £2.43	*Age* =		
House call fee = £2.78	min = 1	.33	.33
GP density = .462	10	.09	.09
Medical card ratio = .370	20	.02	.02
and when the following qualities	30	.01	.01
obtain:[b]	40	.01	.01
sex = female	50	.00	.01
eligibility = Category II	60	.01	.01
VHI cover = no	70	.02	.02
Other help = no	max = 95	.47	.45
Other probabilities apply when	*Eligibility* =		
variables are changed, one by one	Category I	.01	—
(the others held constant as	Category III	.01	—
above) to the values and/or	*VHI cover* = yes	.01	—
qualities indicated.	*Distance to GP*		
	min = under 1 mile	.01	—
	max = more than 10 miles	.01	—
	GP fee		
	min = £0	.01	—
	max = £7	.00	—
	House Call Fee		
	min = £0	.00	—
	max = £10	.01	—
	GP Density =		
	min = 0.429	.01	—
	max = 0.555	.02	—
	Other help = yes	.00	—
	Medical Card ratio		
	min = 0.232	.01	—
	max = 0.586	.00	—

Notes: [a]See Table 7.25. [b]For 5% version, applies only to variables in the model.

Table 7.27: *Logistic regressions of any immunisations in 1980 (Dichotomous Variable) on selected independent variables, children aged under 16 years only*[a]

	Full Model	5% Version
$\bar{R}^{2[b]}$	0.133	0.161
N	560	560
Equation χ^2	96.61**	86.62**
Intercept[c]	1.446	0.698*
	(0.39)	(5.35)
Sex Female	0.372	—
	(1.58)	
Age	−0.695**	−0.672**
	(28.75)	(32.64)
Age Squared ÷ 1,000	30.739**	30.037**
	(14.33)	(15.95)
Category I	−0.224	—
	(0.13)	
Category III	−0.773	—
	(3.45)	
No VHI	−0.414	—
	(1.29)	
Distance to GP	−0.058	—
	(0.53)	
GP Fee	0.029	—
	(0.04)	
House Call Fee	0.031	—
	(0.19)	
Other Help	0.184	—
	(0.16)	
GP Density	0.185	—
	(0.00)	
Medical Card Ratio	−1.231	—
	(0.57)	
Children in Household	−0.039	—
	(0.17)	
Boy-I-No VHI[d]	0.890	—
	(1.30)	
Girl-I-No VHI[d]	1.847**	1.456**
	(8.44)	(14.57)
Joint Tests:		
Age	(63.52)**	(73.62)**

Notes: [a]χ^2 in parentheses beneath parameter estimates. [b]$\bar{R}^2$ adjusted for degrees of freedom. [c]Intercept term in Full Model includes: sex = male; eligibility = Category II; VHI cover = no; other help = no. [d]"Girl", "Boy" = age 5-15.
Significance: *$0.01 < p \leqslant 0.05$. **$p \leqslant 0.01$.

Table 7.28: *Probability of any immunisation in 1980, children aged 0-15 only, based on logistic regression*[a]

| | | Probabilities | |
		Full Model	5% Version
Baseline probability applies when the following variables are set equal to their means, as below:[b]	Baseline probability*	.06	.06
	*Other probabilities***		
Age = 8.29	Sex = male	.08	—
Distance to GP = 2.61	*Age =*		
GP fee = £2.84	min = 1	.57	.51
House call fee = £3.32	4	.21	.18
GP density = .460	7	.08	.07
Medical card ratio = .366	10	.05	.05
Persons in household aged	13	.05	.05
under 16 = 2.51	max = 15	.07	.07
and when the following qualities	*Eligibility =*		
obtain:[b]	Category I	.25	—
sex = female	Category III	.03	—
eligibility = Category II	*VHI cover* = yes	.09	—
VHI cover = no	*Distance to GP*		
**Other probabilities* apply when	min = under 1 mile	.07	—
variables are changed, one by one	max = more than 10 miles	.05	—
(the others held constant as	*GP fee*		
above) to the values and/or	min = £0	.06	—
qualities indicated.	max = £6	.07	—
	House call fee		
	min = £0	.06	—
	max = £10	.08	—
	GP density =		
	min = 0.429	.06	—
	max = 0.555	.06	—
	Medical Card ratio		
	min = 0.232	.07	—
	max = 0.568	.05	—
	Persons in household aged under 16		
	min = 1	.07	—
	max = 8	.05	—
	Other help = yes	.07	

Notes: [a]See Table 7.27. [b]For 5% version, applies only to variables in the model.

Table 7.29: *Logistic regressions of any cervical cancer smear ("Pap") Test in 1980 (Dichotomous Variable) on selected independent variables, women aged over 15 years only*[a]

	Full Model	5% Version
$\bar{R}^{2[b]}$	0.118	0.131
N	999	999
Equation χ^2	104.10**	98.10**
Intercept[c]	–7.035**	–7.004**
	(10.33)	(11.62)
Age	0.203**	0.204**
	(12.75)	(13.49)
Age Squared ÷ 1,000	–2.730**	–2.735**
	(16.52)	(17.70)
Category I	0.461	
	(1.54)	
Category III	0.374	
	(1.46)	
No VHI	–0.250	
	(0.73)	
Distance to GP	0.043	
	(0.40)	
GP Fee	0.025	
	(0.06)	
House Call Fee	0.018	
	(0.09)	
Other Help	0.414	
	(1.35)	
GP Density	17.188**	17.040**
	(12.43)	(12.44)
Medical Card Ratio	–10.672**	–10.617**
	(16.88)	(17.53)
Consultant Density-GP Density Interaction	–12.087**	–11.183**
	(7.64)	(6.90)
Number of Adult Females in Household	–0.728**	–0.751**
	(11.75)	(12.68)
Joint Tests:		
Age	(23.48)**	(26.04)**
GP Density	(14.48)**	(14.15)**

Notes: [a]χ^2 in parentheses beneath parameter estimates. [b]$\bar{R}^2$ adjusted for degrees of freedom. [c]Intercept term in Full Model includes: eligibility = Category II; VHI cover) no; other help = no.

Significance: *$0.01 < p \leqslant 0.05$. **$p \leqslant 0.01$.

Table 7.30: *Probability of cervical cancer smear ("Pap") test in 1980, women aged over 15 only, based on logistic regression* [a]

		Probabilities	
		Full Model	5% Version
Baseline probability applies when the following variables are set equal to their means, as below:[b]	Baseline probability*	.09	.12
Age = 44.61	Other probabilities**		
Distance to GP = 2.59	*Age =*		
GP fee = £2.51	min = 16	.03	.05
House call fee = £2.87	20	.05	.07
GP density = .461	30	.09	.12
Medical card ratio = .368	40	.10	.14
Women in household = 1.54	50	.07	.09
and when the following qualities	60	.03	.04
obtain:[b]	70	.01	.01
Eligibility = Category II	max = 95	.00	.00
VHI cover = no	*Eligibility =*		
Other help = no	Category I	.13	—
**Other probabilities* apply when	Category III	.13	—
variables are changed, one by one	*VHI cover =* yes	.11	—
(the others held constant as	*Distance to GP*		
above) to the values and/or	min = under 1 mile	.08	—
qualities indicated.	max = more than 10 miles	.10	—
	GP fee =		
	min = £0	.09	—
	max = £7	.10	—
	Women in household		
	min = 1	.13	.17
	max = 7	.00	.00
	House Call fee		
	min = £0	.09	—
	max = £10	.10	—
	GP density		
	min = 0.429	.06	—
	max = 0.555	.27	—
	Consultant density		
	min = 0	.45	.36
	max = .387	.08	.07
	Other help = yes	.13	—
	Medical Card ratio		
	min = 0.232	.30	.37
	max = 0.586	.01	.01

Notes: [a]See Table 7.29. [b]For 5% version, applies only to variables in the model.

Table 7.31: *Logistic regressions of any blood pressure test in 1980 (Dichotomous Variable) on selected independent variables, persons aged over 15 years only*[a]

	Full Model	5% Version
$\bar{R}^{2[b]}$	0.132	0.141
N	825	825
Equation χ^2	176.57**	169.67**
Intercept[c]	3.289	-4.760**
	(0.30)	(50.23)
Sex Female	0.603**	0.605**
	(14.21)	(14.59)
Age	0.106**	0.102**
	(19.10)	(18.44)
Age Squared ÷ 1,000	-0.698**	-0.666**
	(8.23)	(7.80)
Category I	0.866*	0.815**
	(14.35)	(13.62)
Category III	-0.250	
	(0.80)	
No VHI	-0.445*	
	(3.95)	
Distance to GP	0.005	
	(0.01)	
GP Fee	0.107	0.139**
	(2.28)	(6.64)
House Call Fee	0.023	
	(0.30)	
Other Help	0.016	
	(0.00)	
GP Density	-16.656	
	(1.46)	
Medical Card Ratio	-19.318	
	(1.86)	
Persons in Household	-0.079*	-0.080*
	(3.73)	(3.88)
Medical Card Ratio-GP Density Interaction	42.960	
	(1.85)	
Joint Tests:		
Age	(65.44)**	(64.99)**
GP Density	(2.24)	
Medical Card Ratio	(1.86)	

Notes: [a]χ^2 in parentheses beneath parameter estimates. [b]$\bar{R}^2$ adjusted for degrees of freedom. [c]Intercept term in Full Model includes: sex = male; eligibility = Category II; VHI cover = no; other help = no.
Significance: *$0.01 < p \le 0.05$. **$p \le 0.01$.

Table 7.32: *Probability of blood pressure test in 1980, persons aged over 15 only, based on logistic regression*[a]

		Probabilities	
		Full Model	5% Version
Baseline probability applies when the following variables are set equal to their means, as below:[b]	Baseline probability*	.43	.45
	Other probabilities**		
Age = 47.46	Sex = male	.29	.31
Distance to GP = 2.59	Age =		
GP fee = £2.34	min = 16	.10	.11
House call fee = £2.64	20	.13	.15
GP density = .462	30	.23	.25
Medical card ratio = .372	40	.35	.37
Persons in household = 3.79	50	.45	.48
and when the following qualities	60	.53	.55
obtain:[b]	70	.57	.58
sex = female	max = 95	.51	.54
eligibility = Category II	Eligibility =		
VHI cover = no	Category I	.64	.65
Other help = no	Category III	.37	—
**Other probabilities* apply when	VHI cover = yes	.54	—
variables are changed, one by one	Distance to GP		
(the others held constant as	min = under 1 mile	.43	—
above) to the values and/or	max = more than 10 miles	.44	—
qualities indicated.	GP fee		
	min = £0	.37	.37
	max = £7	.56	.61
	House Call Fee		
	min = £0	.42	—
	max = £10	.47	—
	GP Density =		
	min = 0.429	.41	—
	max = 0.555	.39	—
	Persons in household		
	min = 1	.49	.51
	max = 14	.25	.27
	Other help = yes	.44	—
	Medical Card ratio		
	min = 0.232	.38	—
	max = 0.586	.43	—

Notes: [a]See Table 7.31. [b]For 5% version, applies only to variables in the model.

hand, specialist density is *negatively* and significantly related to pap tests. The higher is the Medical Card ratio, the more likely a person is to have a physical examination or a blood pressure test (the effects are small), and the less likely a woman is to have a pap test (the impact is great).

These statistics certainly indicate the presence of some problems. Too many people go too long without being seen by a GP. This is especially true of men aged 15–44, who also fail to have blood pressure tests in adequate numbers; of persons with Category II eligibility, who also fail to have physical examinations and blood pressure tests; and persons in households headed by the unemployed, farmers, or fishers. The results indicate a problem in the North-Eastern and North-Western Health Board areas where preventive care is less than elsewhere. There is a problem, as well, in getting working class women access to cervical cancer smear tests.

Not all of these characteristics show up as significant in the regressions, presumably because they are so strongly correlated with other variables. The statistics suggest a case for extending free GP care to the two-thirds of the population who now must pay for consultations, those in Categories II and III. This idea will be discussed further, Chapter 8.

In general, the aged (persons aged 65 and over) use prevention-oriented care more than the rest of the population. Hence it might appear that their situations are more satisfactory in this respect. This may not be correct. Only 3.8 per cent of aged men and 1.4 per cent of aged women report not having seen a GP in five years (including never). Irish health officials can take some satisfaction in the low level of these statistics. But there is evidence, to be cited presently, that outreach to the aged is none the less, inadequate. Fewer than a fifth of the aged received physical examinations in 1980. While there may be some doubt about the cost-effectiveness of annual physical examinations for the whole population, there is less about routine examinations of the aged. Only 3.2 per cent of aged men, and 2.0 of aged women, report immunisations. These figures also seem too low, in light of the dangers posed by influenza to many aged. Medical authorities increasingly advocate a range of adult immunisations. Of aged men, 60.3 per cent had blood pressure tests and of aged women the figure was still higher at 71.4 per cent; but *all* persons in these years of age should have annual blood pressure tests. And while hysterectomies have reduced the numbers of women aged 65 and over at risk from cervical cancer, the number getting smear tests, 2.5 per cent, seems far too low.

A more telling study of the outreach of the medical care system to aged persons at risk is reported in Walsh (1980), which discusses what seems to be the first and only study of unrecognised treatable illness in any Irish population. Walsh and his team surveyed an elderly and, evidently, poor population in North Dublin. These persons were actually called upon in person, by doctors, and, with their permission, given medical examinations. The results are important and shocking. In 105 persons, there were 174 cases of undiagnosed treatable illnesses ranging from incontinence, visual impairment, mental impairment to hypertension and congestive heart failure. In addition to these, there was a large number of cases of previously diagnosed conditions not currently being treated or controlled. In some cases the person did not have a Medical Card to which she or he was entitled, and in other cases the person was not entitled to a Medical Card. Commenting on the latter, Dr. Walsh states,

One feels that a more lenient attitude should be taken, especially as regards savings and pensions that exceed the stated limits, when assessing eligibility for Medical Cards of retired people because of the high prevalence of illness in this age group and of the obvious suffering endured by those who lose out on essential services.

A possible implication is that free GP services might well be extended to the entire aged population, a move which would not be extremely expensive. However, even this would not eliminate the problem. The 105 persons examined by Walsh were not, in general, persons "lost" to the health care system, or persons who failed in all cases to see GPs, or who were unknown to public health nurses. The findings point to a need for routine physical examinations for the aged, and perhaps others particularly at risk, especially those who are not institutionalised and who are living alone.

Conclusions

The results reported in this chapter are too many and too diverse to be meaningfully summarised in a concluding paragraph or two. A few concluding observations will have to suffice. One is that, once again, the significance of the physician in influencing other utilisation is underlined. General practitioners, and in many instances, specialists as well, have such a strong influence over utilisation that other influences are completely overshadowed.

Our analysis and that of others point to important problems in the area of routine screening, early detection and preventive care. Age was one important factor. Children seem not to receive adequate immunisation or, especially, routine dental care. The aged would profit from systematic, annual physical examinations. Social class also appears to be a factor. It strongly influences dental care, and for women, it influences utilisation of cervical cancer smear tests. Throughout the study we have found that members of farming and fishing families have received less medical care, controlling for other influences, than other members of the population. This is a problem requiring closer examination. We have also found that persons living in the North-Western and North-Eastern Health Board areas are less likely to obtain preventive care than persons in central and southern parts of Ireland, and this, too, is a problem deserving attention.

Some of these problems will receive further attention in the next chapter, where we offer concluding comments and recommendations arising out of the study as a whole.

Chapter 8

CONCLUSIONS AND RECOMMENDATIONS

The Irish medical care system has served the needs of the Irish people. It has changed as times have changed, providing new, improved and expanded services. It has kept pace with the science and technology of medical care. It has earnestly sought to make "state of the art" care available to all, wherever they live, and whatever their incomes.

Today, there is need for further change. While the quality of medical care is generally very good, there are some weak spots which require attention. A conscious and honest effort is made to provide needed care to all, but in places there are problems with the amount and/or distribution of resources, with outreach to particular portions of the population, and with the patterns of eligibility for state-financed medical care. These problems deserve attention. The most urgent problems facing the Irish medical care system, and indeed almost every medical care system in Europe and North America, are the rapid growth and increasingly irrational allocation of medical care expenditures. The problems which generated this cost inflation and irrational mix are still in place, generating even more as these words are read. If none of the other problems is addressed, these must be, and indeed, in some way will be.

The author recognises that some readers will turn to this chapter without reading the preceding chapters in which the supporting evidence and analysis are developed in detail. Therefore, an effort has been made to make this chapter self-contained. But in fairness to our thesis, and indeed to our readers, it must be emphasised that this chapter cannot really stand alone, and that our argument is made in the volume as a whole, and not in a single, concluding chapter.

We will review four sets or types of problems in turn: weak spots in the quality of care and in outreach; problems in the amount and distribution of resources; anomalies in eligibility requirements; and exploding and irrational expenditures. We will then review four models for fundamental reform of the system. We conclude with our own vision for the Irish medical care system of the future, and needed first steps toward its achievement.

A. Problem Areas

To simplify the discussion, problem areas have been sorted into four categories. Most of the problems that fall into one category affect other categories, and the classification should be viewed as primarily an expositional convenience.

1. Weak Spots in the Quality of Care

As we saw in Chapter 4, reviews of general practice in Ireland by the GPs themselves, published in the 1970s, contained expressions of concern. The Gowan Report concluded, "There are some indications especially from referral rates, that the level of acute medical care is more haphazard than in the United Kingdom, and Irish doctors still having a too-ready recourse to direct hospital admission to solve their patients' problems." (Gowan, 1972). Another authoritative survey of Irish general practice concluded, "The isolation of the Irish general practitioner, both geographically and intellectually, needs urgent attention ..." (Shannon, 1976).

The required strengthening involves group and team practice and greater use of non-doctor personnel, including clerical staff, technicians, nurses, para-medical aides, midwives and social workers. No financial incentives exist, in either General Medical Services methods of remuneration, or in the structure of VHI reimbursement, which would encourage any of these changes. Improvements in this area will strengthen medical care and in the long run save money as well.

These changes are easier to accomplish in more densely populated urban and suburban areas, but they are more vital in rural areas, especially in remote places, where doctors are more likely to be isolated. If group practice is impossible in some less populated regions, some means of routine physician interaction should be devised.

The use of "physician extenders" to economise on scarce physician time will require education of the general public. It would be no gain for patients to be seen, for example, by a nurse practitioner and *then* to be seen by a physician. While this process of education may take several years, that is no reason not to begin it.

Another weak spot in primary care is the evident failure of outreach to the aged poor, and possibly to other disadvantaged or handicapped populations, outside of institutions. Routine physical examinations for this group in the population are likely to be cost-effective (though some may wish a research basis for this conclusion) and as important as examinations of school children. While adequate care is available, usually without charge, to the aged and to other at-risk members of the population, it is evident that we cannot rely on self-reporting of suspected illnesses in this group. Regular physical examinations of the aged have a high priority in the development of the health services; only one aged person in five had an examination in 1980.

Other weaknesses in outreach suggested in our study (see Chapter 7) include the following. Persons with Category II eligibility used significantly less primary care, as evidenced by the large numbers who had not seen a GP in five years (including never), and had not had a physical examination or a blood pressure test in 1980, or had their children immunised. This weakness seems to argue for extending free GP care to all. Working class women are much less likely to have cervical cancer smear tests and lower class children are much less likely to see their dentists. Preventative care seems less in the North-Eastern and North-Western Health Board areas, and among members of households headed by unemployed persons. Members of farming and fishing families seem to have significantly less utilisation of most kinds of medical care, controlling for other influences. All of these problems require attention.

A possible weak spot in secondary care concerns specialists. An Irish Medical Association Working Party has argued that public patients

> ... are less likely to have an operation performed by a consultant surgeon. They are more likely to receive their day-to-day medical attention from resident staff.... Patients attending out-patients' departments are treated less well, first because of long waiting and poor physical conditions, and secondly because they are often seen by residents who, in our opinion, may not be competent to deal with their problems (Mulcahy, *et al.,* 1975).

The IMA group has alleged three problems in this short quotation: inequality of care as between public and private patients; poor conditions in out-patient departments; and, most serious of all, incompetence to carry out their routine duties by junior hospital doctors. The third allegation should be investigated by physicians, and appropriate remedial action, relating to medical education, selection of residents, supervision, or any other aspect, should be taken. The second allegation can be reviewed by non-physicians. Physical conditions can be improved, even in older hospitals. Long waiting times are a function of the supply of physicians, dealt with in the next subsection.

The equity issue is a fundamental one. There seems to be substantial agreement among the political parties and the general public in Ireland that the same *quality* of care should be available to all, rich and poor, urban and rural, male and female, young and old. This consensus is lacking on whether this basic equality should extend to amenity levels or to waiting times. But the Working Party's allegation goes beyond these to the question of quality of care. Since this implies a fundamental defect in the structure of the Irish medical care system, it requires a structural response, and will be dealt with further in a later section.

Another possible weak spot in the quality of care at secondary level is the fact that some people are served by hospitals which are too small to provide an adequate medical staff. This problem will be discussed in the next subsection.

A final weak spot in the quality of care is the low ratio of dentists to population. A long-term programme, both to increase the numbers of dentists, and to increase dental utilisation, is required. The supply of Health Board dentists in particular needs attention.

2. Amount and Distribution of Resources

In general, problems of amount and distribution of medical care resources are minor. While Ireland has smaller ratios of both physicians and acute hospital beds to population than most other European countries, there are more than enough of these resources, and the low ratios are a credit to the efficiency of the Irish system, rather than a reflection against it. Statistics are scanty, but there appear to be too few physician extenders or para-medical personnel in Ireland, meaning that physicians are often over-qualified for many of their tasks. In future, expansion of these non-doctor personnel should substitute, in part, for growth in the stock of physicians. There do appear to be too few dentists.

The Irish system is decentralised, and hence Department officials have little control over many aspects of resource distribution. There are, none the less, some distributional questions requiring attention.

There is no indication that Ireland has too few doctors, though there may be problems with distribution. Table 4.5 in Chapter 4 shows that in 1975 (the most recent year for which full information was available), general practitioners per 10,000 population ranged from 4.3 (in the Mid-Western area) to 6.0 (in the Midland area). The Midland figure is 25 per cent higher than the national average. Only the Mid-Western (at 90 per cent) and North-Western (at 94) had less than 95 per cent of the national average ratio.

Consideration of the medical care needs of the aged increases the significance of regional disparities somewhat. In 1980, those aged 65 and over have, on average, 78 per cent more GP utilisation than the rest of the population and 62 per cent more than the overall average. If we re-calculate the GP-population ratios for 1975, treating each aged person as 1.62 persons, the adjusted ratios are: Ireland as a whole, 4.5 GPs per 10,000 population; Eastern Health Board area, 4.7, or 104 per cent of the national average; Midland, 5.6, 124 per cent; Mid-West and North-West, 4.0, 89 per cent; North-East, 4.3, 96 per cent; Southern, 4.2, 93 per cent; and Western, 4.4, 98 per cent. Only the Midland, Mid-West and North-West ratios seem to require attention. Significant variation in GP-population ratios can deprive some of timely needed care; and, as we have seen, it helps account for unacceptably long time in GP waiting rooms in some under-served areas, and for compensatory physician-induced demand in areas with relatively high physician densities.

We have no data on the distribution of specialists as such, but the distribution of consultants for 1981 is available. There is considerably more variation in this ratio than for GPs. In the Eastern Health Board area, which had almost exactly half of the country's consultants (496 of 993), the ratio was 4.2 per 10,000 population. In the Southern area, the ratio was 3.1 per 10,000. In the rest of the country, the average was 1.9, and the range was from 1.5 (North-Eastern) to 3.0 (Western). While this pattern is explained, in part, by the concentration of more specialised hospital facilities in Dublin, and secondarily in Cork and Galway, the disparities appear excessive and some regions seem distinctly underserved.

In this connection, the comments by the IMA Working Party, quoted above, should be recalled. The IMA group claimed that out-patient clinic waiting times were frequently excessive. While we lack data on this point, waiting times are presumably greatest in those areas with low ratios of specialist consultants, and presumably junior doctors working under them, to population.

Table 4.13 in Chapter 4 indicates wide disparities in the regional distribution of social workers and physiotherapists. The Eastern Health Board area had 311 of Ireland's 601 social workers in 1979, or 0.35 per 1,000 population, as against 0.09 per 1,000 for the rest of the country, taken as a whole. The Eastern region also employed 194 of 363 physiotherapists, or 0.17 per 1,000, as compared with 0.08 per 1,000 for the rest of the country.

Regarding dentists, there are problems both with overall numbers, especially of Health Board dentists, and with regional distribution, which favours the Eastern and Southern Health Board areas. The following are the numbers of persons served by each dentist: Eastern area, 2,700 persons; Southern area, 2,800 persons; and the rest of the country, 4,900 persons. It also shows eligible persons per Health Board dentist to be 4,200 in the Eastern area, 4,000 in the Southern area and 6,700 in the rest of the country. These are extremely large differences. There is a relationship between the low overall numbers and the geographic mal-distribution. While dentists have far less opportunity than doctors to generate demand for their own services to compensate for high ratios of population, excess demand for dental care gives dentists considerable lattitude in locating their practices. This does not adequately explain, however, the mal-distribution of salaried Health Board dentists. According to Table 4.2 in Chapter 4, Ireland and Britain had the lowest ratios of dentists to population in 1976 in the European Community. At 0.27 per thousand, the Irish ratio compared badly with the (unweighted) average of the other member states, at 0.48. To have raised Ireland's 1975 ratio of dentist to population to the level of that of the next highest country, Belgium (at 0.31 per 1,000), would have required 127 more dentists in Ireland in that year. The greatest need, however, is for Health Board dentists in the areas outside the Eastern and the Southern.

At in excess of 5.5 acute hospital beds per 1,000 population, Ireland has more than enough hospital beds. Only two regions had fewer than four per thousand, a ratio used elsewhere as a target maximum: the North-Eastern, at 3.85; and the North-Western at 3.51. Most of the North-Eastern region's population live within range of the many large County Dublin hospitals in the Eastern region (though at 10 per cent, a larger proportion of people in the North-Eastern region than anywhere else had to wait a month or longer to be admitted to hospital). The North-West, with its low population density, large proportion of aged population, and low ratio of beds to population, is the area most clearly underserved by general hospital facilities.

In 1968, the Fitzgerald Report recommended a policy that general hospitals have at least 300 beds, and argued that those with fewer than 200 beds are incapable of adequately meeting public needs. In 1979, eleven years later, only 13 of Ireland's 158 hospitals, accounting for 25 per cent of total acute beds, met the 300-bed standard, and 133 hospitals, accounting for approximately half of the country's acute beds, did not meet the 200-bed standard and the North-Western and South-Western and South-Eastern had none which meet the 300-bed one.

Finally, we can note that in some areas, inadequate long-stay geriatric facilities mean that these patients use acute hospital beds, at high cost.

3. Eligibility

Elsewhere in this chapter, structural changes in eligibility patterns are suggested, including the extension of free general practitioner services to all. In this section we do not deal with such structural changes, but rather focus on anomalies in eligibility standards. We suggest three changes in the current arrangements.

First, we suggest that all eligibility standards, for Medical Cards and for Category II, be indexed to a national earnings index, and adjusted periodically, perhaps quarterly.[76] This would achieve two objectives. It would reduce the extent of gradual erosion of benefits in the period between adjustments. At present, these adjustments are large and discontinuous. It would also separate the correction of eligibility standards to adjust for inflation from real changes in those standards, reducing the confusion now existing between the two and taking the former out of the political process.

Second, we suggest that Category I entitlement be made a legal right for those meeting eligibility standards, while providing that Health Board Chief Executive Officers (CEOs) could continue to issue Medical Cards at their discretion to those not meeting those standards. At present, Category I eligibility is not a legal right, according to income, but is at the discretion of Health Board CEOs, while that for Category II is a legal right. In spite of agreement among CEOs on generally applicable guidelines for eligibility, it is possible for different standards to apply in the various Health Board areas. In a small country, there is no reason for horizontal inequities to exist in the form of regionally different standards for Medical Cards. This is all the more important as Medical Cards are increasingly used to qualify for non-medical benefits, e.g., free school bus services.

The third suggested change concerns Category II eligibility, which is determined quite differently from Category I. In effect, the unit considered for Category I is the family; that for Category II is the earner. This creates several anomalies and can account for different treatment of families with the same incomes. The appropriate revision is to make the family the basic unit in determining Category II eligibility. Eligibility should depend on family income, including earnings of both spouses and any other family members, and including unearned (i.e., property) income as well as labour income and an adjustment should than be made for family size.

4. Exploding and Irrational Expenditures

Even one who does not read their language will understand and appreciate the word people in the Federal Republic of Germany have used to describe their medical care crisis: "*Kostenexplosion*". The rapid expansion of both utilisation

---

[76]Thanks to G. Hughes, who pointed out to me the superiority of an earnings index for this purpose over the Consumer Price Index, which I had previously proposed.

and price in recent years has not been limited to Ireland, but has affected, at least, all of Western Europe and North America. The details of the cost explosion in Ireland were laid out in Chapter 5.

There is a sense, however, in which the problem is more accurately described as one of economic inefficiency or irrationality, rather than of inflation or costs *per se*. Had the rise in costs been accompanied by widely perceived improvements in the range, reach, extent and quality of medical care, comparable for example to those which occurred when most infectious diseases were conquered in developed countries, there would be substantially less concern. But the cost increases have occurred with no corresponding gains. Barrett (1979) suggests the possibility of decreasing or even negative returns to further expenditures on the Irish health services. Moreover, the most rapid increases in outlays appear not to have occurred in the medical care areas most in need of expansion — preventative care, primary care, community care — but in the sectors which seem already to absorb too many resources — especially hospitals.

In other words, drawing on our analysis in Chapter 2, it is fair to say that the marginal contribution of medical care expenditures to human welfare in Ireland may now be less than the marginal contribution of other expenditures; and it is almost certain that the marginal contribution of medical care expenditures in Ireland is non-uniform across the system. Our analysis shows that there is no mechanism in Ireland which assures an efficient outcome and that existing mechanisms are often perverse to that goal.

Changes are required. The main objectives of these should be to bring increased efficiency and rationality. This means (1) reducing or eliminating uneconomic utilisation; and (2) shifting to lower cost forms of utilisation. Note that the former goal is expressed in terms of uneconomic, and not unnecessary, utilisation. As was noted in Chapter 6, the notion that there is a dichotomy between "necessary" and "unnecessary" utilisation is based on a simplistic and excessively mechanical interpretation, both of medicine and of economics. Much excessive utilisation of medical care may be of *some* medical value, or be undertaken with some positive probability of medical value; but that does not make it worth its cost. The same resources, devoted to medical care elsewhere in the system, might yield significantly more medical value; and it is possible that the same resources shifted outside of medical care, to nutrition, education, highway safety, etc., might yield significantly more social return. The second goal entails, among other things, a shift from costly in-patient hospital care to out-patient care (i.e., a reduction in admitting rates); a shift, within out-patient care, from hospital-based and specialist care to community-based, primary care, especially by general practitioners; and a shift, within primary care, from physician to non-physician care, wherever such shifts are appropriate. Ultimately, this entails a reduction in the number of acute hospital beds.

The heart of the problem lies in the incentive structure facing consumers (the demand side) and providers (the supply side). The nature of these incentives was spelt out in detail in Chapter 3, and summarised in Chapter 5 (in the sub-section,

"The incentive structure"); the reader is referred to those places for a fuller discussion of the problem. What appears here is, hence, a summary of a summary, in effect.

The main incentive problem is that those who make resource-using decisions concerning medical care — patients and providers — frequently do not individually bear the economic costs of those decisions. Hence they are not led systematically to compare the probable benefits of medical care services with their social costs. This incentives problem has a demand side and a supply side.

The demand side refers to the influence of price and other terms on patient demand for medical care. As we saw in Chapter 2, there is a nearly universal tendency for people around the world to deal with the unpredictability of their medical care needs by arranging for some kind of health insurance, either public or private, and either compulsory or voluntary. In this context, the provision of free or subsidised medical care by government or through government financing should simply be considered as compulsory, public insurance. By bringing down the point-of-purchase price of medical care services, in many cases to nothing, insurance increases the demand for those services. This problem is referred to as that of "moral hazard," which is defined as the general tendency of insurance to increase the likelihood of a contingency insured against, in this case medical care utilisation.

It is to be emphasised that the tendency to over-use medical care services because of reduced (or nil) point-of-purchase prices is not the result of government provision *per se*. It is a universal phenomenon that arises in wholly private, market-based medical care systems as well as in wholly public, national health services. It is a characteristic of medical care, not of socialism.

The solution most commonly offered to moral hazard is some form of cost-sharing, under which the patient pays at the point of use some part of the cost of providing the care, service, or product. Cost-sharing is often attractive to policy makers because it can achieve other objectives than combatting moral hazard. It can help hard-pressed health services in raising revenue, a far from unimportant property, in this age of fiscal crisis. It can also, it is asserted, help make patients and physicians more cost-conscious, by reminding them that medical care resources are not free. In addition, it can help in asserting social priorities among types of medical care services, an advantage to be discussed below.

There are a number of types of cost-sharing, most of them variants or combinations of the following: (1) *Deductible*. The patient pays all costs, up to a ceiling, figured on either a time or case basis. Beyond that ceiling, the third-party payor (public or private insurance) pays the cost. The VHI applies this approach to cost-sharing for out-patient care; the Health Services apply it to pharmaceutical prescriptions for persons in Categories II and III. (2) *Flat rate charge for each unit of service*. A nominal charge — say, 50p for each visit to the GP — is imposed, irrespective of number of services or their cost. A flat rate charge is a variant of the deductible. The former is applied to each unit of service, while the latter is applied, as noted, on a time or case basis. (3) *A maximum limit on benefits.* This form of co-payment is usually found only in private insurance; its purpose is to limit the liability of the insurer. (4) *Percentage charges.* The patient is required to pay some set percentage, e.g., 15 per cent.

These four types can exist in combination. For example, there may be a deductible, beyond which the patient pays a percentage, up to a maximum money amount which the pateint has to pay.

The various forms of cost sharing serve different purposes. Deductibles in private insurance limit administrative costs by avoiding large numbers of small claims. In public provision, they serve the equity objective of aiding only persons with large expenses. From an incentive standpoint, they discourage use except when it is clearly important. Their contribution to reducing moral hazard is questionable, however. After the deductible is reached, they make no contribution to this objective. Before it is reached, sums concerned are usually small and incentive effects are small as well. Flat rate charges and percentage charges apply on every unit and can continue to influence utilisation at all levels of use. Flat rate charges are administratively simpler and are appropriate where cost variation is small. The maximum limit on benefits serves only the business needs of the insurer, and unless supplemented by some kind of public or private catastrophic coverage, can leave people vulnerable to economic ruin arising from large medical care costs.

In spite of the attractions of cost-sharing, there is a large body of opinion which is either sceptical of the alleged gains or is opposed to general application of the technique. This point of view, which the author shares, is based primarily on two considerations. First, physicians make most utilisation decisions, and cost sharing merely punishes the patient for the physician's lack of cost consciousness. While physicians who act as "agents" of their patients (see Chapter 2) may take into account patient cost in making such utilisation decisions, imposing costs on patients can be an indirect, inefficient, unsatisfactory and unfair way of attempting to change physician behaviour. Second, the single area where cost-sharing might have an influence on utilisation is in the patient-initiated, first physician contact, for a suspected illness, or for preventative care. Within that area, the greatest impact would be on initial contacts by lower income persons. "Nothing should be done which would discourage people from early access to professional services ... Attempts to exempt the poor from cost-sharing are never wholly successful and insofar as they are successful they further stigmatize the poor" (World Health Organisation, 1979). There may be important places for cost-sharing within a medical care system, as will be noted presently; but as a general technique for limiting utilisation it is liable to have the undesirable effect of limiting mainly or only the types of care which we least want to limit, *viz.,* self-initiated primary care.

In addition to the general problem of moral hazard, we find on the demand side another important genus of problem, where a system imposes fees or charges in a manner that does not correspond with social priorities or costs. In many instances, the structure of prices in the Irish system is such as to encourage utilisation of the higher-cost resources rather than the lower-cost ones. There are instances in which the Irish incentive system encourages in-patient hospital care over out-patient care, specialist care over GP care and physician care over non-physician care. Subsidies to private care and, indirectly, to VHI, have encouraged overexpansion of both, which makes national medical care costs higher than they should be. These demand-side anomalies are discussed at length in Chapter 5. One useful contribution of cost sharing can be to shift utilisation from high-cost and/or low-priority uses to their opposites. For example, if it is desirable to encourage the expansion of primary care relative to secondary, that objective might be achieved by reducing the price of GP services, perhaps to nil, for the portion of the population who currently must pay, while imposing charges, perhaps nominal, flat-rate fees, on out-patient specialist care, or in-patient hospital care, for the same population.

The supply side refers to the influence of remuneration techniques and other incentives on resource-using medical care utilisation decisions made by providers. It is generally conceded in health economics that supply side incentives are more crucial than demand side incentives in influencing utilisation. Two arenas dominate the discussion: physician remuneration; and hospital budgeting or reimbursement.

Physician remuneration has been discussed frequently in this volume. The general argument, supported both by theory and by considerable statistical evidence, is that the fee-for-service method of physician remuneration in general use in Ireland not only fails to make physicians cost-conscious but on the contrary provides them with incentives for utilisation beyond levels which are efficient and economical. Modification of the fee-for-service system is at the heart of any serious effort to control costs and bring economic rationality to the Irish medical care system.

The main alternative to fee-for-service is capitation, under which physicians are paid according to the number of patients they have, rather than the number of times they see them, or the number of services they provide. There is considerable evidence (see Chapters 2 and 5) on a world-wide basis that capitation reduces utilisation and further that it reduces pharmaceutical prescribing rates as well.

In the Irish context, one difficulty (in addition to possible physician opposition) confronts any attempt to apply capitation to general practitioner care. Capitation is not applicable to physician services purchased for a fee at the point of use. Hence as the Irish medical care services are organised at present, it could apply only to Category I care, and not to Categories II and III care. In the Netherlands, GPs are remunerated on a capitation basis for public patients and on a fee-for-service basis for private patients; thus there is precedent for such an arrangement. Some observers have expressed fears that if physicians were to be paid on a capitation basis for Category I patients and on a fee basis for Categories II and III patients, that would create (or perpetuate) two classes of care. GPs, it is alleged, would spend less time with lower income, Category I patients, because consultations with them would bring in no cash income.

It should be noted that similar allegations are made concerning the present system, under which the GMS (Payments) Board pays GPs for services to Category I patients, at fee levels considerably below those prevailing for private patients. Capitation might,however, aggravate this effect, particularly where physicians have target incomes. To combat this effect, it would be necessary that patients on whose behalf capitation payments might be made be able to change GPs easily, thus bringing market forces into play. Patients who felt they were not adequately cared for could then deny their doctors their own and family members' annual capitation fees, which might be a serious penalty.

The only certain way to insure one class of GP care is to pay GPs in the same way for all patients. There are strong arguments for the application of capitation remuneration to the whole population and not merely to persons covered by Medical Cards. Not only would such a technique avoid the tendency of capitation remuneration to create two classes of care, but it would extend the desirable incentive effect of the reform to the whole population. There are two ways in which capitation remuneration could be extended to patients in Categories II and III. One would be to extend free GP care to the entire population. There are other arguments for this change, to be discussed later. But it is not necessary to provide free GP care in order to adopt capitation remuneration. The second technique would be for patients (or the VHI, on their behalf) to pay GPs on a capitation basis. Not only would such a reform alter provider incentives in a decidedly favourable direction, but it would shift demand incentives in favour of primary care, an objective which is desirable in its own right.

There are remuneration techniques intermediate between fee-for-service as currently practised and capitation as described. One is to pay physicians on a *case basis*. The other is to pay them on the basis of *prospectively negotiated ceilings* on total physician remuneration.

Under the case basis, physicians would be paid per case, rather than per unit of service. If desired, fees could vary, according to case diagnosis. Under this technique, a doctor would receive the same amount for each case, or each case with a particular diagnosis, regardless of the number of consultations, and regardless of the mix of services provided at those visits. Cases requiring more-than-average and less-than-average care and attention would average out. In effect, physicians would be paid for their output — treatment of a given problem — rather than their input — resources used; hence their remuneration would more closely resemble that of other producers in the marketplace.

Under prospectively negotiated ceilings, representatives of physicians would negotiate with third-party payors (the Department of Health, or the GMS, and the VHI) prior to each year a ceiling on overall payments in that year for general practitioners' and possibly other classes of physicians' services. As this technique is now applied in Germany, the current year's expenditures are used, together with a growth factor (8 per cent in Germany). If physicians provide more services than can be paid for within the ceiling, in a three-month period, each doctor's reimbursement is cut back uniformly, *pro rata* (Stone, 1980). The advantage of this technique is that the costs of physician services are limited and can be precisely budgeted. It seems to have worked reasonably well in Germany.

The disadvantage is that it provides no incentive to limit utilisation (as opposed to outlay), and indeed may encourage enhanced utilisation (if doctors seek to offset prospective cuts in fee levels) and hence increase forms of utilisation correlated with physician utilisation.

Another alternative is the reorganisation of medical care delivery into pre-paid group plans (PPGPs) such as health maintenance organisations (HMOs), under which patients purchase all medical care, and not merely physician services, on a capitation basis. Pre-paid group plans and HMOs will be discussed later.

Methods by which hospitals are budgeted or reimbursed are as important as, or more important than, the ways in which physicians are remunerated. Hospitals are the main resource users in the Irish medical care system; and while physicians determine the extent of patient use of hospitals, they have less control over the per day or per case cost of that care.

Simplifying considerably, there are four ways in which hospitals' incomes can be determined: (1) *Retrospective reimbursement of costs*. Hospitals are paid, either by patients or by third party payors, according to activity and costs. For example, the state can pay hospitals on a patient-day basis, adjusted perhaps for severity of case mix. This is the rough equivalent of paying physicians on a fee-for-service basis. It assures hospitals that whatever costs they incur will be reimbursed, and thus provides them with no motive to economise. It encourages resource-utilising, rather than resource-saving, decisions. (2) *Prospective budgeting on an individual hospital basis*. Hospitals receive annual budgets from the state or other third party payors. They have an opportunity to explain and defend their budgets, and to use whatever political strength and/or negotiating skill they possess. While prospective budgeting is generally thought to be superior, on economic grounds, to retrospective reimbursement, when it takes the form of review on an individual hospital basis, it may provide virtually the same result: whatever costs are incurred are reimbursed and incentives to economise are lacking.

The other two techniques provide for no negotiation between payor and hospital, and are hence impersonal, arms'-length techniques. (3) *Prospective budgeting on a per capita basis*. Hospitals receive budgets according to the size of the populations to be served, as adjusted, perhaps, for age composition, other structural properties bearing on potential hospital use, and possibly differences in each area's morbidity patterns from the national average. In short, hospitals are paid according to formulae. Variants of such a system are used in centralised systems and national health services. They encourage efficient resource utilisation by hospitals by imposing on them, in effect, the full costs of all resource use. Any unneeded expenditure adds to hospital costs without adding to revenues; any economy reduces costs without reducing revenues. Because this method can provide very different income amounts from those provided under either of the first two methods, a transition from these to formulae-based budgeting needs to be gradual. (4) *Diagnosis-related groups*. The final method reimburses hospitals on the basis of activity, but on a case basis, rather than a costs-incurred, or patient-day, basis. In the US, where this method is used to reimburse hospitals for care of the aged under a social security system, hospitals are paid an amount equal to the average per case cost of all hospitals, adjusted for case diagnosis (under 437 separate diagnosis-related groups, or DRGs).[77] Like the formula system, this one separates hospitals' resource-using decisions from factors influencing their incomes, and hence rewards them for economies and penalizes them for inefficiency.

As noted in Chapter 5, the Department of Health makes its budget decisions affecting hospitals on an *ad hoc* basis in ways which are, to the analyst, obscure.[78] It is difficult to evaluate the present technique precisely because its incentive and allocational implications are not obvious without further research. Other scholars are strongly urged to take up this subject, which seems to the present writer to be the most important single item on the Irish health economics research agenda. The present system appears to resemble the second model, above; arms'-length methods, such as the third and fourth above, would be likely to provide far stronger incentives for efficient utilisation. Any change to such methods would have to be very gradual, and would probably have to be linked to further decentralisation of administrative decision making.

In addition to altering the incentive structure on the demand and supply sides, authorities can seek to control medical care costs by two additional techniques, both discussed in greater detail elsewhere in this study.

The first is the imposition of firm cash limits on annual expenditures. Cash limits are easiest to impose where the system is centralised, as under a national health service. They are hardest to impose where the system is decentralised, market and insurance-based. In Ireland, cash limits could be applied even within currently government-financed aspects of medical care only if the current method of GP remuneration were modified, by adoption of capitation, or by moving to a system of prospectively negotiated ceilings.

The second is by adoption of medical audit and peer review. Medical audit is normally conducted by a third party payor (the State or the VHI), and involves review, by physicians, of services provided or ordered by physicians, to determine whether they are medically necessary, efficacious and cost-effective.[79]

---

[77]"Outliers," cases which deviate significantly from the norms, are reimbursed at cost. Separate norms have been established for urban and rural hospitals. Several years are allowed for transition.

[78]It is appropriate to reiterate what was said in footnote 63 to Chapter 5, namely that the procedure is not obscure because of any disposition of the Department of Health to make it so, or to withhold from the public or researchers vital information concerning the procedures or the outcomes. Instead, the procedures are *ad hoc* and are inherently difficult to model without specific research into the statistical determinants of budgetary allocations.

[79]Cost-effectiveness analysis compares the costs of alternative ways of achieving similar results, or compares results for identical cost. As noted in Chapter 2, true cost-benefit studies are not ordinarily possible in the area of health and medical care, because there is no acceptable measure of "benefit" comparable with cost. Where an Irish Medical Association Working Party is quoted, below, as advocating the use of cost-benefit analysis, it is assumed that they really mean cost-effectiveness analysis.

Peer review is normally based in hospitals (where it is often called bed utilisation review, though more than bed use is at issue) and in medical societies. It, too, involves evaluation of services provided or ordered by physicians. In some countries, it involves the writing of guidelines or standards, to state currently preferred methods of treatment, lengths of hospital stay, and the like. Experience in other countries suggests that these review procedures do not save much money, but that they can be useful in bringing uniformity in standards and policing for less competent or careful practitioners.

B. Models for Reform

In this section we review and assess four alternative models which have been or might be offered for the Irish medical care system: the insurance model; the incremental growth model; the competitive prepaid group plan model; and the national health service model. After each is discussed, we will conclude this section with an overall assessment.

1. *The Insurance Model.* A number of years ago, an Irish Medical Association Working Party, consisting of four prominent specialist consultants, developed a discussion document on the feasibility of a "compulsory specialist and hospital insurance scheme" as an alternative to the present system (Mulcahy, *et al.*, 1975). While the proposed scheme does not seem to have been strongly advanced in recent years, it does provide a worked-out example of an insurance-centred scheme, similar to some found in Western Europe, designed by Irish physicians for the Irish situation.

What is set out is evidently not a complete system, and is called "compulsory institutional and specialist insurance system." It is silent on such subjects as general practitioner care and pharmaceutical medicines. It is fair to assume that its authors tacitly accepted continuation of the current scheme for these: fee-for-service remuneration of GPs; free GP care and medicines for the Medical Card population, financed through the General Medical Services (Payments) Board; and payment of somewhat higher GP fees from their own resources by other patients.

The operative part of the written proposal is brief and can be quoted in full:

1. A standard premium is to be paid by each person or family, along the lines of the present VHI arrangement. For the indigent the premium would be paid by the state. For the middle income group the premium might be paid partly by the individual and partly by the state, and for the high income group by the person or family themselves. Premium payments might be subject to relief of income tax as exists at present with VHI premiums.
2. Patients requiring special accommodtion could pay an extra premium.
3. A schedule of fees would be established and would be fixed in relation to all patients, whether receiving standard or private treatment. This schedule of fees would require to be reviewed annually.
4. Out-patients' services as we know them now would be abolished and patients

would see consultants in their hospital or private offices. A clear schedule of fees for out-patient consultations would exist for such visits.

5. The income from insurance premiums would require to cover maintenance costs of hospitals and payment of all staff. The capital cost of building and the equipping of hospitals would require to be funded by the state. Services for the chronic ill, for geriatric and some psychiatric patients, and for other special cases would also require to be supported by central funds.

6. The system would involve a change from the present Voluntary Health Insurance/client relationship to a Health Insurance/Hospital/Doctor relationship.

7. The system would incorporate medical audit, cost benefit analysis and peer review to ensure optimum use of hospital facilities, the most useful and efficient employment of limited resources, and the avoidance of abuse of the schedule-of-fee system. A compulsory insurance system would facilitate medical audit and cost-benefit analysis, and would also facilitate the supervision of standards of medical treatments.

8. Waiting lists would probably not exist under such a system.

The authors state that the scheme resembles those in place in Belgium and in Canada.

There are some attractive features of this insurance model. One is that distinctions among patients would disappear. For example, all patients would evidently become private patients, in effect, of consultant specialists. At present, as noted in Chapter 4, and discussed earlier in this chapter, public and private patients receive somewhat different care, to the disadvantage of the former.

Another attractive feature of the proposed model is part 7, above, which calls for medical audit, cost-benefit analysis, and peer review.[80] At present the last of these is rare and limited in its application in Ireland, and the first two are wholly absent. Their purpose in the present proposal is to assure that costly, time-consuming, and sometimes possibly hazardous medical and surgical procedures are medically necessary and useful, are efficacious and are the most cost-effective treatments available. As noted in Chapter 4, the VHI state that medical audit is useful mainly to deal with fraud, which they believe to be rare in Ireland.[81] However, that is a limited view of medical audit, and this part of the Working Party scheme should not be dismissed without careful investigation. What seems appropriate is a research project, examining the range of treatments in Ireland for the same diagnosis, including lengths of hospital stays, to determine whether indeed no need, apart from fraud, exists for this kind of review.

---

[80]As noted in footnote 79, above, it is assumed that the authors have in mind cost-effectiveness rather than cost-benefit analysis.

[81]The VHI may be correct that fraudulent claims are rare in Ireland. However, Mr. Tom Ryan, chief executive of the Voluntary Health Insurance Board, recently criticised and questioned the legality of what he described as a widespread practice of hospitals charging VHI subscribers semi-private room rates when they are actually accommodated in public wards (*Irish Times*, October 18, 1984).

In spite of these two attractive features, the insurance model is in general an unconstructive suggestion. It does nothing, really, to deal with the sources of either cost inflation or irrational allocation in Irish medical care. The present incentive structure is retained: physicians are remunerated on a fee-for-service basis, and indeed this is extended into areas where it does not now exist. On the basis of experience elsewhere, reviewed in Chapters 2 and 6, one might predict an increase in utilisation, especially of surgery and other in-patient procedures, as a consequence of a shift to the insurance model. Similarly, there is no change in patient incentives. Moral hazard, which is a problem in market-type medical care systems where care is free or nominally priced at the point of purchase, would persist.

Later in this section, a modified version of Working Party's insurance proposal will be suggested, which will deal with some of these incentive objections.

2. *The Incremental Growth Model.* A second model would aim the Irish Medical care system toward the goal of a system with all services free at the point of use, as an ultimate goal; and would move toward that goal incrementally, by providing free, one by one, services heretofore charged for. This was previously the policy of the Irish Congress of Trade Unions and was set forth and defended in Cassells (1980). Revised Congress policy will be noted presently. The incremental growth model seems also to be a description of the actual development of the Irish system in recent years, as further extrapolated into the future. Thus, even though it is no longer advocated by Congress, it is worth a review in this section.

Under the incremental growth model, Congress established as its "first priority" a "free hospital service for the entire population," which, it stated, "could be achieved by the abolition of the income limit for limited [Category II] eligibility ..." (Ibid.)

For a number of years, the Irish Congress of Trade Unions has been on record as advocating a national comprehensive health service which is free for all at the point of use, a position which underpins both its old and its new policies. Congress's approach was to press for incremental changes which, bit by bit, would move the health services toward that long-run goal. Within the structure of incremental change, Congress chose to concentrate on the income limit for Category II. From the mid-1970s, the approach was to seek increases in the upper-income limit for eligibility. In 1980, Congress adopted the position that there should be no upper-income limit, i.e., that Category III should be abolished and Category II eligibility should be extended to all (other than those covered under the more liberal Category I). As seen in Chapter 4, the major difference between the present Categories II and III concerns consultant specialist services, which are available free to those covered under the former but not to those under the latter. Hence the main effect of the ICTU proposal would be extend free consultant services to the approximately 15 per cent of the population not entitled to these at the present.

This proposal also has some attractive features. It moves the health services in the direction of comprehensive care, free to all. At present, all persons, whatever their incomes, have a right to free hospital care; and those in Categories I and II have free consultant services while in hospital. Thus the proposal would close the last gap in coverage of expensive hospital care for all in Ireland. It would make it unnecessary for anyone in the country to buy Voluntary Health Insurance cover, though of course those wishing private as opposed to public care would still do so. Since the large majority of people in Category III might be expected to continue to prefer private care, and not to avail of the new service, the proposal need not be expensive to administer.

None the less, the disadvantages of this approach outweigh its advantages. Like the IMA Working Party proposal, it envisions no fundamental change in the incentive structure of the Irish medical care system. It does involve three changes, none of them fundamental, in these incentives. First a reduction in the private use of specialist services involves a marginal shift from fee-for-service to salary remunertion. Second, it increases slightly the moral hazard inherent in the system, to the extent that services once charged for, to uninsured persons in Category III, are now provided free. Uninsured persons in Category III are few, however. These two incentive changes are in opposite directions, and as each is small, the net change is still smaller, and of uncertain direction.

The third incentive change inherent in the incremental growth model is a change in the relative costs of primary care from GPs and hospital care, both in- and out-patient. This is a rather more serious consequence than the two just cited. Persons in Category III would join those in Category II in finding it cheaper to use hospital services than GP care, thus encouraging a further shift away from community care and toward hospital care.

There are other objections to the proposal. An important one is distributional. The essence of the proposal is to shift services already provided from the private fee category to the public, free category. Thus public funds for medical care would be used in a way that results in no net increase in resources for medical care. To the extent that persons in Category III avail of these services, the money they save on medical care is released for other purposes — holidays, auto-mobiles, recreation and other private goods. When it is recalled that those in Category III are the (approximately) top 15 per cent of the income distribution, it will be seen that the proposal involves an effective upward redistribution of disposable income.

If Ireland is ever to move from a multi-tiered system in which some benefits are means-tested, to a system in which basic care is free to all, then just exactly this type of upward redistribution of income will be necessary at some point in time. Its regressive redistributional consequences can be neutralised, however, by financing such expension out of savings arising out of cutting back on the many and substantial subsidies to private care. We will return to this subject later in the chapter.

A final criticism is of the contention cited above, that a free hospital service for the entire population is a "first priority". It is argued that there are higher priorities. These will also be discussed later in the chapter.

Congress now advocates (Irish Congress of Trade Unions, 1984) a comprehensive national health service. They do not spell out the features of such a sercice, but call for a government White Paper on the subject. The national health service model is discussed later in this section. Congress states that, "in the phasing in of a national health service, free primary care should have priority," and they call for capitation remuneration of primary care doctors.

3. *The Competitive Pre-Paid Group Plan Model*. Pre-paid group plans (PPGPs) operate in the private sector. They are organisations established for the purpose of providing comprehensive medical care to their clients. Pre-paid group plans either employ doctors or they are associations of doctors. Depending on their size and method of organisation, they may also employ other health professionals and ancillary personnel. They usually own and operate x-ray and pathology facilities. Some even own their own hospitals, or are owned by hospitals, which amounts to the same thing. For a set annual pre-paid fee, comparable to an insurance premium, PPGPs undertake to provide for all of a patient's medical care needs. Services they do not themselves provide are purchased by them for their patients.

The best known and most common type of PPGP in the United States, where this form of arrangement was first begun and where it enrols about 10 per cent of the population, is the Health Maintenance Organisation, or HMO. Health Maintenance Organisations are private businesses, owned by doctors, engaged in the corporate practice of medicine. Other PPGPs are owned differently, but most other features are similar.

Two characteristics of HMOs and other PPGPs stand out: they have an incentive to keep their clients healthy. And they have an incentive to use resources efficiently.

Pre-paid group plans emphasise preventative care and periodic, routine examinations. It is in their economic interest to avoid delay in diagnosing illness, as delay may require more and more expensive treatment.

When PPGP patients are seen by a primary care physician, that physician may prescribe medicines, or refer the patient to a specialist, or order x-rays or tests, or send the patient to hospital, just as in any ordinary pattern of organisation. But when the doctor does so, the cost is borne by the PPGP. Indeed, as many HMOs are organised, the cost is covered from a budgeted fund for that physician. Thus the PPGP and, usually, the physician herself or himself, bear a cost when resource-using decisions are made.

It will be noted that this sub-section is entitled, "*The competitive* pre-paid group plan model." Many attractive features of this technique depend essentially on the patient having alternatives to the PPGP, possibly including conventional (insurance-cum-fee-for-service) care, other PPGPs and other arrangements. Since the patient pays an annual fee and leaves all care in the hands of PPGP physicians, a profit seeking monopoly PPGP might mis-use that trust. It might not provide all needed care, saving money at the expense of the patient's health. Or it might leave the patient to sit long hours in waiting rooms of primary care physicians and specialist out-patient clinics. Or, if it had the unchecked economic power, it might squander resources and simply increase the level of the annual charge.

In the United States, the experience with PPGPs, and in particular HMOs, has been consistently very good, according to evaluation studies.[82] Cost savings are in the range of 20–33 per cent and are concentrated in hospitalisation. The health of HMO clients seems actually to be better than that of similar populations receiving more conventional care, as measured by work-days lost due to ill health. Consumer satisfaction, according to surveys, is high. In the US, HMOs operate in a very competitive, market type of environment.

It is worth noting that American HMOs realise their savings entirely from the effects of altered provider incentives. There are no deductibles or co-payments whatever; one's pre-payment premium covers everything. This should create considerable moral hazard, especially by comparison with private insurance, which in the US inevitably involves both deductibles and co-payment; but moral hazard is obviously not an important factor. This is evidence for the proposition that provider incentives are vastly more important than consumer incentives in the quest for economy and rationality in the provision of medical care.

Competing "Consumer Choice Health Plans", or CCHPs, a type of PPGP, are the central reform proposed for the US by conservative Stanford University economist Alain Enthoven, in his book, *Health Plan* (1979), cited in Chapter 5, above. Enthoven has sufficient faith in the market that he proposes only that enrolment in a CCHP be made available as an option to all consumers, as an alternative to private insurance and fee-for-service care. He is confident that the economic superiority of CCHPs would readily be established through competition. An Irish equivalent of this proposal would call for the creation of health plans which, like HMOs, CCHPs and other PPGPs, would guarantee to provide all needed care, in exchange for a predetermined advance capitation payment. Persons in Category I could choose to enrol with such a health plan, as an alternative to care as now provided; the Health Board would pay the capitation fee in full, and would have no other responsibility to the patient (other than, perhaps, monitoring the quality of care provided by the plan). Persons in Categories II and III would have partial payments made in their behalf by the state, and would pay the balance themselves, as an alternative to purchasing VHI cover.

A more thorough going reform would substitute such plans for all existing care, for all patients. Such a scheme would amount in effect to a modification of the IMA Working Party proposal, above. It would achieve most of that plan's advantages, and specifically it would remove the differences which now exist between care of public and private patients; and it would do so while avoiding

---

[82]Luft (1978) reviews approximately 50 evaluation studies of PPGPs in the preceding two decades and finds costs savings ranging from 10 to 40 per cent, attributable in the main to hospital utilisation 25 to 45 per cent lower for similar populations using conventional, fee-for-service care. See also Enthoven (1979).

most of that plan's disadvantages, and specifically its uneconomic incentive patterns. The result would be a voucher type of medical care system, one in which (a) the annual cost could be determined in advance, as based on the pre-paid fee levels; and (b) the incentive structure would be revised, to provide a strong incentive in favour of resource savings.

Who would organise PPGPs? Groups of physicians, for private gain; hospitals; voluntary organisations; employers; possibly the VHI; or even Health Boards themselves. Plans could be organised by private, public, or non-profit voluntary bodies. Presumably, the state would have to pass on capitation fee levels and keep an eye on the quality of care. As the Irish system is so hospitals-oriented, and as most of PPGPs' savings are in the hospitals area, there would appear to be considerable latitude for profitable PPGPs in Ireland.

Pre-paid group plans are attractive in particular to those who favour market-type, or capitalistic, arrangments, the private practice of medicine, and decent-ralisation. In the conventional practice of medicine, as found in Ireland today, and in many other countries, the market yields distorted, inefficient, uneconomic results, as described in Chapter 2 and as shown throughout this study. Pre-paid group plans can revive the market and restore to it the potential for efficiency.

4. *The National Health Service Model.* There is much loose talk which equates a "national health service" with the provision of all care free to the user at the time of use. The meaning of national health service is rather more precise. As usually employed in the relevant literature, it refers to a centralised, non-market system in which resource-using decisions are made administratively at the macro level, and made, as now, by physicians, through referral, prescribing, etc., decisions, at the micro level. Primary care physicians are paid on a capitation basis. This creates no provider incentive to over-use, such as physician-induced demand. Indeed, it has been argued that it may have another type of uneconomic consequence, namely that primary care physicians, who bear the (time) cost of revisits, have a greater tendency to refer patients to specialists or others, just to get rid of them, though our findings (in Chapter 6) cast doubt on that thesis. Other physicians (for example, specialists and junior hospital doctors) may be paid by capitation, or they may be salaried, a situation which already prevails in Ireland, with respect to public patients. All services are provided on a free or heavily-subsidised basis to patients and the market is not used at all to ration care or resources.

In the NHS model, there is an opportunity to apply effective cash limits, as was discussed above. Because in such a centralised system it is possible to deter-mine total medical care spending in advance, and as well to determine its regional and functional allocation, it is possible to limit spending, and its growth, to any level. This is not possible under decentralised models, such as the present Irish scheme, the insurance model, or the incremental growth model. (It would be possible, however, in the PPGP model.)

To summarise then, the most salient characteristics of the NHS model are (a) free or heavily subsidised care to all members of the population;[83] (b) effective cash limits; and (c) an incentive structure which does not encourage excessive utilisation.

Britain of course uses a version of the NHS model and, indeed, is in effect the originator of the model. And Britain stands out in international comparisons as one of the very few countries whose medical care expenditures have not exploded in recent years. It is one of the crowning ironies of this subject area that the British "National Health", put in place by socialists committed to equity, has become the most effective device, due to its centralisation, for controlling cost expenditures on medical care.

Italy has also adopted a national health service in recent years, for the purpose of rationalising and controlling expenditures. One important feature of the changeover is shift from fee-for-service to capitation remuneration of primary care GPs. The changeover provides an example of a natural experiment, because we have an opportuntiy to observe utilisation differences arising out of different systems, where the popultion served and the physician population are essentially unchanged. In areas where the change from fee-for-service to capitation has taken place, consulting rates have fallen (Abel-Smith and Maynard, 1978).

C. First Steps to Reform: A Personal View

As noted in Chapter 1, the author hopes someday for cost-conscious, health-conscious, consumer-centred Irish health care system in which needed care of equal quality is provided to all, without the imposition of fees or charges on the occasion of use.

This is a long-run target. The need now is for efficiency and economy. It is to be emphasised strongly that these two objectives are not in conflict.

Two quite different models can realise the long-run objectives aduced above, and at the same time achieve enhanced efficiency through substantial change of incentives.

One is a voucher system, based on provision of care by pre-paid group plans, or PPGPs, as discussed in the previous section. In most parts of the country, people could choose from among a number of alternative plans; in less densely settled areas, there might be only one plan, but quality of care and cost standards established in the more competitive areas could be applied to these monopoly plans. Plans could be profit-seeking, except in rural, monopoly areas, or non-profit. Economies would be achieved in this system through imposition of the costs of their decisions on the decision makers themselves, the primary care physicians, through their outright ownership of the plans, in the case of HMOs, or through some kind of profit-sharing and internal budgeting system. In addition, medical care costs would cease to be open-ended, as now.

---

[83]This refers to care as public patients. Typically private care is also available, without subsidy.

The group plan would be an ideal locus for the practice of group medicine, the use of medical auxiliaries, expanded use of social workers and use of a team concept in primary care, developments which are meritorious in their own right, irrespective of financing reforms.

A beginning could be made with optional PPGP selection by consumers, with the state paying fully for people in Category I and partially for those in Categories II and III. Further development of the health services could take the form of (1) expansion in the numbers of PPGPs available; (2) increase in the range and quality of services they provide, as medical science develops; and (3) increase in the portion of the capitation fee paid by the state. Thus development would be wholly evolutionary.

The other model is the national health service type of scheme. It would derive its economies, on the one hand, from use of capitation remuneration and other important incentive reforms (which would be less important, however, than the incentive reforms in the previous model), and, on the other hand, from the use of absolute budget ceilings, combined with administrative allocation of resources at a macro level. It seems likely that administrative allocation would significantly increase the efficiency of resource use in the Irish medical care system, as compared with the result of today's combination of distorted market allocation and *ad hoc* administrative allocation. If knowledgeable people, including a significant number of doctors, sat down to plan the use of medical care resources, and to apply them according to need and likely return, can it be doubted that the result would be a substantial improvement over the present system?

Needless to say, what is described above is the skimpiest of outlines. The development of new forms of medical care delivery and finance is a major study in itself. The choice is essentially a social one, in which political and ideological preferences, as well as economic ones, will play a major role.

If either a PPGP-voucher system or a naional health service is described as a long-run target, what are the steps which should be taken now? The following package of changes, designed for more or less immediate adoption, is consistent with both of the above target models, and with the present system of *ad hoc*, iterative and expedient development. In other words, no choice regarding radical restructuring of the medical care system would be implied by the adoption of the following plan.

The plan consists of ten points. Some points involve greater exenditure; some involve reductions. It is beyond the scopc of the present study to estimate precisely the exchequer implications of the proposals, but it is not the spirit of the plan that it either save or cost money. Instead, it is meant to involve simultaneously a redistribution in the use of public money, and a change in the incentive structure facing patients and providers. For this reason, the precise levels of new fees and charges have been left unspecified. The intended net exchequer effect is nil.

1. Provide everyone with free general practitioner care and remunerate GPs

on a capitation basis. (The former would be contingent on the latter.) As part of the package, give GPs some income security, provide them with paid medical leave and annual holiday leave, and pensions, according to years of practice in the scheme. Some increases in GP incomes may be necessary as well, to over-come doctors' reluctance to go over to a capitation scheme. Because GP fees are a small part of present medical care costs, such income increases, if necessarily, need not be unduly costly. It must be relatively easy for consumers to change from one GP to another, in order that the market provide some discipline. Our estimates, reported above in Chapter 5, are that private expenditure on general practitioner care in 1980 was £19.7m. The exchequer cost of this proposal may be more or less than that, though little if any social cost (e.g., increased percentage of GNP devoted to medical care) is envisioned. After some period of adjustment, increased availability of primary care should bring some budgetary savings in secondary and tertiary care, while the use of capitation remunmera-tion will lower overall GP utilisation, and should hence bring some savings, e.g., a reduction in over-prescribing and reduced future need for GPs.

2. Impose charges for out-patient hospital and consultant specialist services on those persons in Category II who currently receive these free. The charges may not necessarily be so high as to cover full costs. Charges at approximately the current level of private GP fees would, more or less, off set the exchequer costs of free GP services to those with Category II and III eligibility.

3. Impose charges for in-patient hospital care on persons in Categories II and III. Charges should be significantly less than the full bed-day costs, but should be high enough to assert social priorities in favour of out-patient over in-patient care and of primary care where possible. Therefore, consideration should be given to the desired incentive effects. For example, a flat fee per admission would discourage unnecessary one-day admissions for investigations, though it would do nothing to discourage excessively long stays.

The first three points, taken together, are intended to shift both provider and patient incentives in the direction of lower cost care and primary care in parti-cular.

4. Reduce the remaining subsidies to private care, especially hospital care; charge private hospital patients the costs of all services provided to them; abandon tax relief for VHI premiums. This point has three purposes; (1) it is meant to save money, to help finance the first point; (2) it will improve equity; state money should be used to finance the kind of care availble to all, not to subsidise care which is superior, from any standpoint, for any kind of elite; and (3) it will improve efficiency, by raising the price of high-cost medical care services, relative to lower-cost services.

5. Establish systems of medical audit in Health Boards and the VHI, and peer review machinery amongst physicians and within hospitals, as suggested by the IMA Working Party.

6. Create financial incentives for establishment of group practice, use of physician auxiliaries, etc. If fee-for-service is retained, even for a transition

period, one important incentive would be for third-party payors (the GMS (Payments Board and the VHI) to pay GPs when patients are seen only by nurse practitioners, medical auxillaries, or other non-doctor colleagues. If capitation is adopted, a larger list limit could be allowed GPs who work in groups and use ancillary staff. Help with capital costs for the establishment of medical centres would also be important.

7. Enable the creation of pre-paid group plans, and establish capitation rates which the state would pay on behalf of patients in each category of eligibility.

8. Encourage the expansion of dental resources, especially in the Health Boards. Ideally, dentists and dental auxiliaries would practise in the medical centres referred to above; and dental care would be included in the list of services provided by PPGPs.

9. Expand the conception of, and increase resources devoted to, health education. Health education must have a central role in an up-to-date health care system. We cannot spell out this role fully in the present study, which is devoted to medical care; health education requires a study in itself. But three important responsibilities of health education can be noted. First, primary responsibility for care of their own health must be laid at the feet of individuals. They need to be better informed. Hence health education must be informational and not only persuasive. Second, as noted earlier, the public will need to be educated to accept the substitution in many contexts of nurse practioners and medical auxiliaries for physicians and to deal with other non-doctor staff. And third, people need educating in cost-consciousness. This includes understanding the costs to them of their own lifestyle decisions, as well as the cost to them and society at large of medical care.

10. Finally, the Irish health services are in need of considerably expanded funds for research. We do not refer to basic medical research; others more qual-ified than this writer to address that issue will have to speak to it. Instead, our concern is with three other kinds of research. First is research into what might be labelled generally as prevention. The Department of Health should have a continuing research concern with air quality, occupational health and safety, prevention of poisoning in the home, road safety and other aspects of prevention. Second is improved collection of epidemiological data, which is the necessary foundation on which both improved prevention and improved care must rest. This too should be a continuing concern of the Department. There should be more routine collection of morbidity data from general practitioners, as well as periodic in-depth studies. And third, Ireland needs health economists and other social scientists trained in such disciplines as social policy analysis relating to health and medical care. As this is written, there are no health economists, *per se*, in Ireland.[84] One could not read this study from beginning to end without con-

[84]Since this was written, Mr. Eamon O'Shea, who had completed an M.S. in Health Economics at the University of York, took up a position at the Institute of Public Administration, with duties including but not limited to work in health economics. In addition, there are a number of econom-ists without specific health economics training who work at times in health-related areas.

cluding that there is a vast research agenda, which needs to be addressed by economists and other social scientists, so that we can be informed when we address the vital policy issues which arise in this area, rather than merely guessing, or being guided only by our pre-conceptions. That there are no health economists to study systematically and regularly a sector using as much as a tenth of GNP is, or should be, a scandal. Doctors, too, need to know some health economics; and for that reason, it is argued that trained health economists should be on medical as well as arts and commerce faculties in Irish universities.

These ten points are in addition to the miscellany of changes discussed earlier in the chapter, such as more hospital beds for the North-West region, basing Category II eligibility on the family unit, arms'-length budgeting of hospitals, and better outreach for primary care.

These proposals, we will readily concede, reflect opinion as well as analysis. Yet the author began the present study in 1979 with none of these views. They arose out of the study — the review of the structure of the system; discussions with physicians and others who participate in it; the conduct of a major nation-wide survey; statistical analysis of the results of that study; and review of the international health economics literature in search of what is relevant.

Others, addressing the same problems, might develop different lists. Let them do so. That would mean two things. It would mean that they were addressing important problems and it is unlikely that any harm could come of that. And it would show once again that economics, like medicine, is an inexact science.

REFERENCES

AARON, H. J. and W. B. SCHWARTZ, 1984. *The painful prescription: Rationing hospital care*, Washington, D.C., The Brookings Institution.

ABEL-SMITH, B., 1983. "Medical consumption — value for money?" Trinity Trust/School of Pharmacy, Annual Lecture, Dublin.

ABEL-SMITH, B. and P. GRANDJEAT, 1978. *Pharmaceutical Consumption: Trends in Expenditure, Main Measures Taken and Underlying Objectives of Public Intervention in this Field*, Brussels: Commission of the European Community.

ABEL-SMITH, B. and A. MAYNARD, 1978. *The Organisation, Financing, and Cost of Health Care in the European Community*, Brussels, Commission of the European Community.

ACTON, J. P., 1973. *Demand for Health Care Among the Urban Poor, with Special Emphasis on the Role of Time*, Santa Monica, Calif., Rand Corporation.

ALDRICH, J.H. and F.D. NELSON, 1984. *Linear Probability, Logit, and Probit Models*, Beverly Hills and London, Sage Publications.

ANDERSEN, R. and L. BENHAM, 1970. "Factors affecting the relationship between family income and medical care consumption". In H.E. Klarman, (ed.), *Empirical Studies in Health Economics*, Baltimore and London; The Johns Hopkins Press.

ANDERSON, R.R., D. HOUSE and M.B. ORMISTON, 1981. "A Theory of physician behavior with supplier-induced demand", *Southern Economic Journal*, 48.

ARROW, K.J., 1963. "Uncertainty and the welfare economics of medical care", *American Economic Review*, 53.

AUSTER, R., I. LEVESON and D. SARACHEK, 1969. "The reproduction of health, an exploratory study" *Journal of Human Resources*, 6.

BARRETT,S., 1979. "Social and economic aspects of the health services", *Irish Banking Review*, March.

BARRINGTON, R., 1973. *The Shaping of Policy on the Irish Health Services, 1961 to 1970*. Minor thesis, Master of Arts, Department of Ethics and Politics, University College, Dublin.

BERBER, M., 1974. "A survey of the clinical activity in a Dublin general practice", *Irish Medical Journal*, 67.

BEST, G. and R. SMITH, 1980. "The economic evaluation of health policy". Discussion paper 78, Birkbeck College, University of London.

BICE, T.W., R. EICHHORN and P.D. FOX, 1972. "Socio-economic status and use of physician services: a reconsideration", *Medical Care*, 10.

BICE, T.W., *et al.*, 1973. "Economic class and use of physician services", *Medical Care*, 11.

BICE, T.W. and K.L. WHITE, 1969. "Factors related to the use of health services: an international comparative study", *Medical Care*, 7.

BLACK, Sir D., *et al.*, 1980. *Inequalities in Health: Report of a Research Working Group*, London: Department of Health and Social Services.

BONAMOUR, P., 1983. "Le cout de la mort", *Journal d'Economie Medicale*, 1.

CASSELLS, P. 1981. "Health Services". In D. Nevin, (ed), *Trade Union Priorities in Social Policy*, Dublin: Federated Workers Union of Ireland.

289

CLARKSON, J.J., 1982. "Dental Manpower in Ireland", *Journal of the Irish Dental Association*, Jan–Feb.

CULYER, A.J., 1971. "The Nature of the Commodity, 'Health Care' and its Efficient Allocation", *Oxford Economic Papers*, 23.

CULYER, A.J., 1976. *Need and the National Health Service*. London: Martin Robertson.

CULYER, A.J. 1980. "Health services in the mixed economy". In Lord Roll of Ipsden, (ed.), *The Mixed Economy*, Salford: British Association for the Advancement of Science.

CUYLER, A.J. and A. MAYNARD, 1977. See NESC No. 29.

CURRY, J., 1978. "Variation in the assessment of farm income in social administration", *Irish Journal of Agricultural Economics and Rural Sociology*, Vol. 7.

DAVIS, K. and L.B. RUSSELL, 1972. "The substitution of hospital out-patient care for in-patient care", *The Review of Economics and Statistics*, 54.

DEAN, G., H. DOWNING and E. SHELLEY, 1981. "First admissions to psychiatric hospitals in south-east England in 1976 among immigrants from Ireland", *British Medical Journal*, 282 (6 June).

DEPARTMENT OF FINANCE, 1984. *Comprehensive Public Expenditures Programme*, Dublin: Stationery Office.

DEPARTMENT OF HEALTH, 1980, 1981. *Statistical Information Relevant to the Health Services*, Dublin: Stationery Office.

DOWLING, B., 1978. "Alternatives in health care financing". Paper read to Dublin Economics Workshop Conference on Economic Policy, Renvyle, Co. Galway, 6 October.

ENTHOVEN, A.C., 1980. *Health Plan*, Reading, Massachusetts and London: Addison-Wesley Publishing Co.

EUROSTAT, 1977, 1980. *Social Indicators for the European Community*, Luxembourg: Statistical Office of the European Communities.

EVANS, R.G., 1974. "Supplier-induced demand: some empirical evidence and implications". M. Perlman, (ed.), *The Economics of Health and Medical Care*. London: Macmillan.

EVANS, R.G., 1976. Book review (of M. Perlman, (ed.), *The Economics of Health and Medical Care*, London, 1974). *Canadian Journal of Economics*, August.

EVANS, R.G., E.M.A. PARISH and F. SULLY, 1973. "Medical productivity scale effects, and demand generation", *Canadian Journal of Economics*, 6.

FELDSTEIN, M.S., 1967. *Economic Analysis for Health Service Efficiency*, Amsterdam: North Holland Pub. Co.

FELDSTEIN, M.S., 1970. "The rising price of physicians' services", *Review of Economics and Statistics*, 52.

FELDSTEIN, M.S., 1971. "An econometric model of the Medicare system", *Quarterly Journal of Economics*, 85.

FELDSTEIN, M.S., 1971a. "Hospital cost inflation: a study of non-profit price dynamics", *American Economic Review*, 61.

FELDSTEIN, M.S., 1974. "Econometric studies in health economics". In M.D. Intrilligator and D.A. Kendrick, (eds), *Frontiers of Quantitative Economics*, Vol. 2., Amsterdam: North-Holland.

FELDSTEIN, P.J., 1979. *Health Care Economics*, New York: John Wiley & Sons.

FUCHS, V.R., 1974. *Who Shall Live?* New York: Basic Books.

FUCHS, V.R., 1978. "The supply of surgeons and the demand for operations", *Journal of Human Resources*, 13.

FUCHS, V.R. and M. KRAMER, 1972. *Determinants of Expenditures for Physicians' Services in the United States, 1948–1968*. Washington, D.C., Department of Health, Education, and Welfare Publications, National Bureau of Economic Research, Occasional Paper 117.

GENERAL MEDICAL SERVICES (PAYMENTS) BOARD, 1981. *Report, Year Ending 31 December 1980*, Dublin.

GORMLEY, M., 1980. *Guide to the Irish Health Services*, Galway: Emerald Printers.

GOWEN, J.F. 1972. (Recorder, the Research Committee, South of Ireland Faculty, the Royal College of General Practitioners). "A report from general practice in Ireland", *Irish Medical Journal*, 64, (1 April).

GRONAU, R. 1974. "Wage Comparisons — A Selectivity Bias", *Journal of Political Economy*, Nov–Dec.

HECKMAN, J.J., 1976. "The common structure of statistical models of truncation, sample selection, and limited dependent variables and a simple estimator for such models", *Annals of Economic and Social Measurement*, 5.

HELD, P.J. and L.M. MANHEIM, 1980. "The effect of local physician supply on the treatment of hypertension in Quebec", *The Target Income Hypothesis*, Washington, D.C., Department of Health, Education and Welfare, publication HRA-80-27.

HENSEY, B., 1979. *The Health Services of Ireland*, Dublin: Institute of Public Administration.

HIXSON, J.S., *et al.*, 1980. *The Target Income Hypothesis and Releated Issues in Health Manpower Research*, Washington, D.C.: Department of Health, Education and Welfare, publication HRA-80-27.

HSMO, 1974. *Morbidity Statistics from General Practice*, London: Second National Study, 1970–71.

JOINT COMMITTEE ON STATE-SPONSORED BODIES, 1980. *Report: The Voluntary Health Insurance Board*, Dublin: Prl. 8899, (26 March).

KAIM-CAUDLE, P.R., 1969. *Dental Services in Ireland*, Dublin: The Economic and Social Research Institute, Broadsheet Series, No. 1.

KAIM-CAUDLE, P.R., 1970a. *Pharmaceutical Services in Ireland*, Dublin: The Economic and Social Research Institute, Broadsheet Series, No. 3.

KAIM-CAUDLE, P.R., 1970b. *Ophthalmic Services in Ireland*, Dublin: The Economic and Social Research Institute, Broadsheet Series, No. 4.

KELLY, V., 1976. "Hospital stay in Ireland and the United States — a comparison", *Irish Medical Times*.

KIRKE, P., 1981. "Perinatal and infant mortality in Ireland and selected countries: Variations in underlying factors", *Irish Medical Journal*, 74:8.

KIRKE, P. and T. BRANNICK, 1981. "Perinatal and infant mortality in Ireland and selected countries: Present levels and secular trends", *Irish Medical Journal*, 74:8.

LEWIS, H.G., 1974. "Comments on Selectivity Bias in Wage Comparisons", *Journal of Political Economy*, Nov.–Dec.

LUFT, H.S., 1978. "How do Health Maintenance Organisations achieve their 'savings'?", *New England Journal of Medicine*, 298 (June 15).

LUFT, H.S., J.P. BUNKER and A.C. ENTHOVEN, 1979. "Should operations be regionalized? The empirical variation between surgical volume and mortality", *New England Journal of Medicine* 301 (December 20).

MAY, J.J., 1975. "Utilization of health services and the availability of resources", In R. Andersen, J. Kravits and O.W. Anderson, (eds) *Equity in Health Services*, Cambridge, Mass.: Ballinger Publishing Co.

MAYNARD, A., 1976. *Health Care in the European Community*, London: Croom Helm.

MAYNARD, A., 1979. "Pricing, demanders and the supply of health care", *International Journal of Health Services*, 9.

MAYNARD, A., 1980. "Health care evaluation, incentives, and the training of doctors", Mimeographed. University of York.

MAYNARD, A., and A. LUDBROOK, 1980. "Budget allocation in the National Health Service", *Journal of Social Policy*, 9.

McCARTHY, C. and W.J.L. RYAN (eds.), 1982. *Applied Economic Problems*, Dublin: Helicon Ltd./Confederation of Irish Industry.

McCORMICK, J.S. and S.P. ALLWRIGHT, 1977. "A comparison of general practice in Britain and Ireland", *Journal of the Royal College of General Practitioners*, 27 (May).

McPHERSON, K., J.E. WENNBERG, O.B. HOVIND and P. CLIFFORD, 1982. "Small-area variations in the use of common surgical procedures: an international comparison of New England, England and Norway", *New England Journal of Medicine*, Nov. 18.

MEDICO-SOCIAL RESEARCH BOARD, 1977. *Annual Report*, Dublin.

MEDICO-SOCIAL RESEARCH BOARD, 1981. *Activities of Irish Psychiatric Hospitals and Units 1980*, Dublin.

MEDICO-SOCIAL RESEARCH BOARD, 1982. *Annual Report,* Dublin.

MEDICO-SOCIAL RESEARCH BOARD, 1982. *Termination of Pregnancy, England* 1983, *Women from the Republic of Ireland,* Dublin.

MITCHELL, J.B., J. CROMWELL and B. DUTTON, 1981. *Physician Indued Demand for Surgical Operations,* Washington, D.C.: US Dept. of Health and Human Services, Health Care Financing Administration, publication No. 03086.

MICHEL, C., 1978. *The Cost of Hospitalization: Microeconomic Approach to the Problem,* Brussels: Commission of the European Communities.

MONSMA, G.N. Jnr., 1970. "Marginal revenue and the demand for physicians' services", In H.E. Klarman, (ed.), *Empirical Studies in Health Economics.* Baltimore, Johns Hopkins Press.

MULCAHY, R., I. GRAHAM, N. HICKEY and L. DALY, 1980. "Socio-economic factors and coronary heart disease", Paper read to the British Cardiac Society, London (April 1).

MULCAHY, R., V. KELLY, E. TEMPANY and D. TYRRELL, 1975. *Discussion Document* by an Irish Medical Association Working Party on the feasibility of a Compulsory Specialist and Hospital Insurance Scheme as an Alternative to the Present Irish System. Dublin.

MUSGRAVE, R.A., 1959. *The Theory of Public Finance,* McGraw Hill.

NESC NO. 29, 1977. *Some Major Issues in Health Policy,* (Text by A.J. Culyer and A.K. Maynard), Dublin: National Economic and Social Council.

NESC NO. 38, 1978. *Universality and Selectivity: Social Services in Ireland,* Dublin: National Economic and Social Council.

NESC NO. 53, 1983. *Economic and Social Policy 1980–83: Aims and Recommendations,* Dublin: National Economic and Social Council.

NESC NO. 73, 1983. *Health Services: The Implications of Demographic Change,* Dublin: National Economic and Social Council.

NEWHOUSE, J.P., 1970. "A model of physician pricing", *Southern Economic Journal,* 37.

NEWHOUSE, J. and C.E. PHELPS, 1976. "New estimates of price and income elasticities of medical care services". In R. Rossett, (ed.), *The Role of Health Insurance in the Health Services Sector,* New York.

NOWLAN, D., 1977. "A guide to the Health Services: as good as the next", Special Supplement, *Irish Times* (6 July).

O'DONOVAN, D.K., 1976. "The Medical Research Council of Ireland", *Irish Medical Journal,* 69:11 (26 June).

O'HAGAN, J. and M. KELLY, 1984. "Components of growth in current public expenditure on education and health", *The Economic and Social Review,* Vol. 15.

O'HARE, A. and D. WALSH, 1979. *Activities of Irish Psychiatric Hospitals and Units,* 1977, Dublin: Medico-Social Research Board.

OFFICE OF HEALTH ECONOMICS, 1979. *Scarce Resources in Health Care,* London.

PAULY, M., 1980. *Doctors and their Workshops,* Chicago: University of Chicago Press.

PAULY, M. and M.A. SATTERTHWAITE, 1980. "The effect of provider supply on price", In Hixson, *et al.,* above.

PHELPS, C.E. and J.NEWHOUSE, 1975. "Co-insurance, the price of time, and the demand for medical services", *Review of Economics and Statistics,* 57.

PINDYCK, R.S. and D.L. RUBINFELD, 1976. *Econometric Models and Economic Forecasts,* International Student Edition, McGraw Hill.

POLICY AND PLANNING UNIT, 1980. *Inequalities in Health,* London: Department of Health an-d Social Services.

RAPOPORT, J., R.L. ROBERTSON and B. STUART, 1982. *Understanding Health Economics,* Rockville, Maryland: Aspen Systems.

RASKIN, I.A., R.M. COFFEY and P.J. FARLEY, 1980. "Controlling health care costs: an evaluation of strategies", *Evaluation and Program Planning,* 3.

RAWLS, J., 1972. *A Theory of Justice,* New York: Oxford University Press.

REINHARDT, U., 1978. "Comment". In W. Greenberg, (ed.), *Competition in the Health Care Sector: Past, Present and Future.* Washington: Bureau of Economics, Federal Trade Commission.

RUTTEN, F.F.H., 1978. *The Use of Health Care Facilities in the Netherlands – An Econometric Analysis*, Doctoral dissertation, University of Leiden, Netherlands.

SAMUELSON, P., 1954. "The pure theory of public expenditure", *Review of Economics and Statistics*, 36.

SHANNON, W., 1976. "The General practitioner in Ireland — present state and future needs", *Irish Medical Journal*, 69:11.

SHELLEY, E., *et al.*, 1979. "Farmer's lung: a study in North-West Ireland", *Irish Medical Journal*, 72 (30 June).

SLOAN, F.A. and R. FELDMAN, 1978. "Competition among physicians", In W. Greenberg, (ed.), *Competition in the Health Care Sector: Past, Present and Future*. Washington: Bureau of Economics, Federal Trade Commission.

STATIONERY OFFICE, 1966. *The Health Service and their Future Development*, White Paper laid by the Government before each house of the Oireachtas.

STATIONERY OFFICE, 1968. White Paper laid by the Government before each house of the Oireachtas.

STATIONERY OFFICE, 1984. *Building on Reality 1985–1987*, Dublin.

STONE, D.A., 1980. "Health care cost containment in West Germany". Discussion Paper (mineo.) DP-3, University Health Policy Consortium. Boston, MA.

SWEENEY, G.H., 1982. "The market for physicians' services: theoretical implications and an empirical test of the target income hypothesis", *Southern Economic Journal*, 48.

THEIL, H., 1978. *Principles of Econometrics*, Amsterdam: North-Holland Publishing Co.

TUSSING, A.D., 1978. *Irish Educational Expenditures: Past, Present and Future*. Paper 92. Dublin: The Economic and Social Research Institute.

TUSSING, A.D., 1980a. "What kind of health service do we really need?" Annual Conference, Irish Private Hospitals and Nursing Homes Association, Dublin: The Economic and Social Research Institute, Memorandum Series, No. 140.

TUSSING, A.D., 1980b. "Health education in public policy", In *Whither Health Education?*, Dublin: Health Education Bureau.

TUSSING, A.D., 1981a. "Poverty and the development of the health services". In Sister Stanislaus Kennedy, *One Million Poor? The Challenge of Irish Inequality*, Dublin: Turoe Press.

TUSSING, A.D., 1981b. "Supply-demand interdependence in the delivery of medical care". Paper read to Irish Association of University Teachers of Economics, Annual Conference, Wexford, April 5.

TUSSING, A.D., 1982a. "Financing the health services", In C. McCarthy and L. Ryan, (eds.) *Applied Economic Problems*, Helicon Ltd./Confederation of Irish Industry, Dublin: Pre-published in *New Exchange*, Spring, 1982.

TUSSING, A.D., 1982b. "Health, education, and redistribution to the poor", In P. Berwick and and M. Burns, *Conference on Poverty, 1981: Papers of the Kilkenny Conference*, 6th–8th November, 1981. Council for Social Welfare, Blackrock, Co. Dublin.

TUSSING, A.D., 1982c. "Health, health policy and poverty", In L. Joyce and A. Cashin (compilers) *Poverty and Social Policy*, The Irish National Report presented to the Commission of the European Communities, Dublin: Institute of Public Administration.

TUSSING, A.D., 1982d. "Fee for service or capitation?", *Irish Medical Times*, November 12.

TUSSING, A.D., 1983a. "Physician-induced demand for medical care: Irish General Practitioners", *The Economic and Social Review*, April.

TUSSING, A.D., 1983b. "Why the Irish Health Service needs to be radically reformed", Seminar for Labour Party Councillors, Dublin, 14 May.

TUSSING, A.D., 1983c. "The agency role of the physician in Ireland, Britain, and the USA", Paper read to Annual Meeting, American Political Science Association, Chicago, September 1.

TUSSING, A.D., 1984a. "Physician behaviour in Ireland", Paper read to Health Economists' Study Group, Birmingham, January 5.

TUSSING, A.D., 1984b. "Efficiency and control of Irish medical care expenditures," in K.A. Kennedy (ed.), *Public Social Expenditures – Value for Money?*, proceedings of a conference, November 20, Dublin: The Economic and Social Research Institute.

TUSSING, A.D., 1984c. "A study of utilisation of preventative medical care." Paper read to conference, Health Education Bureau, Athlone, November 23.

TUSSING, A.D. and M. A. WOJTOWYCZ (forthcoming). "Physician density and return visits: Physician-induced demand by Irish General Practitioners."

VAN DER GAAG, 1978. *An Econometric Analysis of the Dutch Health Care System*, Doctoral dissertation presented to University of Leiden, Netherlands.

WALSH, J.B., 1980. "Previously unrecognised treatable illness in an Irish elderly population", *Irish Medical Journal*, 73 (February).

WALSH, J.J. and M.C. BAILEY, 1979. "Air pollution — where we stand". In W.K. Downey and G. Ni Uid (Compilers) *Air Pollution - Impacts and Control*, Proceedings of a Seminar, Galway, November 1978, National Board of Science and Technology, Dublin.

WARD, J.B., C. HEALY and G. DEAN, 1978. "Urban and rural mortality in the Republic of Ireland", *Irish Medical Journal*, 17 (28 February)

WHELAN, B.J., 1979. "RANSAM: A random sample design for Ireland", *The Economic and Social Review*.

WILENSKY, G.R. and L.F. ROSSITER, 1980. "The magnitude and determinants of physician initiated visits in the United States", Presented to World Congress on Health Economics, Leiden University, Netherlands (September 8–11).

WILEY, M.M., 1984. *The Irish Dental Care System: Utilisation, Financing, and Policy Options for the Future*, Unpublished doctoral dissertation, The Florence Heller Graduate School, Brandeis University, Waltham, Massachusetts, USA.

WORKING PARTY OF THE GENERAL MEDICAL SERVICE, 1984. *Report*, Dublin: Stationery Office.

WORLD HEALTH ORGANIZATION, 1979. *Sharing Health Care Costs*, Report of an international seminar held at Wolfsberg, Switzerland, March 20–23, 1979. Professor Brian Abel-Smith, general rapporteur. US Department of Health, Education, and Welfare, Publication No. (PHS) 79-3256. Washington.

WORLD HEALTH ORGANIZATION, 1982. *Control of Health Care Costs in Social Security Systems*. Copenhagen: Report on a Workshop.

Appendix I

STATISTICAL TABLES
1980 ESRI NATIONAL HOUSEHOLD SURVEY OF MEDICAL
CARE UTILISATION AND EXPENDITURES

The Appendix Tables report on the findings of the national household survey of health care utilisation and expenditures, conducted by the author and The Economic and Social Research Institute, as described in Chapter 1. A summary version of the survey questionnaire, with means and frequencies, is found in Appendix III. A list of tables follows this introduction and precedes the tables. Some explanation of the tables is required.

Tables A.1 through A.6 report on medical care utilisation; and Tables A.7 through A.9 report on utilisation of health professionals other than doctors or dentists. In these tables, we report, for each type of utilisation, (1) the number of units of utilisation — e.g., the number of general practitioner consultations, or the number of prescription items — per year, per 1,000 persons; (2) the percentage of persons with any utilisation — e.g., the percentage of persons who had any consultations with a general practitioner; and (3) the average number of units of utilisation among those who had any utilisation — e.g., the average number of GP consultations in 1980 among those who had any such consultations at all. Of these three, the first is a product of the second and third, in effect.

Medical care utilisation (A.1–A.6) includes general practitioner consultations, specialist consultations, out-patient visits, dentist visits, prescription items, hospital discharges, hospital nights and prescription items per GP consultation. "Hospital discharges" is a measure of the number of times a person was in hospital as an admitted in-patient. Where a stay in hospital began in one year and ended in another (began in 1979 and ended in 1980, or began in 1980 and ended in 1981), the stay is dated according to the date of discharge rather than the date of admission. "Hospital nights" refers to the annual average number of days in hospital — in effect, the average length of a stay in hospital, multiplied by the average number of stays (discharges). "Prescription items per GP consultation" is based on the general practitioner and prescription data elsewhere in the same tables. These tables also report the numbers of persons in our sample in each of the categories; the total number reported varies slightly from table to table, according to the response rates to the various questions in the sample.

Tables A.7 through A.9 report on utilisation of health professionals other than

Table A.1: *Medical care utilisation by sex and age of patient*

Sex and age	General practitioner consultations			Specialist consultations			Out-patient visits			Dentist visits			Prescription items			Hospital discharges			Hospital nights			Prescription Items per GP consultation			Persons in sample [a]	
	Per year, per 1,000	% with any	Per year, persons with any	Per year, per 1,000	% with any	Per year, persons with any	Per year, per 1,000	% with any	Per year, persons with any	Per year, per 1,000	% with any	Per year, persons with any	Per year, per 1,000	% with any	Per year, persons with any	Per year, per 1,000	% with any	Per year, persons with any	Per year, per 1,000	% with any	Per year, persons with any	Per year, per 1,000	% with any	Per year, persons with any	Number	%
All Males	3,186	61.3	5.20	368	12.3	2.98	438	14.0	3.14	601	23.6	2.54	3,963	53.1	7.46	122	9.7	1.26	1,791	9.7	18.45	.813	52.1	1.56	1,865	49.4
0-14	2,595	63.9	4.06	314	12.8	2.45	251	11.2	2.25	657	25.9	2.54	2,127	53.5	3.98	121	10.1	1.20	1,375	10.1	13.61	.577	53.0	1.09	600	15.9
15-44	2,107	51.1	3.94	360	10.2	3.54	526	13.6	3.86	821	31.2	2.63	1,744	43.4	4.02	74	5.9	1.26	805	5.9	13.64	.546	42.4	1.29	705	18.7
45-64	3,940	63.9	6.16	440	13.7	3.22	408	15.6	2.61	267	13.2	2.02	5,757	55.8	10.32	137	10.8	1.27	2,333	10.8	21.58	.984	54.1	1.82	343	9.1
65+	7,443	83.2	8.94	429	15.9	2.69	720	20.2	3.57	254	9.5	2.68	13,439	79.5	16.90	255	19.3	1.32	5,298	19.3	27.47	2,062	77.8	2.65	216	5.7
All Females	4,036	70.8	5.70	450	14.1	3.18	545	13.5	4.05	821	30.1	2.72	5,116	62.8	8.14	161	11.2	1.43	2,165	11.2	19.33	.962	62.0	1.55	1,090	50.6
0-14	2,407	66.3	3.63	252	11.3	2.22	253	10.5	2.40	826	33.5	2.46	1,948	56.1	3.47	121	8.0	1.51	2,037	8.0	25.48	.569	55.3	1.03	601	15.9
15-44	3,362	66.2	5.08	586	17.3	3.38	593	15.2	3.91	1,158	40.3	2.84	3,678	57.2	6.43	215	15.1	1.42	2,069	15.1	13.69	.795	56.4	1.41	707	18.7
45-64	5,331	73.4	7.26	441	12.4	3.56	941	16.5	5.69	640	19.3	3.23	7,854	67.7	11.59	139	11.3	1.23	2,542	11.3	22.41	1,445	67.4	2.14	337	8.9
65+	7,892	89.8	8.79	552	14.3	3.86	579	11.7	4.96	139	7.1	1.96	12,675	87.0	14.57	135	8.1	1.66	2,232	7.9	28.40	1,686	85.3	1.98	264	7.0
All Persons	3,616	66.1	5.47	410	13.3	3.09	492	13.7	3.59	712	26.9	2.64	4,546	58.0	7.83	142	10.5	1.35	1,980	10.5	18.93	.888	57.1	1.56	3,775	100.0

[a] Detail may not add to total because of rounding.

Table A.2: *Medical care utilisation by health services entitlement category and VHI Cover*

Entitlement and VHI Cover	General practitioner consultations			Specialist consultations			Out-patient visits			Dentist visits			Prescription items			Hospital discharges			Hospital nights			Prescription Items per GP consultation			Persons in sample[a]	
	Per year, per 1,000	% with any	Per year, persons with any	Per year, per 1,000	% with any	Per year, persons with any	Per year, per 1,000	% with any	Per year, persons with any	Per year, per 1,000	% with any	Per year, persons with any	Per year, per 1,000	% with any	Per year, persons with any	Per year, per 1,000	% with any	Per year, persons with any	Per year, per 1,000	% with any	Per year, persons with any	All	% with any	Non-zero only	Number	%
All VHI	2,270	64.2	3.54	473	15.8	3.00	367	13.0	1.00	1,046	41.8	2.51	3,206	54.7	5.86	128	10.2	1.25	1,151	10.2	11.28	.929	53.1	1.75	956	25.5
All non-VHI	4,084	66.8	6.11	388	12.4	3.13	536	14.0	1.00	596	21.8	2.73	5,014	59.2	8.47	146	10.6	1.38	2,266	10.5	21.48	.875	58.5	1.50	2,794	74.5
All I	6,082	77.3	7.87	426	12.6	3.37	644	14.6	4.42	593	18.2	3.25	8,087	72.4	11.17	171	11.9	1.44	3,347	11.8	28.37	1.185	72.1	1.64	1,227	32.7
VHI	3,725	78.6	4.74	329	14.1	2.33	417	11.2	3.74	813	30.8	2.64	4,000	74.3	5.39	100	9.9	1.00	748	9.9	7.52	.775	71.9	1.08	57	1.5
non-VHI	6,197	77.2	8.02	430	12.6	3.42	655	14.7	4.44	583	17.6	3.31	8,286	72.3	11.46	174	12.0	1.46	3,474	11.9	29.22	1.205	72.2	1.67	1,170	31.2
All II	2,540	60.4	4.21	394	12.3	3.19	478	13.4	3.56	637	25.9	2.46	2,652	50.4	5.26	136	9.9	1.37	1,449	9.9	14.58	.693	49.3	1.41	1,832	48.9
VHI	2,373	64.6	3.67	568	15.3	3.71	486	12.6	3.87	840	33.0	2.55	2,760	53.3	5.18	165	11.4	1.45	1,381	11.4	12.13	.936	51.7	1.81	364	9.7
non-VHI	2,582	59.4	4.35	351	11.6	3.02	476	13.7	3.48	587	24.2	2.43	2,625	49.7	5.28	129	9.6	1.35	1,466	9.6	15.30	.633	48.7	1.30	1,468	39.1
All III	2,152	61.7	3.49	430	16.7	2.57	276	13.1	2.10	1,078	44.5	2.42	3,386	53.0	6.39	108	9.7	1.11	1,018	9.7	10.49	.891	51.2	1.74	692	18.5
VHI	2,028	61.9	3.27	431	16.4	2.62	285	13.5	2.12	1,197	48.8	2.45	3,441	53.1	6.48	108	9.6	1.12	1,064	9.6	11.11	.947	51.5	1.84	536	14.3
non-VHI	2,578	60.8	4.24	428	17.9	2.40	243	11.9	2.05	670	29.4	2.28	3,199	52.5	6.09	109	10.1	1.07	861	10.1	8.49	.700	50.4	1.39	156	4.2
All Persons	3,627	66.1	5.48	411	13.3	3.10	495	13.7	3.60	704	26.9	2.63	4,565	58.0	7.86	142	10.5	1.35	1,990	10.5	18.95	.891	57.1	1.56	3,750	100.0

[a]Detail may not add to total because of rounding.

Table A.3: Medical care utilisation by Health Board Area of residence

Health Board Area	General practitioner consultations			Specialist consultations			Out-patient visits			Dentist visits			Prescription items			Hospital discharges			Hospital nights			Prescription items per GP consultation			Persons in sample[a]	
	Per year, per 1,000	% with any	Per year, persons with any	Per year, per 1,000	% with any	Per year, persons with any	Per year, per 1,000	% with any	Per year, persons with any	Per year, per 1,000	% with any	Per year, persons with any	Per year, per 1,000	% with any	Per year, persons with any	Per year, per 1,000	% with any	Per year, persons with any	Per year, per 1,000	% with any	Per year, persons with any	All persons	% with any	Persons with any	Number	%
Eastern	3,559	68.1	5.23	539	16.1	3.36	640	18.8	3.41	895	35.0	2.56	4,928	59.9	8.22	125	10.2	1.23	1,398	10.1	13.86	1.000	58.3	1.71	1,198	31.7
Midland	3,780	57.3	6.60	188	8.3	2.25	200	9.1	2.19	273	18.5	1.36	5,935	52.4	11.32	114	10.5	1.09	2,094	10.5	19.99	.830	52.4	1.58	174	4.6
Mid-Western	3,853	66.5	5.80	242	12.1	2.00	273	11.6	2.35	620	14.5	4.29	3,833	59.3	6.46	133	10.1	1.32	1,395	10.1	13.84	.694	58.2	1.19	303	8.0
North-Eastern	3,403	66.3	5.13	376	14.6	2.58	608	16.1	3.79	861	29.8	2.89	4,956	56.7	8.73	177	13.0	1.37	3,058	13.0	23.56	1.021	56.3	1.81	389	10.3
North-Western	3,956	66.8	5.92	205	10.1	2.02	289	9.2	3.14	295	13.7	2.15	5,368	58.1	9.24	133	10.2	1.30	1,355	10.2	13.28	.992	58.1	1.71	221	5.9
South-Eastern	3,831	68.3	5.61	315	13.8	2.28	346	10.4	3.31	741	25.2	2.94	3,399	56.6	6.00	145	11.9	1.23	1,987	11.9	16.75	.718	56.1	1.28	421	11.2
Southern	3,409	63.4	5.38	576	12.5	4.60	609	12.4	4.91	759	29.1	2.61	4,545	56.7	8.02	169	9.9	1.71	2,733	9.9	27.65	.924	55.4	1.67	607	16.1
Western	3,640	65.0	5.60	262	9.4	2.78	344	8.6	3.99	457	20.0	2.28	3,810	58.4	6.52	135	9.2	1.47	2,226	9.2	24.30	.694	58.3	1.19	462	12.2
Ireland	3,616	66.1	5.47	410	13.3	3.09	492	13.7	3.59	712	26.9	2.64	4,546	58.0	7.83	142	10.5	1.35	1,980	10.5	18.93	.888	57.1	1.56	3,775	100.0

[a]Detail may not add to total because of rounding.

Table A.4: *Medical care utilisation by Employment Status of head of household*

Employment status	General practitioner consultations			Specialist consultations			Out-patient visits			Dentist visits			Prescription items			Hospital discharges			Hospital nights			Prescription items per GP consultation			Persons in sample[a]	
	Per year, per 1,000	% with any	Per year, persons with any	Per year, per 1,000	% with any	Per year, persons with any	Per year, per 1,000	% with any	Per year, persons with any	Per year, per 1,000	% with any	Per year, persons with any	Per year, per 1,000	% with any	Per year, persons with any	Per year, per 1,000	% with any	Per year, persons with any	Per year, per 1,000	% with any	Per year, persons with any	All persons	% with any	Persons with any	Number	%
Employed (including self-employed)	2,825	63.6	4.44	396	13.7	2.89	411	13.6	3.03	777	30.9	2.51	3,155	54.3	5.82	137	10.1	1.36	1,655	10.1	16.44	0.747	53.4	1.40	2,723	72.2
Unemployed, seeking work	3,271	62.7	5.22	216	11.6	1.86	504	11.5	4.39	873	16.6	5.27	2,684	56.5	4.75	119	8.8	1.35	1,852	8.8	20.99	0.662	55.5	1.19	240	6.4
Retired	7,010	78.2	8.96	725	15.0	4.83	182	18.3	6.45	400	14.2	2.81	10,662	73.2	14.57	183	14.0	1.31	3,754	14.0	26.90	1.471	72.5	2.03	388	10.3
Household duties, full-time	5,392	74.1	7.28	267	9.7	2.76	411	11.8	3.48	342	14.7	2.33	8,983	69.9	12.85	139	9.9	1.40	2,772	9.9	27.97	1.367	68.5	2.00	236	6.3
Other[b]	3,194	78.4	4.11	80	5.7	1.22	76	5.8	1.16	924	45.5	2.07	2,800	66.0	4.21	36	3.3	1.02	492	3.3	13.44	1.110	51.4	1.53	187	5.0
All Persons	3,616	66.1	5.47	410	13.3	3.09	492	13.7	3.59	712	26.9	2.64	4,546	58.0	7.83	142	10.5	1.35	1,980	10.5	18.93	0.888	57.1	1.55	3,774	100.0

Notes: [a] Detail may not add to total because of rounding. [b] Includes 14 household heads not working because of long-term sickness or disablement.

Table A.5: *Medical care utilisation by occupation of head of household*

Occupation	General practitioner consultations			Specialist consultations			Out-patient visits			Dentist visits			Prescription items			Hospital discharges			Hospital nights			Prescription items per GP consultation			Persons in sample[a]	
	Per year, per 1,000	% with any	Per year, persons with any	Per year, per 1,000	% with any	Per year, persons with any	Per year, per 1,000	% with any	Per year, persons with any	Per year, per 1,000	% with any	Per year, persons with any	Per year, per 1,000	% with any	Per year, persons with any	Per year, per 1,000	% with any	Per year, persons with any	Per year, per 1,000	% with any	Per year, persons with any	All persons	% with any	Persons with any	Number	%
Professional, manager, or employer	2,322	64.4	3.61	427	15.9	2.68	315	14.0	2.25	1,126	44.2	2.55	3,712	52.9	7.01	130	10.7	1.22	1,229	10.5	11.66	1.022	51.4	1.99	610	16.2
Salaried employee or intermediate non-manual worker	3,232	64.4	5.02	581	16.3	3.56	497	13.5	3.67	888	38.7	2.30	4,001	54.8	7.31	195	13.0	1.50	3,599	13.0	27.69	0.893	53.9	1.66	405	10.8
Other non-manual worker	3,702	68.8	5.38	563	12.1	4.66	556	16.1	3.45	676	26.3	2.57	4,568	57.5	7.94	123	10.0	1.23	1,249	10.0	12.50	0.901	56.7	1.59	381	10.1
Skilled manual worker	4,146	67.2	6.17	415	16.1	2.57	676	16.4	4.12	771	24.7	3.12	4,776	61.1	7.82	162	11.0	1.47	1,840	11.0	16.73	0.764	60.1	1.27	569	15.1
Semi-skilled or unskilled manual worker	4,900	72.1	6.80	379	12.2	3.09	782	16.3	4.78	519	17.8	2.92	6,205	66.3	9.35	149	11.1	1.34	2,852	11.1	25.68	1.084	65.4	1.66	826	21.9
Farmer, agricultural worker, or fisherman	3,138	60.8	5.16	294	10.1	2.92	229	9.0	2.55	524	20.5	2.55	3,746	53.8	6.97	116	8.8	1.32	1,424	8.8	16.22	0.701	53.3	1.32	975	25.9
All persons	3,612	66.0	5.47	411	13.3	3.09	493	13.7	3.59	712	26.9	2.65	4,546	58.0	7.84	142	10.5	1.35	1,984	10.5	18.93	0.887	57.1	1.56	3,767	100.0

[a] Detail may not add to total because of rounding.

Table A.6: Medical care utilisation by age head of household completed full-time education

Age Completed Education	General practitioner consultants			Specialist consultants			Out-patient visits			Dentist visits			Prescription items			Hospital discharges			Hospital nights			Prescription items per GP consultation			Persons in sample[a]	
	Per year, per 1,000	% with any	Per year, persons with any	Per year, per 1,000	% with any	Per year, persons with any	Per year, per 1,000	% with any	Per year, persons with any	Per year, per 1,000	% with any	Per year, persons with any	Per year, per 1,000	% with any	Per year, persons with any	Per year, per 1,000	% with any	Per year, persons with any	Per year, per 1,000	% with any	Per year, persons with any	All persons	% with any	Persons with any	Number	%
Under 14	5,473	72.4	7.56	370	14.5	2.55	1,216	15.4	7.92	936	17.4	5.38	6,563	65.9	9.95	156	11.7	1.34	3,567	11.7	30.58	0.865	64.1	1.35	222	5.9
14	3,962	65.0	6.10	396	10.0	3.94	491	13.8	3.56	566	21.1	2.68	5,058	56.9	8.89	131	9.6	1.36	2,062	9.6	21.41	0.885	56.3	1.57	1,476	39.4
15	3,641	64.1	5.68	288	12.3	2.33	349	13.2	2.64	492	21.3	2.31	4,757	55.5	8.58	141	11.1	1.27	1,246	11.1	11.23	0.894	55.1	1.62	408	10.9
16	3,266	66.2	4.93	391	13.1	2.98	390	13.3	2.92	663	25.5	2.60	3,765	60.3	6.24	163	10.3	1.58	2,653	10.2	26.05	0.827	58.5	1.41	669	17.8
17	3,288	66.9	4.91	494	19.7	2.51	382	13.7	2.79	903	33.3	2.71	2,813	55.6	5.06	144	11.3	1.27	1,229	11.3	10.87	0.648	55.2	1.17	280	7.5
18	2,756	64.3	4.28	481	17.0	2.83	566	12.9	4.39	955	39.9	2.40	5,078	56.2	9.04	115	9.8	1.17	1,283	9.8	13.03	1.088	55.6	1.96	355	9.5
19	4,729	74.2	6.37	700	25.5	2.75	291	9.1	3.20	917	33.0	2.77	5,342	60.3	8.87	156	13.1	1.19	1,150	13.1	8.78	0.979	60.3	1.62	73	1.9
Over 19	2,234	69.6	3.21	518	17.3	3.00	454	15.6	2.91	1,266	55.6	2.28	2,775	60.5	4.59	165	13.1	1.25	1,235	13.1	9.40	1.072	58.0	1.85	264	7.0
All Persons	3,621	66.1	5.47	412	13.3	3.10	493	13.7	3.60	715	27.0	2.65	4,562	58.0	7.86	142	10.5	1.35	1,956	10.5	18.68	0.891	57.1	1.56	3,748	100.0

[a]Detail may not add to total because of rounding.

doctors or dentists, namely opticians, audiometrists, midwives, nurses, social workers, chiropodists, psychologists, physio- or occupational therapists, and others.

Tables A.10 through A.15 report on preventative care utilisation, i.e., most recent general practitioner consultation, and whether one had the following in 1980: a physical examination when one was not ill or pregnant and did not think or suspect he or she was; an immunisation for any disease; a blood pressure test; and/or a cervical cancer smear ("pap") test (for adult women).

Tables A.16 through A.27 report on private (i.e., household) medical care expenditures, by major type. Figures are for the year 1980; that is, they relate to annual outlays, rather than unit charges. Tables A.16 through A.21 report on the averages of these per household, whilst Tables A.22 through A.27 report on the averages per person. Expenditures made by employers on behalf of their employees are not included. The reported amounts are gross, in the sense that VHI or, in the case of prescription medicines, Health Board reimbursements are not deducted.

Note that tables are organised by characteristics of head of household, and expenditures are for all persons in the household (in the case of average per household), or for all persons in the household divided by number of persons in the household (in the case of average per person). Households headed, for example, by persons with Category I eligibility (Medical Cards) may include persons with other categories of eligibility.

Tables A.28 through A.35 report on referral behaviour by doctors. Tables A.28 and A.29 report on the further care or treatment ordered, prescribed, or suggested, per most recent visit, respectively, to general practitioner or specialist. The figures in the tables are percentages, and they show, *inter alia*, that 23.5 per cent of all most recent visits to general practitioners, and 39.0 per cent of all most recent visits to specialists, resulted in a return visit being arranged. Tables A.30 through A.35 report on whose idea the most recent utilisation was, in the case of general practitioner or specialist consultations, out-patient hospital visits, dentist visits, and hospital admissions, and who prescribed pharmaceutical medicines. Respondents were asked (with slight variations in the form of the question, according to the type of utilisation): "About the most recent time each member was seen by a general practitioner in 1980: Whose idea was it, or who first suggested that they see the doctor? Was it — a return visit; a household member's idea; the general practitioner's idea; another doctor's idea; other; or don't know, or no visit in 1980?"

Tables A.36 and A.37 are concerned with the characteristics of persons in the three entitlement categories in the public health services, and with persons covered or not covered by Voluntary Health Insurance (VHI). Table A.36 reports on entitlement and VHI cover by age and sex, and Table A.37 reports on these by Health Board area of residence. Figures reported are, in all cases, percentages.

Table A.38 reports on average annual numbers of general practitioner consultations, by the usual fee charged by the general practitioner for a consultation in the GP's office or surgery, by Health Board area.

The remaining tables, A.39 through A.42, report on various hospital statistics from the survey. Tables A.39 and A.40 report on the numbers of beds in patients' hospital rooms, by patients' ages and sexes, and by category of health services entitlement and VHI cover. A room with only one bed is usually referred to as "private" accommodation; two to four as "semi-private"; and five or more as "public ward". Table A.41 reports on the Health Board area locations of hospitals, together with Health Board area places of residence of patients. Entries in the main diagonal show those patients who stayed in hospitals within their own Health Board areas. Other entries reflect instances in which patients living in one Health Board area travelled to other Health Board areas for in-patient hospital services. For example, in our sample of 394 hospital admissions in 1980, 19 persons who lived in the North-Eastern Health Board area stayed in (were discharged from) hospitals in the Eastern Health Board area, as compared with 30 who lived in and stayed in hospitals in the North-Eastern Health Board area. Of 394 hospital stays (discharges), 44, or 11 per cent, involved persons from one Health Board area using in-patient services in another; of the 44, 35 stayed in hospitals in the Eastern Health Board area.

Table A.42 reports, for each person discharged from hospital in 1980, how long he or she had to wait to be admitted, by category of entitlement and VHI cover. Only 7.8 per cent had to wait more than a month, and only 1.6 per cent more than a year. Health services entitlement and VHI cover do not appear to matter.

Table A.7: *Utilisation of health professionals other than doctors or dentists, by type of health professional, 1980*

Type of health professional	Per year, per 1,000	% with any	Per year, persons with any
Optician (vision examination)	118	10.0	1.19
Audiometrist (hearing examination)	21	1.6	1.30
Midwife[a]	41	1.8	2.31
Nurse	350	2.7	13.09
Social worker	10	0.4	2.05
Chiropodist	72	2.4	2.97
Psychologist	13	0.4	2.93
Physio- or occupational therapist	35	0.7	4.90
Other	8	0.2	3.50
Total, all health professionals	633	16.1	3.97

[a]Rates figured on women aged 18–44 rather than whole population.

Table A.8: *Utilisation of health professionals other than doctors or dentists, 1980, by patients' sex and age, VHI Cover and Category of Health Services Entitlement and Health Board area of residence*[a]

Patient characteristic	Per year, per 1,000	% with any	Per year, persons with any
Sex and Age			
All Males	504	12.6	4.01
0–14	221	13.0	1.71
15–44	148	7.1	2.10
45–64	326	15.3	2.13
65+	2,727	25.1	10.85
All Females	759	19.2	3.94
0–14	278	12.2	2.28
15–44	523	17.6	2.98
45–64	959	26.6	3.60
65+	2,230	30.4	7.33
VHI Cover and Entitlement Category (I, II, or III)			
All VHI	374	18.3	2.04
All non-VHI	723	15.2	4.76
All Category I	1,225	21.0	5.83
VHI*	377	21.6	1.74
non-VHI	1,267	21.0	6.04
All Category II	323	12.6	2.64
VHI	321	19.5	1.65
non-VHI	335	10.9	3.08
All Category III	382	16.2	2.35
VHI	418	17.5	2.39
non-VHI	259	11.8	2.19
Health Board Area			
Eastern	586	16.9	3.46
Midland	762	16.9	4.51
Mid-Western	713	21.6	3.30
North-Eastern	1,043	19.6	5.32
North-Western	1,978	14.4	13.73
South-Eastern	356	18.1	1.97
Southern	335	11.0	3.04
Western	309	11.4	2.71
All Persons	633	16.1	3.97

[a]For list of types of health professionals, see Table A.7.
*Absolute levels too low to establish meaningful rates.

Table A.9: *Utilisation of health professionals other than doctors or dentists, by employment status, occupation and age completed full-time education of head of household*[a]

Head of household characteristic	per year, per 1,000	% with any	Per year, persons with any
Employment status			
Employed (including self-employed)	436	14.2	3.07
Unemployed, seeking work	448	13.6	3.30
Retired	1,999	26.0	7.70
Household duties, full-time	674	22.4	3.01
Other	190	13.4	1.36
Occupation			
Professional, manager or employer	618	17.5	3.54
Salaried employee or intermediate non-manual worker	584	17.0	3.43
Other non-manual worker	616	14.4	4.28
Skilled manual worker	483	16.7	2.89
Semi-skilled or unskilled manual worker	890	16.4	5.43
Farmer, agricultural worker, or fisher	543	14.3	3.78
Age Completed Full-Time Education			
Under 14	610	15.5	3.94
14	823	15.6	5.26
15	367	18.8	1.95
16	614	14.6	4.20
17	284	14.1	2.01
18	777	15.3	5.07
19	252	11.2	2.25
Over 19	380	21.8	1.75
All persons	633	16.1	3.97

[a]For a list of types of health professionals, see Table A.7.

Table A.10: *Preventative care utilisation by sex and age of patient, 1980*

| Sex and Age | Most recent general practitioner consultation (% distribution) | | | | | Per cent with following utilisation in 1980 | | | |
	Within last 4 weeks	Within last 12 months	Within last 2 years	Within last 5 years	More than 5 years or never	Physical exam. when not ill	Immunisation (any disease)	Blood pressure test	Pap smear test[a]
All Males	22.2	40.0	18.3	9.8	9.7	8.5	6.7	22.1	—
0–14	20.7	44.4	20.4	7.4	7.1	2.0	15.5	1.9	—
15–44	14.5	37.6	20.0	14.2	13.7	9.6	2.5	15.6	—
45–64	26.5	38.4	16.6	9.1	9.4	12.2	2.2	46.6	—
65+	44.8	38.5	9.3	3.7	3.8	17.2	3.2	60.3	—
All Females	28.0	43.4	16.0	6.9	5.7	7.7	6.8	31.8	9.8
0–14	20.5	46.4	20.3	7.4	5.4	2.6	17.3	1.2	—
15–44	22.1	44.8	18.0	8.3	6.8	6.5	1.8	32.2	14.8
44–64	34.2	39.6	13.3	5.4	7.5	10.2	2.1	54.4	6.6
65+	53.0	37.4	4.3	4.0	1.4	19.1	2.0	71.4	2.5
All Persons	25.3	41.7	17.0	8.4	7.6	8.1	6.7	27.1	9.8

[a]Rates based on women aged 18 and over.

Table A.11: *Preventative care utilisation by VHI cover and health services entitlement, 1980*

VHI Cover and Category of Entitlement (I, II, or III)	Most recent general practitioner consultation (% distribution)					Per cent with following utilisation in 1980			
	Within last 4 weeks	*Within last 12 months*	*Within last 2 years*	*Within last 5 years*	*More than 5 years or never*	*Physical exam. when not ill*	*Immunisation (any disease)*	*Blood pressure test*	*Pap smear test[a]*
All VHI	21.6	43.8	18.4	7.9	8.4	7.7	7.7	24.7	15.2
All Non-VHI	26.5	41.0	16.6	8.5	7.4	8.2	6.4	27.9	8.0
All Category I	38.0	40.0	10.5	6.8	4.8	11.1	6.2	38.8	5.7
VHI*	30.7	51.7	10.9	1.3	5.4	6.4	4.0	27.7	7.1
non-VHI	38.3	39.4	10.5	7.1	4.7	11.4	6.4	39.4	5.6
All Category II	18.5	42.4	20.3	9.3	9.5	6.5	6.6	21.7	10.2
VHI	21.0	44.8	18.5	7.2	8.5	9.5	6.6	29.4	9.5
non-VHI	17.9	41.8	20.7	9.8	9.8	5.7	6.6	19.8	10.4
All Category III	20.3	42.7	20.5	8.9	7.5	7.0	7.9	20.4	19.3
VHI	20.9	42.1	19.2	9.1	8.7	6.8	9.0	21.1	22.6
non-VHI	18.4	44.6	24.8	8.5	3.7	7.9	4.2	18.0	9.4
All Persons	25.3	41.7	17.0	8.4	7.6	8.1	6.7	27.1	9.8

*Numbers too small to establish meaningful rates. [a]Rates based on women aged 18 and over.

Table A.12: *Preventative care utilisation by Health Board area, 1980*

Health Board area	Most recent general practitioner consultation (% distribution)					Per cent with following utilisation in 1980			
	Within last 4 weeks	Within last 12 months	Within last 2 years	Within last 5 years	More than 5 years or never	Physical exam. when not ill	Immunisation (any disease)	Blood pressure test	Pap smear test[a]
Eastern	25.2	43.7	19.6	6.7	4.9	7.1	8.4	26.0	14.5
Midland	33.1	24.2	27.8	7.8	7.0	8.7	2.0	38.1	21.1
Mid-Western	22.4	45.3	14.9	7.3	10.1	10.0	8.5	28.4	4.0
North-Eastern	29.3	37.5	12.4	6.1	14.7	3.9	8.5	24.5	9.4
North-Western	21.1	46.0	9.9	12.6	10.4	1.7	5.6	25.9	10.6
South-Eastern	28.8	40.3	14.0	9.8	7.1	4.9	9.3	24.9	8.3
Southern	22.7	41.5	16.4	8.4	10.9	7.4	3.5	26.5	7.3
Western	22.4	43.8	19.2	11.9	2.7	19.7	4.2	29.6	1.0
Ireland	25.2	41.7	17.1	8.3	7.7	8.1	6.7	27.0	9.8

[a]Rates based on women aged 18 and over.

Table A.13: *Preventative care utilisation by employment status of head of household, 1980*

Employment status	Most recent general practitioner consultation (% distribution)					Per cent with following utilisation in 1980			
	Within last 4 weeks	Within last 12 months	Within last 2 years	Within last 5 years	More than 5 years or never	Physical exam. when not ill	Immunisation (any disease)	Blood pressure test	Pap smear test[a]
Employed (including self-employed)	21.3	43.2	18.8	8.8	7.9	6.5	7.2	22.0	11.9
Unemployed, seeking work	22.6	40.4	15.8	11.5	9.7	3.7	16.8	17.4	23.8
Retired	41.5	37.1	7.6	5.5	8.3	17.8	1.6	53.4	4.0
Household duties, full-time	34.7	39.9	13.3	6.7	5.4	11.5	2.0	40.8	3.1
Other[b]	10.4	68.1	16.0	5.3	0.3	15.5	7.6	20.1	5.7
All persons	25.2	41.7	17.1	8.3	7.7	8.1	6.7	27.0	9.8

[a]Rates based on women aged 18 and over. [b]Includes 14 household heads not working because of long-term sickness or disablement.

Table A.14: *Preventative care utilisation by occupation of head of household, 1980*

Occupation	Most recent general practitioner consultation (% distribution)					Per cent with following utilisation in 1980			
	Within last 4 weeks	Within last 12 months	Within last 2 years	Within last 5 years	More than 5 years or never	Physical exam. when not ill	Immunisa- tion (any disease)	Blood pressure test	Pap smear test[a]
Professional, manager, or employer	22.6	42.8	18.0	8.6	8.1	7.6	9.3	24.6	14.3
Salaried employee or intermediate non-manual worker	24.6	41.4	18.2	7.1	8.8	6.8	5.8	26.6	13.7
Other non-manual worker	22.4	46.9	15.2	7.9	7.6	6.7	9.2	24.8	14.0
Skilled manual worker	28.3	39.9	17.4	9.3	5.1	9.5	5.8	25.5	8.4
Semi-skilled or imski unskilled manual worker	32.0	40.5	14.9	6.5	6.1	9.8	6.3	30.7	7.8
Farmer, agricultural worker, or fisher	20.5	41.0	18.7	9.9	9.9	6.9	5.5	27.1	6.1
All persons	25.2	41.6	17.1	8.3	7.7	8.0	6.7	27.0	9.8

[a]Rates based on women aged 18 and over.

Table A.15: *Preventative care utilisation by age head of household completed full-time education, 1980*

Age completed education	Most recent general practitioner consultation (% distribution)					Per cent with following utilisation in 1980			
	Within last 4 weeks	Within last 12 months	Within last 2 years	Within last 5 years	More than 5 years or never	Physical exam. when not ill	Immunisation (any disease)	Blood pressure test	Pap smear test[a]
Under 14	33.9	39.2	16.6	5.0	5.3	13.9	5.6	29.3	1.7
14	25.4	40.2	17.8	9.4	7.3	8.4	5.9	27.4	7.4
15	26.0	38.7	17.3	9.5	8.5	6.1	7.4	28.4	9.6
16	25.8	41.0	18.1	7.0	8.1	5.8	6.7	24.6	9.6
17	19.0	48.7	16.6	7.4	8.3	7.6	10.8	24.5	11.5
18	21.9	42.5	15.6	10.0	10.0	11.1	6.8	31.0	13.6
19	30.1	51.0	13.9	1.9	3.1	2.1	3.0	20.2	25.6
Over 19	23.6	48.0	14.9	6.5	6.4	8.6	8.8	26.8	19.5
All Persons	25.2	41.7	17.1	8.3	7.7	8.1	6.8	27.0	9.7

[a]Rates based on women aged 18 and over.

Table A.16: *Private medical expenditures, by type, 1980: average per household, by sex and age of head of household (£)*

Sex and age of household head	GP fees	Specialist fees	Out-patient hospital charges	Dentists' fees and charges	Prescription medicines	Non-prescription charges	In-patient hospital charges including specialist	Other health professionals	Cost of eyeglasses	Other medical expenditures	Total
All Males	24.57	9.14	1.12	19.18	36.44	12.28	24.24	3.62	8.11	0.54	139.25
Under 45	36.46	15.62	1.21	19.71	42.54	16.46	27.18	4.00	6.85	0.23	170.24
45–64	21.41	5.88	1.15	25.50	38.11	10.99	29.17	3.95	11.03	0.31	147.50
65+	7.31	2.38	0.90	7.35	21.95	6.53	10.19	2.35	5.51	1.54	66.01
All Females	7.91	2.23	0.82	7.39	12.10	4.98	5.19	1.67	3.44	0.36	46.09
Under 45	4.03	7.08	—	17.54	4.43	3.02	—	2.11	1.99	—	40.19
45–64	12.41	1.67	2.31	14.21	20.15	6.99	13.35	2.63	5.24	0.60	79.57
65+	6.27	1.63	0.19	1.99	9.29	4.29	1.88	1.09	2.77	0.30	29.69
All households	20.69	7.53	1.05	16.43	30.77	10.58	19.80	3.17	7.02	0.50	117.54

Table A.17: *Private medical expenditures, by type, 1980: average per household, by VHI cover and category of health services entitlement of head of household (£)*

VHI cover and entitlement category (I, II, or III) of household head	GP fees	Specialist fees	Out-patient hospital charges	Dentists' fees and charges	Prescription medicines	Non-prescription charges	In-patient hospital charges including specialist	Other health professionals	Cost of eyeglasses	Other medical expenditures	Total
All VHI	28.82	19.00	2.92	38.06	45.98	13.02	53.70	7.29	13.31	1.18	223.28
All non-VHI	18.04	3.79	0.44	9.38	25.80	9.79	8.74	1.82	4.97	0.28	83.04
All Category I	4.58	1.23	0.16	2.77	5.72	5.80	1.60	1.33	3.59	0.23	27.01
VHI*	2.70	5.65	—	10.14	3.10	4.32	—	3.45	4.48	—	33.84
non-VHI	4.64	1.09	0.17	2.54	5.81	5.85	1.65	1.26	3.56	0.23	26.79
All Category II	28.96	5.94	0.80	16.30	43.74	12.96	17.79	3.38	6.84	0.31	137.04
VHI	22.36	9.98	1.20	18.79	41.57	9.72	28.56	6.52	11.29	0.14	150.14
non-VHI	31.08	4.65	0.67	15.51	44.44	14.00	14.34	2.37	5.42	0.36	132.84
All Category III	36.60	27.49	3.95	49.23	55.39	15.66	70.44	7.17	16.13	1.73	283.79
VHI	36.84	28.50	4.77	57.16	54.07	16.79	82.05	8.46	16.17	2.23	307.05
non-VHI	35.75	24.01	1.15	21.92	59.95	11.80	30.51	2.70	15.97	—	203.76
All households	20.69	7.53	1.05	16.43	30.77	10.58	19.80	3.17	7.02	0.50	117.54

Note: VHI cover and/or category of entitlement of household head may not pertain to all household members.
*Absolute levels too low to establish meaningful averages.

Table A.18: *Private medical expenditures, by type, 1980: average per household, by Health Board area (£)*

Health Board area	GP fees	Specialist fees	Out-patient hospital charges	Dentists' fees and charges	Prescription medicines	Non-prescription charges	In-patient hospital charges including specialist	Other health professionals	Cost of eyeglasses	Other medical expenditures	Total
Eastern	29.11	7.62	1.70	24.00	41.97	14.79	29.37	4.08	8.55	0.20	161.39
Midland	11.06	3.32	0.68	3.85	21.88	5.34	10.39	2.62	6.38	0.19	65.70
Mid-Western	15.66	7.60	0.21	4.76	20.91	6.63	8.67	1.90	5.29	0.38	72.00
North-Eastern	20.13	6.87	1.00	20.02	31.96	7.26	16.24	5.86	7.41	0.03	116.79
North-Western	12.95	6.76	1.47	4.95	21.59	10.56	7.02	1.66	3.50	0.15	70.61
South-Eastern	14.94	2.96	0.42	13.93	19.81	10.26	11.61	2.90	8.68	2.73	88.25
Southern	21.94	13.39	0.82	16.24	36.55	7.96	14.20	2.41	6.07	0.51	120.09
Western	14.38	6.70	0.73	16.02	17.96	11.04	32.04	1.58	5.72	—	106.16
Ireland	20.69	7.53	1.05	16.43	30.77	10.58	19.80	3.17	7.02	0.50	117.54

Table A.19: *Private medical expenditures, by type, 1980: average per household, by employment status of head of household (£)*

Employment status of household head	GP fees	Specialist fees	Out-patient hospital charges	Dentists' fees and charges	Prescription medicines	Non-prescription charges	In-patient hospital charges including specialist	Other health professionals	Cost of eyeglasses	Other medical expenditures	Total
Employed (including self-employed)	27.86	10.91	1.43	23.43	41.56	13.40	27.01	4.06	8.83	0.70	159.20
Unemployed, seeking work	21.04	2.51	0.21	4.36	12.98	10.35	—	0.98	2.49	0.24	55.17
Retired	6.23	2.07	0.25	4.80	12.90	4.98	10.32	2.71	4.69	0.10	49.05
Household duties, full-time	6.86	1.61	0.93	4.37	8.61	4.94	8.50	1.03	3.60	0.27	40.72
Other[a]	3.20	0.16	0.01	5.14	9.83	5.65	0.48	0.05	0.35	0.01	24.87
All Households	20.69	7.53	1.05	16.43	30.77	10.58	19.80	3.17	7.02	0.50	117.54

[a]Includes 14 household heads not working because of long-term sickness or disablement.

Table A.20: *Private medical expenditures, by type, 1980: average per household, by occupation of head of household (£)*

Occupation of household head	GP fees	Specialist fees	Out-patient hospital charges	Dentists' fees and charges	Prescription medicines	Non-prescription charges	In-patient hospital charges including specialist	Other health professionals	Cost of eyeglasses	Other medical expenditures	Total
Professional, manager, or employer	28.09	18.96	3.81	38.06	45.10	13.65	73.78	7.78	12.47	0.63	242.33
Salaried employee or intermediate non-manual worker	22.41	8.44	0.65	25.36	37.24	12.93	28.88	4.00	10.30	0.14	150.37
Other non-manual worker	19.11	1.35	0.31	16.44	26.49	13.62	2.29	1.32	5.53	0.34	86.81
Skilled manual worker	24.45	10.14	1.68	9.22	33.40	8.55	12.07	3.39	6.84	0.02	109.75
Semi-skilled or unskilled manual worker	19.38	1.70	0.28	5.41	26.13	10.20	3.76	1.29	4.36	0.44	72.95
Farmer, agricultural worker, or fisher	15.53	6.42	0.21	13.46	24.09	8.15	8.90	2.32	5.43	0.96	85.46
All Households	20.77	7.56	1.05	16.49	30.88	10.61	19.88	3.18	7.04	0.50	117.97

Table A.21: *Private medical expenditures, by type, 1980: average per household, by age head of household completed full-time education (£)*

Age household head completed education	GP fees	Specialist fees	Out-patient hospital charges	Dentists' fees and charges	Prescription medicines	Non-prescription charges	In-patient hospital charges including specialist	Other health professionals	Cost of eyeglasses	Other medical expenditures	Total
Under 14	20.79	2.27	0.21	7.89	22.99	12.20	0.93	1.86	4.58	0.55	74.26
14	16.37	2.12	0.45	8.90	26.27	9.90	10.62	1.44	4.69	0.79	81.54
15	18.57	2.27	0.73	13.60	21.07	10.69	7.87	2.40	4.97	0.26	82.43
16	23.75	9.56	0.78	16.90	35.46	11.02	21.66	3.69	9.47	0.29	132.58
17	24.63	21.83	0.21	24.12	28.47	9.63	38.63	3.97	6.74	0.04	158.27
18	25.03	13.10	2.75	29.25	41.12	9.81	52.10	7.56	10.23	0.37	191.33
19	62.06	31.59	10.27	35.00	112.45	16.32	38.51	2.57	5.96	—	314.73
Over 19	23.46	17.36	2.73	37.34	39.51	13.28	31.19	6.63	15.20	0.52	187.23
All households	20.82	7.58	1.06	16.51	30.97	10.64	19.94	3.19	7.07	0.50	118.29

Table A.22: *Private medical expenditures, by type, 1980: average per person, by sex and age of head of household (£)*

Sex and age of household head	GP fees	Specialist fees	Out-patient hospital charges	Dentists' fees and charges	Prescription medicines	Non-prescription charges	In-patient hospital charges including specialist	Other health professionals	Cost of eyeglasses	Other medical expenditures	Total
Households with male heads	6.06	2.16	0.25	4.14	9.58	3.10	6.53	0.92	2.15	0.11	35.00
Under 45	8.39	3.63	0.23	4.68	10.00	3.68	6.57	0.86	1.65	0.04	39.74
45–64	5.25	1.15	0.19	4.57	9.39	2.44	8.01	0.87	2.64	0.06	34.58
65+	2.99	1.06	0.39	2.27	9.13	3.11	3.91	1.14	2.26	0.32	26.69
Households with female heads	4.44	0.90	0.35	3.90	6.67	2.78	3.44	1.18	1.98	0.27	25.91
Under 45	2.52	3.54	—	12.71	2.95	2.28	—	2.01	1.99	—	28.00
45–64	6.70	0.49	1.06	6.58	10.06	3.47	10.13	1.59	2.31	0.60	43.00
65+	3.61	0.63	0.05	0.90	5.57	2.51	0.57	0.82	1.81	0.15	16.62
All households	5.68	1.86	0.28	4.08	8.90	3.02	5.81	0.98	2.11	0.15	32.88

Table A.23: *Private medical expenditures, by type, 1980: average per person, by VHI cover and category of health services entitlement of head of household (£)*

VHI cover and entitlement Category (I, II, or III) of household head	GP fees	Specialist fees	Out-patient hospital charges	Dentists' fees and charges	Prescription medicines	Non-prescription charges	In-patient hospital charges including specialist charges	Other health professionals	Cost of eyeglasses	Other medical expenditures	Total
All VHI	7.84	4.72	0.69	9.57	13.78	3.48	14.64	1.93	3.27	0.27	60.19
All non-VHI	4.98	0.93	0.14	2.29	7.31	2.87	2.93	0.68	1.73	0.11	23.97
All Category I	1.29	0.39	0.04	0.70	1.74	2.12	0.54	0.69	1.48	0.14	9.12
VHI*	0.83	1.88	—	4.86	0.73	1.80	—	1.12	1.94	—	13.16
non-VHI	1.31	0.34	0.04	0.56	1.77	2.13	0.56	0.68	1.47	0.14	8.99
All Category II	8.55	1.66	0.26	4.71	13.46	3.64	6.01	0.94	2.02	0.09	41.34
VHI	7.90	3.53	0.31	7.91	16.15	3.36	8.59	1.89	3.32	0.12	53.07
non-VHI	8.76	1.07	0.24	3.69	12.59	3.73	5.19	0.64	1.60	0.08	37.58
All Category III	8.31	6.03	0.91	10.34	13.63	3.54	18.25	1.85	3.98	0.34	67.18
VHI	8.43	6.10	1.11	11.33	13.01	3.77	21.64	2.07	3.41	0.44	71.30
non-VHI	7.88	5.81	0.24	6.93	15.77	2.77	6.57	1.10	5.97	—	53.03
All persons	5.68	1.86	0.28	4.08	8.90	3.02	5.81	0.98	2.11	0.15	32.88

Note: VHI cover and/or category of entitlement of household head may not pertain to all household members.
*Absolute levels too low to establish meaningful averages.

Table A.24: Private medical expenditures, by type, 1980: average per person, by Health Board area (£)

Health Board area	GP fees	Specialist fees	Out-patient hospital charges	Dentists' fees and charges	Prescription medicines	Non-prescription charges	In-patient hospital charges including specialist	Other health professionals	Cost of eyeglasses	Other medical expenditures	Total
Eastern	7.97	2.09	0.44	6.53	11.64	4.18	8.15	1.20	2.41	0.04	44.65
Midland	3.06	0.74	0.17	0.92	6.55	2.15	2.21	0.72	1.82	0.04	18.39
Mid-Western	6.01	1.29	0.04	1.07	7.29	1.92	1.61	0.70	2.29	0.38	22.59
North-Eastern	5.23	1.51	0.22	4.34	9.06	1.64	3.03	2.04	2.40	0.01	29.48
North-Western	3.38	1.42	0.24	1.27	8.19	3.53	1.02	0.36	0.94	0.04	20.40
South-Eastern	3.32	0.81	0.07	3.08	5.54	3.13	3.93	1.01	1.92	0.04	23.44
Southern	5.87	3.24	0.40	3.46	10.15	2.18	3.52	1.01	2.17	0.62	31.94
Western	4.14	1.89	0.15	4.18	5.41	2.99	14.32	0.41	1.82	0.17	35.30
Ireland	5.68	1.86	0.28	4.08	8.90	3.02	5.81	0.98	2.11	0.15	32.88

Table A.25: *Private medical expenditures, by type, 1980: average per person, by employment status of head of household (£)*

Employment status of household head	GP fees	Specialist fees	Out-patient hospital charges	Dentists' fees and charges	Prescription medicines	Non-prescription charges	In-patient hospital charges including specialist	Other health professionals	Cost of eyeglasses	Other medical expenditures	Total
Employed (including self-employed)	7.01	2.53	0.38	5.73	10.97	3.30	6.92	1.01	2.16	0.20	40.19
Unemployed, seeking work	4.54	0.49	0.04	0.77	2.78	2.14	—	0.34	0.83	0.06	11.97
Retired	3.07	0.82	0.06	1.71	6.04	2.61	3.96	1.46	2.20	0.03	21.96
Household duties, full-time	3.89	0.70	0.23	1.13	4.62	2.65	6.32	0.71	2.07	0.14	22.47
Other[a]	0.58	0.17	0.00[b]	0.62	1.75	1.87	0.20	0.04	0.19	0.00[b]	5.15
All persons	5.68	1.86	0.28	4.08	8.90	3.02	5.81	0.98	2.11	0.15	32.88

[a]Includes 14 household heads not working because of long-term sickness or disablement. [b]Less than 0.005.

Table A.26: *Private medical expenditures, by type, 1980: average per person, by occupation of head of household (£)*

Occupation of household head	GP fees	Specialist fees	Out-patient hospital charges	Dentists' fees and charges	Prescription medicines	Non-prescription charges	In-patient hospital charges including specialist	Other health professionals	Cost of eyeglasses	Other medical expenditures	Total
Professional, manager or employer	7.34	4.68	0.90	8.73	14.74	3.98	24.32	2.31	3.95	0.11	71.06
Salaried employee or intermediate non-manual worker	6.98	2.48	0.46	7.22	12.56	3.44	8.78	1.70	3.19	0.11	46.92
Other non-manual worker	5.69	0.31	0.60	5.37	7.45	4.31	0.41	0.35	1.70	0.06	25.70
Skilled manual worker	5.80	2.44	0.38	2.94	8.31	2.60	2.12	1.14	1.89	0.01	27.64
Semi-skilled or unskilled manual worker	4.79	0.45	0.06	1.33	6.56	2.88	0.84	0.34	1.32	0.25	18.83
Farmer, agricultural worker, or fisher	4.92	1.45	0.04	2.54	6.89	2.16	2.00	0.61	1.54	0.21	22.36
All Persons	5.70	1.87	0.28	4.10	8.94	3.03	5.83	0.99	2.12	0.15	33.00

Table A.27: *Private medical expenditures, by type, 1980: average per person, by age head of household completed full-time education (£)*

Age household head completed education	GP fees	Specialist fees	Out-patient hospital charges	Dentists' fees and charges	Prescription medicines	Non-prescription charges	In-patient hospital charges including specialist	Other health professionals	Cost of eyeglasses	Other medical expenditures	Total
Under 14	5.76	0.42	0.02	1.72	7.40	3.18	0.09	0.62	2.24	0.27	21.72
14	3.99	0.58	0.10	1.93	6.46	2.71	4.48	0.33	1.20	0.16	21.96
15	5.41	0.52	0.18	2.92	5.39	2.91	1.13	1.08	1.59	0.08	21.23
16	6.20	2.12	0.13	3.49	9.64	2.89	4.86	1.03	2.81	0.11	33.26
17	8.17	5.56	0.03	6.03	10.00	2.84	17.51	1.30	1.69	0.01	53.16
18	7.94	3.53	0.86	9.12	14.30	3.45	12.10	2.37	2.98	0.06	56.70
19	14.38	7.00	1.83	6.46	26.89	3.23	8.03	0.57	1.45	—	69.83
Over 19	6.90	4.35	0.99	10.93	15.05	4.72	6.26	2.33	5.39	0.42	57.33
All persons	5.72	1.88	0.28	4.10	8.96	3.04	5.85	0.99	2.12	0.15	33.10

Table A.28: *Profile of a visit with the doctor (general practitioner): Further care or treatment ordered, prescribed, or suggested, per most recent visit, by VHI cover and Health Services entitlement, 1980 (per cent)*

VHI Cover and Category of Entitlement (I, II, III)	Return visit	Refer to another doctor	Refer to other professional	Prescribe medicine(s)	Non-prescription medicine(s)	Surgical, nursing, other device	Out-patient dept.	Hospital admission	Other	Total visits in sample
All VHI	17.6	8.5	2.6	70.4	8.2	1.8	8.2	5.1	1.3	612
All Non-VHI	25.5	6.6	2.4	79.4	3.9	1.3	10.7	5.3	1.3	1,869
All Category I	34.9	5.6	3.6	84.1	3.4	1.6	9.8	6.2	1.6	948
VHI*	42.6	3.3	3.3	92.3	3.3	1.6	5.7	6.3	4.9	45
non-VHI	34.5	5.7	3.7	83.7	3.5	1.6	9.9	6.2	1.4	903
All Category II	17.8	8.0	1.6	73.2	6.7	1.0	11.6	4.6	1.1	1,106
VHI	17.8	8.8	2.5	65.7	14.4	0.7	10.8	5.6	0.8	235
non-VHI	17.8	7.8	1.4	75.2	4.6	1.0	11.7	4.4	1.1	871
All Category III	13.3	8.0	2.1	72.1	3.7	2.1	6.8	4.7	1.2	427
VHI	14.0	9.0	2.7	70.9	4.4	2.4	6.3	4.6	1.3	332
non-VHI	10.0	4.4	0.0	76.9	0.8	1.0	8.1	5.6	1.5	95
All persons	23.5	7.1	2.5	77.2	4.9	1.4	10.0	5.3	1.3	2,481

*Absolute numbers too small to establish meaningful rates.

Table A.29: *Profile of a visit with the doctor (specialist): Further care or treatment ordered, prescribed, or suggested, per most recent visit, by VHI Cover and Health Services entitlement, 1980 (per cent)*

VHI Cover and Category of Entitlement (I, II, III)	Return visit	Refer to another doctor	Refer to other pro-fessional	Prescribe medicine(s)	Non-prescription medicine(s)	Surgical, nursing, other device	Out-patient dept.	Hospital admission	Other	Total visits in sample
All VHI	40.1	10.5	0.2	21.7	1.3	2.6	13.8	16.4	5.9	152
All non-VHI	38.3	15.9	3.2	30.1	2.3	4.9	28.7	22.6	5.2	345
All Category I	38.1	21.9	4.5	31.0	3.2	7.1	36.8	27.7	4.5	155
VHI*	37.3	31.8	0.0	30.9	0.0	0.0	9.1	5.5	13.6	8
non-VHI	38.2	20.8	4.6	31.5	3.5	7.8	37.8	29.2	3.9	147
All Category II	39.4	12.8	1.3	27.4	1.3	3.1	22.6	18.6	6.6	226
VHI	41.2	11.5	0.0	27.1	0.0	2.0	18.2	21.7	6.6	56
non-VHI	39.0	13.3	1.9	27.3	1.9	3.5	24.1	17.9	6.2	170
All Category III	38.8	6.9	3.9	23.3	1.7	2.6	10.3	15.5	4.1	116
VHI	39.9	7.5	4.0	18.6	2.5	3.0	11.2	14.8	4.2	88
non-VHI	37.4	5.2	3.9	39.6	0.0	0.0	5.9	18.0	2.6	28
All persons	39.0	14.1	2.9	27.7	2.1	4.3	24.0	20.9	5.1	497

*Absolute numbers too small to establish meaningful rates.

Table A.30: *Whose idea was most recent GP consultation?[a] – Per cent distribution by VHI Cover and Category of Health Services entitlement*

VHI Cover and Category of entitlement (I, II, or III)	Return visit	Household member's idea[a]	GP's idea	Another Doctor's idea	Other	Total doctor's ideas[b]	Total No. in sample
All VHI	19.8	75.3	3.4	0.2	1.3	23.4	609
All non-VHI	31.5	62.9	4.2	0.6	0.9	36.3	1,863
All Category I	39.8	53.9	4.6	1.2	0.6	45.6	946
VHI*	34.5	60.6	2.5	2.5	0.0	39.5	45
non-VHI	40.0	53.5	4.7	1.1	0.6	45.8	901
All Category II	24.2	71.0	3.5	0.1	1.2	27.8	1,101
VHI	24.5	70.7	3.3	0.0	1.5	27.8	232
non-VHI	24.1	71.1	3.5	0.1	1.1	27.7	868
All Category III	15.8	79.1	3.7	0.2	1.2	19.7	426
VHI	15.2	79.7	3.7	0.0	1.4	18.9	332
non-VHI	17.9	76.8	3.9	0.8	0.6	22.6	94
All persons	28.7	65.8	4.0	0.5	1.0	33.2	2,472

[a]Includes patient, parent, etc. [b]Sum of return visit, GP's idea and another doctor's idea.
*Absolute numbers too small to establish meaningful rates.

Table A.31: *Whose idea was most recent specialist consultation? – per cent distribution by VHI Cover and Category of Health Services entitlement*

VHI Cover and Category of entitlement (I, II, or III)	Return visit	Household member's idea[a]	GP's idea	Another Doctor's idea	Other	Total doctor's ideas[b]	Total No. in sample
All VHI	30.7	15.1	45.8	6.3	2.2	82.9	152
All non-VHI	24.5	9.9	53.9	7.3	4.4	85.7	348
All Category I	24.6	7.1	56.6	6.6	5.2	87.8	155
VHI*	13.6	21.8	50.9	13.6	0.0	78.1	8
non-VHI	25.2	6.3	56.9	6.2	5.5	88.3	147
All Category II	28.4	11.0	50.4	8.5	1.6	87.3	225
VHI	39.9	13.2	39.6	7.4	—	86.9	55
non-VHI	24.8	10.4	53.9	8.9	2.1	87.6	170
All Category III	25.5	18.4	47.2	4.7	4.2	77.4	116
VHI	26.9	15.8	48.5	5.0	3.7	80.4	88
non-VHI	21.0	26.7	42.9	3.9	5.5	67.8	28
All persons categorised	26.5	11.5	51.6	7.0	3.3	85.1	496

[a]Includes patient, parent, etc. [b]Sum of return visit, GP's idea and another doctor's idea.
*Absolute numbers too small to establish meaningful rates.

Table A.32: *Whose idea was most recent out-patient visit? – Per cent distribution by VHI Cover and Category of Health Services entitlement*

VHI Cover and Category of entitlement (I, II, or III)	Return visit	Household member's idea[a]	GP's idea	Another Doctor's idea	Other	Total doctor's ideas[b]	Total No. in sample
All VHI	16.8	22.8	44.6	13.0	2.7	57.6	125
All non-VHI	24.3	11.7	47.8	13.2	2.9	61.0	394
All Category I	25.2	9.6	48.3	14.1	2.7	52.4	181
VHI*	43.1	22.4	34.5	0.0	0.0	34.5	6
non-VHI	24.6	9.1	48.8	14.6	2.8	63.4	175
All Category II	25.0	11.9	48.5	12.2	2.5	51.0	245
VHI	21.0	13.3	52.1	13.5	—	65.6	45
non-VHI	25.9	11.5	47.6	11.9	3.1	59.5	200
All Category III	10.9	30.8	39.8	14.3	4.2	44.0	91
VHI	12.3	29.3	39.5	14.2	4.7	53.7	72
non-VHI	5.8	36.5	40.9	14.5	2.3	55.4	19
All persons categorised	22.6	14.4	46.9	13.2	2.9	60.1	517

[a]Includes patient, parent, etc. [b]Sum of GP's idea and another doctor's idea.
*Absolute numbers too low to establish meaningful rates.

Table A.33: *Whose idea was most recent Dentist visit? – Per cent distribution by VHI Cover and Category of Health Services entitlement*

VHI Cover and Category of entitlement (I, II, or III)	Return visit	Household member's idea[a]	Dentist's idea	Another Doctor's idea	Other	Total doctor's ideas[b]	Total No. in sample
All VHI	25.4	68.1	1.0	0.5	5.0	1.5	394
All non-VHI	26.6	64.3	1.6	0.6	6.9	2.2	594
All Category I	26.7	62.7	2.2	1.7	6.7	3.9	213
VHI*	25.4	72.1	2.5	0.0	0.0	2.5	18
non-VHI	26.8	61.9	2.1	1.9	7.3	4.0	195
All Category II	25.3	66.5	1.2	0.0	7.0	1.2	470
VHI	19.0	74.9	0.3	0.0	5.8	0.3	118
non-VHI	27.4	63.7	1.5	0.0	7.4	1.5	352
All Category III	27.1	67.6	1.1	0.6	3.6	1.7	305
VHI	28.8	65.4	1.3	0.7	3.8	2.0	258
non-VHI	17.5	80.2	0.0	0.0	2.4	0.0	47
All persons	26.1	66.0	1.4	0.6	5.9	2.0	988

[a]Includes patient, parent, etc. [b]Sum of dentist's idea and another doctor's idea.
*Absolute numbers too low to establish meaningful rates.

Table A.34: *Who prescribed most recent pharmaceutical medicine? – Per cent distribution by VHI Cover and Category of Health Services entitlement*

VHI Cover and Category of entitlement (I, II or III)	GP	Another doctor	Other	Total doctor's ideas[a]	Total in sample
All VHI	93.3	5.6	1.0	98.9	532
All non-VHI	95.0	4.7	0.4	99.7	1,659
All Category I	96.0	4.0	0.0	100.0	889
VHI*	97.9	2.1	0.0	100.0	42
non-VHI	95.9	4.1	0.0	100.0	847
All Category II	93.7	5.5	0.8	99.2	921
VHI	92.1	7.4	0.5	99.5	193
non-VHI	94.2	5.0	0.9	99.2	728
All Category III	93.0	5.8	1.2	98.8	370
VHI	93.3	5.2	1.5	99.5	288
non-VHI	92.0	8.0	0.0	100.0	82
All persons categorised	94.5	4.9	0.5	99.3	2,180

[a]Sum of GP and another doctor.
*Absolute numbers too low to establish meaningful rates.

Table A.35: *Whose idea was most recent hospital admission?[a] – Per cent distribution by VHI Cover and Category of Health Services entitlement*

VHI Cover and Category of entitlement (I, II, III)	Household member's idea[a]	GP's idea	Another doctor's idea	Other	Total doctors' idea[b]	Total in sample
All VHI	10.7	52.7	22.4	14.1	75.1	99
All non-VHI	7.4	60.5	21.4	10.8	81.9	294
All Category I	3.7	73.7	16.4	6.2	90.1	144
VHI*	19.4	57.4	15.5	7.7	72.9	6
non-VHI	3.1	74.4	16.4	6.1	90.8	138
All Category II	11.2	50.9	24.2	13.7	75.1	182
VHI	9.7	61.4	24.5	4.4	85.9	41
non-VHI	11.7	47.6	24.1	16.5	71.7	141
All Category III	9.8	46.8	26.0	17.4	72.8	67
VHI	10.7	44.8	21.7	22.8	66.5	51
non-VHI*	6.9	55.3	39.7	0.0	93.0	16
All persons	8.3	58.5	21.7	11.6	80.2	392

[a]Includes patient, parent, etc. [b]Sum of GP's idea and another doctor's idea.
*Absolute numbers too low to establish meaningful rates.

Table A.36: *Entitlement under the Health Services and VHI cover, per cent by age and sex, 1980*

Sex and age	With VHI Cover			Without VHI Cover			All		
	I	*II*	*III*	*I*	*II*	*III*	*I*	*II*	*III*
Males	1.3	9.0	13.9	28.9	42.7	4.2	30.3	51.8	18.0
0–14	0.6	8.7	18.6	23.8	42.5	5.8	24.4	51.3	24.5
15–44	2.0	9.4	13.7	20.7	49.5	4.6	22.7	58.9	18.3
45–64	0.4	9.6	13.4	29.0	45.6	2.0	29.2	55.5	15.3
65+	2.4	7.6	1.9	69.4	17.0	1.7	71.8	24.5	3.7
Females	1.7	10.4	14.7	33.4	35.6	4.2	35.1	46.1	18.8
0–14	0.7	8.6	22.1	25.1	39.4	4.1	25.8	47.8	26.3
15–44	2.5	12.8	14.7	21.5	43.1	5.4	24.1	56.1	21.5
45–64	0.8	12.2	12.6	39.6	31.6	3.2	40.7	43.9	16.0
65+	3.2	6.0	0.6	75.8	12.2	2.2	78.7	18.3	3.0
All persons	1.5	9.7	14.3	31.2	39.2	4.2	32.7	48.9	18.4

Detail may not add to 100 per cent because of rounding.

Table A.37: *VHI Cover and Health Services entitlement, by Health Board area, 1980 – Per cent distribution*

VHI Cover and Category of entitlement (I, II, III)	Health Board area								
	Eastern	Midland	Mid-Western	North-Eastern	North-Western	South-Eastern	Southern	Western	Ireland
All VHI	34.3	21.6	7.0	32.4	10.2	20.4	25.7	22.2	25.5
All non-VHI	65.7	78.4	93.0	67.6	89.8	79.6	74.3	77.8	74.5
All Category I	19.8	38.8	46.0	38.6	41.6	35.3	26.6	51.3	32.7
VHI*	1.7	0.4	0.7	1.7	0.5	1.9	1.1	2.4	1.5
non-VHI	18.1	38.4	45.3	36.9	41.1	33.4	25.5	48.9	31.2
All Category II	53.9	53.6	44.7	37.6	49.9	50.3	51.0	41.5	48.8
VHI	10.0	14.9	3.9	12.5	3.2	8.2	9.6	13.1	9.7
non-VHI	43.9	38.7	40.8	25.1	46.7	42.1	41.4	28.4	39.1
All Category III	26.3	7.6	9.3	23.8	8.5	14.4	22.4	7.2	18.5
VHI	22.6	6.3	2.4	18.2	6.5	10.3	15.0	6.7	14.3
non-VHI	3.7	1.3	6.9	5.6	2.0	4.1	7.4	0.5	4.2
All Persons[a]	100.0	100.0	100.0	100.0	100.0	100.0	100.0	100.0	100.0
Distribution[b]	31.8	4.6	8.1	10.4	5.9	11.1	15.8	12.3	100.0[a]

[a]Detail may not add to total because of rounding. [b]Per cent of sample living in each Health Board area.
*Except for Ireland (last column), absolute levels too small to establish meaningful rates.

Table A.38: *General practitioner consultations, by usual GP fee, by Health Board area*

Health Board area	Nil (medical card)[a]			1p–£2.99			£3.00–£3.99			£4.00–£4.99			£5.00–£5.99			£6.00+			All persons		
	Per year, per 1,000	Per cent with any	Per year, persons with any	Per year, per 1,000	Per cent with any	Per year, persons with any	Per year, per 1,000	Per cent with any	Per year, persons with any	Per year, per 1,000	Per cent with any	Per year, persons with any	Per year, per 1,000	Per cent with any	Per year, persons with any	Per year, per 1,000	Per cent with any	Per year, persons with any	Per year, per 1,000	Per cent with any	Per year, persons with any
Eastern	5,236	73.5	7.13	2,957	59.9	4.93	3,077	62.7	4.91	3,377	68.7	4.92	2,639	64.7	4.08	2,498	83.8	2.98	3,559	68.1	5.23
Midland	6,568	62.7	10.48	—	—	—	1,763	51.5	3.42	2,057	55.7	3.69	—	—	—	—	—	—	3,780	57.3	6.60
Mid-Western	5,528	66.7	8.29	7,043	70.5[b]	9.99	2,486	59.5	4.18	2,195	72.8	3.01	1,882	53.8	3.50[b]	6,500[b]	100.0[b]	6.50[b]	3,853	66.5	5.80
North-Eastern	3,943	71.3	5.53	2,578	84.2	3.06	2,767	59.3	4.67	3,385	62.7	5.40	3,448	68.5	5.03	—	—	—	3,403	66.3	5.13
North-Western	6,126	78.5	7.80	3,482	66.7	5.22	2,344	47.4	4.94	2,209	60.7	3.64	1,648	63.9	2.57	—	—	—	3,960	66.8	5.92
South-Eastern	5,994	76.2	7.87	2,027	56.8	3.57	2,567	60.0	4.28	2,830	69.5	4.07	2,709	60.6	4.47	1,000[b]	50.0[b]	2.00[b]	3,831	68.3	5.61
Southern	4,495	68.4	6.57	6,806	47.2	14.41	2,024	49.9	4.06	3,129	66.4	4.71	3,282	68.2	4.81	—	—	—	3,408	63.4	5.37
Western	4,728	69.3	6.83	3,471	70.6	4.92	3,054	64.7	4.72	1,949	53.1	3.67[b]	1,500[b]	100.0[b]	1.50[b]	3,000[b]	50.0[b]	6.00[b]	3,640	65.0	5.60
Ireland	5,616	71.1	7.26	3,698	66.6	5.56	2,677	58.9	4.55	2,995	65.9	4.55	2,691	64.8	4.15	2,577	79.4	3.25	3,616	66.1	5.47

Notes: [a]Persons with nil fees for reasons other than Medical Card excluded. [b]Fewer than 10 persons in category in sample.

Table A.39: *Number of beds in hospital room, by sex and age of in-patient, 1980, per cent distribution*

Sex and age	Only 1	Number of Beds 2–4	5 or more	Total patients[a]
All Males	6.0	12.8	81.3	100.0
0–14	4.6	9.3	86.2	100.0
15–44	6.3	12.9	80.8	100.0
45–64	10.8	17.2	72.0	100.0
65+	2.9	12.9	84.2	100.0
All Females	14.0	19.6	66.5	100.0
0–14	17.8	17.5	64.8	100.0
15–44	16.5	22.9	60.6	100.0
45–64	4.9	21.9	73.2	100.0
65+	11.4	0[b]	88.6	100.0
All Persons	10.8	16.1	73.1	100.0

[a]Detail may not add to total because of rounding. [b]Less than 0.05 per cent.

Table A.40: *Number of beds in hospital room, by Category of Health Services entitlement and VHI cover, 1980, per cent distribution*

Eligibility and VHI cover	Only 1	Number of Beds 2–4	5 or more	Total patients[a]
All VHI	27.0	22.5	50.5	100.0
All non-VHI	5.5	14.0	80.4	100.0
All Category I	5.7	9.0	85.3	100.0
VHI*	0[b]	6.5	93.5	100.0
non-VHI	5.9	9.1	85.0	100.0
All Category II	9.9	19.8	70.3	100.0
VHI	29.1	29.3	41.6	100.0
non-VHI	3.8	16.8	79.4	100.0
All Category III	22.8	23.1	54.1	100.0
VHI	26.2	19.1	54.7	100.0
non-VHI*	12.4	35.2	52.4	100.0
All Persons	10.8	16.1	73.1	100.0

[a]Detail may not add to total because of rounding. [b]Less than 0.05 per cent.
*Absolute levels too small to establish meaningful rates.

Table A.41: *Health Board area location of hospital and Health Board area residence of patient, 394 hospital admissions, 1980*

Health Board area location of hospital	Health Board area of residence								
	Eastern	Midland	Mid-Western	North-Eastern	North-Western	South-Eastern	Southern	Western	Total
Eastern	120	5	1	19	2	5	1	2	155
Midland	0	12	0	1	0	0	0	0	13
Mid-Western	0	0	29	0	0	0	0	0	29
North-Eastern	0	0	0	30	6	0	0	0	36
North-Western	0	0	0	0	15	0	0	2	17
South-Eastern	0	0	0	0	0	45	0	0	45
Southern	0	0	1	0	0	0	59	0	60
Western	0	1	0	0	0	0	0	38	39
Total	120	18	31	50	23	50	60	42	394

Table A.42: *Length of wait to get into hospital as in-patient, by Category of Health Services entitlement and VHI cover, 1980, per cent distribution*

	Up to 48 hours	*Up to a month*	*Up to a year*	*More than a year*	*Total persons*[a]
All VHI	70.8	22.5	4.5	2.2	100.0
All non-VHI	73.4	18.4	6.7	1.4	100.0
All Category I	70.7	22.1	5.4	1.9	·100.0
VHI*	50.3	49.7	0.0	0.0	100.0
non-VHI	71.5	20.9	5.6	2.0	100.0
All Category II	78.6	16.5	4.9	0[b]	100.0
VHI	79.0	14.8	6.2	0[b]	100.0
non-VHI	78.5	17.0	4.4	0[b]	100.0
All Category III	71.2	22.2	4.7	1.9	100.0
VHI	69.4	25.3	5.2	0[b]	100.0
non-VHI*	76.2	13.4	3.0	7.4	100.0
All Persons	72.8	19.4	6.2	1.6	100.0

[a]Detail may not add to total because of rounding. [b]Less than 0.05 per cent.
*Absolute levels too low to establish meaningful rates.

Appendix II

CALCULATION OF TABLE 6.1

Column (1) of Table 6.1 reports the per cent of each type of utilisation deemed to be the responsibility of (ordered, suggested, referred, or prescribed by) a general practitioner. The figures are taken from Appendix Tables A.30 through A.35. In line 1, return visits are treated as the GP's idea. Out-patient hospital (line 3) and dentist (line 5) figures are calculated on the basis of non-return visits only.

Column (2) reports the per cent of each type of utilisation deemed to be the responsibility of a doctor other than the patient's GP, usually a specialist. These figures are also taken from Appendix Tables A.30 through A.35. On line 2, return visits are treated as the other doctor's idea. As in Column (1), out-patient hospital (line 3) and dentist (line 5) figures are calculated on the basis of non-return visits only.

GP's adjusted share, Column (3) is calculated as follows. For general practitioner services, the adjusted share is 100 per cent. In other words, all of the cost of GP services is attributed to GPs. For specialists (line 2), the adjusted GP share is 51.6 per cent, from Column (1), plus 51.6 per cent of return visits (26.5 per cent), from Table A.31 for a total of 65.2 per cent. When a GP refers a patient to a specialist, the GP as gatekeeper is deemed responsible in Column (3) not only for the first but for the second, third, etc., specialist visits.

For the remaining types of utilisation in Column (3), the proportion for which GPs are directly responsible, as indicated in Column (1), is augmented by 65.2 per cent of the proportion for which another doctor was reported to be responsible, as indicated in Column (2). This adjustment is based on the estimate, as mentioned in the preceding paragraph, that GPs are deemed responsible for 65.2 per cent of specialist visits. GPs, as gatekeepers to the system, are indirectly responsible for the services prescribed by the specialists to whom the GP referred patients.

Column (4) brings forward totals from Table 5.5.

The adjusted shares in Column (3) are applied to total medical care expenditures in Column (4) to yield the estimates of GP responsibility in Column (5). Public sector data on hospital and specialist expenditures are not broken down as in Table 6.1, so it was necessary to weight the shares using private sector data from the author's survey (see Table 5.4). The weights used are: specialist out-patient, 23.6 per cent; hospital out-patient, 3.6 per cent; and hospital in-patient, 72.8 per cent. (Because the range of GP's adjusted share for these three lines is small, from 65.2 per cent to 72.6 per cent, the result is not very sensitive to the particular weights adopted.)

No data were collected on doctor responsibility for the "other" category of utilisation and expenditure (line 7). In Column (5), GP responsibility is treated as nil, because of lack of information.

For calculation of overhead, see Table 5.5, note (d). GP share of overhead expenditure is assumed to be the same in proportion as GP share of all other items combined (66.8 per cent).

Appendix III

SUMMARY OF SURVEY QUESTIONNAIRE, WITH MEANS AND FREQUENCIES

Note: Letter "H" by question number indicates data were collected for entire household (either aggregate or head of household only); otherwise, data were collected on each individual. There were 1,069 households, and (using the re-weighted data) 3,775 persons in the survey.

1H.	*Number of persons in household.*	
	Mean = 3.5	
1a.	*Sex.*	
	Male = 1,866 Female = 1,909	
1b.	*Age.*	
	Mean = 31.2	
1c.	*Relationship to head of household.*	
	Self	1,072
	Spouse	659
	Son/daughter	1,819
	Son-in-law/daughter-in-law	58
	Other relative	153
	Not a relative	14
2H.	*Employment status of head of household.*	
	Employed (including self-employed)	665
	Unemployed, seeking work	47
	Retired	175
	Household duties, full-time	122
	Not working because of long-term sickness or disablement	56
	Other	4
3H.	*Occupation group of head of household.*	
	Professional, manager, or employer	165
	Salaried employee, or intermediate non-manual worker	122
	Other non-manual worker	105
	Skilled manual worker	153
	Semi-skilled or unskilled manual worker	240

	Farmer, farmer's relative, or farm manager; other agricultural worker or fisherman	280
	Unknown	4
4H.	*Age head of household completed full-time education.*	
	Mean = 15.6	
5.	*Category of Health Services entitlement.*	
	Category I	1,227
	Category II	1,833
	Category III	692
	Missing data	23
6.	*VHI Cover.*	
	Yes	969
	No	2,802
	Missing data	3
7H.	*Distance from home to GP.*	
	Up to one mile	452
	Up to two miles	121
	Up to three miles	135
	Up to five miles	156
	Up to ten miles	167
	Over ten miles	32
	Missing data	6
8H.	*Usual GP fee – surgery, your home.*	
	Surgery.	
	No fee	433 households
	Mean (>0 only)	£3.79
	Home.	
	Mean (>0 only)	£5.44
9H.	*Does GP fee include all or most prescription medicines and pills?*	
	Yes	17
	No	635
	No fee	433
10.	*Most recent time each member was seen by GP.*	
	Within past 4 weeks	948
	Within past 12 months	1,570
	Within past 24 months	644
	Within past 5 years	314
	Longer ago than that (or never)	289
	Missing data	10
11.	*How many times each member seen by GP in 1980.*	
	Nil	1,280
	Mean (>0 only)	5.5
12.	*Place of each member's most recent GP visit.*	
	Member's home	477

Doctor's office/surgery	1,982
Another place	35
No visit/missing data	1,281

13. *Whose idea was each member's most recent GP visit?*

Return visit	710
A household member's idea	1,640
The GP's idea	99
Another doctor's idea	13
Other	24
Don't know/no visits/missing data	1,289

14H. *Total household expenditure on GP fees in 1980.*

None	463 households
Mean (all 1,069 households)	£20.69
Mean (>0 only)	£36.50

15. *At most recent GP visit, further treatment or care prescribed, suggested, or ordered by doctor.*

Yes

15a.	*Return visit arranged.*	586
15b.	*Referred to another doctor.*	177
15c.	*Referred to a health professional other than a doctor (such as dentist, optician, midwife).*	61
15d.	*Prescribed medicine.*	1,927
15e.	*Suggested/ordered non-prescription medicine.*	122
15f.	*Prescribed/suggested other device, appliance item (excluding contraceptives).*	35
15g.	*Referred to hospital for out-patient service or treatment.*	249
15h.	*Referred to hospital for admission.*	133
15i.	*Other.*	32

16. *Any visits to specialist?*

Yes	500

17. *How many?*

Mean (>0 only)	3.1

18. *Whose idea was each member's most recent specialist visit?*

Return visit	132
A household member's idea	57
A GP's idea	257
Another doctor's idea	35
Other	19
Don't know/no visits/missing cases	3,275

19H. *Total household expenditure on (out-patient) specialist fees.*

None	898 households
Mean (all 1,069 households)	£7.53
Mean (>0 only)	£47.07

20. *At most recent specialist visit, further treatment or care prescribed, suggested, or ordered by doctor.*

				Yes
	20a.	*Return visit arranged.*		194
	20b.	*Referred to another doctor.*		70
	20c.	*Referred to a health professional other than a doctor.*		15
	20d.	*Prescribed medicine.*		138
	20e.	*Suggested/ordered non-prescription medicine.*		11
	20f.	*Prescribed/suggested other device, appliance, item (excluding contraceptives).*		21
	20g.	*Referred to hospital for out-patient service or treatment.*		120
	20h.	*Referred to hospital for admission.*		106
	20i.	*Other.*		25

21. *Any visits to hospital out-patient department?*
Yes 517

22. *How many?*
Mean (>0 only) 3.6

23. *Whose idea was each member's most recent specialist visit?*
Return visit 117
A household member's idea 75
A GP's idea 244
Another doctor's idea 68
Other 15
Don't know/no visits/missing cases 3,255

24. *Total 1980 household expenditure on out-patient hospital services.*
None 1,001 households
Mean (all 1,069 households) £1.05
Mean (>0 only) £16.51

25. *Any dentist visits?*
Yes 1,017

26. *How many?*
Mean (>0 only) 2.6

27. *If any visits, were dentures or bridgework supplied?*
Yes 106

28. *Was household member referred by dentist to a doctor, a dental specialist, or an orthodontist in 1980?*
Doctor 5
Dental specialist 15
Orthodontist 19
More than one of these 1
None of these 929
No visits/missing cases 2,760

29. *Whose idea was each member's most recent dentist visit?*
Return visit 260
A household member's idea 656
A GP's idea 14
Another doctor's idea 5

	Other	61
	Don't know/no visit/missing cases	2,779
30.	*Treatment provided at each member's most recent dentist visit [enter only one].*	
	Check-up only	780
	X-ray(s)	12
	Filling(s)	418
	Extraction(s)	232
	Dentures/bridgework	95
	Other	58
	Don't know/no visit/missing cases	2,780
31.	*Fee charged by dentist for each member's most recent visit in 1980.*	
	No visit	2,758 persons
	No fee	391 persons
	Don't know/no response	163 persons
	Fee paid (>0)	463 persons
	Mean (>0 only)	£16.02
32H.	*Total 1980 household expenditure on dentists' fees.*	
	None	711 households
	Mean (all persons)	£16.43
	Mean (>0 only)	£49.06
33.	*How many prescription items each member received in 1980.*	
	None	1,584 persons
	Mean (>0 only)	7.8
34.	*Who prescribed each member's most recent prescription item*	
	GP	2,073
	Another doctor	107
	Other	12
	Don't know/no prescription/missing cases	1,583
35H.	*Total 1980 household expenditures on prescription and on non-prescription medicines.*	
	a. *Prescription medicines.*	
	None	488 households
	Mean (all households)	£30.77
	Mean (>0 only)	£56.61
	b. *Non-prescription medicines.*	
	None	233 households
	Mean (all households)	£10.58
	Mean (>0 only)	£13.53
36.	*Is any member in hospital now?*	
	Yes	22 persons
37.	*How long has member been in hospital?*	
	Mean (> 0 only)	20.8 days
38.	*Who referred member to hospital or first suggested he or she be admitted?*	
	A household member's idea	0

	A GP's idea	12
	Another doctor's idea	4
	Other	3
	Don't know/missing cases	3
39.	*Number of beds in member's room.*	
	Only 1	4
	2 to 4	2
	More than 4	12
	Don't know/Missing cases	4
40.	*Length of wait for admission.*	
	48 hours or less	11
	Up to a month	4
	Up to a year	2
	More than a year	2
	Don't know/missing cases	3
41.	*Name and locality of hospital.*	
42.	*Members in hospital for at least an overnight stay in 1980.*	
	Yes	394
43.	*How many times in hospital (discharges) in 1980?*	
	Mean (>0 only)	1.4
44.	*Who referred member to hospital or first suggested he or she be admitted?*	
	A household member's idea	32
	A GP's idea	230
	Another doctor's idea	85
	Other	46
	Don't know/missing data	1
45.	*Length of member's stay.*	
	Mean (>0 only)	18.9
46.	*Number of beds in member's room.*	
	Only one	37
	2 to 4	59
	More than 4	264
	Don't know	34
47.	*Length of wait for admission.*	
	48 hours or less	272
	Up to a month	71
	Up to a year	18
	More than a year	4
	Don't know	29
48.	*Name and locality of hospital.*	
49.	*Total 1980 household expenditures on in-patient hospital care, including specialist fees and any other related charges, as well as hospital room charges.*	
	None	985
	Mean (all households)	£19.80

Mean (>0 only)   £251.98

50. *Any consultations, examinations, or treatment from health care professionals other than doctors or dentists.*

Yes   608 persons

Mean, all kinds (>0 only)   4.0 visits

		Yes	Mean (>0 only)
a.	*Optician*	371	1.2
b.	*Audiometrist*	62	1.3
c.	*Midwife*	11	2.4
d.	*Nurse*	101	15.0
e.	*Social worker*	19	2.1
f.	*Chiropodist*	92	2.9
g.	*Psychologist*	17	2.6
h.	*Physio- or occupational therapist*	26	4.8
i.	*Other*	8	3.8

51H. *Total 1980 household expenditures on health care professionals other than doctors or dentists.*

None   857 households

Mean (all households)   £3.17

Mean (>0 only)   £15.98

52. *Members supplied with eyeglasses.*

Yes   350 persons

53. *How many pairs of eyeglasses.*

Mean (>0 only)   1.2

54H. *Total 1980 household expenditures on eyeglasses.*

None   856 households

Mean (all households)   £7.02

Mean (>0 only)   £35.23

55. *Members supplied with hearing aids.*

Yes   8

56. *How many hearing aids.*

Mean (>0 only)   1.0

57H. *Total 1980 household expenditures on hearing aids.*

None   1,068 households

Mean (>0 only)   £280.00

58.-61. *In 1980 did member have:*

		Yes
58.	*Complete physical examination when not ill, injured, pregnant?*	305
59.	*Immunisation for any disease?*	254
60.	*Blood pressure test?*	1,019
61.	*Cervical cancer smear ("pap") test (adult women only)?*	121

62H. *Any 1980 household medical expenditure not asked in previous questions.*

None   1,045 households

	Mean (all households)	£0.50
	Mean (>0 only)	£22.27

63H. *Any other body or organisation (such as employer) that helps household with medical care costs.*

Yes   75

64H. (Asked for respondant only, not other household member.)

How long a wait in GP's waiting area and/or examination room (most recent visit).

Up to 30 minutes   573
Up to 60 minutes   278
Up to 2 hours   108
More than 2 hours   37
Don't know/no response   73

65H. *Did any member of household make gifts to doctor (excluding cases where doctor is close friend or relative)?*

Yes   29
Money   14
Something else   15
Value — mean (>0 only)   £9.31

348 ESRI PUBLICATIONS

Books:

Economic Growth in Ireland: The Experience Since 1947
Kieran A. Kennedy and Brendan Dowling
Irish Economic Policy: A Review of Major Issues
Staff Members of ESRI (eds. B. R. Dowling and J. Durkan)
The Irish Economy and Society in the 1980s (Papers presented at ESRI Twenty-first Anniversary Conference)
Staff Members of ESRI
The Economic and Social State of The Nation
J. F. Meenan, M. P. Fogarty, J. Kavanagh and L. Ryan
The Irish Economy: Policy and Performance 1972-1981
P. Bacon, J. Durkan and J. O'Leary
Employment and Unemployment Policy for Ireland
Staff Members of ESRI (eds., Denis Conniffe and Kieran A. Kennedy)
Public Social Expenditure – Value for Money? (Papers presented at a Conference, 20 November 1984)

Policy Research Series:

1. *Regional Policy and the Full-Employment Target*   M. Ross and B. Walsh
2. *Energy Demand in Ireland, Projections and Policy Issues*   S. Scott
3. *Some Issues in the Methodology of Attitude Research*   E. E. Davis *et al.*
4. *Land Drainage Policy in Ireland*   Richard Bruton and Frank J. Convery
5. *Recent Trends in Youth Unemployment*   J. J. Sexton

Broadsheet Series:

1. *Dental Services in Ireland*   P. R. Kaim-Caudle
2. *We Can Stop Rising Prices*   M. P. Fogarty
3. *Pharmaceutical Services in Ireland*   P. R. Kaim-Caudle
assisted by Annette O'Toole and Kathleen O'Donoghue
4. *Ophthalmic Services in Ireland*   P. R. Kaim-Caudle
assisted by Kathleen O'Donoghue and Annette O'Toole
5. *Irish Pensions Schemes, 1969*   P. R. Kaim-Caudle and J. G. Byrne
assisted by Annette O'Toole
6. *The Social Science Percentage Nuisance*   R. C. Geary
7. *Poverty in Ireland: Research Priorities*   Brendan M. Walsh
8. *Irish Entrepreneurs Speak for Themselves*   M. P. Fogarty
9. *Marital Desertion in Dublin: An Exploratory Study*   Kathleen O'Higgins
10. *Equalization of Opportunity in Ireland: Statistical Aspects*
R. C. Geary and F. S. Ó Muircheartaigh
11. *Public Social Expenditure in Ireland*   Finola Kennedy
12. *Problems in Economic Planning and Policy Formation in Ireland, 1958-1974*
Desmond Norton
13. *Crisis in the Cattle Industry*   R. O'Connor and P. Keogh
14. *A Study of Schemes for the Relief of Unemployment in Ireland*
R. C. Geary and M. Dempsey
with Appendix   E. Costa
15. *Dublin Simon Community, 1971-1976: An Exploration*   Ian Hart
16. *Aspects of the Swedish Economy and their Relevance to Ireland*
Robert O'Connor, Eoin O'Malley and Anthony Foley
17. *The Irish Housing System: A Critical Overview*
T. J. Baker and L. M. O'Brien

18. *The Irish Itinerants: Some Demographic, Economic and Educational Aspects*
M. Dempsey and R. C. Geary

19. *A Study of Industrial Workers' Co-operatives*
Robert O'Connor and Philip Kelly

20. *Drinking in Ireland: A Review of Trends in Alcohol Consumption, Alcohol Related Problems and Policies towards Alcohol*
Brendan M. Walsh

21. *A Review of the Common Agricultural Policy and the Implications of Modified Systems for Ireland*
R. O'Connor, C. Guiomard and J. Devereux

22. *Policy Aspects of Land-Use Planning in Ireland*
Frank J. Convery and A. Allan Schmid

23. *Issues in Adoption in Ireland*
Harold J. Abramson

Geary Lecture Series:

1. *A Simple Approach to Macro-economic Dynamics* (1967)
R. G. D. Allen
2. *Computers, Statistics and Planning-Systems or Chaos?* (1968)
F. G. Foster
3. *The Dual Career Family* (1970)   .
Rhona and Robert Rapoport
4. *The Psychosonomics of Rising Prices* (1971)
H. A. Turner
5. *An Interdisciplinary Approach to the Measurement of Utility or Welfare* (1972)
J. Tinbergen
6. *Econometric Forecasting from Lagged Relationships* (1973)
M. G. Kendall
7. *Towards a New Objectivity* (1974)
Alvin W. Gouldner
8. *Structural Analysis in Sociology* (1975)
Robert K. Merton
9. *British Economic Growth 1951-1973: Success or Failure?* (1976)
R. C. O. Matthews
10. *Official Statisticians and Econometricians in the Present Day World* (1977)
E. Malinvaud
11. *Political and Institutional Economics* (1978)
Gunnar Myrdal
12. *The Dilemmas of a Socialist Economy: The Hungarian Experience* (1979)
János Kornai
13. *The Story of a Social Experiment and Some Reflections* (1980)
Robert M. Solow
14. *Modernisation and Religion* (1981)
P. L. Berger
15. *Poor, Relatively Speaking* (1983)
Amartya K. Sen
16. *Towards More Rational Decisions on Criminals* (1984)
Daniel Glaser

General Research Series:

1. *The Ownership of Personal Property in Ireland*
Edward Nevin
2. *Short-Term Economic Forecasting and its Application in Ireland*
Alfred Kuehn
3. *The Irish Tariff and The E.E.C.: A Factual Survey*
Edward Nevin
4. *Demand Relationships for Ireland*
C. E. V. Leser
5. *Local Government Finance in Ireland: A Preliminary Survey*
David Walker
6. *Prospects of the Irish Economy in 1962*
Alfred Kuehn
7. *The Irish Woollen and Worsted Industry, 1946-59: A Study in Statistical Method*
R. C. Geary
8. *The Allocation of Public Funds for Social Development*
David Walker
9. *The Irish Price Level: A Comparative Study*
Edward Nevin
10. *Inland Transport in Ireland: A Factual Study*
D. J. Reynolds
11. *Public Debt and Economic Development*
Edward Nevin
12. *Wages in Ireland, 1946-62*
Edward Nevin

111. *Worker Priorities, Trust in Management and Prospects for Workers' Participation*
                                                            Christopher T. Whelan
112. *The Impact of Energy Prices on the Irish Economy during 1973-1981*
                                                                      E. W. Henry
113. *Schooling and Sex Roles: Sex Differences in Subject Provision and Student Choice in Irish Post-Primary Schools*
                            D. Hannan, R. Breen and B. Murray, D. Watson, N. Hardiman,
                                                                    K. O'Higgins
114. *Energy Crops, Forestry and Regional Development in Ireland*
                                            Frank J. Convery and Kathleen Dripchak
115. *Aggregate Supply, Aggregate Demand and Income Distribution in Ireland: A Macro-sectoral Analysis*   John Bradley and Connell Fanning
116. *Social Mobility in the Republic of Ireland: A Comparative Perspective*
                                    Christopher T. Whelan and Brendan J. Whelan
117. *Attitudes towards Poverty and Related Social Issues in Ireland*
                                    E. E. Davis, Joel W. Grube and Mark Morgan
118. *A Study of New House Prices in Ireland in the Seventies*
                                                                    Ian J. Irvine
119. *Education and the Labour Market: Work and Unemployment Among Recent Cohorts of Irish School Leavers*
                                                                    Richard Breen
120. *Payroll Tax Incidence, the Direct Tax Burden and the Rate of Return on State Pension Contributions in Ireland*
                                                                  Gerard Hughes
121. *Crime Victimisation in the Republic of Ireland*
                                        Richard Breen and David B. Rottman
122. *Medium-term Analysis of Fiscal Policy in Ireland: A Macroeconometric Study of the Period 1967-1980*
                John Bradley, Connell Fanning, Canice Prendergast and Mark Wynne
123. *The Irish Wealth Tax A Case Study in Economics and Politics*
                                        Cedric Sandford and Oliver Morrissey
124. *Aspects of Freight Transport in Ireland*
                                                                    Jack Short
125. *Small-Scale Manufacturing Industry in Ireland*
                                        Kieran A. Kennedy and Tom Healy

126. *Irish Medical Care Resources: An Economic Analysis*
                                                              A. Dale Tussing